COLLÈGE DE FRANCE – CNRS
CENTRE DE RECHERCHE D'HISTOIRE
ET CIVILISATION DE BYZANCE

MONOGRAPHIES 45

INHERITANCE, LAW AND RELIGIONS IN THE ANCIENT AND MEDIAEVAL WORLDS

edited by

Béatrice Caseau & Sabine R. Huebner

Cet ouvrage a bénéficié du soutien du Labex RESMED (ANR-10-LABX-72) dans le cadre du programme Investissements d'avenir ANR-11-IDEX-0004-02.

ACHCByz
52, rue du Cardinal Lemoine – 7500'
www.achcbyz.com
2014

ISBN 978-2-916716-52-7
ISSN 0751-0594

Composition et infographie
Artyom Ter-Markosyan Vardanyan

TABLE OF CONTENTS

A CROSS-CULTURAL APPROACH TO SUCCESSION AND INHERITANCE IN THE ANCIENT AND MEDIAEVAL MEDITERRANEAN

Béatrice Caseau and Sabine R. Huebner

Socio-historical scholarship on the family has been flourishing in recent decades among scholars of the ancient and medieval world. Scholarly attention turned above all to the definition of the 'family', families of the social elite, family memories, family networks, the structure and organization of the *oikos/domus*, and representations of the family. We propose to work on patterns of and conflicts over succession and inheritance in a cross-cultural comparative perspective, a topic which so far has received surprisingly little attention by historians and anthropologists interested in the family, but which lies, we believe, at the heart of all family strategies affecting household composition, intergenerational relations, and the organization of old age care.

By studying inheritance and succession patterns for a society, region, or locality, we obtain a new grasp on family dynamics and learn more about cultural and social expectations ingrained in a society, such as women's rights and status, organization of family support networks, and the potential for intergenerational conflict. When the law provided for equal sharing between children, in what ways and to what effect could parents favor one child over others? What conflicts could arise among siblings? What was the place of girls in the distribution of the patrimony? How could the elderly generation assert their role in the family by using their property as leverage for securing old age support from their heirs? We know of various forms of succession and inheritance patterns for ancient and pre-modern societies laid out in the legislation and often adjusted to and modified in everyday practice.

The last two decades have seen the publication of a number of studies on wills and inheritance in the classical world, such as those by Rubinstein (1993) on classical Athens or Champlin on Roman wills (1991), or the set of papers on property transmission in the Mediterranean medieval world edited under the direction of Joelle Beaucamp and Gilbert Dagron (1998). However, inheritance and succession strategies among the common population, peasants, laborers, small traders, and craftsmen, which indubitably constituted about 95 percent of all ancient and medieval societies, have been almost entirely neglected in scholarship. Kreller's groundbreaking study (1919) on inheritance and succession in Greco-Roman Egypt,

Inheritance, Law and Religions in the Ancient and Mediaeval Worlds, ed. by B. Caseau and S. R. Huebner (Centre de recherche d'Histoire et Civilisation de Byzance, Monographies 45), Paris 2014.

for example, for which we have probably the richest source of information on the social strata below the elite, was published almost a century ago, and no one has ever advanced an update or extension of the topic.

Moreover, the interconnection of family and household forms, on the one hand, and succession and inheritance patterns, on the other hand, has not been discussed at all, even though such a diachronic comparative study is certainly to be desired.

Across societies of the ancient Mediterranean, the next of kin from the male line usually inherited. The system of primogeniture in ancient Israel let only the eldest son inherit. In ancient Egypt the firstborn male was granted a double share and the right to succeed to his father's office and household headship, while his brothers and sisters received a smaller share of their father's estate. Greek and Roman societies, however, did not recognize the right of the firstborn. Children usually inherited equally, but girls often received their share of movable property as a dowry, while their brothers often inherited land – whether they kept their patrimony undivided or divided it up was another question and depended on the number of brothers, the size of the estate, whether it was a rural or urban setting, and custom. Legitimate children were entitled to inherit but fathers often found a way to provide a share of their inheritance to their illegitimate children. A widow was usually barred from inheriting from her husband but was granted a lifelong usufruct that secured her old age. Whether daughters could inherit at all varied from society to society. A dowry given to them at their wedding usually represented their premortem share in their father's estate. If they had not yet been married, their father's heirs made provision for their maintenance and a dowry. In the absence of sons, daughters generally succeeded to their father's patrimony but were obliged to marry one of their father's kinsmen. In the absence of children, brothers or fathers' brothers inherited. If children had died but had left grandchildren, those inherited in their stead. No matter how the succession was organized, however, more or less serious internal conflicts within the family were often the result. Wills were challenged.

Ancient and medieval societies based legal succession on the degree of family relations, but they also introduced some testamentary freedom which allowed the bequeathal of goods and properties to institutions or to persons other than relatives. What conflicts could arise when a childless bequeather, for example, chose to adopt a person outside the family as heir (e.g. testamentary adoption) or decided to leave his assets to an institution, such as a monastery or a waqf?

Considering the role of religion is a particularly fascinating aspect when studying inheritance and succession conflicts. Bequests to religious institutions disregarding succession rules based on the degree of kinship often caused difficulties over inheritance, but sometimes religious leaders by their active involvement in family affairs also helped to resolve family disputes.

In this volume, based on a conference held in March 2013 at the Institute of Byzantine Studies at the Collège de France, in Paris, a number of distinguished ancient and medieval historians engage with the subject, spanning the period from archaic Greece up to the late Middle Ages, taking into account jurisprudence and legal cases in the civil laws of the Greeks, the Romans, and the Byzantines, and studying the religious laws of pagans, Jews, Christians, and Muslims.

The book is organized by themes. The first section deals with the inheritance rights of illegitimate children and with the unequal treatment of women. The chapter by Maria Nowak concerns Greco-Roman Egypt and shows the rights of illegitimate children to inherit in that region. She concludes that, in the Hellenistic period, extramarital offspring could inherit and that they were also mentioned in wills written by Roman soldiers. The question of illegitimate children is also the topic chosen by Judith Evans Grubbs for the late Roman period. The legislation changed from the time of Constantine to that of Justinian: Constantine had refused senators the right to transmit property to children born to lowborn women, but Justinian wanted to allow parents to provide for their illegitimate children – a man could leave up to half of his property to his natural children if he had no legitimate ones.

The unequal right of women to inherit is the topic of the three following articles. Lahcen Daaif shows how donations to a waqf could help provide funds to girls and bypass the Islamic law. Yves Sassier shows how, in the absence of a male heir, succession was organized in the county of Nevers in the 13th century. Cameron Sutt shows how estates were divided in Arpad-era Hungary, with special attention to the place of daughters within the inheritance system in the 13th century.

The next section is devoted to kinship conflict over inheritance. Brenda Griffith-Williams deals with inheritance rights of adoptive sons and of daughters, in ancient Athens, and the difficulty for heirs from matrilineal kinship to inherit. Sabine R. Huebner's article focuses on family conflicts over inheritance in Greco-Roman Egypt. It shows that in that region, daughters received dowries but also inherited a share of their father's estate. Documents preserved on papyri show different cases of family members fighting in court over inheritance, siblings but also parents and children, guardians and wards. Nicholas Kalospyros studies inheritance issues in Philo of Alexandria, while Giles Rowling studies inheritance disputes appearing in the 2nd century Babatha archive.

The following section deals with how the Christian authorities encouraged giving part of one's estate to the poor or to religious institutions. Religious ideas of caring for the poor by making them heirs appear in the will of Gregory of Nazianzus, studied by Fotis Vasileiou. Jean-Claude Cheynet uses records from ecclesiastical tribunals to study conflicts between families and monasteries, when a donation was made to a religious institution in a will.

Conflicts arose in ruling families, when the succession also involved transmitting power.

Amber Gartrell tackles the succession strategy of Augustus, whose succession was marred with scandals and even deaths. Christian Settipani studies how imperial power was transmitted inside the imperial family, during the Byzantine iconoclastic era. Conflicts or preventive measures to avoid conflicts led to exile, confiscation of properties, or even executions. Gerhard Lubich deals with the Merovingian period and shows how family murders and civil wars were part of the inheritance process.

The last section is devoted to the forms of testaments and the practice of law. Heinz Barta writes on the form of testaments in ancient Greece and Ptolemaic Egypt. He deals with the question of the influence of the Greek form of testaments on the Roman practice. Carlos Sanchez-Moreno Ellart discusses the forms of Roman testaments and the rule to have either five or seven witnesses. He studies both forms in Roman law and in barbarian law codes. James Howard-Johnston presents an 11th century document, the *Peira*, made of compiled decisions of the Byzantine judge Eustathios Romaios.

This collection of articles does not aim to provide a thorough study of all aspects of conflicts over inheritance but to throw light on different aspects of family conflicts over inheritance. It examines gender issues, the evolution of law, and the influence of religions in partitive inheritance. This volume is based on a jointly organized international conference hosted at the Collège de France, in Paris, in March 2013. We firstly would like to thank all participants of this conference who made valuable substantive contributions by presenting papers or serving as chairpersons and the institutions, which provided generous funding: on the French side, the LABEX RESMED, 'Religions en Méditerranée', the Research Center "Orient & Méditerranée" (UMR 8167), the Institut Byzantin at the Collège de France and the University of Paris-Sorbonne, and for the German side, the German Research Foundation (DFG). We wish to thank Jean-Claude Cheynet, head of the Research Center and of the LABEX RESMED, for welcoming this Franco-German research project. We wish to thank as well Constantin Zuckerman for accepting this book in the collection of the 'Monographies du Centre de recherche d'histoire et civilisation de Byzance, Collège de France – CNRS.' Our gratitude goes to Artyom Ter-Markosyan and Fotis Vasileiou for harmonizing the notes of the articles, and to Artyom Ter-Markosyan for his patient and very professional typesetting work. Finally, our thanks go to the institutions, which provided the funds to publish this book: the LABEX RESMED, the Associations des amis du Centre d'histoire et de civilization de Byzance and the University of Paris-Sorbonne.

ILLEGITIMATE CHILDREN, GENDER ISSUES

THE HEREDITARY RIGHTS OF THE EXTRAMARITAL CHILDREN IN LIGHT OF THE LAW OF PAPYRI*

Maria Nowak

Introduction

My article aims to present the hereditary situation of extramarital children in Graeco-Roman Egypt, between the first and third centuries AD. I intend to discuss whether the legal status of *apator*, *chrematidzon metros*, etc.[1] was inferior to that of legitimate offspring. First I shall discuss the regulations concerning extramarital children present in jurisprudential sources, specifically the *Gnomon of Idios Logos*; second, I will examine papyri which provide information about the succession of illegitimate offspring.

Gnomon of Idios Logos

One of the most important juridical sources regarding non-formal families and illegitimate children in the legal practice of Graeco-Roman Egypt is the *Gnomon of Idios Logos*,[2] (preserved in *BGU* V 1210, and very fragmentarily in *P. Oxy*. XLII 3014), a second-century document containing either abstracts of imperial *mandata* or a case-book of the proceedings

* I am greateful to Tomasz Derda (University of Warsaw) and Paul Schubert (University of Geneva) for their valuable comments and suggestions. I would also like to thank Sofie Waebens (University of Leuven) for remarks on military problems and Jesse Simon for correcting English. All remaining errors and inaccuracies are mine. The present article is an effect of my research in the framework of the project financed by SCIEX.

1. For the terminology see A. Calderini, Apatores, *Aegyptus* 33, 1953, pp. 358–369; H. C. Youtie, ΑΠΑΤΟΡΕΣ: Law vs. Custom in Roman Egypt, in *Le monde grec; pensée, littérature, histoire, documents; Hommages à Claire Préaux*, J. Bingen, G. Cambier, G. Nachtergael (eds.), Brussels 1975, pp. 723–740; in Latin sources: B. Rawson, *Spurii* and the Roman view of illegitimacy, *Antichthon* 23, 1989, pp. 10–41, pp. 14–15.

2. The text was published as *BGU* V 1210 by W. Schubart in 1919. The edition was followed by the commentary by W. Uxkull-Gyllen (*BGU* V.2). The further editions: Th. Reinach, *Un code fiscal de* l'Égypte romaine: Le Gnomon de l'Idiologue, *NRHD* 43, 1919, pp. 583–636 (Greek text and translation) and *NRHD* 44, 1920, pp. 5–134 (commentary); *Jur. Pap.* 93; *FIRA* I 99 (partly); *Pap. Primer*[4] 54; S. Riccobono, *Gnomon dell'Idios Logos*, Palermo 1950 (Greek text, translation, commentary); J. Mélèze Modrzejewski, Gnomon de ideologue, in *Les lois des Romains*, P. F. Girard, F. Senn (eds.), Napoli 1977, pp. 12–49 (text and translation).

Inheritance, Law and Religions in the Ancient and Mediaeval Worlds, ed. by B. Caseau and S. R. Huebner (Centre de recherche d'Histoire et Civilisation de Byzance, Monographies 45), Paris 2014.

that took place before the *idios logos*, the official responsible for, among other things, *bona vacantia*, and a judge in succession disputes.[3] The 'prototype' of the *Gnomon* as a manual for the *idios logos* was created before the second century, probably during the reign of Augustus. It contains, among other things, information regarding personal status and the law of succession in Graeco-Roman Egypt. Among these norms, we find direct and indirect references to hereditary rights and *testamenti factio passiva* of children born out of wedlock. The rules concerning such children in the *Gnomon* are not systematized, but they may nonetheless be divided into three groups: children of mixed unions between non-Romans, illegitimate offspring of Romans, and the children of soldiers.

First, in paragraph 11 we are informed of a woman named Krenea, who could not inherit from her children, *BGU* V 1210, l. 44: ια. γυνὴ Κρηνέα τέκνον οὐ κληρ[ο]νομεῖ, '11. Krenea does not inherit from (her) child'. The rule is unclear and perhaps fragmentary; there is no clear suggestion as to whether the *Gnomon* refers to all her children — both legitimate and illegitimate — or only to the latter; and if so, we cannot be certain whether the rule applied to testamentary or intestate succession. The other sources do not supplement our knowledge in this matter. The next paragraph concerns children born of Krenea and a *xenos*, who are entitled to the succession after both of them, *BGU* V 1210, l. 45-46: ιβ. τὰ ἐκ Κρηνέας κα̣ὶ̣ ξένου γενόμενα τέκνα τοὺς γονεῖς ἀμφοτέ[ρ]ους κληρονομεῖ, '12. children born of a woman from Kyrene and *xenos* inherit from both parents'. Again the meaning of the quoted passage is not obvious: the rule might express the hereditary privilege granted for the offspring of unions that were not formal marriages on account of the marital prohibition; or, rather, it might indirectly state that the union of these two groups of people living in Egypt could marry and produce legitimate offspring who could inherit from them. If the former interpretation is correct, then this would have been a privilege granted to the children born of informal unions. However, the interpretation of the above passage is not obvious, as the prohibition of marrying a person belonging to a different social group was not a rule; mixed marriages were casuistically regulated. For instance, evidence from papyri proves it is possible that a citizen of Ptolemais could marry an foreign woman and that, moreover, such a marriage would grant a wife citizenship;[4] a man from Naukratis, on the other hand, was not allowed to marry an Egyptian (*W. Chr.* 27 [Antinoopolis, after AD 161]). Marriages between Greeks and Jews were not numerous, but they did happen (*P. Ent.* 23 [Magdola, 218 B.C.]).[5]

Another paragraph referring to the hereditary rights of illegitimate children is the one which restricts *testament factio passiva* of Alexandrian wives; they could inherit via testament only one third of their husbands property, or as much as their common children (*BGU* V 1210, l. 29-32). The conclusion to be drawn from this passage is that only legitimate children of Alexandrians were protected in the succession after their fathers, for the advantage of the illegitimate ones is not even mentioned.

3. On *idios logos*, see R. Swarney, *The Ptolemaic and Roman idios logos*, Toronto 1970.

4. J. Mélèze Modrzejewski, Dryton le crétois et sa famille ou les mariages mixtes dans l'Égypte hellénistique, in H. van Effenterre (ed.), *Aux origines de l'Hellénisme. La Crète et la Grèce. Hommage à Henri van Effenterre*, présenté par le Centre G. Glotz, Paris 1984, pp. 353–377.

5. J. Mélèze Modrzejewski, *Le droit grec après Alexandre*, Paris 2012, pp. 43–45; C. Fischer-Bovet, Ethnic identity and status: comparing Ptolemaic and Early Roman Egypt, in *Identity and identification in Antiquity* (forthcoming).

Paragraph 13 deals with the law on the status of children born of an *aste* — a woman who was a citizen of one of three (later one of four) cities in Egypt — and a *xenos*. In this case, the children follow the status of their father, that is the lower status, and do not inherit from their mother (*BGU* V 1210, l. 47-48: ιγ. τὰ ἐξ ἀστῆς καὶ ξένọυ γενόμενα τέκνα ξένα γεịνεται καὶ οὐ κληρονομεῖ τὴν μητέρα, '13. children born of a citizen woman and *xenos* are born as *xenoi* and they do not inherit from their mother'). The children are here considered illegitimate, for a marriage between these two social groups was not legally recognised, at least not by the laws that applied to the citizens of Egyptian *poleis*.[6] However, we should not forget that a child born of such a union could be recognised as legitimate by its father's community.[7] We find a very similar decision in paragraph 38, where the hereditary rights of children born of the union of an *aste* and an Egyptian are concerned.

Furthermore the legal and hereditary situation of extramarital children of Roman citizens is discussed in the *Gnomon*.[8] One such example is a rule on incestuous unions, found in paragraph 23, which penalises such relations between Romans with the confiscation of their property,[9] *BGU* V 1210, l. 70-72: κγ. οὐκ ἐξὸν Ῥωμαίοις ἀδελφὰς γῆμαι οὐδὲ τηθίδας, ἀδελφῶν θυγατέρας συνκεχώρηται. Παρδαλᾶς μέντοι ἀδελφῶν συνελθόντων \τὰ ὑπάρχοντα/ ἀνέλαβεν, '23. It is not allowed for Romans to marry either their sisters or aunts, it is allowed to marry brothers' daughters. Pardalas confiscated properties of siblings who had intercourse'. The situation of children is not discussed directly, but the other sources provide the information that such offspring were considered illegitimate (G. 1.64), thus they were not their parents' heirs.[10] The consequences were even more significant, as the confiscation of parental property would have affected testamentary succession: parents whose property was confiscated could no bequeath it to their children.

In addition to the situation of children born of incestuous union between Romans (which are poorly attested in papyri[11]) the *Gnomon* regulates hereditary rights of children born of Romans and non-Romans who were not granted *conubium*, as well as the children of soldiers. There is no doubt that the latter (or at least most them) were illegitimate,

6. For instance, to become an Alexandrian one had to be the legitimate child of Alexandrian, P. M. Meyer, Papyrus Cattaoui, II. Kommentar, *Archiv* 3, 1906, pp. 67–105, p. 81. As Delia observed, it is impossible to state whether to produce legitimate offspring Alexandrian had to marry an Alexandrian woman or any *aste* of other Greek cities. D. Delia, *Alexandrian citizenship during the Roman principate* (= *American classical studies* 23), Atlanta 1991, p. 54.

7. This phenomenon was quite common in Greek world. The fact that men from one *polis* were privileged to take a wife of whatever origin did not necessarily mean that the union was recognized as a legitimate one in wife's community. D. Ogden, *Greek bastardy in the Classical and Hellenistic periods*, Oxford 1996, p. 290.

8. For the reasons for illegitimacy of Roman children see: Rawson, *Spurii* (quoted n. 1), p. 18.

9. This was not the unique penalty, since persons involved in incestuous unions were deported to the island as those guilty of adultery. Before Augustus the penalty was even more sever, since the offenders were punished with death. A. Berger, *Encyclopedic dictionary of Roman law*, Philadelphia 1955, *s.v. incestum*; J. F. Gardner, *Women in Roman law and society*, London 2012, p. 23.

10. On the other hand, the brother-sister marriages were accepted among non-Romans, J. Rowlandson, R. Takahashi, Brother-sister marriage and inheritance strategies in Greco-Roman Egypt, *Journal of Roman Studies* 99, 2009, pp. 104–139 (with further literature).

11. *I.a.* see the protocol of the prosecution in such a case before *praefectus Aegyptii*, *BGU* IV 1024 (Hermopolis Magna, AD 360).

for *conubium* was only given to soldiers after their service (G. 1.57); the children would thus have been excluded from intestate succession — at least from their Roman parent — as only marital children could be intestate heirs of their parents (G. 3.2). The prohibition of disposing *mortis causa* the property between Greeks and Romans (in certain periods it was possible by *fideicommissa*, that is a formless request addressed to an heir or any other person profiting from inheritance to do something to the advantage of the third person[12]) was the rule, expressed also in the *Gnomon*: *BGU* V 1210, l. 56-58: ιη. τὰ\ς/ κατὰ πίστιν γεινομένας κληρονομίας ὑπὸ Ἑλλήνων \εἰς/ ⟦ὑπὸ⟧ Ῥωμαίους ἢ ὑπὸ Ῥωμαίων \εἰς/ Ἕλληνας ὁ θεὸς Οὐεσπασιανὸς [ἀ]νέλαβεν, οἱ μέντοι τὰς πίστεις ἐξωμολογησάμενοι (*l.* ἐξομολογησάμενοι) τὸ ἥμισ[υ ε]ἰλήφασι. '18. Divus Vespasian confiscated inheritances left as trusts (made) by Greeks to Romans and by Romans for Greeks. Yet, those who confessed having accepted such trusts kept a half.'[13] Such a rule must have affected the hereditary rights of a significant number of illegitimate children with at least one Roman parent for, in such cases, the general rule was that children followed the lower status either according to *ius civile* or *lex Minicia*;[14] thus the principle quoted above would have applied to them.

In addition to these norms restricting the hereditary rights of illegitimate Roman children, in the text of the *Gnomon* there are also some norms granting them hereditary privileges. These rules, however, mostly concern children born to Roman soldiers. Paragraph 34 excludes the limitations of *testamenti factio passiva* in case of *testamentum militis*, allowing soldiers to make a will in whatever form and language they wished (which would be valid within one year after their discharge); more importantly, it allowed them to bequeath their property to whomever they wanted, but only if they could inherit, *BGU* V 1210, l. 96-98: λδ. τοῖς ἐν στρατείᾳ καὶ ἀπὸ στρατείας[15] οὖσι συνκεχώρηται διατίθεσθα[ι] καὶ κατὰ Ῥωμαικὰς καὶ Ἑλληνικὰς διαθήκας καὶ χρῆσθαι οἷς βούλωνται ὀνόμασι, ἕκαστον δὲ τῷ ὁμοφύλῳ[16] καταλείπειν καὶ οἷς ἔξ[εσ]τιν. '34. It was agreed that those in army and those after their military service can make a Roman will or a Greek will and to apply the words as they wish, it is allowed for them to bequeath (their property) to anyone of their rank'. The last part of the paragraph must relate to mostly soldiers' children who were not Romans on

12. Of course, the succession *mortis causa* in any form was possible only between Roman citizens and the only exception to this rule (introduced by Augustus) was *fideicommissum*.

13. G. II 285. According to Gaius *peregrini* could acquire through *fideicommissa* until the time of Hadrian. *Gnomon*, on the other hand, mentions that trusts left to Greeks were confiscated from the time of Vespasian. There are two possible interpretations of these passages. Either it was Vespasian who introduced the confiscation of the property left to peregrines and Hadrian only maximized its effects, or Vespasian's constitution concerned only the trusts between Romans and Greeks (not all peregrines). The prohibition is attested also by Pausanias (8.43.5).

14. For the status of children born of different mixed unions in Roman Egypt see: R. BAGNALL, Egypt and *lex Minicia*, *Journal of Juristic Papyrology* 23, 1993, pp. 25–28, p. 27.

15. The expression ἀπὸ στρατείας was the subject of wide scholarly discussion. The problem is whether the rule expressed in *Gnomon* applied to both soldiers and veterans or to soldiers. It is highly probable, however, that it concerned solely soldiers. M. AMELOTTI, *Il testamento romano attraverso la prassi documentale. I: Le forme classiche di testamento*, Firenze 1966, pp. 83–89.

16. For the interpretation of this word see: R. ALSTON, *Soldier and society in Roman Egypt. A social history*, London 1995, p. 57.

account of being born to a woman who was not a citizen.[17] Such an interpretation of the above passage is supported by the Gaian text explaining that restrictions concerning *testamenti factio passiva* did not apply to *testamentum militis* (G. 2.110), and also by a constitution of Alexander Severus (C. 6.21.5).[18] It is worth noting that the rule discussed here would have softened the one concerning *fideicommissa*.

The next paragraph states that soldiers' natural children could inherit (together with collaterals) from them when no will was made. This decision is an abstract of Hadrian's edict, also attested in a copy preserved on papyrus (*BGU* I 140 = *Sel. Pap.* II 213 [AD 119, Alexandria?]). The law allowed children born to soldiers during their period of military service to ask for *bonorum possessio* from their fathers at the same class as testators' collaterals, that is *unde cognati*, the third group of persons who could request *bonorum possessio* from the deceased in *ius honorarium*. The same rule — albeit, with much less precision — is repeated in *P. Bad.* IV 72 (Ankyron, AD 117–118). The papyrus concerns two children, a son and a daughter, who inherited some property from their father, a legionary soldier; Fr. B ctr., ll. 21-23: ἔξεστι δ̣ὲ κ̣αὶ τοὺς [ἐν λεγεῶ]νι στρατευομένους κληρονομεῖσθαι ὑπὸ τέ[κνων], 'it is allowed for soldiers in legions to be inherited by their children.'[19] It does not explain what type of succession it refers to, thus we can only presume it is intestate succession; moreover, it mentions only the children of legionary soldiers, whereas the other two sources do not differentiate between military units. In practical terms, the edict recognised the blood relationship between fathers and their children with respect to hereditary rights, but natural children could only obtain possession of goods belonging to the inheritance if no marital children or agnatic relatives — that is, related through parental power — existed.[20] On the other hand, from the time of Julius Ursus, *praefectus Aegypti* (AD 79/80?), veterans' daughters who had been granted Roman citizenship were not entitled to succession from their Egyptian mothers, *BGU* V 1210, l. 140-141: νδ. θυγατρὶ μ[ι]σσικίου Ῥωμαίᾳ γεν[ομ]ένη Οὖρσος οὐκ [ἐπέτρε]ψε κληρον[ομ]ῆσαι τὴν μητέραν (*l.* μητέρα) Αἰγ[υπ]τίαν οὖσαν, '54. Ursus did not permit a veteran's daughter who became a Roman to inherit from her mother, being Egyptian'.

The above paragraphs do not provide a coherent picture of the hereditary situation of extramarital children in Egypt. In some cases, decisions preserved in the *Gnomon of Idios*

17. Children from veterans discharged from the *auxilia* and fleet (and the *equites singulares augusti*, but they do not appear in Egypt) received the Roman citizenship upon their fathers' discharge from the army (until AD 140, when auxiliary veterans were no longer granted the *civitas liberorum* privilege). S. E. PHANG, *The marriage of Roman soldiers (13 B.C. — A.D. 235): law and family in the imperial army*, Leiden 2001, passim.

18. Ulpianus attributed the rule releasing soldiers' wills from all formal requirements to Trajan (D. 29.1.1 *pr.*). The same text is repeated perhaps in *P. Fay.* 10. AMELOTTI, *Il testamento romano* (quoted n. 15), pp. 82–83.

19. The most interesting problem in this document is the civil status of legionary soldiers' children, which will not be discussed here. S. WAEBENS, *P. Bad.* IV 72 and the inheritance problems of soldiers' illegitimate children in Roman Egypt (forthcoming).

20. Such legal situation could encourage some people to safeguard their children rights. This is the case of a Latin contract between Demetria and Gaius Valerius Gemellus (*FIRA* III 20 = *Ch.L.A.* 295 = *P. Mich.* VII 442 [Cezarea, 2nd c. AD]). The document states that Demetria was Gemellus' wife before his military service and their common children were born during this marriage, that is before their father's military service. PHANG, *The marriage* (quoted n. 17), pp. 47–49.

Logos are also known from other legal sources; this is mostly the case for those paragraphs that concern Romans or their children. Much more complicated are the passages which do not deal with Romans, but rather with the non-Roman inhabitants of Egypt. These parts of the text also raise questions regarding the nature of the regulations, specifically whether these rules were introduced by the Romans, or if they were promulgated during the Ptolemaic period and merely adopted by the Romans. The former interpretation would suggest that Roman rulers were interested in the illegitimacy and hereditary rights of their subjects, regardless of whether or not they were Roman citizens.[21] The paragraphs might reflect the judgments given as a result of legal proceedings that took place before different *idioi logoi;* it is, however, certain that we are not dealing with the official text of laws, and thus the *paragraphoi* cannot be interpreted in isolation from the documents of legal practice which might explain the rules expressed in the *Gnomon*.

Papyri

The information presented in the *Gnomon* may be supplemented with evidence from papyri, especially testaments mentioning extramarital children. These might help to determine the rights and abilities of such children in terms of succession, as well as their real situation in legal practice. The most important question is whether parents were unrestricted in appointing their illegitimate children heirs and leaving them legacies. Sources concerning the testamentary succession of illegitimate children of both Romans and non-Roman inhabitants of Roman Egypt are few; however, they may help us to determine not only the hereditary situation of extramarital children, but also the scale of testamentary freedom in the legal practice of Roman Egypt.

The limits of testamentary freedom — non-Roman wills to the advantage of extramarital children

The testamentary rules concerning non-Romans are not obvious. Before examining attestations of extramarital children succeeding their parents in the papyri, questions concerning the limits of testamentary freedom must first be addressed. One document expressing a principle of testamentary freedom is a protocol of dispute which took place before Blesius Marianus, prefect of *Cohors I Flavia Cilicum equitata*, acting as *iudex datus* (*M. Chr.* 84 = *SPP* XX 4 = *CPR* I 18 = *Jur. Pap.* 89 [Ptolemais Euergetis, AD 124]).[22] The parties of the dispute are the testator's father and the testamentary heir. The father wanted to revise his son's will, arguing that children born of *agraphoi gamoi* were not allowed to make a will if their

21. The opposite opinion, Rawson, *Spurii* (quoted n. 1), p. 12.

22. H. J. Wolff, *Written and unwritten marriages in Hellenistic and postclassical Roman law*, Pennsylvania 1939, pp. 60–61; J. Crook, *Legal advocacy in the Roman world*, London 1995, pp. 74–75; U. Yiftach-Firanko, *Marriage and marital arrangements: A history of the Greek marriage document in Egypt, 4th Century BCE — 4th Century CE* [= *Münchener Beiträge zur Papyrusforschung und antiken Rechtsgeschichte* 93], München 2003, pp. 82–91.

father was still alive. In such a case the father was an heir. However, his opponent claimed that the will was valid, for 'the law of Egyptians'[23] allowed one to dispose of their property in whatever way he wanted, as long as the will was composed properly.[24]

> *M. Chr.* 84, l. 15-20: [κ]αὶ τοῦ Ἀμμωνί[ου διὰ] Μαρκιανοῦ ῥήτορος ἀποκριναμένου ṭὸ[ν] τῶν Αἰγυπτίων νόμον διδόναι ἐξουσίαν πᾶσι τοῖς διατιθεμένοις καταλείπειν [ο]ἷς βούλο[ντ]αι τὰ ἴδια, ἑαυτὸν μέντοι ἀνεψιὸν ὄντα τοῦ τετελ[ε]υτηκότ[ο]ς καταλ[ε]λεῖφθαι σὺν ἑτέρῳ υἱῷ τοῦ ἀντιδίκου κλ[ηρ]ονόμον [κ]αὶ τὴν δι[α]θήκην πλήρη ἔχειν τὸν τῶν μαρ[τύ]ρων ἀρι[θμό]ν.
>
> Ammonios said via Marcianus, rhetor, that the law of Egyptians allows those making a will to leave their own (things) as they wish; him being the cousin of the one who passed away and another son of the adversary were appointed heirs and the number of testamentary witnesses is complete.

It seems quite plausible that the testamentary freedom was indeed the rule among the non-Roman population of Roman Egypt; nevertheless there were a few exceptions. One of them is suggested in the document quoted above, as the father of the testator claimed that sons born of *agraphos gamos* were not entitled to make wills during their fathers' lifetime. Exceptions to testamentary freedom appear also in the *Gnomon of Idios Logos* (cf. paragraphs 5, 6, 10, 14, 15, 112). However, the most intriguing question is whether the inhabitants of Roman Egypt made wills to the advantage of their extramarital children freely, or if they were restricted in this respect.

The former seems to be the case in a second-century will composed for a woman, Taarpaesis *alias* Isidora (*P. Köln* II 100 [Oxyrhynchos, AD 133]). The text is well preserved and detailed. The testatrix appears to be a relatively wealthy woman, for she possesses at least two houses and more than ten *arourai* of land.[25] She appointed her three children, Ptolemaios, Berenike and Isidora (also called Apollonarion) heirs, and they are described with the words: τοὺς τρεῖς χρηματίζοντας μητρὸς ἐμοῦ, 'officially known as my children', which means that the children were of a father who was not Taarpaesis' husband.[26] We have no information concerning any other offspring of the testatrix, thus we may assume that the illegitimate children were her only progeny.[27] Moreover, the testament was properly opened and executed,

23. On the term, J. Mélèze Modrzejewski, La loi des Égyptiens: le droit grec dans l'Egypte romaine, dans *Proceedings of the XVIII International Congress of Papyrology*, Athens 1988, pp. 383–399.

24. That is at *agoranomos*, *BGU* V 1210, l. 33-34: Δ[ι]αθῆκαι, ὅσα μὴ κατὰ δημοσίους χρηματισμοὺς γείνωνται, ἄκυροί εἰσι, 'the wills which were not composed as public documents, are void'. M. Nowak, Dryton's wills reconsidered, *Revue Internationale des droits de l'antiquité* 59, pp. 241–251.

25. According to Alan Bowman five *arourai* were enough to feed an average family: A. Bowman, *Egypt after the pharaos. 332 BC—AD 642*, London 1986, p. 238.

26. The term χρηματίζων μητρός is characteristic for the Oxyrhynchite nome and it signifies the one 'officially named as a son of...', that is illegitimate son of a woman whose name appeared in genitive after the expression. Ogden, *Greek bastardy* (quoted n. 7), p. 335. Daughters could be described with the same term, but their number is much lower. M. Malouta, Fatherless and formal identification in Roman Egypt, in S. R. Hübner, D. M. Ratzan (eds.), *Growing Up Fatherless in Antiquity*, Cambridge 2009, pp. 120–138, p. 124.

27. According to Youtie these children were common children of the testatrix and her partner also appearing in the will as the beneficiary of some bequeaths. Such a conclusion is based on the onomastic grounds. Youtie, ΑΠΑΤΟΡΕΣ (quoted n. 1), p. 727.

for the document is the official copy confirmed by the witnesses' signatures during the opening of the will;[28] thus the provisions to the advantage of testatrix' extramarital children would have been put into effect.

Perhaps a similar example is *PSI* XII 1263 (Oxyrhynchos, AD 166–167), a copy of a will composed for a woman named Sintheus. As in the above-mentioned case of Taarpaesis, Sintheus also appoints her sons heirs. Here as well, the sons appear with no indication of their father's name. They are described only as 'her sons': καταλείπω κληρον[όμους] τοὺς υἱούς μου Σαραπίωνα καὶ [Διογένην], 'I appoint as my heirs Sarapion and [Diogenes], my sons'. The sons were named after their maternal grandfather and great-grandfather, which might suggest their extramarital status. Again, the extramarital status of these children (if they really were such) had little effect on their ability to inherit *via* their mother's will, at least when no legitimate children were involved. This will also probably took effect, for it is a copy.[29] If there were any difficulties in bequeathing to the advantage of these illegitimate children (or in the limitations of testamentary freedom) they are not visible.

We find a slightly different approach in a first-century will composed for Soeris, probably an Egyptian woman, from Oxyrhynchos (*P. Oxy.* I 104 [Oxyrhynchos, AD 96]). The testatrix appoints her son, Areotos, heir; he is also described as: χρηματίζων μητρὸς ἐμαυτῆς τῆς Σοήριος, 'officially known as Soeris' children'. In contrast to the previous document, however, this one explicitly informs us that, at the moment when the will was composed, the testatrix had a husband (who was not Areotos' father)[30] and a daughter born of this marriage. She bequeathed some minor legacies to them, but the son was appointed as the main successor.

The rights of the testatrix' husband were safeguarded by bequeathing him the right to dwell in — and also to rent to a third party — the house left to the heir; moreover, the son, being the heir, was obliged to pay back a debt that his mother owed to her husband in accordance with a secure-deed made through a bank. The heir was also bound to pay a legacy to his step-sister, born of the testatrix' husband; the woman was granted the right of dwelling in the same house in the event of her divorce, but the privilege was restricted only to the right of dwelling. Unfortunately, there is no secure method to determine the reasons for these provisions; we cannot be sure if they were the result of laws forcing testators to respect the rights of the members of their formal families, or if they arose from some other circumstances which we do not know, for example a marital agreement securing the hereditary rights of the spouse and marital offspring.

In order to understand the situation more clearly, we need to look at marital agreements from both the Hellenistic and Roman periods,[31] which can provide additional information. A significant number of these contracts contain provisions concerning the succession of common offspring in the event of the death of either spouse. In many cases these contracts aimed to safeguard the hereditary rights of future or already born marital children, as in the following examples.

28. M. Nowak, The function of witnesses in the wills from late antique Egypt, dans P. Schubert (ed.), *Actes du 26e Congrès international de papyrology, Genève, 16-21 août 2010*, Genève 2012, pp. 573–580, p. 575.

29. The commentary to *PSI* XII 1263.

30. Youtie, ΑΠΑΤΟΡΕΣ (quoted n. 1), p. 725.

31. For the full list of such contracts see: Yiftach-Firanko, *Marriage* (quoted n. 22).

P. Gen. I 21 (Arsinoites, 2nd c. BC): ἐὰν δέ τις ạὐτῷν ἀνθρώπινόν τι πάθῃ καὶ τελευτήσ̣[ηι], ἔστω τὰ καταλεπόμενα ὑπάρχοντα τοῦ ζῶντος αὐτῶν καὶ τῶν τέκνων τῶν ἐσομένων αὐτοῖς ἐξ ἀ[λ]λήλων.

If one of them [spouses] suffers human fate and dies, the remaining estate shall belong to the surviving spouse and their future children.

P. Oxy. III 496, l. 10-11 (Oxyrhynchos, AD 127): ẹ̀ạ̀ṿ δ̣[ὲ] . . . . .η̣ ṭịṿạ τῶν γαμούντω [ν τελευτῆσαι -ca.?- ἐχέτω ὁ γαμῶν] τὴν κατὰ τῶν ἑαυτοῦ ἐξου[σί]αν ἃ̣ ἐὰν αἱρῆται ἐπιτελε[ῖ]ν καὶ οἷς ἐὰν βούλη[ται] μερίζε[ιν], ἐὰν δὲ μηδὲν [ἐ]πιτελέσῃ εἶναι καὶ αὐτὰ μετὰ τελευτὴν αὐτοῦ τῶν ἐξ ἀλλή[λ]ων [τ]έκνω[ν].

But either husband or wife should chance to die, the husband shall have power over his own property to make any further provisions he pleases and to divide it among whom he will; but if he makes no further provisions the property shall after his death belong to their children. (tr. *P. Oxy.* III)

The clauses in these different papyri vary, but they appear in many documents of this type from both the Hellenistic and Roman periods.[32] Normally, if a provision becomes an element of a contract, there is a reason for this. The appearance of such contractual provisions suggests that the parties involved wanted to secure the succession of their common marital children. This leads to the conclusion that illegitimate children would inherit from their parents together with the legitimate offspring, unless they were excluded contractually.[33]

The above supposition is also supported by the fact that a number of marital agreements prohibit extramarital offspring, as in the oldest dated Greek text from Egypt.

P. Eleph. 1, l. 8-9 (Elephantine, 310 B.C): μὴ ἐξέστω δὲ Ἡρακλείδηι γυναῖκα ἄλλην ἐπεισάγεσθαι ἐφ᾽ ὕβρει δημητρίας μηδὲ τεκνοποιεῖσθαι ἐξ ἄλλης γυναικὸς μηδὲ κακοτεχνεῖν μηδὲν παρευρέσει μηδεμιᾶι Ἡρακλείδην εἰς Δημητρίαν.

Let it not be permitted to Herakleides to bring in another woman as an outrage to Demetria, nor to have children by another woman, nor to deal deceitfully in any way on any pretense, Herakleides against Demetria' (tr. *P. Eleph.*)

The contract states that if the husband is not obedient to its terms, he should pay his newly married wife double the amount of the dowry. *P. Eleph.* 1 is not a unique example of such a provision, and we find it in a few documents composed between the fourth and first centuries B.C.[34] If we keep in mind the previously discussed contractual decision concerning

32. I.e. *CPR* I 28 (Ptolemais Euergetis, AD 110), *BGU* I 183 (Sokopaiu Nesos, AD 83), *BGU* I 251 (Sokopaiu Nesos, AD 81), *BGU* I 252 (Ptolemais Euergetis, AD 98), *BGU* IV 1098 (Alexandria, 19-15 BC), *P. Freib.* III 26 (Philadelphia, 178 B.C.), *P. Freib.* III 29 (Philadelphia, 178 B.C.), *P. Freib.* III 30 (Philadelphia, 179-178 B.C.), *P. IFAO* III 5 (Oxyrhynchites, 2nd c. AD), *P. Mich.* V 343 (Tebtynis, AD 54-55), *SB* XVI 12334 (Philadelphia, 2nd c. AD), *SB* XXIV 16256 (Arsinoites, AD 117-118), *P. Oxy.* III 497 (Oxyrhynchos, 2nd c. AD).

33. Ogden, *Greek bastardy* (quoted n. 7), pp. 340–341.

34. *SB* XII 11053 (Tholtis, 267 B.C.), *P. Freib.* III 30 (Philadelphia, 179-178 B.C.), *P. Giss.* 29 (Krokodilopolis, 173 B.C.), *P. Tebt.* III.2 974 (Tebtynis, 2nd c. B.C.), *Tebt.* I 104 (Kerkeosiris, 92 B.C.).

marital children's succession, the prohibition of extramarital children fits perfectly with the supposition that such children were not excluded from the succession after their parents.

A Hellenistic testament written in Pathyris in the second-century B.C. (*SB* XVIII 13168 [Pathyris, 123 B.C.]) proves that extramarital children (if not excluded contractually) could have some hereditary rights. The testator, Pachnubis, leaves his property to his wife, Ταθώτηι Ἀρυώτου Περσίνῃ ἧ̣ι σύ[νειμι] γυναικὶ κατὰ νόμους, 'Tathotis daughter of Haruotes, the Persian, my wife wedded according to the laws', while his two sons born of another woman, τοῖς ἐμοῖς υἱοῖς τοῖς ἐξ ἐμοῦ καὶ ἄλλης γυνα[ικός], receive only one bed and one mattress. There are two facts worth mentioning. First, we cannot be certain whether the sons were illegitimate or not (although such a supposition is supported by the strong distinction between the wife — who is described as the one married according to law — and the boys' mother, called simply 'the other woman'). Second, the meaning of the disposition for the sons is very unclear, for there are no exact parallels; one possible interpretations is that the testator wanted to leave his entire property to his wife, but he had duties towards his sons.

The *Legal Code from Hermopolis West* casts further light on the hereditary rights of illegitimate children in Graeco-Roman Egypt. This is the casebook of Egyptian law, a manual used by judges to decide cases, perhaps originating from the eighth century B.C. The text, as it has been preserved, was composed in the third century B.C; we possess both the Demotic version of the Code and its Greek translation. The latest Greek copy comes from Oxyrhynchos in the second-century AD (*P. Oxy*. XLVI 3285).[35] The text contains information on different legal matters, *inter alia*, on succession. In this respect we do not find any differentiation between legitimate and extramarital offspring[36] (the only child whose position was better than others' was the oldest son, no matter whether legitimate or not).

In such a context it is worth recalling the well-known passage by Diodorus, who claimed that there was no concept of bastardy among the Egyptians, with the only exception of priestly families, whose offspring was produced with one wife only (Diod. 1.80.3-4).[37] It is also important to note the Demotic contracts — composed both before and after Alexander — which, much like the Greek marital agreements, safeguarded the hereditary rights of common future and/or already existing children. Through such contracts, husbands could exclude from succession all other children born to them.[38]

From all of the documents quoted above, we may assemble the following picture. When Greeks started settling in Egypt, they probably met with the Egyptian custom that included illegitimate children in intestate succession equally with legitimate ones (if there was, in fact, any differentiation at all). The situation was further complicated by the fact that the new settlers came from a variety of places where the problem of hereditary rights was approached

35. G. Mattha, G. R. Hughes, *The Demotic legal code of Hermopolis West*, Cairo 1975; S. L. Lippert, Codex Hermopolis, in R. Bagnall et alii ed., *The Encyclopedia of Ancient History*, Oxford 2012.

36. P. W. Pestman, *Marriage and matrimonial property in ancient Egypt: A contribution to establishing the legal position of the woman*, Leiden 1961, p. 48; Ogden, *Greek bastardy* (quoted n. 7), p. 331.

37. Calderini, Apatores (quoted n. 1), p. 359; Youtie, ΑΠΑΤΟΡΕΣ (quoted n. 1), p. 732, Ogden, *Greek bastardy* (quoted n. 7), p. 330.

38. Pestman, *Marriage* (quoted n. 36), p. 48.

in different ways.[39] Thus, the easiest way to safeguard the rights of children begotten during marriage was the contractual one. The existence of such contractual provisions up to the Roman period suggests that neither Ptolemies nor Romans introduced the general rule prohibiting either testamentary or intestate succession — or both — of illegitimate children. It seems that hereditary rights of children were restricted only by the decisions of their parents.

Soldiers' children

We must also ask whether the rules concerning soldiers' children expressed in the *Gnomon* are visible in the legal practice of Roman Egypt. As I have demonstrated in the first part of this article, soldiers were free to appoint whoever they wanted as an heir. This rule is confirmed also in *P. Cattaoui recto* (*BGU* I 114 = *FIRA* III 19 b, col. IV, l. 1-15 [Alexandria?, AD 114–142]).[40] An Alexandrian woman, Chrotis, described her son as having been born to her from the union with an Alexandrian citizen, Isidoros, who became a soldier serving in *auxilia*. Her claim, however, is not clear; Meyer thought that she wanted her son not to pay a tax on the inheritance, and for this she wanted him to be recognized as a legitimate child of his father.[41] It is obvious that the boy was appointed heir by his father in the will composed during his military service; the official decided that the boy could not be recognised as a legitimate child of his father, for the military laws forbade this, but κληρονόμον δὲ αὐτὸν ἔγραψεν νομί[μως], 'he appointed him heir lawfully'. Moreover, Meyer has suggested that Isidoros was already a Roman when he composed his will;[42] if this is correct, the document would be an example of testamentary succession between a Roman and a non-Roman in practice (the exception mentioned in the *Gnomon of Idios Logos*, paragraph 34).

A unique text of a Roman will preserved almost entirely on wax tablets (*FIRA* III 47 [Alexandria, AD 142]) provides further information.[43] Antonius Silvanus, the testator and *eques alae primae Thracum Mauretanae*, appointed his son the sole heir. His son, Marcus Antonius Satrianus, was certainly an extramarital child, for his mother Antonia Thermutha was not (and could not be) the testator's wife, since he was a soldier. However, the text does not specify the legal bonds between the father and his son; Antonius Silvanus even behaves as if the boy was his legitimate son, since not only does he leave him the inheritance, but also appoints him a tutor.[44] The most intriguing question is whether or not Silvanus' son and heir

39. For instance, in Athens after 'Pericles' law', illegitimate children were excluded completely from succession after their parents, while in Tegeia they were granted the inheritance if there was no marital offspring (H. J. Wolff, Marriage law and family organization in ancient Athens, *Traditio* 2, 1944, pp. 43–95, pp. 69, 89), while the inscriptions from Gortyn do not even contain a term for the bastardy (Ogden, *Greek bastardy* [quoted n. 7], p. 264).

40. Meyer, Papyrus Cattaoui (quoted n. 6), pp. 80–83.

41. Meyer, Papyrus Cattaoui (quoted n. 6), p. 81.

42. Meyer, Papyrus Cattaoui (quoted n. 6), p. 81.

43. What is interesting is the fact that testator being a soldier made his will according to rules governing the regular testament, so it is highly probable that he wanted to have a will valid not only during his military service but also after his *missio*. Amelotti, *Il testamento romano* (quoted n. 15), p. 86.

44. The similar example is to be found in Drusilla's dossier (the full list of documents belonging to this dossier see: P. Schubert, *P. Gen.* I 74 et le process de Drusilla, *ZPE* 130, 2000, pp. 211–217, pp. 215–217).

would have been considered a Roman. Dieter Liebs has suggested that Antonia Thermoutha might be a Roman (her *nomen* suggests so)[45] and that the son born of her would have followed his mother's status. According to Liebs, this supposition is justified by the fact that the son was appointed heir in a will composed to be valid also after the father's military service.[46] This is, however, only speculation, for we know that the boy could have acquired citizenship together with his father,[47] thus even if the will was composed in order to serve its purpose also after Silvanus' military discharge, it would have obtained such an effect. And, as illustrated in the previous example, if Silvanus had died during his service, the fact that his son was not a Roman would not prevent testamentary succession. Unfortunately, we cannot be sure whether Silvanus' will took effect, for it is preserved as an original; thus these questions must remain unanswered.

A different example is the famous will of a Roman veteran, Gaius Longinus Castor, who appointed his two slave-women, Marcella and Kleopatra, his heirs, freeing them at the same time. He subsequently distributed his property *via* legacies among the sons of these women (either slaves or already manumitted); he also appoints them as his heirs in case of the death of the heirs in the first degree. Moreover, he manumits his slave-girl leaving her a legacy too. According to James Keenan, these slave-women were Gaius Longinus Castor's concubines, and their children were his offspring.[48] Contrary to the examples discussed above, the will was composed not for a soldier, but for a regular Roman citizen (albeit a veteran). Another difference is that neither the concubines nor the children were explicitly described as such.[49] Gaius Longinus Castor tried to hide this fact in his will by introducing his family as a group of slave men and women. By contrast, another second century Latin will written for a Roman citizen, Caius Hostilius Clemens (*Ch.*L.A X 427 [provenance unknown, 2nd c. AD]) contains *heredis institutio* appointing *liberii mei naturales*,[50] that is, it names the testator's illegitimate children as heirs. However, the papyrus is poorly preserved and the context remains unknown. There are two conclusions that may be drawn from these papyri. First, the illegitimate children appear in their fathers wills, and the fathers do not

---

She was married to a Roman soldier who died leaving a will in which he left his estate to his children as well as he appointed tutors for them (*M. Chr.* 88, l. 24-27 [Arsinoites, AD 128-129]).

45. However, not even the possession of *tria nomina* could be a proof of Roman citizenship, for there is plenty of examples proving that not only Romans had them. A. Mócsy, Die Namen der Diplomempfänger, dans W. Eck, H. Wolff (eds.), *Heer und Integrationspolitik*, Köln, Wien 1986, pp. 437–466.

46. D. Liebs, Das Testament des Antonius Silvanus, römischer Kavallerist in Alexandria bei Ägypten, aus dem Jahr 142 n. Chr., dans K. Märker (ed.), *Festschrift für Weddig Fricke zum 70. Geburtstag*, Freiburg 2000, pp. 113–128, p. 121.

47. See n. 18.

48. J. G. Keenan, The will of Gaius Longinus Castor, *Bulletin of the American Society of Papyrologists* 31 (1994), pp. 101–107.

49. Keenan, The will of Gaius (quoted n. 48), p. 105.

50. However, this adjective could mean biological children as opposed to adopted ones. Rawson, *Spurii* (quoted n. 1), p. 14. On the other hand, there are a fair number of Latin papyri proving that the description *liber naturalis* was applied to extramarital children. One of those is *P. Diog.* 1 (Contrapollonospolis Magna, AD 127), *testatio* composed for an auxiliary soldier, Marcus Lucretius Clemens. He declared his son born of Octavia Tamusta, l. 11-13: *ut possit post honestam missionem suam ad epicrisin suam adprobare filium suum naturalem esse*, 'in order to be able to prove (after his honorable discharge) in *epikrisis* that his son is his natural son'.

seem to be restricted in bequeathing to the advantage of their children, even if those children were not Romans. Second, in legal documents the parents could either describe these children as legitimate offspring, or they could skip underling the blood relationship altogether; thus it is not an easy task to trace extramarital offspring in papyri.

Intestate succession

The positive assumption concerning the rights of extramarital children on the grounds of succession and the relevance of blood bonds in Graeco-Roman Egypt is supported also by sources related to non-testamentary succession. In *PSI* XV 1532 (Oxyrhynchos, AD 100–117) a man declared his property which he had inherited from his brother — who is explicitly described as χρηματιζων μητρὸς τῆς αὐτῆς. The man, related to his brother through illegitimacy, was his sole heir. Also *P. Oxy.* LV 3798 (Oxyrhynchos, AD 144) proves the succession rights of a non-formal family. The document confirms a return of loan: Gaius Veturius Gemellus and Lucia Veturia alias Thermouthion, children of a veteran and Artemis, acknowledged that they received repayment, with interest, of three hundred drachmae that were lent to Agathus Daemon by their mother. The mother died intestate and the declarants were her only heirs. There can be no doubt that children were born during their father's service, that is before he received *ius conubii* towards their mother. Despite this fact, they were their mother's legitimate heirs. An even more intriguing problem is *status civitatis* of the two heirs. According to the editors, it is possible that they were not Roman citizens, for their father, an auxiliary soldier, was discharged after AD 140, when Antoninus Pius deprived auxiliary veterans of the privilege of receiving the citizenship for children born during their service; however, the exact date of Gaius Veturius Gemellus' (the father's) discharge is unknown.[51] The supposition seems correct, for Romans could not inherit after peregrines. Moreover, they did not have any hereditary rights towards their mothers estates until *sc. Orphitianum* (AD 178).[52] Thus the papyrus offers further evidence that, in local legal practice, children (illegitimate or not) were entitled to succession after their parents.

One final text confirming the hereditary rights of extramarital children is *P. Diog.* 18 (Philadelphia, AD 225), a petition requesting the nomination of a tutor. The children in question were the sons of one woman, but each of them had a different father and one was declared *apator*. Moreover, all three sons were non-testamentary heirs of their mother, hence, once again, the status of the children did not affect their rights. Because the document was composed after the *constitutio Antoniniana*, there could be no doubt that it concerned the succession between Romans. It was written after *sc. Orphitianum* which granted *bonorum possessio unde legitimi* (excluding all other persons belonging to this class) to all children, no matter whether they were marital or extramarital, D. 38.17.1.2: *Sed et vulgo quaesiti admittuntur ad matris legitimam hereditatem*, 'But also illegitimate children are admitted to the intestate succession after their mother.'[53]

51. For the discussion on the children's status see the commentary *P. Oxy.* LV 3798: *P. Oxy.* LV, pp. 79–80.
52. *P. Oxy.* LV, p. 80.
53. See also *P.S.* 4.10.1; I. 3.4.3.

Conclusions

Ultimately, the surviving documents are too few to offer a complete picture of the situation of extramarital children with regard to succession in Graeco-Roman Egypt, but some details may nevertheless be inferred. First, it is more than plausible that non-Roman testators who had no marital children and/or spouses could freely bequeath to the advantage of their extramarital offspring, unless it was excluded by contractual provisions. The marital agreements suggest an interesting conclusion: perhaps, at least in the Hellenistic period, illegitimate children were entitled to succession after their parents equally with the legitimate ones; however, this could vary depending on the social group. Second, we can observe that extramarital children played an important role in the wills of women and Roman soldiers. This may also have been the case regarding non-testamentary succession, where illegitimate children were entitled to succession after their mothers and fathers who served in the Roman army. We do not find many documents composed by regular Roman men openly bequeathing something to the advantage of their natural children.

ILLEGITIMACY AND INHERITANCE DISPUTES IN THE LATE ROMAN EMPIRE

Judith Evans Grubbs

In 454 Marcian, emperor in the eastern Roman Empire, sent a law to his praetorian prefect Palladius which has come down to us under the title 'on the Marriages of Senators' (*de matrimoniis senatorum*). Palladius, 'always eager to hold to the correct path of justice in concluding all lawsuits,' had asked Marcian to clear up an ambiguity in a law of the emperor Constantine from more than a century earlier. One particular phrase in Constantine's law had created doubt and confusion and 'the back-and-forth arguing of litigators' (*litigatorum contentio alterna*) who had tried to interpret the unclear language to the benefit of the party they represented, resulting in inconsistent judgments in court cases. In his response to Palladius' request, to be posted where it could 'come to the notice of all,' Marcian intended to put an end to such lawsuits once and for all.[1]

The law of Constantine which had caused such confusion and litigation is found in the Theodosian Code, where it was the third Constantinian law placed under the title 'On Natural Children and their Mothers' (*CTh* 4.6.3, *de naturalibus filiis et matribus eorum*):[2]

> *Senatores seu perfectissimos, vel quos in civitatibus duumviralitas vel quinquennalitas vel flamonii vel sacerdotii provinciae ornamenta condecorant, placet maculam subire infamiae et peregrinos a Romanis legibus fieri, si ex ancilla vel ancillae filia vel liberta vel libertae filia, sive Romana facta seu Latina, vel scaenica vel scaenicae filia, vel ex tabernaria vel ex tabernari filia vel humili vel abiecta vel len-*

1. Marcian, *Novel* 4, given April 4, 454 at Constantinople. Texts of the laws discussed are in Th. Mommsen and P. M. Meyer (eds.), *Theodosiani Libri XVI cum Constitutionibus Sirmonidanis et Leges Novellae ad Theodosianum Pertinentes*, volume 1.2, Berlin 1904, for the Theodosian Code) and volume 2 (for the Sirmondian Constitutions and post-Code 'new laws' between 438-468); P. Krueger (ed.), *Corpus Iuris Ciuilis vol. II: Codex Iustinianus.* Dublin and Zurich 1967, for the Code of Justinian; A. Watson (ed.), *The Digest of Justinian. Latin Text edited by Theodor Mommsen with the aid of Paul Krueger, English translation edited by Alan Watson*, Philadelphia 1985, for the Digest. All translations are my own unless otherwise noted.

2. *CTh* (= *Codex Theodosianus*) 4.6.3, *de naturalibus filiis et matribus eorum* (Mommsen's text reproduced from Y. Lassard and A. Koptev, *The Roman Law Library* [http://webu2.upmf-grenoble.fr]. The first law under this title is lost; of the second only the fragmentary ending is preserved (see below). Cf. also *CJ* (= *Codex Justinianus*) 5.27.1, a slightly changed version which omits the final sentence.

Inheritance, Law and Religions in the Ancient and Mediaeval Worlds, ed. by B. Caseau and S. R. Huebner (Centre de recherche d'Histoire et Civilisation de Byzance, Monographies 45), Paris 2014.

onis vel harenarii filia vel quae mercimoniis publicis praefuit, susceptos filios in numero legitimorum habere voluerint aut proprio iudicio aut nostri praerogativa rescripti, ita ut, quidquid talibus liberis pater donaverit, sive illos legitimos seu naturales dixerit, totum retractum legitimae suboli reddatur aut fratri aut sorori aut patri aut matri. Sed et uxori tali quodcumque datum quolibet genere fuerit vel emptione collatum, etiam hoc retractum reddi praecipimus: ipsas etiam, quarum venenis inficiuntur animi perditorum, si quid quaeritur vel commendatum dicitur, quod his reddendum est, quibus iussimus, aut fisco nostro, tormentis subici iubemus. Sive itaque per ipsum donatum est qui pater dicitur vel per alium sive per suppositam personam sive ab eo emptum vel ab alio siue ipsorum nomine comparatum, statim retractum reddatur quibus iussimus, aut, si non existunt, fisci viribus vindicetur. Quod si existentes et in praesentia rerum constituti agere noluerint pacto vel iureiurando exclusi, totum sine mora fiscus inuadat. Quibus tacentibus et dissimulantibus a defensione fiscali duum mensuum tempora limitentur, intra quae si non retraxerint vel propter retrahendum rectorem provinciae interpellaverint, quidquid talibus filiis uel uxoribus liberalitas impura contulerit, fiscus noster inuadat, donatas vel commendatas res sub poena quadrupli severa quaestione perquirens. Licinniani autem filius, qui fugiens comprehensus est, compedibus vinctus ad gynaecei Carthaginis ministerium deputetur. Lecta xii k. aug. Carthagine Nepotiano et Facundo conss. (21 July 336).

In his law Constantine had forbidden senators, *perfectissimi* (the highest rank of equestrians), the leading members of municipal councils (*duumviri* and *quinqueviri*), and holders of provincial priesthoods to 'consider among the number of legitimate children' offspring born to them from lowborn or disreputable women either during their lifetime or in their will. Men holding those positions who tried to benefit such children were to be penalized by loss of citizenship (they were reduced to the status of *peregrini*, non-citizen foreigners) and by the stain of legal infamy, even if they had previously received permission from the emperor (via an imperial rescript) to recognize the children. Whatever a man had left to these children, whether he called them *legitimi* or *naturales*, was to be given instead to his legitimate offspring or, if he had none, to his siblings or parents. Anything he had given to the children's mother (here called an *uxor*, although from the law's viewpoint such women were not legitimate wives), was also to be taken away; moreover, women who asserted their right to the property, described here as infecting the minds of their men with 'poisons,' were to be tortured.[3] Constantine's law provided a detailed list of the women whose children were forbidden to receive anything from their high-ranking fathers. They included: slavewomen and their daughters, freedwomen and their daughters, actresses (*scaenicae*, 'showgirls') and their daughters, tavern-keepers and their daughters, a 'humble and lowly' (*humilis vel abiecta*) woman, the daughter of a pimp or gladiator, and a woman who sold merchandise in public (*quae mercimoniis publicis praefuit*).

It was the words *humili vel abiecta* that had caused all the uncertainty and litigation that Palladius now asked Marcian to resolve. What exactly did they mean? Had Constantine intended to ban unions between men of rank and poor but freeborn women, and thereby forbid the inheritance rights of children born from those unions? Surely not, said Marcian: 'Who would think that Constantine of renowned memory, when he forbade that the nuptial

3. All of the women listed in the law were either slaves or *humiliores* ('more lowly'), who at this period could be subjected to torture in order to elicit information (or, as here, to force them to surrender what they had been given). *Venena* could refer to magical practices as well as poison.

couches of senators be contaminated by the filth of polluted women, had placed the gifts of fortune before the good things given by nature and had preferred wealth, which the vicissitudes of chance can take away as well as bestow, to free birth (*ingenuitas*) which, if it has once been inborn, cannot be taken away?'[4] Instead, Marcian decreed, the phrase 'humble and lowly' simply repeated and summed up the categories of women already listed: slave women, freed women, actresses and so on. Marcian's reasoning was influenced by new Christian ideas about poverty that had developed in the almost 120 years since Constantine, but he was probably right that poor but respectable women of free birth were not included in Constantine's ban.[5]

It is important to note that Marcian was responding to widespread confusion about the meaning of Constantine's law and who was affected by it. There had been lawsuits, and different judges had given different decisions, leading to appeals that had eventually made their way to the praetorian prefect (who was the final court of appeal in the late Empire) and even to the Emperor himself. Clearly, although the women concerned might be 'humble and lowly,' the men who had children by them were not, and they or their families had the money and influence (both were needed) to pursue the matter up to the highest court. As with other late Roman legislation regarding inheritance and the validity of marriages, Marcian's law was not a spontaneous decree of the emperor, but a response to a specific case (or cases).[6]

The legislation of Constantine and the emperors following him on 'natural' children and their mothers has been much discussed, particularly in the Romanist scholarship of the twentieth century.[7] Here I will focus only on what the laws tell us about conflicts over

4. *Quis arbitretur inclitae recordationis Constantinum, cum geniales senatorios toros contaminari pollutarum mulierum faece prohiberet, fortunae munera bonis naturalibus praetulisse et diuitiis, quae uarietas casuum tam potest adimere quam tribuere, postposuisse ingenuitatem, quae auferri non potest, si semel nata sit?* (MARCIAN *Novel* 4 lines 25-28 in MOMMSEN–MEYER v. 2). Translation from J. EVANS GRUBBS, *Law and Family in Late Antiquity: The Emperor Constantine's Marriage Legislation*, Oxford 1995, pp. 292–293.

5. On new Christian ideas about poverty see P. BROWN, *Through the Eye of a Needle: Wealth, the Fall of Rome, and the Making of Christianity in the West, 350-550 AD*, Princeton 2012. See below on Constantine and freeborn concubines.

6. Recent studies, particularly by Caroline Humfress, have stressed that most fourth and fifth century imperial laws were responses to specific cases. This is clear in the post-*Theodosian Code* laws (such as Marcian's *Novel* 4), whose preambles, setting out the reasons for the law's enactment, have been preserved in full. C. HUMFRESS, Cracking the Codex: Late Roman Legal Practice in Context, *Bulletin of the Institute of Classical Studies* 49, 2006, pp. 241–254. Unfortunately the laws preserved in the Codex Theodosianus were edited by Theodosius' compilers to give only the general gist of the original law, shorn of details of individual cases (although see below on the 'son of Licinnianus' in *CTh* 4.6.2 and 3).

7. E.g. F. M. DE ROBERTIS, La condizione sociale e gli impedimenti al matrimonio nel Basso Impero. *Annali della Facoltà dei Giurisprudenza della Università di Bari* 2, 1939, pp. 45–69; M. SARGENTI, Il diritto privato nella legislazione di Costantino. Problemi e prospettive nella letteratura dell'ultimo trentennio, in *Atti dell'Accademia Romanistica Costantiniana, Convegno I* (= *AARC* I), Florence, 1975, pp. 229–332, at 261–272; C. VAN DE WIEL, La légitimation par mariage subséquent, de Constantin à Justinien. Sa réception sporadique dans le droit byzantin, *RIDA* 25, 1978, pp. 307–350; M. NIZIOLEK, *Legal Effects of Concubinage in Reference to Concubine's Offspring in the Light of Imperial Legislation of the Period of Dominate* (*sic*), Warsaw, 1980 (with review by W. LITEWSKI in *BIDR* 1982, pp. 303–318); M. NAVARRA, Testi Costantiniani in materia di filiazione naturale, *AARC* VII, 1988, pp. 459–475; G. LUCHETTI, *La legittimazione dei figli naturali nelle fonti tardo imperiali e Giustinianee*, Milan, 1990; EVANS GRUBBS, *Law and Family* (quoted n. 4), pp. 283–304; T. A. J. MCGINN, The Social Policy of Emperor Constantine in *Codex Theodosianus* 4,6,3, *Tijdschrift voor Rechtsgeschiedenis* 67, 1999, pp. 57–71; K. HARPER, *Slavery in the Late Roman World AD 275-425*, Cambridge UK 2011, pp. 442–460. This is by no means a complete list.

the inheritance rights of illegitimate children. Although *CTh* 4.6.3 is often described as a marriage law, its real concern was inheritance, specifically the right of senators and others to give during their lifetimes, or leave in their will, property to their children by lowborn women. Amidst all their harsh, prescriptive rhetoric, late Roman laws on the children called *naturales* reveal that there were many men of high rank who desired to benefit their illegitimate children by lowborn women, and who were willing to go to great lengths to see that their children inherited.

Concubines and their offspring before Constantine

Roman law had never recognized marriage between a free person and a slave, and marriage between senators and freedwomen or actresses had been prohibited ever since 18 BCE, when the first emperor Augustus, as part of his program to restore traditional morality and encourage marriage and childbearing, had banned marriage between someone of senatorial status and a former slave. After this a senator (or his son or his grandson) who wanted a monogamous relationship with a freedwoman would have to have her as a concubine, unless he had received permission to marry her by imperial *indulgentia*.[8] Before Constantine, however, men below senatorial status could legally marry freedwomen, and we know of many marriages between men and their former slaves both from the legal sources and from funerary inscriptions. But for men who held a position of social dignity, marriage to a freedwoman would not be considered appropriate, because there was too great a disparity in status and enslavement carried with it a certain moral and social 'stain' (*macula*) that would shame an elite family.[9] Thus long before Constantine's law, the women it lists (those of servile origins or inappropriate occupation) had been considered unsuitable marriage partners for men holding imperial priesthoods or provincial or municipal offices, and epigraphic evidence shows that often such men, even though they could have married a freedwoman, preferred to live in concubinage with her instead.[10]

In Roman terms, *concubinatus* was a long-term monogamous relationship between a man and a woman of lower rank.[11] Although married men might and often did have casual sexual relations with their slaves, this was not the same thing as keeping a concubine. A fragment of another law of Constantine said that a man could not have a wife and a concubine at the same time, but this merely codified what had already been Roman practice.[12] The most common

8. *Dig.* (= *Digest*) 23.2.44 pr (Paulus, 1st book on the *lex Julia et Papia*); *Dig.* 23.2.31 (Ulpian, 6th book on the *lex Julia et Papia*). The Augustan marriage legislation is referred to collectively as the *lex Julia et Papia*.

9. On the the *macula servitutis* see H. Mouritsen, *The Freedman in the Roman World*, Cambridge UK 2011, pp. 10–35; also Harper, *Slavery* (quoted n. 7), pp. 203–348 on the dishonor of slavery.

10. S. Treggiari, *Concubinae*, *Papers of the British School at Rome* 49, 1981, pp. 59–81.

11. On *concubinatus* pre-Constantine, see Treggiari, *Concubinae* (quoted n. 10),; B. Rawson, Roman Concubinage and other *de facto* Marriages, *TAPA* 104, 1974, pp. 279–305; and T. A. J. McGinn, Concubinage and the *lex Iulia* on Adultery, *TAPA* 121, 1991, pp. 335–375. For the later Empire see A. Arjava, *Women and Law in Late Antiquity*, Oxford, 1996, pp. 205–217. Concubinage with one's own slave was also not uncommon, but should be distinguished from more casual exploitation of female slaves, since Roman *concubinatus* was supposed to be a monogamous, albeit non-marital, relationship.

12. *CJ* 5.26.1 (*ad populum*, 326). This may be from the now missing *CTh* 4.6.1; see below.

and acceptable type of *concubinatus* was between a man and his own freedwoman (*liberta*). The Roman jurist Ulpian, writing in the early third century, even thought that it was more suitable for a man to have his *liberta* as a concubine than to marry her.[13] Moreover — and this is relevant for understanding the impact of Constantine's law — whereas Roman law forbade gifts between spouses during the duration of a marriage, gifts to a concubine were valid before Constantine.[14]

A relationship with a concubine might come before marriage, when a young man wanted a steady sexual partner but was not yet ready for the financial responsibilities, or after the death of a wife, if he already had adult children and did not want to complicate the succession. The young (and not yet saintly) St. Augustine is an example of the first situation; the emperor Vespasian an example of the second. Sometimes a man might forgo marriage entirely to live with a concubine, as did Libanius, the fourth century teacher of rhetoric.[15] This last group, men who never married, were the most likely to have illegitimate children by a concubine whom they would want to make their heirs, an inheritance strategy that Constantine now outlawed.

In Roman law, only legitimate children were *sui heredes* — 'automatic heirs' who inherited if he died without a will and who had to be included in the will in order for it to be valid. Illegitimate children would only receive something if their father specifically bequeathed it to them in his will. If a man had other legitimate children from a legal marriage, he would be unlikely to make an illegitimate child his heir, although he might leave the child a legacy. If he had no legitimate children, however, he might well want to make his illegitimate child his heir, or one of his heirs.[16] Adoption (strictly speaking, adrogation) was even possible, although a patron/father would need permission from the emperor, which would not be granted unless there were a good reason, for instance that the man was elderly and had no legitimate children — in other words, needed a heir.[17] If there were legitimate offspring, they might contest a will which favored an illegitimate child.[18]

We know of a case from around the year 200 CE where a concubine's child was made co-heir along with a legitimate granddaughter. The father, Cocceius Cassianus, was a senator and evidently a widower, who was said to have 'loved' his concubine Rufina 'with full honor' (*honore pleno dilexerat*). Cassianus called Rufina's daughter his *alumna* (foster child), but it was evident that she was his illegitimate (*vulgo quaesita*) daughter. When he died leaving his estate to both his granddaughter and to Rufina's daughter as co-heirs, the right of the illegitimate girl to inherit was challenged, probably by the granddaughter. The case came

13. *Dig.* 25.7.1pr; cf. Marcellus, *Dig.* 23.2.41.1, who thought that unlike other concubines, the *liberta* could be said to have the honor of a *materfamilias*.

14. Treggiari, *Concubinae* (quoted n. 10) pp. 62–63; E. Karabélias, Rapports juridiques entre concubins dans le droit romain tardif (donations, actio furti, successions) in *AARC* VIII, Naples, 1990, pp. 439–453.

15. On Vespasian, see Suetonius, *Divus Vesp.* 3. For Augustine and Libanius, see below.

16. J. Gardner, *Family and Familia in Roman Law and Life*, Oxford 1998, pp. 259–269.

17. Cf. *CJ* 8.47.3 (286), where Diocletian and Maximian deny permission to the petitioner Marcianus for lack of good reason. J. F. Gardner, The Adoption of Roman Freedmen, *Phoenix* 43, 1989, pp. 236–257, at 248–252. In the Republic, permission would be granted by the *centuria curiata*.

18. Under the *lex Falcidia*, at least one fourth of the estate had to go to the *sui heredes* by will; otherwise they could bring a suit of 'undutiful will.'

before the emperors Septimius Severus and Caracalla (reigned 197-211).[19] The matter was complicated by the fact that Rufina the concubine was freeborn, and so she could have married Cassianus legally. In this she was unusual: more often, concubines were of servile origin, or perhaps a freedwoman's daughter who was freeborn but still of low social class. It was because Cassianus could have married Rufina that his failure to do so rendered the relationship suspicious: was it really *concubinatus*, an acceptable union between two people of disparate status that simply lacked the honor and benefits of legal marriage, or was it *stuprum*, the term for illicit sex (which included not only adultery but also sexual relations with a respectable unmarried woman)? If so, it would be inappropriate, even immoral, to allow her child to inherit. However, the emperors evidently considered the relationship to have been *concubinatus* rather than *stuprum*, and the daughter of Rufina (and clearly, of Cassianus also) was able to inherit her share under Cassianus' will.

As an *ingenua*, Rufina ranked above the slaveborn *liberta* who was the preferred kind of concubine, but she was presumably not one of the *honestiores* (who would include decurions and their families and above, but not freeborn plebeians).[20] She may have been the daughter of a former slave, and thus of low enough birth that she would be considered unsuitable as a senator's wife. The disparity in status between Cassianus and Rufina, and the fact that Cassianus had been married and had at least one child earlier in life, evidently made concubinage a better alternative. It may be that Cassianus had entered the relationship not intending to sire any more potential heirs, but his affection for Rufina, and for her daughter, made him change his mind. Whatever the case, ambiguity regarding the nature of the relationship remained.[21]

Interestingly, this was not the only time that Septimius Severus was asked to rule on the nature of a union between a senator and a woman of lower rank. The senator Pontius Paulinus had given gifts to a freedwoman with whom he was living, and the question was raised whether he had married her in contravention of the Augustan law or had her as a concubine. The emperor decided that she was a concubine, 'because she had not been considered with the *affectio* of a wife' and therefore she could receive the gifts. It is noteworthy that Ulpian, the jurist who relates this case, disapproved of the emperor's decision.[22] His (minority) opinion adumbrates the later legal attitude of Constantine, under whose law neither Rufina's daughter nor Paulinus' concubine eould have received anything.

The point I would like to make here is that these third century cases from the *Digest* show that the right of a high-ranking man to benefit his concubine or her child by him was being

19. *Dig.* 34.9.16.1 (Papinian, 8th book of *Responsa*); see McGinn, Concubinage (quoted n. 11), pp. 354–357; and Gardner, *Family and Familia* (quoted n. 16), pp. 258–259 (who assumes that it was the granddaughter who challenged the will). For the difference between *vulgo quaesiti* and *naturales*, see below.

20. We do not actually know anything about Rufina's status except that she was freeborn. Scholars generally assume that she was of low birth, but see McGinn, Concubinage (quoted n. 11), p. 357 n.95. *Dig.* 25.7.3 (Marcian, 12th book of *Institutiones*) says that a lowborn (*obscuro loco nata*) *ingenua* may be a concubine, but many scholars doubt that the passage as we have it is completely pre-Justinianic.

21. On the ambiguity surrounding the appropriateness of a freeborn concubine, see Treggiari, *Concubinae* (quoted n. 10), pp. 71–77.

22. *Dig.* 24.1.3.1 (Ulpian, 32nd book on Sabinus). *Affectio* here means not 'affection' but *affectio maritalis*, the feeling one has toward a spouse, on which see Treggiari, *Concubinae* (quoted n. 10), pp. 62–64. Ulpian's was a minority opinion: ibid. p. 75.

challenged more than a century before Constantine's law, probably by the man's relatives who resented the loss of any of his property to a non-marital relationship. How often such challenges arose is unknown, but the two Severan cases suggest they were not uncommon. Inheritance disputes were the bread and butter of Roman law, and when a wealthy estate was at stake, interested parties would be unlikely to ignore what they felt was an unjust will.

Constantine's Legislation

Two laws of Constantine that are not connected with the legislation of 336 repeat the classical legal doctrine that the child of a free man and a slave woman is a slave. They are of interest because they refer to particular situations and, although no names are given, they seem to have been responding to actual cases.

The first of these laws, dated 319 (at a time when Constantine was emperor only in the West), declares that 'Although it seems unworthy for men who do not possess any rank (*dignitas*) to descend to sordid marriages (*conubia*) with slave women, it is nevertheless not at all prohibited by the laws; but marriage (*conubium*) with servile persons is not possible and from a union (*contubernium*) of this type slaves are born.'[23] The law goes on to condemn decurions (town councillors) — men of local *dignitas* — who have fled their municipal responsibilities and taken refuge on the estates of a powerful man, where they are cohabiting with the estate owner's slave. Such a union is not *conubium* but *contubernium*. The decurion and the slavewoman are both to be harshly punished (the decurion by deportation to an island and confiscation of his property, the slavewoman by condemnation to the mines), but this is because the man has abandoned his legal obligations to his *curia* and not because of the non-marital relationship which, as the law says, is not in itself illegal. The second law, from 331, rejects claims to freedom by children of a freeborn man and his slavewoman, even if they have lived for sixteen years in freedom with their parents (*parentibus*, which here must signify the free father as well as the slave mother). 'For by common law (*ius commune*) it is necessary that a child follow its mother's condition, so that, even if a slavewoman has ascended to her master's bed, she bears to her lord not the offspring of free men, but of slaves.'[24] This law was evidently in response to an inquiry (from Junius Bassus, praetorian prefect in the west) about whether such children could claim freedom by the prescription of time (*praescriptio temporis*) according to the Roman idea of *favor libertatis*.[25] The answer was no, since there had been no preceding presumption of freedom — in other words, the father must have known his children were slave-born, and could have freed them legally. The query probably arose from a case where a man died without freeing his *naturales* children, and after his death they tried to claim not only freedom but also his estate.

23. *CTh* 12.1.6 (to Patroclus, office unknown, 319); Evans Grubbs, *Law and Family* (quoted n. 4), pp. 278–280.

24. *CTh* 4.8.7 (to the praetorian prefect Junius Bassus, 331); Evans Grubbs, *Law and Family* (quoted n. 4), pp. 280–283.

25. N. Lenski, Constantine and Slavery: *Libertas* and the Fusion of Roman and Christian Values, *AARC* XVIII, 2012, pp. 235–260, at 252–254.

Neither the law of 319 nor the law of 331 conflicted with the classical Roman legal distinctions between slave and free birth. Both laws imply, however, that there were people who did not recognize the rule that a child of a free man and a slave woman (even his own slave woman) could not be their father's heirs. Constantine's law of 336 took this rule even further, by expanding the number of children who could not inherit.

Constantine innovated in three important ways. First, he extended the ancient Augustan ban on marriage between those of senatorial status and former slaves to apply also to the provincial and municipal elites, a considerably larger group, and at the same time he expanded the category of women whom such elites were forbidden to marry to include the daughters of freedwomen and other women of low status who had not been explicitly covered before.[26] This expansion of the Augustan marriage restrictions is not explicitly stated in *CTh* 4.6.3, but it is assumed: if the children of such unions may not be considered legitimate then *ipso facto* the unions are not *iustum matrimonium*. One of Constantine's two earlier laws on natural children and their mothers must have explicitly banned marriages between men of rank and lowborn women. Of these, *CTh* 4.6.1 is entirely lost and we have only the ending of *CTh* 4.6.2, which like *CTh* 4.6.3 was read out at Carthage in 336. The original law may have been from 326, a year which saw Constantine enact several other measures concerning marriage and adultery.[27]

Under Constantine's legislation, a slavewoman (*ancilla*) and her daughter (*ancillae filia*), both of whom as slaves would always have been ineligible for marriage to any free man, are listed along with a freedwoman (*liberta*), who would not have been able to marry a senator (or a near descendant of a senator) in the male line under the Augustan law but could marry any free man outside the senatorial order, and the daughter of a freedwoman (*libertae filia*), who (assuming she was born after her mother's manumission), would have been an *ingenua* and able to marry anyone, including a senator.[28] Actors and their children had also been forbidden to marry members of the senatorial order under the Augustan legislation. Prostitutes and pimps (*lenones*) were prohibited from marrying all freeborn people (including, of course, senators) under earlier law; Constantine extends the ban to include their daughters.[29] Tavern-keepers (*tabernariae*) and their daughters, gladiators' daughters, and women who sold merchandise in public would likely be slaves or former slaves also, but the lawmaker appears more concerned with their or their parents' sordid occupation. Taverns and inns (*cauponae*) were linked in both the popular and legal mind with prostitution, and like prostitutes, gladiators were *personae infames*.[30] The inclusion of women in charge of public merchandise might appear incongruous, but they could also be associated with prostitution and Roman elite society

26. McGinn, Social Policy (quoted n. 7).

27. de Robertis, La condizione sociale (quoted n. 7) p. 52; Evans Grubbs, *Law and Family* (quoted n. 4), pp. 296–299. Harper, *Slavery* (quoted n. 7), pp. 443–448 sees *CTh* 4.6.1, *CJ* 5.26.1, and the law referred to by Zeno in *CJ* 5.27.5 (see n. 34) as all part of a large body of legislation on marriage, adultery and concubinage of 326 (on which see Evans Grubbs, *Law and Family* (quoted n. 4), pp. 350–352.

28. The law qualifies the *liberta* as 'either having been made a Roman or a Latin.' This refers to the rules for fully legal manumission under the *lex Aelia Sentia* (of Augustan date): a woman not freed according to the law (for instance, one freed before she reached age 30) would become a Latin, not a Roman citizen.

29. *Dig.* 23.2.44.1-7 (Paulus, 1st book on the *lex Julia et Papia*).

30. *Dig.* 23.2.43 pr.-9 (Ulpian, 1st book on the *lex Julia et Papia*); Evans Grubbs, *Law and Family* (quoted n. 4), pp. 290–291.

looked down in general on banausic pursuits, which were thought unfitting for free people. Such women, like tavern-keepers, were 'analogues' for prostitutes.[31] The *humilis vel abiecta* woman is mentioned after *tabernariae* and their daughters; conceivably the terms might modify only *tabernaria* and *tabernari filia*, but both ancient and modern commentators on the law have argued over whether they constitute a discrete category.[32] Essentially, all these women, if not slaves or former slaves themselves, were closely associated with slave activities and the sexual availability of slaves.[33] Thus Marcian was correct in his interpretation that Constantine had not intended to ban marriage with freeborn women of good behavior. In fact, another law of Constantine, now lost, had said that if a man married his *freeborn* concubine, any children they had had before the marriage would be legitimated. This is the first instance in Roman law of post-natal legitimation (as opposed to the later adrogation of an illegitimate child).[34]

Secondly, Constantine went further than an expansion of Augustus' prohibition of marriage: by forbidding a man to give anything to such a concubine or her children, he penalized the long-standing custom of concubinage between high-ranking men and lowborn women (which Augustus' legislation had implicitly allowed) and took away the man's right to benefit his concubine and her children financially. Constantine's third innovation was the most far-reaching and had the longest-lasting effect: he redefined the meaning of the term *naturales*.

In classical law, the word *naturalis* when used to describe a child had several meanings.[35] It could be used to denote a man's biological children as opposed to those whom he adopted, or children whom he had emancipated from *patria potestas*, and who had then been adopted into another family but retained ties with their natal family. But jurists also used the word *naturalis* to refer to certain illegitimate, slaveborn children. Slaves legally had no parents or other relations, but Roman jurists realized that former slaves did have biological kinship ties; for instance, Roman incest rules forbidding marriage between a man and his daughter were applied to former slaves too.[36] There were two kinds of slaveborn *filii naturales*:

31. T. A. J. McGinn, The Legal Definition of Prostitute in Late Antiquity, *Memoirs of the American Academy in Rome* 42, 1997, pp. 73–116 on legal and social analogues for prostitutes. Cf. *Sententiae Pauli* 2.24.11 (a legal text more or less contemporary with Constantine's law).

32. I do not enter here into the ancient question of the meaning of *humili vel abiecta* (the subject of the lawsuits Marcian's law was intended to solve and a topic of debate among 20th century Romanists). Evans Grubbs, *Law and Family* (quoted n. 4), pp. 292–293 and McGinn, Legal Definition (quoted n. 31), pp. 82–85 for earlier literature.

33. Cf. M. Morabito, Droit romain et réalités sociales de la sexualité servile in J. Poumarède and J.-P. Royer (eds.), *Droit, histoire et sexualité*, Lille 1987, pp. 3–20, on 'la persistance au Bas-Empire d'une solide mentalité esclavagiste' (p. 11) in this law.

34. We know of this law only through a law of Zeno (*CJ* 5.27.5) that revived it in 477. The original ruling may have been part of the missing *CTh* 4.6.1 (see above). Both Constantine's law and Zeno's revival of it were temporary measures, meant only for those who were already living in concubinage with a freeborn woman.

35. On the use of *naturalis* in the pre-Constantinian jurists, see H. J. Wolff, The Background of the Post-Classical Legislation on Illegitimacy, *Seminar* 3, 1945, pp. 21–45; M. Niziolek, Meaning of the Phrase *Liberi Naturales* in Roman Law Sources up to Constantine's Reign, *RIDA* 22, 1975, pp. 317–344; and Luchetti, *La legittimazione* (quoted n. 7), pp. 1–64. See also E. Hermann-Otto, *Ex Ancilla Natus: Untersuchungen zu den 'Hausgeborenen' Sklaven und Sklavinnen im Westen des römischen Kaiserreiches*, Stuttgart 1994, pp. 83–88 for careful distinction of the different types of *naturales*, especially slaveborn, with many legal and epigraphic examples.

36. *Dig.* 23.2.14.2 (Paulus, 35th book *ad Edictum*), where a *naturalis* (i.e. slaveborn) freedman father cannot marry his *vulgo quaesita* (freeborn but illegitimate) daughter; cf. *Dig.* 23.2.8 (Pomponius, 5th book *ad Sabinum*): such bans are due to *mores*, not *leges*.

1) children born to freedpeople before their manumission; 2) children of a slave woman and a free man, usually the mother's master.

A close reading of the pre-Constantinian legal sources reveals that in all cases where the word *naturalis* is used in regard to illegitimacy (rather than to biological relationship before adoption or emancipation), the *naturalis* was born a slave.[37] Different terms were used for the children of non-marital relationships when the mother was free at the time of the child's birth: these were designated *spurii* or *vulgo quaesiti*, words that imply the product of a promiscuous relationship.[38] This pre-Constantinian distinction between *naturales*, who were slaveborn, and *spurii*, who were freeborn illegitimates, has gone largely unnoticed by legal scholars. In the pre-Constantinian period the mother of a *spurius* might be a concubine (often a freedwoman) in a monogamous, non-marital union with the child's father, and no moral opprobrium attached to the children themselves.[39] Although *spurii* were at a disadvantage compared to legitimate children because they did not have a legal *paterfamilias* and therefore did not have automatic inheritance rights from their (biological, not legal) father as *sui heredes*, their status as freeborn (*ingenui*) placed them above *naturales* in the Roman legal and social hierarchy. *Naturales*, as slaveborn, would even after manumission bear the *macula servitutis*. They were also barred from holding public office, specifically that of decurion.[40] *Spurii* were not, although legitimate candidates would be preferred to them.[41] Before Constantine, both *naturales* (assuming they had been freed) and *spurii* could receive gifts from their biological father during his lifetime or in his will, though they would not be made heirs except in the absence of legitimate children. The *Digest* records several cases of illegitimate children receiving legacies or even being made co-heirs. Often the children were *naturales* conceived in slavery; usually they were children of the testator and his slave.[42]

Constantine's law conflates the terms *naturales* and *spurii*, and treats all children of relationships between the men and women listed in *CTh* 4.6.3 in the same way, regardless of their birth status or that of their mothers.[43] In classical law, children born while their mother was

37. It is supported by epigraphic evidence, especially from Rome, where *naturales* are clearly slaveborn and *spurii* (designated as 'son/daughter of Spurius') are freeborn but fatherless.

38. *Dig.* 1.5.23 (Modestinus, 1st book of *Pandecta*); Gaius, *Inst.* (= *Institutiones*) 1.64.

39. On the legal and social attitude toward *spurii/vulgo quaesiti* before Constantine, see B. Rawson, *Spurii* and the Roman View of Illegitimacy, *Antichthon* 23, 1989, pp. 10–41. An exception to this lack of moral stigma might be the children of incestuous unions (described by the jurists as *nefariae nuptiae*), although even in that case the children were not penalized until late antiquity: see P. Moreau, Rome: The Invisible Children of Incest, in V. Dasen and T. Späth, eds., *Children, Memory and Family Identity in Roman Culture*, Oxford 2010, pp. 311–329.

40. Under the *lex Visellia* of 24 CE: *CJ* 9.21.1 (Tetrarchy, 300? CE); Mouritsen, *The Freedman* (quoted n. 9), pp. 73–74. There were some public roles available to freedmen, particularly that of Augustalis.

41. *Dig.* 50.2.3.2 (Ulpian, 3rd book *de Officio Proconsulis*); cf. *Dig.* 50.2.6 pr (Papinian, 1st book of *Responsa*); *Dig.* 50.2.9 pr (Paulus, 1st book of *Decreta*). The question of the eligibility of *spurii* for curial office seems to have arisen often, and was clearly still relevant in Justinian's time, as the inclusion of these passages in the *Digest* shows.

42. *Dig.* 28.6.45 (Paulus, 12th book of *Responsa*); *Dig.* 40.5.40 pr. (Paulus, 15th book of *Responsa*); *Dig.* 42.8.17.1 (Julian, 49th book of *Digesta*). Of course, if a father made no provision for an illegitimate child, he or she had no legal claim.

43. However, the classical use of *naturalis* to denote a legitimately conceived biological child is still found in postclassical epitomes of classical sources: see Luchetti, *La legittimazione* (quoted n. 7), pp. 34–43. The term *spurius* is also used in late Roman pre-Justinianic sources to describe children of other kinds of non-marital unions: e.g., *CTh* 4.12.3 (320 or 326); *CTh* 3.12.2 (355).

in slavery would be *naturales*, but children of a freedwoman concubine (assuming they were born after she had been manumitted) would be freeborn *spurii*, not *naturales*. In Constantine's law and in later legislation following on it, all children of the women listed are considered *naturales*. Just as their mothers, even if not slaveborn themselves, are associated with the activities and sexual availability of slaves, so their children are considered on the same level as those born in slavery. Attempts by their father to pass them off as *legitimi* or to obtain permission from the emperor to adrogate them or make them heirs, are firmly rejected.[44]

Constantine's law was intended to raise the dignity of the new elite that he had created, especially in the east, with the foundation of Constantinople and the expansion of the imperial bureaucracy throughout the Empire.[45] The great increase in positions available within the imperial government (including far more provincial governorships after Constantine's predecessor Diocletian divided up existing provinces) and the establishment of a second Senate in Constantinople created opportunities for many 'new men,' especially in the eastern Empire.[46] These men came primarily from the curial elites and included those whose origins and previous occupations would have rendered them unsuitable for high status offices.[47] Ablabius, Constantine's praetorian prefect and right-hand man, was of quite undistinguished birth and had begun his career on the staff of the governor of Crete. Supposedly one of his mother's relations was the proprietress of a tavern (though one of the more expensive sort) and also practiced as a midwife.[48] Optatus, consul in 334 and Constantine's first appointment to the newly revived rank of patrician, was even said to be the son of a tavern-keeper's daughter and to have gotten his start as tutor to the son of Licinius, Constantine's one-time co-emperor and rival.[49] These biographical details come from sources hostile to Ablabius and Optatus,

44. NAVARRA, Testi Costantiniani (quoted n. 7), pp. 468–475, thinks Constantine did not prohibit the possibility of *adrogatio* via imperial rescript for the children of *CTh* 4.6.3; it was only when the fathers tried to pass them off as legitimate without permission from the emperor or obtained a rescript through fraudulent means that they were absolutely forbidden to give the children anything. I do not agree; on the contrary, all personal rescripts were to be rejected. This doesn't mean that men with influence or patrons at court could not get a special exception: see below on the case of Libanius.

45. SARGENTI, Il diritto private (quoted n. 7), pp. 268–271; EVANS GRUBBS, *Law and Family* (quoted n. 4), pp. 287–289; MCGINN, Social Policy (quoted n. 7).

46. P. HEATHER, New Men for new Constantines? Creating an imperial elite in the eastern Mediterranean, in P. MAGDALINO, ed., *New Constantines: The Rhythm of Imperial Renewal in Byzantium, 4th–13th Centuries*, Aldershot 1994, pp. 11–33.

47. EVANS GRUBBS, Law and Family (quoted n. 4), pp. 287–289. For the social origins of the early senators of Constantinople see Libanius, *Oratio* 42, written in defense of Libanius' secretary Thalassius, whose application to join the Senate in Constantinople had been denied on the grounds of his father's occupation (owner of a shield-making factory). On this speech see P. PETIT, Les sénateurs de Constantinople dans l'oeuvre de Libanius, *L'antiquité classique* 26, 1957, pp. 347–382, and A. F. NORMAN, *Antioch as a Centre of Hellenic Culture as Observed by Libanius*, Liverpool 2000, pp. 145–167.

48. Libanius, *Or.* 42.23; Eunapius, *Vitae Philosophorum* 463-464 in W. C. WRIGHT, ed., *Philostratus and Eunapius: Lives of the Sophists*, Cambridge, MA and London 1921 (reprinted 1968), pp. 385–389. Eunapius was extremely hostile toward Ablabius, who had brought about the death of Sopater, a Neoplatonist theurgist.

49. Libanius, *Or.* 42.23, see also NORMAN, *Antioch* (quoted n. 47). One of Libanius' targets in *Or.* 42 is Optatus' nephew and namesake, a senator under Theodosius I and Arcadius, who had blackballed Thalassius' application to the Senate in Constantinople (n. 47). For doubts about the reliability of Libanius in this highly polemical speech, see R. A. KASTER, *Guardians of Language: The Grammarian and Society in Late Antiquity*, Berkeley and Los Angeles 1988, pp. 419–421.

and should be taken with a grain of salt, but it is not coincidental that they see kinship with a tavern-keeper as automatically disqualifying someone from a position of honor; this reflected a long-held elite prejudice that is also found in Constantine's law.[50] In any case, it is clear that the numbers of senators grew enormously in the years after the foundation of Constantinople, and that the senatorial elite in the fourth century (more so in the east than in the west) owed more to imperial patronage and personal wealth than to distinguished lineage.

Ironically, according to a number of ancient and modern writers, Constantine himself was the product of a quasi-marital union between his father Constantius and the lowborn Helena, and his first-born son Crispus may also have been a concubine's child. Scholars have long debated whether Helena, who according to Ambrose had once been a *stabularia* (the social equivalent of a *tabernaria*) was wife or concubine, and there has been similar uncertainty over whether Constantine's relationship with Crispus' mother Minervina was legal marriage or concubinage. The evidence is ambiguous and contradictory and has been examined at great length by modern scholars.[51] But as we have seen, such ambiguity and uncertainty existed also in Roman legal debates before Constantine. It all depended on the relative status of the two partners and on their intentions (or at least the man's intention) in entering the relationship — as far as such intentions could be determined by third parties.[52] Moreover, the nature of a relationship could change over time: *concubinatus* might become marriage if the partners began to regard themselves as married (as long as there were no legal impediments), but on the other hand, if a man married to a lowborn woman were elevated to senatorial rank, what had been considered a socially acceptable marriage might become unacceptable and be perceived as *concubinatus*, particularly by those without first-hand knowledge of the man's intentions.[53] This is in fact what seems to have happened in the case of Helena, and perhaps also Minervina (though very little is known about her or her status). After Constantius was named Maximian's Caesar and elevated to the Tetrarchy, his marriage to the lowborn Helena would no longer have been appropriate or politically expedient, and later writers (as well as many modern scholars) would understand it to have been concubinage, especially as Constantius then married Theodora, the daughter of Maximian's wife. Similarly, Constantine, whether after Minervina's death or after separation from her, also made a dynastic marriage with Maximian's daughter Fausta in 307. Whatever the nature of their relationship before the elevation of her partner, in retrospect Helena (and probably Minervina) was perceived as a concubine. Just so would unions between those who advanced socially and politically under Constantine and lowborn women be seen as inappropriate and degrading, and the women's children would be considered unsuitable to follow in their father's footsteps.

50. Indeed, Libanius and Eunapius may have included this detail to show (subtly) that Constantine did not apply his own legal standards to his friends and appointees.

51. On the relationships and the still on-going debate about the status of Helena and Minervina, see EVANS GRUBBS, *Law and Family* (quoted n. 4), pp. 306–307 and scholars cited there. Good recent treatment of the evidence and useful family tree in E. HERMANN-OTTO, *Konstantin der Grosse*, Darmstadt, 2009, pp. 134–139 and 202-203. Helena as *stabularia*: Ambrose, *de Obitu Theodosiani* 42.

52. And this could be quite difficult: see TREGGIARI, *Concubinae* (quoted n. 10), p. 63.

53. According to Justinian, the early third-century jurist Ulpian had wondered whether the elevation to senatorial status of a man married to his own freedwoman would result in the marriage's dissolution (*CJ* 5.4.28, to the praetorian prefect Johannes, 531 or 532).

Like Augustus 350 years earlier, Constantine was trying to impose social and moral standards on his new aristocracy, and to ensure that the children of current office-holders, who were expected to follow their fathers in taking on curial or provincial duties, were of appropriate birth status. An additional goal may have been to cut down on litigation regarding the inheritance rights of concubines and their children; as we saw above, such litigation clearly occurred when the man involved was wealthy and of high rank. Constantine's law would have had little impact on the unions of those below curial status, who had little property to leave and were unlikely to infiltrate the upper ranks of imperial society, although evidently *humiliores* of substance would have been affected had anyone wanted to challenge their wills.[54] It was not a moral measure intended to discourage concubinage and illegitimacy, but an attempt to prevent the property of Constantine's new elite (many of whom had benefited from imperial largesse) from passing into the hands of their lowborn children or (especially) the children's mother.[55] This ban on benefiting *naturales*, as they were now called, would have caused more distress to both the fathers and their children than a law (like that of Augustus) that simply prohibited legal marriage.

The penalties for disobeying the law were severe: not only were any gifts or bequests made to natural children and their mothers to be confiscated and given to legitimate family members, but a man of rank who tried to benefit his illegitimate family lost his social and legal position, and his lowborn concubine could be tortured. If legitimate heirs kept quiet about the illicit legacies or passed on gifts to the illegitimate children (probably through *fideicommissa*, trusts), the property was to be taken by the imperial fisc. This suggests that legitimate family members, such as the man's parents or siblings, or perhaps family friends, might actually collude in passing on property to his natural children. If anything, Constantine's law would have increased inheritance disputes within families, as some legitimate heirs could challenge or denounce attempts to benefit illegitimate relatives, and would also encourage informers — long the bane of elite Roman society.[56]

At the end of Constantine's law, reference is made to a certain base-born 'son of Licinnianus' who had managed to achieve a position of rank through the use of an imperial rescript, but had been captured while fleeing, forced back into his original status, and was to be put to work in the imperial weaving mills at Carthage. This son of Licinianus (*sic*) appears also in the fragmentary *CTh* 4.6.2, enacted less than three months earlier, which reveals that this man had undeservedly 'ascended the height of *dignitas* by means of a most sacred rescript': that is, despite his low (evidently slave) birth he had achieved a position of honor after petitioning the emperor and receiving a favorable reply. The culprit was to be deprived of his property, 'whipped and

54. Harper, *Slavery* (quoted n. 7), pp. 452–453, believes that in addition to the measures in *CTh* 4.6.3 aimed specifically at the senatorial, provincial and municipal elites, Constantine (in another law, now lost) banned all men from passing on their property to illegitimate children. It is true that the truncated versions of the post-Constantinian laws preserved in the Theodosian and Justinianic Codes speak more generally of the illegality of property transfers to *naturales*, but the full version of Marcian's *Novel* 4 and Justinian's *Novel* 89 indicate that the laws were not concerned about those below curial rank, who would have been *humiliores* like the women they lived with. Moreover, the sanctions against benefiting *naturales* would only come into play if a third party (presumably a relative but perhaps an unrelated informer) brought a legal challenge.

55. Navarra, Testi Costantiniani (quoted n. 7), contra earlier scholars who saw *CTh* 4.6.3 as a general ban on concubinage.

56. Cf. Tacitus, *Annales* 3.25-28 on the Augustan legislation and informers.

bound with fetters' and reduced to his original status.[57] Just who this son of Licinnianus was and what connection, if any, he had with Constantine's former co-ruler and enemy Licinius (who had been put to death after his defeat by Constantine twelve years earlier, along with his legitimate son) is obscure. If the emperor Licinius had an illegitimate son, he is otherwise unknown. Possibly the 'son of Licinnianus' in Constantine's laws was an impostor claiming connections with the former emperor, like the false Neros who had arisen in past centuries. But it is more likely that he was a different person altogether, who had managed to obtain an imperial rescript allowing him to inherit from his father despite his slave birth. It may have been this particularly shocking case of usurpation of status that inspired Constantine's harsh measure in the first place.[58] The punishment of internment in the Carthaginian weaving mills and the fact that both *CTh* 4.6.3 and its predecessor *CTh* 4.6.2 were read aloud at Carthage (evidently in the forum or perhaps in the *curia*, where the town council would meet) indicates that the son of Licinnianus was a native of the area, which would rule out any child of the former eastern emperor Licinius.[59] Without the full text of *CTh* 4.6.2 or *CTh* 4.6.3 (whose preface, which would have explained the reason for the law's enactment, was omitted in the abbreviated version of the law preserved in the *Codex Theodosianus*) we cannot know what prompted the emperor to act. However, the 'son of Licinnianus,' whoever he was, is a rare example of a reference to an individual in the *Codex Theodosianus*, whose compilers were instructed to delete unnecessary verbiage and leave only the generalized gist of the laws they collected.[60]

Case Study: Libanius

Apart from the fragmentary papyri records of Greco-Roman Egypt, ancient historians do not have the sort of archival material or legal case transcripts available to those who study later periods.[61] However, we do know in detail of one particular fourth-century case, that of the famous teacher of rhetoric, Libanius of Antioch, who fought very hard for the right to pass on his property to his illegitimate son Cimon. Libanius belonged to the curial class of Antioch, and although his profession gave him immunity from the duties and burdens usually expected of *curiales*, as a member of the local elite he was affected by Constantine's law. After his fiancée (and cousin) died, Libanius never married, but instead entered a monogamous union with a slaveborn concubine, which lasted until her death almost four decades later.[62]

57. *CTh* 4.6.2, read at Carthage (like *CTh* 4.6.3) on April 29, 336.

58. Sargenti, Il diritto privato (quoted n. 7), pp. 266–267; Evans Grubbs, *Law and Family* (quoted n. 4), pp. 284–286.

59. Theodosius' compilers must have taken the texts of *CTh* 4.6.2 and 4.6.3 from a Carthaginian source: J. Matthews, *Laying Down the Law: A Study of the Theodosian Code*, New Haven, 2000, esp. pp. 280–293; J. N. Dillon, *The Justice of Constantine: Law, Communication, and Control*, Ann Arbor MI 2012, p. 33. Other copies of Constantine's laws sent to other provinces would not have included the instructions regarding the son of Licinnianus.

60. On the instructions to the compilers see Matthews, *Laying Down the Law* (quoted n. 59), pp. 53–84.

61. See for instance T. Kuehn, *Illegitimacy in Renaissance Florence*, Ann Arbor MI 2002, which uses not only Florentine archives but also *consilia* (opinions in support of one side of a dispute) written by contemporary jurists who drew on Roman law (particularly Justinian's).

62. On her status, see Libanius, *Ep.* 188.5 (in Norman's Loeb edition) and *Or.* 1.278; and cf. Eunapius, *Vitae Philos.* 496 (Loeb).

They had one son, Cimon (also called Arabius or Arrhabius), whom Libanius cherished and had educated in rhetoric, although ultimately Cimon rejected rhetoric for a career in law.

Libanius was well aware of the legal prohibition on making Cimon his heir, and both his 'Autobiography' (*Oratio* 1) and several of his letters to friends discuss his attempts to gain exemption from the law for his son. He had hoped for a dispensation from the emperor Julian, a friend and fellow pagan, but Julian had been killed before this could happen.[63] Libanius was pleased when in 371 the western emperor Valentinian I modified Constantine's law so that a father could leave one-fourth of his property to an illegitimate child if there were no other legitimate heirs and one-twelfth of his property if there were, and he was delighted when Valens, Valentinian's brother and co-emperor in the East, adopted Valentinian's law, albeit grudgingly.[64] Unfortunately, Valentinian's law was rescinded about ten years later by his successor Theodosius I, but Libanius was able to use his personal influence to gain an exception for Cimon.[65]

Libanius says that he had friends who would have given Cimon anything left to them by Libanius in his will — exactly the sort of dodge that Constantine's law was trying to prevent. However, he adds that there were others who would have brought charges against this roundabout way of making Cimon heir, 'as it was against the law.' Indeed Libanius had many personal enemies who could have seen this as a way to injure him after his death through the dishonor and impoverishment of his son. But in his struggle to enable his wealth to go to Cimon, Libanius had support from the town council of Antioch. This was because although as a teacher of rhetoric Libanius himself was exempted from curial responsibilties, Cimon as his heir would be liable. The council approached the emperor and obtained permission for Cimon to inherit, much to Libanius' joy and relief.[66] But Cimon did not want actually to serve in the *curia*, which brought financial burdens and personal risk, and was instead angling to get an appointment in the imperial administration that would confer senatorial status and immunity from such obligations.[67] The Senate in Constantinople, however, rejected Cimon's nomination for the governorship of Cyprus, precisely on the grounds of his mother's low birth.[68] On his way back to Antioch from Constantinople after this humiliation, Cimon injured his leg in a fall and soon died. Cimon's mother, the nameless concubine, had died not long before, so Libanius was left utterly bereft.[69]

Libanius' grief at his son's death was compounded by the injury to both his and his son's honor; in describing Cimon's rejection by the Senate he more than once refers to the *hybris*

63. Cf. *Ep*. 121.6-7 (Norman), where Libanius is hoping for help from Julian's successor Jovian, though he doesn't really expect it (and didn't receive it).

64. *Or*. 1.145. The law is *CTh* 4.6.4 (to the prefect of Rome Ampelius, 371). For a different approach to *CTh* 4.6.4, see J. TATE, Inheritance Rights of Nonmarital Children in Late Roman Law, *Roman Legal Tradition* 4, 2008, pp. 1–36, at 10–20.

65. *Or*. 1.195-6. Theodosius' law is not extant but cf. *CTh* 4.6.5 (Honorius, 397) which refers to 'the laws of Constantine and our father.'

66. *Or*. 1.195-6.

67. *Ep*. 169 (Norman) to Tatianus. Libanius also was against Cimon's cooption by the town council, and tried unsuccessfully to get an exemption for Cimon.

68. *Epp*. 175, 176, and 179 in Norman; see Norman's Note on this incident in his Loeb vol. 2, 462-464. For the similarly humiliating rejection of Libanius' secretary Thalassius, see PETIT, Les senateurs (and above n. 47).

69. *Or*. 1.278-83; *Epp*. 182, 183, 187, 188 (Norman).

(insult, injury) Cimon suffered.[70] In fact, he blamed the Senate's decision for Cimon's death, and claimed that Cimon died 'from grief in consequence of the insult (*hybris*) he suffered.'[71] Libanius' love for his son is palpable and he had no doubt that Cimon should be his heir, despite his concubine's ineligibility as a marriage partner.

Libanius' case was far from unique; we might compare the relationship of Libanius' younger contemporary, Augustine, with his son by a concubine, Adeodatus ('given by God'). Like Cimon's mother, Augustine's concubine (whom he never names, just as Libanius never names his concubine) was not of the status suitable for a man of curial class. The difference is that unlike Libanius, Augustine was willing, albeit reluctantly, to put aside his concubine in order to marry a wealthy girl.[72]

Naturales and Inheritance after Constantine

The vacillations in the law regarding natural children and their mothers over the two centuries after Constantine also reveal how controversial the law was, and how important its provisions were to those affected. As noted above, Constantine's law was mitigated in 371 by Valentinian and Valens, but their law was overturned by Theodosius I. After Theodosius' death in 395 and the now permanent division of the Empire into two halves, different policies evolved in the East and West in regard to the rights of illegitimate children; in general, eastern laws were more favorably disposed to *naturales*. In 397, the western emperor Honorius reiterated the policy of Constantine and of Honorius' father Theodosius I, but eight years later his nephew Theodosius II, now emperor in the East, returned to the more generous law of Valentinian I and Valens (so that in the absence of legitimate heirs, a man could leave up to a fourth of his property to natural children and their mother, but only a twelfth if there were legitimate children).[73] Since Theodosius II was a very young boy at the time his law was passed, we can assume it was not made at the emperor's own initiative, but was a response (crafted by Theodosius' consistorium and his quaestor) to petitions or lawsuits from men without legitimate offspring or from the *naturales* themselves.

That such petitions and litigation continued in both halves of the Empire is clear from the last two laws surviving under the title *de naturalibus filiis et matribus eorum* in the Theodosian Code. These were probably not the only laws on the subject over the next two and a half decades; on the contrary, the incomplete state of the Code as we have it makes it extremely likely that there was other legislation that has not survived.[74] A fragmentary law of the western

70. *Or.* 1.279: *hybreon*; Ep. 175 (Norman): *hybristo*; *Ep.* 188.5 (Norman): *hybreos*; cf. also *Or.* 1.257 on Thrasydeus' earlier attack on Cimon: *hybrize*.

71. *Ep.* 188.5, trans. Norman.

72. *Conf.* IV.2 and VI.15; see D. Shanzer, *Avulsa a latere meo*: Augustine's Spare Rib - Confessions 6.15.25, *JRS* 92, 2002, pp. 157–176.

73. Honorius' law: the fragmentary *CTh* 4.6.5 (to Petronius, the Vicar of Spain, 397). Law of Theodosius II: *CTh* 4.6.6 (to Anthemius, the praetorian prefect, 405). The version in the *Codex Justinianus* (*CJ* 5.27.2) differs and shows signs of a Justinianic revision, especially as it makes provision (of $1/24^{th}$) to the *concubina* even if there are no surviving children.

74. Just how many early 5th century laws are missing, and what they said, is controversial. A. Arjava, Ein verschollenes Gesetz des Codex Theodosianus über uneheliche Kinder (*CTh* 4, 6, 7a) in *ZSSR:RA* 115, 1998,

emperor Valentinian III (again, a very young child) is especially interesting because it points up the implications of Constantine's redefinition of the term *naturales* (on which see above):

> 'We order that the name of *naturales* be placed on those who, procreated without the honorable celebration (or celebrity)[75] of marriage, have been brought to light by a legitimate joining (*legitima coniunctio*). However, it is clear *ipso iure* that slaves are born from the womb of a slave-woman (*ex ancillae utero*), although because of the force of nature it is not possible to take away the name of *naturales* even from these. In hereditary matters however ...'[76]

Before Constantine's legislation, the term '*naturales*' would have been applied *only* to those 'born from the womb of a slavewoman'; the children of unmarried free mothers would have been *spurii*. Less than a century later, Valentinian III's law only grudgingly allows that slaveborn children can be called *naturales* also. His extremely fragmentary and enigmatic law seemingly revises the definition of *naturales* again, by granting that appellation to children from a *legitima coniunctio* that does not have all the characteristics of legal marriage. But what are these characteristics? Evidently the law was looking for some visible sign of *affectio maritalis*, the intent to be married. This could have been a traditional wedding ceremony, or the exchange of dowry and prenuptial gifts (with the dowry coming from the bride's family and the prenuptial gifts from the groom's), or the drawing up of *tabulae nuptiales* (a marriage contract).[77] Without such a manifestation of marital intent, according to Valentinian's law, the union was a *legitima coniunctio* but the children were *naturales* rather than legitimate themselves. And as *naturales*, they would be subject to the restrictions on inheritance that were then in force in the western half of the Empire — apparently (though this is not certain) the policy of Constantine and Honorius rather than the more liberal law of Theodosius II in the East.[78]

414-418. Arjava suggested a missing *CTh* 4.6.7a, an eastern law which the eastern *CTh* 4.6.8 then repeals, but see TATE, Inheritance Rights (quoted n. 64), pp. 24–34.

75. ... *sine honesta cele[bratione] matrimonii*, adopting Mommsen's reconstruction of the missing letters. But M. SARGENTI, Il matrimonio nella legislazione di Valentiniano e Theodosio, in *Studi sul diritto del tardo impero*, Padua 1986, 239-258 (originally published in *AARC* IV, Perugia, 1981, pp. 201–222) points out that this should be *cele[britate]*, meaning 'public knowledge' rather than referring to an actual ceremony of marriage (p. 252).

76. *CTh* 4.6.7, to the praetorian prefect Bassus. The date does not survive, but must be 426 or 427. The rest of the law as printed in Mommsen's edition of the *Code* is actually not from the surviving manuscript of the *Code* (T), or from the Breviarium of Alaric (from which many laws missing in the damaged manuscript T have been restored). It is from a law in the *lex Romana Burgundionum*, a compilation made for Romans living in the Burgundian kingdom, and we should not assume that it reflects Valentinian III' s original law. SARGENTI, Il matrimonio (quoted n. 75), p. 248; TATE, Inheritance Rights (quoted n. 64), pp. 21–22.

77. See further J. EVANS GRUBBS, Marrying and Its Documentation in Later Roman Law, in P. REYNOLDS and J. WITTE, Jr. (eds.), *To Have and To Hold: Marrying and Its Documentation in Western Christendom, 400-1600*, Cambridge, UK, 2007, pp. 43–94, esp. pp. 64–72 and pp. 85–94. *CJ* 5.4.21 (undated but also to Bassus), probably from the same law originally as *CTh* 4.6.7, makes an exception for soldiers, who are free to marry *sine aliqua sollemnitate matrimoniorum* (without any public celebration of marriage), as long as their wives are free-born. TATE, Inheritance Rights (quoted n. 64), pp. 25–27 for the possibility that *CTh* 4.10.3 (also to Bassus, dated 30 March 426) was part of the same law, which would give *CTh* 4.6.7 a date of 426.

78. See above on the western laws. The problem is that there were other laws now lost, such as that of Theodosius I (see n. 65). One law in the Theodosian Code evidently allowed one-eighth to *naturales* when there were legitimate children: see the *Interpretatio* to *Novel* 22 of Theodosius II (MOMMSEN–MEYER vol. 2, p. 53). Possibly this was in the missing part of *CTh* 4.6.7: see Mommsen's note to *CTh* 4.6.7 in MOMMSEN–MEYER vol. 1.2, p. 178.

The paradoxical concept of a legitimate union resulting in illegitimate children provoked an eastern law about a year later, in which Valentinian's uncle Theodosius II declared that just because prenuptial gifts, dowry, a ceremony (*pompa*), or other physical manifestation of marriage was absent, 'no one should reckon on account of this that a marriage that has otherwise been entered into correctly lacks validity or that the rights of legitimate offspring can be taken away from the children born from it.' However, Theodosius also stressed that even such an undocumented marriage had to be between those 'equal in honor' (*inter pares honestate personas*) who were not prohibited from marrying by law.[79] Thus both Theodosius II in the east and Valentinian III in the west were requiring some sort of evidence of marital intent when a union was between social unequals.[80] Theodosius also reiterated the law made under his name more than twenty years earlier (*CTh* 4.6.6, which had itself repeated the policy of *CTh* 4.6.4 of Valentinian). At the same time, Pope Leo I was receiving similar requests for clarification from Christians. The pope's *responsa*, although couched in biblical justifications, followed Roman law in differentiating marriage and concubinage.[81]

Publication of the *Theodosian Code* by Theodosius II in 438 would have drawn new attention to the imperial policy on *naturales*, and therefore spawned new litigation in the courts, as parents of illegitimates sought to provide for them and were opposed either by relatives or informers bringing prosecutions.[82] Whereas the laws preserved in the *Theodosian Code* were abridged by Theodosius' compilers and shorn of details that would have revealed the reasons for their enactment, imperial *novellae* ('new laws') passed after the Code's publication are preserved in full. Several of these *novellae* were prompted by appeals from (presumably wealthy) individuals who wanted clarification — or mitigation — of the Roman rules of inheritance.[83] Sometimes these appeals came to the emperor's attention by way of his praetorian prefect, as happened in the case of Marcian's law clarifying Constantine's category of *humiles uel abiectae* women.

Twelve years before Marcian's law, Theodosius II himself responded to a *suggestio* from his praetorian prefect, Apollonius, who had come up with a way for illegitimate children to inherit from their fathers and take on a respectable, if burdensome, role in society. By the fifth century the town councils (*curiae*) were having an increasingly difficult time replenishing their numbers, as curial office became more onerous and the wealthiest and most

79. *CTh* 3.7.3 (to the praetorian prefect Hierius, 20 February, 428). This may have originally been part of the same law as *CTh* 4.6.8 and *CTh* 3.5.13, both of which have the same date and addressee. See, however, SARGENTI, Il matrimonio (quoted n. 75), pp. 245–247, who sees *CTh* 3.7.3 and 3.5.13 as part of a law on marriage, whereas *CTh* 4.6.8 was part of another law on succession.

80. SARGENTI, Il matrimonio (quoted n. 75), pp. 253–257; EVANS GRUBBS, Marrying and its Documentation (quoted n. 77), p. 88; R. ASTOLFI, Lo '*status*' delle '*personae*' e la forma del matrimonio nella legislazione del tardo impero, *AARC* XVIII, Rome 2012, pp. 151–181, at p. 161–170. I do not discuss here the short-lived Novel 6 of Majorian (valid only in the West), which required dowry for a valid marriage and legitimate children, on which see EVANS GRUBBS, Marrying and its Documentation pp. 70–71.

81. EVANS GRUBBS, Marrying and its Documentation (quoted n. 77), pp. 89–91.

82. As the last law in the title '*De naturalibus*,' *CTh* 4.6.8 (Theodosius II, 428) would have had validity over earlier laws, in both halves of the Empire, unless and until new measures were enacted.

83. E.g., *Novels* 21.1 and 21.2 of Valentinian III (446); on which see HUMFRESS, Cracking the Codex (quoted n. 6), pp. 247–253; *Novel* 5 of Marcian (to the pr. prefect Palladius, 455). On advocates in late antiquity, C. HUMFRESS, *Orthodoxy and the Courts in Late Antiquity*, Oxford 2007, pp. 9–132.

influential members of the curial class (*potentiores*) obtained immunity by entering the imperial administration (as Libanius' son Cimon had tried to do decades earlier, without success.) Apollonius had been saddened both by the plight of cities that lacked men of wealth and patriotism to pay for their upkeep, and by the unfortunate situation of *naturales* who were prevented from inheriting by earlier laws ('some rather harsh, others more humane'). In response, Theodosius decided that, in the absence of any legitimate children, a *naturalis* son who became a member of his local town council could inherit from his father.[84] Less than three months later he extended his new policy to include illegitimate daughters who married town councillors.[85] The idea, said the emperor, was to benefit both parties: *naturales* could inherit, and the *curiae* would be replenished by new blood.[86]

Although Theodosius II was the first to enshrine such a policy in a general law, people must have been making such arrangements for some time already in order to get around the law's restrictions, as the case of Libanius and his Cimon illustrates. Presumably the only people who might object to Theodosius' law would be family members likely to inherit otherwise, so the law required that there be no legitimate children who would otherwise be heirs, and allowed the testator's parents or grandparents to claim a fourth of the estate. The interests of other relatives (e.g., the testator's siblings or other agnates) were subordinated to the needs of illegitimate children and of the town councils. Not surprisingly, this drew objections. In 470 a case came to the attention of the eastern emperor Leo: a notable of the city of Bostra in Arabia had declared in a public spectacle (perhaps the theatre) that he wished to enroll his *naturalis* son Philocalus in the *curia*, and Philocalus had taken a place among the *principales* of Bostra. But the father then died intestate, and Philocalus' right to inherit was challenged by his father's relatives. Leo decided that even though his father had not stated in writing his desire for his son to succeed him, Philocalus was to inherit and he and his children were now obligated to serve in the *curia*. This decision created an important precedent.[87]

Sixth century laws of the eastern Empire continued to address the inheritance rights of *naturales*. Anastasius declared that if a man had no existing children from a legal marriage but had children by a woman living with him 'in a wife's place' (*uxoris loco*), he could make them his heirs or transfer his property to them in any way he liked, as long as dotal documents were drawn up. The same also was true for any children he had officially adopted (adrogated) after receiving permission from the emperor. Thus concubinage could be changed into marriage by documentation and children born before the marriage would inherit as legitimate heirs. Unlike the temporary measure of Constantine (revived, also for a limited period, by Anastasius' predecessor Zeno), Anastasius' law did not restrict post-marital legitimation

84. *Novel* 22.1.3-9 of Theodosius II, 16 Dec. 442. A quarter of the estate was to be preserved for the man's parents or grandparents (the 'Falcidian Fourth'), so they would not bring charges of 'undutiful will.'

85. *Novel* 22.2.11 (also to Apollonius, 9 March 443). LUCHETTI, *La legittimazione* (quoted n. 7), pp. 65–172 on legitimation *per oblationem curiae*.

86. *Novel* 22.1.3. Theodosius' original law encouraged all those with children, not just *naturales*, to dedicate them to the *curia*; but the much abbreviated version found in the *Code of Justinian* (*CJ* 5.27.3) refers only to *naturales*.

87. *CJ* 5.27.4 (470), referred to as a precedent by Justinian in *Novel* 89.2 (542). LUCHETTI, *La legittimazione* (quoted n. 7), pp. 115–125. To me, the laws suggest that Philocalus, and other *naturales* offered to the *curiae* by their fathers, were not always willing to undertake curial duties as the price of their inheritance.

to the children of freeborn concubines, and was intended to have effect in the future also. The father's wish, declared Anastasius, was to supersede challenges from the man's agnate or cognate relatives or others who relied on 'some sort of clever and subtle pretext of laws or constitutions' to try to get the deceased's property for themselves.[88] This went too far for Anastasius' successor Justin, who said that although the cases of legitimation that had occurred as a result of Anastasius' law could stand, in the future 'all should know that they must seek legitimate posterity' and petitions to subvert imperial law by obtaining a rescript allowing them to adrogate *naturales* were banned.[89] Evidently many men had been taking advantage of the liberality of Justin's predecessor and had made their illegitimate children heirs, perhaps without even bothering to marry the children's mother if they could obtain an rescript. Justin had no tolerance for such 'unjust lustful desires' nor for the clever and deceitful machinations such men used to obtain imperial permission.

Justinian's Reforms

The final edition of Justinian's *Code* in 534 included a slightly modified version of Constantine's law of 336 and a greatly abridged version of Marcian's *novella* of 454.[90] In the meantime both the Augustan and the Constantinian restrictions on marriage between high-ranking men and lowborn women had been increasingly attenuated, particularly by Justinian himself. His predecessor and uncle, Justin, had removed the ban on marriage between senators and former *scaenicae* (actresses) or their daughters, aspiring to imitate the benevolence of God by showing mercy to the weakness of the female sex. (His contemporary Procopius famously claimed that Justinian himself, desirous of marrying the former showgirl Theodora, had instigated his uncle's law.)[91] The children by such marriages were declared legitimate and able to succeed to their father, even if there were other children from a previous marriage.

88. *CJ* 5.27.6 (517); see van de Wiel, La légitimation (quoted n. 7), pp. 324–326 and Luchetti, *La legittimazione* (quoted n. 7), pp. 202–216, who punctuate *CJ* 5.27.6 differently than Krueger. Since the law was overturned at least in part by Justin (see following note), the text in *CJ* 5.26.6 does not completely reflect the original law. See also *CJ* 2.7.23.4 (506), which says that those who have married without dotal documents but *mutuo contrahendi matrimonium animo* can declare their marital intentions before a lawyer of the fiscus, whether or not there are already children from the union. This does not legitimate the already born children, however, according to Astolfi, Lo '*status*' delle '*personae*' (quoted n. 80), pp. 173–174.

89. *CJ* 5.27.7 (519). Justin particularly objected to Anastasius allowing legitimations through subsequent marriage to occur in the future; he believed this discouraged legal marriage and enabled illicit lust.

90. Constantine's law: *CJ* 5.27.1. The entire text of *CTh* 4.6.3 is preserved in the *CJ* version, with alterations made to reflect changes in status and office-holding in the intervening 200 years (e.g. '*Latina*' is omitted, since Justinian had abolished Latin status; '*peregrinos*' becomes '*alienos*'). Marcian's law: *CJ* 5.5.7. The law is shorn of its preface and of any evidence that it was prompted by legal disputes over the meaning of Constantine's law. Note that the two laws are placed under different titles in the *Codex Justinianus*: Constantine's is under the title *de naturalibus liberis et matribus eorum et ex quibus casibus iusti efficiuntur* (the last five words a revealing addition to the *CTh* title on natural children), whereas Marcian's is under *de incestis et inutilibus nuptiis*.

91. *CJ* 5.4.23 pr (between 520-523); Procopius, *Anecdota* IX.47-52. D. Daube, The Marriage of Justinian and Theodora: Legal and Theological Considerations, *Catholic University Law Review* 16, 1967, pp. 380–399; and D. French, Maintaining Boundaries: The Status of Actresses in Early Christian Society, *VChr* 52, 1998, pp. 293–318, at pp. 312–317.

Dotal documents were required for such a marriage, however, in order to have written evidence of marital intent.[92] Justinian later decreed that if a man married to his own *liberta* was later elevated to senatorial rank, the marriage remained valid; the emperor vehemently admonished the 'most cruel sanction' of the Augustan law against senatorial/libertine marriages 'to be silent.'[93] In 539 he allowed all men, of whatever rank, to marry freedwomen as long as they had marriage documents; children born before the documents were drawn up were to be considered freeborn legitimate heirs.[94]

Justinian gradually dismantled all remaining impediments to the ability of *naturales* to inherit from their fathers. First he increased the maximum amount they could receive in the absence of legitimate children to one-half of their father's property (double the one-fourth allowed by previous emperors).[95] Then he said that if a man had lived in concubinage (*consuetudo*) with a free woman whom he was permitted to marry and had children by her, and then married her with dotal instruments (which demonstrated that the union was now intended to be marriage) and had additional children, those born before the marriage had the same inheritance rights as those born after. A year later, he had to issue another law stating that even if there were no children born after the marriage, those born before could still inherit. This clarification was in response to the 'empty subtlety' of those who had willfully misinterpreted the previous law; presumably other relatives or interested parties (or their lawyers) were trying to exploit the legal loophole.[96]

Not long after, a case came to Justinian's attention: a certain man whose legitimate son was dead wished to make his son's *naturalis* son heir to all his property. Was he restricted from doing so by the law allowing *naturales* to receive at most one-half in the absence of other children? No, Justinian decided, an illegitimate grandson could inherit fully from his grandfather, because the reason for limiting the amount natural sons received was to 'rein in paternal vice' and the father at fault here was already dead.[97] This shows just how far the law on natural children, and imperial ideology, had evolved since Constantine's original law of 336. Constantine had not been interested in improving the morality of the high-ranking men whose unions with lowborn women he restricted; his concerns were with maintaining social honor and traditional status distinctions, as well as cracking down on a particularly egregious case of status usurpation (the son of Licinnianus). Justinian, on the other hand, was concerned with promoting legal marriage and with alleviating the condition of natural children (though not at the expense of morality). And it was a specific case that had come to him on appeal that prompted his law.

Up to this point the mitigation of earlier inheritance restrictions had applied only to the illegitimate children of free women, usually freeborn concubines. But by 531 Justinian was

92. On documents and marital intent, see C. Castello, Lo strumento dotale come prova del matrimonio, *SDHI* 4, 1935, pp. 208–224; van de Wiel, La légitimation (quoted n. 7), pp. 341–344; Evans Grubbs, Marrying and its Documention (quoted n. 77), pp. 74–94.

93. *CJ* 5.4.28 (531 or 532). '... taceat Papiae legis crudelissima sanctio' (*CJ* 5.4.28.3).

94. *Novel* 78.3.

95. *CJ* 5.27.8 (528).

96. *CJ* 5.27.10 (529); *CJ* 5.27.11 (530). Justinian thus reinstates the law of Anastasius (*CJ* 5.27.6, 517, n. 88) that his uncle Justin had repealed (*CJ* 5.27.7, 519, n. 89); cf. Astolfi, Lo '*status*' delle '*personae*' (quoted n. 80), p. 176.

97. *CJ* 5.27.12 (531).

extending his generosity to cover slave children and their mothers also. In that year he passed a law saying that if an unmarried man had kept his *ancilla* 'in the name of concubine' and had maintained this relationship until he died, after his death the slave concubine and her children by him would *not* become the property of his heirs but would be free — a reversal of the classical legal situation in which a man's slaves, whatever their relationship with him, would have belonged to his heir unless he explicitly freed them.[98] And, the emperor added, if a man had designated his slave (*servus*) as his son (*filius*) in the public records (*acta*), it was to be understood that he intended to free the boy, who was to receive Roman citizenship.[99] In his *Institutes*, Justinian claimed a precedent for this rather extraordinary measure in the elder Cato, who allegedly said that slaves adopted by their master are by that very act freed. The emperor stressed, however, that this did not give the freed slave the *ius filii* — the full legal status of a son.[100]

Justinian continued to make new policies regarding the inheritance rights of *naturales* in the *Novellae* ('new laws') enacted after his Code's publication. In 535 he said that a man without legitimate children but with children from a slave (concubine) could free them and if they became *curiales* they could inherit three-fourths of the estate; previously this benefit (begun by Theodosius II a century earlier) had not been available to the slaveborn.[101] *Novel* 18 of 536, a long law aimed at improving the inheritance rights of children in general, devotes a chapter explicitly to *naturales* (here called *physikoi* in Greek). This is because, the emperor says, he was being constantly bothered by the petitions of weeping children begging for relief from the current laws — an indication that disputes and litigation over the rights of illegitimate children were still a problem, despite (or because of) all the legislation of the past two centuries. He also wants to please God and do acts worthy of Him. Justinian therefore expanded his previous measure which had allowed a man to leave up to one-half of his property to his *naturales* in his will if he had no legitimate children (and up to one-twelfth if he had), so that now even if he died intestate, his illegitimate children and their mother (assuming she was a free concubine) could share up to one-sixth of the estate. But it was necessary that the children and concubine have lived in his home with him, and that there have been only one concubine — in other words, that this was a family in all but law. Justinian also felt obliged again to state that a man could free his slave concubine and her children and marry her, and the slaveborn children would have the same inheritance rights as those born after the marriage. Evidently there were still cavilling lawyers and their clients who questioned whether this after-the-fact legitimation applied to cases where the concubine had been a slave.[102]

98. *CJ* 7.15.3 (531); cf. the Greek version at *CJ* 6.4.4.3. In such a case, however, they would not inherit or receive anything more than their liberty. On this law see Ev. KARABÉLIAS, La pratique du concubinat avec une femme libre, affranchie ou esclave dans le droit post-classique, in *AARC* VII, Naples 1988, pp. 183–201 at pp. 195–198. Classical law had exempted a man's slave concubine and her *naturales* children from being sold to pay his debts: *Dig.* 42.5.38 pr (Paulus, 1st book of *Sententiae*); cf. *Dig.* 20.1.8 (Ulpian, 73rd book on the Edict).

99. *CJ* 7.6.1. This has the same date and addressee as *CJ* 7.15.3 and was in all probability originally part of the same law. *CJ* 7.6.1 is a long constitution abolishing Latin status.

100. Justinian, *Institutiones* 1.11.

101. *Novel* 38.2.1. Theodosius II's law: n. 84-85 above.

102. *Novel* 18.5 (to the pr. prefect Johannes) and *Novel* 18.11, referring to *CJ* 5.27.10 and 11 (see at n. 96). This law also expanded the 'Falcidian Fourth' (the amount that had to be left to *sui heredes* under a will) from

Justinian returned to the subject of natural children in 538. He knew men who had intended to draw up marriage documents with their concubine to legitimize their children, but the concubine had died before they could do so, and the children remained *naturales* (here called *nothoi* in Greek). Another man loved his illegitimate children and wanted to legitimate them, but did not think their mother was worthy of being a legal wife (it is enough to say that, the emperor adds). In another case a father wanted to legitimate his children, but their mother had unexpectedly inherited from a cognate relative and her children, because they did not want their father to get usufruct of their legacy, had hidden her in order to prevent the marriage (evidently these were adult children). To remedy all these real-life situations where the father's wishes to follow the law had been thwarted, Justinian decided that a man could consider his children by a free concubine to be legitimate even if he did not marry their mother. A man who wished to do this needed to petition the emperor or, if he died before doing so but his will made it clear he wanted them to be legitimated, his children themselves needed to supplicate and show the emperor the will.[103] This no doubt encouraged an increase in weeping suppliants, despite Justinian's previous attempts to reduce their numbers.

The final act came in 542. *Novel* 89 begins by rehearsing the evolution of legal attitudes toward illegitimates over the centuries: once Roman law didn't even care about them, and they were considered 'alien to the republic.' But Constantine ('of pious memory') first began making laws about *naturales*, and gradually emperors came to have more merciful opinions, with some allowing the children to receive part of their father's estate and others looking for ways to free the children from the earlier law (i.e. Constantine's) and enable them to succeed to him in full. Justinian intends to complete and combine these merciful measures in his law. This is because originally, before written laws, all children were born free and legitimate, and only with the advent of wars, lawsuits, and lusts did some become slaves and illegitimate.[104]

Novel 89 proceeds to summarize and reconfirm Justinian's previous measures that improved the lot of *naturales*, and to clarify somewhat ambiguous areas. Adoption (i.e. *adrogatio*) of *naturales* by petition to the emperor, which had once been thought acceptable, was

one-fourth to one-third. For Justinian's earlier policy, see *CJ* 5.27.8 (n. 95). On Justinian's justification of his innovations as '*imitatio dei*,' see C. F. PAZDERNIK, Justinian's *Novels* and the Law of Succession: A Chapter in the Transformation of Law and Society with Special Reference to *Ius Naturale*, in *Confrontation in Late Antiquity*, ed. L. JONES HALL, Cambridge 2003, pp. 47–59.

103. *Novel* 74 pr-2 (538). *Novel* 74.3 reiterates the ban on the adoption of *naturales*/*nothoi*, and *Novel* 74.4.1 says that men endowed with high dignity (senators and *illustres*) had to provide a prenuptial gift and other appurtenances of honorable marriage when they married their concubine, so that it would be clear that marriage was intended. *Novel* 74.5 responds to pleas of women deceived by men they thought were their husbands, who later ejected them, sometimes along with their children; see R. VIGNERON, La politique moralisatrice de Justinien à l'égard des séducteurs, in R. FEENSTRA et al., eds., *Collatio Iuris Romani: Études dédiées à Hans Ankum*, Amsterdam 1995, vol. II, pp. 583–592. Such women must have been of low social and economic status, as they had no dowry and were used as temporary companionship by men until they could find a wife with a dowry.

104. *Novel* 89 pr-1 (to Johannes, 542). On the (not always accurate) historical 'sketches' in the prefaces to Justinian's *Novels*, see M. MAAS, Roman History and Christian Ideology in Justinianic Reform Legislation, *DOP* 40, 1986, pp. 17–31; cf. PAZDERNIK, Justinian's *Novels* (quoted n. 102), pp. 53–54 on the preface to *Novel* 89. These *novellae* were of course written by Justinian's famous quaestor, Tribonian, and demonstrate his style and philosophizing tone, but do reflect the outlook and purposes of the emperor himself.

now banned since it did not sufficiently consider *castitas*.[105] In cases where a man died intestate with no legitimate offspring or wife (or other close heirs) but had lived monogamously with a free concubine, she and their children may receive together one-sixth of his property. But if he had children by several women (which would be fornication) then they and their children may not benefit. If he died intestate leaving both legitimate (presumably from a previous legal marriage) and illegitimate children, the illegitimate children could not inherit, but their legitimate half-siblings were to take care of them financially.[106] None of these benefits, however, was to be enjoyed by those children who were not even worthy of the name of *naturales/nothoi*, those born from 'wicked or incestuous or legally condemned embraces' — children of incest or adultery, or of unmarried free women not in a concubinage relationship with a man of higher rank. They were not even to be reared (!).[107] Here Justinian clarifies what became the distinction between *naturales* and *spurii* in medieval and later law, whereby *spurii* are the condemned and repudiated offspring of illicit and unholy unions.[108]

And finally, the law concluded, 'certain things written in a constitution of Constantine of pious memory to Gregorius about such children' (i.e. *naturales*) were no longer to be considered; they were obsolete and Constantine, wishing to discourage high officeholders from having illegitimate children, had removed from them 'the gentleness of imperial generosity.'[109] (Justinian cannot resist a subtle criticism here of his 'pious' predecessor.) And in another law of the same year which presented a variety of measures concerning marriage and divorce, the emperor returned again to the subject of unions with women of low status, specifically the identity of the *abiectae* about whom Marcian had been consulted. Neither Constantine's law nor Marcian's interpretation of it were to be valid any longer, Justinian said: if men wanted to marry such women, they could; those who held high *dignitas* needed to have dotal documents to prove their intentions.[110]

Justinian's objectives in his legislation ran completely counter to that of earlier centuries. In their laws Augustus and Constantine had both put establishing and maintaining social distinctions above encouraging marriage; Justinian on the other hand wished to promote monogamous marital unions above all, even if that meant legalizing unions between widely disparate classes. But it was important that marital intent (*affectio*) be present, and therefore in cases that in the past would have been assumed to be *concubinatus* rather than marriage, external manifestations (primarily a dotal contract) were necessary. When it was impossible for

105. *Novel* 89.11.2, confirming *Novel* 74.3 (quoted n. 103). This is because under the pre-Constantinian rules, a man could have adopted a natural child without marrying his mother; Justinian wants to promote legal marriage. This refers to the law of Anastasius (*CJ* 5.27.6), amended by Justin (*CJ* 5.27.7) so as not to allow adrogation without marriage (see n. 88-89).

106. *Novel* 89.12. Likewise, if he had illegitimate children by an earlier relationship with a concubine, and after her death he made a legitimate marriage, his children by the marriage were to support the illegitimate children (whom he had never legitimated).

107. *Novel* 89.15. Ph. Moreau, *Incestus et prohibitae nuptiae: L'inceste à Rome*, Paris 2002, pp. 362–366.

108. Luchetti, *La legittimazione* (quoted n. 7), pp. 53–57. Later law: see Kuehn, *Illegitimacy in Renaissance Florence* (quoted n. 61), pp. 33–86; J. Witte, Jr., *The Sins of the Fathers: The Law and Theology of Illegitimacy Reconsidered*, Cambridge 2009, pp. 49–103. It is not the same as the *naturales/spurii* distinction of classical law, on which see above at n. 37.

109. *Novel* 89.15.

110. *Novel* 117.6.

a union to be interpreted as marriage, as when a man had lived with a slave concubine and her children without freeing them, Justinian at least wanted to ensure their freedom after he died.

But to trace a straight trajectory of Roman imperial law on *naturales* from Constantine, the enactor of harsh restrictions, to Justinian, the abolisher of almost all restrictions, would not only disregard the evidence of legal vacillations in the fourth and fifth centuries (seen imperfectly through the laws of the Theodosian Code), but also ignore the role played by individual litigants. Men anxious to secure the inheritance rights of children born out of wedlock were countered by relatives and others who did not want ancestral properties to go to *naturales* who were legally not family. Petitioners buffeted emperors with pleas to make exceptions for their child, or they paid legal professionals to make clever arguments against such exceptions. Behind the rhetoric of the laws we can sense the dramas and machinations of real people, people like Libanius or Philocalus of Bostra or the anonymous fathers and children who petitioned Justinian, or even the mysterious 'son of Licinnianus' mentioned at the end of Constantine's law. In my opinion, all of the modifications to Constantine's law in the two succeeding centuries, culminating in the extensive reforms of Justinian giving natural children from monogamous relationships the same rights as their legitimate siblings, arose from real-life cases. Even Constantine's original ruling was influenced by a particular individual, although he also had additional reasons of policy.[111] The laws of late Roman emperors on *naturales* are much more than a series of often contradictory and conflicting rulings (though that is how they appear to anyone who has worked through them!). They are the end product of contentious legal disputes over inheritance, disputes whose traces are otherwise unfortunately unknown.[112]

111. And Justin's removal of the ban between senators and actresses was prompted by a specific case, that of his nephew Justinian, if we may believe Procopius; see n. 91.

112. I would like to thank Antti Arjava and Susan Treggiari for corrections and advice on a draft of this paper. Any mistakes that remain are of course my own.

L'ÉGALITÉ ENTRE HOMMES ET FEMMES DANS LES *WAQFIYYĀT* MAMELOUKES

UN DÉFI À LA LOI ?

Lahcen Daaïf

L'institution du waqf (pl. *awqāf*) a connu un essor fulgurant à l'époque mamelouke en Égypte[1], particulièrement au cours de la période burjite (1382-1517)[2] qui s'est distinguée par une riche production littéraire notamment historiographique, juridique et notariale.

La ville du Caire à elle seule, sous les Mameloukes, comptait un nombre imposant de mosquées et de collèges. D'après al-Maqrīzī (m. 845/1442), il y avait à son époque 158 monuments religieux dont 88 mosquées, mais au XIXe siècle on dénombrait 264 édifices religieux, ce qui représente une augmentation de plus de 67 % en moins de cinq siècles[3]. Les revenus considérables dont bénéficiaient ces édifices leur venaient des *awqāf* d'immeubles et de terres cultivées. Les propriétés foncières étaient en grande partie converties en biens de mainmorte, *waqf* dont les Mameloukes eux-mêmes tiraient de considérables avantages, mettant à mal la situation économique du pays[4]. Déjà au XIVe siècle, le cadastre signale 2 163 villages qui étaient constitués soit en *waqf*, soit en concessions foncières (*iqṭāʿāt*), soit les deux à la fois, ou partagés entre *waqf*, *iqṭāʿ* d'un côté et propriétés particulières de l'autre. Les religieux et les étudiants qui en profitaient avaient en outre droit à des donations que l'État rechignait parfois à leur accorder[5].

L'amplification du phénomène était telle que ses répercussions néfastes sur l'organisation et les obligations de l'État décidèrent celui-ci à recourir à des subterfuges encore plus néfastes

1. La base de données *Comparing Arabic Legal documents* (= CALD), mise en place depuis 2009 dans le cadre du projet européen *Islamic Law Materialized* (= ILM) par l'équipe de recherche de la section arabe de l'*institut de Recherche et d'Histoire des Textes* (= IRHT), renferme plus de 3300 documents dont deux tiers consistent en des actes légaux. Ceux de la période mamelouke en constituent les trois-quarts dont 41 *waqfiyya*-s et 15 *istibdāl*-s (acte de substitution d'un bien de mainmorte à un autre).

2. Cf. al-Maqrīzī, *al-Mawāʿiẓ wa-l-iʿtibār fī ḏikr al-ḫiṭaṭ wa-l-āṯār*, éd., A. F. Sayyid, Londres, al-Furqān Islamic heritage foundation 2002-2004, V vol., vol. IV, p. 178.

3. A. Darrāǧ (éd.), *Ḥuǧǧat waqf al-Ašraf Barsbāy*, *Institut français d'archéologie orientale* (= IFAO), Le Caire 1963, p. 13.

4. Surtout après la mort du sultan Barqūq (m. 800/1397), cf. al-Maqrīzī, *al-Mawāʿiẓ* (cité n. 2), p. 178.

5. Darrāǧ, *Ḥuǧǧat* (cité n. 3), p. 16.

Inheritance, Law and Religions in the Ancient and Mediaeval Worlds, ed. by B. Caseau and S. R. Huebner (Centre de recherche d'Histoire et Civilisation de Byzance, Monographies 45), Paris 2014.

pour remédier à la situation financière désastreuse du pays, d'où une fiscalité injuste et vénalité des charges généralisée. Plusieurs tentatives ont été entreprises d'une manière soutenue sans qu'aucune n'aboutisse à un résultat concret. Nul doute que la plus représentative d'entre elles qui visaient à rééquilibrer le budget de l'État, était de prélever une taxe sur les rentes des *awqāf* dans le cadre des préparatifs de guerre sur trois siècles successifs, VIIIe/XIVe, IXe/XVe et Xe/XVIe siècles[6]. Elles furent toutes sans suite, principalement à cause de la résistance des cadis et des oulémas, toutes écoles juridiques confondues[7]. Le sultan al-Ẓāhir Sayf al-Dīn Barqūq (m. 800/1397) soutint une solution plus radicale lorsque, suite au besoin urgent d'affronter les armées de Tamerlan, il envisagea la suppression pure et simple des *awqāf* (*ibṭāl al-awqāf*) en vue de mettre fin à cette situation qui appauvrissait l'État. Mais il eut affaire, lui aussi, à la résistance des oulémas et surtout des cadis qu'il avait consultés et qui refusèrent de sanctionner par une fatwa sa décision[8].

Dans la mesure où les actes de waqf publiés sont en nombre limité, il ne pourra être question d'approche statistique dans les lignes qui suivent. Notre intérêt portera exclusivement sur les actes qui tiennent compte de la clause égalitaire dans la distribution des revenus d'un waqf, clause dont on présentera et traduira quelques modèles. Mais afin de mettre en lumière les raisons qui sous-tendent ce souci d'égalité entre les deux lignées de la descendance des fondateurs de ces waqfs, nous proposons une analyse sociohistorique en prenant en considération le groupe social auquel ils appartenaient.

Waqfiyya : présentation et analyse

Les *waqfiyyāt*, sing. *waqfiyya*[9] sont des actes légaux par lesquels sont immobilisés en biens de mainmorte les propriétés mobilières, immobilières ou foncières au profit de personnes désignées (waqf *ahlī* ou *ḏurrī*) ou de fondations pieuses tels qu'hôpital, mosquée, medersa, zawiya etc. ou au profit des pauvres et des nécessiteux (waqf *ḫayrī*)[10]. Ces *waqfiyyāt*[11] sont très longues et peuvent être rédigées sur plusieurs pages. Celles établies pour des princes et des personnalités in-

6. *Ibid.*, p. 15 ; M. Abū Zahra, *Muḥāḍarāt fī l-waqf*, Maṭba'at 'A. Muḫaymar, Le Caire 1959, p. 20-24.

7. L'une des premières tentatives fut celle entreprise par le Sultan al-Ẓāhir Baybars (m. 667/1277) qui s'était résolu à exproprier les bénéficiaires des waqfs *ahlī* au profit de l'État, mais il eut affaire à une résistance de savants religieux à la tête desquels se tenait le grand imām Šāfi'ite, Muḥyī l-Dīn al-Nawawī qui mourut la même année. Voir l'une de ses lettres échangées avec le sultan à ce sujet dans al-Suyuṭī, *Ḥusn al-muḥāḍara fī tārīḫ Miṣr wa-l-Qāhira*, éd. M. A. Ibrāhīm, Le Caire 1968, II vol., vol. II, p. 101-103. Rappelons que le sultan Baybars fut le premier à avoir institué la judicature des quatre écoles juridiques sunnites : ḥanafisme, mālikisme, šāfi'isme, ḥanbalisme, cf. al-Suyuṭī, *Ḥusn al-muḥāḍara*, II, p. 96.

8. Al-Maqrīzī, *al-Mawā'iẓ* (cité n. 2), p. 178 ; Abū Zahra, *Muḥāḍarāt* (cité n. 6), p. 23.

9. Au Maghreb et en Andalousie elle est désignée sous le nom de *rasm al-taḥbīs*, cf. D. S. Powers, A court case from fourteenth-century North Africa, *Journal of the American Oriental Society* 110, 1990, p. 230.

10. Al-Maqrīzī, *al-Mawā'iẓ* (cité n. 2), p. 175-176, qui le désigne sous le nom d'*al-aḥbās* ; voir aussi S. Denoix, Pour une exploration d'ensemble d'un corpus. Les waqfs mamelouks du Caire, dans *Le Waqf dans l'espace islamique, outil de pouvoir socio-politique*, éd. R. Deguilhem, *L'Institut Francais d'Études Arabes de Damas*, Damas 1995, p. 29-44, p. 30-31.

11. Beaucoup de ces *waqfiyyāt* sont conservées au Caire dans les archives nationales, ministère des *awqāf*, *Dār al-waṯā'iq al-qawmiyya*, *Dār al-kutub* et au patriarcat copte, cf. M. M. Amin, *Catalogue des documents d'archives du Caire de 239/853 à 922/1516*, IFAO, Le Caire 1981, p. XIII, aussi D. Crecelius, The Organization of Waqf Documents in Cairo, *International Journal of Middle East Studies* 2, 1971, p. 266-277, p. 271-277.

fluentes, qui par ailleurs sont les plus nombreuses, forment des opuscules entiers dont le nombre de pages varie de vingt à cinquante, atteignant parfois soixante-dix, voire six cents pages[12]. Elles se sont beaucoup plus affinées au fil du temps et se sont enrichies d'amples détails, topographiques, descriptifs, architecturaux et juridiques. Mais en général, les *waqfiyyāt* sont faites sur un même modèle, fidèle en tous points à celui qu'en proposent les juristes dans les manuels notariaux (*kutub al-šurūṭ*), notamment ceux rédigés par des auteurs contemporains[13]. Ce modèle obéit au même plan composé de plusieurs sections, reproduites dans quasiment le même ordre, et rédigées souvent dans un langage juridique identique, exception faite de quelques expressions et formules isolées qui changent en fonction de lieux ou d'époques éloignées[14].

Une *waqfiyya* peut avoir pour objet un ou plusieurs biens-fonds à la fois (*ʿayn*, pl. *aʿyān mawqūfa*), notamment celles qui concernent les biens immobilisés par des sultans, princes ou gouverneurs[15]. Quel que soit leur nombre, ces biens-fonds sont présentés et décrits séparément, chaque bien étant suivi des conditions fixées par le fondateur de waqf dans la distribution des revenus qu'il génère aux bénéficiaires déterminés ou indéterminés. De la sorte, une *waqfiyya* est susceptible de mettre l'accent sur l'égalité entre ses bénéficiaires hommes et femmes dans une section relative à un bien-fonds déterminé, et ne pas en tenir compte dans une autre section portant sur un autre bien-fonds. Toutefois, c'est bien la même règle qui prévaut dans toutes les sections constitutives d'une *waqfiyya*, à moins que le *wāqif* ne se contente de répéter la même clause dans chacune des sections de la *waqfiyya* pour renvoyer aux conditions préalablement évoquées dans la première section.

Il n'en va pas autrement du nombre des bénéficiaires qui peut largement varier d'une *waqfiyya* à l'autre. Dans le cadre d'un waqf, une *waqfiyya* peut désigner pour un ou plusieurs biens immobilisés, un ou plusieurs bénéficiaires à la fois qui ne sont pas systématiquement de la famille proche du *wāqif*. En effet, des personnes sans aucun lien de parenté consanguine ou utérine avec le *wāqif* peuvent figurer dans l'acte. Ce sont généralement des personnes avec lesquelles ce dernier a un lien particulier, tels un ami très proche, un client (*mawlā*) ou esclave affranchi (*ʿabd maʿtūq*) ; ou des personnes pour lesquelles il témoigne une grande considération d'ordre religieux ou spirituel, comme une figure pieuse (*ṣāliḥ*), un savant religieux (*ʿālim*), ou un chef de file d'une confrérie religieuse (*šayḫ ṭarīqa*) à laquelle le *wāqif*

12. Pour ne citer que des exemples déjà édités, voir Ṣ. al-Munağğid (éd.), *Kitāb waqf al-Qāḍī ʿUṯmān b. Asʿad b. al-Munağğā*, *Institut français du Proche-Orient*, Damas 1949, en 20 pages ; ou Darrāğ, *Ḥuğğat* (cité n. 3), en 69 pages. Voir aussi la première *waqfiyya* d'al-Ḥasan b. Muḥammad b. Qalāwūn sur sa medersa à al-Rumyla qui atteint les 600 pages dans sa forme originale et approche les deux cents pages dans l'édition qu'en a faite H. N. al-Ḥarithy, *The Waqf document of Sultan al-Nāṣir Ḥasan B. Muḥammad b. Qalāwūn for his Complex in al-Rumaila*, Bibliotheca Islamica 45, Beyrouth – Berlin 2001, p. 1-186 ; de même que celle d'al-Ašraf Qāytbāy (m. 901/1496) en 235 folios, cf. D. Behrens-Abouseif, Qāytbāy's Foundation in Medina, the *Madrasah*, the *Ribāṭ* and the *Dashīshah*, *Mamlūk Studies Review* II, 1998, p. 62.

13. Notamment al-Ğarawānī (m. 788/1386), *al-Kawkab al-mušriq fīmā yaḥtāğ ilayhi l-muwaṯṯiq li-ʿālim al-šurūṭ*, éd. S. Saghbini, Berlin 2010., p. 134-170, et al-Asyūṭī (m. 880 ?/1475 ?), *Ğawāhir al-ʿuqūd wa-muʿīn al-quḍāt wa-l-muwaqqiʿīn wa-l-šuhūd*, éd. M. ʿAbd al-Ḥamīd M. al-Saʿdanī, Beyrouth, Dār al-Kutub al-ʿilmiyya, s.d. II vol., vol. I, p. 257-302.

14. Sur la structure variée de ces documents voir al-Asyūṭī, *Ğawāhir al-ʿuqūd* (cité n. 13), p. 256-257. Aussi Denoix, Une exploration (cité, n. 10), p. 30-31.

15. Comme la medersa à al-Rumyla dans la *waqfiyya* d'al-Ḥasan b. Muḥammad b. Qalāwūn, cf. al-Ḥarithy, *The Waqf document* (cité n. 12), p. 1-186, suivie d'une autre *waqfiyya* sur cette même medersa, p. 186-227.

serait affilié. Ces personnes sont tout aussi bien susceptibles de figurer comme bénéficiaires par le constituant d'un waqf dans des actes de waqf conformément à la loi religieuse[16]. Cette disposition s'applique davantage encore aux actes dressés pour des Mamelouks dont l'ascendance ignorée, de par leur capture dès l'enfance, est supplantée par des liens de patronage et de fraternité (*ḫušdaš*) : dans la maison militaire c'est le maître qui est leur père (*wālid*) de substitution[17], tandis que lui voit en eux ses enfants (*awlād*)[18].

Les revenus d'un bien de mainmorte peuvent être assignés à deux types de bénéficiaires séparément : une partie est convertie en waqf *ḏurrī*, destinée à des personnes nommément inscrites dans la *waqfiyya*, l'autre est convertie en waqf charitable (*ḫayrī*), tel l'entretien ou la gestion d'un lieu religieux ou public. Lorsque les deux types de bénéficiaires s'associent sur un waqf ou une portion de waqf, il s'agit alors d'un waqf *muštarak*. Pour illustrer ce dernier cas par un seul exemple, il suffit d'évoquer l'un des biens-fonds constitutifs de la *waqfiyya* de Barsbāy dont les revenus sont pour moitié destinés à sa descendance à parts égales entre les hommes et les femmes, et pour moitié à l'école d'al-Ašrafiyya[19].

Le même principe d'égalité entre les hommes et les femmes est formulé à l'endroit des bénéficiaires par le *wāqif* dans le même moule expressif et dans un ordre similaire, comme en témoignent de nombreuses *waqfiyyāt*[20].

Sans nous astreindre à suivre l'ordre des éléments juridiques de la *waqfiyya*, intéressons-nous de près à la troisième partie, dans laquelle le *wāqif* (le fondateur du waqf) fixe les conditions (*šurūṭ*) à observer pour la gestion et la distribution des profits générés par le waqf. Succédant à l'énumération des biens mobiles ou immobiles du *wāqif*, ces conditions sont caractérisées par une précision minutieuse et un considérable souci de détail qui règlementent tous les aspects du fonctionnement et de la conservation du waqf[21].

Mais avant d'aborder plus en détails ces conditions, rappelons que dans une *waqfiyya*, il est fait mention, en premier lieu, du statut légal du waqf à travers la formule consacrée qui se décline sous plusieurs formes dont voici la plus commune :

> « *waqfan šarʿiyyan wa-ḥabsan dāʾiman marḍiyyan lā yubāʿu aṣlu ḏālika wa-lā yūhabu wa-lā yumlaku wa-lā yurhanu*[22] [....] :

16. Voir par exemple, al-Ḫaṣṣāf, *Aḥkām al-awqāf*, Beyrouth 1999, p. 57-61 : une maison pour loger des personnes déterminées ; p. 80-83 : le *wāqif* immobilisant les revenus de sa propriété foncière au bénéfice de la descendance d'une autre personne.

17. M. Eychenne, Le *bayt* à l'époque mamelouke. Une entité sociale à revisiter, *Annales Islamologiques* 42, 2008, p. 275-295, p. 275, sur les liens pérennes d'amitié et de solidarité, p. 291-293.

18. M. H. Benkheira, A. Giladi, C. Mayeur-Jaouen, J. Sublet, *La famille en islam d'après les sources arabes*, Les Indes savantes, *Etudes sur l'Asie*, Paris 2013, p. 20, 22.

19. Il s'agit de la section 11 de la *waqfiyya* de Barsbāy qui est un waqf *muštarak*, cf. Darrāǧ, *Ḥuǧǧat* (cité n. 3), p. ٤٠-٤١.

20. Comme la *waqfiyya* d'Ibn Tūġān al-Ḥasanī datée de 870/1465, et celle d'al-Qāḍī ʿUṯmān b. Asʿad b. al-Munaǧǧā (m. 641/1243) (cf. *supra*, note 12).

21. Les divers types de conditions en fonction de l'objet du waqf sont exposés par al-Asyūṭī, *Ǧawāhir al-ʿuqūd* (cité n. 13) : les conditions communes : p. 257-259 ; conditions à fixer pour le waqf d'une mosquée, voir p. 259-271 ; conditions pour le waqf d'une medersa, voir p. 272-277 ; conditions pour le waqf d'un hôpital, voir p. 277-282 ; conditions pour une zawiya de confrérie soufie, p. 282-290.

22. Sur les entrées introductives des waqfs, suivant la nature de son objet et le rang social du *wāqif*, voir al-Asyūṭī, *Ǧawāhir al-ʿuqūd* (cité n. 13), p. 256-257.

Un bien de mainmorte légal et une immobilisation permanente qui satisfait aux règles de la loi. Les fondations originelles de ce bien ne sauraient être ni vendues, ni données, ni acquises, ni hypothéquées, ni héritées [.....] »

Après quelques formules rituelles d'usage, le *wāqif* énumère alors une série de conditions minutieuses qui doivent être observées, pour gérer jusque dans ses moindres détails le waqf et répartir ses revenus non seulement entre les bénéficiaires parmi sa famille et sa descendance, mais aussi entre les pauvres et les nécessiteux dans le cas d'un waqf de charité ou d'un waqf combinant les deux types de bénéficiaires (waqf *muštarak*).

Entre *waqfiyya* d'un musulman et d'un non-musulman *ḏimmī*

Bien que nous ne nous intéressions ici qu'aux *waqfiyyāt* établies pour des musulmans, ne perdons pas de vue que certaines *waqfiyyāt* établies pour des chrétiens sont susceptibles d'insister également sur cette égalité entre les hommes et les femmes pour les mêmes raisons que les musulmans. L'éventualité de la gestion du waqf par un musulman, en cas d'absence d'un chrétien (*naṣrānī*) milkite est à envisager. À défaut de ces conditions d'égalité exigées par le *wāqif*, l'administrateur (*nāẓir*) ou le *qāḍī* musulman seraient en droit d'appliquer la loi coranique dans la distribution des revenus entre les hommes et les femmes d'un waqf fondé par un chrétien. À preuve la *waqfiyya* de Sinaï n° 259[23] dans laquelle le *wāqif*, un melkite du nom de Sulaymān b. Bišāra b. Fahd, pose les mêmes clauses d'égalité que celles stipulées dans les *waqfiyyāt* musulmanes :

> « [....] *min awlādihi wa-awlād awlādihi wa-ḏurriyatihi wa-naslihi wa-ʿaqibihi al-ḏukūr wa-l-ināṯ min walad al-ẓahr wa-l-baṭn bi-l-sawiyya baynahum lā yufaḍḍal ḏakar minhum ʿalā unṯā wa-lā unṯā ʿalā ḏakar* :
>
> [...] parmi ses enfants, les enfants de ses enfants, sa descendance, sa postérité et sa progéniture masculine et féminine qu'elle soit de sa descendance masculine ou féminine[24], à égalité entre eux, sans préférer un garçon à une fille, ni une fille à un garçon[25] ».

Et bien évidemment, lorsqu'il s'agit d'un prêtre melkite immobilisant une propriété foncière en waqf, comme c'est le cas de Maqārī b. Musallam[26] qui s'est assuré la possession de plusieurs bien-fonds durant sa vie, la *waqfiyya* ne stipule pas les mêmes conditions de partage

23. Il s'agit du troisième acte dans le document du Sinaï n° 259, entièrement déchiffré par nos soins dans la base CALD.

24. Littéralement : qu'elle soit enfant du dos ou du ventre (respectivement descendant du père ou descendant de la mère). D'autres mots équivalents sont usités dans le langage du Coran et de la tradition prophétique : *raḥim* pour les femmes et *ṣulb* pour les hommes, voir la fine analyse qu'en fait M. H. Benkheira, Le vocabulaire arabe de la parenté dans les sources anciennes, *La famille* (cité n. 18), p. 56-57.

25. Les actes de waqf du patriarcat copte renferment quelques *waqfiyyāt* chrétiennes qui fixent ces mêmes conditions pour la descendance du *wāqif*, comme l'acte Coptic Part. Archive D 417, en cours de déchiffrement dans la base CALD.

26. Le personnage de Maqārī b. Musallam apparaît dans plusieurs actes légaux conservés dans les archives du monastère de Sainte Catherine au Mont Sinaï, dont voici quelques numéros d'inventaire : 252, 262, 264, 264, 271, 275, 283, 286, 287, 290, 291, 292, 293, 297, 298, 306, 307, 308, 309, 312, 1064. Ils sont tous en cours de déchiffrement dans la base CALD.

des revenus, et par conséquent ne fait pas mention d'égalité entre les hommes et les femmes étant donné qu'elle allait de soi. En témoigne la *waqfiyya* Sinaï n° 275[27] dans laquelle le prêtre Maqārī, en immobilisant en waqf son bien-fonds au profit des prêtres du monastère Sainte-Catherine du Mont Sinaï (Ṭūr Sīnā'), n'a pas fait état d'une clause d'égalité entre les deux sexes. Il en est de même de la *waqfiyya* Sinaï n° 249, enregistrée dans le tribunal šāfi'ite de Gaza, dans laquelle le prêtre (*qiss*) Mubārak b. Baraka b. Sābā ? immobilise l'intégralité de sa maison située à Gaza au profit des prêtres résidant dans ce même monastère du Mont Sinaï, mais sans la moindre spécification de clause égalitaire[28].

Il y aurait lieu de rappeler que d'un point de vue juridique, toutes les conditions, sans exception, susceptibles d'être fixées par un *wāqif* musulman peuvent l'être aussi par un *wāqif ḏimmī*[29] : « Effectivement, répondit al-Ḫaṣṣāf (m. 261/875), il [le *ḏimmī*] est statutairement semblable au musulman en ce qui relève des conditions d'un *wāqif*. Car, tout ce qu'il est permis au musulman de fixer comme conditions [dans sa *waqfiyya*] est aussi permis au *ḏimmī* »[30].

Principe d'égalité entre hommes et femmes dans les conditions du *wāqif*

Dans les waqfiyyāt *familiales* (ahlī *ou* ḏurrī)

Aborder la question de l'égalité entre les deux sexes dans les actes de waqf, c'est d'abord traiter principalement des waqfs familiaux (*ahlī* ou *ḏurrī*), dans la mesure où les waqfs charitables ne sont concernés que quand ils renferment un waqf *muštarak*, ce qui n'est pas souvent le cas. La longue *waqfiyya* du sultan al-Nāṣir Ḥasan Muḥammad b. Qalāwūn (m. 741/1341), par exemple, ne prévoit aucune partie *muštaraka*, alliant le waqf *ḫayrī* dont elle traite à un waqf familial (*ahlī*)[31]. Par contre, la fameuse *waqfiyya* du Sultan al-Ašraf Barsbāy (m. 841/1438), quant à elle, consacre la 22e section (*kitāb*) exclusivement à sa descendance (*Awqāf ḫāṣṣa bi-l-ḏurriyya*)[32]. En effet, cette section se distingue des nombreuses autres sections qui ont trait aux waqfs *ḫayrī* dont les bénéfices sont affectés principalement à la grande mosquée d'al-Ašrafiyya (*al-Ǧāmi' al-Ašrafī*[33]). Après avoir énuméré ses divers biens situés dans la région

27. L'acte de waqf au nom de Maqārī b. Musallam, daté du 26 *rabī' al-ṯānī* 894/29 mars 1489 est à la marge de l'acte de vente d'un immeuble dont il est l'acheteur. Cet acte est entièrement déchiffré par nos soins dans la base CALD.

28. Entièrement déchiffré par nos soins dans la base CALD ; voir les indications dans le catalogue édité par D. S. Richards, Documents from Sinai Concerning Mainly Cairene Property, *Journal of the Economic and Social History of the Orient* 38, 1985, p. 225-293, p. 228-229.

29. Le cas du Zoroastien (*maǧūsī*) est sujet à caution, à tout le moins d'après al-Ḫaṣṣāf, *Aḥkām* (cité n. 16), p. 292. Mais il l'intègre toutefois dans les gens de la *ḏimma* au même titre que les chrétiens et les juifs, cf. *ibid.*, p. 287, 288, Un *ḏimmī* peut bénéficier des revenus d'un waqf d'un musulman, cf. al-Ḫaṣṣāf, *ibid.*, p. 291, 294 ; al-Asyūṭī, *Ǧawāhir al-'uqūd* (cité n. 13), p. 250.

30. Al-Ḫaṣṣāf, *Aḥkām* (cité n. 16), p. 292. Voir aussi R. Peters, WAḲF, *Encyclopédie de l'Islam*, 2e éd., XI, p. 66.

31. Al-Ḥarithy, *The Waqf document* (cité n. 12), p. 1-186.

32. Darrāǧ, *Ḥuǧǧat* (cité n. 3), p. 61-63 ; Abū Zahra, *Muḥāḍarāt* (cité n. 6), p. 25-26.

33. Darrāǧ, *Ḥuǧǧat* (cité n. 3), de la première à la huitième section, il est question des waqfs dont les revenus sont destinés à *al-Ǧāmi' al-Ašrafī*, p. 1-34 ; voir aussi la 16e section, p. 48 ; la 20e, p. 59-60 ; la 24e, p. 67-69. D'autres

du Caire qu'il immobilise au profit de sa descendance, Barsbāy, suivant les diverses formules d'usage déjà consignées dans les manuels notariaux[34], pose les règles de priorité à respecter entre les générations successives de sa descendance comme suit :

« Tout ceci est constitué en waqf par le *wāqif* au profit de ses enfants encore de ce monde, puis au profit de ceux que Dieu fera naître d'eux, les garçons et les filles en cela égaux, puis au profit de leurs enfants, qu'ils descendent de sa progéniture masculine ou féminine, puis au profit de la descendance de ces derniers, à parts égales entre les garçons et les filles, qu'ils descendent de sa progéniture masculine ou féminine. Ceci de sorte que la première génération occulte toujours [en termes d'héritage] la suivante (*taḥǧib al-ṭabaqa l-ʿulyā minhum al-suflā*). Lorsque l'un des héritiers de la première génération trépasse en laissant derrière lui pour héritier un enfant, un petit-enfant ou un arrière petit-enfant descendant de sa progéniture masculine ou féminine qu'il s'agisse d'une ou de plusieurs personnes, il héritera de ce dernier, même s'il est de la dernière génération (*wa in safal*) selon les conditions et l'ordre explicités précédemment[35] ».

Ce sont ces mêmes conditions que l'on trouve fixées dans d'autres *waqfiyyāt* mameloukes, telle la *waqfiyya* Cairo National Archive 27 datée de 721 de l'hégire, sachant que celle de Barsbāy, elle, est datée de 841 de l'hégire.

Les formules qui reviennent systématiquement pour exprimer ces conditions de distribution des profits à parts égales entre les hommes et les femmes (mentionnées tantôt au pluriel tantôt au singulier), se déclinent soit sous une forme générale, comme dans Cairo National Archive 27 : « *al-ḏukūr wa-l-ināṯ bi-l-sawiyya baynahum* : les garçons et les filles à parts égales entre eux »,[36] et dans Cairo National Archive 223 (datée de 903 de l'hégire) : « *al-ḏakar wa-l-unṯā fīhi sawāʾ*: Le garçon et la fille [traité] en cela en égaux »[37]. Soit sous une forme davantage détaillée, plus particulièrement en ce qui concerne les droits des générations ascendantes par rapport à celles descendantes. À cet égard, la *waqfiyya* Cairo National Archive 27 suffit à donner un aperçu de ce souci de précision. Elle fut établie pour l'officier supérieur de l'armée mamelouke Abū Saʿīd Baktamar b. ʿAbd Allāh lorsqu'il était le bénéficiaire de son propre waqf de son vivant :

> « *Yantafiʿu bi-ḏālika l-intifāʿ al-šarʿī intifāʿ miṯlihi bi-miṯl ḏālika ʿalā l-waǧh al-šarʿī ṯumma min baʿdihi ʿalā awlādihi l-ḏukūr wa-l-ināṯ bi-l-sawiyya baynahum yastiqullu bihi l-wāḥid ʿinda nfirādihi ḏakaran kān aw unṯā wa-yaštariku fīhi l-iṯnān famā fawqahumā ʿinda l-iǧtimāʿ bi-l-sawiyya baynahum lā yufaḍḍal ḏakarun ʿalā unṯā wa-lā unṯā ʿalā ḏakar* :
>
> Il tire légalement bénéfice de ce bien-fonds comme il convient à tout un chacun dans cette situation juridique, conformément à l'usage légal, puis après lui le bénéfice ira à ses enfants à parts égales

sections traitent des waqfs constitués au bénéfice d'autres lieux de culte, telles la grande mosquée de Siryāqos dans la banlieue du Caire (la 23e section, p. 63-67) ; une zawiya située dans un lieu désertique (la 14e section, p. 45-47). Sur la *waqfiyya* de Barsbāy, voir aussi les remarques pertinentes de ABŪ ZAHRA, *Muḥāḍarāt* (cité n. 6), p. 26.

34. On en trouve d'ores et déjà les éléments de base au IIIe/IXe siècle, chez al-ḪAṢṢĀF, *Aḥkām* (cité n. 16), p. 62-79. Voir aussi al-ĞARAWĀNĪ, *al-Kawkab al-mušriq* (cité n. 13), p. 147ق-148ق et p. 147ب-148ب; al-ASYŪṬĪ, *Ǧawāhir al-ʿuqūd* (cité n. 13), p. 263-264.

35. DARRĀĞ, *Ḥuǧǧat* (cité n. 3), p. 62.

36. M. M. AMIN, « Waṯāʾiq waqf al-sulṭān al-Nāṣir Muḥammad b. Qalāwūn », dans *Taḏkirat al-nabīh fī ayyām al-Manṣūr wa-banīh*, Markaz taḥqīq al-turāṯ, Le Caire 1982, III vol., vol. II, p. 349.

37. M. M. AMIN, *Catalogue des documents d'archives du Caire*, p. 449.

entre les garçons et les filles. En cas d'un unique héritier, qu'il soit fille ou garçon, il en tirera seul le bénéfice, mais en cas de deux héritiers ou plusieurs, ils se le partageront équitablement ; le garçon ne doit pas être préféré à la fille, ni la fille au garçon[38] ».

Ou encore dans la *waqfiyya* Cairo National Archive 223 [39] et dans Cairo Ministry of Waqf 571[40] (datée de 870/1465), la *waqfiyya* de l'officier mamelouk Yaḥyā b. Ṭūġān al-Ḥasanī :

> « *Al-ḏakar wa-l-unṯā fī ḏālika sawā' yastaqillu bihi l-wāḥid 'inda l-infirād wa-yaštariku fihi l-iṯnān 'inda l-iǧtimā' bi-l-sawiyya* :
>
> Le garçon et la fille doivent être traités en cela en égaux. Lorsqu'il n'y a qu'un unique héritier il en devient le seul bénéficiaire, et se le partagent équitablement [s'y associent] lorsqu'ils sont deux ».

Dans ces trois dernières *waqfiyyāt*, de longs développements se poursuivent dans des paragraphes donnant lieu à de nombreux détails compartimentant les générations entre elles et délimitant les droits de chacune par rapport à celle qui la précède ou lui succède. Comme le contenu de ces paragraphes est rédigé à l'identique, nous en proposons pour modèle celui de la *waqfiyya* de Muḥammad b. Qalāwūn, dont voici la traduction :

« Après eux [les revenus iront] à leurs enfants, puis[41] aux enfants de leurs enfants, ensuite à leur descendance et postérité, garçons et filles descendant des mères ou des pères. La première génération occulte toujours la suivante ainsi que cela sera explicité plus loin. Cela dit, à la mort de l'une des personnes désignées qui aurait laissé derrière elle un enfant, un petit-enfant (*walad* sans précision de sexe) et davantage, ce sont ses frères et sœurs qui se partageront les bénéfices du waqf à parts égales, en sus des bénéfices qui leur revenaient [ailleurs][42]. Si cette personne n'a ni frère, ni sœur, sa quote-part (*naṣībuhu*) ira alors à son fils, puis à son petit-fils, et ensuite à sa descendance suivant l'explication mentionnée plus haut. Si elle n'a laissé ni enfant, ni petit-enfant, ni aucune descendance, [sa quote-part] ira aux générations (*ṭabaqāt*) les plus proches [de la sienne[43]].

Outre les enfants bénéficiaires directs de son waqf, le *wāqif* peut prendre l'initiative de fixer au préalable les mêmes conditions d'égalité pour les enfants d'un de ses enfants bénéficiaires garçon ou fille. Dans cette même *waqfiyya* du Sultan al-Ašraf Barsbāy (m. 841/1438), éditée en abrégé (*ḥuǧǧa manšūra*)[44], outre les sections dédiées aux conditions dans lesquelles

38. Amin, (cité n. 36), p. 349.
39. Amin, (cité n. 37), p. 449.
40. S. Conermann et S. Saghbini, *Awlād al-Nās* as Founders of Pious Endowments: The *Waqfiyah* of Yaḥyā Ibn Tūġān al-Ḥasanī of the Year 870/1465, *Mamlūk Studies Review* VI, 2002, p. 21-50, p. 44.
41. Les juristes insistent particulièrement sur le sens de la préposition *ṯumma* que nous rendons ici par « puis ». Placée entre plusieurs générations, elle exprime un ordre de succession (*tartīb bayna l-aǧyāl*) contrairement à la préposition *wāw* qui exprime l'association (*ǧam'*) de plusieurs générations dans un revenu de waqf. Voir Ibn Abī l-Dam, *Kitāb Adab al-qaḍā', wa-huwa l-durrar al-manẓūmāt fī l-aqḍiyya wa-l-ḥukūmāt*, éd. M. M. al-Zuḥaylī, Damas 1982., p. 546-547, al-Asyūṭī, *Ǧawāhir al-'uqūd* (cité n. 13), p. 252.
42. N'oublions pas qu'au sein des familles qui bénéficient des revenus d'un waqf pluriel (*muštarak*), certains héritiers *ab intestat*, selon leur degré de parenté avec le *wāqif* héritent en même temps d'autres biens de celui-ci suivant les règles successorales du *fiqh*.
43. Amin, (cité n. 36), p. 349-350. À ce niveau, les deux autres *waqfiyyāt* sont assez similaires.
44. Darrāǧ, *Ḥuǧǧat* (cité n. 3), partie arabe, p. ١-٦٩.

l'accent est mis sur le partage à parts égales entre la descendance masculine et féminine du *wāqif*, Barsbāy rappelle que les mêmes règles de partage doivent être observées entre les descendants de sa fille Fāṭima Sutayta à laquelle il concède exclusivement un bien immobilier situé au Caire[45]. Il s'ensuit que la descendance de celle-ci doit se plier à ces conditions pour pouvoir prétendre en tant que bénéficiaires, à une partie des revenus générés par ce waqf. Cependant, si Fāṭima s'avère dans l'impossibilité d'enfanter, les bénéfices de la fondation iront à la descendance de Barsbāy par ses autres enfants, suivant les mêmes conditions d'égalité entre les deux sexes énoncées au préalable[46]. Sous cet angle, ce waqf peut être considéré "suspensif"[47], parce qu'en premier lieu, il est limité dans le temps, étant établi au bénéfice de Fāṭima, et qu'ensuite, dans le cas où elle s'avérerait sans descendance, il sera attribué aux héritiers de Barsbāy, à savoir à sa descendance assurée par ses autres enfants.

La charité du waqf soumise à l'égalité entre les deux sexes

Ainsi que nous l'avons évoqué précédemment dans les *waqfiyyāt* établissant un waqf *ḫayrī*, les conditions fixées par le *wāqif* servent à gérer la distribution des bénéfices au profit des lieux religieux et institutions publiques à moins que le *wāqif* n'ait prévu une section relative à un waqf *muštarak* ou à un waqf *ahlī* comme dans la *waqfiyya* de Barsbāy. Toutefois, même dans le cadre d'un waqf *ḫayrī* il est possible pour le fondateur de waqf, dans la section réservée au waqf familial ou *muštarak*, de poser la condition d'égalité entre les hommes et les femmes bénéficiaires sans qu'ils soient nécessairement des membres de sa famille, ni qu'ils aient un quelconque lien de parenté avec lui. En effet, il arrive que cette clause d'égalité tienne une place majeure dans les conditions fixées par le *wāqif* quant à la distribution d'une portion des revenus de son waqf *ḫayrī* aux pauvres et aux nécessiteux. En d'autres termes et bien que ce soit rare, la clause d'égalité figure même dans des actes de waqfs où les bénéficiaires ne sont pas nommément désignés.

Dans la *waṯīqat* waqf Masrūr b. ʿAbd Allāh al-Šiblī al-Ǧimdār, datée de 760/1358, il est précisé que seuls les pauvres en retraite pieuse (*al-ǧiwār*) dans les deux villes saintes de l'islam, La Mecque et Médine, qui soient d'obédience sunnite à l'exclusion des deux sectes zaydite et rāfiḍite, peuvent se voir bénéficier de la charité de son waqf à parts égales entre les hommes et les femmes : « *wa-ilā l-muǧāwirīn bihimā al-ḏukūr wa-l-ināṯ al-sunniyyīn ġayr al-zaydiyya wa-l-rawāfiḍ bi-l-sawiyya*[48] ».

Curieusement, les manuels notariaux ne proposent pas de formulaire mentionnant l'égalité entre les hommes et les femmes lorsque les revenus du waqf sont affectés en général aux pauvres et aux nécessiteux[49].

45. Darrāǧ, *Ḥuǧǧat* (cité n. 3), p. 37 [feuillet 45].

46. Darrāǧ, *Ḥuǧǧat* (cité n. 3), p. 38 [feuillet 45].

47. Le caractère supposé suspensif de ce waqf n'en fait pas, une fois réversible aux propriétaires héritiers, une propriété ordinaire et aliénable. Il garde son statut de waqf mais au bénéfice d'une autre lignée du constituant du waqf. Pour plus de développement sur ce sujet, cf. Cl. Cahen, Réflexions sur le waqf ancien, *Studia Islamica* 14, 1961, p. 37-56, p. 44 et suivantes.

48. Il s'agit de la *waqfiyya* : Cairo *Aḥwāl šaḫṣiyya* 39, cf. Ibrāhīm ʿAbd al-Laṭīf, « Waṯīqat waqf Masrūr Ibn ʿAbd Allāh al-Šiblī al-Ǧimdār » *Maǧallat kulliyyat al-Ādāb*, Ǧāmiʿat al-Qāhira, XXI, 1 (1959), p. 133-185, p. 150.

49. Nulle mention d'égalité entre les deux sexes dans les sections traitant des waqfs *ḫayrī* dans al-Asyūṭī, *Ǧawāhir al-ʿuqūd* (cité n. 13), p. 263, 270-271, 286, 287-288, 290-291, notamment le formulaire modèle proposé

Les waqfiyyāt *indifférentes à l'égalité et anti-égalitaires*

Beaucoup de *waqfiyyāt*, vraisemblablement les plus nombreuses, passent sous silence cette mention d'égalité entre les deux sexes, qui d'ailleurs n'est pas toujours mise en avant dans les manuels notariaux contemporains[50]. Au vu du nombre restreint des *waqfiyyāt* que nous avons consultées[51], il nous a paru évident que l'égalité est souvent stipulée comme clause par des fondateurs de waqf appartenant au groupe social des politiques : sultan, officier de l'armée, émir, gouverneur etc.[52] Certes ils représentent la portion la plus écrasante dans les *waqfiyyāt* mameloukes archivées, suivie de loin d'autres groupes sociaux, d'abord les dignitaires religieux, puis l'élite civile et enfin les commerçants[53]. Les *waqfiyyāt* établies pour des groupes sociaux indéterminés ou autres que politique ne semblent pas faire mention de cette clause d'égalité[54]. Bien évidemment, ne sont pas concernées par cette clause les *waqfiyyāt* dans lesquelles la volonté du *wāqif* fait dépendre cette condition du choix de l'administrateur (*nāẓir*), ce qui est rarement le cas dans les actes commandités par des « politiques », la distribution des revenus du waqf étant faite conformément à la règle coranique (Coran, IV:11), à savoir que la part de l'homme vaut le double de celui de la femme : « *En ce qui concerne vos enfants, Dieu vous prescrit d'attribuer au garçon une part égale à celle de deux filles* ».

En cas de conflit entre héritiers, le juge fera appliquer la loi coranique, autrement dit le profit du waqf avantagera l'homme au détriment de la femme. Toute plainte risque de ne pas avoir l'effet juridique escompté à moins de faire appel à des témoins en nombre pour faire entendre que le silence du *wāqif* ne signifie pas un partage selon la règle coranique.

D'autres *wāqifs* enfin, insistent clairement sur la préférence masculine, en rappelant que le partage du *ray'* du waqf doit se faire selon la loi divine, c'est-à-dire que l'homme a droit au double de ce qui revient à la femme. C'est dans le même ordre d'idées que sont réparties les parties constitutives du waqf du grand *qāḍī* 'Uṯmān b. As'ad b. al-Munağğā (m. 641/1243) qui constitua en waqf plusieurs biens-fonds (en 634/1237) à la fois au profit de ses enfants et sa descendance, et au profit des institutions religieuses. Ce *wāqif*, qui est d'obédience ḥanbalite – ce qui pourrait justifier, en partie du moins, sa préférence pour la règle coranique – ne se

---

pour les waqfs *ḫayrī*, p. 294-295. Al-Ğarawānī, *al-Kawkab al-mušriq* (cité n. 13), recourt à des expressions qui renvoient au choix du *wāqif* ou de l'administrateur, p. 135ب, 139ب, 139ق, cf. sur le waqf *ḫayrī* (*al-birr wa-l-qurubāt*) proprement dit : p. 149-150ب, 149-150ق. Le formulaire proposé par Šihāb al-Dīn al-Nuwayrī, dans son encyclopédie n'en tient pas compte non plus, pas même dans la partie traitant du waqf *ahlī* où la préférence est donnée à la règle coranique, cf. al-Nuwayrī, *Nihāyat al-arab fī funūn al-adab*, éd. M. R. Muruwwa *et alii*, Beyrouth 2004, XXXIII vol., vol. IX, p. 103-104.

50. Bien qu'il y ait fait parfois allusion, c'est la règle coranique qui est souvent mentionnée par al-Asyūṭī, *Ğawāhir al-'uqūd* (cité n. 13), voir note précédente.

51. Plus exactement 41 *waqfiyyas* disponibles dans la base de données CALD.

52. Sur le cumul des fonctions des émirs mamelouks, cf. Denoix, Une exploration (cité, n. 10), p. 36.

53. Denoix, Une exploration (cité n. 10), p. 35.

54. Citons par exemple les waqfs *ḫayrī* suivants : Jérusalem Ḥaram 833 (747 de l'H) établi pour une femme du Maghreb du nom de Fāṭima b. Muḥammad al-Ḥusbābī ?; Jérusalem Ḥaram 617 (759 de l'H) établi pour 'Uṯmān b. Hurayf ?, un homme pieux ; Jérusalem Ḥaram 020 (768 de l'H), établi pour Ğa'far b. Muḥammad al-Saffār, cf. L. Donald, *A Catalogue of the Islamic Documents from al-Ḥaram aš-Šarīf in Jerusalem*, Beyrouth & Wiesbaden 1984, p 318-319.

55. Al-Munağğid, *Kitāb waqf* (cité n. 3), p. 30-31

contente pas de mentionner la différence d'héritage entre les hommes et les femmes, mais opte, à trois reprises, pour une citation du verset coranique « *li-l-ḏakar miṯlu ḥaẓẓ al-unṯayayn* : *au garçon une part égale à celle de deux filles* » qu'il incorpore dans chaque condition énoncée[55].

Recours au tribunal pour réclamer justice contre l'exclusion des femmes

Si le fondateur d'un waqf est en droit d'immobiliser différents biens de mainmorte au profit de ses enfants, en désignant séparément un bien pour chacun d'eux, il peut tout aussi immobiliser en partie ou dans sa totalité un bien au seul profit de sa descendance mâle à condition d'en préciser clairement les modalités et les conditions dans sa *waqfiyya*. Mais quelles que soient les précautions juridiques prises en ce sens pour prévenir d'éventuels conflits futurs entre les bénéficiaires, les cours de justice n'étaient pas moins amenées à trancher de nombreux litiges familiaux de cette nature[56].

Il est donc certainement arrivé que cette clause d'égalité fasse l'objet de plusieurs plaintes dans un tribunal mamelouk. Nous en voulons pour preuve le document Jérusalem Ḥaram 025 publié par Donald Little[57], dans lequel on apprend que le juge supérieur (*qāḍī l-quḍāt*) du Ḥaram al-Šarīf a reçu une requête (*qiṣṣa*) au sujet d'un waqf situé dans la ville de Nābulus dont les bénéficiaires étaient tous des hommes de la descendance du *wāqif*. Ces derniers décidèrent de recourir à la justice pour faire respecter la volonté de leur aïeul qui, selon eux, avait bien stipulé dans sa *waqfiyya* que seule sa descendance masculine est en droit de tirer profit du *ray*ʿ de son waqf, à l'exclusion de sa descendance féminine.

L'affaire en est arrivée là, suite à la contestation par une tierce personne, non nommée dans le document hélas, qui faisait répandre le bruit que le *wāqif* avait au contraire stipulé dans sa *waqfiyya* qu'il immobilisait son bien-fonds au profit de sa descendance mâle et femelle à égalité entre eux. Le juge de Nābulus a alors délivré son jugement dans un *marsūm* où il déclare que le dernier mot dans cette affaire revient au défunt *wāqif*. Or la volonté de ce dernier telle qu'elle avait été consignée dans sa *waqfiyya*, réexaminée par le juge doit être respectée, à savoir que seuls les hommes, à l'exclusion des femmes, peuvent jouir des profits tirés du waqf selon les conditions que le *wāqif* avait scrupuleusement établies. On se doute bien à quelle branche parentale appartient la personne anonyme qui avait fait courir la rumeur contre les monopolisateurs des revenus du waqf. Il s'agit vraisemblablement, d'un des descendants de la lignée matrilinéaire du *wāqif*, mais il est tout aussi probable que ce soit l'un des époux des femmes descendantes de ce dernier qui avaient été exclues de son testament de waqf.

Ce procès qui semble ne concerner de prime abord que deux parties qui ne se connaissent pas est en réalité un litige familial autour d'un héritage comme il y en avait tant à cette époque.

56. On en trouve trace dans les documents légaux qui nous sont parvenus ainsi que dans les avis juridiques émis par les juristes, et consignés par écrit dans de grands recueils juridiques appelés *nawāzil* ou *fatāwā*. Voir les données tirées d'al-WANŠARĪSĪ, *al-Miʿyār al-Muġrib*, et développées par POWERS dans A court case (cité n. 9), p. 229-254, *ibid.*, *Fatwās* as sources for legal and social history: A dispute over endowment revenues from fourteenth-century Fez », *al-Qanṭara* 11, 1990, p. 348-394, p. 295-341.

57. L. DONALD, Five Petitions and Consequential Decrees from Late Fourteenth Jerusalem, *al-Maǧalla al-ʿArabiyya li-l-ʿUlūm al-Insāniyya* 54, 1996, p. 353.

Droit normatif et volonté du wāqif

La question de l'égalité entre les hommes et les femmes en droit successoral islamique ne saurait être abordée sans rappeler la différence de moitié qui sépare la femme de l'homme. L'on est donc en droit de s'interroger sur le statut juridique de cette égalité entre les deux sexes confirmée dans certaines *waqfiyyāt*, comme sur la nature de son rapport avec les règles successorales qui avantagent les hommes sur les femmes. Faut-il y voir une condition outrageuse envers la loi religieuse, voire une mesure qui transgresse le cadre légal délimité par celle-ci ? La réponse est sans nul doute négative. Les manuels notariaux tout comme les ouvrages de *fiqh* sont unanimes quant à accorder cette disposition au *wāqif* dans la formulation de ses conditions.

Il faut rappeler que les prescriptions coraniques en matière de droit successoral ne sont pas prises en compte systématiquement dans les conditions que fixe le fondateur dans la distribution des revenus (*ray'*) de son waqf *ahlī* au profit de sa descendance, des personnes connues ou inconnues, ou de son waqf *ḫayrī* au profit des pauvres et des nécessiteux.

Comme l'a fait observer à juste titre Hennigan, les traditions prophétiques, souvent mises en avant par les juristes pour fonder religieusement l'institution du waqf, tant dans les ouvrages de *fiqh* que dans les manuels notariaux (*kutub al-šurūṭ*), sont principalement de deux catégories : les traditions représentant le waqf sous forme d'aumône (*ṣadaqa*) et celles qui en recommandent le *tasbīl*, c'est-à-dire le fait d'en fructifier les revenus de bienfaisance (*tasbīl al-ṯamara*)[58].

Les hadiths rapportés du Prophète tout comme les propos attribués à ses Compagnons sont unanimes à considérer les revenus d'un waqf comme une aumône (*ṣadaqa*), un acte charitable pieusement accompli par le *wāqif*, même lorsqu'il en destine les revenus à sa propre descendance. Les juristes se réfèrent souvent à la tradition prophétique transmise par le deuxième calife 'Umar b. al-Ḫaṭṭāb dans laquelle le Prophète lui recommande d'immobiliser le fonds (*aṣl*) et d'affecter les revenus à des œuvres de bienfaisance (*tasbīl*)[59]. Les quatre écoles juridiques sunnites, par delà leurs divergences mineures sur le partage à parts égales entre les hommes et les femmes, sont d'avis commun que les conditions fixées par le *wāqif* constituent l'épine dorsale de l'acte de waqf, et qu'à ce titre elles doivent être minutieusement respectées[60].

58. Il y a une troisième catégorie dite *amsakta*, relativement aux traditions mentionnant le verbe *amsaka* (immobiliser le bien principal). L'auteur la considère comme une catégorie tardive, parce qu'elle concerne les traditions postérieures aux traités de waqf des deux grands juristes ḥanafites qui furent les premiers spécialistes en la matière : Al-ḪAṢṢĀF (m. 261/875) et Hilāl al-RA'Y (m. 245 ou 249/859 ou 863). Ces traditions sont recensées dans les recueils de hadiths du IVe et Ve/Xe et XIe siècles (tels *Kitāb al-Sunan al-kubrā* d'al-BAYHAQĪ (m. 458/1066) et *al-Sunan* d'al-DĀRAQUṬNĪ (m. 385/995)). Cf. P. C. HENNIGAN, *The Birth of a Legal institution. The Formation of the Waqf in Third-Century A. H. Ḥanafī Legal Discourse*, Brill, Leyde – Boston 2004, p. 110-111.

59. « *Ḥabbis al-aṣl wa-sabbil al-ṯamara* : immobilise le fonds et donne les revenus en aumône », cf. H. LAOUST, *Le précis de droit d'Ibn Qudāma*, Beyrouth 1950, p. 123-124 ; Al-ḪAṢṢĀF, *Aḥkām* (cité n. 16), p. 8 ; A. al-ḪALLĀL, *Kitāb al-Wuqūf min masā'il al-imām Aḥmad b. Ḥanbal al-Šaybānī*, éd. 'Abd Allāh b. A. b. 'A. al-Zayd, Riyad, Maktabat al-ma'ārif, 1989/1410, II vol., I, p. 201-202 ; al-SARAḪSĪ, *al-Mabsūṭ*, Beyrouth 1989, XXXI vol., vol. XII, p. 30-31; al-ṬARĀBULUSĪ, *Kitāb al-Is'āf fī aḥkām al-awqāf*, Maṭba'a Hindiyya, Le Caire 1902, p. 6 ; al-ASYŪṬĪ, *Ǧawāhir al-'uqūd* (cité n. 13), p. 249 ; al-ĞARAWĀNĪ, *al-Kawkab al-mušriq* (cité n. 13), p. 134ق; voir aussi le sous-chapitre consacré à cette question par HENNIGAN, *The Birth of a Legal institution* (cité n. 58), p. 70-82.

60. Cette divergence s'illustre dans la controverse entre les juristes šāfi'ites et ḥanafites sur les conditions du *wāqif*, controverse suscitée par la consultation du sultan al-Nāṣir Ḥasan b. Muḥammad b. QALĀWŪN, rapportée par al-MAQRĪZĪ, *al-Mawā'iẓ* (cité n. 2), p. 118-123.

De là, les conditions qu'il revient au *wāqif* de fixer sont valides à partir du moment où elles ne transgressent pas les règles de la loi religieuse et n'entrent pas en contradiction avec les fondamentaux de la religion musulmane. Citons les exemples les plus souvent donnés pour illustrer ce principe. L'origine illicite des revenus d'un bien de mainmorte invalide *stricto sensu* l'établissement d'un waqf, de même que le fait d'affecter les revenus d'un waqf à une activité économique ou commerciale interdite (par ex. vente du vin, élevage porcin etc.)[61] ; un animal domestiqué ne saurait être désigné ni objet d'un waqf, ni non plus bénéficiaire de son *ray'* aussi fort que soit le lien affectif qui le lie au *wāqif* sauf dans le cadre d'une institution ; un enfant apostat (*murtadd*) peut faire l'objet d'une exclusion suivant la volonté du *wāqif* et perdre ainsi sa place d'héritier dans une *waqfiyya* parmi ses frères et sœurs musulmans[62]. Pareillement, est considéré comme acte préjudiciable tout waqf établi par une personne aux capacités mentales défaillantes, ce qui frappe de nullité (*fāsid*) la *waqfiyya* quand bien même elle serait ratifiée par un tuteur légal. Dans le même ordre d'idées, un *wāqif* qui, dans sa maladie de mort, immobilise en waqf l'ensemble de son bien ou une partie dépassant le tiers est dans l'obligation d'obtenir le consentement de ses héritiers légaux, au risque de voir le waqf ramené, par décision du juge, après sa mort, au tiers (*ṯuluṯ*) prescrit par la loi religieuse[63].

Néanmoins, l'ardeur dont faisaient preuve ces fondateurs de waqf (*wāqifūn*), en particulier dans l'établissement d'un waqf familial (*ḏurrī*), afin que les revenus de leurs biens-fonds immobilisés au profit de leur descendance soient partagés à parts égales entre les hommes et les femmes n'en demeure pas moins un moyen déguisé qui vise à contourner les prescriptions successorales (*'ilm al-farā'iḍ*) de la *šarī'a* qui avantagent les hommes sur les femmes. D'un autre côté, cependant, cette possibilité qu'offrent effectivement les règles moins strictes du waqf de contourner le droit successoral est tout aussi un moyen efficace pour les *wāqifs* désireux de transmettre en toute sécurité la totalité de leurs biens-fonds à leur famille à travers leur descendance masculine uniquement. Par conséquent, la même raison vaut pour les deux types de fondateurs de waqf, égalitaire et non égalitaire. À elle seule, cette interprétation ne peut suffire à expliquer cette volonté caractéristique dont font preuve quelques fondateurs de waqf à voir leurs biens en partie ou dans leur totalité équitablement partagés entre leurs descendances, masculine et féminine. On sait en effet qu'un moyen juridique supplémentaire pourrait être emprunté pour atteindre le même objectif, à savoir le legs par testament (*waṣiyya*) ou par donation (*hiba*) qui sont aussi efficaces pour transmettre *inter vivos* une propriété. À tout le moins partiellement, étant donné que ces deux institutions juridiques ne laissent qu'une mince marge légale à l'expression de la volonté du testateur ou du donateur comparée à celle dont bénéficie le *wāqif* pour constituer un waqf pour sa descendance. C'est en ce sens que le waqf présente un net avantage pour le *wāqif* et constitue une sorte d'alternative à ces deux modes de transmission de biens en islam.

Il y a donc bel et bien une volonté affichée par le *wāqif*, qui s'exprime incontestablement à travers cette égalité qu'il exige entre les deux lignées de sa descendance. Cette aspiration à

61. al-ASYŪṬĪ, *Ǧawāhir al-'uqūd* (cité n. 13), p. 250.

62. Al-ḪAṢṢĀF, *Aḥkām* (cité n. 16), p. 290-291; al-ṬARĀBULUSĪ, *Kitāb* (cité n. 59), p. 106; al-ASYŪṬĪ, *Ǧawāhir al-'uqūd* (cité n. 13), p. 250.

63. Ce genre de cas a donné lieu à de nombreux litiges traités par la justice mamelouke, cf. al-ṬARĀBULUSĪ, *Kitāb* (cité n. 59), p. 35.

l'égalité dont il témoigne semble transcender la largesse d'ordre légal qui s'offre à lui dans le cadre d'une *waqfiyya*. Sans exagérer le trait interprétatif, on peut supposer une autre raison au fait d'inclure dans la descendance légataire la postérité féminine au même titre que la postérité masculine : un souci d'équité qui serait plutôt solidaire d'une conception différente de la famille en général et de la descendance en particulier. Au lieu d'une lignée patrilinéaire assez représentative de la conception de la descendance telle qu'elle est largement déterminée dans les textes culturels et religieux de l'islam comme des religions monothéistes par ailleurs, la descendance pour ces *wāqifs* se conçoit autrement. Elle pose une double lignée, patrilinéaire et matrilinéaire : les hommes et les femmes sans préférence discriminatoire, bien que cela puisse ne concerner parfois qu'une section de la *waqfiyya* portant sur une portion déterminée du bien de waqf. Comme nous en avons fait état plus haut, gardons-nous d'oublier que cette tendance égalitaire est répandue principalement dans les *waqfiyyāt* établies pour l'élite politique la plus en vue, autrement dit pour l'aristocratie militaire, laquelle, rappelons-le au passage, n'est pas d'origine arabe, mais turque au sens large du terme et circassienne[64]. Il faut donc tenir compte de cette réalité socio-historique des fondateurs de waqf partisans de l'égalité, puisqu'elle participe à coup sûr de cette disposition égalitaire qui les caractérise quant à assurer à leur descendance féminine un rang social enviable et des revenus confortables qui les mettraient à l'abri du besoin.

Pour apporter une explication supplémentaire à cette disposition, il y aurait lieu de se référer à deux autres aspects majeurs dans la vie d'un Mamelouk : d'une part, son éducation religieuse qui, depuis sa capture et son arrivée dans l'enceinte familiale de son patron jusqu'à son affranchissement au sein du sultanat mamelouk, s'est peu à peu réduite jusqu'à disparaître au profit de la formation militaire (*furūsiyya*) ; de l'autre ses liens matrimoniaux quasi exclusivement noués avec des femmes de même origine que lui, les mariages avec les femmes locales étant rares, à la différence des fils de Mamelouks qui s'unissaient fréquemment à celles-ci dès la première génération[65]. De par son parcours, son adoption, et son insertion dans un réseau familial à multiples liens électifs forts au détriment des liens biologiques, ce *wāqif* mamelouk se serait fait une conception différente de la famille, et à travers elle, une conception de la descendance qui n'est pas en tous points fidèle à l'image prétendue dominante de la famille médiévale où le volet agnatique (parents mâles du côté paternel) constitue le noyau dur[66]. Il se pourrait donc que ces liens électifs noués depuis l'enfance durant sa formation et joints à la restriction des liens de mariage aux femmes de la même origine ethnique aient œuvré à l'élaboration de cette conception de la descendance à double lignée dans l'esprit du Mamelouk détenteur du pouvoir. Mais bien sûr cette conception est mise en place en vue de protéger les biens contre la fragmentation par héritage et surtout contre toute éventuelle confiscation *post mortem*[67]. Sous cet angle, on peut se présenter le problème autrement : en raison de l'absence de la ligne ascendante dans la généalogie d'un Mamlouk, la patrilinéarité s'en serait

64. Incluant les Mamelouks de diverses origines, kiptchaqe, tatare, moghole, arménienne etc., cf. D. AYALON, Mamlūk, *Encyclopédie de l'Islam*, 2e éd. VI, p. 299-301.

65. AYALON, Mamlūk (cité n. 64), p. 299.

66. Sur la parenté et son lexique en islam, voir M. H. BENKHEIRA, Le vocabulaire arabe de la parenté (cité n. 24), p. 55-58.

67. Voir les développements de ABŪ ZAHRA, *Muḥāḍarāt* (cité n. 6), p. 25-27.

trouvé affectée dans la ligne descendante, puisqu'elle est mise sur un même pied d'égalité que la matrilinéarité, mais sans que cela ait des conséquences notables sur le système patriarcal en vigueur dans la société mamelouke médiévale. La particularité de la situation sociale du Mamelouk – à la fois son éducation religieuse minimale et l'impact de sa famille d'accueil au sens large (l'élite militaire) comme au sens strict (la maison du maître) en tant qu'entité sociale visible – conjuguée à son souci de transmettre par voie héréditaire ses biens, a présidé à cette conception égalitaire entre les deux lignées de sa descendance. Ce sont donc ces liens de solidarité, de camaraderie et de clientèle, tissés tout au long de son parcours militaire et doublés d'un lien de mariage accentuant le degré d'appartenance à une ethnie non arabe, qu'il faut, semble-t-il, créditer d'un rôle déterminant dans la formulation de la conception de la descendance à double lignée.

La récurrence des crises politiques de même que la lutte pour le pouvoir, qui ont été à l'origine de successions constantes et rapides à la tête de l'État mamelouk, doivent être prises en considération dans la compréhension des objectifs visés par cette clause égalitaire dans les *waqfiyyāt* des princes et des sultans. Appelée à se dissoudre dans la société musulmane arabophone dès la deuxième génération, la descendance de ces derniers est quasiment exclue de l'institution militaire en faveur de nouvelles générations d'arrivants mamelouks fraîchement capturés. Or, dans la mesure où l'on sait que c'est bien de cette institution que proviennent les nouveaux dirigeants politiques mamelouks, il est donc exclu pour le Mamelouk d'élite d'envisager un successeur de sa propre descendance au sein du pouvoir politique par décret sultanien ou quelque autre testament politique[68]. Compte tenu de ces données historiques, nous privilégions l'hypothèse suivante : conscients de leur incapacité à transmettre leur statut de pouvoir par héritage à leur descendance, ces dirigeants politiques se rabattaient en contrepartie sur la transmission de leur richesse matérielle accumulée par le biais des actes de waqf dans le but d'assurer ainsi une pérennité du capital économique à défaut d'une pérennité du capital symbolique[69]. Toutefois, cette transmission héréditaire emprunte chez bon nombre d'entre eux la voie égalitaire entre les deux lignées de leur descendance, féminine et masculine. De ces deux capitaux autrefois réunis dans la même personne mamelouke détentrice de pouvoirs politique et militaire, en l'occurrence le *wāqif*, seul le capital économique, à la faveur des règles souples que permet l'institution du waqf, s'avère transmissible par voie héréditaire sans désavantager la femme au profit de l'homme.

C'est toute l'époque mamelouke en réalité qu'il convient d'invoquer pour fonder ce principe d'égalité en mettant en lumière l'évolution du statut de la femme dans la société mamelouke, et tout particulièrement au sein de l'élite politique. À l'appui de nombreux documents d'archive et de sources historique, juridique et littéraire de cette époque, plusieurs études récentes ont mis au jour le rôle actif de la femme dans l'économie urbaine (notamment à Jérusalem, Damas, Le Caire) et partant, le poids social de plus en plus accru dont

68. Sur le système militaire mamelouk, cf. D. AYALON, Mamlūkiyāt, *Jerusalem Studies in Arabic and Islam* 2, 1980, p. 322-339 ; aussi D. AYALON, *The Mamlūk military society. Collected studies*, Variorum Reprints, Londres 1979.

69. N'ayant épargné ni les savants religieux, ni les mystiques soufis, ni les puissants et notables, l'on ne s'étonnera pas de voir que le modèle héréditaire intéressait aussi les Mamelouks qui y recouraient à travers les waqfs qu'ils fondaient en nombre pour transmettre leurs biens, fait observer C. MAYEUR-JAOUEN, dans « Portraits de familles avec saints », *La famille* (cité n. 18), Paris 2013, p. 311-390, p. 374.

elle jouissait dans ses rapports à l'homme au sein de la famille et de la société mamelouke en général[70]. Ainsi les rapports entre l'homme et la femme, tout au long de cette période, ont connu un changement considérable à la faveur de nombre de facteurs dont l'indépendance économique de la femme constitue à n'en pas douter le facteur majeur[71]. À la lumière de ces éléments, il y a lieu, sinon d'ancrer, du moins de mettre en relation cet état de choses avec le modèle matrimonial que présentait l'élite mamelouke. Dès lors le statut réel de la femme ne saurait être envisagé indépendamment de l'avènement des Mamelouks au pouvoir dont le système politique bannit toute transmission héréditaire.

Conclusion

Bien que l'on ne dispose pas encore d'études historique et juridique suffisantes sur l'ensemble des *waqfiyyāt* originales de l'époque mamelouke pour établir des statistiques fiables entre les fondateurs de waqf partisans de l'égalité entre les deux sexes et ceux qui s'y opposaient en recourant à la règle coranique, on peut d'ores et déjà affirmer que ce sont évidemment ces derniers qui l'emportent en nombre sur les premiers.

C'est en poussant plus loin l'investigation pour identifier les descendants des *wāqif*s que l'on pourra trancher de la pertinence de notre hypothèse au sujet des raisons sous-tendant la conception égalitaire de la descendance. Ce qui pour le moment ne saurait souffrir le moindre doute est que le waqf, aux règles bien plus souples que dans les deux autres institutions juridiques (*waṣiyya*, *hiba*), a permis à ces fondateurs de waqf d'assurer, au travers tout aussi bien que sous couvert d'un acte charitable, une transmission héréditaire de leurs biens en posant comme condition juridique le principe d'égalité entre leurs descendances féminine et masculine. Pour ce faire, cette élite mamelouke, à l'inverse de la majorité des *wāqif*s, s'est invariablement tenue à une conception cognatique de la descendance au sein d'une culture largement acquise à la conception agnatique majoritaire dans l'aire islamique de cette époque. Par la restriction de ses liens matrimoniaux qui ont participé à façonner sa vision de la famille et de la femme – vision elle-même résultante des contraintes de l'institution du sultanat –, l'élite mamelouke a certainement contribué, d'une manière dont il reste encore à déterminer les contours, à l'amélioration certaine du statut social de la femme, voire de son statut juridique[72].

70. Surtout Y. Rapoport, *Marriage, Money and Divorce in Medieval Islamic Society*, Cambridge 2005, Id., Divorce and the Elite Household in Late Medieval Cairo, *Continuity and Change* 16, 2001, p. 201-218 ; A. Giladi, Toutes les femmes d'al-Saḫāwī : quelques remarques sur le *Kitāb al-nisā'* (« Le Livre des femmes »), comme source de « l'Histoire intime » des sociétés musulmanes médiévales, *Les non-dits du nom. Onomastique et documents en terres d'Islam*. Mélanges offerts à Jacqueline Sublet, *Institut français du Proche-Orient*, éd. C. Müller et M. Roiland-Rouabah, Damas – Beyrouth 2013, p. 547-566.

71. Rapoport, *Marriage* (cité n. 70), p. 82-88.

72. Sur les femmes, les mères, les sœurs et les filles des princes mamelouks, et leur rôle politico-social prépondérant, on consultera avec profit l'étude de H. M. S. 'Abd al-nabī, « al-Zawāǧ fī usar salāṭīn al-mamālīk » *Annales Islamologiques* 42, 2008, (partie arabe) p. ٢٥-٤٧.

CONFLIT DE SUCCESSION ENTRE HERITIERES ET SENTENCE DU PARLEMENT ROYAL AU XIIIe SIECLE : LA PARTITION DU GRAND COMTÉ DE NEVERS-AUXERRE-TONNERRE (TOUSSAINT 1273)

Yves Sassier

Dans les plus anciens registres du Parlement de Paris, figure une sentence rendue en novembre de l'année 1273 dans le cadre d'un conflit successoral concernant un ensemble territorial important, le grand comté de Nevers-Auxerre-Tonnerre situé aux marges occidentales du duché de Bourgogne. Un an plus tôt, la succession avait été ouverte par le décès de la comtesse Mathilde de Nevers. Mariée à un fils du duc Hugues IV de Bourgogne, celle-ci avait eu trois filles et laissait donc trois héritières : Yolande, l'aînée, épouse de Robert, héritier du comté de Flandre (le futur Robert III de Flandre), Marguerite, la seconde, épouse de Charles Ier d'Anjou, roi de Sicile, et Aélis, la benjamine, épouse de Jean, issu de la lignée des comtes de Chalon. L'arrêt, inventorié en 1863 par Edgard Boutaric au premier volume de son *Inventaire des actes du Parlement de Paris*[1], relate que Jean de Chalon et Aelis ont cité à comparaître devant le roi l'aînée et son mari afin que l'on procède au partage de l'héritage dont semblaient s'être emparés Yolande et son époux. Un document inédit que nous avons trouvé à la *Bibliothèque nationale* dans la collection Baluze[2] signale de fait trois hommages rendus quelques mois plus tôt, en mai 1273, par Robert de Flandre à l'évêque d'Auxerre : le premier pour le comté d'Auxerre, le second et le troisième pour deux châtellenies, Coulanges et Donzy, situées à l'intérieur des limites de l'ancien *pagus Altissiodorensis*. Peut-être est-ce pour riposter à cet hommage que, s'il faut en croire le texte de l'arrêt, Jean de Chalon est venu, quelque temps avant de citer en justice Yolande et son mari, prêter hommage au roi Philippe III le Hardi pour l'ensemble

1. E. Boutaric, *Inventaire des actes du Parlement de Paris*, t. 1, 1863, p. 328, 2e col. n° 171. Publié par M. Quantin, *Recueil de pièces pour faire suite au cartulaire général de l'Yonne*, 1873, p. 340 et 341, n° 678.

2. B. N., *Coll. Baluze*, t. 74, *fol.* 416, qui donne pour référence le 4e registre de la Chambre des Comptes de Nevers, *fol.* 46 r : (...) *Deinde dictus comes Nivernensis fecit memorato episcopo homagium ligium de comitatu Autissiodorensi et de omni terra in diocesi Autissiodorensi constituta ad dictum comitem pertinente.* Mentionné dans Y. Sassier, *Recherches sur le pouvoir comtal en Auxerrois du* X^{e} *au début du* XIIIe *siècle*, Auxerre-Paris, 1980, p. 218 et n. 207-208.

Inheritance, Law and Religions in the Ancient and Mediaeval Worlds, ed. by B. Caseau and S. R. Huebner (Centre de recherche d'Histoire et Civilisation de Byzance, Monographies 45), Paris 2014.

des biens relevant de la succession de la comtesse Mathilde[3]. Riposte à laquelle pourrait ainsi s'être prêté le roi lui-même, pour des raisons non indiquées mais que l'on peut deviner : l'empressement de l'aînée à s'emparer de l'ensemble, et probablement aussi la perspective d'une puissance accrue de ces comtes de Flandre à la fidélité incertaine ont pu quelque peu indisposer et inquiéter en haut lieu ! En présence du roi, Jean et Aelis ont demandé, dit le texte de l'arrêt, « le partage desdits comtés de Nevers, d'Auxerre et de Tonnerre, de toutes les autres terres où qu'elles puissent être situées, ainsi que de leurs produits et revenus, selon les coutumes des lieux en lesquels se trouvent lesdites terres »[4]. De leur côté Yolande et son mari ont soutenu que les trois comtés « n'en formaient qu'un seul ne pouvant être divisé et devant leur revenir pour cause de primogéniture »[5]. Les autres terres, ajoutaient les défendeurs, devaient aussi revenir à Yolande au titre du droit d'aînesse, *salva competenti provisione de dictis terris secundum consuetudinem locorum Aelesi et ejus marito* (sauf à ce que celle-ci pourvoie de façon convenable et suffisante Aelis et son mari sur lesdites terres conformément à la coutume des lieux). Du côté des demandeurs, donc, une action en partage fondée sur la coutume des lieux ; du côté adverse, une demande en réponse, se prétendant elle aussi conforme à la coutume des lieux, visant à la reconnaissance de l'unité de l'héritage, de son caractère « impartable », dirait-on en Normandie, et à l'application stricte au grand comté du droit d'aînesse.

Ce conflit successoral, un conflit purement judiciaire, dont le règlement rapide par cette voie judiciaire témoigne du prodigieux essor de la justice royale au cour de ce siècle, est intéressant à divers points de vue : d'abord parce qu'il pose la question du statut et de l'intégrité d'un assez vaste ensemble territorial – les trois comtés en question formant géographiquement un tout parfaitement continu et cohérent – qui s'était constitué vers les années 1050-1060 et avait connu une direction le plus souvent, mais pas toujours, unitaire depuis environ deux siècles. Ensuite parce qu'il pose la question du sort d'une succession en l'absence d'héritier mâle et en présence de plusieurs héritières, et requiert des juges royaux qu'ils se prononcent sur une alternative : reconnaissance d'un droit d'aînesse entre héritières portant sur la totalité, comme le soutient ici l'aînée, et s'accommodant de correctifs destinés à ne pas déshériter complètement les puînées en leur réservant des biens pris, non sur les trois comtés, mais sur d'« autres terres » ? Consécration, à l'inverse, de l'égalité entre héritières que semblerait ici soutenir la puînée, ou celle consistant à tendre vers une certaine égalité, s'accommodant par exemple d'une sorte de droit de préciput en faveur de l'aînée ? Enfin, cette affaire est intéressante parce qu'elle nous montre les deux parties invoquant, en vue de solutions diamétralement opposées, les coutumes des lieux, ce qui pose la question de l'état de la coutume, de son stade de formation, et surtout de son applicabilité à un héritage quelque peu

3. Quantin, *Recueil de Pièces* (cité n. 1), p. 341 : *Cum dominus Johannes de Cabilone, miles, receptus fuisset in homagium domini regis de parte Aalesin, uxorem suam, contingente in omnibus terris ad Yolendim comitissam Nivernensem et Margaretam reginam Sicile, sorores suas, ex successione Mathildis, quondam comitisse Nivernensis, matris sue, devenerant* (...)

4. Suite du texte note précédente : (...) *iidem dominus Johannes et Aalesis, ejus uxor, postmodum fecerunt conveniri coram domno regedictam Yolandim et dominum Robertum de Flandria, ejus maritum qui dictas terras tenebat, et petierunt partagium in Nivernen., Altissiod. et Tornod. comitatibus et in aliis terris ubicumque sitis, secundum consuetudines locorum in quibus dicte terrae sitae sunt* (...).

5. Ibid. : *Dicta Yolandis et ejus marito ex adverso dicentibus dictos tres comitatus esse unum comitatum, ac tunc non debere dividi, imo ad dictam Yolendim tanquam primogenitam, secundum locorum consuetudines, pertinere.*

hors normes puisqu'on est en présence d'une quasi-principauté, d'un ensemble territorial faisant de son détenteur l'un des sept ou huit plus puissants titulaires d'*honores* du royaume.

Ce sont ces divers aspects qui sont au cœur du *casus* qui nous intéresse ici. Evoquons d'abord la question de l'unité de ces trois comtés que j'ai abordée dans une contribution publiée en 2008 et consacrée à « la succession au comté de Nevers aux XIe-XIIIe siècles »[6], un article qui n'évoquait qu'en conclusion, et de façon très succincte, le jugement de 1273, car il était pour l'essentiel axé sur les XIe et XIIe siècle. Résumons donc le bilan dressé dans cette récente contribution. C'est au XIe siècle que se forme, non sans soubresauts, ce que l'on peut appeler le grand comté de Nevers à la suite de deux mariages : le premier a lieu vers 1023-1025 entre Renaud, fils et successeur de Landri, comte de Nevers depuis la fin du Xe siècle, et une fille du roi Robert le Pieux, et il apporte à Renaud le comté d'Auxerre qui relevait du duc de Bourgogne. Cette ancienne appartenance du comté aux ducs de Bourgogne sera la cause d'une guerre opposant en 1040 ce comte Renaud, premier du nom, qui y perdra la vie, à son beau-frère le duc de Bourgogne Robert, fils puîné du roi Robert le Pieux, qui s'emparera quelques années durant, jusqu'autour de 1050, du comté d'Auxerre. Mais le jeu des rapports de forces et des alliances[7] fait que le comté reviendra, vers 1050-1055, au fils aîné et principal héritier du comte Renaud, le comte Guillaume Ier de Nevers. Quant au comté de Tonnerre, il est acquis grâce au mariage de ce même comte Guillaume Ier avec l'unique héritière de ce comté, autour de l'année 1155, et un chroniqueur du XIIe siècle, auteur d'un récit sur l'origine des comtes de Nevers, présente Guillaume Ier comme celui qui rassembla les trois comtés en un seul : *unum de tribus componens*, comme si l'union avait été définitivement acquise.

En réalité, ce que dit le chroniqueur ignore une première partition qui eut lieu du vivant même de ce comte entre ses trois fils : Renaud, le deuxième à porter ce nom, eut le comté de Nevers qu'il semble avoir gouverné en association avec son père ; le second, nommé Guillaume, eut le Tonnerrois, et le troisième, Robert, évêque d'Auxerre, semble avoir été aussi comte de cette cité, même si, dans le cas présent, la partition n'était évidemment pas programmée pour se perpétuer. Mais le comte Guillaume Ier, qui avait fait ce partage, survécut à ses trois fils et, de nouveau, administra le tout. À la mort du vieux comte, en 1098, c'est l'un des deux fils de Renaud II, le comte Guillaume II, qui obtint l'ensemble des trois comtés en évinçant du Tonnerrois une héritière légitime de son oncle et homonyme, héritière contre le mari de laquelle il dut, l'année suivante, en 1099, mener une guerre pour faire prévaloir sa revendication. On pourrait alors penser que l'on s'est orienté vers une stratégie successorale alliant aînesse forte et priorité à la parenté agnatique, mais il faut faire ici plus que nuancer. Droit d'aînesse, sans nul doute, assorti de l'évidente volonté des comtes successifs, pendant plusieurs générations, de faire prévaloir une solution unitaire pour au moins deux des trois comtés : Nevers et Auxerre formeront désormais un ensemble homogène et indivisible revenant à l'aîné. Et cela durera jusqu'en 1273, du moins si l'on fait abstraction d'une vingtaine d'années, entre 1200 et 1221, durant lesquelles – mais la situation n'était pas prévue pour être définitive – il y aura deux comtes distincts à Nevers et à Auxerre. Nevers et Auxerre forment donc bien un seul lot revenant systématiquement à l'aîné quelque soit le nombre de

6. « La succession au comté de Nevers (XI-XIIIe s.) », *Making and Breaking the Rules: Succession in Medieval Europe, c. 1000 – c. 1580.* (Colloque Londres, 6-8 avril 2006, The Institute of Historical Research.), 2007, p. 221-232.

7. Evoqué dans SASSIER, *Recherches* (cité, n. 2), p. 45-48.

puînés. En revanche, lorsque le comte Guillaume II se fait moine sur la fin de sa vie, en 1147, il reproduit le schéma successoral adopté par son aïeul Guillaume Ier en réservant le comté de Tonnerre au deuxième de ses trois enfants, Renaud, dont la mort au combat, lors de la désastreuse bataille du Mont Cadmos un an plus tard, permettra le retour du comté aux mains du seul aîné. Il semble d'ailleurs que, désormais, la solution de l'unité ait prévalu puisqu'à la génération suivante le comte Guillaume IV, malgré la présence de deux frères, donc de trois héritiers potentiels pour les trois comtés, fut le seul détenteur du tout, et puisqu'à sa mort sans héritier le plus âgé de ses deux frères puînés, Guy, obtint seul aussi les trois comtés.[8]

Aînesse forte et agnation se sont donc finalement imposées très vite, dès la fin du XIe siècle s'agissant des deux comtés de Nevers-Auxerre – et l'on peut vraiment, ici, parler de stratégie lignagère –, de façon plus heurtée, et plus hasardeuse, s'agissant du comté de Tonnerre qui, en outre, sera affecté, dans le dernier quart du XIIe siècle, de 1176 à 1192, au douaire d'une comtesse, veuve du comte Guy de Nevers.

Puis, à partir de 1181 et jusqu'en 1272, la succession par agnation, que l'on aurait pu croire être passée en coutume, disparaît avec la mort du comte Guillaume V, malgré la présence d'un dernier agnat, Renaud, frère du comte Guy et oncle du dernier comte, qui ne mourra qu'en 1191. L'ère des héritières commence avec quatre générations d'héritières : Agnès de Nevers (m. 1183), sœur du comte Guillaume V, Mathilde de Courtenay (m. 1257), sa fille Agnès de Donzy, décédée très tôt (1226), et sa petite fille Mathilde (m. 1272) ; des héritières filles uniques qui se suivent en ligne directe jusqu'à la mort de la dernière de celles-ci, Mathilde, fille de la comtesse Agnès et du comte de Saint-Pol, Guy de Chatillon. Par la force des choses c'est une ère d'unité des trois comtés qui débute en 1181, et aussi une ère d'implication du roi, en tant que seigneur dont relève directement la cité de Nevers et, sinon la cité d'Auxerre qui se trouve dans la mouvance de l'évêque, tout au moins le *castrum* protégeant cette cité, dans le choix des futurs époux[9]. Je n'évoquerai ici que les deux premiers mariages, celui d'Agnès, sœur et héritière de Guillaume V, le dernier comte issu par les hommes de Landri, avec Pierre de Courtenay, un prince capétien, cousin germain de Philippe Auguste, futur prétendant au trône de Constantinople (il finira sa vie, après une entreprise ratée visant à conquérir ce trône, dans les prisons du despote d'Epire). En 1182, Pierre épouse Agnès et devient comte de Nevers-Auxerre, puis des trois comtés après récupération, en 1192, du douaire de sa belle-mère, qu'il administre jusqu'en 1200 pour le compte de son épouse, puis de sa fille unique Mathilde. En 1199, il perd une guerre contre l'un de ses indociles vassaux, Hervé de Donzy, et doit, l'année suivante, après arbitrage du roi, se résigner au mariage de sa fille avec le vainqueur et à l'abandon aux nouveaux époux du comté de Nevers, conservant à titre viager ceux d'Auxerre et de Tonnerre[10]. C'est là l'unique entorse, elle aussi vouée à n'être que provisoire, à cette stratégie unitaire, puis à ce fait unitaire, qui ont en somme duré depuis la mort du comte Renaud de Tonnerre au cours de la 2e croisade, en 1148, jusqu'en 1273 : 125 ans, largement le temps qu'il faut, en apparence du moins, pour consolider en coutume ce fait unitaire et expliquer juridiquement que la comtesse Yolande ait pu avoir de telles prétentions sur l'ensemble du grand comté et faire hommage à l'évêque d'Auxerre pour le comté et les châtellenies de l'Auxerrois.

8. Sur tout cela voir l'article mentionné *supra*, n. 6.
9. Sur la question complexe des mouvances auxerroises, SASSIER, *Recherches* (cité, n. 2), chapitre III, p. 177-223.
10. SASSIER, *Recherches* (cité, n. 2), p. 173-174.

Il n'est pas inintéressant de comparer cette évolution à celle des comtés champenois tenus par la maison de Blois depuis les années 1020. C'est assez lentement, et somme toute assez tardivement, que s'y est imposée la solution de l'unité politique de toute la Champagne puisque, jusqu'en 1125 au moins et même peut-être au-delà, semble avoir prévalu l'idée que l'aîné, héritier des comtés de Blois, Chartres et Châteaudun, devait aussi détenir des biens, voire certains comtés qui formeront par la suite, avec les comtés de Troyes, de Vitry et de Bar-sur-Aube, le grand comté de Troyes : l'aîné tient, en même temps que les comté de Blois et de Chartres, les comtés de Meaux et de Provins, limitrophes de celui de Troyes, tandis que le puîné tient le comté de Troyes. Au cours des années 1120, la mort sans héritier d'un comte de Troyes permet à la branche aînée, représentée par le comte Thibaud IV de Blois et de Chartres, de mettre la main sur l'ensemble des territoires champenois, et c'est en 1152, avec l'avènement du comte Henri Ier le Libéral, fils aîné de Thibaud IV (Thibaud II comme comte de Troyes), que la stratégie successorale change pour faire de l'ensemble des comtés champenois un tout indivisible aux mains du seul aîné qui portera aussi le titre de *comes palatinus*, de comte du Palais (du roi de France) que se réservait jusque-là le comte de Blois en titre[11]. Unité, donc, qui s'imposera jusqu'à l'annexion de la Champagne, en 1285, au domaine du roi de France. De même constate-t-on l'exclusion, à l'extrême fin du XIIe siècle, des deux filles et plus proches héritières naturelles du comte palatin Henri II, fils aîné et successeur d'Henri Ier au profit du plus proche parent agnatique, son frère puîné, Thibaud III[12]. À la mort de Thibaud III, sa veuve, Blanche de Navarre, avec le soutien du roi Philippe Auguste, et non sans devoir soutenir une guerre contre l'époux d'une des héritières évincées, assurera à son fils Thibaud IV l'ensemble du comté champenois[13]. La solution est ici tout à fait différente de ce qui s'est passé à Nevers en 1181, où la fille du précédent comte l'a emporté sur son oncle paternel. Mais on le voit : la solution de l'unité semble bien s'être imposée, à une courte génération près, à peu près au même moment en Champagne et en Nivernais.

Pourtant, et j'en viens maintenant à la solution imposée par le parlement royal en 1273, c'est la partition qui a prévalu : après enquête sur les coutumes des lieux, il a été décidé que chacun des trois comtés constituait un *comitatus per se*, et que, les sœurs étant trois, chacune des dites sœurs présentes au procès aurait un de ces trois comtés[14]. Il n'est pas simple, eu égard au fait que les arrêts de la cour royale ne sont pas motivés, de cerner la raison profonde de cette sentence. D'un strict point de vue juridique (nous évoquerons plus tard le point de vue politique, qui fut peut-être le plus déterminant), l'unité n'a pas lieu d'être, a-t-on peut-être pensé en cours royale, puisque chacun de ces trois ensembles relève de seigneurs différents : le Nivernais relève féodalement du roi, le comté d'Auxerre relève féodalement de l'évêque de cette cité, malgré la mouvance royale sur le château comtal et la mouvance

11. Sur cette longue période, M. Bur, *La formation du comté de Champagne (v. 950 – v. 1150)*, Nancy, 1977. Sur le changement qui marque l'avènement du comte Henri Ier le Libéral, Th. Evergates, *The Aristocracy in the County of Champagne, 1100 – 1300*, University of Pennsylvania Press, 2007, p. 83.

12. Evergates, *The Aristocracy* (cité n. 11), p. 34 et s.

13. Evergates, *The Aristocracy* (cité n. 11), p. 36 et s.

14. Quantin, *Recueil de Pièces* (cité n. 1), p. 341 : *Tandem, super premissis factis in questis et intellectis consuetudinibus locorum, quia clarum repertum fuit quod dicti tres comitatus quilibet est comitatus per se, et dicte sorores numeros inttres, judicatum fuit quod quelibet dictarum sororum, que in judicio fuerunt coram nobis, haberet unum de comitatibus predictis integrum* (...).

du duché de Bourgogne sur un faubourg d'Auxerre situé sur la rive droite de l'Yonne, tandis que le comté de Tonnerre est dans la mouvance de l'évêché de Langres. L'argument est tout à fait plausible, même si le même constat peut être fait pour la Champagne voisine qui relève de multiples seigneurs féodaux : du roi de France pour Meaux et Provins, du duc de Bourgogne pour Troyes, de l'archevêque de Reims pour les châteaux de la Marne, du duc de Lorraine et de l'évêque de Langres pour les comtés et forteresses de l'est champenois. Il est cependant plus probable que c'est la « féminité » des héritières potentielles qui a permis la solution adoptée par la cour royale. Le principe de l'application de l'aînesse forte, valant aussi bien entre filles qu'entre mâles, vaut sans doute pour certains très grands fiefs : au siècle précédent elle avait prévalu pour l'Aquitaine dévolue en son entier à Aliénor, malgré la présente d'une sœur. L'on a de même, pour des successions nobles moins importantes, des régions comme l'Anjou où la Bretagne, où l'on voit la fille aînée recueillir le patrimoine ancestral au détriment de ses sœurs[15]. Mais d'autres régions du royaume tendent à atténuer de droit d'aînesse et privilégient le partage, non sans, dans certaines situations, accorder, sinon un préciput au sens technique du terme, tout au moins un choix préférentiel à l'aînée. C'est ainsi qu'en Normandie où l'aînesse a triomphé très tôt pour le duché et les grands fiefs à partir d'un principe d'indivisibilité, le fief de haubert, le fief de chevalerie, « impartable » entre frères, devient « partable » entre sœurs. Toutefois, lorsqu'il existe dans une succession autant de fiefs nobles qu'il existe de sœurs, le principe du non-partage de chacun de ces fiefs l'emporte de nouveau et l'aînée vient la première dans le choix de son fief[16]. Dans la Champagne voisine, les travaux de Theodore Evergates ont bien montré que, si l'indivisibilité du grand comté champenois assure, tout au moins entre descendants mâles, la totalité de l'*honor* comtal à l'aîné, s'est très tôt imposé pour les fiefs nobles dépendant du comté un principe d'égalité entre héritiers, avec le grave risque d'une fragmentation à l'infini qui, parce qu'elle portait aussi sur des forteresses parfois importantes que détenaient les lignages nobles et posait donc le problème de l'unité du commandement militaire, a fini par inquiéter le pouvoir comtal[17]. Deux ordonnances comtales promulguées en 1212 et en 1224 avec l'accord des principaux barons du comté ont eu le souci de veiller à la non-partition des ouvrages défensifs et, plus généralement, de la capacité de défense de chaque seigneurie du comté – c'est évidemment, ici, l'intérêt du pouvoir comtal que l'on sauvegarde lorsqu'il s'agit de maintenir l'intégrité du système défensif d'une seigneurie dépendante. La première de ces ordonnances nous intéresse ici parce qu'elle concerne le cas où la succession échoit à plusieurs héritières : dans une succession où il n'y a qu'un château ou qu'une résidence fortifiée, le château ou la maison-forte, ainsi que les droits et revenus attachés au château et à la justice de son ressort et les fiefs pour lesquels est dû le service militaire au maître de la fortification, reviendront dans leur totalité à la fille aînée, le reste des terres et les revenus de ces terres étant également partagés entre les autres sœurs jusqu'à égaler le revenu de l'aînée. Dans une succession où il y a plusieurs châteaux, l'aînée des filles prend le prin-

15. J.-L. Thireau, « Les successions dans l'ouest de la France à l'époque féodale », *Making and Breaking the Rules : Succession in Medieval Europe, c. 1000 – c. 1580.* (Colloque Londres, 6-8 avril 2006, The Institute of Historical Research.), 2007, p. 249-269, principalement p. 260.

16. R. Besnier, « Les filles dans le droit successoral normand », *Tijdschrift voor rechtsgeschiedenis*, 1930, p. 488-506.

17. Evergates, *The Aristocracy* (cité n. 11), chap. 6, p. 119 et s., principalement p. 121-122.

cipal des châteaux et ses sœurs choisissent, selon l'ordre des naissances, les autres châteaux ou résidences fortifiées[18]. C'est cette solution, d'abord propre aux fratries d'héritières, que, douze ans plus tard, en 1224, une ordonnance du comte palatin Thibaud IV étendra aux successions entre frères, mais en l'aménageant pour, quelque soit le cas de figure, concéder en outre à l'aîné un droit sur la terre située dans le district de son château[19].

Si j'ai tant parlé du partage des fiefs champenois, c'est parce que c'est une solution assez proche du partage champenois entre filles en cas de pluralité de châteaux que l'on a appliquée au grand comté de Nevers. D'une part, nous l'avons vu, le grand comté n'a pas eu le traitement d'une principauté, mais celui d'un agrégat d'entités distinctes, comme si chaque comté s'était trouvé ravalé au rang de l'entité châtelaine champenoise. Peut-être y a-t-il à cela – je l'ai évoquée au début de mon intervention – une raison politique : il n'était sans doute pas de l'intérêt du roi de favoriser la mainmise d'une très puissante maison, celle de Flandre, et de l'héritier de cette maison, sur cet ensemble de trois comtés. Et le parlement pouvait d'autant dire le droit que le cas d'espèce qu'il examinait – l'ouverture d'une succession entre plusieurs héritières de même rang – ne s'était jamais présenté dans la succession des comtes de Nevers.

D'autre part, le Parlement a invité l'aînée, Yolande, à choisir la première, ce qu'elle a fait en acceptant le plus riche et le mieux pourvu des trois comtés, celui de Nevers ; puis la cour royale, tenant compte encore de l'ordre des naissances, a attribué d'autorité le moins riche des deux autres en revenus, le comté d'Auxerre, à la demanderesse, Aelis, dernière dans l'ordre des naissances, en supposant que si la seconde dans l'ordre des naissances, absente, avait eu à choisir entre Tonnerre et Auxerre, elle aurait probablement pris le plus riche des deux en droits et revenus, celui de Tonnerre. Mais il l'a fait de façon provisoire, dans l'attente que se manifeste la seconde fille, Marguerite de Sicile, qui pourra alors exprimer son choix et, éventuellement, se faire attribuer le comté d'Auxerre.[20]

Voila l'affaire – une affaire somme toute très banale, si on la compare, notamment, à celle, beaucoup plus sombre, qui verra bientôt la comtesse Yolande de Nevers et de Flandre mourir tragiquement, étranglée sur l'ordre de son mari pour avoir peut-être voulu modifier l'ordre de succession au profit de leur fils en faisant disparaître son beau-fils, né d'un premier mariage de Robert de Flandre. Ce qu'il convient de noter tout de même, c'est que contrairement à ce qui est déjà, très probablement(il conviendrait, comme l'a fait Théodore Evergates pour la Champagne voisine, d'explorer l'histoire des familles nobles de chacun des trois comtés vers la fin du XIIe et au XIIIe siècle et de repérer quelques successions entre sœurs pour en être totalement sûr), la coutume de ces trois comtés où, d'après les coutumes rédigées au XVIe siècle, les fiefs nobles connaissent un partage strictement égal entre filles sans le moindre

18. EVERGATES, *The Aristocracy* (cité n. 11), p. 122.

19. EVERGATES, *The Aristocracy* (cité n. 11), p. 122.

20. QUANTIN, *Recueil de Pièces* (cité n. 1), p. 341 : *Et dictum fuit de Yolandi et ejus marito ut quem vellent de dictis comitatibus predictis integrum, cum pertinentiis suis, qui acceptarunt comitatum Nivernensem. Et quia regina Sicilie, soror secunda natu, in judicio non fuerat, nec aliquid petieret, et suppositum fuerit quod si petiisset et pro ipsa judicatum fuisset forsitan comitatum Tornodorensem acceptasset, ut pote meliorem et in redditibus pinguiorem comitatu Altissiodorensi et pertinenciarum ejusdem deliberata fuit Aalesi, uxori dicti domini Johannis, ita quod, cum dicta domina Margareta, regina Sicile, venerit et partem suam petere voluerit ac obtinuerit, sit in ejus optione accipiendi illum quem maluerit de comitatibus Altissiod. et Tornod.*

droit de préférence au profit de l'aînée[21], le partage de 1273 n'a apparemment pas été un partage égalitaire : l'intégrité de chacun des *honores* comtaux a été respectée. Je précise : « celle de chacun des honores comtaux », et uniquement de ceux-ci, car le parlement s'est également intéressé aux « autres terres » pouvant former la succession, qui peuvent se trouver réparties dans l'ensemble du royaume, tout au moins dans sa partie nord : celles-ci ont été divisées de façon égale (*equaliter*) entre les héritières, ce qui éloigne des solutions champenoises, et ce qui correspond à ce que sera au XVIe siècle la coutume du Nivernais, de l'Auxerrois et du Tonnerrois, comme de nombreuses autres régions du nord et du centre-est en matière de partage des fiefs nobles entre filles[22] ; Cela semble bien montrer – ou plutôt confirmer, car il est admis que le moment-clé se situe entre les années 1150-1230 – que pour ces biens plus ordinaires que sont les « autres terres »,les coutumes sont déjà cristallisées au XIIIe siècle. Notons en tout cas que ces « autres terres » n'ont pas servi à compenser l'inégalité de traitement née des disparités de valeurs entre les trois comtés. L'on sait enfin que ces entités comtales ne subiront jamais le sort des fiefs qui en dépendent, ce qui signifie que deux coutumes successorales coexistent en Nivernais, Auxerrois et Tonnerrois comme un peu partout : l'une applicable à l'entité comtale qui préserve l'unité de l'*honor*, l'autre applicable aux fiefs qui en dépendent, où l'aînesse entre garçons qui réserve le château ou la maison forte et le terrain attenant au premier né doit s'accommoder de formules de partages tendant à rétablir une certaine égalité entre héritiers, et où l'aînesse disparaît entre filles au profit de la stricte égalité.

21. Ancienne coutume d'Auxerre, Bourdot de RICHEBOURG, *Nouveau coutumier général...*, 1724, t. 3, p. 583, titre *des fiefs, droits et profits féodaux*, art. CCLV : « Entre filles, soit en ligne directe ou collatérale, n'y a point de droit d'aisneesse, mais y auront autant l'une que l'autre ». Coutume de Nivernais, *id.*, *Ibid.*, t. 3, p. 1162, chap. XXXV : de droit d'aînesse, art. III : « En succession de femme droit d'aînesse n'a point de lieu, ne pareillement entre filles venans à la succession ». Le comté de Tonnerre suivait au XVIe siècle la coutume du baillage de Sens (Bourdot de Richebourg t. 3, p. 561), laquelle contenait un article (Bourdot de Richebourg, t. 3, p. 522, art. CCIV) rédigé dans les mêmes termes que l'article CCLV ci-dessus de l'ancienne coutume d'Auxerre.

22. QUANTIN, *Recueil de Pièces* (cité n. 1), p. 341 : *Omnes vero alie terre, ubicumque sint site, sive sint baronie, sive castellanie, sive vavasorie, inter dictas sorores equaliter dividantur.*

PARENTELA, KINDRED, AND THE CROWN: INHERITANCE PRACTICES IN ÁRPÁD-ERA HUNGARY

Cameron Sutt

The last century of the Árpád dynasty in Hungary was one of immense change. The lower nobility forced the Golden Bull, a charter specifying their privileges, upon Andrew II, and the oligarchs established their power to the further detriment of the crown. When the dynasty ended around 1300, the Angevin kings struggled to destroy the power of these same oligarchs. In the midst of these political changes, the Hungarian nobility struggled to maintain their status. A key component to their struggle was inheritance custom, custom that often pitted families against their kin and kin against the crown. This paper will explore how these elements shaped inheritance among the nobility in the Árpád era.

Much of what we understand about medieval Hungarian customs comes to us from the early sixteenth-century legal treatise of Stephan Werbőczy, the *Tripartitum opus iuris consuetudinarii inclyti regni Hungariae*.[1] It is difficult to understate the importance of Werbőczy's work, both in Hungarian legal history and in the historiography of Hungarian social history. Werbőczy has been called a Hungarian Bracton, and his influence arguably exceeds that of the English jurist.[2] Werbőczy's collection of the customary laws of the kingdom, compiled in 1514 and approved the Diet three years later, had an astonishing run of importance in the legal thinking of the Hungarian kingdom, its importance only fading slightly with the liberal era of the nineteenth century.[3]

Werbőczy presented the *Tripartitum* as a collection of customary law, but scholars have become more and more aware of the influence of Werbőczy's agenda in the composition itself. First of all, Werbőczy portrayed the Hungarian clans, or kindreds, as one with an ubreakable solidarity, the betrayal of which was among the gravest of crimes.[4] Erik Fügedi,

1. All citations of the *Tripartitum* in this text come from J. M. Bak, P. Banyó and M. Rady, *Tripartitum opus iuris consuetudinarii inclyti regni Hungariae* (Laws of the Kingdom of Hungary 5), Idyllwild, CA 2005.

2. L. Péter, The primacy of *consuetudo* in Hungarian law, in *Custom and law in central Europe*, ed. by M. Rady, Cambridge 2003, p. 101.

3. L. Péter, The Irrepressible authority of the Tirpartitum, in *Tripartitum* (quoted n. 1), pp. xvii–xxiii.

4. T. Klaniczay, La corte di Mattia Corvino e il pensiero accademico, in *Matthias Corvinus and the humanism in Central Europe*, ed. by T. Klaniczay and J. Jankovics, Budapest 1994, pp. 165–174, pp. 104–105 (I: 39).

Inheritance, Law and Religions in the Ancient and Mediaeval Worlds, ed. by B. Caseau and S. R. Huebner (Centre de recherche d'Histoire et Civilisation de Byzance, Monographies 45), Paris 2014.

in his seminal study, *The Elefánthy*, demonstrated that the solidarity towards the kindred was tempered by numerous factors, and kindreds were frequently divided by inter-clan rivalries.[5] Also, the *Tripartitum* has something of an ideological agenda which is most evident in the Prologue. Werbőczy used the work to describe the relationship between the crown and the nobility as he saw it, which is to say he supported the lower nobility. In his description of the rights and obligations of the nobility vis-à-vis the crown, he argued that the two estates (to be a bit anachronistic) were connected in a reciprocal relationship in which each derived its authority and privileges from the other. Thus, it was from the crown that the nobility owed their existence because it was the king who had created the nobility through the granting of land. At the same time, Werbőczy argued that the nobility elected the king, and in this way there was to be now intervening institution or individual between the king and the 'people.'[6] Werbőczy's political paradigm fails on several points.[7] First, the idea of an elective monarch was clearly fiction. Also, Werbőczy portrayed the nobility as a legally uniform entity with his famous phrase *una eademque libertas*, though in reality significant differences existed between those of the noble status in the sixteenth century.[8] In a similar vein, Werbőczy completely ignored the so-called 'conditional nobles' who held estates from the church.[9] He also insisted that legal cases were regularly referred from the lower courts of the county to the king's courts giving the nobility a right, and regular access, to a sort of appeals process. Scholars have shown this appeals process as something of a fiction. Others have pointed out that Werbőczy concept of custom was rather unimaginative and even contradictory.[10]

Despite such issues, the *Tripartitum* does provide a wealth of information regarding customary law as it was practiced in the sixteenth-century kingdom of Hungary. Werbőczy came from a noble, if not wealthy, family in northeastern Hungary that provided for him with an education though he does not seem to have completed more than a few years in university in Cracow, deciding instead to focus on a career as a notary.[11] As a young man he obtained a position as notary in the royal chancellery, and within ten years he held both the position of protonotary to the justiciar as well as the protonotary of Transylvania.[12] As protonotary Werbőczy obtained extensive legal experience because notaries and protonotaries of the Jagiełło kings performed most of the judicial functions needed in the court. Members of the chancellery, having mostly studied in Italy, had been heavily influenced by humanist ideals

5. E. Fügedi, *The Elefánthy: The Hungarian nobleman and his kindred*, Budapest 1998. See also M. Rady, Erik Fügedi and the Elefánthy kindred, *The Slavonic and East European Review* 77, 1999, pp. 295–308.

6. M. Rady, Stephen Werbőczy and his *Tripartitum*, in Bak, Banyó, and Rady, *The Customary law*, pp. xxxvii–xxxix. Fügedi, *The Elefánthy* (quoted n. 5), p. 19. M. Rady, *Nobility, land and service in medieval Hungary*, New York 2000, p. 8.

7. For the following, see Rady, Stephen Werbőczy (quoted n. 6), xxxvii-xxxix.

8. E. Fügedi, Kinship and privilege: The social system of medieval Hungarian nobility as defined in customary law, in J. M. Bak, *Nobilities in Central and Eastern Europe: kinship, property, and privilege*, Budapest 1994, pp. 72–73.

9. Rady, Stephen Werbőczy (quoted n. 6), xxxviii.

10. D. Ibbetson, Custom in the *Tripartitum*, in *Custom and Law in Central Europe*, ed. by M. Rady, Cambridge 2003, pp. 16–22.

11. A. Kubinyi, István Werbőczy als Politiker in der Zeit vor Mohács, in... *The Man of many devices, who wandered full many ways... Festschrift in honor of János M. Bak*, ed. by B. Nagy and M. Sebők, Budapest 1999, p. 559. Rady, Stephen Werbőczy, p. xxix.

12. Kubinyi, István Werbőczy (quoted n. 11), p. 564.

from the time of Matthias Corvinus (r.1458-1490), and the study of law had fallen into disfavor to the extent that royal judges sought to show themselves as humanistic scholars rather than legal experts, leaving the notaries to fulfill the legal duties.[13] Werbőczy therefore had extensive legal experience to draw upon when composing the *Tripartitum*.

This legal experience shows clearly in the *Tripatitum*, and the work provides a wealth of information regarding the customary law as it was practice in the sixteenth-century kingdom of Hungary. Though not always a completely accurate depiction of reality, the *Tripartitum* does provide a useful framework for studying inheritance practices for earlier periods. What we see in the *Tripatitum* is that the customs of inheritance in sixteenth-century Hungary centered on the status of the property in question, be it real estate or moveable property. Real estate was of course the focus of most inheritance issues, and Werbőczy tells us that it was categorized according to its source of origin – it was viewed as either that obtained through royal donation, or that obtained as part of the family's ancestral land.[14] Ancestral land was that held by the kindred, a term that is admittedly odd in English, but is perhaps the best translation of the terms *genus* or *generatio* found in the sources.[15] The kindred was dominated by the institution of *aviticitas* which was the community of males who considered themselves to have descended from a common ancestor, or *avus*.[16] The relationship of property to the kindred was the most important factor in determining inheritance rights, Since ancestral land was the property of the kindred, it could never legally be alienated from the kindred, and many of the regulations found in the *Tripartitum* were designed to make sure that the lands did not pass to 'strangers' (*extraneo*). To this end, when the patriarch died, the ancestral land was divided equally among his sons. These divisions then created further branches in the kindred, even creating new kindreds of their own.[17] Werbőczy was greatly concerned with protecting the integrity of the ancestral land and the rights of minor sons in the event that the death of the father. In such cases a guardian had to be found who would protect the rights of the son(s) and the rights of the kindred.[18] Ideally, the father should appoint a guardian in a will, but lacking that, other members of the kindred could serve as guardian. Under no circumstances could cognates serve as guardian for fear that the property would be alienated from the kindred.[19] If the patriarch died with no sons, the property passed to the next agnate. If no agnate could be found, the property would escheat to the corwn since, as explain by Werbőczy, all nobility originated with the crown through the donation of land.[20]

13. Gy. Bónis, *A jogtudó értelmiség a Mohács előtti Magyarországon*, Budapest 1971, pp. 310–312. T. Klaniczay, La corte di Mattia Corvino e il pensiero accademico, in T. Klaniczay and J. Jankovics, eds, *Matthias Corvinus and the humanism in Central Europe*, Budapest 1994, pp. 165–174.

14. E.g. Bak, Banyó and Rady, *Tripartitum* (quoted n. 1), pp. 52–53, 76–77, 126–127 (I:5, 21, 57, 58)

15. See the translator's notes in Fügedi, *The Elefánthy* (quoted n. 5), p. 5.

16. Fügedi, *The Elefánthy* (quoted n. 5), pp. 20–21. E. Fügedi, The *avus* in the mediaeval conceptual framework of kinship in Hungary, *Studia Slavica. Academiae Scientiarum Hungaricae* 25, pp. 137–142. E. Fügedi, Some characteristics of the medieval Hungarian noble family, *Journal of Family History* 7, 1982, pp. 29–31.

17. Rady, *Nobility* (quoted n. 6), 30.

18. To my count, Werbőczy discussed guardianship in at least twenty chapters. See also Fügedi, *The Elefánthy* (quoted n. 1), pp. 22–23.

19. Bak, Banyó and Rady, *Tripartitum* (quoted n. 1), pp. 198–199 (I:116.3).

20. Bak, Banyó and Rady, *Tripartitum* (quoted n. 1), pp. 58–59 (I:10).

While sons were to be provided for in the *Tripartitum*, Werbőczy mandated that fathers could not favor sons at the expense of the rights of the kindred.[21]

Individuals could obtain land through means other than inheritance, typically through either purchase or through an extraordinary royal donation. In each of these cases, the customary rules of inheritance differed significantly from those regarding the ancestral lands of the kindred. In the case of purchased lands, the *Tripartitum* maintained that the one who purchased the land had the final say in their disposition since he obtained them by means of his military service, explaining that the money used to purchase the lands was itself obtained by such service.[22] Since he obtained these lands through his own efforts, other members of the kindred had no right whatsoever to them. As Werbőczi put it, 'while the others gave themselves up to sluggishness, negligence and idle ease, [he] was acquiring goods and property rights with ceaseless service and the shedding of his blood or by other service and virtues.'[23]

Such was the customary law regarding ancestral property and the kindred as recorded in the *Tripartitum*. For earlier periods, the picture is far less clear. What is clear, though, is that inheritance practices up through the fourteenth century were shaped by several competing interests within Hungarian society. On the one hand the crown sought to increase its access to land through escheat. The kindred naturally wanted to maintain its potential access to ancestral lands and therefore sought to reduce the practice of escheat. At the same time, the needs of the kindred were at odds with the more immediate family of the *parentela*, particularly the desire of fathers to pass properties directly to their sons.

The earliest laws of the kingdom, those attributed to Stephen I (r. 1000-1038), indicate that the *parentela* initially had the legal upper hand. A *decretum* from Book I allowed men to bequeath their property freely to wives, sons, daughters, 'relatives' (*parentes*) or the church.[24] In another, widows were allowed to pass their property to either their sons or their daughters without mention of other kin.[25] The rights of the kindred first appears explicitly only in the legislation of Coloman from the beginning of the twelfth century. In the *decretum*, lands 'given by St. Stephen' are to be passed to any heir 'in natural succession.'[26] The reference to Saint Stephen was a common expression that referred to the far distant past, and therefore is thought to refer to ancestral lands, and the generic term 'in natural succession,' evidently refers to the rights of the kindred.[27] In contrast, those lands 'given by other kings,' in other words donated lands, are to pass first to sons, and then to brothers of the deceased. The distinction between ancient, ancestral land belonging to the kindred and donated land belonging to the *parentela* is thought to be a compromise between the needs of the crown to have property to disperse to supporters on the one hand with the need of the landhold-

21. Bak, Banyó and Rady, *Tripartitum* (quoted n. 1), pp. 126–129 (I: 58).

22. Bak, Banyó and Rady, *Tripartitum* (quoted n. 1), pp. 52–53, 126–127 (I: 5 and 57).

23. *...caeteris torpor & negligentiae desidiaeque deditis) continue serviendo sanguinis sui effusione vela liter servitiis aut virtutibus suis....* Bak, Banyó and Rady, *Tripartitum* (quoted n. 1), pp. 110–111 (I: 44).

24. Stepehn I:6. J. Bak, Gy. Bónis, J. Sweeney, *Decreta regni mediaevalis Hungariae 1000-1300* (Laws of the Kingdom of Hungary I/1), Idyllwild, CA, p. 3.

25. Stephen I:26. Bak, Bónis, and Sweeney, *Decreta 1000-1300* (quoted n. 24), 6.

26. Coloman 20. Bak, Bónis, and Sweeney, *Decreta 1000-1300* (quoted n. 24), 26.

27. Rady, *Nobility* (quoted n. 6), p. 188, n.67.

ing elite to maintain the integrity of their possessions on the other.[28] As Martyn Rady has pointed out, this 'compromise' was essentially impossible to maintain since the oral nature of most of the land agreements and records meant that the distinction between ancestral and acquired lands became impossible to maintain.[29] During the thirteenth century, the position of the landowners had strengthened, and the Golden Bull of 1222 allowed landowners without sons to dispose of land by testament, and the land only escheated to the crown if the owner died intestate and had 'no relatives at all.'[30] In the *decretum* of 1267, however, the kindred's rights were recognized, and the law specified that land would go to 'relatives and clansmen' (*cognate et generationes*) rather than escheat.[31] By the end of the thirteenth century, the power had shifted away from the kindred to the *parentela*, and the *decretum* of 1290 gave landowners significant latitude in their choice of inheritors. The testator could pass down his properties 'either to his kindred, or any one of his relatives, or to his wife, or to churches... or to whomever he wishes.'[32] The laws of the thirteenth century indicate the common striving by the nobles against the king's right to escheat, but they also show the conflict between the immediate family unit, the *parentela*, and the broader family of the kindred.

A turning point in the relationship of the kindred and the right of escheat came in the fourteenth century when the Angevin kings secured their position over the oligarchs. Beginning in the 1320s, Charles I (r. 1301-42) issued the first of the so-called 'new donations' (*novae donations*), and his successor, Louis the Great (r. 1342-82), only increased their use. These royal land grants came with the stipulation that the land was to be passed from father to sons, and it also required that the other males in the kindred were excluded from the property.[33] The action of the Angevin kings was no doubt decisive, and the rights of the sons in the first instance became the norm from the latter part of the fourteenth century.[34] The kings clearly desired these changes because they had a greater chance at obtaining lands through escheat than when the whole of the agnates had to be eliminated. At the same time, much of these changes were brought by request of the nobility in order to focus inheritance upon their sons.[35] Yet the matter was not settled for good. When the issue of inheritance came up at the Diet of 1351, Louis specifically forbad the practice of free disposition, ordering that property should pass to '*fratres, proximos et generationes*.'[36] While the decree of 1351 gave the kindred the legal authority that eventually found its way into the *Tripartitum*,

28. E. WALDAPFEL, Nemesi birtokjogunk kialakulása a középkorban, *Századok* 65, 1931, pp. 144–150. RADY, *Nobility* (quoted n. 6), 25.

29. RADY, *Nobility* (quoted n. 6), 25.

30. *nullam penitus generationem* BAK, BÓNIS, and SWEENEY, *Decreta 1000-1300* (quoted n. 24), p. 32.

31. BAK, BÓNIS, and SWEENEY, *Decreta 1000-1300* (quoted n. 24), 41.

32. BAK, BÓNIS, and SWEENEY, *Decreta 1000-1300* (quoted n. 24), 44.

33. P. ENGEL, Nagy Lajos ismeretlen adományreformja, *Történelmi* Szemle 39, 1997, pp. 137–157. RADY, *Nobility* (quoted n. 6), 100-101.

34. RADY, *Nobility* (quoted n. 6), 101.

35. RADY, *Nobility* (quoted n. 6), 102. For a discussion of origins of the edict see J. BAK, Louis I and the lesser nobility in Hungary, in *Louis the Great: King of Hungary and Poland*, ed. by S. B. VARDY, G. GROSSCHMID, L. DOMONKOS, New York 1986, p. 69.

36. J. BAK, P. ENGEL, and J. SWEENEY, *Decreta regni mediaevalis Hungariae 1301-1457* (Laws of the Kingdom of Hungary I/2), Salt Lake City 1992, p. 8.

the decree of 1351 had to be reissued on several occasions, and several charters show that it was sometimes ignored in practice, indicating that the ultimate triumph of the kindred was far from a linear progression.[37]

The question remains, what customs of inheritance were actually in practice prior to the Angevin reforms. No consensus is forthcoming because the charter record is ambiguous. Perhaps not surprisingly, the great majority of charters recording the inheritance and division of properties from the thirteenth century record divisions among members of the kindred rather than among sons. Certainly in a charter from 1282 dividing a certain 'inherited property' named Bel, the division of the property is between what appear to be several branches of the same kindred. The main parties are several sets of cousins, but the connections between the groups of cousins is not entirely clear.[38] Similarly, the canons of Vasvár recorded a division of a property among two sets of *consanguinei* in 1254, and it is not possible to establish how the families were related.[39] Numerous such charters record only that a certain *terra* or *possessio* was divided among such unspecified kinsmen (*consanguinei*, *cognaciones*, *proximi*, *genera*, or sometimes *generatio*).[40] In a lesser clan, the property might be only one village. Such was the case in 1260 when the members of the Zounuk kindred (*de genera Zounuk*) divided up the village Bagon among themselves. All of them were residents of the same village.[41] In other instances, the properties could quite extensive and dispersed among several recognized locales.[42] These divisions frequently occurred among *fratres*, but in the Hungarian usage, this term could mean any relative in the agnatic line. Cousins were usually referred to as *fratres patruelis*, but they too could simply be termed *fratres*. The expression, *fratres carnualis* was typically used for men sharing a father while *fratres uterinis* referred to those sharing a mother.[43]

When divisions did take place, the participants made certain that the properties were divided equally among those involved, be they brothers, cousins or more distant relatives. Family members had a very real idea of the value of properties, and in order to avoid controversy, participants were very deliberate in making sure each portion was equal. A frequent means of making sure the divisions were fair and acceptable was through the use of arbiters from within the kindred itself.[44] A charter issued by the chapter at Esztergom in 1271 recorded the division of several significant estates among cousins of the Kachin kindred. After the division had been made, one of the arbiters pointed out that a property received by one cousin was inferior, and so he was compensated by his other cousins with portions from their property.[45] If the individuals were from rather insignificant clans, then the arbitration might be conducted by local

37. Rady, *Nobility* (quoted n. 6), 101.
38. G. Wenzel, *Codex Diplomaticus Arpadianus Continuatus*, Pest 1871, vol. 9, p. 342.
39. Wenzel, *Codex Diplomaticus* (quoted n. 38), vol. 7, pp. 375–376.
40. Wenzel, *Codex Diplomaticus* (quoted n. 38), vol. 7, pp. 473–474, 537–538; vol. 8, p. 364; vol. 9, pp. 96, 97, 535–536, 364. G. Fejér, *Codex Diplomaticus Hungariae Ecclesiasticus ac Civilis*, Buda 1829, vol. 4, book 2, pp. 440–441; vol. 4, book 3, pp. 45–46, 704–705; vol. 8, book 1, pp. 165–168.
41. Wenzel, *Codex Diplomaticus* (quoted n. 38), vol. 7, pp. 537–538.
42. Fejér, *Codex Diplomaticus*(quoted n. 40) , vol. 8, book 3, pp. 704–705
43. Fügedi, Some characteristics (quoted n. 16), pp. 30–31.
44. E.g. Wenzel, *Codex Diplomaticus* (quoted n. 38), vol. 9, p. 342.
45. Wenzel, *Codex Diplomaticus* (quoted n. 38), vol. 8, p. 353.

men considered particularly honest or perhaps by local canons.[46] If, on the other hand, the clan was prominent and the properties large and numerous, then of course much more powerful individuals would be drawn in to give the force of their position to the deal struck.[47] In any case, since peace was dependent upon all agreeing upon the division, if the properties involved were large, they were frequently split equally among all members. Villages might be split in two or three equal portions with an eye to exact equality among the different portions. So, for example in 1256 brothers split a property in half including the monastery that they likewise split in half. Similarly, one wonders exactly what was meant by the two relations of Beelgégen who split a fishpond in half in 1312.[48] Sometimes, in contrast to such vague conditions, the charters are very exact in their enumeration of the property divisions. When two brothers, Egidio and Iwanka, divided their father's properties in 1336, it included a castle with two separate residences. Egidio received the *magnam palatium* with the cellar and stone mill while Iwanka received the less significant *palatium* that contained the cistern and an abandoned cellar. The brothers agreed, however that the tower, the bulwark, the gate, and the road leading to the castle should be held in common with each brother having usage rights to these three.[49] After all, what good is a *magnum palatium* if you can't enter or leave the castle it's located in?

At times a father might pass the lands under his direct control to his sons, and they would control them together as a *frérèche*. This practice was described by Werbőczy, and by the sixteenth century at least, the eldest son was to manage the estates.[50] This sharing of estates by brothers can be seen in some charters from the thirteenth century. In 1289, a son and two grandsons of Paulus of the Guthkeled kindred divided property among themselves (Fig. 1). The elder Paulus had at least two sons, Laurencius and Detricus. Detricus had two sons, Mathya and Paulus. By the time the charter was drawn up in 1289, the elder Paulus had died, and it seems that his son Detricus had as well since he nowhere took part in the proceedings, and his spoke on their own behalf. In addition, Detricus' two sons held all of the elder Paulus' property communally with their uncle Laurencius.[51] The property they shared included ancestral, purchased and otherwise acquired lands, and the charter recorded the division between Laurencius and his nephews.[52] The inherited property was split equally between Laurencius and his nephews, though its usage remained shared. At the same time, the nephews were forced to hand over a purchased property to their uncle.[53] It is interesting to note that Detricus was unable pass any lands directly to his sons from among the inherited lands that belonged to the *frérèche*.

46. *Proborum virorum... communitatis*. WENZEL, *Codex Diplomaticus* (quoted n. 38), vol. 9, p. 536. FEJÉR, *Codex Diplomaticus* (quoted n. 40), vol. 9, book 6, p. 30-32.

47. For example, the when members of the Hont-Pázmány clan divided properties of Zselíz, numerous noblemen were brought in, including the palatine from the great Csák clan. WENZEL, *Codex Diplomaticus* (quoted n. 38), vol. 10, p. 233.

48. WENZEL, *Codex Diplomaticus* (quoted n. 38), vol. 9, p. 97. fishpond, FEJÉR, *Codex Diplomaticus* (quoted n. 40), vol, 8, book 1, p. 474.

49. FEJÉR, *Codex Diplomaticus* (quoted n. 40), vol, 8, book 4, p. 203.

50. FÜGEDI, Some characteristics (quoted n. 16), p. 30. See BAK, BANYÓ and RADY, *Tripartitum* (quoted n. 1), pp. 104–113 (I. 40-45).

51. *communiter vsque modo possessis*. WENZEL, *Codex Diplomaticus* (quoted n. 38), vol. 9, p. 505.

52. WENZEL, *Codex Diplomaticus* (quoted n. 38), vol. 9, p. 505.

53. WENZEL, *Codex Diplomaticus* (quoted n. 38), vol. 9, p. 505.

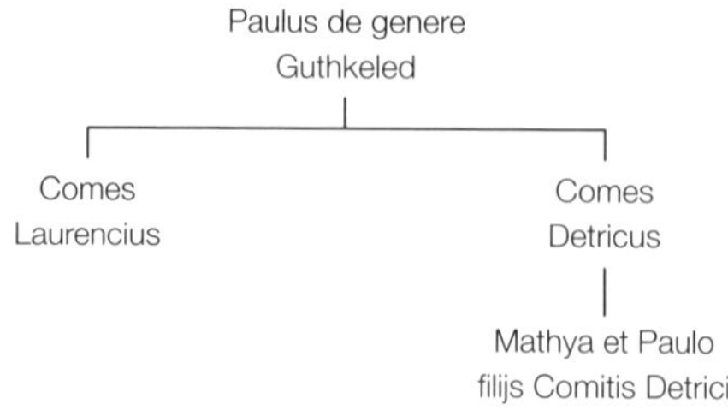

Fig. 1. Parties involved in a land division of 1289.

In a similar manner, a pair of charters from roughly the same period records a disputed division between two brothers and their uncle over 'inherited, purchased and acquired' properties.[54] In both of these cases, brothers shared the properties held by their deceased father until such time as they formally divided them amongst themselves and formed their own new branches of the kindred.

Other cases from the same period indicate that divisions among brothers were not always safe from the intervention of the kindred. Pál Engel reported a case from the first quarter of the fourteenth century in which brothers had divided the patrimony amongst themselves by 1325 at the latest. In 1327 they were forced to draw up a new charter recording another division, but this time the two brothers split the properties with two heretofore unrecorded cousins.[55] Both the reason the cousins were shut out of the division in the first instance and the reason they were later included is not completely understood, but it does indicate the power of the kindred could hold.

At the same time several examples show that in some instances the *parentela*'s rights superseded those of the kindred, and fathers would dispose of their property directly to their sons individually. In other words, the sons did not share the patrimony as part of a *frérèche*. For example, two brothers split up their father's male and female slaves after his death in 1300.[56] The will of *Comes* Nicolas from 1231 designated that both ancestral and purchased properties be split among his sons, and these properties were quite significant.[57] In a charter from 1279, the two sons of Henry, the Ban of Slavonia split between them sizeable properties, again both inherited and purchased, including castles.[58] Inherited castles also appear as the main objects of the patrimony left for the two sons of Petrus of Sumus in 1336.[59]

54. Wenzel, *Codex Diplomaticus* (quoted n. 38), vol. 10, pp. 121, 345.

55. Engel, *Nagy Lajos* (quoted n. 33), pp. 141–142.

56. I. Nagy, A. Ipolyi, and D. Véghely, *Codex Diplomaticus Patrius*, Budapest 1880, vol. 7, pp. 23–25.

57. Fejér, *Codex Diplomaticus* (quoted n. 40) , vol. 3, book 2, pp. 227–230.

58. Fejér, *Codex Diplomaticus* (quoted n. 40), vol. 5, book 2, pp. 593–595. The two sons, Nicolas and Magister Johannes were only described as *fratres*, but other charters make it clear they were both sons of Bán Henry. See Fejér, *Codex Diplomaticus* (quoted n. 40), vol. 7, book 5, p. 467.

59. Fejér, *Codex Diplomaticus* (quoted n. 40), vol. 8, book 4, pp. 202–204.

How do we explain this inconsistency of inheritance practice in which sometimes the *parentela* took precedence and sometimes the kindred? Marty Rady listed several possible explanations. First, perhaps the inheritance rules varied from one kindred to the other. I do not find this explanation likely simply because in the rare examples when charters explicitly referenced inheritance rules, nowhere do they refer to the laws of a particular kindred. In fact, what explicit evidence we have regarding laws of inheritance refer to kingdom-wide rules. For example a charter from 1296 records the division of several significant estates among cousins, and at one point the charter makes the point that the division among these was done 'by right of birth, or inheritance' (*iure geniture hereditariaue*) with no reference to distinct kindred rules.[60] In the will of *Comes* Nicolas mentioned above part, the youngest son was given his father's *domus* 'as is the custom in Hungary' (*vt mos est in Hungaria*).[61] Interestingly, this custom survived into the sixteenth century and is recorded by Werbőczy.[62]

A second possibility posited by Rady is that land divisions depended on whether the land was worked communally by the family prior to the division.[63] Communal ownership of property was common in the thirteenth century, and as described above, it is accepted in the *Tripartitum*.[64] We have seen that sons could possess their father's property communally as part of a *frérèche*, but to say that this communal ownership after the death of the patriarch resulted from the rights of the *parentela* is to confuse cause with result. In other words, there is no reason for thinking that the sons had precedent over the kindred merely because they received the land together as a single unit. Rather, we should understand that when fathers did prejudice the kindred to favor their sons, they did so by giving their sons the property to own communally. Land was held in common not only among sons, but among various members of a kindred. Kindred members continued to retain some of the property in communal ownership even after divisions among its members. In most instances, communal rights to property made the most sense for all parties involved. For example, when forests or a river are among the divided property, all the parties retained access.[65] Or when two brothers with rather insignificant holdings divided them among themselves, they retained the communal ownership of the residence (*locus sessionalis*), presumably because it made the most sense financially to stay together in that location rather than having one of them build another elsewhere.[66] In other instances, it is difficult to see why particular properties were kept communal in ownership if the charter does not specifically state the reason.[67]

Rady argued that a third possible reason some *parentelae* could ignore the kindred – the fathers bribed judges to circumvent the law.[68] We should avoid thinking in terms of rigid legal

60. Wenzel, *Codex Diplomaticus* (quoted n. 38), vol. 10, p. 234.
61. Fejér, *Codex Diplomaticus* (quoted n. 40), vol 3, book 2, p. 228.
62. Bak, Banyó and Rady, *Tripartitum* (quoted n. 1), pp. 106–107 (I: 40.2).
63. Rady, *Nobility* (quoted n. 6), 100.
64. Bak, Banyó and Rady, *Tripartitum* (quoted n. 1), pp. 106–107 (I: 40).
65. Fejér, *Codex Diplomaticus* (quoted n. 40), vol, 8, book 1, p. 165.
66. Wenzel, *Codex Diplomaticus* (quoted n. 38), vol. 8, p. 247.
67. See for example, Wenzel, *Codex Diplomaticus* (quoted n. 38), vol. 8, pp. 43–44, 353; vol. 9, pp. 505–506; Nagy *Codex Diplomaticus Patrius* (quoted n. 56), vol. 6, pp. 207–208. Fejér, *Codex Diplomaticus* (quoted n. 40), vol. 5, book 2, pp. 593–595.
68. Rady, *Nobility* (quoted n. 6), 100.

customs. Inheritance practices in the thirteenth century depended greatly upon the individual power and authority of the testator in question. When the testator or even the *parentela* was strong vis-à-vis the kindred, then land was passed to sons. Certainly all of the examples given above in which the father was able to freely dispose of his property to his sons, the *parentela* was one of substantial means. One was the Bán of Slavonia whose son Nicolas would later himself be Bán. Another involved numerous properties, including at least two castles that were split among the sons. The third also had numerous properties including several residences. Gyula Kristó has pointed out that the power of the 'oligarchs' in the latter half of the thirteenth century was based upon the independent properties of the *parentela* and not upon the kindreds as previously thought.[69] These great families that vied with royal power at the end of the thirteenth century were able to evade the requirements imposed upon them by their kindred and were able to create their own 'petty kingdoms' to use the phrase common in Hungarian historiography.[70] While the power of the oligarchs continued to rise in relation to their kindreds, generally, the power relationship between branches of the kindred were almost certainly a fluid affair. Such changing fortunes of families versus their other kin could explain how property could originally be given to sons, only later to be challenged by the kindred. The changing fortunes of a *parentela* and its kindred would explain the situation described by Pál Engel discussed above.[71] The *Tripartitum* specifically allowed for revisiting property divisions in the event that one son took advantage of his power to grab all the property.[72] Engel sought for a legal justification for the change in course between the relatives, but it could just as easily be explained in terms of shifting power relationships between the various branches of the kindred.

Another source of the tension between the kindred and the *parentela* was the inheritance customs of daughters. Again we turn to Werbőczy to provide a framework for understanding how women fit within the system. The relative insignificance of the female line shows itself in his disinterest in enumerating the mother's relatives. Indeed, they are all simply referred to as *proximi*.[73] Women received property at the time of their marriage in the form of a gift from their husbands. This was called the *dos*, or *dotalitium*, and according to the *Tripartitum*, it was based upon the size of the groom's estates. The bride was to receive *dotalitium* in either cash or in 'moveable and marketable chattels' upon the death of her husband.[74] We should think of the *dotalitium* as something akin to the *Morgengabe* since Werbőczi specifically associated it with the loss of 'virginity and consummation of the marriage.'[75] Unlike *Morgengabe*, however, the *dotalitium* was paid to women upon their succeeding marriages with the rate halving with each marriage, so that at a second marriage, a woman received half of her original *dotalitium*, upon a third, she received one-quarter, and so on until the fifth

69. I. Bolla, Az Aranybulla-kori társadali mozgalmak a Váradi Regestrum megvilágításában, *Annales Universitatis Scientiarum Budapestinensis de Rolando Eötvös Nominatae. Sectio historica* 1, 1957, p. 92. As Gyula Kristó put it: *a tartományuraság* családi (és nem nemzetségi) alapon jött létre, in Gy. Kristó, *A feudális széttagolodás Magyarországon*, Budapest 1979, p. 149.

70. Kristó, *A feudális széttagolodás* (quoted n. 69), p. 149.

71. Engel, *Nagy Lajos* (quoted n. 33), 141-142.

72. Bak, Banyó and Rady, *Tripartitum* (quoted n. 1), pp. 112–113 (I: 46.1).

73. Fügedi, Some characteristics (quoted n. 16), 30-31.

74. Bak, Banyó and Rady, *Tripartitum* (quoted n. 1), pp. 176–177 (I: 95).

75. Bak, Banyó and Rady, *Tripartitum* (quoted n. 1), pp. 175–176 (I: 93).

or sixth marriage whereupon Werbőczi confessed 'her dower will be reduced to a very small amount.'[76] Because of this declining scale, Erik Fügedi preferred to think of the *dotalitium* as more of a widow's pension.[77]

Daughters were also to inherit from their father upon his death, but they were excluded from the ancestral estates of the kindred. Instead, they received goods valued at one-quarter of the property of their father. The filial quarter was the total amount provided for all of a man's daughters, so that if he had more than one, the girls would have to share the quarter amongst themselves. The filial quarter was determined from the 'common estimation,' of their father's lands, usually one-tenth of its total value.[78] Normally, daughters were forbidden from receiving the quarter in the form of real estate, but Werbőczy did acknowledge that girls could receive their portion in land in the case of *defectis semine*. In such instances, the daughter was to receive the quarter, so that they were provided for until their marriage, after which members of the girl's kindred had the right to redeem it. The land, in other words, was not to remain in the hands of the daughter so as to protect the kindred from its alienation.[79] If, on the other hand, the daughter were to marry a landless man, then according to the *Tripartitum* she would be able to retain property in order to maintain her noble status.[80] The general prohibition against paying the filial quarter in land extend to purchased and acquired lands as well because, in the words of Werbőczy,

'this kingdom of Hungary, with the lands subjected to it, lies amidst and indeed in the jaws of enemies, and has always been protected and defended by the sword and by arms;... Since girls and women do not and cannot wield arms... such goods do not belong to the right of the female line.'[81]

The rules governing women's inheritance in the *Tripartitum* were clearly designed to make certain that the ancestral estates would not come into the possession of a stranger, that is a non-agnate, and they show that a woman's primary role was to produce sons who could then further maintain the interests of the kindred.

The earliest record of the filial quarter in Hungary appears in the privileges issued by Andrew II in 1222 known as the Golden Bull.[82] The *decretum* states that if any of the *servientes regis* (the upper stratum of soldiers) were to die without male heirs, then their daughter would inherit one-quarter of their property.[83] It is generally agreed that the origins of the

76. *Dos sua in tantum minuetur ut admodum exigua sit futura*. Bak, Banyó and Rady, *Tripartitum* (quoted n. 1), pp. 178–179 (I: 96.1).

77. Fügedi, Some characteristics (quoted n. 16), p. 31.

78. Bak, Banyó and Rady, *Tripartitum* (quoted n. 1), pp. 172–173 (I:89). P. Banyó, Birtoköröklés és leánynegyed. Kísérlet egy középkori jogintézmény értelmezésére, *AETAS* 2000, p. 79.

79. Bak, Banyó and Rady, *Tripartitum* (quoted n. 1), pp. 90–91 (I: 29.5-6). Banyó, Birtoköröklés (quoted n. 78), p. 79.

80. Bak, Banyó and Rady, *Tripartitum* (quoted n. 1), pp. 90–91 (I:29.7).

81. *...quia regnum istud Hungariae cum partibus sibi subiectis in medio faucibus hostium situm & positum est quod gladio semper & armis tutari defendisque solet... . Mulieres autem & puellae armis militare cum hostibusque decertare non solent neque possunt... ob hoc bona ipsa iuri foemineo non deserviunt*. Bak, Banyó and Rady, *Tripartitum* (quoted n. 1), pp. 74–75, (I: 18, 19).

82. M. Rady, The filial quarter and female inheritance in medieval Hungarian law, in Nagy and Sebők eds, *The Man of many devices*, p. 424. A. Murarik, *Az ősiség alapintézményeinek eredete*, Budapest 1938, p. 165.

83. Bak, Bónis, and Sweeney, *Decreta 1000-1300* (quoted n. 24), p. 32.

practice can be found in the Roman Lex Falcidia, but the means by which it entered Hungary is less certain.[84] Antal Murarik, who demonstrated the quarter's Roman provenance, argued that it arrived shortly before the Golden Bull under the influence of the Hungarian legal scholar at Bologna, Paulus Hungarus, who had returned to Hungary in 1221.[85] Such a late arrival to Hungary is unlikely since the Golden Bull seems to assume that the practice was understood and had been in wide use by the time of its composition.[86] In fact, it has been argued that the absence of *decreta* dealing with the quarter in the thirteenth century indicates that it was regulated by customary law.[87] Since similar institutions were present in both Polish and Latvian regions, the origins of the filial quarter in Hungary in all likelihood are to be found in broader Roman legal ideas.[88]

Regardless of the origins, by the time of Werbőczy's *Tripartitum*, as we have seen, women were forbidden from receiving the quarter in land so as to protect the interests of the kindred. However, the issue appears to have been rather confused during the last of the Árpád era and the beginning of the Angevins.[89] The *decretum* of 1290 specifically forbad allowing land to pass to non-kinsmen through either the *dos* or the filial quarter.[90] From approximately the same time, however, another *decretum* specifically declared that in the absence of a male heir, the quarter shall be given in land to either the man's daughter or his sister in order to prevent it all going to the king in escheat.[91] This latter legislation can be interpreted in several ways. It may be understood that the law only took effect if the kindred had completely died out, but it is more likely that the law was stating the royal prerogative of escheat to the detriment of the kindred.[92] The confusion in the early legislation touching on the filial quarter points to the continual tension among the three parties interested in inheritance – the *parentela*, the crown, and the kindred. The kindred had an interest in preventing quarter payments in the form of land so as to retain the land within the kindred. At the same time, the crown and the *parentela* were more interested in cutting out the kindred. The varied and confused practice of the filial quarter during the Árpáds and early Angevins can only be understood when viewed in light of this three-way struggle.

The back-and-forth nature of royal decrees regarding the property to be given for the filial quarter is matched by the charter evidence. Péter Banyó has shown that from the thirteenth to the fifteenth century, lands composed approximately half of the daughters' quarters that are recorded, so that of the fifty-nine examples found in the thirteenth century, only twenty-six consisted of moveables.[93] Banyó rejects any of the general theories that Hungarian histori-

84. MURARIK, *Az ősiség* (quoted n. 82), pp. 166–183. BÓNIS, *Középkori jogunk elemei*, p. 95.

85. MURARIK, *Az ősiség* (quoted n. 82), pp. 185–188.

86. J. HOLUB, La 'quarta puellaris' dans l'ancien droit Hongrois, in M. ROTONDI ed., *Studi in memoria di Aldo Albertoni*, Milan 1938, vol. 3, pp. 281–282.

87. BANYÓ, Birtoköröklés (quoted n. 78), p. 81.

88. Gy. BÓNIS, *Einflüsse des römischen Rechts in Ungarn* (Ius Romanum Medii Aevi 5/1), Milan 1964, p. 97.

89. For most of what follows, see BANYÓ, Birtoköröklés (quoted n. 78), pp. 80–83.

90. BAK, BÓNIS, and SWEENEY, *Decreta 1000-1300* (quoted n. 24), p. 45 (1290:23).

91. BAK, BÓNIS, and SWEENEY, *Decreta 1000-1300* (quoted n. 24), p. 74 (1300:18); for dating of the *decretum*, see p. 134.

92. BANYÓ, Birtoköröklés (quoted n. 78), p. 80.

93. BANYÓ, Birtoköröklés (quoted n. 78), pp. 83–84.

ography has put forward to explain these cases. Some have posited that land was given when families were short of cash, but this is not likely in so many cases, especially when they involve the rather powerful families such as the Drugeth and Ónodi Cudar.[94] A second explanation relies upon the *Tripartitum*'s allowance for male members of the kindred to redeem the quarter after the marriage of its recipient. Since the first mention of this practice only occurs in the fifteenth century, this is also unlikely.[95] The third possibility is that the land given came from the father's acquired properties and not the ancestral ones, but Banyó has effectively demonstrated that not to be the case.[96] In essence, scholars search in vain for a theory that explains even the majority of the cases. Banyó argued that each issuance of the filial quarter varied with the particular situation of that family at that time. Sometimes the family had enough land to pass it to the daughter as part of her quarter. If the family had little land, then the quarter would have consisted solely of moveables. We must also remember that issues such as the affection a mother felt for her daughter or that brothers felt for their sister surely played a role in these decisions though those sorts of motivation are impossible to recover from the sources.[97] The increasing desire of fathers to keep their properties intact and in the hands of their offspring at the expense of the kindred also must have been important, and this desire contributed to the appearance of a new practice under the Angevins – the prefection of daughters.

Since the decree of 1351 shut off any legal avenue for keeping property within the *parentela* of those men dying without sons, the Angevin kings introduced the prefection (*praefacio*) of daughters. The practice allowed a daughter to receive the become the legal heir of her father through the special grace of the king. She would then establish her own kindred, and the land would not be divided among the kindred of her father. Charles I seems to have begun the process when he issued a special charter of *praefacio* in 1332.[98] Louis I expanded the practice, and by the end of the fourteenth century it had become regularized and accepted into Hungarian customary law. The kindred naturally opposed the practice, and by the time of Sigismund (r.1387-1437), it was not allowed as long as agnates within four degrees could be found.[99]

Perhaps unsurprisingly, divisions of lands frequently occasioned violence or were the result of violence among members of the kindred. Phrases such as *contencionem habuerunt, hostiliter inimicabiliterque agebatur*, or *lis et contencio fuisset* appear with some frequency in the charters. Changes in the family could invalidate a previously-agreed upon land division, so that dissention rose up in the family. Such was the case in the last half of the thirteenth century when four brothers from the prominent Aba clan had equally divided the lands left to them by their father. All was well until one of the brothers died and 'a great weed' had grown up among them leading to both contention and the drawing up of a new charter of division.[100] Contention could lead to more significant violence as in the case in 1300 when two families of the same kindred divided the ancestral lands, but one family was dissatisfied, and they would not

94. Banyó, Birtoköröklés (quoted n. 78), p. 84.
95. Banyó, Birtoköröklés (quoted n. 78), p. 84.
96. Banyó, Birtoköröklés (quoted n. 78), pp. 85–86.
97. Banyó, Birtoköröklés (quoted n. 78)s, p. 89.
98. J. Holub, Középkori fiúsítások, *Turul*, 1927, pp. 84–85.
99. Holub, Középkori fiúsítások (quoted n. 98), p. 84.
100. Wenzel, *Codex Diplomaticus* (quoted n. 38), vol. 10, p. 71.

give up the property according to the formal division. Several offers of financial compensation were made, but each was rejected.[101] Instead, as the charter put it, the troublesome family followed a path of 'destruction, fire, loss, death, captivity' such that it moved the other members against them and they were forced to pay for the 'spirit of rebellion' with the very same property they so desired.[102] In fact, a common strategy seems to have been the forcible occupation of land by one party though in the charters I have not found that the strategy produced much success.[103] This is probably due to the nature of the source material. Those forced to give back land they had occupied would also be more likely to be forced to agree to a written agreement confirming the transfer whereas anyone whose violence was successful would not then also need a charter confirming their rights. Or it may simply be a case of the victors writing the history in that they would not likely include in any charter they had drawn up wording suggesting they based their claim upon force as well as law. In fact, we may suspect that violence was actually quite an effective means of defending ones perceived hereditary rights since several types of violence became accepted enough to be recorded in the *Tripartitum*. The first of these was the *repulsio* which allowed for a defendant to resist the bailiff's efforts to evict him from an estate if he met the bailiff with drawn sword. In such a case, the defendant could force a retrial though, according to Werbőczi, this tactic could only be used once. Any succeeding attempts would result in treason charges with the possible loss of all the defendant's estates. [104] Another legitimization of force to establish hereditary rights in the *Tripartitum* is the *reoccupatio*. Quite simply, the *reoccupatio* gave any litigant evicted from an estate the right, within one year, to return and himself evict by force his once legal opponent thus forcing a retrial.[105] The acceptance of both the *repulsio* and the *reoccupatio* as legal procedures are clearly attempts to regularize and thereby limit practices which had a long history in Hungary as have seen.[106]

To conclude this brief study of inheritance practices under the Árpáds, we have frequently seen reflections of the later customs as recorded in Werbőczi's *Tripartitum*. Maintenance of the integrity of the ancestral land was of primary importance and members of the kindred took great pains to make sure any division produced equal portions for each party involved. Daughters' path to inheritance and their access to property were likewise controlled, at least theoretically, by the rights of the kindred. The picture of inheritance rules as they actually existed in the thirteenth and early fourteenth centuries is complicated further by extra-legal factors such as the power of individuals within the kindred or their capacity for violence. As for the place of daughters within the system, the amount of land available or the capacity for affection played a role among other factors. Perhaps most importantly, inheritance customs must be viewed in light of the three-way struggle between the crown, the kindred and the *parentela*, the situation changing as the power relationship between each changed.

101. Wenzel, *Codex Diplomaticus* (quoted n. 38), vol. 10, p. 396.

102. *Destruccionum, incendiorum, dampnorum, mortis, captiuacionis*. Wenzel, *Codex Diplomaticus* (quoted n. 38), vol. 10, p. 397.

103. See for example, Fejér, *Codex Diplomaticus* (quoted n. 40), vol.4, book 3, p. 45-46.

104. M. Rady, Hungarian Procedural Law and Part Two of the *Tripartitum*, in Rady ed., *Custom and Law*, p. 69.

105. Rady, Hungarian Procedural Law (quoted n. 104), p. 68.

106. Rady, Hungarian Procedural Law (quoted n. 104), p. 69.

KINSHIP AND CONFLICTS OVER INHERITANCE

MATRILINEAL KINSHIP IN ATHENIAN INHERITANCE DISPUTES: TWO CASE STUDIES

Brenda Griffith-Williams

Introduction

Any inheritance system, especially one that combines a fixed order of succession with an element of testamentary freedom, creates the potential for conflict between those of a dead person's family and friends who benefit from his estate and those who do not. In a predominantly patrilineal system such as that of classical Athens there is scope, in particular, for conflict between the deceased's relations on his father's side and those related to him through his mother. The main part of this paper examines two cases of conflict between patrikin and matrikin which are known to us from the forensic speeches of Isaios, a fourth-century logographer (speechwriter) who appears to have specialized in inheritance disputes. To put these case studies into context, I begin with a brief survey of the relevant features of Athenian inheritance law.[1]

A typical male citizen of classical Athens wanted not only to pass on his land and other possessions to his heir, or heirs, but also to leave a successor who would keep his *oikos* alive and carry out the funeral and annual commemorative rituals on his behalf.[2] Ideally his successor would be a natural, legitimate son, who had an unquestioned right to inherit his father's estate, excluding any daughters or other family members, and could not be disinherited; but Athenian law made it possible to create an 'artificial heir', either by adoption or by succession through a female line.

1. The term 'Athenian law' applies, in this paper, to the law of Athens in the fourth century BC. It would be misleading to speak of 'Greek law', since each *polis* (city state) of ancient Greece had its own legal system. To the extent that we know about inheritance law in other *poleis* (notably Gortyn and Sparta) it differed in some important respects from that of Athens.

2. It the deceased left no direct descendants, responsibility for the funeral fell to his next of kin, or, in an extreme case, to any available friends; but it is likely that only direct descendants were obliged to carry out the commemorative rituals in subsequent years. Cf. B. Griffith-Williams, *A commentary on selected speeches of Isaios*, Leiden 2013, pp. 73–74.

Inheritance, Law and Religions in the Ancient and Mediaeval Worlds, ed. by B. Caseau and S. R. Huebner (Centre de recherche d'Histoire et Civilisation de Byzance, Monographies 45), Paris 2014.

A law attributed to the sixth century legislator, Solon, allowed a man without natural legitimate sons to dispose of his property as he chose, provided he was of sound mind, unimpaired by old age, drugs or disease, and not acting under the influence of a woman or under constraint.[3] The original scope and effect of Solon's law are unclear, but in the fourth century it was interpreted as permitting the creation of a son and heir by adoption, either *inter vivos* or by will.[4] If the adoptive father had a daughter, the adopted son would normally be expected to marry her.

A man who adopted *inter vivos* would introduce his adopted son to his phratry, and enrol him in his deme, as if he had been a natural legitimate son. Once these formalities were completed, the adopted son lost his legal relationship with his natural father (though not with his mother),[5] and had the same legal status as a natural legitimate son of his adoptive father, including the right of direct entry onto the father's estate after his death. In the event of a dispute about the adoption, the son would be expected to produce witnesses who could testify that he had been properly introduced into his father's phratry and enrolled in his deme. On the other hand, a son adopted by will could not take possession of the estate without submitting a claim to the court. Once his claim was approved, he would be registered in the appropriate phratry and deme as his adoptive father's son. Even if the deceased left no legitimate descendants of either sex, natural or adopted, it was possible for one of his surviving kinsmen, with the agreement of the rest of the family, to be enrolled in his phratry as his son and heir.[6] If an Athenian died leaving no legitimate sons, natural or adopted, but did leave a daughter, she became an *epiklēros*, and could be claimed in marriage by her father's next of kin.[7] The father's estate then passed to the son or sons of the *epiklēros* two years after he or they reached puberty.[8]

Given all these possibilities, it seems unlikely that many Athenians died without leaving either a male heir or a daughter who could be expected to produce one; but when that did happen, or when an adoption was successfully disputed, the dead man's estate passed to one of his collateral relations. The order of succession, which was prescribed by law, did not completely exclude those related to the deceased through his mother, but it did put them at a disadvantage. Homopatric brothers (that is, brothers by the same father as the deceased) came first, followed by sisters by the same father, and then cousins related to the deceased through his father. So, as we shall see from the first of our two case studies, even homometric siblings of the deceased (that is, half-brothers or sisters by the same mother) were in a lower position than his patrilineal cousins.

3. The law is cited at [Dem.] 46.14.

4. L. Rubinstein, *Adoption in IV. Century Athens*, Copenhagen 1993, provides a comprehensive account of Athenian adoption law and practice.

5. Isa. 7.25: 'but no-one is adopted out of his mother's family'.

6. The origins of this practice, which is known by modern scholars as 'posthumous adoption', are obscure, but it appears to have been a matter of custom rather than law. Cf. Griffith-Williams, *A commentary*, (quoted n. 2), pp. 203–205.

7. Close kin marriage, including many unions that would nowadays be considered incestuous, was common in classical Athens. The only prohibited degrees of kinship were parent and child, and brother and sister by the same mother.

8. For full discussion of the Athenian epiklerate, see L. Gernet, Sur l'épiklérat, *Revue des Études Grecques* 33, 1921, pp. 337–379; and E. Karabélias, *L'épiclérat attique: recherches sur la condition juridique de la fille épiclère athénienne*, Athens 2002.

Although the law allowed an adoptive father complete freedom of choice, most attested Athenian adoptions involve an adopter and adoptee who were already related by blood or through marriage. (This may be taken as an indication that an Athenian would, typically, not have wanted his property, and responsibility for his family cults, to pass outside his wider circle of kinsmen.)[9] It is likely that many of the Athenians who adopted chose their next of kin (that is, the person who would have inherited in any event if the adopter had left no descendants);[10] but when the adopted son was a more distant kinsman, or a complete outsider to the family, there was a risk that the adoption would be contested by someone higher in the order of intestate succession. In particular, as our second case study shows, if an Athenian chose to adopt a member of his mother's family, the adoption would be vulnerable to challenge by a surviving patrilineal kinsman.

The patrilineal bias in the Athenian order of succession reflected the patrilineal structure of Athenian families. A married woman retained some ties with her paternal *oikos*, and her children might enjoy affectionate relations with her father and brothers,[11] but they belonged to the *oikos* of her husband, their father. When the marriage ended, whether through death or divorce, she would expect to return to her father's *oikos* or, if he was already dead, to come under the protection of another male relative, typically a brother or an adult son. There was also a strong expectation that a widow or divorced woman would remarry as soon as possible, especially if she was still of childbearing age; but any children of her previous marriage would normally remain in their father's *oikos* and inherit his estate. An orphan – that is, a child whose father had died, whether or not the mother was still alive – would remain under the protection of a guardian (normally a paternal uncle or other relation of the child's father) who was responsible for maintaining the estate until the child came of age. So a widow or divorced woman who remarried would become stepmother (Greek *mētruia*) to her new husband's children from any previous marriage of his, but he would not normally take on the rôle of a modern stepfather to any older children of hers.

Of course, not every Athenian family conformed to the normal pattern. As Sabine Hübner has pointed out,[12] we know from Isaios's speeches of two Athenians, Astyphilos and Apollodoros, whose unusually close ties of affection with their stepfathers led to conflict over their respective estates between their patrilineal next of kin and a matrilineal kinsman to whom they were more closely related by blood. In both cases Isaios's client was a matrilineal kinsman of the dead man whose estate was at issue; the speeches he wrote for them give us an insight into the obstacles they faced in claiming the estate, and the strategies they could employ to make the best of their position.

9. Cf. GRIFFITH-WILLIAMS, *Oikos*, family feuds and funerals: argumentation and evidence in Athenian inheritance disputes, *Classical Quarterly* 62, 2012, p.148.

10. RUBINSTEIN, *Adoption*, (quoted n. 4), pp. 79–80.

11. On the traditionally strong bond in ancient Greece between mother's brother and sister's son, and between mother's father and daughter's son, see J. BREMMER, The importance of the maternal uncle and grandfather in archaic and classical Greece and early Byzantium, *Zeitschrift für Papyrologie und Epigraphik* 50, 1983, pp. 173–186.

12. S. R. HÜBNER, Callihroe's dilemma: remarriage and stepfathers in the Greco-Roman east, in S. R. HÜBNER and D. M. RATZAN ed., *Growing up fatherless in antiquity*, Cambridge 2009, p. 65.

Case 1: On the estate of Astyphilos (Isaios 9)

The speaker of Isaios 9, whose name we do not know, claims the estate of Astyphilos, his homometric half-brother, who died abroad on military service. The speaker explains that he himself came home from military service to find Astyphilos's cousin, Kleon, in occupation of Astyphilos's estate. Kleon told him that his son had been adopted by Astyphilos in a will which he had deposited with his maternal uncle, Hierokles, before leaving Athens for Mytilene. From a legal point of view, the speaker's first problem is to establish his own right to inherit the estate. His opponent, Kleon, is a first cousin of Astyphilos on his father's side, so even if the court found that Astyphilos did not leave a valid will, it would be Kleon who would have the stronger claim to inherit as next of kin. The speaker deals with this rather perfunctorily by asserting, early in the speech, that Kleon's father, Thoudippos, has been adopted into a different family, so that Kleon and his son no longer have a legal relationship with Astyphilos. He brings no evidence about the adoption of Thoudippos, relying on the confident assertion that the estate belongs to 'no-one else but me' (Isa. 9.1, 24).[13] The rest of the speech is devoted to an attack on the purported will.

The speaker's main line of attack is the allegation that the will is a forgery, produced in collusion between Kleon and Hierokles, and he produces witnesses to support his story that Hierokles offered to sell a forged will to the highest bidder, in return for a share in the estate. As he tells this story he emphasizes his feelings of bitter betrayal by Hierokles, who is his own maternal uncle as well as Astyphilos's.[14] But he also describes a family quarrel dating back to an earlier generation, saying that Astyphilos's father, Euthykrates, had died as the result of a fight with his brother Thoudippos, Kleon's father, over the division of their paternal estate. Euthykrates, on his deathbed, solemnly enjoined his relatives never to allow any of Thoudippos's family to come near his tomb, and when the young Astyphilos heard about this he never spoke to Kleon for the rest of his life, thinking that it would be impiety to do so (Isa. 9.20). This reminds us of the religious dimension in the Athenian inheritance system; as the speaker forcefully argues later in the speech (Isa. 9.36-37), Astyphilos would no more have entrusted the commemorative rituals to the son of his lifelong enemy than he would have wanted him to inherit his property.

Astyphilos's widowed mother remarried while Astyphilos was still a small child, and she took him with her to the household of her new husband, Theophrastos. Although this is not explicitly stated, it appears that Theophrastos was also Astyphilos's guardian, which would explain why the orphaned Astyphilos became, in effect, a member of his stepfather's family. The speaker introduces himself in his opening sentence as the homometric half-brother of Astyphilos, but he does not dwell on the matrilineal basis of their relationship. He refers to Astyphilos seven times as 'my brother' (Isa. 9.2, 4, 7, 24, 29, 30, 34), twice using the phrase 'my brother's property', as if to underline the point that he and Astyphilos were, effectively, brought up as homopatric brothers, not in separate households as would normally have been expected for homometric half-siblings. He brings testimony to confirm that both he and his

13. On Isaios's reticence about the adoption of Thoudippos, see Griffith-Williams, *A commentary* (quoted n. 2), p. 153.

14. According to C. Cox, *Household interests: property, marriage strategies and family dynamics in classical Athens*, Princeton 1998, p. 124, this is 'one of the rare instances of a public dispute between nephew and maternal uncle'.

father, Theophrastos, were on terms of close affection with Astyphilos. Witnesses testify that the two boys were brought up and educated together (Isa. 9.28); that Theophrastos cultivated Astyphilos's paternal estate and doubled its value, handing the property over in good order when Astyphilos came of age (Isa. 9.28-29); that it was Theophrastos who chose a husband for Astyphilos's sister and gave her in marriage (Isa. 9.29); that Theophrastos always took both of the boys together to the religious ceremonies (Isa. 9.30); and that the speaker never had a quarrel with Astyphilos, with whom he was brought up from infancy (Isa. 9.30).[15] At the very end of the speech, he reminds the judges once more that he was brought up and educated with Astyphilos, and was his brother.

So there are two aspects of the narrative about family relations in Isaios 9: on the one hand, Astyphilos treated Kleon's branch of the family as his enemies, while, on the other hand, he enjoyed close ties of gratitude and affection with his stepfather and half-brother. What are we to make of this story? It is, of course, not even worth trying to establish how much of it was true, but we can usefully consider why Isaios thought it appropriate for his client to tell this kind of story at all. Some modern scholars have described the story, and the evidence he brings to support it, as 'non-legal' or 'extra-legal': not relevant to the legal issue of the validity of Astyphilos's will, but simply designed to appeal to the judges at an emotional level and elicit their sympathy for the speaker. A full account of the scholarly debate would be beyond the scope of this paper, but, for reasons I have set out in more detail elsewhere,[16] I think it is wrong to see the evidence about family relations in this speech as irrelevant to the legal issue. In order to win his case, the speaker of Isaios 9 needs to persuade the judges that Astyphilos did not adopt Kleon's son. His allegation about the forged will is supported by his story about the quarrel between Astyphilos and Kleon and his picture of domestic harmony in the household of Theophrastos. This story would not be persuasive on its own, but it is, nonetheless, relevant to the speaker's legal case because it explains why Astyphilos was unlikely to have adopted Kleon's son and more likely to have wanted his estate to go to his half-brother.

As I have also pointed out elsewhere,[17] evidence about a testator's relationships with his beneficiaries and others in the family is still used in contested inheritance cases in the modern English courts, and for similar reasons: because it may arouse suspicion about the authenticity of a will. In the Athenian context it also has a more specific purpose: to help to overcome the disadvantage suffered by a claimant whose relationship with the deceased was matrilineal. The idea that Astyphilos had chosen to adopt the son of a patrilineal first cousin, who would have been legally his next of kin if Kleon's father had not been adopted out of the family, would probably have seemed perfectly natural to most of the judges, and they would not have expected the orphaned Astyphilos to have had much contact with his stepfather's family. Indeed, Kleon, who was the second speaker at the trial, probably intended to exploit this expectation by arguing that Astyphilos would not have wanted his estate to go to a mere homometric half-brother. The detailed account of Astyphilos's relations with Theophrastos and the speaker, making the point that this was a family that did not conform to the regular

15. On the significance of the witness testimony in this speech, see B. Griffith-Williams, 'Those who know the facts': witnesses and their testimony in Isaios 9, *Acta Antiqua Academiae Scientiarum Hungaricae* 48, 2008, pp. 253–261.

16. Griffith-williams, *Oikos*, (quoted n. 9), pp. 145–162.

17. *Ibid.*, pp. 157–158.

Athenian pattern, would have been an effective way of forestalling this, especially since the speaker's account is supported by witnesses. A modern court would undoubtedly expect to hear evidence of more recent relations within the family, but, in a culture where enmity was inherited, the speaker's story may have appeared all the more convincing because the quarrel was so deeply rooted.

A clear implication of this story, and one that may well have influenced some of the judges at an emotional rather than a rational level, is that the rigid application of the law might in certain circumstances be unfair to a matrilineal kinsman. But the speaker is not asking the judges to ignore the law and give him the estate in defiance of Astyphilos's will; his aim is to convince them that the document produced by Kleon is not genuine, because it does not express Astyphilos's true wishes. As a last resort, in case they do not believe the accusation of forgery, he makes the point that if Astyphilos did make a will in favour of the son of his sworn enemy, he cannot have been in his right mind, and so the will would in any event be invalid under Solon's law.

Case 2: On the estate of Apollodoros (Isaios 7)

The circumstances of our second case, Isaios 7, are somewhat different, but some features of the speech are strikingly similar to Isaios 9. Thrasyllos, the speaker, claims the estate of his mother's homometric half-brother, Apollodoros, saying that Apollodoros adopted him *inter vivos*. He is opposed by one of Apollodoros's female first cousins on his father's side, who claims the estate as next of kin, and who is represented in the legal action by her husband, Pronapes. It seems that Apollodoros did not actually complete the formalities of the adoption himself because, after introducing Thrasyllos to his phratry as his adopted son, he died before the meeting of his deme at which he was planning to enrol him, so Apollodoros's fellow demesmen completed the formalities on his behalf. This irregularity did not necessarily make the adoption invalid, as some scholars have argued,[18] but it probably gave Thrasyllos's opponents the pretext they needed to contest the adoption. Even if they did not deny that it took place as Thrasyllos described, they could have argued that the adoption was not valid under Solon's law because Apollodoros was a confused old man acting under the influence of a woman, his half-sister, and that it was Thrasyllos himself, rather than Apollodoros, who urged the demesmen to carry out the enrolment in the event of Apollodoros's death.[19] Thrasyllos counters these objections with witnesses who testify that Apollodoros made his intentions perfectly clear to his fellow demesmen, who duly enrolled Thrasyllos, according to Apollodoros's instructions, after his death.

Isaios evidently did not think that this account of the adoption, persuasive as it seems, would be sufficient on its own to make his client's case. So, like the speaker of Isaios 9, Thrasyllos tells a story of a long-lasting family quarrel. He says that Apollodoros's father, Thrasyllos senior, died on the Sicilian expedition of 415/3 BC, leaving a substantial fortune. Apollodoros was still a child, so his uncle Eupolis (the survivor of his father's two brothers) became his

18. See, especially, W. Wyse, *The speeches of Isaeus*, Cambridge 1904, p. 549: 'When Apollodoros died, the adoption was certainly incomplete ...'. But cf. L. Moy, *Étude sur les plaidoyers d'Isée*, Paris 1876, p. 218: 'Nous aurons l'occasion de voir, dans ce plaidoyer, quelles étaient les formalités nécessaires pour la validité de l'adoption.'

19. Cf. Isa. 6 and 8, both of which feature narratives about the exploitation of vulnerable old men by relatives eager to gain possession of their property.

guardian, but Eupolis mismanaged the estate and defrauded Apollodoros of a large amount of property.[20] Apollodoros's mother had remarried, and her second husband, Arkhedamos, took pity on Apollodoros, brought him up in his own household, and, when he came of age, helped him take successful legal action against Eupolis. Such a large amount of money was involved that there was no possibility of a reconciliation between Eupolis and Apollodoros, who became even closer to his stepfather's family. When Arkhedamos was taken prisoner of war, Apollodoros repaid his kindness by contributing to his ransom, and later helped him out of some financial difficulties. In due course, after Arkhedamos had died, Apollodoros became his half-sister's *kurios*, making arrangements for her marriage in a provisional will which he left before setting off on military service in the Corinthian War of 394-386 BC. Apollodoros survived the war, and had a son whom he loved and brought up as his heir. But some years later the son died unexpectedly, leaving Apollodoros an old man with no-one to care for him and manage his affairs, or to continue his *oikos* after his death and carry out the funeral and commemorative rituals. Naturally enough, it was to his half-sister that he turned in his distress, and, with her approval, he adopted her son. He would certainly not have wanted his property to go to the wife of Pronapes, whose father was his enemy Eupolis.

Adopting a sister's child was apparently not uncommon in classical Athens (Isaios 7 is one of six examples known to us from the Attic orators)[21] but it was most likely to be seen as appropriate when there was no suitable candidate for adoption who was related to the adoptive father on his father's side. That was certainly true in at least two cases. The speaker of Isaios 6 explains precisely the circumstances in which Philoktemon made a will adopting his sister's son: Philoktemon, although married, had no children; his two brothers had already died childless; and he had two sisters, one of whom had never had a son despite being married to Khaireas for many years. But his other sister, the wife of Phanostratos, had two sons, of whom Philoktemon adopted the older, Khairestratos (Isa. 6.6). In the other example, the speaker of Isaios 3 asks rhetorically whether Pyrrhos, by adopting his nephew Endios (the speaker's brother), was trying to exclude some closer relation. This he emphatically denies: no-one was more closely related to Pyrrhos than the speaker and his brother Endios, because Pyrrhos had no brother or brother's sons, and they were his sister's sons (Isa. 3.72).

What makes Apollodoros's position different from these is that the sister whose son he adopted was not a sister of the full blood but a homometric half-sister. Apollodoros had no brothers, so, if he and his sister had shared the same father, she and her offspring would have inherited his estate as his next of kin when he died leaving no natural or adopted offspring. But because they were related only through their mother, it was Apollodoros's cousins on his father's side who were his next of kin, not the half-sister and her son. And in most Athenian families, as we have seen, a homometric half-brother and sister would have been brought up in separate households, with little opportunity to develop a close, affectionate relationship.

20. Allegations of fraud or mismanagement by children's guardians were apparently not uncommon in Athens; cf., e.g., Dem. 27 and 28, Dem. 38.3, Lys. 32, Lys. 10.5, Isa. 5.10, Isa. 8.42. This is perhaps not surprising, given that the guardian was often the child's paternal uncle or other paternal kinsman, who would have inherited the estate if the deceased had died childless.

21. The others are Isa. 3 (Endios adopted by Pyrrhos), Isa. 6 (Khairestratos adopted by Philoktemon), Isa. 11 (sister's daughter adopted by Hagnias), Isa. 11.41 (sister's daughter adopted by Theophon), Isa. 11.49 and [Dem.] 43 (Makartatos adopted posthumously by Makartatos). Cf. [Dem.] 44, where Leokrates adopted the son of his sister's daughter.

It is quite possible that Pronapes and his wife claimed that they had been prepared to give Apollodoros one of their own sons for adoption; and, if they did say this, it would have seemed perfectly reasonable to the judges. So the story of the quarrel between Apollodoros and Eupolis, and the argumentation used in the speech, are designed to explain why Apollodoros acted as Thrasyllos says he did, and not in accordance with Athenian norms. As we saw in relation to Isaios 9, the story is relevant to Thrasyllos's legal case because it makes it more likely that the adoption really was carried out in accordance with Apollodoros's wishes.

Like the speaker of Isaios 9, Thrasyllos exploits the fact that his blood relationship to the deceased is closer than that of his opponent. He refers to his mother four times as Apollodoros's sister (Isa. 7.9, 14, 17, 43) without mentioning that they were in fact half-siblings (although that would have been clear enough from his narrative), and almost at the end of his speech he urges the judges to remember that he is Apollodoros's nephew while his opponent is a cousin (Isa. 7.45).

Thrasyllos repeatedly stresses Apollodoros's affection for his half-sister, and for his stepfather Arkhedamos (Thrasyllos's maternal grandfather), but, in contrast to the speaker of Isaios 9, he does not claim that he himself had a particularly close personal relationship with Apollodoros. This does not necessarily mean that his relations with Apollodoros were actually hostile – after all, they belonged to different generations, and probably had less opportunity for contact than the two half-brothers in Isaios 9 – but it may be that the absence of a positive bond enabled his opponents to portray Thrasyllos as an outsider who took advantage of Apollodoros at a time when he was especially vulnerable. Thrasyllos is able to counter this with a positive account of his own character: his exemplary treatment of his parents, and his services to the *polis*, were known to Apollodoros and explain Apollodoros's choice of Thrasyllos as his adopted son.

Conclusion

Each of these speeches makes a plausible case for a claimant who might at first have appeared to be at a disadvantage because his relationship to the deceased was matrilineal. Each speaker tells a story that contains both positive and negative arguments in support of his contention that his deceased relative would not have wanted his estate to pass, in the regular way, to his closest patrilineal kinsman. The negative argument seems to have been at least as important as the positive: it was not sufficient for a claimant to show that he (or his close kin) had been on good terms with the deceased; he was also expected to prove that the deceased had actively quarrelled with his patrilineal kinsmen and would not have wanted them to inherit his estate.

We do not know the result of either of these cases, or precisely what factors influenced the judges who heard them in reaching their decisions. Some of them may have been sympathetic to Isaios's clients from the outset, because they knew of similar situations within their own families or communities. Some, even if they were initially inclined to favour the patrilineal claimant, may have been persuaded to change their minds, while others may have remained hostile or sceptical. They all faced the difficult task, after hearing both parties to the dispute, of deciding whether Astyphilos's half-brother was really the victim of a wicked conspiracy, or an unscrupulous impostor; and whether Thrasyllos was really the honest citizen he claimed to be, or a materialistic opportunist as his opponents probably portrayed him.

'IT IS A DIFFICULT MATTER TO BE WRONGED BY STRANGERS, BUT TO BE WRONGED BY KIN IS WORST OF ALL' INHERITANCE AND CONFLICT IN GRECO-ROMAN EGYPT

Sabine R. HUEBNER

INTRODUCTION

Ways of passing on property and patterns of succession are at the center of determining a society's means for social reproduction. Jack Goody, one of the most influential cultural anthropologists of the 20th century, has been at the forefront of developing theories and methodologies on studying inheritance and succession in cross-cultural comparison.[1] Goody coined the term 'diverging devolution' for the entire process of transmitting property from one generation to the next via gifts, dowries and post-mortem inheritance. The timing, manner and quantity of this devolution of property to heirs determine the organization of the family, household and interpersonal relationships between family members.[2] Inheritance customs and modes of property transmission thereby define marriage patterns and family and household compositions. Inheritance patterns moreover affect intergenerational, gender and sibling relationships and are always associated with negotiations about rights and obligations of kin. Conflicts between respective heirs are intrinsic to different types of inheritance.[3]

According to Goody, in premodern times partible inheritance for sons and the dowry as premortem inheritance settled on a daughter at her wedding day were the major forms of inheritance for women in all Mediterranean societies.[4] Since Goody first proposed his theory, however, studies on early modern and modern Mediterranean societies have found more and more micro-regions with varying patterns that contradict a common Mediterranean form of inheritance. In these micro-regions anthropologists have found, for instance, patterns of

1. J. GOODY, 'Strategies of Heirship,' *Comparative Studies in Society and History* 16, 1973, pp. 3–20; J. GOODY, J. THIRSK and E. P. THOMPSON (eds.), *Family and Inheritance: Rural Society in Western Europe, 1200–1800*, Cambridge 1976; cf. C. HANN, 'Reproduction and Inheritance: Goody Revisited,' *Annual Review of Anthropology* 37, 2008, pp. 145–158.
2. J. GOODY, *The Oriental, the Ancient and the Primitive: Systems of Marriage and the Family in the Pre-industrial Societies of Eurasia*, Cambridge 1990, p. 15.
3. M. GULLESTAD and M. SEGALEN (eds.), *Family and Kinship in Europe*, London 1997, p. 157.
4. GOODY, 'Strategies of Heirship' (cited in n. 1).

Inheritance, Law and Religions in the Ancient and Mediaeval Worlds, ed. by B. CASEAU and S. R. HUEBNER (Centre de recherche d'Histoire et Civilisation de Byzance, Monographies 45), Paris 2014.

radical partible inheritance where all children, sons as well as daughters, inherited equally, while in other regions the rule was impartible inheritance combined with primogeniture of the eldest son. In some regions the patriarch of the household retained his position of authority and power until he died; in others the old father retired at a certain point, usually at the marriage of the eldest son and heir.

Inheritance patterns in the ancient Mediterranean

According to classical Athenian law, sons succeeded to their father's estate at a certain point during their father's lifetime, not just upon his death. Sons usually inherited equally; daughters received, however, a dowry at their wedding, which could be considered their share of the inheritance. However, if a man had a daughter and no sons, the daughter became an *epikleros* at her father's death and would be married to one of her father's nearest male relatives: a brother or a nephew. The patrimony would pass through her to her male offspring.

According to Roman law, all children (male and female, including adopted) inherited from their father. If children had died before the paterfamilias, their offspring succeeded in their place to their grandfather's inheritance. If the deceased had no children, his nearest agnates would inherit, meaning brothers and sisters, or nephews.

With regard to ancient Egypt we have evidence from the New Kingdom and the Late Period that in intestate successions radical partible inheritance was the norm. All children, sons as well as daughters, received equal shares of their paternal and maternal patrimony. Partible inheritance usually meant that if more than one child survived in each generation, estates became progressively smaller. As a consequence, siblings in ancient Egypt often held their inherited patrimony jointly to avoid excessive fragmentation of their property. The eldest son acted as trustee and administrator of the property for the community of heirs, organizing the farming or leasing of the land and allocating to each of the siblings their respective revenues. If the patrimony was to be divided among the siblings because the family had grown too large for the house, or the siblings feared conflict, the eldest son received a double share of the patrimony and could choose his share first before the remainder was split between the other siblings.

The last time the inheritance system in Roman Egypt was studied explicitly was almost 100 years ago.[5] This is all the more surprising given that we are much better informed about inheritance practice in Roman Egypt than in any other region of the Roman Empire. Even if the most common form of property devolution, intestate inheritance, usually did not tend to generate written documentation, if conflict arose, we then have petitions to judges, lawsuit proceedings and contractual settlements between heirs. We are even better informed about testamentary dispositions.

One thing becomes clear immediately when studying all of these documents: customs and forms of devolution varied depending on the ethnicity of the testator under question. For Roman citizens in Egypt, Roman law applied, with all the implications expounded earlier. For

5. Hans Kreller's study titled *Erbrechtliche Untersuchungen auf Grund der gräco-ägyptischen Papyrusurkunden* was published in 1919. See specifically for inheritance tax in Egypt: W. Eck, 'Zur Erhebung der Erbschafts- und Freilassungssteuer in Ägypten im 2. Jh. n. Chr.,' *Zeitschrift für Papyrologie und Epigraphik* (=*ZPE*) 27, 1977, pp. 201–209.

Greeks in Hellenistic times, an amalgam of Greek and indigenous Egyptian customs and laws seems to have been at play, while in Roman times the indigenous customs seem to have prevailed. The population of Roman Middle and Upper Egypt as documented in our papyri bequeathed property to their children without regard to gender or marital status. While classical Athenian society had known a retirement of the father around his 60th birthday or when his son got married, succession in Roman Egypt normally happened at the death of the testator, as in Rome, where the patriarch, as long as he lived, stayed in power and managed the entire family estate.[6]

In a previous study I have shown the close connections between patterns of inheritance, urban or rural environment and prevalent patterns of domestic organization in Roman Egypt.[7] Property in rural families was, for instance, often held 'jointly and undivided' (κοινὸν καὶ ἀδιαίρετον) between siblings, while siblings in the city divided their parental estate right after their parents' death. This also meant that brothers in the countryside often continued to live together under one roof long into adulthood, even if their parents had already died and they themselves were already married with children. Cousins thus grew up like brothers and sisters. The eldest of the brothers in a joint household acted as head and represented the family to the outside world. Only at a later point, and sometimes never at all, did brothers formally divide their property and set up individual households for their families. The cause for such division might have been tensions between brothers' wives but also the growing number of family members getting too big for their paternal house.

Let us have a more detailed look at some of these contractually laid down divisions. My first example, a division of property between two brothers, comes from mid third century Tebtunis. Herodes, also called Lourios, and his brother Sarapammon had inherited grain lands, 7 arouras in the village of Kerkeosiris, another 7 arouras near the village of Tebtunis and another 1 aroura near the village of Kerkesis, making a total of 15 arouras. All three villages were not too far from each other and all were located in the Arsinoite nome. Lourios and Sarapammon state in their respective document that, having kept their grain land undivided for some time, they then decided to split each piece of land in two equal shares. They determined that each of them would receive exactly one half share of each respective piece of land. That means, instead of giving one brother the 7 arouras in Kerkeosiris and the other the 7 arouras in Tebtunis, each brother received a half share in Kerkeosiris and another half share in Tebtunis. They further declared that from then on each of them was free to administer and dispose of his respective 7½ arouras of grain land in whatever way he chose. The brothers had also jointly inherited a house in the metropolis Arsinoe, but Lourios had already sold his half share to his brother Sarapammon. The two brothers did not give the reason why they decided to split up their property at this point which they had hitherto held undivided. Farming two adjoining pieces of land jointly was surely more economical than if each brother farmed his own half share, above all since about 14 arouras of grain land was the average size of landholding in the region. The brothers after their division, however, with their respective 7½ arouras were far below the

6. Rarely, parents set up a retirement contract with their children transferring their entire property during their lifetime in exchange for old-age maintenance. Examples: *P.Mich.* 5.321 from Tebtunis, 42 CE; *P.Mich.* 5.322 from Tebtunis, 46 CE. See S. R. Huebner, *The Family in Roman Egypt: A Comparative Approach to Intergenerational Solidarity and Conflict*, Cambridge 2013, pp. 124–140.

7. Huebner, *Family in Roman Egypt* (cited in n. 6).

average, and probably were hardly able to live with their respective families above subsistence level.[8] It is unlikely that tension between the brothers led them to divide up their property since they decided to leave another 2 arouras near the village of Tebtunis, which had likewise come to them as an inheritance, undivided as common property.[9]

Three other brothers, Horion, Eudaimon and Eulogios, from early fourth century Oxyrhynchus formally divided their paternal inheritance right after their father's death in order to avoid conflict, as they stated. By contrast to the two brothers above, they did not divide every piece of land or real estate into equal shares: one of the brothers received cash, while the two others each received various plots of land.[10]

Sisters in Roman Egypt usually joined their brothers in their efforts to keep the paternal estate undivided. However, if the sister was already married and lived elsewhere, some division of property became necessary, as for instance in the following case from first century CE Tebtunis in the Arsinoite nome. The 31-year-old Marempsemis and his married 35-year-old sister Tamarres[11]

8. See for landholding in Roman Egypt: J. F. OATES, 'Philadelphia in the Fayum during the Roman Empire,' *Atti XI Congresso internazionale di papirologia, Milano 1965*, Milan 1966, pp. 454–457; J. F. OATES, *Landholding in Philadelphia in the Fayum (A.D. 216)*, Toronto and Amsterdam 1970, pp. 385–387; J. ROWLANDSON, *Landowners and Tenants in Roman Egypt: The Social Relations of Agriculture in the Oxyrhynchite Nome*, Oxford 1996; J. ROWLANDSON, 'Land and Landholding in Graeco-Roman Egypt,' *The Encyclopedia of Ancient History* 7, 2012, pp. 3874–3875. Cf. for later Roman Egypt: R. S. BAGNALL, 'Landholding in Late Roman Egypt: The Distribution of Wealth,' *Journal of Roman Studies* 82, 1992, pp. 128–149.

9. Division of property, 4 February 248 CE: *P.Tebt.* 2.319 (cf. Hunt, A.S. Sel. pap., v. 1, no. 53; Meyer, P.M. Juristische Papyri, no. 53). APIS translation: '*To Aurelius Maximus also called Hermaiskos, priest, Archidikastes, and superintendent of the chrematistai and the other courts, from Marcus Aurelius Herodes also called Lourios, of Antinoe, and from Marcus Aurelius Sarapammon and however else he is styled. Whereas Aurelius Sarapammon and Lourios have come by succession of inheritance into possession of grain lands about the village of Kerkeosiris in the division of Polemon in the Arsinoite nome, viz. 7 arouras in two parcels, and near the village of Tebtunis in the same division in the place called Karion 7 arouras likewise, and near the village of Kerkesis 1 aroura, making a total of 15 arouras, which have hitherto been undivided, and they have now decided to divide these on the understanding that each should distinguish his own share, Aurelius Lourios and Aurelius Sarapammon now agree that they have divided the aforesaid arouras, and that of the 7 arouras near the village of Kerkeosiris each of them has received 3 1/2 arouras, of the 7 arouras near the village of Tebtunis each of them has received 3 1/2 arouras, and of the land near the village of Kerkesis each of them has received one half, so that each of them may henceforth possess and own the part that has fallen to him, viz. 7 1/2 arouras, and administer and dispose of them, each in whatever way he chooses; and that Aurelius Sarapammon has entire control of his property near the village of Theogonis, viz. 3 out of 6 arouras, because Lourios has sold his half share; and they have left as common property the 2 arouras belonging to them near the village of Tebtunis in the place called Pagagoros, until some decision shall be reached about them, and further settlement shall be made by them about whatever other property they find to appertain to the estate. And Aurelius Lourios shall not proceed against Aurelius Sarapammon on account of the house in the metropolis, having sold the half share belonging to him: and so on. The 5th year of the Philippi, Mecheir 9.*'

10. Division of an inheritance, 326 CE (an agreement between three brothers to divide): *P.Princ.* 2.79. APIS translation: '*In the consulship of our lords Constantine Augustus for the seventh time and Constantius the most noble Caesar for the first time, [month], [day]. Aurelii Horion and Eudaimon and Eulogios, three sons of Dionysios, son of Dioskorides, . . . our above mentioned father Dionysios departed his life, and we, his children, . . . we refrain from conflict with each other and division . . . [l. 5] it is agreed that we three make a division of our own shares for ourselves . . . and to Eudaimon 75 talents in silver for having a share . . . the arouras that exist in our father's name around the village of Senepta . . . to yield however much, or the two of us, Horion and Eudaimon, for a third . . . with a share being claimed by us, half a share, and however much there is of arouras . . .*'

11. Tamarres's 38-year-old husband was acting as her guardian.

decided to divide jointly held parcels of land that they had inherited from their parents. In the conclusion of their contract both parties gave assurance that they would not proceed against the other on any account with respect to the shares that each of them had received. If either of the contracting parties violated any of the aforesaid provisions, the breaker of the contract was to forfeit to the party abiding by it twice the amount of the damage and expenses and a fine of 200 drachmas of silver, and to the treasury a like sum, and the contract would be no less valid.[12]

While all the customs described above for Roman Egypt conformed to indigenous Egyptian rather than Greek inheritance practice, a particular Greek custom that Greek settlers probably had brought with them to Egypt was the entitlement of daughters to a dowry.

12. Division of property, Tebtunis (Arsinoites), 11 July 46 CE: *P.Tebt.* 2.383. APIS translation: '*The sixth year of Tiberius Claudius Caesar Augustus Germanicus Imperator, the 17th of the month Gorpiaios, Epeiph 17, at Tebtunis in the division of Polemon of the Arsinoite nome. Marepsemis also called Patareis, aged about 31, having a scar on his forehead to the left, and Tamarres, aged about 35, having a scar on her left temple, both children of Paopis, Tamarres acting with her guardian, her husband Psenkebkis son of Onnophris, aged about 38, having a scar ..., agree with each other that they have divided between them by mutual consent through this agreement from the present time for ever the vacant area surrounded by walls which they both own, and a vacant area called Achenes' (?) in a different parcel, and the third share owned by them of a priest's lodging called ..., which has two storeys and is common and undivided, situated within the outer (wall of...) the great, greatest god, all at the aforesaid village of Tebtunis, on the conditions that Marepsemis has obtained for his share the aforesaid third share of the aforesaid two-storeyed priest's lodging called ... of which the adjacent areas are on the south another priest's lodging belonging to Marsisouchos son of Marepsemis, on the north and open space and the entrance and exit of the temple, on the west the priest's lodging of ... son of Marsisouchos, on the east the priest's lodging of Marres and his partners, while Tamarres has on her side obtained for her share the aforesaid vacant area enclosed with walls, of which the measurements are from south to north 11 cubits, from west to east 5 1/2 cubits, the measurements of the aforesaid vacant area called Achenes' in another parcel being from south to north ... cubits two palms, from west to east 5 1/2 cubits, and the adjacent areas are for the area surrounded by walls on the south and east the entrance and exit of Marsisouchos son of N.N. and his partners, on the north a royal road, on the west the areas owned by Lusimachos son of Didumos, and for the aforesaid area called Achenes' on the south the areas called after Chousous owned by Psenkebkis son of Pakebkis, on the north the aforesaid entrance and exit into which the aforesaid Tamarres and her assigns and heirs shall open a door from the ... an entrance and exit leading from ..., and the said Tamarres and her assigns and heirs shall enter and go out through the exit leading to the north and east, on the west a public road, on the east the house of the aforesaid Marsisouchos son of N.N. Each of the contracting parties therefore and their assigns and heirs shall possess and own the shares which each has received from the present day forever ... and neither shall proceed against the other on any account in respect of the shares which each of them has received. If either of the contracting parties violates any of the aforesaid provisions, the breaker of the contract shall forfeit to the party abiding by it twice the amount of the damage and expenses and as a fine 200 drachmas of silver, and to the Treasury a like sum, and the contract shall be no less valid. The wife of Marepsemis, Thomsais daughter of Marepsemis, aged about 30, having a scar on her right ..., with Marepsemis himself as guardian, consents to this division, and neither brings nor will bring any accusation, nor will any representative of hers do so. The signatories are, for Marepsemis, Psoiphis son of Onnophris, aged about 26, having a scar on his forehead to the left, and for the rest, Marepsemis also called Kaleos, son of Marepsemis, aged about 38, having a scar ... (2nd hand) I, Marepsemis also called Patareis son of Paopis, agree to divide the belonging third share, as stated above, of the two-storeyed pastophorion. My wife Thonpseis daughter of Marepsemis with me as guardian consents to the division and will not proceed against ... as written above. Psoiphis son of Onnophris has written for them because they do not know letters. (3rd hand) I, Tamarres, daughter of Paopis, with my husband Psenkebkis son of Onnophris as guardian agree to divide and I have received the aforementioned share of the aforementioned (vacant areas) surrounded by walls and vacant areas in another parcel (called) Achanes' and I will do each thing as stated above. Marepsemis has written for them because Psenkebkis can only write Egyptian and the other does not know letters. (4th hand; Demotic) Psenkebkis (son of) Onnophris. (1st hand) The sixth year of Tiberius Claudius Caesar Augustus Germanicus Imperator, Epeiph 17. Registered through Eutuchides the overseer of the record-office of Tebtunis and Kerkesouchon Oros. I, Kronion, have signed with him, the sixth year of Tiberius Claudius Caesar Augustus Germanicus Imperator, Epeiph 17. Verso: Division of Marepsemis; Division of Tamarres.*'

Fathers in classical Athens had given their daughters dowries comprising money, jewellery, furniture and clothes, but no real estate to avoid the fragmentation of land and property. During her marriage the dowry was administered by the woman's husband; it functioned as an insurance policy in case of divorce or the death of her spouse. Dowries were unknown in Egypt in Pharaonic times, probably because all children regardless of their sex had equal rights to inherit. However, in Hellenistic times the practice of endowing a daughter became more widespread in Egypt also. In Roman Egypt we then find a combination of practices: daughters usually received a dowry but also held a right to a share in the parental inheritance, including houses and land. Dowries and inheritances complemented each other: the value of the dowry, consisting mainly of female goods, was subtracted from the later share in the parental property. The result of dowries and the right to inherit in Egypt was that in the second century CE two-thirds of land in the Fayum villages was in the hands of women.[13]

A special form of inheritance was the usufruct where the recipient was granted the rights to the use of property as long as he or she lived, but not the power to sell it. The right of usufruct was often given to the surviving widow, who did not inherit from her husband but was simply repaid the sum of her dowry by her husbands' heirs, to provide her with maintenance for the remaining years of her life. Afterwards the property would fall to her late husband's heirs.

When a certain Herodion died in mid first century Tebtunis, his three sons inherited his four slaves, two female and two male, of whom one was lame. The eldest brother received a female slave, including her future offspring, and the second eldest brother received the healthy male slave. The youngest of the three brothers received the other female slave and the lame slave including their offspring. At first sight it might seem that the youngest son received more than his brothers. The contract goes on, however, to determine that this female slave was to stay with the young men's mother and serve her for the rest of her life, as their father had set out in his will.[14] In this way, although Herodion's three sons were the main beneficiaries, he had made arrangements to guarantee his widow care in her old age.

If a person died childless, his or her belongings would fall back to the natal family; a wife or husband did not inherit. If there were children, however, the natal family lost all rights to the property of the deceased, which could be much to their annoyance. Conflicts between the

13. D. W. HOBSON, 'Women as Property Owners in Roman Egypt,' *Transactions of the American Philological Association* 113, 1983, pp. 311–321; D. W. HOBSON, 'House and Household in Roman Egypt,' *Yale Classical Studies* 28, 1985, pp. 211–229; K. GEENS, *Panopolis: A Name Capital in Egypt in the Roman and Byzantine Period*, doctoral dissertation, 2 vols, Katholieke Universiteit, Leuven 2007. Cf. the situation in Sparta, where women could inherit as well and two-fifths of land was in female hands (S. HODKINSON, 'Animal Husbandry in the Greek Polis,' in C. R. WHITTAKER, ed., *Pastoral Economies in Classical Antiquity*, Cambridge 1988, pp. 35–74).

14. *P.Mich.* 5.323, Tebtunis, 47 CE. APIS translation: '*The seventh year of Tiberius Claudius Caesar Augustus Germanicus Imperator, the twenty-ninth of the month Xandikos, the twenty-ninth of Mecheir, in Tebtynis in the division of Polemon of the Arsinoite nome. Haryotes, about thirty-five years old, with a scar below his left jaw, and Kronion, about thirty years old, with a scar on his left forearm, and Haryotes the younger, also called Arabarches, about twenty-seven years old, with a scar above his left eyebrow, the three sons of Herodion, acknowledge that they have divided among themselves by mutual agre[e]ment, by a division at the present time, from the present day forever, the four slaves that belong to them by inheritance from their father, Thermoutharion and Sambous and Heraklas and Heraklous, who is lame; and that Haryotes the elder has received as his share Sambous with the slave offspring that shall come from her, and Kronion has received as his share the aforesaid Heraklas, and Haryotes the younger, also called Arabarches, has received as his share the aforesaid slaves, Thermoutharion and the lame Heraklous, with the slave offspring that shall come from them; and they agree that the service*

siblings and the children of the deceased thus do not seem to have been rare. Children who were still minors at their father's death would be appointed a guardian who was responsible for administering the orphans' property, to provide the children with daily maintenance from their patrimony's revenues and to turn over the estate with a full accounting when the children reached majority.[15] Conflicts between uncles and their siblings' children were further aggravated by the fact that the late parents had often appointed their brothers to act as guardians for their minor orphans.[16] This meant that uncles were supposed to act as trustees of an estate that would in fact have fallen to them if their deceased siblings had not had children.

In the following case from late second century Oxyrhynchus we hear of a conflict between two sisters and their maternal uncle about the inheritance of their maternal grandfather. The grandfather, Zoilos, had bequeathed dowries to his two granddaughters, but left the property under the control of their maternal uncle, his son, until the girls married.[17] Only years later, when apparently both women had already been married for several years, did they finally reach a settlement with their uncle about the property assigned to them in their grandfather's will.[18]

---

of the slave Thermoutharion to the mother of the contracting parties, Taorseus, daughter of Haryotes, which was assigned to her by their father, for as long as she shall live, shall continue. Each of the contracting parties, therefore, and his heirs and assigns shall own and possess the shares they have received from the present day forever indisputably, and no one of the contracting parties shall proceed against what the others have received in any way. If any of the contracting parties violates any of the aforesaid provisions, the one who does not abide by the contract shall pay the one who does abide by it double the amount of the damages and expenses and a fine of fifteen hundred silver drachmai, and a like amount to the treasury. Nonetheless, in addition to the terms of the contract remaining valid, it shall be just as they have of their own free will agreed about everything. The signatures of the three contracting parties are in their own hands. The contract shall be valid everywhere.'

'*(2nd hand) I, Haryotes, son of Herodion, have joined in making a division at the present time, and have received as my share the aforesaid slave, Sambous, and I will do everything as aforesaid.*

'*(3rd hand) I, Kronion, son of Herodion, have joined in making a division at the present time, and have received as my share the aforesaid slave, Heraklas, and I will do everything as aforesaid.*

'*(4th hand) I, Haryotes the younger, also called Arabarches, son of Herodion, have joined in making a division at the present time, and have received as my share the two aforesaid slaves, Thermoutharion and Heraklous, who is lame, and I will do everything as aforesaid.'*

15. R. P. Saller, *Patriarchy, Property and Death in the Roman Family*, Cambridge 1994, pp. 183–185; J. Evans Grubbs, *Women and the Law in the Roman Empire: A Sourcebook on Marriage, Divorce, and Widowhood*, London and New York 2002, p. 23.

16. E.g. *P.Mich*. 18.789 after 190 CE (maternal uncle acting as guardian for two minor girls who inherited some property from their maternal grandfather).

17. *P.Mich*. 18.789 after 190 CE.

18. *P.Mich*. 18.789 after 190 CE. APIS translation: '*Calpurnia and Apia also called Theodora, both daughters of Gai[- - -], their mother being Theodora, from the city of Oxyrhynchus, each with her husband as guardian, Calpurnia with Apion, son of Apollonios, son of Sarapion, his mother being Saraeus, by adoption daughter of Diogenes, son of Sarapion, from the same city, and Apia also called Theodora with Chosion, son of [- - -]on, also called Chosion, his mother being Thaisous, from the same city, to our maternal uncle Dioskourides, son of Zoilos, son of Dioskourides, of the Hadrianicphyle and the Olympian deme, one of the class of victors at the sacred games who are exempt from taxation, former gymnasiarch and former high priest of the lords Augusti and of all the gods of the same city of the Oxyrhynchites, neokoros of the great Sarapis of the Hellenic Sarapeium in the same city, greeting. Since your father, who is our maternal grandfather, Zoilos, son of Dioskourides, son of Hermes, his mother being Theodora, from the same city of Oxyrhynchus, by means of the sealed testament which he drew up through the office of the public notary in the same city in the 27th year, Tybi, which was unchanged when he died and (then) opened, in addition to the other things that he stipulated for us, wished, upon the condition that you set aside the income from the property belonging to us as indicated by this testament until we marry husbands and that after our marriage for another two(?) years you pay to us, whatever husbands we marry, instead of [- - - and of - - -.'*

We have another case of conflict between an uncle and his late brother's children from early second century Karanis. A man had died, leaving a widow and two minor children, and the latter inherited his entire property, comprising houses, furniture and grain supplies. The man's brother, however, was unhappy with this situation and laid claim to his deceased brother's estate with violence. The widow, however, did not let her husband's brother pilfer her children's property. In a petition to the prefect of Egypt she claimed that the brother even broke into their house at night and stole all movable household items 'like a thief.'[19]

In another petition from late third century Oxyrhynchus it was not the widow but the orphaned daughter herself who petitioned the prefect for recovery of her inheritance.[20] Aurelia Didyme's mother and two maternal uncles had inherited equal shares of their paternal property and had held the goods jointly. The property comprised a house, slaves, furnishing, and immovable and movable goods. The three siblings had continued living together in their natal home, apparently even though the sister, the petitioning woman's mother, had a child. She might have moved back to her natal home when her husband died or she divorced him. When she died, however, her two brothers conspired to defraud their orphaned niece of her rightful inheritance. Aurelia Didyme starts her petition with the words: 'It is a difficult matter to be wronged by strangers, but to be wronged by kin is worst of all.' And she goes on:

19. Petition to a prefect, 119–124 CE, *P.Mich.* 9.525. APIS translation: '*To Titus Haterius Nepos, prefect of Egypt, from Sarapous, daughter of Petnes, son of Tithois, from the village of Karanis in the Arsinoite nome. My husband Peteeus from the same {same} village died leaving two orphan children, Theon and . . . nais, and property in grains and houses and furniture, all of which . eos, the brother of my aforesaid husband, lays claim to with violence. Moreover, . . . he entered the house by night and stole every thing that was in the house like a thief(?). Wherefore I brought in the archephodos of the village, who made a written deposition that it was the aforesaid brother who broke in. Therefore I have appealed(?) to you . . . asking . . . that you hear me against . . . that I may be the object of your benevolence. Farewell.*'

20. *P.Oxy.* 34.2713 from 297 CE. For a German translation, see: A. Papathomas, Literarische und rhetorische Elemente in *P.Oxy.* XXXIV 2713, *Archiv für Papyrusforschung* 52, 2006, p. 246f. Cf. Evans Grubbs, *Women and Law* (cited in n. 15), p. 54. English translation: J. Rowlandson, *Women and Society in Greek and Roman Egypt: A Sourcebook*, Cambridge 1998, p. 75: '*To Aristius Optatus, most distinguished prefect of Egypt, from Aurelia Didyme, daughter of Didymos, from the . . . most glorious city of the Oxyrhynchites. It is a difficult matter to be wronged by strangers, but to be wronged by kin is worst of all. My mother's father Dioskoros had three children in all – Theon, Dioskoros, and Ploutarche, my mother – who inherited from him when he died. After some time, my mother also died, while I was under-age and already an orphan. My lord prefect, you know well that the race of women is easy to despise, because of the weakness of our nature. For all the things from the inheritance devolving upon us (for it was a single household and one family) were in the house there in which they were living – that is, the slaves, the immovables, the furnishings, and movable goods were all there undivided. In the meantime, my mother's brothers from the same mother plotted together with useless and foolish stupidity, intending to cheat me. Each one grabbed whatever he wanted of the slaves and all the rest, paying no attention to me whatsoever, but, so to speak, even pushing me off from the third part of the inheritance that falls to me. Now, at any rate, I have recovered, due to your ever-alert spirit, and I am beginning to realise that I should approach no one but you, the benefactor and guardian of me and everyone else. Thus I hurry to ask you, since you have seen me bereft, to command, whenever it seems good to you, that my uncles, brothers of my mother, be compelled to return to me what belongs to me, as heiress of my mother, together with the increments from that time until now from the slaves and rents and everything else. I shall eternally confess my gratitude to your spirit, once I take back my inheritance from my mother through your trustiness and your nobility. Farewell.*'

'*(2nd hand) I, Aurelia Didyme, submitted this petition. I, Aurelius Thonis, wrote for her because she does not know letters.*'

For all the things from the inheritance devolving upon us (for it was a single household and one family) were in the house there in which they were living – that is, the slaves, the immovables, the furnishings, and movable goods were all there undivided. In the meantime, my mother's brothers from the same mother plotted together with useless and foolish stupidity, intending to cheat me. Each one grabbed whatever he wanted of the slaves and all the rest, paying no attention to me whatsoever, but, so to speak, even pushing me off from the third part of the inheritance that falls to me.

In another case from second century Karanis we hear of a young man whose mother had left him two houses with courtyards in the village of Karanis. His maternal uncle, however, laid claim to the houses and 'attacked [him] in an arrogant way.'[21]

While according to Roman law the guardian for an orphaned child had to be male and was often the father's closest male relative, according to indigenous Egyptian custom the mother also could take on the guardianship for her children after their father's death.[22] In the papyri we find evidence for numerous mothers acting as guardians of their fatherless children.[23] One result of mothers being in control of their orphaned children's property meant that a minor orphan lived with the fear that his mother might spend his father's estate, alone or with her new partner, before he or she was able to assume the inheritance.[24] Parents in Roman Egypt were socially and morally expected to nominate their children as heirs, and disinheritance was accepted only when children had failed to render the appropriate duty.[25] However, it was well known that some parents could be led astray and wrongfully disinherited their own children, pressured for instance by a second spouse. In this case the will was to be declared void because it contradicted the claims of filial and parental piety.[26] On the other hand, children who had really not shown the expected obedience and respect and had behaved with ingratitude towards their elderly parents were not entitled to inherit anything from them if the parents had explicitly wished so.

21. Petition, 2nd century CE (SB 22.15831). APIS translation: '*From Heron, son of Horos, from the village of Karanis. Having come to the two houses and the two courtyards in the village which devolved upon me from an inheritance of my deceased mother, Taarpagathes, daughter of Petheus, my mother's uncle(?), Chairemon, together with [- - -], attacked me in an arrogant way [- - -].*'

22. This follows S. R. Huebner, 'Callirhoe's Dilemma: Remarriage and Stepfathers in the Graeco-Roman East,' in: S. R. Huebner and D. M. Ratzan (eds.), *Growing Up Fatherless in Antiquity*, Cambridge 2009, pp. 61–82. See also O. Montevecchi, 'Una donna prostatis del figlio minorenne in un papiro del IIa,' *Aegyptus* 61, 1981, pp. 113–115; T. J. Chiusi, 'Zur Vormundschaft der Mutter,' *Zeitschrift der Savigny-Stiftung für Rechtsgeschichte: Romanistische Abteilung* 111, 1994, pp. 175–91; R. Van Bremen, *The Limits of Participation: Women and Civic Life in the Greek East in the Hellenistic and Roman Periods*, Amsterdam 1996, pp. 228–230; Evans Grubbs, *Women and Law* (cited in n. 15), pp. 254–257; H. J. Wolff, *Das Recht der griechischen Papyri Ägyptens in der Zeit der Ptolemäer und des Prinzipats I. Bedingungen und Triebkräfte der Rechtsentwicklung*, Munich 2002, p. 78, n. 31.

23. E.g. *SB* 16.12720 (142 BCE; cf. Rowlandson, *Women and Society*, cited in n. 20, no. 125; R. S. Bagnall and P. Derow, *The Hellenistic Period: Historical Sources in Translation*, Oxford 2004, no. 123); *SB* 5.7568 (36 CE); *BGU* 8.1813 (62 CE); *P.Oxy.* 2.265 (81–95 CE); *P.Oxy.* 6.898 (123 CE); *P.Oxy.* 3.496 (127 CE); *P.Oxy.* 3.497 (early 2nd century CE).

24. Cf. Huebner, 'Callirhoe's Dilemma' (cited in n. 22).

25. Cf. W. Eck, 'Zum neuen Fragment des sogenannten testamentum Dasumii,' *ZPE* 30, 1978, pp. 277–279; E. Champlin, 'Miscellanea Testamentaria,' *ZPE* 62, 1986, pp. 253–255.

26. Cf. Huebner, *Family in Roman Egypt* (cited in n. 6), pp. 89–91.

Conclusions

We have to conclude that the general pattern – partible inheritance for sons and the dowry as premortem inheritance settled on a daughter at her wedding day – claimed by Goody for all Mediterranean societies did not apply to Roman Egypt. Ideally, in Roman Egypt all children, daughters as well as sons, succeeded to their father's estate. Daughters did receive dowries but also shared in the inheritance, including land and real estate. Land as would be expected in an agrarian society was the most valued and most often documented asset bequeathed. Research in recent decades on various societies of the preindustrial Mediterranean has shown that the modes of inheritance influenced decisively the way the family was organized and which kin shared a common residence. For Roman Egypt the partible inheritance system meant that, in land-working families, siblings often held their inherited patrimony jointly to avoid fragmentation of their paternal land.

We have seen different kinds of conflicts arising between family members from an inheritance, such as conflicts among siblings about the division of their parental property. Family members who had been sharing a household before were suddenly proceeding against each other in court. If division of the patrimony became necessary, many siblings therefore decided to lay down contractually the arrangements they had made between themselves and promised to abstain from further legal proceedings against each other about the matter. Conflicts between a ward and his or her guardian about the management of the former's inheritance also seem to have been common, especially if the guardian, being biased, should have been disqualified from this duty. If the guardian was the paternal uncle of the ward, for example, he would have been in line to inherit from his brother before the latter had children. Sometimes even the mother who had acted as guardian had embezzled her own children's patrimony before they came of age. In the papyri we also occasionally encounter conflicts between parents and their children if one of the parties has neglected its expected duties of intergenerational support, though formal disinheritance as the most drastic measure seems to have been very rare. The adoption of an heir in Roman Egypt was – as in many other Mediterranean societies – a means of coping with the discrepancies that arose between ideals for succession and demographic realities. From these and other sources that allow us a glimpse into interfamilial conflict over family property we have an impression of the loss, *hurt* and heightened *emotions* caused by these divisions between family members.

BABATHA'S ARCHIVE: INHERITANCE DISPUTES IN SECOND CENTURY ROMAN ARABIA

Giles Rowling

At some time after the establishment of the territory of the former kingdom of Nabataea as the Roman Province of Arabia in 106 CE and not later than 125 CE Yehudah son of Eleazar Khthousion and Babatha daughter of Simon, both of whom were Jews resident in Maoza, a town at the southern point of the Dead Sea, married under a *ketubba* or Jewish marriage agreement written in Aramaic.[1] In it Yehudah took Babatha as his wife 'according to the law of Moses and the Judeans', and acknowledged an indebtedness for Babatha's dowry of 400 zûzîn or denarii, and apparently charged all his property to secure its repayment.[2] He undertook that in the event that he predeceased her she should have the right of residence in his house and maintenance out of his estate until his heirs should be minded to make repayment.[3] There appear to have been no children of the marriage between Babatha and Yehudah.

An undertaking that 'All property which I have is surety for your marriage contract', that is the dowry, was implied in marriage agreements as an 'unstated condition imposed by the Court' by the provisions of the Mishnah, a collection of rabbinic legal materials reduced to

---

Papyrological abbreviations:

P. Yadin	N. Lewis (ed), *The Documents from the Bar Kokhba Period in the Cave of Letters: Greek Papyri*, Jerusalem, 1989. Y. Yadin, J. C. Greenfield, A. Yardeni and B. A. Levine (eds), *The Documents from the Bar Kokhba Period in the Cave of Letters: Hebrew, Aramaic and Nabatean-Aramaic Papyri*, Jerusalem 2002.
P XḤev/Se	H. M. Cotton and A. Yardeni, *Aramaic, Hebrew and Greek Documentary Tests from Naḥal Ḥever and Other Sites*, with an Appendix containing alleged Qumran Texts (The Seiyâl Collection II). Oxford 1997 [Discoveries in the Judaean Desert, XXVII].

---

1. *P. Yadin* 10; the families of Babatha and Yehudah are set out in the Table appended to this paper; the Table is abridged and adapted from that published by N. Lewis in Id. (ed.), *The Documents from the Bar Kokhba Period in the Cave of Letters: Greek Papyri*, Jerusalem 1989.
2. Lines 6-7 and 17-8; the papyrus is defective at this point but that Babatha had such a charge is supported by the provisions of the Mishnah (*mKet* 4.7) for which see below.
3. Lines 15-16.

Inheritance, Law and Religions in the Ancient and Mediaeval Worlds, ed. by B. Caseau and S. R. Huebner (Centre de recherche d'Histoire et Civilisation de Byzance, Monographies 45), Paris 2014.

writing in about 200 CE but dating from earlier.[4] Whether, as has been argued, the contents of the contemporary Jewish legal documents are 'the best evidence we have ... for the state of Jewish law and the authority exercised by the rabbis at the time', in any event Babatha's marriage agreement, although damaged so that its contents are to some extent the result of inference, appears to accord closely with the law as later declared in the provisions of the Mishnah.[5]

Babatha had been previously married to Jesus, son of another Jesus, who had predeceased her; they had a son, yet another Jesus, but so far as we know, no other children.

We cannot say when this Jesus to whom Babatha was married died but it must have been before 124 CE because in that year the City Council of Petra appointed Ἀbdobdas and John son of Eglas as guardians of her son Jesus; at some date between then and 132 CE John of Eglas died and his son Simon was appointed 'second guardian' apparently in place of his father by that Council.[6]

Yehudah had also previously married Miriam. Nothing in the papyri forming Babatha's archive shows explicitly whether Yehudah had divorced her or whether he remained married to her. In a record of a summons brought by Babatha against Miriam she refers to Yehudah as ἀνδρός μου καί σου ἀ[πογενουμένου]'my and your deceased husband' and Miriam appears to refer to him in similar terms.[7] Miriam apparently continued to live in the Province. Yehudah and Miriam had a daughter Shelamzion, but apparently no other children. In 120 CE by a marriage agreement written in Greek and expressed to be made according to 'the laws', Yehudah gave Shelamzion, his daughter, to be married to Judah Cimber.[8] The agreement concluded with a Greek expression πίστει ἐπηρωτήθη καὶ ἀνθωμολογήθη ταῦτα οὕτως καλῶς γείνεσθαι which was apparently intended to be the equivalent of a *cautio* or Latin record of a question and answer making the agreement enforceable as a formal oral Roman law contract of *stipulatio*.[9] Gaius, writing in the second century CE, records that a stipulation might be made by a question and answer using the words 'FIDE PROMITTIS? FIDE PROMITTO' even where the parties were not Roman citizens, and further says that the question and answer might be expressed in Greek 'si modo Graeci sermonis intellectum habeant' giving as examples 'veluti hoc modo:... ὁμολογεῖς: ὁμολογῶ· πίστει κελεύεις: πίστει κελεύω'.[10] In *vadimonia* in the form of tablets from Puteoli and Capua of the first century BCE a form of *cautio* recording a *stipulatio* appears in the form 'fide rogavit ... fide promisit', to which the form of *cautio* in Shelamzion's marriage agreement appears to correspond.[11]

4. *mKet* 4. 7-12; all translations from the Mishnah are from that of J. NEUSNER, *The Mishnah: a New Translation*, New Haven and London 1988.

5. H. M. COTTON, The Rabbis and the Documents, in *The Jews in a Graeco-Roman World*, ed. M. GOODMAN, Oxford 1998, pp. 167–79, 172.

6. *P. Yadin* 12; see *P. Yadin* 27, ll 6-8.

7. *P. Yadin* 26, ll 7-8 and 14-15. In what appears to be a fragmentary copy of a petition to the Governor of the province in Babatha's proceedings against Miriam, she apparently refers to Yehudah as ἀν]δρὸς α[ὐτῆς] καὶ ἐ[μ]οῦ ἀπογενομέ[νου: *P. Yadin* 34, l 5.

8. *P. Yadin* 18.

9. *P. Yadin* 18, ll 27-28 and 66-7; J. G. OUDSCHOORN, *The Relationship between Roman and Local Law in the Babatha and Salome Komaise Archives: General Analysis and Three Case Studies on Law of Succession, Guardianship and Marriage*, Leiden 2007, pp. 150–155

10. *Inst* 3. 92-3.

11. G. CAMODECA (ed), *Tabulae Pompeianae Sulpiciorum* 4, ll 7-8; 13, ll 7-8; and 14, p 3, ll2-3, Rome 1999.

A few days after the marriage Yehudah settled property at En Gedi, a courtyard and surrounding buildings, upon Shelamzion, one half immediately and the other half upon his death.[12] It appears from an earlier transaction by which Yehudah had, with the authority of his father Eleazar, charged it, that this courtyard was previously the property of his father.[13]

Babatha appears to have had some means of her own because not only did she bring in to her marriage with Yehudah a dowry of 400 zûzîn or denarii, apparently four times the dowry prescribed by the Mishnah as the dowry of a widow, but in a census held in the Province in 127 CE she registered four date plantations at Maoza which she owned in her own right.[14] Furtherin 128 CE she was able to lend 300 denarii to Yehudah, repayable on demand, for the repayment of which Yehudah granted her a right of execution over all his property present and future: γε[ινο]μένης δὲ τῆς πράξεως τῇ αὐτῇ Βαβαθᾳ ... ἀπό τε Ἰούδου καὶ τῶν ὑπαρχόντων αὐτοῦ πάντῃ πάντων, ὧν τε ἔχει καὶ ὧν ἂν ἐπικτήσηται κυρίως.[15] The document contains a similar *cautio* for a *stipulatio*. We cannot say how Babatha acquired her property but it may have been by gift from her former husband Jesus or from her father Simon. It appears from a deposition in proceedings to which she was a party apparently of 130 CE that during his lifetime Yehudah had registered in Babatha's name three further date plantations also situated at Maoza.[16]

No later than 124 CE while Yehudah was still alive Babatha embarked upon litigation against one of the guardians of her son Jesus claiming that they were paying him insufficient maintenance to enable him to live in an appropriate standard of living and offering to take over management of the estate, giving security by way of a charge over her own property. This appears from copies of her petition of 124 CE to the Governor of the province, her summons to John of Eglas one of the guardians of 125 CE, and her deposition in the proceedings of 125 CE.[17] She was presumably already married to Yehudah since he was her guardian in relation to the proceedings. Babatha had in her possession three copies in Greek of a formula for the *actio tutelae*, a Roman law action available against tutors or guardians after their tutorship had ended, and no doubt she intended that proceedings under that action be brought after their tutorship had ended.[18] The proceedings against the guardians continued but without any conclusion, and as late as 132 CE Babatha was receiving on behalf of her son Jesus the same amount of maintenance that she had previously complained was insufficient, as appears from a copy of a receipt given by her to Simon the substituted guardian.[19]

No later than June 130 CE Yehudah died without having repaid the 300 denarii that he had borrowed from Babatha. His heir or heirs appear not to have decided to repay to Babatha her dowry or the debt sinceshe then took possession of three date plantations formerly the property of Yehudah by way of distraint, claiming the right to do so under both her charge for the repayment of her dowry and her right of execution for repayment of the debt of 300

12. *P. Yadin* 19, ll 11-15 and 15-16.

13. *P. Yadin* 11, ll 3-5 and 15-17; H. M. Cotton, Courtyard(s) in Ein Gedi: P.Yadin 11, 19 and 20 of the Babatha Archive, *Zeitschrift für Papyrologie und Epigraphik* 112, 1996, pp. 197–201, 199.

14. *mKet* 1. 2; 4. 7 and *P. Yadin* 16.

15. *P. Yadin* 17, ll 33-7.

16. *P. Yadin* 24, fragment a, ll 4-6.

17. *P. Yadin* 13, ll 19-23; *P. Yadin* 14, ll 26-7; *P. Yadin* 15, ll 20-26.

18. *P. Yadin* 28-30; Gaius, *Inst.* 1.191.

19. *P. Yadin* 27, ll 8-11.

denarii, and in September 130 CE sold the then current year's date crop from those plantations to one Simon, by a transaction made in two separate instruments, one of sale by her and one of purchase by Simon, asserting in the instrument of sale κατέχω αὐτὰ ἀντὶ τῆς προικός μου καὶ ὀφιλῆς.[20] Both the documents contain a Greek equivalent of a *cautio* for a *stipulatio*, in the form πίστεως ἐπερωτημένης καὶ ἀνθομολογημένης.[21]

In September 130 CE Besas, guardian of the orphans, the number and names of whom we do not know, of Jesus son of Eleazar Khthousion, accordingly the deceased brother of Yehudah, summoned Babatha before the Governor of the province concerning an unspecified date plantation which he alleged had devolved upon the orphans through their father and was held by Babatha by force: ἀνήκοντα τοῖς αὐτοῖς ὀρφανοῖς ὃν βίᾳ διακρατῖς.[22] Presumably at the same time, he made a deposition in which he refers to date plantations at Maoza registered in her name by Yehudah and appears in a damaged text to have asserted that they devolved upon the orphans from their father Jesus: δίκεον ὀρφαν[ῶν ... τ]ῶν αὐτῶν εἰδῶν ἐξ ὀνό[ματο]ς Ἰησούο[υ πατρὸς αὐτῶν].[23] He required her to disclose by what right she held the plantations, and gave notice that in default of her doing so he would register them in the names of the orphans. In July 131 CE Julia Crispina, described as ἐπίσκοπος or supervisor of the orphans, herself summoned Babatha, because Besas was ill, concerning those date plantations, asserting that they did not devolve on her and that she held them by force: ὑπαρχόντων τῶν αὐτῶν ὀρφαν[ῶ]ν βίᾳ διακρατῖς ἃ οὐκ ἀνῆκέν σοι; in an answer Babatha denied that she held them by force.[24]

There may also have been a dispute between Besas and Julia Crispina on behalf of the orphans and Shelamzion daughter of Yehudah because in 130 CE by a release they ceded or surrendered to her property, that is a courtyard and rooms at En Gedi, that had descended to her from the property of Eleazar Khthousion her grandfather: ὁμολογοῦμεν συνκεχωρηκέναι σοι ἐξ ὑπαρχόντων Ἐλεαζάρου τοῦ καὶ Χθουσίωνος, Ἰούδου πάπου σου αὐλὴν σὺν παντὶ δικαίοις αὐτῆς ἐν Ἠνγαδοῖς καὶ πᾶσιν ἐν αὐτῇ οἰκίαις.[25] They agreed to register it for her at her request and at her expense. The document also concludes with a Greek equivalent of a *cautio* for a *stipulatio* in the same form as that in the documents relating to Babatha's sale of the date crop to Simon.[26] It has been shown from the descriptions of the adjoining properties that this courtyard described as descending from her grandfather Eleazar, is not the courtyard that had been given to her by her father Yehudah in 128 CE.[27]

A dispute also arose between Babatha and Miriam, the other wife of Yehuda and in 131 CE Babatha summoned Miriam before the Governor of the province for a statement why she had seized the contents of the house of Yehudah, and in reply Miriam sought an order that Babatha not approach the property of Yehudah because she alleged Babatha had no claim against him regarding his estate.[28]

20. *P. Yadin* 22, ll 9-10 and see the counterpart *P. Yadin* 21, ll 11-12.
21. *P. Yadin* 21, ll 27-8 and *P. Yadin* 22, ll 29-30.
22. *P. Yadin* 23, ll 6-7 and 16-17.
23. *P. Yadin* 24, ll 7-8.
24. *P. Yadin* 25, ll 9-10 and 41-2; ll 17-19 and 51-2.
25. *P. Yadin* 20, ll 6-9 and 27-30; the text is a composite of the versions in the Inner and Outer texts.
26. *P. Yadin* 20, ll 16-17 and 40.
27. *P. Yadin* 19; H. M. Cotton, Courtyard(s) in Ein-gedi (quoted n. 13), pp. 197–201 (fn 13) 200.
28. *P. Yadin* 26, ll 6-8 and 12-17.

At this point the record of the proceedings ceases because in 132 CE there broke out the Revolt raised by Simon Bar Kokhba against the Roman authorities, and Babatha must have fled with her archive to the so called Cave of Letters in the Wadi Hever on the West Bank of the Dead Sea near En Gedi where her archive and that of a relation Salome Komaïse were found in 1961 CE.

The archive gives rise to several interesting legal points and issues.

First, although the litigation concerned Jewish families and I suggest Jewish law, all the litigation in which Babatha was involved was litigation before the Roman Governor of the Province, and we have no record of any other court there, and contractual documents involved are framed with an eye to treating claims under them as if they were claims under Roman law contracts. These agreements appear significant for the manner in which the Roman authorities treated claims made under law other than Roman law by inhabitants of a Province.

I turn first to the question of why Yehudah should have made the settlement upon his daughter Shelamzion shortly after her marriage to Judah Cimber. According to the Mishnah, following the rule set forth in *Num* 27. 8-9, a daughter of the deceased took as heir in default of sons of the deceased and in priority to his brothers.[29] In *Num* 36.5-9 it is ruled in the context of the allotment of land among the tribes of Israel that daughters were to take in default of sons only where they married within one of the clans of their tribe, so that (vv 7 and 9) land should not be transferred from one tribe to another. The primary rule is represented in the Mishnah as 'the son takes precedence over the daughter; ... the daughter takes precedence over [surviving] brothers' and it is also provided that the 'offspring of the daughter take precedence over the brothers' of the deceased, but there is no trace there of the rule set forth in *Num* 36.[30] One may assume that the rule was of no further utility and certainly we have no knowledge of the tribe or tribes to which Shelamzion and her husband Judah Cimber belonged or indication in the documents that tribal affiliations were then of any significance in this respect. Under the Roman law of intestate succession daughters, as long as they remained in the *potestas* of their father, as well as his sons were *sui heredes* and entitled to share in his estate.[31] However neither Yehudah nor any of his family appear to have been Roman citizens but *peregrini* and the Roman law rules of succession being *iuris civilis* were inapplicable to them.[32] Certainly nothing in the disputes over the inheritances indicates that any of the parties relied upon them.

Thus according to the Mishnah, unless a son were born to a marriage of Yehudah, Shelamzion would have been his heir, taking the obligation to pay the dowries of his two wives Babatha and Miriam and other debts in so far as they had not been paid. There is nothing to suggest that a son was born to either of his marriages, but at the time of the marriage of Shelamzion to Judah Cimber it cannot have been clear that there would be no son, and if there were, then any son would, on the footing that Mishnaic law applied, become heir to Yehudah to the exclusion of Shelamzion with the result that she would receive nothing from his estate. The effect of the gift to her was to make provision for her out of his estate whether or not she remained heir,

29. *mBB* 8. 2.
30. *mBB* 8. 2.
31. Gaius, *Inst*. 2. 156.
32. J. A. C. Thomas, *Textbook of Roman Law*, Amsterdam 1976, p. 479; see Ulpian 22. 2.

and that is the most reasonable explanation for it.[33] This interpretation is supported by the fact that in 120 CE Simon, the father of Babatha, gave all his property at Maoza to his wife Miriam subject to conditions so that she would take at his death if she were then married to him, a probable reason for doing this being to make provision for her since by the provisions of the Mishnah, a wife could not inherit from her husband; and by the fact that, in 129 CE Salome Grapte made an immediate gift of property at Maoza, a date plantation and half of a courtyard with accompanying rooms, to her daughter Salome Komaïse, perhaps again to make provision for her in the case that she would not be heir to either of her parents.[34]

I turn now to the release by which Besas and Julia Crispina as guardians of the orphans ceded or surrendered to Shelamzion a courtyard and rooms at En Gedi, the property of her grandfather Eleazar the father of Yehudah.[35] We do not know whether there were any legal proceedings or even a dispute between Besas and Julia Crispina as against Shelamzion. If the statement in it is correct, then the property had passed to her from the estate of Eleazar Khthousion her grandfather through her father Yehudah.[36] We do not know which the elder was or when either Eleazar or Jesus died, but it appears that Yehudah and Jesus were the heirs of Eleazar and if either predeceased Eleazar his offspring would take the shares of their father in the estate, since it is provided in the Mishnah that offspring have the precedence of their parent.[37] It is a possible interpretation that Shelamzion took the courtyard as heir of Yehudah, but we cannot on the material available explain why she took that courtyard or what the effect of the cession or surrender was. A possible interpretation of this document is that the share of Yehudah in Eleazar Khthousion's estate was or included the courtyard and rooms at En Gedi, and Besas and Julia Crispina were acknowledging that it had passed to Shelamzion; it was apparently common for such an inheritance to remain undivided, and perhaps this cession reflects an agreement between Yehudah and Jesus as heirs of their father Eleazar Khthousion or Shelamzion as the heir of Yehudah and the guardians of the heirs of Jesus to partition the inheritance, but one cannot be more definite.[38]

On that footing the estate of Eleazar would pass to Shelamzion on the one hand and to Jesus' orphans on the other, and it was the contents of the share of the orphans that Besas and Julia Crispina were attempting to get in by legal proceedings against Babatha. In that case Besas and Julia Crispina were in effect contending that the Groves were not part of the share of Yehudah in the estate so that he had no right to register them in the name of Babatha and she derived no right to them, and was holding them by force.

If indeed the cession or surrender made in July 130 by Besas and Julia Crispina in favour of Shelamzion and the legal proceedings brought by them against Babatha in December that year were connected and the dispute giving rise to them concerned property devolving from Eleazar Khthousion to the brothers Yehudah and Jesus, then the claims of Besas and Julia

33. H. M. Cotton and J. C. Greenfield, Babatha's Property and the Law of Succession, *Zeitschrift für Papyrologie und Epigraphik* 104, 1994, pp. 211–224, p 219.

34. *P. Yadin* 7; *P XḤev/Se* 64; *mBB* 8. 1; see Cotton and Greenfield, Babatha's (quoted n. 33), pp. 211–224 (fn 32), 218 and 219–220.

35. *P. Yadin* 20.

36. Lines 28-30.

37. *mBB* 8. 2.

38. H. M. Cotton, Courtyard(s) in Ein-Gedi (quoted n. 13), pp. 199–200.

Crispina on behalf of the orphans were not as heirs to Yehuda but as heirs to Jesus and the dispute must have been over whether certain property of which Yehudah was apparently the owner, some of which he registered in the name of Babatha, was in truth his or was in the event the property of Jesus. If their claims were correct then registration of property in her name should have given her no rights.

This position is to some extent supported by expressions used in the summons and deposition of Besas and in the summons of Julia Crispina all of which claim the property of the orphans devolving from their father which did not devolve on Babatha; and in the cession or surrender to Shelamzion referring to the property as devolving on her from her grandfather Eleazar.[39]

On this view it appears that Shelamzion was indeed the heir to Yehudah, and I suggest that this is not disproved by the claims made by Besas and Julia Crispina on behalf of the orphans against Babatha. It seems that the documents are best explained by taking the dispute to have been whether certain plantations were the property of Yehudah and later of Babatha. However in the present state of the documentation it is not appropriate to express any greater certainty.

The nature of the dispute between Babatha and Miriam, wives of Yehudah, appears to be over their respective rights to execute against property forming part of the estate of Yehudah after his death. No document available to us shows conclusively whether Yehudah had divorced Miriam, presumably before his marriage to Babatha, or she remained his wife at the time of his death. Nor have we any copy or extract from Miriam's marriage agreement. The only relevant material in the material available to us is the expressions used by both Babatha and Miriam referred to above in the fragmentary copy of Babatha's petition and the record of her summons against Miriam.[40] There does not appear to have been any prohibition under the then Jewish or Roman law against Jewish men contracting polygamous marriages, but although the expressions to which I have referred may mean that Yehudah had not divorced Miriam and was married concurrently to both Babatha and Miriam, it has been argued that those expressions cannot be used to argue for polygamous marriages because they can bear 'a plausible alternative interpretation of serial monogamy'.[41] Each of Babatha and Miriam seems to have seized property forming part of the estate of Yehudah, Babatha three date plantations and Miriam the whole contents of his house τὰ π[άν]τα ἐν τῇ οἰκίᾳ Ἰούδου Ἐλεαζάρου Χθουςίωνος ἀνδρός μου καὶ σου ἀ[πογενομένου.[42] In her documents relating to her sale in 130 CE of the then current crop of those plantations, Babatha had stated her claim to seize them was to recover her dowry and also 300 denarii lent to Yehudah in 128 CE, and in her reply to Babatha's summons, Miriam sought an order that Babatha should not approach the property forming part of his estate asserting that Babatha had no claim against Yehudah concerning his property μηδέναν λόγον ἔχιν σε πρὸς τὸν αὐτὸν Ἰούδαν περὶ τῶν ὑπαρχόντων αὐτοῦ.[43] Miriam disputed Babatha's right to execute against the estate of Yehudah but it

39. *P. Yadin* 23, ll 6-7; *P. Yadin* 24, ll 7-8; *P. Yadin* 25, ll 9-10 and 41-42; and *P. Yadin* 20, ll. 6-8 and 27-29

40. See above fn 7.

41. R. Katzoff, Polygamy in P. Yadin?, *Zeitschrift für Papyrologie und Epigraphik* 109, 1995, pp. 128–132, 132; for the view that Miriam was a 'living, undivorced wife' of Yehudah at the time of his marriage to Babatha, see Lewis, *Documents from the Bar Kokhba Period* (quoted n. 1), p. 22.

42. *P. Yadin* 26, ll 6-7.

43. *P. Yadin* 26, ll 15-7.

does not appear that Babatha also disputed the right of Miriam to do so. Although we have no document setting out the rights of Miriam, since she had been the wife of Yehudah her dowry would be repayable to her and she would have by the provisions of the Mishnah if not by her marriage contract, a security over all the then property of Yehudah just as did Babatha, but, on the other hand, she would have no rights of inheritance.[44] If she were divorced by Yehudah she would remain entitled to the recovery of her *ketubba* and nothing suggests that she would not retain her right to recover it and her right of execution for it over his property after his death.[45] Babatha's summons was not to require Miriam to give up the contents of Yehudah's house but to justify her seizure of them. I suggest that Miriam remained entitled, whether or not she had been divorced from Yehudah, to make execution just as Babatha had done. We cannot however say whether it was on that basis that she had seized the contents of the house but on the material available to us that would have been a possible reason for it. Here then we have, apparently, two rival claims to recover a *ketubba* and to execute upon Yehudah's property to recovery it. The Mishnah[46] provides that where a man had married two wives and died, the first wife took precedence over the second. However the material we have does not show that Miriam relied on this provision but I do not think we know how their rival claims would have been worked out.

Unfortunately the litigation in which Babatha was involved in the Province of Arabia with Miriam, the guardians of her son Jesus, and the guardians of the orphans of Yehudah's brother Jesus, was, so far as the records we have show, incomplete: there is no document in the archive, judgement or agreement, by which any of the litigation was concluded. We cannot therefore say exactly what the rights of the various parties were but can only draw inferences from those documents that are available. I have, however, attempted to infer from those documents, and what we know of the Jewish law from the Mishnah, what were those rights under the law that they appear to have regarded as binding.

The Families of Babatha and Yehudah

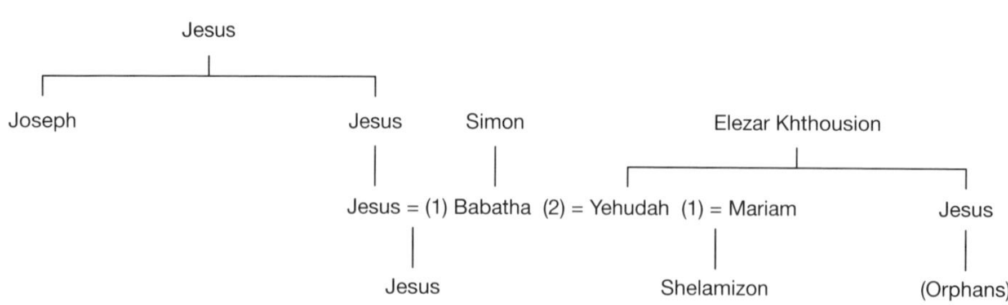

44. *mKet* 4. 7, *mBB* 8. 1.
45. *mKet* 5. 1.
46. *mKet* 10. 1.

TOWARDS THE ALLEGORY OF IDEALIZED *OIKOS*:

NUCLEAR AND EXTENDED FAMILY VERSIONS, SUCCESSION AND INHERITANCE ISSUES AND THEIR COGNATES IN PHILO JUDAEUS

Nicholas A. E. KALOSPYROS

Beyond the notion of allegory and allegoresis as hermeneutic techniques we could trace interesting elements concerning nuclear and extended family structure and relationships (esp. marriage, parents and children, extended kin, gender roles) in the numerable treatises of the Jewish-Hellenistic philosopher Philo of Alexandria, so as to verify the thematic view of family-*oîkos* in the Graeco-Roman world, under the keen spectrum of a prolific author and post-Platonic allegorist. The perception of family-beyond-household bounds, along with the study of relevant inheritance and succession conflicts and family cognates in the Philonian world, seems like an epitome of the Biblical creation, whilst at the same time enables us to form linguistic and stylistic devices of recognizing his theory of family membership in Hellenistic antiquity. My paper aspires to set off the archaiognostic reading of an allegorical hermeneutic tradition including the formation of idealized *oîkos* and its succession patterns, upon the philological documentation which is necessary for the establishing of such a study direction. The allegorical reduction of *oîkos* amounts to the bridging of the gap between the natural creation and the realm of universal nature amidst the unique nature (*physis*) of humanity. *Oîkos*, then, is metaphorically elevated above any other typical *thesmos physeos*, just like each one of the Ten Commandments is called. Philologically speaking and in Philo's terms, we have reached the literary scope of transcendental expression in Graeco-Judaean literature.

Undoubtedly, through the ages and as attested by the existence of mankind, the entity of family transcended various experimentations to view it exclusively either as a historical definition or as a notion corresponding to the legal categories of relationship or ownership; life itself developed the prerequisites of belonging to a community. Thus, the processing of such a transcendental phenomen of life deserves an equally unique in its origin and methodology mode of conception, which could increase our scientific intuition towards respective terms and relevant cognates deriving from *oîkos*, whose notion, usually denoting the family unit in

Inheritance, Law and Religions in the Ancient and Mediaeval Worlds, ed. by B. CASEAU and S. R. HUEBNER (Centre de recherche d'Histoire et Civilisation de Byzance, Monographies 45), Paris 2014.

Classical Greece, arose new in each generation without, even in terms of agnatic succession, ceasing to include imperishable natural as well as personal association with moral terms and political obligations.[1] Allegory forms an important factor of interpreting facts or imagery deliberately, and as such it would prove of great importance if intelligible as a literary device to examine the borders of family in ancient world; especially when mastered by a prolific author like Philo of Alexandria (born c. 25/20 BC, died c. AD 50), also known as Philo Judaeus.[2]

Although the Philonic corpus, full of perplexed combinations of biblical thought and philosophical doctrines, seems notoriously difficult for the uninitiated reader, we may acknowledge an otherwise latent character of sublime singularity towards the unique validity of *oîkos-familia* in the context of post-classical thought and religious culture anticipating early Christianity; unless we direct our research to Philo's lifelong decision to express an impassioned protest against the degradation and confusion of having to leave a life of contemplation for political duties[3] by writing treatises, which likewise reveal extensive familiarity with the exegesis tradition of the Septuagint, i.e. the *Old Testament*, it would be difficult to approach Philo's philosophical ideas. Convinced[4] of the supremity of the Middle Platonism — with current Stoicism — in his native Alexandria, and of his ancestral faith, he presented himself a devoted follower of Moses, yet not a Hebrew Moses, but a Hellenized philosopher, a vivid personification of an intertwined reconciliation between Jewish scripture[5] and Greek philosophy in the Graeco-Roman world through allegorical exegesis.[6]

Our challenge is then fulfilled between juristic tendencies, crabbed by their nature, and attempts leading to the idealization of a nostalgic past in a conservative mood and to the exploitation of moral values and ethical codes necessary for erecting ancient ideals in a fading society.

1. On the narrower legal sense of the term see G. Thür & R. Osborne, Oikos, in *Brill's New Pauly Encyclopaedia of the Ancient World. Antiquity* 10, H. Cancik and H. Schneider (eds.), Leiden—Boston 2007, col. 69-71. Of course, women and daughters could not found or continue an *oîkos*.

2. I quote from the edition prepared in the Series 'Loeb Classical Library' (Cambridge, Mass. & London, England: Harvard University Press), with English Translation by F. H. Colson and G. H. Whitaker, vol. I-X, 1929-1962 and the two last volumes *Suppl.* I-II (1953), Translated by R. Marcus.

3. So E. R. Goodenough, *The Politics of Philo Judaeus: Practice and Theory*, With a general bibliography of Philo by H. L. Goodhart and E. R. Goodenough, New Haven 1938 [photogr. reprod., Hildesheim 1967], p. 73; cf. *Spec.* (= De specialibus legibus I, II, III, IV '*The Special Laws*') 3. 1ff.

4. In *Opif.* (= De opificio mundi '*On the Account of the World's Creation given by Moses*') 16 Philo reveals his Platonic epistemology; cf. *QE* (= Quaestiones et solutiones in Exodum I, II '*Questions and Answers on Exodus*') 2. 90, *Gig.* (=De gigantibus) 54, *Her.* (= Quis rerum divinarum heres sit '*Who is the Heir of Divine Things*') 111 and *Abr.* (= De Abrahamo '*On Abraham*') 119.

5. On the kind of philological commentary of the Scripture in Philo see V. Nikiprowetzky, *Le commentaire de l'Écriture chez Philon d'Alexandrie. Son caractère et sa portée* (*Observations philologiques*) (Arbeiten zur Literatur und Geschichte des hellenistischen Judentums; 11), Leiden 1977 and on Philo's reception of the concepts of natural law and the relativizing of the Torah see M. Konradt, Tora und Naturgesetz: Interpretation graeca und universaler Geltungsanspruch der Mosetora bei Philo von Alexandrien, in *Juden in ihrer Umwelt: Akkulturation des Judentums in Antike und Mittelalter*, M. Konradt & R. C. Schwinges (eds.), Basel 2009, pp. 87–112.

6. G. E. Sterling, Platonizing Moses: Philo and Middle Platonism, *The Studia Philonica Annual* 5, 1993, pp. 96–111. See also A. Kamesar (ed.), *The Cambridge Companion to Philo*, Cambridge 2009 and M. Hadas-Lebel, *Philo of Alexandria: A Thinker in the Jewish Diaspora*. Studies in Philo of Alexandria 7. Leiden—Boston 2012 on the notion of Philo's Judaism; Hadas-Lebel introduces the notion of 'practice and ethics', showing that Philo combined halachic observance with an individualistic and spiritual interpretation of the laws.

Therefore, crucial issues such as the social structures of household and kinship in Palestine and the Graeco-Roman world, the self-contained *familia* and its very restricted membership, entirely separate and discrete, and the kind of biological connection between the persons engaged, or their obligations towards the paterfamilias who had *patria potestas* within the family over the persons of his children and descendants and usually of his wife as well, being virtually autonomous, are significant only if undergone allegorical expectations and metaphoric applications.

Pomeroy in his attempt to define family in classical and Hellenistic Greece,[7] that had a wider range of manifestations than it has in the modern Western world, sought after a protean definition, whereby the words 'public' and 'private' seem problematic to correspond exactly to the ancient frame and conception of *polis*, phratry and genos, quasi- or pseudo-kin groups;[8] on the other hand, public, domestic/public, and domestic/private, and, perhaps, legal and linguistic *syggeneia* and *anchisteia* may form a second group of denotations, while a third rubric of definition is concerned with *oîkos* embracing not only human beings but also property issues and so translated as family, household or estate.[9] But how would he react in the case of proposing a fourth factor of viewing family as an eloquent mystical image of existence before divine will of instructing this certain way of personal and interpersonal identity? We are warned not to intellectualize the historical complements of society: 'The Roman *familia* was not an end in itself but a means to an end. It was merely one among a number of legal mechanisms devised in order to serve the real end, i.e. the promotion of the welfare and contentment of the families, of whatever composition, of which Roman society was constituted, and through that the harmony of the society as a whole'.[10] In the traditional Mediterranean culture, under the concrete circumstances of Roman authority and rabbinic tradition, the family proffers a sphere available to metaphoric usage; it is within family that the individual is inserted into social life.[11] Barton studied the radical realignments of Roman emotional life through its volatile equilibrations by associating moral values, such as honour, with the justification of the patriarchal society with its social obduracies, concealing sterner realities and acting as a rhetorical concealment,[12] whilst shame, forming a delicate system of reciprocities, caused an occasional anguish.[13] The contradictory social and moral aspects were sometimes glossed over in particular ideals; for instance, the ideal of *concordia* usually covered severe realities like arranged marriages, violence within family and casual divorce. Since the real family of the Roman epoch 'suffered tension, betrayal, conflict, and indifference',

7. On family in the course of Greek history see also C. B. PATTERSON, *The Family in Greek History*, Cambridge, MA & London, UK 1998, and H.-J. GEHRKE, Family. IV: Greece and Rome. A: Greece, in *Brill's New Pauly* (cf. n. 1), 5, col. 334-338.

8. S. B. POMEROY, *Families in Classical and Hellenistic Greece. Representations and Realities*, Oxford 1997, pp. 17–66.

9. This latter could remind us of the classical understanding of family according to Aristotle's *Pol.* 1252b 10-12 and 1323a 5-6.

10. J. F. GARDNER, *Family and* Familia *in Roman Law and Life*, Oxford 1998, p. 279. On family in ancient Rome see M.-L. DEISSMAN-MERTEN, Family. IV: Greece and Rome. B: Rome, in *Brill's New Pauly* (cf. n. 1), 5, col. 338-343.

11. S. GUIJARRO, The Family in First-Century Galilee, in *Constructing Early Christian Families. Family as Social Reality and Metaphor*, H. MOXNES (ed.), London 1997, pp. 42–65 (here p. 62).

12. J. LENDON, *Empire of Honour*, Oxford 1997, pp. 24–25.

13. C. A. BARTON, *Roman Honor. The Fire in the Bones*, Berkeley—Los Angeles—London 2001.

experienced also by Victorian and modern family,[14] and since the symbol of the community and mutuality in the first Christian communities as family is one that pervades the literature,[15] the ideology of the family-formation (childbirth, brotherhood, *oîkos*, community of a household)[16] serves as the historical garment of the social impact of Roman rule upon the Jewish family;[17] however largely restricted to the elite,[18] Philo had to connect it with the ancestral laws of his compatriots, in order to serve the cultural homogeneity of his fellow-countrymen.

Philo's allegorical description[19] is grounded on two major convictions: in the first place, the theoretic promotion of parallel and analogical comparison between the world patent sense, riping for birth after the pattern of incorporeal,[20] and the symbols making ideas visible:

14. S. DIXON, *Childhood, Class and Kin in the Roman World*, London—New York 2001, p. 113.

15. J. M. LIEU, *Christian Identity in the Jewish and Graeco-Roman World*, Oxford—New York 2004, pp. 166–169. I. RICHARZ, *Oikos, Haus und Haushalt. Ursprung und Geschichte der Haushaltsökonomik*, Göttingen 1991, pp. 35–39 discussed domestic life in the *Old* and the *New Testament*. On the family in early Christianity see G. S. NATHAN, *The Family in Late Antiquity. The Rise of Christianity and the Endurance of Tradition*, London—New York 2000.

16. Childhood, family and status continue to be in the centre of public interest as they interact; see S. DIXON, The Sentimental Ideal of the Roman Family, in *Marriage, Divorce, and Children in Ancient Rome*, B. RAWSON (ed.), Canberra—Oxford 1991, pp. 99–113.

17. A. TROPPER, The economics of Jewish Childhood in Late Antiquity, *Hebrew Union College Annual* 76, 2005, pp. 189–233 and *idem*, Childhood in Light of the Demographics of the Jewish Family in Late Antiquity, *Journal for the Study of Judaism* 37, 2006, pp. 299–343 studied the economic structure, childhood, and child minding of Jewish family in late antiquity, dealing with evidence based on rabbinic literature. L. J. ARCHER, *Her Price is Beyond Rubies: The Jewish Woman in Graeco-Roman Palestine*, Sheffield 1990, pp. 69–101 emphasized on the familial and son-centred character of Jewish education in the Graeco-Roman period.

18. M. WILLIAMS, The Jewish Family in Judaea from Pompey to Hadrian — the Limits of Romanization, in *The Roman Family in the Empire* (*Rome, Italy, and Beyond*), M. GEORGE (ed.), Oxford 2005, pp. 159–182, along with S. SAFRAI, Home and Family, in *The Jewish People in the First Century*, vol. II, S. SAFRAI & M. STERN (eds.), Assen 1976, pp. 728–792; S. J. D. COHEN, The Jewish Family in Antiquity, *Brown Judaic Studies* 289, Atlanta 1993; also T. ILAN, *Jewish Women in Greco-Roman Palestine: An Inquiry into Image and Status*, Tübingen 1995.

19. On allegorical interpretation the passage *Ios.* (= De Iosepho '*On Joseph*') 6 [II. 46] is important. On allegory in *Ios.* as an allegorical biography see F. FRAZIER, Une « biographie allégorique » chez Philon? Sur l'emploi de l'interprétation allégorique dans le *De Josepho*, in *L'allégorie de l'antiquité à la Renaissance* (Colloques, congrès et conférences sur la Renaissance européenne 43), B. PÉREZ-JEAN and P. EICHEK-LOJKINE (eds.), Paris 2004, pp. 255–286. On allegory in general (classical theories of and usage in literature) see P. ROLLINSON, *Classical Theories of Allegory and Christian Culture*, Pittsburgh—Sussex 1981; C. WALDE, Allegory, in *Brill's New Pauly* (cf. n. 1), 1, col. 517-519; and *L'allégorie de l'antiquité à la Renaissance*. ROLLINSON, *ibid.*, p. 9 wrote that Philo separates and distinguishes his text and the meanings he elucidates from myth and poetry, and he (p. 7) observed that Philo's attitude towards the text of the *Old Testament* is remarkably similar to Plutarch's account of pagan gods; on Philo's practices see *ibidem*, 7-10. J. PÉPIN, Remarques sur la théorie de l'exégèse allégorique chez Philon, in *Philon d'Alexandrie, Lyon 11-15 Septembre 1966* (Colloques Nationaux du Centre National de la Recherche Scientifique), Paris 1967, pp. 131–167 and *idem*, *La tradition d'allégorie: de Philon d'Alexandrien a Dante*, Paris 1987 (esp. on allegorical tradition) commented on the theory of the allegorical exegese in Philo; for a general discussion of Philo's allegorical method see I. CHRISTIAENSEN, *Die Technik der allegorischen Auslegungswissenschaft bei Philon von Alexandrien* (Beiträge zur Geschichte der biblischen Hermeneutik; 7), Tübingen 1969 and H. A. WOLFSON, *Philo. Foundations of Religious Philosophy in Judaism, Christianity, and Islam*, vol. I, 3rd print. rev., Cambridge, MA 1962, pp. 115–138, involving anthropomorphisms and actually discarding the entire historical setting of the story. R. WILLIAMSON, *Jews in the Hellenistic World: Philo* (Cambridge Commentaries on Writings of the Jewish and Christian World; 1.i), Cambridge 1989, pp. 144–175 and D. DAWSON, *Allegorical Readers and Cultural*

> 'Now these are no mythical fictions, such as poets and sophists delight in, but modes of making ideas visible, bidding us resort to allegorical interpretation guided in our renderings by what lies beneath the surface (δείγματα τύπων ἐπ' ἀλληγορίαν παρακαλοῦντα κατὰ τὰς δι' ὑπονοιῶν ἀποδόσεις)' (*Opif.* 157 [I. 125]);

in the second place, the indispensable eternal verity of the ancestral God, at which men cannot but be gratified:

> 'God is an author in whose works you will find no myth or fiction, but truth's inexorable rules all observed as through graven on stone. [...] And even as the mind, with its ear tuned to the poems of God, is glad, so the speech, being in tune with the conceptions of the understanding, and, if we may so speak, lending its ear to them, cannot but rejoice' (*Det.*= Quod deterius potiori insidiari soleat '*That the Worse is Wont to Attack the Better*' 125 [II. 285-286]).

The proper perception of underlying multifaceted symbols enables human mind to understand divine things latent in Scripture[21] and to be accustomed to a symbolic discourse associated with the future:[22]

> 'These are the contents of the ordinance taken literally. But another meaning also is indicated of the mystical character which symbols convey (αἰνιγματώδη λόγον ἔχων τὸν διὰ συμβόλων); words in their plain sense are symbols of things latent and obscure' (*Spec.* 1. 200 [VII. 215]).

It is obvious that he believed in his allegorical exegesis unfolding the mystery[23] of beings and institutions, for he should manage to incorporate into his interpretation of his Jewish faith as many of the divine things he saw in the world of secular thought and civilization around him, whilst the language of the Pentateuch constituted the language of symbolism (in Greek terminology: *ainigma*, *ainissesthai*, *ainigmatodes*, *deigma* and *hypodeigma*).[24]

Revision in Ancient Alexandria, Berkeley—Los Angeles—Oxford 1992, pp. 73–126 on Philo reading Scripture allegorically. Greek philosophy supplies a language of reason used by Philo as exegete to examine the deeper meaning present in the Scriptures themselves; the task of the Philonic scholars is therefore to concentrate on the exegetical themes, without severing them from the scriptural passages as a set of independent ideas.

20. 'The world patent sense was ripe for birth after the pattern of the incorporeal' (*Opif.* 36 [I. 27]).

21. See *Spec.* 4. 192 (*dianoia*) and *Prob.* (= Quod omnis probus liber sit) 80, to seek the correct interpretation of the Hebrew Scriptures.

22. D. I. Sly, *Philo's Alexandria*, London & New York 1996, p. 136, believes that allegory was Philo's way of making the Scripture contemporary and relevant, since the two levels of reading Scripture satisfied his need to be both traditional and current; it was the means by which he derived from Scripture spiritual principles that could appeal to an age of anxiety. On the connection of symbol and allegory see A. Rolet (ed.), *Allégorie et symbole : voies de dissidence ? de l'Antiquité à la Renaissance*, Rennes 2012. (Interférences)".

23. Cf. *Fug.* (= De fuga et inventione '*On Flight and Finding*') 79.

24. D. Robertson, *Word and Meaning in Ancient Alexandria: theories of Language from Philo to Plotinus*, Hampshire 2008, pp. 9–28 on the creative mixture of Stoic and Platonic strands conveyed to us through Philo's language. On Philo's language as stylistic device of hermeneutics see K. Otte, *Das Sprachverständnis bei Philo von Alexandrien* (*Sprache als Mittel der Hermeneutik*) (Beiträge zur Geschichte der Biblischen Exegese; 7), Tübingen 1968.

With his allegorical and futher anagogical exegesis in socio-cultural and political assimilation and acculturation[25] he could accommodate Judaism to the dominant culture, without abandoning its distinctive traditions and practices, and interpret competing and congenial forces amidst the relationships in which persons operated.[26] Jewish literature already offered a suitable substratum for the similitude of lifelike instances. Perhaps more than any other of the *Old Testament* pseudepigrapha the Greek Life of Adam and Eve can still serve as an example; this postbibical text brings together motifs drawn from ancient myths that address the deepest human needs: above all, the promise of life beyond death through access to the tree of life.[27]

In Philo family metaphors did create a new sense of belonging, beyond hierarchical order[28] and power relationships, emphasizing equality in the sight of the Creator:[29] the law formed the core of Jewish identity and being the focus of weekly instruction in the synagogue, it was thence transmitted to the home.[30] As Barton states it, 'Philo uses the powerful idiom of kinship ties to speak metaphorically about religious and philosophical allegiance, and in particular to convey certain *priorities*: the mental over the physical, thought over sense, nature over culture, piety over lawlessness, the love of God over idolatry, and so on. The metaphorical uses of kinship convey a 'programme' which touches on issues religious, philosophical, ethical and social and for which the heroes serve as focal instances, representing the truth in

25. J. BOUFFARTUGUE, 'La structure de l'âme chez Philon: terminologie scolastique et métaphors', in *Philon d'Alexandrie et le langage de philosophie: actes du colloque international organize par le Centre d'Études sur la philosophie hellénistique et romaine de l'Université de Paris XII-val de Marne* (*Créteil, Fontenay, Paris, 26-28 octobre 1995*) (Monothéisms et philosophie), C. LÉVY (ed.), Turnhout 1998, pp. 59–75 set an opinion, that, in spite of awkwardnesses and forgery not that inevitably the extensive use of the allegorical interpretation involves, Philon knew to integrate the terminology and the Greek metaphors relating to clothing of the heart in an anthropology fundamentally faithful to Biblical teaching.

26. D. R. EDWARDS, *Religion & Power. Pagans, Jews, and Christians in the Greek East*, Oxford · New York 1996, pp. 7–14 and J. DYCK, Philo, Alexandria and Empire. The politics of allegorical intrpretation, in *Jews in the Hellenistic and Roman Critics*, J. R. BARTLETT (ed.), London—New York 2002, pp. 149–174.

27. M. B. ELDRIDGE, *Dying Adam with his Multiethnic Family. Understanding the Greek Life of Adam and Eve* (Studia in Veteris Testamenti Pseudepigrapha; 16), Leiden—Boston—Köln 2001 and M. DE JONGE and J. TROMP, *The Life of Adam and Eve and Related Literature*, Sheffield 1997. 'The Rabbis consider the Torah the blueprint God consulted to create the world (MAvoth 3:14). The imagery used here may have had more ancient roots. Philo describes in parable-like form how an architect plans the structure of the city he is going to build. Thus, it is with the 'logos', the realm of rational powers, that God created the world' (E. OTTENHEIJM, Learning and Practising: Uses of an Early Jewish Discourse in Matthew (7:24-27) and Rabbinic Literature, in *Dying Adam with his Multiethnic Family. Understanding the* Greek Life of Adam and Eve (Jewish and Christian Perspective Series; 17), M. POORTHUIS, J. SCHWARTZ and J. TURNER (eds.), Leiden—Boston 2009, pp. 45–64 [here, p. 59]). This 'logos' parallels the blueprint of an architect, comparing God to an architect and the logos with the 'idea' or blueprint in *Opif.* 15-25 and *Aet.* (= De aeternitate mundi '*On the Eternity of the World*') 2.

28. Cf. *Post.* (= De posteritate Caini '*On the Posterity of Cain and His Exile*') 109 [II. 389-391] and *Ebr.* (= De ebrietate '*On Drunkenness*') 131 [III. 387].

29. On metaphorical language and its usage in culture see G. LAKOFF & M. JOHNSON, *Metaphors We Live By*, Chicago 1980; J. SOSKICE, *Metaphor and Religious Language*, Oxford 1985; and P. MACKY, *The Centrality of Metaphors to Biblical Thought: A Method for Interpreting the Bible* (Studies in the Bible and Early Christianity 19), Lewiston 1990.

30. J. M. G. BARCLAY, The Family as the Bearer of Religion in Judaism and Early Christianity, in *Constructing Early Christian Families. Family as Social Reality and Metaphor*, H. MOXNES (ed.), London 1997, pp. 66–80 (here, p. 70); cf. *Hypoth.* (= Hypothetica / Apologia pro Iudaeis '*Hypothetica / Apology for the Jews*') 7.14.

these areas to a quintessential degree. The force of the metaphor lies in the *shock* which comes from the identification of what is normally valued negatively, with the sphere of the holy: the wise man is the one who quits his ancestral home, the Levite is like the homicide. It may be no coincidence, therefore, that in the Gospel stories about Jesus and the disciples, stories of kinship enmity and teaching about the subordination of family ties are not infrequent. It is highly likely that, as in Philo, such stories and teaching carry a significant metaphorical load with strong social corollaries'.[31] Considering Philo's Platonizing view of God's word as the visualization of heavenly ideas — i.e. literal implications, symbolisms, intrinsically indeterminate, creative invention, and abstraction visualized in literary implication and allegorical rereading — in the multidynamic[32] rhetorical vehicle[33] of allegoresis,[34] we justify Borgen's remark that Philo by his allegorical interpretation worked upon a rewriting of Biblical events and laws in acquaintance with the Greek-speaking world.[35]

It is self-evident that the first step to the conjunction of the family unit is the matching of the two sexes, the masculine and the feminine one. Both sexes in Philo appear substantially in symbolic utterances. His Moses, for example, is a perfect illustration of the ideology of masculinity evident in a wide range of Greco-Roman literature; moreover, with Philo's Moses, perfect masculinity is commensurate with divinity, but both remain relative to the 'asexual masculinity' of God.[36] The masculine character of mind (*nous*) allows a collation to the rational virtue:

31. S. C. Barton, The Relativisation of Family in the Jewish and Graeco-Roman Traditions, in *Constructing Early Christian Families. Family as Social Reality and Metaphor*, H. Moxnes (ed.), London 1997, pp. 81–100 (here, p. 88).

32. For example, J. van der Watt, *Family of the King: Dynamics of Metaphor in the Gospel according to John* (Bible Interpretation Series; 47), Leiden 2000 commented on the dynamics of metaphor in the Gospel according to John.

33. *Metaphor, Allegory, and the Classical Tradition* (*Ancient Thought and Modern Revisions*), G. R. Boys-Stones (ed.), Oxford 2003 edited various essays on considering philosophical approaches to allegory next to rhetorical discussions of metaphor; by placing studies of classical theory alongside analyses of literary practice that draw on the terms of contemporary theory, the chapters included aim to contribute to a fairer picture of classical approaches to language.

34. On allegoresis, being analogous to 'allegory' as a figurative, metaphorical manner of speech, defined as metaphorical exegesis and hermeneutic technique, see J. C. Joosen & J. H. Waszink, Allegorese, in *Reallexikon für Antike und Christentum*, Bd. 1 (Aund-Bauen), T. Klauser (ed.), Stuttgart 1950, pp. 283–293; and H. Cancik-Lindemaier and D. Mohr-Sigel, Allegoresis, in *Brill's New Pauly* (cf. n. 1), 1 (A-Ari), col. 511-516. Especially on Jewish allegoresis see I. Heinemann, *Altjüdische Allegoristik*, Breslau 1936 and A. Goldberg, Das schriftauslegende gleichnis im Midrasch, *Frankfurter Judaistische Beiträge* 9, 1981, pp. 1–90. F. Graf, Allegorism: II. History of Religions and Mythology, in *Brill's New Pauly Encyclopaedia of the Ancient World. Classical Tradition* 1, M. Landfester (ed.) and co-ed. by H. Cancik & H. Schneider, col. 98-103 discussed allegorism in mythology and the history of religion: he believes that allegorical exegesis of the Bible constitutes the core of allegorism (*ibidem*, pp. 95–96), esp. in Biblical all-utterances of the creation; Philo furnished large parts of the Mosaic books with an ethical-moral allegorism.

35. P. Borgen, *Philo of Alexandria: An Exegete for his Time* (Supplemets to Novum Testamentum; 86), Leiden—Boston—Köln 1997, pp. 46–79. We should note down that concerning Christian typology the salvific events of the *New Testament* have already their forerunners and announcers in the *Old Testament*.

36. C. M. Conway, Gender and divine relativity in Philo of Alexandria, *Journal for the Study of Judaism* 34, 2003, pp. 471–491. M. L. Satlow, 'Try to be a man': the rabbinic construction of masculinity, *Harvard Theological Review* 89, 1996, pp. 19–40 notes that the rabbinic understanding of manliness as a cultural transformation is amply attested in contemporaneous non-Jewish sourves drawn esp. from the elite intellectual circles of Greece and Rome; some of their fundamental assumptions are found in Philo, *Contempl.* (= De vita contemplative '*On the Contemplative Life or Suppliants*') 68-69 and *Fug.* 51-52.

> 'In the first place the victim of the whole-burnt-offering is a male because the male is more complete, more dominant than the female, closer akin to causal activity, for the female is incomplete and in subjection and belongs to the category of the passive rather than the active. So too with the two ingredients which constitute our life-principle, the rational and the irrational; the rational which belongs to mind and reason is of the masculine gender, the irrational, the province of sense, is of the feminine. Mind belongs to a genus wholly superior to sense as man is to woman; unblemished and purged, as perfect virtue purges, it is itself the most religious of sacrifices and its whole being is highly pleasing to God' (*Spec.* 1. 200-201 [VII. 215]).[37]

On the contrary, the female sex[38] is irrational and akin to bestial passions, such as fear, sorrow, pleasure and desire,[39] the beguiling pleasure outwitting and misleading the mind:[40]

> 'Because a wife is a selfish creature, excessively jealous (φίλαυτον ἡ γυνὴ καὶ ζηλότυπον οὐ μετρίως) and an adept at beguiling the morals of her husband and seducing him by her continued impostures. [...] For he who is either fast bound in the love lures of his wife or under the stress of nature makes his children his first care ceases to be the same to others and unconsciously has become a different man and has passed from freedom into slavery' (*Hypoth.* 11. 14-17 [IX. 443]).[41]

Then, we should query in which way could an allegorist endure woman as misfortune and the ontologically secondary status of the gendered human being,[42] as far Gilabert i Barberà wonders if Philo expresses the patently misogynous view that man's progressive degradation goes hand in hand with the increasing sexualization of the story of the fall.[43] However complicated

37. Cf. *Ebr.* 72 [III. 353] and *Opif.* 77 [I. 61-63] also *Leg.* (= Legum allegoriae I, II, III '*Allegorical Interpretation of Genesis*') 3. 49-50 [I. 333-335]); 188 [I. 429]); 221 [I. 451].

38. R. Radice, Il femminile come 'concetto allegorico' in Filone di Alessandria, *Ricerche Storico-Bibliche* 6, 1994, pp. 167–177 wrote on the allegorical conception of the female in Philo. A. Wasserstein, Philo's Portrayal of Women — Hebraic or Hellenic?, in '*Women Like This*': *New Perspectives on Jewish Women in the Greco-Roman World* (Society of Biblical Literature: Early Judaism and its Literature), A.–J. Levine (ed.), Atlanta 1991, pp. 41–66 studied Philo's portrayal of women, typical of Judaism or of Hellenism. On family and woman in Philo see E. R. Goodenough, *An Introduction to Philo Judaeus*, 2nd ed., Oxford 1962, pp. 126–127; Philo lays great stress upon the sanctity of the family, but displays a low opinion of women throughout, his own popular rather than Greek philosophical background (for instance in Plato and among the Stoics).

39. Cf. *Sobr.* (= De sobrietate '*On the Prayers and Curses Uttered by Noah When He Became Sober*') 23 [III. 457] ('Because we declare that in the beloved wife we have a figure of pleasure and in the hated wife a figure of prudence. For pleasure's company is beloved beyond measure by the great mass of men, because from the hour of their birth to the utmost limits of old age she produces and sets before them such enticing lures and love-charms (δελέατα καὶ φίλτρα ἐξ ἑαυτῆς ἐπαγωγότατα ἐνδιδούσης); while for prudence, severe and august as she is, they have a strange and profound hatred, as foolish children hate the most wholesome but most distasteful directions of their parents and those who have the charge of them' and *QG* (= Quaestiones et solutiones in Genesim I, II, III, IV '*Questions and Answers on Genesis*') 4. 15, [Suppl. I. 288].

40. Cf. *Leg.* 3. 59-64 [I. 341-343].

41. The passage in discussing the Essenes avoiding marriage and giving birth to children and on female arrogance.

42. On this sort of misogyny see D. Boyarin, *Carnal Israel: Reading Sex in Talmudic Culture*, Berkeley 1993, pp. 78–80, 231–234.

43. P. Gilabert i Barberà, '...Però la dona ho esguerrà tot': el *De opificio mundi* de Filó d'Alexandria (LIII-LXI) o els fonaments grecs d'una fita en la història da la misogínia occidental, *Anuari de Filologia: Studia*

it might seem, in Philo's world view three female personifications of conceptual constructs are included: wisdom, with decidedly male attributes;[44] sense perception, with female attributes;[45] and nature, which is male as the rational, active craftswoman who forms the various parts of the cosmos, and female in her semi-immanence and her material sphere of activity. In addition, Harrison observed that through allegorization Philo depicts the spiritual quest as if it had been a primarily human than rather gender-defined experience; feminine qualities such as desire and receptivity are portrayed by Philo as negative when associated with the senses but positive when associated with the mind.[46] Although wisdom and sense perception are important for Philo insofar as they relate to the human mind, nature is a figure independent of the mind[47] and the earth is compared to a mother whom earlier men called Demeter and Pandora.[48]

The other pole of the natural conjunction to reproduction, the masculine gender, is represented by reflection to the positive element of activation; to draw again our attention to the former Philonic recognition, sense-wife is attracted to her lawful husband, i.e. Adam-mind:

> '(*Gen*. ii. 21-22) and *QG* 1. 52 [Suppl. I. 30] on giving the name of Life to the first created woman. What is the 'side' which He took from the earth-born man; and why did He mould the side into woman? The literal sense is clear. For by a certain symbolical use of 'part' it is called a half of the whole, as both man and woman, being sections of Nature, become equal in one harmony of genus, which is called man. But in the figurative sense, man is a symbol of mind, and his side is a single sense-faculty. And the sense-perception of a very changeable reason is symbolized by woman. [...] Accordingly the lawgiver says that woman was made from the side of man, intimating that woman is a half of man's body' (*QG* 1. 25, [Suppl. I. 14-15])[49]

Graeca et Latina 13, 1990, pp. 55–84 (here, p. 76). D. T. RUNIA, *Philo of Alexandria* On the Creation of the Cosmos according to Moses. *Introduction, Translation and Commentary* (Philo of Alexandria Commentary Series; 1), Leiden · Boston · Köln 2001, pp. 359–361, commenting on *Opif.* 151-152, wrote about Philo's attitude towards women and sexuality, after D. I. SLY, Philo's Perception of Women, *Brown Judaic Studies* 209, Atlanta 1990, pp. 109, 219, and D. WINSTON, Philo and the Rabbis on Sex and the Body, *Poetics Today* 19, 1998, pp. 41–62. T. ILAN, *Jewish Women* (quoted n. 18), studied the status of Jewish women in Graeco-Roman Palestine. The role of women in Jewish religion and worship was rather one of passive onlooker than active participant, and it was esp. women that were associated to magical tradition of Hellenistic Palestine (on this see L. J. ARCHER, The Role of Jewish Women in the Religion, Ritual and Cult of Graeco-Roman Palestine, in A. *Images of Women in Antiquity*, A. CAMERON and A. KUHRT (eds.), rev. ed. London 1993, pp. 273–287 [and 311-312 App., Corr., Addenda]); on the same issue see also R. PATAI, *Sex and Family in the Bible and the Middle East*, New York 1959.

44. Cf. *Fug.* 51 [V. 37]; but *Fug.* 188f. [V. 113f.] on sense-perception under the name of woman.

45. Cf. *Migr.* (= De migratione Abrahami '*On the Migration of Abraham*') 206 [IV. 253].

46. N. V. HARRISON, The Feminine Man in Late Antique Ascetic Piety, *Union Seminary Quarterly Review* 48, 1994, pp. 49–71.

47. According to S. L. MATTILA, Wisdom, Sense Perception, Nature, and Philo's Gender Gradient, *Harvard Theological Review* 89, 1996, pp. 103–129.

48. Cf. *Opif.* 133 [I. 105]. D. T. RUNIA, Etymology as an allegorical technique in Philo of Alexandria, *Studia Philonica Annual* 16, 2004, pp. 101–121 on etymology as an allegorical technique in Philo, influenced by Stoic models, and on the etymology of Hebrew names.

49. On the passage see the commentary of R. RADICE, *Allegoria e paradigmi etici in Filone di Alessandria* (*Commentario al* 'Legum allegoriae') (Centro di Ricerche di Metafisica/Collana Temi metafisici e problemi del pensiero antico. Studi e testi; 79), Milano: 2000, pp. 384–385. Cf. also *Cher.* (= De Cherubim '*On the Cherubim, and the Flaming Sword, and Cain the First Man Created Out of Man*') 41 [II. 33].

and, therefore, man should take care of woman as of a necessary part of him,[50] whereas woman should exercise her duty to serve him as a whole,[51] to support him in deep devotion[52] and to conceive the seeds of virtue[53] demanded by fertile souls destined for noble actions:

> 'But we may also allegorize such parts of the subject as admit of being studied in a figurative sense. We should know, then, that nature's right reasoning has the functions both of a father and a husband, though the conceptions attached to each are different (ἐπινοίαις διαφόροις). It acts as a husband because it deposits the seed of virtue in the soul as in a fertile field. It acts as a father because its nature is to beget good intentions and noble and worthy actions, and then to foster its offspring with the water of the truths which education and wisdom abundantly supply. The mind is likened on the one hand to a virgin, on the other to a woman either in widowhood, or still united to a husband. As a virgin it keeps itself pure and uncorrupted from the the malignant passions, pleasures and desires and griefs and fears. Over this virgin mind the father who begat it has assumed authority. But when, like a wife, it dwells with virtuous reasoning as its worthy mate, that same reasoning promises to take charge of it and impregnates it husband-like with thoughts of highest excellence. But the soul, which is bereaved of its birth-tie with sound sense or its marriage-tie with right reasoning, is widowed of all that is most exvellent and, deserted by wisdom because it has chosen a life of guilt, must stand bound by the decision which it has made to its own undoing. It has none to heal its errors, no reasoning of wisdom (τὸν κατὰ σοφίαν λόγον), either to live with it as its husband or to act as its father and begetter' (*Spec.* 2. 29-31 [VII. 323-325]).[54]

Furthermore, we cannot and should not exclude the female option to rival the men in piety,[55] beyond the 'recognition' of female beauty being misleading and seducive.[56]

There is already a metaphoric context in the *Old Testament*, especially in the linguistic frame of the Septuagint. In the first chapter of *Genesis* the creation of 'male' and 'female' is recorded, through a meaning sliding from *'iššâ* 'woman' to its other meaning 'wife'; in verse 23 Adam refers to 'woman', in verse 24, an etiological aside, the same word is used to mean 'wife', and throughout the rest of the Hebrew Bible, as Satlow remarks,[57] the word *'iššâ* customarily denotes a 'wife'. The Septuagint γυνή and the Aramaic translation of Onkelos preserve this shift

50. On the creation of the woman-helper to Adam-man (*Gen.* ii. 18) see *Leg.* 2. 1ff. [I. 225ff.] that He had formed the mind before and is about to form its helper, and *Leg.* 2. 5 [I. 227-229] ('in these particulars again, while using terms of outward nature he is conveying a deeper meaning' 'ἀλλὰ καὶ ταῦτα φυσικῶς ἀλληγορεῖ'), for sense and the passions are helpers of the soul and come after the soul.

51. Cf. *QG* 1. *27, [Suppl. I. 16], *Hypoth.* 7. 3 [IX. 425] and *Spec.* 4. 178 [VIII. 119].

52. Cf. *Abr.* 246 [VI. 121].

53. Cf. *Deus* (= Quod Deus immutabilis sit '*On the Unchangeable of God*') 137 [III. 79]. See C. Werman, God's House: Temple or Universe, in *Philo und das Neue Testament: wechselseitige Wahrnehmungen: 1. Internationales Symposium zum Corpus Judaeo-Hellenisticum, 1.-4. Mai 2003, Eisenach/Jena* (Wissenschaftliche Untersuchungen zum Neuen Testament; 172), R. Deines & K.-W. Niebuhr (eds.), Tübingen 2004, pp. 309–320 on the God's house, being temple or universe, an idea deriving from the relative Scriptures from the Land of Israel more than those of the Hellenistic-Jewish diaspora.

54. Cf. *Spec.* 3. 178 [VII. 587-589].

55. Cf. *Mos.* (= De vita Moysis I, II '*On the Life of Moses*') 2. 136 [VI. 515]. On woman's place in and outside household matters, best suitable to indoor life, and her naturally proper behaviour see *Spec.* 3. 169-177 [VII. 581-587].

56. Cf. *Ios.* 269 [VI. 269-271] and *Virt.* (= De virtutibus '*On the Virtues*') 113 [VIII. 231].

57. M. L. Satlow, *Jewish Marriage in Antiquity*, Princeton & Oxford 2001, pp. 57–58, 291 n. 93.

from 'woman' to 'wife'. In this philological context we can locate the categorical imperative of lawful sexuality, which should be excited by unfeigned emotions. Both parts of the above-reflected conjunction do, in fact, require genuine emotions, in order to maintain an authentic tie creating life and its derivatives. Neither the ancient philosophers nor Jewish thinkers omitted to debate the value of emotions: 'Philo started a tradition, which is still found in his Jewish successor Maimonides in the twelfth century, of seeing moderation and eradication of emotion (metriopatheia, apatheia) as ideals for different people. In his view, Aaron and Abraham represent moderation, Moses and Isaac eradication, and Maimonides also adopts Moses as his model'.[58] Such emotions deserve the allegorical reader of *eros*/love[59] as a strengthener of character in the partnership of eternal union,[60] even in abandoning earthly/mundane bonds of wedding or parental relations.[61] These emotions convey an unambiguous intellectualizing-anagogical conception in the direction of transmitting knowledge of the ancestral laws to the posterity, since the husband is the main responsible for the ensuring of tradition[62] — holy for the continuation of Judaism as an ethnic phenomenon. By emphasizing on the image of unity,[63] Philo envisaged a double route to the reduction of virtue: (i) the soul's harmonization to heavenly love:

58. R. Sorabji, *Emotion and Peace of Mind* (*From Stoic Agitation to ChristianTemptation*). *The Gifford Lectures*, Oxford 2000, p. 385.

59. Y. Muffs, *Love and Joy: Law, Language and Religion in Ancient Israel*, Cambridge, MA 1992 discussed terms of love and joy in ancient Israel. A. Brenner, *The Intercourse of Knowledge: On Gendering Desire and 'Sexuality' in the Hebrew Bible* (Biblical Interpretation Series), Leiden 1997 wrote on gendering desire and sexuality in the Hebrew Bible. On *eros* among the Jews see D. Biale, *Eros and the Jews: From Biblical Israel to Contemporary America*, New York 1992. S. Goldhill, The Erotic Experience of Looking: Cultural Conflict and the Gaze in Empire Culture, in *The Sleep of Reason: Erotic Experience and Sexual Ethics in Ancient Greece and Rome*, M. C. Nussbaum and J. Sihvola (eds.), Chicago 2002, pp. 374–399 also wrote on philosophical and literary views about erotic gazing in the 2nd cent. A. D., among them Philo's *Opif.* 166. Furthermore, on words for love in Biblical Greek see J. Barr, Words for Love in Biblical Greek, in *The Glory of Christ in the New Testament: Studies in Christology. In Memory of George Bradford Caird*, L. D. Hurst and N. T. Wright (eds.), Oxford 1987, pp. 3–18.

60. Cf. *QG* 1. *17, [Suppl. I. 11].

61. Cf. *QG* 1. *29, [Suppl. I. 17-18]. See Philo *Legat.* (= Legatio ad Gaium 'De virtutibus prima pars, quod est' *On the Embassy to Gaius* '*The First Part of the Treatise On Virtues*') 72 on the importance of marriage ties in binding families socially together.

62. Cf. *Hypoth.* 7. 14 [IX. 433]. J. M. G. Barclay, *Jews in the Mediterranean Diaspora From Alexander to Trajan* (*323 BCE-117 CE*), Edinburgh 1996, pp. 412–413 wrote that '[...] we may note the importance of the socializing of children within the Jewish tradition, a task which ensured that Judaism would be continued as an ethnic phenomenon. The education of children was already emphasized in the Pentateuch (e.g. *Deut.* 6. 6-7, 20-25; 11. 19; 31. 10-13) and it features prominently among the concerns of later rabbinic Judaism [see O. L. Yarbrough, Parents and Children in the Jewish Family of Antiquity, in Cohen, The Jewish Family (quoted n. 18), Atlanta 1993, pp. 35–59 (here, pp. 41–49)]. [...] Philo indicates that synagogue instruction in the law [...] was passed on by Jewish men to their wives, children and slaves (*Hypoth.* 7. 14) and he also mentions, as a matter taken for granted, that Jews have been trained 'from a very early age' to honor the One God and to observe the laws e.g. *Legat.* 115, 195, 210; *Praem.* (= De praemiis et poenis, De exsecrationibus) 162; *Spec.* 1. 314; 2. 88; 4. 149-50; cf. *Mos.* 1. 31-33. Indeed he speaks of the laws and the 'ancestral customs' as 'engraved' on the soul of every young Jew (*Legat.* 210; *Spec.* 4. 14; cf. 2. 22)'.

63. The Philonic sense of unity embodies an undercurrent Platonic image, e.g. in the idea of intercourse; close to Philo's aspects of imagery seems to be another metaphor used for intercourse: 'the metaphor of fusion [...] justified in Aristophanes' speech in Plato's *Symposium* [192d-e] by the myth that each human being is only half of an original whole and passionately seeks reunion. The terms he uses, with their explicit reference to the smith's techniques of melting and fusing, seem to be unusual in this context; commoner expressions speak of 'mixing' or 'being together'' (S. C. Humphreys, *The Family, Women and Death. Comparative Studies*, 2nd ed., Ann Arbor 1993, p. xxvi).

'(*Gen*. xvi. 2). [...] But with the wife the union was one of the soul harmonized to heavenly love [= ἕνωσις ψυχῆς ἁρμοζομένης ἔρωτι θείῳ]. That is the literal meaning [= τὸ ῥητόν]. But as for the deeper meaning [= τὸ πρὸς διάνοιαν], he who has truthfully entrusted his thoughts [= τοὺς λογισμούς] to wisdom and justice and other virtues, when once he has received the thoughts of wisdom and has tasted marriage with her, remains her mate [= σύνοικος] and husband, even though he provides abundantly for the education of the school [= τῇ ἐγκυκλίᾳ παιδείᾳ]' (*QG* III. *20, [Suppl. I. 207])

and (ii) the outcasting of pleasure — a misguiding and thus venturesome force which falsifies the faculties of life — from the process of begetting true descendants:

'And certainly the first approaches of the male to the female have pleasure to guide (ξεναγὸν ἔχουσιν ἡδονήν) and conduct them, and it is through pleasure that begetting and the coming of life is brought about, and the offspring is naturally at home with nothing sooner than pleasure, delighting in it and feeling distress at pain its contrary' (*Opif*. 161 [I. 127-129]).[64]

He also stated that

'In fact we have a doctrine laid down most profitable to us all, that every craftsman whose work is to produce pleasure can produce no fruit of wisdom. He is neither male nor female, for he is incapable of either giving or receiving the seeds whence spring the growth that perishes not, and the base craft he practises is aimed against human life. He destroys the indestructible and quenches the unquenchable ever-abiding lamps of nature' (*Ebr*. 212 [III. 427-429]).

For the same reason, the circumcision is also coloured allegorically and symbolically:

'For since among the love-lures of pleasure the palm is held by the mating of man and woman, the legislators thought good to dock the organ which ministers to such intercourse, thus making circumcision the figure of excision of excessive and superfluous pleasure (αἰνιττομένοις περιτομὴν περιττῆς ἐκτομὴν καὶ πλεοναζούσης ἡδονῆς), not only of one pleasure but of all the other pleasures signified by one, and that the most imperious' (*Spec*. 1. 9 [VII. 105]).

In the discussion of kinship following accepted marriage, the proper emotional standard of pairing shapes sexual relationship and gender conditions within the family and towards constant distinction of cultural values; for instance, the distance between men's honour and women's shame results not only in a dual pattern, but in a hierarchical system in which the husband has the eminent position, by being closer to God: 'The emphasis upon the unity between husband and wife and (some sort of) equality between them, represents only one aspect of a description of relations between a couple. The relative value of that aspect must be measured against the background of more traditional and deeply

64. Cf. *Congr*. (= De vita contemplative '*On the Contemplative Life or Suppliants*') 12 [IV. 463-465] ('In the present discussion, we must eliminate all bodily unions or intercourse which has pleasure as its object. What is meant is a mating of mind with virtue. Mind desires to have children by virtue, and, if it cannot do so at once, is instructed to espouse virtue's handmaid, the lower instruction').

rooted cultural structures'.[65] It is probable that according to Philo divine law is procreationist and faithful members of the ancestral God should engage in strictly reproductive relations within marriage; otherwise they are at risk of being led by the apostasy-prone nature of their sexual appetite to transgress the sexual regulations outlined explicitly in the Pentateuch.[66] These sexual prohibitions[67] are transformed, by means of the allegorical process of Philonic interpretation, into philosophical concepts[68] resulting from the cultural consent to biological terms; when women bear children, they need the assistance of men to engender them and, however varying the patterns, both women and men contribute to the rearing of dependent children.[69] Allegory turns gender and relationships involved in the reproduction of human beings (marriage, filiation, coparenthood, heterosexual intercourse, pregnancy, parturition) in presuppositions of political identity and social education, since 'in ancient classifications of the body, civic status seem to be more important than biology'.[70] Besides, child-bearing is, consequently, spiritually formed[71] at God's image and cultivation of virtues:

> 'Man and woman, male and female of the human race, in the course of nature come together to hold intercourse for the procreation of children. But virtues whose offspring are so many and so perfect may not have to do with mortal man, yet if they receive not seed of generation from

65. H. Moxnes, What is Family? Problems in Constructing Early Christian Families, in *Constructing Early Christian Families. Family as Social Reality and Metaphor*, H. Moxnes (ed.), London 1997, pp. 13–41 (here, pp. 32–33).

66. See K. L. Gaca, Philo's principle of sexual conduct and their influence on Christian Platonist sexual principles, *Studia Philonica* 8, 1996, pp. 21–39. On Philo's views and detailed rulings deducing from the Sixth Commandment see also S. Treggiari, *Roman Marriage.* Iusti Coniuges *from the Time of Cicero to the Time of Ulpian*, Oxford 1991, pp. 214–215.

67. On Jewish family in Philo's contemporary Alexandria see also A. Reinhartz, Philo's *Exposition of the Law* and Social History: Methodological Considerations, in *Society of Biblical Literature 1993 Seminar Papers* 34, E. H. Lovering Jr. (ed.), Atlanta 1993b, pp. 6–21 (also on adultery and other family topics). On moral crimes and deviations and different forms of incontinence discussed by Philo see *Spec.* 3. 11-82 [VII. 481-527]. For Jewish and Christian slave owning (*Spec.* 2. 123; 2. 67-69; 3. 137-143) and *porneia* see C. Osiek, Female Slaves, *Porneia*, and the Limits of Obedience, in *Early Christian Families in Context. An Interdisciplinary Dialogue* (Religion, Marriage, and Family), D. L. Balch and C. Osiek (eds.), Grand Rapids—Michigan—Cambridge, UK 2003, pp. 264–270. On inceste see P. Moreau, *Incestus et prohibitae nuptiae. Conception romaine de l'inceste et histoire des prohibitions matrimoniales pour cause de parenté dns la Rome antique* (Collection d'Études Anciennes; 62, Série latine), Paris 2002, p. 120 commenting upon R. Fox, *Anthropologie de la parenté*, French transl., Paris 1972 [with S. Dreyfus, Vocabulaire et concepts des études de parenté, pp. 263–292], p. 59; cf. also *Spec.* 3. 14.

68. B. Decharneux, Interdits sexuels dans l'oeuvre de Philon d'Alexandrie dit « le Juif », in *Religion et tabou sexuel* (Université Libre de Bruxelles Institut d'Étude des Religions et de la Laïcité: Problèmes d'Histoires des Religions; 1), J. Marx (ed.), Brussels 1990, pp. 17–31.

69. H. W. Scheffer, Sexism and Naturalism in the Study of Kinship, in *Kinship and Family. An Anthropological Reader* (Blackwell Anthologies in Social and Cultural Anthropology; 4), R. Parkin and L. Stone (eds.), Oxford 2004, pp. 294–308 (here, p. 304).

70. Humphreys, *Family* (quoted n. 63), p. xxv.

71. V. E. F. Harrison, The Allegorization of Gender: Plato and Philo on Spiritual Childbearing, in *Asceticism*, V. L. Wimbush and R. Valantasis (eds.), New York—Oxford 1995, pp. 520–534, commented on spiritual childbearing, androcentrism and the soul; the soul exercises masculine virtues, but at the end, it functions as feminine by receiving seed, becoming pregnant and giving birth.

> another they will never of themselves conceive. Who then is he that sows in them the good seed save the Father of all, that is God unbegotten and begetter of all things?' (*Cher.* 43-44 [II. 35]),[72]

and it is accomplished only under divine permission and configuration.[73]

Marriage has been regarded as an adequate metaphorical image in the ancient pagan world before Jews and Christians; we can argue that from Catullus's epithalamium to a prospective bride and groom[74] and the poem for a recenty married couple written by the prolific liturgical poet (*payytan*) Eleazar Qallir (Qiliri)[75] until the epithalamium composed by the Christian bishop Paulinus of Nola around 405 A. D.,[76] we can read an analogy between this imminent fleshly marriage and the relationship between God and Israel, beyond simple spousal blessing and instruction, Christ's love for the Church, an institution that points toward the transcendent.[77] Satlow rightly pointed out the transition from Roman pagan marriage to the Second Temple Judaism: 'Marriage is a licit outlet for sexual desire; it provides heirs and succor for one's old age; and it furnishes citizens to the state, who both worship the gods and defend the homeland. In these functions, marriage is secular institution. Yet like all else in antiquity, Roman marriage could hardly be labeled 'secular'. Marriage was given by the gods, and anyone entering into one would be foolish not to acknowledge the gods' gift and to pray to them for the success of the marriage. In marriage, as in all else, mere humans asked the gods for their protection. Replace 'gods' with 'God' in the precedent paragraph and the same sentiment held true for the Jews during the Second Temple period. Contemporary Jewish writers in Greek shared these utterly conventional Greek and Roman views — and perhaps even rites — of marriage. Neither Philo nor Josephus date the origins of marriage to Adam and Eve: both seem to understand it as a purely human institution. At the same time, both assumed that spouses propitiated God when they married. Philo, for example, assumes that 'persons who take maidens in lawful matrimony ... have celebrated the bridal sacrifices and feasts' [Philo *Spec.* 3. 80]. Josephus argues that a man should not marry a prostitute because God will not accept her marital sacrifice

72. But cf. *Sacr.* (= De sacrificiis Abelis et Caini '*On the Birth of Abel and the Sacrifices Offered by Him and by His Brother Cain*') 101 [II. 169].

73. Cf. *QG* III. *18, [Suppl. I. 203] and *Migr.* 69 [IV. 171].

74. Catullus 61. 61-75.

75. E. Fleisher, *Hebrew Liturgical Poetry in the Middle Ages*, Jerusalem 1975, pp. 154–64 (the original text of the above mentioned poem) and M. L. Satlow, Slipping Towards Sacrament: Jews, Christians and Marriage, in *Jewish Culture and Society under the Christian Roman Empire* (Interdisciplinary Studies in Ancient Culture and Religion 3), R. Kalmin & S. Schwartz (eds.), Leuven 2003, pp. 65–89 (here, pp. 65–66).

76. D. G. Hunter, *Marriage in the Early Church* (Sources of Early Christian Thought), Minneapolis 1992, pp. 128–40 (the Latin text of Paulinus' epithalamium can be found at *CSEL* 30: 238-245) and Satlow, Slipping Towards Sacrament (quoted n. 75), pp. 66–67.

77. On marriage as Christian and Jewish metaphor see Satlow, Slipping Towards Sacrament (quoted n. 75), pp. 66–68, 72–74, 84–88. See also J. E. Grubbs, *Law and Family in Late Antiquity. The Emperor Constantine's Marriage Legislation*, Oxford 1995, for the study of the Emperor's Constantine legislation on marriage. L. Larsson Lovén & A. Strömberg (eds.), *Ancient Marriage in Myth and Reality*, Cambridge Scholars Publishing 2010 insisted on the idea of marriage in antiquity. On the Medieval idea of marriage see C. Brooke, *The Medieval Idea of Marriage*, Oxford 1989 and K. Cooper, *The Virgin and the Bride: Idealized Womanhood in Late Antiquity*, Cambridge, MA 1996.

[Josephus, *AJ* 4. 245]. Jews, both authors suggest, supplicated their God for protection when they married, and did so in ways that appear to resemble Roman wedding rituals'.[78] Discoveries in the region of the Dead Sea,[79] despite their scanty proportion, are useful to our purpose; according to these data, a Qumran wisdom text relates marriage to *Genesis* ii. 24,[80] with the motif of the help-meet; like the *Ben Sira* 36. 29-30, the Qumran text insists on the authority of the husband over the wife. Baumgarten studying celibacy and marriage wrote that the pairing of male and female is further indicated by the word *re'iyyatov* ('his companion') and the ideal relationship between husband and wife is alluded to in the Ritual of Marriage;[81] this fragmentary, but significant text, shows that women of virtue, rather than being denigrated, were honoured for their longevity within the Qumran community.[82] Moreover, there is an apparent allegorical tradition in Biblical thought, e.g. in *Wisdom of Solomon* and the *Song of Songs* attributed to Solomon,[83] and we can also observe it in the first treatise in the history of Judaism that is devoted completely to the mystical understanding of marriage, the '*Iggereth Hakodesh*', a work originating in the 13th cent. Spanish Judaism and attributed to Moses Nachmanides; both Philo and this treatise relate intercourse to a higher type of knowledge, i.e. metaphysical knowledge.[84] In Philo's opinion it is mind that marries virtue:

78. Satlow, Slipping Towards Sacrament (quoted n. 75), pp. 68–69. For the most complete description of the Jewish marriage from the Second Temple period see *Tobit* 8. 5-8 (a passage based on *Genesis* ii-iii). See also M. L. Satlow, The Metaphor of Marriage in Early Judaism, in *Families and Family Relations as Represented in Early Judaisms and Christianities: Texts and Fictions* (*Studies in Theology and Religion* 2), A. Brenner and J. W. van Henten (eds.), Leiden 2000, pp. 3–32 (here, pp. 8–12).

79. J. C. Collins, Family life, in *Encyclopedia of the Dead Sea Scrolls*, vol. 1, L. H. Schiffman and J. C. Vanderkam (eds.), Oxford 2000, pp. 287–290 (here, p. 288).

80. 4Q416 2.iii.21-iv.1.

81. 4Q502.

82. J. M. Baumgarten, Celibacy, in *Encyclopedia of the Dead Sea Scrolls*, vol. 1, pp. 122–125 (here, p. 124) and J. A. Fitzmyer, Marriage and Divorce, in *Encyclopedia of the Dead Sea Scrolls*, pp. 511–515 (here, p. 512).

83. 'Jewish Greek writers, for example, compare the relationship between an individual and Wisdom in erotic terms. Solomon's desire in *Wisdom of Solomon* (xviii. 2-16) to make the personified Wisdom his mistress, with its manifest erotic overtones, goes far beyond the portrayal of Lady Wisdom in *Proverbs* viii. One of Philo's favorite metaphors is the description of the 'marriage' of one's soul to wisdom (*sophia*) or reason (*logos*) [See Philo *Post*. 78 (making *sophia* a spouse); *Her*. 5-9 (acquiring culture is preliminary to the fullmarriage of the acquisition of virtue), 41, 59 (soul is the legitimate wife); *Fug*. 52 (God begats wisdom, to whom Jacob goes for a bride); *Somn*. (= De somniis I, II) 1. 198-200 ('marriage' of different kinds of thoughts, gives good wise 'offspring', with a similar image at *Abr*. 100-101, where the union is between virtue and thought); *Somn*. 2. 234 (wisdom is spouse); *Spec*. 2. 30 (mind 'wedded' to *logos*); *Contempl*. 68 (women remained virgins to 'wed' *sophia*). Cf. R. A. Horsley, Spiritual Marriage with Sophia, *Vigiliae Christianae* 33, 1979, pp. 30–54]. The idea in both *Wisdom* and Philo relies more on Greek classical and philosophical precedents than on the biblical metaphor of covenant as marriage' (Satlow, *Jewish Marriage* (quoted n. 57), pp. 44, 287 n. 13).

84. M. Harris, Marriage as Metaphysics: a Study of the '*Iggereth Hakodesh*', *Hebrew Union College Annual* 33, 1962, pp. 197–220 (here, pp. 209–217). On the Jewish use of marital metaphors and myths in antiquity see Satlow, *Jewish Marriage* (cited in n. 57), pp. 42–67, whereby it is stated that the relationship between God and Israel was compared to human marriage, and that provided a Jewish idiom for the expression of the 'Stoic' idea that marriage is rooted in nature and part of the fabric of the cosmos; on conclusions drawn upon Jewish marriage in Roman Palestine *ibidem*, pp. 262–264.

'Now in a marriage where the union is brought about by pleasure, the partnership is between body and body, but in the marriage made by wisdom it is between thoughts which seek purification and perfect virtues. Now the two kinds of marriage are directly opposed to each other. For in the bodily marriage the male sows the seed and the female receives it; on the other hand in the marriage within the soul, though virtue seemingly ranks as wife, her natural function is to sow good counsels and excellent words and to inculcate tenets truly profitable to life, while thought, though held to take the place of the husband, receives the holy and divine sowings. Perhaps however the statement above is a mistake due to the deceptiveness of the nouns, since in the actual words employed νοῦς has the masculine, and ἀρετή the feminine form' (*Abr.* 100-101 [VI. 53-55]).

Although his text stresses Jewish penalties, much of it also reflects Greek philosophical doctrine and is aimed at a wider audience.[85] In deducing detailed rulings from the Sixth Commandment, he preaches against 'adultery, the greatest of crimes (μοιχείας, τοῦ μεγίστου τῶν ἀδικημάτων)' (*Ios.* 44 [VI. 165]),[86] which affects the stability and cohesion of *oîkos*.

Philo's allegorical reduction of *oîkos* includes another fundamental condition, the parental relationship, i.e. the ties between parents and children. It concerns a major idiom in terms of which Philo redefines his philosophical preoccupations, a mandatory obligation which transcends family allegiance, familial corollaries, a spiritual kinship in the case of Therapeutai,[87] and various patterns of sociability alternative or complementary to that of the household and those based on marital and kinship ties.[88] The parental relationship is erected upon the indissoluble bound of kinship between parents and between parents and child — in order to eliminate hatred and moral decline[89]—, the inherent superiority of the parent to the child and the hierarchical order of male to female. Among these, four particular aspects are to be raised: 1) The hierarchical structure of the parent-child relationship, which is an expression of the dualistic view of human society. 2) Parents' responsibilities towards their children, which consists of bringing children into the world, nurturing and instructing-educating them. 3) According to the Fifth Commandment,[90] responsibilities of children towards their parents are expressed in obedience, fear, courtesy and care for them in old age; honour towards parents is assimilated to the indebtedness to the Creator.[91] 4) Family affection.[92] The allegorical transformation of the relationship is directed to the utmost nature of God's providence on the world's behalf:

85. Treggiari, *Roman Marriage* (quoted n. 66), pp. 214–215.

86. On the destructive consequences of this God-detested sin cf. *ibid.*, 56 [VI. 171] and also on the words supposed to have been thought by Joseph for avoiding succumbing to temptation: *ibid.*, 45 [VI. 165] ('by debasing (νοθεύων) his bed, his household and his kin'); on its consequences against children and citizens cf. especially *Decal.* (= De Decalogo '*The Decalogue*') 121-131, 168 [VII. 69-73, 91]). Also on adultery cf. *Spec.* 4. 203 [VIII. 135] and on adultery and harlotry exploiting the body's beauty see also *Virt.* 4. 36-40, 112-113 [VIII. 185-189, 231] — the latter towards women prisoners.

87. See *Contempl.* 18 and 72.

88. Barton, The Relativisation of Family (quoted n. 31), pp. 82–88.

89. Cf. *Fug.* 3 [V. 11-13] and *Ebr.* 70 [III. 351-353] ('Therefore we shall kill our 'brother' — not a man, but the soul's brother, the body; that is, we shall dissever the passion-loving and mortal element from the virtue-loving and divine (τοῦ φιλαρέτου καὶ θείου τὸ φιλοπαθὲς καὶ θνητὸν διαζεύξομεν').

90. On the command of *Exod.* xx. 12 'Honour thy father and thy mother, that it may be well with thee' equating to honouring the mind as father of our complex being, and sense as mother, so that we ourselves shall receive good treatment at their hands, see *Det.* 52-54 [II. 237-239].

'For that the Maker should care for the thing made is required by the laws and ordinances of Nature, and it is in accordance with these that parents take thought beforehand for children' (*Opif.* 172 [I. 137]).

In Philo's mind child-bearing is to be allegorically meant in terms of a father, the right reason, and a mother, education[93] or wisdom:[94]

'Now 'father and mother' is a phrase which can bear different meanings. For instance we should rightly say and without further question that the Architect who made this universe was at the same time the father of what was thus born, whilst its mother was the knowledge possessed by its Maker. With His knowledge God had union, not as men have it, and begat created being. And knowledge, having received the divine seed, when her travail was consummated bore the only beloved son who is apprehended by the senses, the world which we see. This in the pages of one of the inspired company, wisdom is represented as speaking of herself after this manner: 'God pobtained me first of all his works and founded me before the ages' (*Prov.* = De providentia I, II '*On Providence*' viii. 22). True, for it was necessary that all that came to the birth of creation should be younger than the mother and nurse of the All' (*Ebr.* 30-31 [III. 333-335]).[95]

Philo remarks that parents by their nature stand on the border-line between the mortal and the immortal side of existence.[96] This double presence of biological kinship and the assimilation of generation to the Generator of All[97] entails a basic contradistinction between the man and to the father, 'for He that openeth the womb is husband, but father of the children is he to whom she is said to bear them' (*Leg.* 3. 181 [I. 425]).[98] Furthermore, the notion of education requires an imperative duty towards ancestral tradition, expressed in a significant passage from his treatise *On the Posterity of Cain and his Exile*:

91. Cf. *Leg.* 3. 10 [I. 307], emphasizing on our inability to recompense or praise as He deserves Him who brought the universe out of non-existence; *Mut.* (= De mutatione nominum '*About Those whose names are Changed and Why They Have Their Manes Changed*') 40 [V. 163]); *Mos.* 2. 44 [VI. 165]; *Mos.* 2. 207 [VI. 551-553] and *Spec.* 2. 226-227 [VII. 447-449].

92. A. Reinhartz, Parents and Children: a Philonic Perspective, in Cohen, The Jewish Family (quoted n. 18), Atlanta 1993, pp. 61–88 discussed the relationship between children and their parents as described in Philo's exposition of the law.

93. On the kind of education cf. *Migr.* 116 [IV. 199] and *Legat.* 5 [X. 5].

94. Cf. *Fug.* 109 [V. 69] on the allegation that the High Priest is not a man but a Divine Word.

95. Cf. *Ebr.* 33-34 [III. 335-337] ('I suggest, then, that the father is reason, masculine, perfect, right reason and the mother the lower learning of the schools, with its regular course or round of instruction. These two stand to us in the relation of parents to children, and it is good and profitable to obey them. Now right reason, the father, bids us follow in the steps of nature and pursue truth in her naked and undisguised form. Education, the mother, bids us give ear to rules laid down by human ordinance, rules which have been made in different cities and countries and nations by those who first embraced the apparent in preference to the true').

96. Cf. *Decal.* 51 [VII. 31-33]; 107 [VII. 61]; 117-120 [VII. 67-69] and, concerning fear towards parents, *Spec.* 2. 237-241 [VII. 455-459].

97. Cf. *Ebr.* 42 [III. 341].

98. On the children borne by Leah and Rachel.

> 'If, then, I inquire of the father who begat me and brought me up, or of those of the same age with him but my elders, in what way God distributed or dispersed or settled the nations, will they answer me with steady certainty, as though they had followed that process of distribution step by step? Assuredly not. They will say 'We too when we were young made diligent inquiry from our parents and persons still older than they, and we ascertained nothing definite; for they had nothing to teach us, seeing that they in their time had applied to others, whom they regarded as knowing, to enlighten their ignorance'. Probably, then, the lawgiver gives the title of father of our soul to right reason, and of elders to the associates and friends of right reason. These were the first to fix the boundaries of virtue. To the school of these it is advisable to go, to learn by their teaching the essential matters. The essential matters are these. When God divided and partitioned off the nations of the soul, separating those of one common speech from those of another tongue, and causing them to dwell apart; when He dispersed and put away from Himself the children of earth, whom the lawgiver calls 'sons of Adam', then did He fix the boundaries of the offspring of virtue corresponding to the number of the angels' (*Post.* 90-91 [II. 377-379]).[99]

From the obligations of children to parents[100] we pass over to the symbols and allegorical terms of kinship. Applying a Platonic remainder of kinship between man's rational soul and the heavenly beings,[101] Philo represents the kinship or family relation that exists between man and the divine, in his concept of *συγγένεια* in the most general sense:[102] man being akin to God because he has been endowed with the gift of the rational faculty[103] in that he possesses διάνοια.[104] The kinship of family relationship *sub specie Dei* is also depicted in terms allegorical favoured:

> '(*Ex.* xxiv. 8b). Why does he say further, 'Behold the blood of the covenant which the Lord commanded you concerning all these words'? (He does so) because the blood is a symbol [= σύμβολον or σημεῖον] of family kinship [= συγγενικῆς οἰκειότητος]. And the form of kinship is twofold: one is that among men, which has its origin in ancestors, while that among souls has its origin in wisdom. Now he did not mention the kinship of ancestor and offspring, because it is also common to irrational animals, but from the other (kind of kinship) as from a root grew wisdom' (*QE* 2. 36, [Suppl. II. 77-78]).

99. G. E. Sterling, The Bond of Humanity: Friendship in Philo of Alexandria, in *Greco-Roman Perspectives on Friendship* (Resources for Biblical Study/Society of Biblical Literature; 34), J. T. Fitzgerald (ed.), Atlanta 1997, pp. 203–223 wrote on the relevant term of friendship in Philo.

100. Let us enumerate some other passages involving the relationship between parents and child are: (i) *Mut.* 206 [V. 249]; (ii) *Spec.* 1. 137-138 [VII. 177-179]; (iii) on the heirs of parents, sons or daughters, the distribution of paternal property, etc. *Spec.* 2. 124-138 [VII. 381-389]); (iv) *Spec.* 2. 254 [VII. 467]; (v) *Aet.* 58 [IX. 225]; (vi) *Prov.* 2. 3-5 [IX. 461].

101. *Timaeus* 47b 8; cf. 35a, 41d.

102. On which see D. T. Runia, *Philo of Alexandria and the* Timaeus *of Plato* (Philosophia Antiqua; 44), Leiden 1986, p. 341. Other texts which stress the kinship between man and God or his Logos are *Spec.* 4. 14; *Praem.* 163; *QG* 2. 45 and 62; *QE* 2. 29.

103. Cf. *Opif.* 77.

104. Cf. *Opif.* 146.

The magnificence of the acknowledgement of Heavenly Father's presence[105] and the resemblance such a relationship bears of mortal ties cannot but be interpreted transcendentally; this interpretation transfigures everyday advantages with metaphoric sense:

> 'For if you should be willing to search more deeply and not confine yourself to the mere surface, you will clearly understand that to trust in God alone and join no other with Him is no easy matter, by reason of our kinship with our yokefellow, mortality, which works upon us to keep our trust placed in riches and repute and office and friends and health and strength and many other things' (*Her*. 92 [IV. 329])

and

> 'For we should have one tie of affinity, one accepted sign of goodwill, namely the willingness to serve God and that our every word and deed promotes the cause of piety. But as for these kinships, as we call them, which have come down from our ancestors and are based on blood-relationship, or those derived from intermarriage or other similar causes, let them all be cast aside if they do not seek earnestly the same goal, namely, the honour of God, which is the indissoluble bond of all the affection which makes us one (πάσης ἑνωτικῆς εὐνοίας ἄλυτος δεσμός ἐστιν). For those who are so minded will receive in exchange kinships of greater dignity and sanctity' (*Spec*. 1. 317 [VII. 283]).

A further comment on that could set forth an additional symbolization: of the high-priest as a symbol of common kinship and relationship of his whole nation ('καὶ τοῦ σύμπαντος ἔθνους συγγενὴς καὶ ἀγχιστεὺς κοινὸς ὁ ἀρχιερεύς ἐστι').[106] Then, only the Levites and those who devoted themselves to the real common Father can leave their mortal kin and depart from mundane kinship.[107] Since 'This is a most noble definition of deathless life, to be possessed by a love of God and a friendship for God with which flesh and body have no concern (ἔρωτι καὶ φιλίᾳ θεοῦ ἀσάρκῳ καὶ ἀσωμάτῳ κατεσχῆσθαι)' (*Fug*. 58 [V. 41]), it remains to conceive the essential allegory of *oîkos* in the Philonic corpus. To this we must develop the cores from the four following passages:

(i)

> 'And speech is our 'father's house (οἶκος)', 'father's' because Mind is our father, sowing in each of the parts of the body the faculties that issue from itself, and assigning to them their workings, being in control and charge of them all; house — because mind has speech for its house or living-room, secluded from the rest of the homestead. It is Mind's living-place, just as the hearthside is man's. It is there that Mind displays in orderly form itself and all the conceptions to which it gives birth, treating it as a man treats a house. And marvel not at Moses having given to speech the title of Mind's house in man; for indeed he says that God, the Mind of the universe, has for His house His own Word' (*Migr*. 3-4 [IV. 133-135]).

105. Cf. *Congr*. 177 [IV. 549-551].
106. *Spec*. 3. 131 [VII. 559]; cf. *Spec*. 4. 159 [VIII. 107-109].
107. Cf. *Fug*. 88-89 [V. 57-59] and *Contempl*. 18 [IX. 125].

(ii)

'So highly does Moses extol the lover of virtue (ἀποσεμνύνει τὸν φιλάρετον) that when he gives his genealogy he does not, as he usually does in other cases, make a list of his grandfathers, great-grandfathers and ancestors in the male anmd female line, but of certain virtues, and this is little less than a direct assertion that a sage has no house or kinsfolk or country save virtues and virtuous actions' (*Abr.* 31 [VI. 19-21]).

(iii)

'But houses and families of many members have theirs [sc. *rewards*] also. For instance the twelve tribes into which the nation was divided had the same number of chieftains connected not only by membership of the same house and family but by a still more real affinity (γνησιωτέρας οἰκειότητος), for they were brothers with the same father (ὁμοπάτριοι), and their grandfather and great-grandfather as well as their father were the founders of the nation (ἀρχηγέται τοῦ ἔθνους)' (*Virt.* 57 [VIII. 347]).

and (iv)

'Am I not a wanderer from my country, an outcast from my kinsfolk, an alien from my father's house? Do not all men call me excommunicate, exile, desolate, disfranchised? But Thou, Master, art my country, my kinsfolk, my paternal hearth (ἡ πατρῴα ἑστία) [...]' (*Her.* 26-27 [IV. 297]).[108]

Reduced as kinsfolk, family, father, nation or destination, God himself or His creative and omnipotent speech (*logos*) should be the epitome of the Biblical creation, i.e. the *oîkos* for created flesh and blood:

'Didst thou not call upon Me as thy house, thy father and the husband of thy virginity?' (*Jer.* iii. 4). Thus he implies clearly that God is a house, the incorporeal dwelling-place of incorporeal ideas, that He is the father of all things, for He begat them, and the husband of Wisdom, dropping the seed of happiness for the race of mortals (σπέρμα τῷ θνητῷ γένει καταβαλλόμενος) into good and virgin soil. For it is meet that God should hold converse with the truly virgin nature, that which is undefiled and free from impure touch; but it is the opposite with us. For the union of human beings that is made for the procreation of children, turns virgins into women. But when God begins to consort with the soul, He makes what before was a woman into a virgin again, for He takes away the degenerate and emasculate passions (τὰς ἀγεννεῖς καὶ ἀνάνδρους ἐπιθυμίας) which unmanned it and plants instead the native growth of unpolluted virtues (τὰς αὐθιγενεῖς καὶ ἀκηράτους ἀρετάς)' (*Cher.* 49-50 [II. 39]).

To gain such an achievement, 'for thou shalt find the house of wisdom a calm and fair haven, which will welcome thee kindly as thou comest to thy moorings in it' (*Fug.* 50 [V. 37]), and to dwell allegorically, 'when the soul has entered into her own house [...] the house then is the soul' (*Leg.* 3. 238-239 [I. 463]), one is expected to render the rhetorical question 'shall

108. Cf. *Her.* 186 [IV. 377] on the other half of didrachmon left to the slavish kind.

the child of my household (ὁ οἰκογενής μου) be my heir, he who is the offspring of the blood-life?' (*Her.* 65 [IV. 315]) by offering a conscious negative answer, for it is incorporeal natures that inherit intellectual things, and by renouncing bodily measures:

> 'Do you not see that Abraham, when he had 'forsaken land and kindred and his father's house', i.e. the body, sense, and speech (*Gen.* xii. 1), begins to meet with the powers of Him that is? For when he has gone out from all his house, the Law says that 'God appeared to him' (*Gen.* xii. 7), showing that He clearly manifests Himself to him that escapes from things mortal and mounts up into a soul free from the encumbrance of this body of ours' (*Det.* 159 [II. 307-309]).

It is by consideration of inner qualities that we should live in a masculine space aligned to the Lord:

> 'The female offspring of the soul is vice and passion, that emasculating influence which affects us in each of our pursuits. The male offspring is health of soul and virtue, by which we are stimulated and strengthened. Of these the men's quarters must be dedicated wholly to God, the women's quarters must be set to our own account, and therefore we have the command 'all that openeth the womb, the males to the Lord'' (*Sacr.* 103 [II. 171]).[109]

Admission to succession and acquisition of inheritance seems more an allegorical matter than that of rabbinical inheritance law amplified and expanded upon Biblical provisions, such as *Nm.* 27, 8-11; 36, 6-7; *Dt.* 21, 16-17, which formulated a linear parentela system favouring male descendants and granting the testator's offspring.[110] Then, legitimate sons and daughters are those inheriting the *oîkos* of God and it is allegiance to God that transcends family ties and legitimates their subordination. We feel that Philo's conception of the city as a social and cultural phenomenon may be inferred from a large number of scattered remarks throughout his works. Runia remarks that Philo's ambivalence towards the city is related to his dual ideological background (Jewish and Greek) and that it anticipates developments in later antiquity; Philo contrasts the ideal and the reality of the city and of the good and the bad city, and frequently juxtaposes city life and solitude.[111] However, the allegorical reduction of *oîkos* enables the bridging of the gap between the natural creation and the realm of universal nature amidst the unique nature (φύσις) of humanity.[112] *Oîkos*, then, is metaphorically elevated above any other typical θεσμός φύσεως, just like each one of the Ten Commandments is called.[113] Philologically speaking, we have reached the literary scope of

109. Cf. *Det.* 28 [II. 221]. Cf. also the passage, whereby Philo discuss Onan's spilling seed on the ground, and thus going beyond all bounds in love of self and love of pleasure in *Post.* 181 [II. 435-437]; and *Migr.* 217 [IV. 259], *Deus* 17 [III. 19] and 19 [III. 19-21].

110. Sh. Shilo, Succession, in *Encyclopaedia Judaica*, vol. 15, Jerusalem 1972, pp. 475–481.

111. D. T. Runia, The idea and the reality of the city in the thought of Philo of Alexandria, *JHI* 61, 2000, pp. 361–379.

112. J. W. Martens, *One God, One Law: Philo of Alexandria on the Mosaic and Greco-Roman Law* (Ancient Mediterranean and Medieval Texts and Contexts/Studies in Philo of Alexandria and Mediterranean Antiquity; 2), Boston—Leiden 2003, pp. 67–81.

113. Cf. *Decal.* 32; *Her.* 168-172; *Congr.* 120. On the meaning and usage of θεσμός and νόμος in Philo see J. W. Martens, *ibid.*, pp. 131–149.

transcendental expression in Graeco-Judaean literature. If we transcend further, it is bound that we will touch upon the early and medieval Christian metaphors for the sanctity of family towards the Kingdom of Heaven.[114] We may conclude that in Philonic philosophy *oîkos* is a principal allegiance: the imprint of divine dwelling among men. In other words, he upgraded transcendentally the entity of family. This philosophical perception awaits allegorical application, in order to highlight the preference of the mental instead of the physical, the love of God instead of idolatry and other mundane bounds, and of divine priorities latent in the Pentateuch instead of literal readings easy to grasp.

114. For example, S. P. Ahearne-Kroll, 'Who are my mother and my brothers?': Family Relations and Family Language in the Gospel of Mark, *JR* 81, 2001, pp. 1–25 worked upon an analysis of the Gospel of Mark in comparison with Epictetus' *Discourses* and Philo's *Contempl.*, showing how the Evangelist relativized family relations and used 'family' as a metaphor for new life within the strategies of goodness found in contemporary philosophical movements.

CHRISTIAN INFLUENCE
OVER PARTITIVE INHERITANCE

FOR THE POOR, THE FAMILY, THE FRIENDS: GREGORY OF NAZIANZUS' TESTAMENT IN THE CONTEXT OF EARLY CHRISTIAN LITERATURE[1]

Fotis Vasileiou

In the spring of 381, the archbishop of Constantinople, Gregory of Nazianzus, president of the ongoing Church Council, withdrew from the conference meetings and retired at home, citing illness.[2] His retreat occurred while the Council was at a critical point; the conflicts between the bishops about the Antiochene schism[3] and the struggle to reach a commonly accepted formula for the Homoousion were raging in front of the curtains and behind them, causing Theodosius I's discontent. Gregory of Nazianzus, the emperor's choice for the seat of Constantinople, although the leading theologian of his times, failed to emerge as a leader of the Nicaeans, especially after the sudden death of Meletios of Antioch. His inflexibility did not facilitate finding a common ground between the opposing views, impelling Theodosius to intervene, while Gregory was still bedridden. Bishops from Egypt and Illyricum were called in Constantinople, in order to provide a renewed impetus to the Council.[4]

It was not the first time that Gregory flew away from a difficult situation. Since his youth, he he had often escaped whenever he felt threatened or when he had to fight in order to reach a goal — it appears that even *Origen's Philokalia* was composed in collaboration with Basil of

1. The research leading to this essay has received funding from the European Union's Seventh Framework Programme (FP7/2007-2013 — MSCA–COFUND) under grant agreement n° 245743 — Post-doctoral programme Braudel-IFER-FMSH, in collaboration with the Laboratoire d'excellence Religions et Sociétés dans le Monde Méditerranéen (*RESMED*). I thank V. Déroche and B. Caseau for their comments. I am also grateful to G. McDowell and A. Kostoulas for reading my paper. All the mistakes are my responsibility.

2. For the Council of Constantinople see C. D. Davis, *The First Seven Ecumenical Councils, Their History and Theology*, Wilmington 1987, pp. 81–133 and R. P. C. Hanson, *The Search for the Christian Doctrine of God. The Arian Controversy 318-381 AD*, Edinburgh 1988, pp. 791–823. On Gregory's role in it, see J. McGuckin, *St. Gregory of Nazianzus: An intellectual Biography*, Crestwood 2001, pp. 350–369.

3. On the Meletian Schism in the Antiochene Church, see Hanson, *Christian Doctrine* (quoted n. 2), pp. 382–384.

4. N. McLynn sees a more political Theodosius, who was and less committed to the Nicaean cause, 'Moments of Truth: Gregory of Nazianzus and Theodosius I', in Sc. McGill, Cr. Sogno, E. Watts (eds.), *From Tetrarchs to the Theodosians. Later Roman History and Culture, 284-450 CE*, Cambridge 2010, pp. 215–239.

Inheritance, Law and Religions in the Ancient and Mediaeval Worlds, ed. by B. Caseau and S. R. Huebner (Centre de recherche d'Histoire et Civilisation de Byzance, Monographies 45), Paris 2014.

Caesarea during one of these flights.[5] This time though things were getting serious for him, the illness that excused him from the Synod was not a diplomatic one. He decided he had to draw up his testament.[6]

What a dramatic scene that would have been! On May 31,[7] the ailing bishop, surrounded by a chorus of seven witnesses[8] (six bishops and one priest),[9] dictated his διαθήκη — most probably to Theodosius, the notarios who was mentioned in the will.[10] It is possible that other members of his band of stalwarts were attending, including close associates like Theophilos, a former slave who was manumitted by Gregory, and his brother Eupraxios, who would be freed after his death according to his will,[11] or the deacon Evagrios, who was rewarded for his loyalty with 'small signs of friendship.'[12]

Gregory dictated his last will and testament to the scribe and he signed after reading it.[13] Then, his nephew, Amphilochios, bishop of Iconium, read and signed it and subsequently all the other witnesses did the same. After Gregory's death, this document was deposited at the Church of Nazianzus, where it was subsequently copied by a certain Ioannis, reader and notarios of this Church;[14] this copy was transcribed multiple times and thus survived to our days.

It is a compelling document. Gregory's is not just the earliest complete testament, but it survived in a unique way too. As Joëlle Beaucamp points out, 'le mode de transmission du texte (...) le distingue de la majorité des testaments de l'époque. La plupart d'entre eux sont connus par les papyrus (...) Mais pour l'Antiquité tardive, le testament de Grégoire de

5. Origen's *Philocalia* was composed at Basil's monastic retreat at Annisa, where Gregory fled after his ordination as a priest by his father in the winter of 361-362. M. Harl, editor of *Philocalia*, argues that Gregory did not participate in the compilation, *Philocalie d'Origène*, *Sources chrétiennes* (= *SC*) 302, Paris 1983, pp. 1–20. McGuckin, pp. 81–84, provides a convincing answer to her arguments, and Ph. Rousseau supports the traditional view, *Basil of Caesarea*, Berkeley-Los Angeles-Oxford 1994, pp. 56–61. N. McLynn, on the other hand, while not finding this story persuasive, does not agree with Harl either, What was the 'Philocalia of Origen', *Meddelanden från Collegium Patristicum Lundense* 19, 2004, pp. 32–43.

6. J. Beaucamp (ed. & french trans.), Le testament de Grégoire de Nazianze, *Fontes Minores* X, L. Burgmann ed., Frankfort 1998, pp. 1–100. English tr. B. E. Daley, Gregory of Nazianzus, London—New York 2006, pp. 184–189.

7. According to Beaucamp, Le testament (quoted n. 6), pp. 77–80, three of the manuscripts mention that the testament was composed one day prior to the calends of January; another one places it one day before the calends of July, while the majority does not specify the month. But in January, Gregory was in Cappadocia and it would be extremely difficult for all these bishops to visit him in the harsh wintertime just to witness his testament. Moreover, he was not bishop of Constantinople on June 30. So, the solution proposed by Baronius appears to be the most appropriate and convincing: a scribe falsely wrote January instead of June.

8. On the number of the witnesses, see C. Sánchez-Moreno Ellart's paper in this volume.

9. His cousin Amphilochius of Iconium, Optimos of Cilician Antioch, Theodosius of Ida, Theodoulos of Apamea, Hilarios of Isauria, Themistios of Adrianople and the priest Chledonios.

10. Testament, l. 60-62. Elaphios, the other notarios mentioned in the will (89-92), must have assisted him in the past.

11. Testament, l. 57-60.

12. Testament, l. 82-84. Most probably this was Evagrios Pontikos, who was Gregory's student and was also ordained deacon by him. On his life and ideas, see A. Guillamumont, *Un Philosophe au Désert. Évagre le Pontique*, Paris 2004; also J. S. Konstantinovsky, *Evagrius Ponticus: The making of a Gnostic*, Farnham 2009.

13. Testament, l. 98-100

14. Testament, l. 122-125.

Nazianze est le seul texte grec de ce genre qui soit conservé, dans son intégralité, par l'intermédiaire de manuscrits.'[15] Yet it has not attracted the attention it deserves, partly because of Gregory's intriguing personality and the power of his pen: scholars are focusing on his orations, poems and epistles, texts that are juicier and more affluent in ideas and arguments, descriptions of relationships and situations, emotions and memories, than the comparatively dry, legal text of his will. But this text, unlike his autobiographical poems and his masterful funeral or theological orations, was not intended to be read or heard by his congregation or the audiences across the empire, and subsequently the literary flair of the testator was not needed. It was a private document addressed to his immediate family and a few close friends and associates, and except for the legal jargon, he spoke freely, directly, without his rhetorical prowess. Here is the best glimpse at Gregory of Nazianzus in his everyday life that we can ever have.

Gregory's last will and testament is largely a written validation of adjustments that he had already made and a confirmation of wishes that he had expressed orally earlier to his family and friends. 'I have already openly revealed my intentions,' wrote Gregory after the declaration of his name, sound mental health, and the validity of his last will and before the statement that his property would be allocated for the relief of the poor of the Church of Nazianzus. Similar expressions were later on used for two important arrangements: the horses and the sheep attached to the estate of Arianzos,[16] which was converted into a monastic establishment, should be given to his heir, Gregory the deacon;[17] in addition, Roussiane, a devoted virgin who was his relative, should continue to receive her annuity.[18] He also confirmed that the purchase of estate of Kanotala, which had been bought from his cousin Amphilochios of Iconium, had been revoked, citing his files for the deed as evidence.[19] Consequently, two of the arrangements that Gregory had made earlier, besides the transition of the main part of his fortune to the Church of Nazianzus for the poor, were aiming to support the ascetic commitment of people who belonged to his inner family and spiritual circle.

In addition, the Nazianzen ordered that the slaves who had been manumitted by his late parents or himself should remain free and their *peculia* not be jeopardized. Kyle Harper notes that 'the confirmation was legally superfluous, but not imprudent given the social vulnerability of freedmen.'[20] It also offers some insights into Gregory's emotional and mental state, I may add. He appears to have worried that orally expressed wishes and orders, no matter how clearly they were formulated, were insufficient. He may have feared that without a written confirmation, his desires would be circumvented, if not by his heirs, then by his nephews and nieces who had been disinherited or others who coveted his property. The Holy Trinity was set as his ultimate guarantor — any of his heirs who did not follow his instructions, and anyone who might contest his will for any reason, would have to face divine justice.

15. Beaucamp, Le testament (quoted n. 6), pp. 1–2.

16. On the location of Arianzos, see Fr. Hild & M. Restle (eds.), *Kappadokien, Tabula Imperii Byzantini* 2, Wien 1981, pp. 150–151.

17. Testament, l. 36-43.

18. Testament, l. 44-46.

19. Testament, l. 78-81.

20. K. Harper, *Slavery in the Late Roman World AD 275-425*, Cambridge 2011, pp. 480–482.

This lack of trust could be traced to a bitter experience that he considered as the beginning of all his misfortunes.[21] The sudden death of Caesarius, his beloved brother, in 368, shocked Gregory and his parents. While he was on his deathbed, the diseased ordered his wealth to be spent on the poor.[22] This became a convenient pretext for his servants to sell up and parcel out his belongings without taking into account either his liabilities to third parties or his family's wishes. Gregory and his parents might have become annoyed by such audacity, but this was not the main reason for their distress. Things became complicated, perhaps even dangerous, when creditors appeared demanding the money they claimed to have lent to Caesarius. It appears that initially Gregory satisfied some of them, but that did not relieve their pressure; the exact opposite must have happened. So, he sought for help from friends and fellow Cappadocians, who held important positions in the imperial bureaucracy.[23] Basil of Caesarea was also involved and sent letters on behalf of the family.[24] Finally, exasperated by the circumstances, Gregory donated the remains of his brother's fortune to the imperial treasury. However, his Testament reveals that a part of that property finally came to his possession.[25]

This experience was too much for him. At the very time when he felt the need to mourn his beloved brother in privacy, he had to parley with creditors and beg imperial officials.[26] Meanwhile, because of this deplorable state of affairs, the good name of his late brother was jeopardized, his family was in danger of losing its prestige and even faced financial ruin, and everyone's peace of mind, not least his own, was disturbed. Moreover, he realized that in times of weakness, one cannot rely on anybody; at best, friends, colleagues, and relatives disappear, or, at worst, they try to take advantage of the situation. In his eyes, Caesarius was abandoned alone, naked, without any friends or supporters to protect him from the pack of dogs who preyed upon his money and estate. He was left alone to stand for him. 'When an oak tree falls, who does not gather wood?' he wonders in an account of these events.[27]

Those emotions were subsequently reinforced, when he felt that Basil of Caesarea, his closest friend, betrayed him.[28] Basil proved himself 'a second father to him, but one far more oppressive', when he cunningly elected Gregory bishop of Sassima.[29] Thereafter, his trust to people was never restored again, and when he felt that death was approaching, he had to seal

21. Gregory recounted the story in his autobiographical poem Εἰς τὸν ἑαυτοῦ βίον (*De vita sua*), l. 365-374; C. Jungck (ed. & trans. german), Heidelberg 1974; C. White (ed. & trans.), Cambridge 1996. On the impact of this event on him when he was composing his Testament, see R. Van Dam, Self-representation in the Will of Gregory of Nazianzus, *Journal of Theological Studies* 46, 1995, pp. 126–127.

22. For a reconstruction of the events following the death of Caesarius, see McGuckin, *Gregory of Nazianzus* (quoted n. 2), pp. 155–165. On Caesarius' life and relationship with Gregory; also R. Van Dam, *Families and Friends in Late Roman Cappadocia*, Philadelphia 2003, pp. 60–65.

23. Gregory of Nazianzus, Ep. 29.

24. Basil of Caesarea, Ep. 32-33.

25. Testament, l. 68-70.

26. His great sadness is expressed in a letter to Philagrios, Ep. 30.

27. *De vita sua*, l. 370-374.

28. For the Sassima incident, see McGuckin, *Gregory of Nazianzus* (quoted n. 2), pp. 168–227; Rousseau, *Basil of Caesarea* (quoted n. 5), pp. 134–139; J. Bernardi, *Saint Grégoire de Nazianze: Le Théologian et son temps* (*330-390*), Paris 1995, pp. 138–142.

29. *De vita sua*, l. 391-392.

his verbal commands with a written testament and set God as his guarantor. Everything had to be crystal-clear because Gregory was alone. He was the last of his line, he was not married, he had no children and his parents and siblings had died long ago. His closest relatives were his nephews and grandnephews, but some of them had been disinherited in a disgraceful way, and his named heir was a manumitted ex-slave. In case of complications, such as an unjust claim or a challenge, who would have the moral right and the power to defend his wishes? So, he had to armor his last will against any possible besieger.

Nourishing the poor

In the Testament, Gregory confirmed the distribution of all his property, with the exception of certain gifts and legacies, to the Church of Nazianzus 'for the service of the poor who are under the care of the aforesaid Church.'[30] This donation was mentioned in one of his poems written a few months after the death of his father.[31] He also confirmed that the caretaking would be supervised by the three administrators he had already selected — he called them πτωχοτρόφους, 'feeders and nourishers of the poor' — Marcellos the deacon and monk, Gregory the deacon and monk, and the monk Eustathios. Gregory the deacon and monk was also named as the sole heir of all his movable and immovable property. His main task was to transfer everything to the Church of Nazianzus.[32]

There is no doubt that Gregory financed a type of institution for the poor in his native town. Still, we do not know when this service started, what portion of his property was disposed for this task or how the poor were relieved, i.e., if only a 'soup kitchen' was operating or if other actions were included, like patient care.[33] The term that Gregory used to describe the three administrators, πτωχοτρόφοι, might reflect the influence of Basil of Caesarea, who used to call his 'new city',[34] the famous 'Basileias', a Πτωχοτροφεῖον.[35] Beaucamp notes that in the *Chronicon Paschale* and in a Novel by Justinian the same term, πτωχοτρόφος, is used to denote the director of a hospital.[36] Nevertheless, in the absence of relevant information from other sources it is safer to assume that nothing so ambitious existed in Nazianzus. The help Gregory offered may have covered the basic needs of the beneficiaries in a much smaller scale than Basil's institution.

Almost all our knowledge about Gregory's heir derives from this document. He had been a slave in the family of the Nazianzen who was manumitted and ordained monk and deacon by his former master. In addition to his responsibilities as executor of his Will, Gregory left to

30. Testament, l. 11-12.
31. Beaucamp, Le testament (quoted n. 6), pp. 48–49.
32. Testament, l. 19-31.
33. On food and bread distribution by the Church, see B. Caseau, Autour de l'autel: le contrôle des donateurs et des donations alimentaires, *Donations et Donateurs dans le monde byzantin*, J.-M. Spieser & E. Yota (eds.), Actes du colloque international de l'Université de Fribourg (13-15 mars 2008), ed. by, Paris, 2012, pp. 47–73.
34. J. Bernardi, Gregory of Nazianzus, *Oration* 43, 63, *SC* 384, Paris 1992.
35. On Basileias, see Rousseau, *Basil of Caesarea* (quoted n. 5), pp. 139–142; S. R. Holman, *The Hungry Are Dying: Beggars and Bishops in Roman Cappadocia*, New York 2001, pp. 74–76.
36. Beaucamp, Le testament (quoted n. 6), pp. 49–50.

his heir a gift of 50 gold coins as a reward for his loyal service — this was the largest amount he bequeathed to anyone. Gregory the deacon and monk along with the monk Eustathios were given the estate at Arianzos with the breeding mares and the sheep attached to it.[37]

Gregory of Nazianzus instituted heir someone who was not a member of his biological family but belonged to his spiritual one. Christianity gave priority to spiritual ties over traditional blood relations; monasteries were in a way a new type of family, based on spiritual bonds and constructed around a spiritual father. Nazianzen often secluded himself seeking contemplation and peace; one can assume that Gregory and Eustathios followed him in these excursions not just as his personal servants, but as his disciples and fellow ascetics. They inherited the estate of Arianzos, which had already been transformed into an ascetic retreat, so as to continue what Gregory had started. In addition, the fact that the heir shared the same name with him and his late father underlined a sense of continuity and stability — Nazianzen never called Gregory the monk and deacon 'a son', but nevertheless he would be the third Gregory to own this particular property.

We should not assume that naming a freedman his heir or bequeathing his properties to the Church was due to the lack of direct descendants and relatives. He had family members He was very close to his niece, Alypiana (in the Testament she was called θυγατέρα, daughter[38]), her husband, Nikoboulos (whom Gregory referred to as 'son' on many occasions[39]) and their children (Nikoboulos the Younger was his pupil and the editor of his epistolary corpus). Moreover, it was not unusual for a freedman to be named heir or coheir by his ex-master.[40] They could be trusted to obey a dying man's last wishes. Also, masters shared mutual feelings of trust and affection with their slaves and *liberti*. In the case of the two Gregories, it seems possible that their common preoccupation with spiritual matters only strengthened their relationship. As will be shown, his decision was in accordance with family tradition and the Christian mentality of his times, and, above all, with his own ideas. Therefore, he should not be considered so much as an innovator in this than someone who followed a pattern and adjusted it to his taste.

Gregory expounded his views on wealth and how a Christian should care for the poor in one of his most popular homilies, 'On the Love of the Poor', delivered in 366 or 367 to promote fund-raising for Basil's of Caesarea *Ptochotropheion*.[41] In a high-leveled theological oration, Gregory places, as Susan Holman puts it, 'the poor at the very centre of all that Church meant to him: the identity of the Christ.'[42] For him, the poor, just like the rich, were created in the

37. Testament, l. 36-43.

38. Testament l. 63.

39. i.e. Ep. 13, 21, 126 etc.

40. E. Champlin, *Final Judgments. Duty and Emotion in Roman Wills, 200 BC — AD 250*, Berkeley 1991, pp. 131–133.

41. Gregory of Nazianzus, *Oration* 14, *PG* 35, c. 855-910. Daley, *Gregory of Nazianzus* (quoted n. 6), pp. 76–97. An extended analysis of Gregory's Oration in McGuckin, *Gregory of Nazianzus* (quoted n. 2), pp. 145–155 and Chr. A. Beeley, *Gregory of Nazianzus on the Trinity and the Knowledge of God: In your Light We Shall See Light*, New York 2008, pp. 254–258. Also, B. J. Matz, Deciphering a Recipe for Biblical Preaching in Oration 14, in Chr. A. Beeley (ed.), *Re-Reading Gregory of Nazianzus. Essays on History, Theology and Culture*, Washington 2012, pp. 45–66.

42. Holman, *The Hungry Are Dying* (quoted n. 35), p. 143.

image of God, and poor and rich are united after baptism in the body of Christ. Their weakness is not due to God's will — He provided equally for everybody — but due to human injustice, which was the womb that gave birth to poverty and wealth, freedom and slavery, the 'common disease.'[43] Christians should imitate God and help their fellow humans who are in a difficult position, as they are a reminder to everyone of the common human condition: before Christ everybody is destitute and in need of His benefaction. However, Gregory did not just ask his audience to be more generous, because he did not consider wealth as a private property to which an individual had an absolute right. He thought of it rather as a God-given trust and considered that its owner is just a temporary steward (οἰκονόμος). The wealthy had the duty to restore, as much as was possible to them, the original equality human beings had before the Fall.[44]

It seems that his family had adopted such an attitude towards the destitute. Caesarius left his property to the poor, while Gorgonia, their older sister, considered that 'her possessions belonged to all the needy, in the same way that each possessed what was his own.'[45] In the funeral oration he pronounced for his father, he said that his parents were competing to outdo each other in almsgiving.[46] Gregory the Elder considered himself as a steward (οἰκονόμος) of foreign property rather than an owner, while his mother was heard many times saying that she wished she could sell herself and her own children as slaves in order to raise money to relieve the impoverished.[47]

Gregory's close friend, Basil of Caesarea, and his family, also excelled in almsgiving; he disposed of his property to help his famine-stricken congregation.[48] Nazianzen praised his parents, Basil the elder and Emmelia, for their πτωχοτροφίαις.[49] Macrina, their first born daughter who devoted herself to virginity, helped and gave shelter in her convent to many starving women during the famine of 368. Under the guidance of his mother, Naucratios, the third child of the family, practiced a kind of asceticism, a key point of which was the caretaking of some poor old man.[50]

There is a striking resemblance between the image of the ideal wealthy Christian the Nazianzen described in the oration 'On the Love of the Poor' and the image he constructed for his father. He even uses the same word, οἰκονόμος, to describe them. One might think that Gregory was exaggerating; after all he was delivering praise for the late bishop. Even if this assumption is correct, this does not mean that the description was fictitious. After all, this oration was delivered before his fellow citizens, the congregation of Nazianzus, people who lived for decades under the bishopric of his father. They knew Gregory the Elder and Nona well, and Gregory was aware that there was no point in attempting to fabricate their memories. He was nevertheless trying to interpret Gregory the Elder's and Nonna's well-known

43. Or. 14. 25, c. 892.

44. On Gregory's perspective on wealth, see B. Coulie, *Les richesses dans l'œuvre de Saint Grégoire de Nazianze*, Louvain 1985.

45. M.-A. Calvet-Sebasti (ed.), Gregory of Nazianzus, *Or.* 8, *SC* 405, 12, Paris 1995. Daley, *Gregory of Nazianzus* (quoted n. 6) pp. 63–75.

46. Or. 18, *PG* 35, c. 1009.

47. Or. 18, c. 1008-1009.

48. Gregory of Nyssa, *On Basil the great*, *PG* 46, c. 805D-808A.

49. J. Bernardi (ed.), Gregory of Nazianzus, *Oration* 43, *SC* 384, 9, Paris 1992.

50. P. Maraval (ed.), Gregory of Nyssa, *Life of Macrina*, *SC* 178, 8-9, Paris 1971.

attitude in accordance with his own views; he transformed his parents into a screen onto which he projected his own ideas. Their charitable activities were reconstructed in such a way as to become a Christian paradigm. In addition, we should not forget that caring for the poor was not just a responsibility for late antique bishops but a foundation of their authority.[51] Gregory the Elder was the head of the Church of Nazianzus for decades and he would have certainly developed some kind of protective net for the needy of the area. When Gregory said that the Church of Nazianzus flourished under his father,[52] he was certainly referring to the ministration of the poor too. Besides, Gregory himself assisted his father and he would have contributed to shaping his actions in favor of the poor.

Gregory constructed the same image for himself too. In his Testament, he appeared more as an οἰκονόμος than an owner. The image he constructed for himself is however different from that of his father, as he appears accountable not to God or his fellow humans who were poverty stricken, but to his parents. Thus, he asked Alypiana's forgiveness for not bequeathing his property to her 'since he had already promised everything to the poor, or, rather, since he was following the promise of his blessed parents, to disregard their intent would be, in his view, neither holy nor trustworthy.'[53] In other words, Gregory was addressing his niece not as a wealthy landowner, patron of the destitute, but as someone who submitted his will to others; he was not making the decisions, he was just obeying like a goodson or a pious ascetic — obedience was considered a great ascetic virtue.[54]

Gregory of Nazianzus expected the same behavior from his heir too. Gregory the deacon and monk had to act as a steward of the property and distribute it to the Church of Nazianzus for the sake of poor — Nazianzen was very explicit on this: he should not forget the fear of God and whom his property should serve. After all, he had 'named him heir for this purpose.'[55]

The Hagiographic Horizon

Abba Poemen (*BHG* 1553z–1555g) got so puzzled when a certain brother asked him what he should do with an inheritance he had received, that he took three days to think it over.[56] When they met again Poemen answered:

'What shall I say to you, brother? If I say, give it to the Church, they will become lunches (ἀριστοποιοῦσι); if I tell you, give it to your relatives, you will not have any reward; if I tell you, give it to the poor, you will be carefree (ἀμεριμνεῖς). Go and do as you like, it is not up to me.'[57]

51. P. Brown, *Poverty and Leadership in Later Roman Empire*, Hanover and London 2002, p. 45 ff.

52. Gregory of Nazianzus, Or. 18, *PG* 35, c. 1004.

53. Testament, l. 64-68.

54. On the value of obedience, see Gr. Gould, *The Desert Fathers on Monastic Community*, Oxford 1993, pp. 52–58.

55. Testament l. 28-30.

56. On Abba Poemen, see St. Ramphos, Πελεκᾶνοι Ἐρημικοί. Ξενάγησι στὸ Γεροντικό, Athens 1994, pp. 389–404. W. Harmless, *Desert Christians. An Introduction to the Literature of Early Monasticism*, Oxford – New York 2004, pp. 206–211, as well as his Remembering Poemen Remembering: The Desert Fathers and the Spirituality of Memory, *Church History* 69.3, 2000, pp. 483–518.

57. J.-C. Guy (ed.), *Apophthegmata partum* (*systematic collection*), 10. 82, 66, *SC* 474, Paris 2003.

This brief story perfectly encapsulates the management options a monk had for his property, as well as their consequences. Ἀκτημοσύνη, the will of owning no personal property, was paramount for an anchorite, and the brother could not keep the fortune without negating his ascetic status.[58] Since he accepted the inheritance,[59] he had to find the best way to abolish it, so he rushed to Poemen for advice. But he did not get a definite answer. Poemen described the three options and let him free to choose for himself. He could donate his property to a bishopric, but he should know that this would not be of much help for the needy. Lunches were helpful, but did not really make a difference in someone's life. What is more, Poemen appears to imply that such a poor management could scandalize the donator and make him lose his ἀμεριμνησία. Only if he distributed his fortune himself to the poor or to his family, he would be carefree, but the latter choice deprived him of any reward.

Poemen was an Egyptian anchorite who detested theological debates and found pleasure in discussing the passions of the soul.[60] His attitude toward the Church's charitable activities could be associated to a certain tension between monastics and the church officials.[61] Gregory, on the other hand, was a bishop, a scholar, a celebrated rhetor and a brilliant theologian. Nonetheless, when composing his last Will, he faced more or less the same options as the questioner. Despite the image that we have of him today, Gregory always considered himself as leading an ascetic life (which he referred to as 'philosophical').[62] In his Testament we can even detect a similar distrust of Church activities: he may have dedicated his property to the Church of Nazianzus, but he did not name her as an heir — despite the fact that Constantine's legislation gave him this right. His immediate heir was Gregory the deacon and monk, who had to transmit this property to the Church, and after that the management of the bequest was to be entrusted to the three πτωχοτρόφοι; it was up to them to decide who should benefit and how. In other words, the bishop of Nazianzus did not have much to do with Gregory's money! It seems that the Nazianzen took this decision primarily because the bishopric of his native town was vacant after the death of his father and his own resignation. When he was composing his will, he did not know who might occupy this position, and, meanwhile, the alarming news of the Apollinaristic activities in the region may have arrived

58. On the value of ἀκτημοσύνη, see D. BRAKKE, Care for the Poor, Fear of Poverty and Love of Money. Evagrius Ponticus on the Monk's Economic Vulnerability, in S. R. HOLMAN (ed.), *Wealth and Poverty in the Early Church and Society*, Grand Rapids 2008, pp. 76–87. Strict compliance with this rule was required only for the anchorites and the holy men and women, as papyrological and archaeological evidence have shown that monks and monasteries owned significant assets, D. CANER, Wealth, Stewardship, and Charitable 'Blessings' in Early Byzantine Monasticism, in *Wealth and Poverty*, pp. 221–242; R. S. BAGNALL, *Monks and Property*: Rhetoric, Law and Patronage in the Apophthegmata Patrum and the Papyri, *Greek, Roman, and Byzantine Studies* 42, 2001, pp. 7–24; J. E. GOEHRING, *Ascetics, Society and the Desert. Studies in Early Egyptian Monasticism*, Harrisburg 1999, pp. 39–52; E. WIPSZYCKA, *Études sur le Christianisme dans l'Égypte de l'antiquité tardive*, Rome 1996, pp. 337–362.

59. In a similar situation, Arsenios (VI. 2) did not accept the inheritance. To the *magistrianos*, who begged him not to tear the testament up, he argued that he had died before the testator.

60. *Apophthegmata partum*, 10. 54, 42-49.

61. On the relations between monks, anchorites and the Church, see M. KAPLAN, *Pouvoirs*(?), *église et saintеté. Essais sur la société Byzantine*, Paris 2011, pp. 149–166; WIPSZYCKA, *Études* (quoted n. 58), pp. 281–336.

62. On Gregory's views on asceticism, see MCGUCKIN, *Gregory of Nazianzus* (quoted n. 2), pp. 87–99.

in Constantinople.[63] Being suspicious and wary, he did everything in his power to control the stewardship of his donation. He was not prepared to allow those ignorant people, who made his life miserable at the Council, decide who would manage his patrimony. In 383, Gregory's cousin Eulalios, with whom he had an excellent relationship, was elected bishop of Nazianzus. Eulalios worked with Gregory on the editing of his Homilies and, as McGuckin reasonably supposes, he must have been cooperating with the three πτωχοτρόφοι and the monk Eustathios to relieve the poor of the area.[64] One wonders if in the intervening years the Nazianzen modified his will, or if he composed another one, so as to include Eulalios or his grand nephew Nikoboulos the Younger.

The *Lausiac History* (*BHG* 1435–1438) recounts a dilemma similar to that of the unnamed monk in the Poemen's saying.[65] When the father of two brothers, Paesios and Elias, died and left them his property, they were considering their alternatives:

'What mode of life shall we adopt, brother? If we adopt the merchant career, which our father followed, then we shall have to die and leave our labours to others. Perhaps we may even succumb to dangers from robbers or on the sea. Come, then, let us embrace monastic life, that we may make a profitable use of our father's riches and not lose our souls.'

In this story, Palladios was trying to answer the question from the point of view of two young laymen. Paesios and Elias had essentially two alternatives: to follow their father's path or not. A worldly career besides commerce was not considered as an option. Their main objection, as it appears in this rationale, was to live in safety and live for themselves. They appear not to be interested in following the paternal footsteps or any family tradition. This detachment is rather impressive, as they are presented to feel absolutely free to choose what they considered as best for themselves. They do not seem restricted or confined in any way; they do not seem obliged to answer to anyone. So they ended up adopting the ascetic lifestyle — a choice that sounds awkward to us, but in late antiquity offered certain advantages to young men and women.[66] The two brothers did not agree with each other in what kind of ascetic life they should adopt and ended up following different paths; the first distributed his part of the paternal inheritance in charity and followed the anchoritic lifestyle, while the other founded a monastery and fed everyone who might pass by. The story ends after the death of the two brothers, with Abba Pambo assuring some young monks that they both were equal before the eyes of God, despite their different mode of *ascesis*, as he dreamt of them in Paradise. It is definitely a story that could inspire the restless youth of late antiquity, who wanted to experience a different life than the one they were being prepared for.

Anthony (*BHG* 140–141), according to his *Life*, also gave his parental property to the poor. In an attempt to imitate the example of the ancient Christians, as was described in the *Acts of Apostles*, and to follow Jesus' command on being perfect, Anthony donated his estate to people

63. In a letter sent to Bosporios in 382, Gregory claimed that he installed Chledonios as a supervisor of the seat of Nazianzus because of the Apollinaristic assaults, Ep. 138.

64. McGuckin, *Gregory of Nazianzus* (quoted n. 2), p. 385.

65. G. J. M. Bartelink (ed.), Palladios of Helenopolis, *The Lausiac History* 14. 1-3, Milan 1974; W. K. L. Clarke (trans.), *The Lausiac History of Palladius*, London 1918.

66. On the promotion of the emancipation of the young people in late antique Christian literature, see F. Vasileiou, *Ποιμένας ἤ Τύραννος. Ὁ πατέρας στὴν χριστιανικὴ λογοτεχνία τῆς Ὕστερης Ἀρχαιότητας*, Ἀθήνα 2013, p. 139 ff.

from his village 'so that they would not bother him or his sister about anything. What remained was sold and the money was given to the poor; he only kept little for his sister.'[67] Later he gave away everything, trusted his sister to some known and faithful virgins, and he left for the desert.

The way he handled his property reveals that Anthony, like Poemen, thought that ἀμεριμνησία was vital for one's spiritual progress. It appears though that getting rid of property was, apparently, not enough for someone to be freed from anxiety; he had to do things in a certain way, so as not to provoke his fellow villagers. Thus, the poor were only given the proceeds from the sale of his liquid assets, while his lands were bequeathed to his neighbors. In that way, he bought off their acceptance to his decisions and avoided disputes.

We can find many analogous cases in the hagiographic literature of late antiquity, since holy men and women followed the example of Anthony and their hagiographers that of Athanasios. Thus the disposal of the inheritance became a *topos* in hagiography, that reveals the importance of voluntary poverty and the expectation that holy men and women would spend in charities any money or assets that came into their possession.[68] Synklitiki (*BHG* 1694–1694a), for instance, after the death of their parents, distributed her patrimony to the poor, and along with her blind sister, left her parental home to settle outside the city of Alexandria in a tomb that belonged to a relative.[69] When he inherited his father, Publius, a good-looking young man of senatorial background, withdrew to an estate about 5.5 km away from his hometown, Zevgma.[70] There he built a small shelter for himself and gave 'home, property, herds, clothing, vessels of silver and bronze and everything else that went with them' to the poor. Soon he became quite famous; many visited him and imitators came later to live under his guidance. Publius' case differs from that of Anthony's or Synklitiki's. Despite Theodoret's initial phrasing, the following passages reveal that Publius actually kept a part of his property that allowed him to have what he considered as essential to his survival and to create a safe zone: a hut and the estate around it, that later evolved to a monastery. He certainly was not living in absolute poverty. On the other hand, he strongly rejected everything he considered as lavish or unnecessary: 'he continually inspected and examined the cells to prevent their containing something stored away in excess of need. They say that he even carried scales with which he examined closely the weight of the bread...'

Faretrios, a Constantinopolitan who also belonged to the senatorial class, followed more or less the same path. He waited for his father to die before donating all his fortune to the monastery of Akoimetoi and become a monk there along with his sons.[71] The abbot of the Akoimetoi monastery, Marcellos, , chose not to take his part of the inheritance, when his own father died and leaving the entire estate to his brother, who was a layman. This might not have ensured any divine reward, but it surely kept him away from family quarrels. Later, when his brother also passed away, he became the only heir of the family fortune, but again he did

67. G. J. M. Bartelink (ed.), Athanasios of Alexandria, *Life of Anthony* 2, *SC* 400, Paris 1994.

68. On the development of this motive in byzantine hagiography, see Th. Pratsch, *Der Hagiographische Topos*, Berlin—New York 2005, pp. 124–125.

69. A. G. Ampelagra (ed.), *Life of Syncletica*, Thessaloniki 2002.

70. P. Cavinet & A. Leroy-Molinghen (eds.), Theodoret of Cyrus, *Philotheos Historia*, *SC* 234, 5, Paris 1977; R. M. Price (trans.), *Theodoret of Cyrus, A History of the Monks of Syria*, Kalamazoo 1985.

71. G. Dargon (ed.), *Life of Marcellos Akoemetos, La vie ancienne de s. Marcel l'Acémète*, *Analecta Bollandiana* 86, 1968, pp. 296–297.

not keep it or bestow it to the monastery he led. Instead, he donated to other monasteries and churches and used a part to feed the needy. This created tension between himself and the other monks, but Marcellos told them that it would be better for them all if they kept their hopes to Jesus. Hypatios (*BHG* 760), founder and abbot of the Rouphinianai monastery in Constantinople, had difficulty accepting inheritances. In his *Life*, we read that a *scholastikos* bequeathed him some *nomismata* and clothing, which Hypatios distributed to other monasteries and to the poor.[72] On a different occasion, he resigned from inheriting from Aetios, a wealthy man who suffered from mental problems (φρενοβλαβής ὤν) and had taken refuge in his monastery. He granted the inheritance to Ourbicios Cubicularius, who had brought Aetios there in the first place.[73] Ourbicios used part of this money to build an oratory and convents at Rouphinianai.[74] In contrast, Savas (*BHG* 1608–1610), after the death of his mother, bestowed the inheritance to his monastery and used it to expand it.[75] Porphyry of Gaza (1570–1572) sent his friend, Marcos, to his native town, Thessaloniki, in order to divide the inheritance with his siblings. When Marcos brought his part back to Jerusalem, Porphyry gave everything to the needy and to monasteries, especially to Egyptian monasteries, which were considered poor.[76] According to his *Life*, he soon gave everything away, and, immersed in poverty, he became σκυτοτόμος, leather artisan, to earn his living.

Similarly to Porphyry, after the death of his parents, Abraham the recluse (*BHG* 5) asked a dear friend to distribute his inheritance to the poor and to the orphans, so that it might not become an obstacle to his prayers — he was already living as a recluse.[77] 'And as he did so, he stayed carefree', as his hagiographer states. But, as in Publius' story, not everything was given away; Abraham's friend wisely kept some for a future need. When Abraham became priest in a village of pagans and asked his trustee to send him back what was left, this proved enough to build a church.[78] Abraham, according to his *Life*, handled the inheritance of his young niece in the same way. The seven-year-old girl brought to live with him after the death of her father, and Abraham ordered her property to be given to the poor, so that she might not to be confined in the care of worldly matters.[79] In this way, he determined the future of Maria, limiting it to the four walls of a cell. Thirteen years later, when she opened the door and exited the convent, she was almost inescapably led to prostitution. As she did not have any other income or a way to make a living for herself in the world, she ended up in a πανδοχεῖον.

Maria is not a unique case. Late antique Christian literature provides us with other similar stories of young females who ended up in prostitution because they had spent every penny they inherited in benevolences. In *Apophthegmata Patrum* we read of someone who, after the death of her parents, transformed her house to a hostel for the monks, using all her resources to host and nourish them.[80] Ioannes Moschos also recounted a similar story of a young Al-

72. G. J. M. Bartelink (ed.), Kallinikos, Life of Hypatios, *Sources Chrétiennes* 177, Paris 1971, 34, p. 220.
73. *Life of Hypatios*, 12. 4-13, pp. 116–120.
74. On Ourbicios' see *PLRE* II, Urbicious 1.
75. E. Schwartz (ed.), Kyrillos of Scythopolis, *Life of Savas*, 25, Leipzig 1939.
76. H. Grégoire & M. A. Kugener (eds.), Mark Deacon, *Life of Porphyry of Gaza*, Paris 1930, 6-10.
77. *Life of Abraham and his niece Maria*, *AASS* Mar. II, pp. 932–937.
78. *Life of Abraham*, p. 933
79. *Life of Abraham*, p. 994
80. *Apophtegmata Patrum* 13, 17.

exandrian woman who spent her entire inheritance to save a desperate bankrupt from committing suicide, and at the end became a prostitute.[81] Maria was finally saved by her uncle, the recluse, who for this occasion not only left his cell, but he disguised himself as a soldier.[82] John the Little was sent by the other desert fathers to the hostess and managed to make her repent and renounce the world, while the third woman was saved by angels, since no man could see her inner purity. These stories, as they came to us, are Christianized — or rather monasticized — adaptations of the motif of the damsel in distress, where a young, beautiful, naïve heroine suffers patiently, waiting for a strong male to save her.

But the majority of the female characters in this literature were not weak or fragile. On the contrary, in late antique Christian literature we meet many women with strong wills who were able to achieve their goals. In the *Life of Synklitiki*, for example, the heroine became an anchorite despite her parents' wish that she marry. And, of course, hagiography provided the example of Thekla (*BHG* 1717–1718),[83] who became a follower of St. Paul, and Macrina (*BHG* 1012), the sister of Basil of Caesarea and Gregory of Nyssa, who transformed her household into an ascetic retreat with the help of her mother.[84] Not surprisingly, women were behind the two most impressive donations of the era. Following the death of her father, Melania the Younger (*BHG* 1241–1242), convinced her husband, Valerius Pinianus to liquidate her enormous property and donate it to bishoprics, ascetics, and monasteries across the Empire.[85] At the end, she still had enough to build a monastery and a nunnery in Jerusalem. Olympias (*BHG* 1374), an aristocratic young woman from Constantinople, who was orphaned and widowed at a very young age, had her property put in trust by Theodosius, after refusing to marry a relative of his.[86] When she regained control, she donated huge amounts to the church of Constantinople and in support of John Chrysostom. Both Melania the Younger and Olympias voluntarily chose to live in poverty, but this poverty, as Wendy Mayer points out, 'is not a reduction to the point of neediness (as is often the case for the economic poor), but rather a removal of all that is superfluous.'[87] This down-to-earth attitude was very similar to Gregory's, who funded the philanthropic activities of the Church of Nazianzus with the part of his property he did not use.

Addressing to Family and Friends

Gregory of Nazianzus was undoubtedly devoted to his family and especially to his parents. For as long as they were alive, he put his own wishes and dreams on hold in order to fulfill their expectations; it is telling that, despite wishing to live in a contemplative solitude away from church affairs, he became assistant bishop to his father and remained in the seat

81. *PG* 87.3, c. 3097-3100.
82. *Life of Abraham*, p. 936.
83. G. Dragon (ed. & trans. french), *Life and Miracles of Thekla*, *SH* 62, Brussels 1978.
84. Gregory of Nyssa, *Life of Macrina*.
85. D. Gorce (ed.), Gerontios, *Life of Melania the Younger*, *SC* 90, Paris 1962.
86. A.-M. Malingrey (ed.), Life of Olympias, *SC* 13 bis, Paris 1968, pp. 406–449.
87. W. Mayer, Poverty and Generosity toward the Poor in the Time of John Chrysostom, in *Wealth and Poverty* (quoted n. 5 8), pp. 140–158.

of Nazianzus until his parents' death.[88] In addition, his family members often appeared in his literary work or inspired it: he wrote funeral orations for his father and two siblings, other orations on behalf of his father or addressing him, and many of his poems referred to them. There he presented himself as the obedient and lawful son who is sacrificed by his father: he was Isaac to his father's Abraham and to his mother's Sarah.[89] Even in the autobiographical poems he wrote as an old man, he used the same imagery when he was referring to his family.

In his Testament he mentions his late parents twice: when he ordered that the slaves that they had emancipated should be respected, along with their legacies, and later on when he apologized to Alypiana for not leaving her a part of his property. This is our well-known Gregory, who obeyed parental orders despite his own desires. But in this same text Gregory also used a different tone. He spoke as someone in authority, as a *paterfamilias* exercising his *patria potestas* over the younger members. In the same sentence where he apologizes to his sweetest daughter Alypiana, he adds: '...I take little notice of the other two (nieces), Eugenia and Nonna, whose way of life is reprehensible.'[90]

Eugenia and Nonna, unknown from other sources, were the other two daughters of Alypius and Gregory's sister, Gorgonia.[91] We do not know how they had provoked their uncle, but it is obvious that the formal disavowal was of great importance to him, since he broke his old habit not to refer to anyone not worth mentioning in his writings. To underline his rejection, Gregory distributed to Alypiana's descendants what was left from Caesarius' fortune, 'silk or linen or woolen garments, or ponies.'[92] Caesarius was definitely a successful and wealthy man and these paraphernalia could be quite valuable, but their primary value was symbolic. By leaving the remains of his beloved brother's inheritance to Alypiana and her family, the Nazianzen completely separated them from Eugenia and Nonna. Alypiana was not shamefully disinherited; she had nothing in common with her sisters. Gregory was obliged to omit his niece, but he still found a way to honor her.

This forceful rejection of his two nieces is a surprise, as it comes from a man who detested controversies throughout his life, and tried to avoid conflicts and confrontations. Of course, the testament would be read after his death, but it is reasonable to assume that the disavowal of Eugenia and Nonna, as other arrangements, was already known. His stance is explained by two reasons. First, this reference is largely due to his effort to safeguard his property from any future assault. This is confirmed by Gregory's statement just a few lines below: 'I wish that neither she (Alypiana) nor her sisters should contest any of these dispositions, either against my heir or against the Church (of Nazianzus).'[93] Given the good relations he had with Alypiana and her family, this seems to be mainly addressed to Eugenia and Nonna. But we should not underestimate his great discontent for their behavior, which seems to be his other motive. The next paragraph supports this view.

88. On Gregory's relationship with his father, VASILEIOU, *Ποιμένας ή Τύραννος* (quoted n. 66), pp. 288–328.

89. On the metaphors Gregory used to describe his parents and himself, see MCGUCKIN, *Gregory of Nazianzus* (quoted n. 2), pp. 13–22.

90. Testament l. 63-64.

91. See *PLRE* I, Stemma 17.

92. Testament, l. 69-70.

93. Testament, l. 70-73.

'Let it be known that my in-law Meletios is in unlawful possession of the property in Apenzinsus, which used to be part of Euphemios's property. On this subject I have already written to Euphemios many times, accusing him of cowardice if he does not reclaim what is his. Now I call on all — rulers and subjects — to recognize that Euphemios is being treated unjustly; it is necessary to restore this property to Euphemios.'[94]

As is the case of Eugenia and Nonna, nothing is known about this Meletios, except that he was married to one of them. Gregory took a stand in a disagreement that did not really exist, since the alleged owner of the estate had not raised any claims, but this was not enough for him: he wanted justice to be served, order to be restored. Moreover, when many of his contemporary bishops were accused of economic mismanagement, Gregory did not want to be associated with squatters. Meletios' behavior could damage his reputation in the long run. His personal integrity also weighed in here. He could not tolerate such a flagrant case of bullying coming from a member of his family, especially when he saw himself as a victim of similar behaviors. Besides, this particular case of usurpation made him anxious about his own estate; Eugenia, Nonna, and their families were obviously not to be trusted. He had to alienate and completely cut them off in order to protect his legacy. It is worth noting though that Euphemios did not escape Gregory's criticism, as he was accused of cowardice — a paradoxical charge indeed coming from a man who preferred flight to confrontation.

No narrations of analogous repudiations by the testator in late antique Christian literature exist . In the well-known case of Melania the Younger, her father Valerius Publicola[95] threatened to disinherit her, but he never carried his threat out. Just before his death, he expressed his deep regret for not letting her embrace the ascetic lifestyle she wished and asked for her forgiveness in tears.[96] John Moschos in his *Patrum Spirituale* (*BHG* 1442–1442) delivered a very similar story about a wealthy man who behaved in a very ugly way to his son, Avivos, because he was pious, 'pure and temperate in all things, who, from his childhood, had not drunk wine [and] it was his intention to withdraw from the world.'[97] His reproach was so severe that kith and kin thought that he would disinherit his son. So when the old man fell ill, 'they resolved to intervene with the father on his son's behalf'. In a scene that echoes the *Life of Melania the Younger*, the penitent father called for his son, apologized to him and in the presence of everyone asked for his forgiveness setting him administrator of his inheritance.

In both stories, the fathers use their inheritance in order to impose their will to their descendants. They do not agree with their values and lifestyle, so they try to blackmail them out of it. We do not know if Gregory did likewise, if he had warned his nieces of his intentions and failed to change them. It seems possible, but he did not mention anything in his Testament or other writings. So he disinherited them. In sharp contrast, testators in hagiography backed down in the end, acknowledged their mistake, and accepted the decision their children made.

We do not know how Gregory was related to the virgin Roussiane, but he undoubtedly felt responsible for her.[98] As we already mentioned, he ensured the amount of money she

94. Testament, l. 73-77.
95. *PLRE* I, Publicola 1.
96. *Life of Melania*, pp. 138–140.
97. *PG* 87.3, c. 3092, 202.
98. Testament, l. 44-56.

was given every year 'in order that she might live decently'. Moreover, he made provisions for her residence. Roussiane could choose where a house suitable for a virgin should be built. For as long as she lived, she would retain ownership of it, but after her death it would be restored to the Church of Nazianzus. Finally, he let her choose 'two serving girls' whom she could set free after her death, 'if it should be agreeable to them', and, if not, they would belong to the Church as well.

Gregory had not expressed his view on slavery in detail, as Gregory of Nyssa did,[99] but he had clearly condemned the institution whenever he mentioned it. For example, in his Oration 'On the Love of the Poor' he regarded slavery along with poverty a result of the human injustice and in contrast to the God-given law and liberty.[100] Modern readers may find it disturbing that he still was a slave-owner himself; some of his slaves were manumitted by his parents or himself, but others were still under his ownership: in his Testament, in addition to his heir Gregory and monk Eustathios, who were freedmen, he also mentioned his servant Theophilus, who was manumitted, and his brother Eupraxios and Theodosios, whom he would set free after his death. To each of them Gregory left a legacy of five gold coins.[101] In Oration 14 he urged his audience to imitate God,[102] but he still owned human beings. Gregory was definitely not the only one who could not live up to his own ideals, but there is more than this here. In a slave-owning society, isolated actions could only make life difficult and complicated for everyone. Moreover, the quality of a slave's life depended not only on his or her status but mainly on the nature of his or her labor and the behavior of his or her master. There is no doubt that the slaves who are mentioned in Gregory's last will are those who had strong ties with him and held important positions in his household and bishopric. They enjoyed a quality of life much better than many free persons who belonged to lower and poorer classes. But we do not know if he owned more that were not mentioned; it is reasonable to assume that he had people to work on his estates. So the ethical and anthropological problem, as Gregory puts it, was one he was facing.

By the end, Gregory remembered some close friends and associates who stood by him in difficult times. Like Anthony, who left Athanasios of Alexandria, Serapion of Thmuis, and his community of disciples one of his cloaks, Gregory distributed his garments to Evagrius the deacon (a shirt, a colored tunic, and two cloaks), Theodoulos the deacon, (a shirt and two colored tunics) and Elaphios the notarios (two colored tunics, three cloaks and a simple robe). At the same time, he bequeathed them a significant amount of money as well: 30 gold coins to Evagrios and 20 each to Theodoulos and Elaphios.[103]

Raymond Van Dam notes that 'the most surprising aspect of Gregory's will was his lack of concern for his own memory.'[104] Truly, late Roman testators, by the end of their last will,[105] used to make provisions about their tombs and monuments, the burial and the commemo-

99. In his famous 'Fourth Oration on Ecclesiastes' Gregory of Nyssa denounced slavery, J. McDonough & P. Alexander (eds.), *Gregory of Nyssa*, Leiden 1962. p. 33.

100. Or. 14, 25, c. 892.

101. Testament, l. 57-62.

102. Or. 14, 25, c. 889.

103. Testament, l. 82-92.

104. Van Dam, Self-representation (quoted n. 21), p. 131.

105. Champlin, *Final Judgments* (quoted n. 40), p. 169.

rative ceremonies, but Gregory did not seem to bother. This is not what we were expecting from a man who thoroughly constructed his image in his literary works and he actually referred to his burial in many of his poems. For example, in epigram 84 he mentioned that he would share the same tomb with his father — as it happened. It is difficult to explain his stance. Maybe he had already made the necessary arrangements when he was taking care of his parents' funeral, or he felt that his fame and social position would ensure him a proper ceremony and rest place. Perhaps his true and earnest belief in the afterlife and divine justice made him indifferent to all these vanities; he was expecting that Jesus would repay those who hurt him and restore his reputation.[106]

Conclusion

As it is shown, Gregory of Nazianzus' last will and Testament is important not only as one of the oldest Byzantine will, but also for a better understanding of the testator himself. Without his usual rhetoric excellence, he created a multi-layered self-image that ranges from the lawful son to the strict head of the family; he appears committed to the wishes and the orders of his late parents, while he is the arbiter of the deeds and behaviors of his nieces and nephews. Following his own ideas and the Christian ideal of his times, he disposed his property for the caretaking of the poor. At the same time, as an aristocrat benefactor, he rewarded with generous legacies close associates and friends, most of whom were liberti or slaves, who would be liberated after his death; in other words, he benefitted those who would have faced severe economic difficulties without his protection.

Soon Gregory recovered and after some official celebration in his honor, he took leave of Constantinople and headed back to his native land. There, once more, he dealt with the problems of the bishopric of Nazianzus, by appointing Chledonios as a surrogate bishop. During the following years he had the chance to take care of his patrimony and his literary legacy. Despite the lack of written testimony, it is a fair, assumption that he supervised the charity activities he financed. With the help of Nikoboulos the younger and Eulalios, his Orations and Epistles were edited. Besides that, he delivered his famous funeral oration for Basil of Caesarea and wrote many poems inspired by the difficult times of the past and the hopes for a future reward.

106. A. Tuilier & G. Bady (eds.), J. Bernardi (trans.), Gregory of Nazianzus, *Personal Poems* II, 1, 8, Paris 2004.

LES CONFLITS D'HÉRITAGE D'APRÈS LES TRIBUNAUX ECCLÉSIASTIQUES (XIe-XVe S.)

Jean-Claude CHEYNET

Gilbert Dagron a évoqué, dans son article « Hériter de soi-même », les conflits d'intérêt qui pouvaient naître du don de tout ou partie d'une fortune pour les œuvres pieuses, en particulier en faveur d'un monastère, mais aussi d'autres établissements religieux[1]. La famille, pour les biens patrimoniaux, et parfois l'Etat, pour les biens donnés par les empereurs, étaient enclins à contester cette perte et s'inquiétaient d'éventuels empiètements des institutions ecclésiastiques.

Les sources, comme toujours dans le monde byzantin, sont limitées. Elles sont concentrées pour l'essentiel dans les archives des monastères de l'Athos, dans la *Peira*[2] du juge Eustathe Rhômaios, dont James Howard-Johnston commente ici plusieurs décisions, dans le recueil des jugements de Dèmètrios Chômatianos, qui bénéficient d'une édition moderne[3], et principalement dans le registre patriarcal pour l'époque des Paléologues, en cours de réédition[4]. Malheureusement les documents de ce registre, conservés à partir de 1315, datent d'une époque

1. G. DAGRON, Hériter de soi-même, dans *La transmission du patrimoine. Byzance et l'aire méditerranéenne*, éd. J. BEAUCAMP et G. DAGRON (Travaux et mémoires, Monographies 11) (désormais BEAUCAMP-DAGRON, *Transmission*), p. 81-99, tout particulièrement p. 94-97. L'auteur montre que, en l'absence de disposition testamentaire et d'héritier direct, un tiers de la fortune du défunt doit aller à l'Eglise. Il rappelle également une novelle de Constantin VII. L'empereur s'étonnait que les législateurs aient attribué la fortune des morts intestats à des parents « qui ne leur étaient rien de leur vivant ... sans réserver à Dieu la moindre part... »

2. *Πεῖρα ἤγουν διδασκαλία ἐκ τῶν πράξεων τοῦ μεγάλου κυροῦ Εὐσταθίου Ῥωμαίου*, cur. J. et P. ZÉPOS, *Jus Graecoromanum. 4*, Athènes 1931 (désormais *Peira*), p. 9-260.

3. G. PRINZING (éd.), *Demetrii Chomateni Ponemata diaphora*, *Corpus Fontium Historiae Byzantinae* 38, Berlin 2002.

4. *Das Register des Patriarchats von Konstantinopel.* 1. *Edition und Übersetzung der Urkunden aus den Jahren 1315-1331*; H. HUNGER, O. KRESTEN, Vienne 1981; 2. *Edition und Übersetzung der Urkunden aus den Jahren 1336-1350*, H. HUNGER, O. KRESTEN, E. KISLINGER, C. CUPANE, Vienne 1995; 3. *Teil, Edition und Übersetzung der Urkunden aus den Jahren 1350-1363*, J. KODER, M. HINTERBERGER und O. KRESTEN, Vienne 2001 (désormais, *Register des Patriarcats* I, II, III). Sur l'intérêt de ces documents, cf. en dernier lieu, *The Register of the Patriarchate of Constantinople. An Essential Source for the History and Church of Late Byzantium*, éd. Ch. GASTGEBER, Ek. MITSIOU, J. PREISER-KAPELLER, Vienne 2013, tout particulièrement la contribution de Ek. MITSIOU, Late Byzantine Female Monasticism from the point of view of the Register of the Patriarchate of Constantinople, p. 161-171. L'auteur fait allusion aux actes n°s 135 et 184.

Inheritance, Law and Religions in the Ancient and Mediaeval Worlds, ed. by B. CASEAU and S. R. HUEBNER (Centre de recherche d'Histoire et Civilisation de Byzance, Monographies 45), Paris 2014.

pendant laquelle l'Empire est appauvri et les patrimoines diminués, surtout durant le dernier siècle avant la chute de Constantinople. Seule, la *Peira* offre un aperçu de la façon dont ces affaires se traitaient au sein de la riche aristocratie du temps des Macédoniens et des Comnènes. Les procès de la *Peira* engageaient des livres, voire des dizaines de livres d'or, alors que le registre patriarcal tranchait des contestations qui dépassaient rarement plus de quelques dizaines d'hyperpères dévalués.

La transmission des biens, sources de revenus mais aussi d'influence, est en effet le principal objectif des familles byzantines[5]. Notons au préalable que l'Etat s'intéressa un temps aux conséquences de la donation de *psychika* sur les patrimoines laïcs modestes, ceux des villageois d'une commune rurale. Basile II craignait que des puissants, métropolites ou évêques, ne cherchent par ce biais à accaparer les petits oratoires, entretenus par la donation de lopins de terre, et à s'introduire subrepticement dans les communes[6]. Un jugement d'Eustathe Rhômaios, rapporté dans la *Peira*, concerne un cas, semble-t-il, de ce type. Bien des hommes pieux du village de Saint-Auxence, situé dans le thème de Chaldie, s'étaient regroupés pour fonder une église et la doter de biens immobiliers destinés à assurer le service par les prêtres. Des laïcs, peut-être des puissants, tentèrent de mettre la main sur l'église et furent déboutés par le juge[7].

Dans les familles, la transmission du patrimoine s'accomplissait en deux phases, au moment du mariage et au moment du décès, le premier étant souvent le plus déterminant[8]. Pour une famille, il s'agit d'éviter que son patrimoine ne soit dispersé au profit de personnes étrangères, notamment chez la belle-famille, à moins que le mariage n'ait produit des fruits. Le second objectif, plus personnel, mais d'une importance fondamentale, est de s'assurer que des prêtres ou des moines prieront pour l'âme du défunt en attendant le Jugement dernier, ce qui impliquait la pérennité de la fondation. En fait, seul Grégoire Pakourianos a connu une complète réussite, puisqu'on prie toujours à Bačkovo pour le salut de son âme. Le testateur, quand il s'agissait du chef de la maisonnée, se préoccupait généralement de l'ensemble de la parenté proche et incluait dans les commémoraisons son épouse, ses enfants, ceux morts prématurément comme ceux qui lui survivaient. Il incluait éventuellement d'autres proches, oncles et tantes, frères ou sœurs, notamment s'ils étaient restés

5. Dans ses *Conseils et récits*, Kékauménos évoque le risque de voir son fils mener une vie dissipée, emprunter et se trouver dans l'impossibilité de rembourser et de payer les intérêts. Il sera traîné devant les tribunaux et même sa mort n'arrêtera pas les poursuites. Sinon, il sera obligé de vendre un bien de famille, préjudice économique, mais surtout moral, car la perte de ce qui a été transmis par son père constitue une honte (*Cecaumeni consilia et narrationes*, éd. et trad. G. G. Litavrin, *Советы и рассказы Кекавмена*, Moscou 1972, p. 190-192).

6. N. Svoronos, *Les novelles des empereurs macédoniens concernant la terre et les stratiotes*, éd. P. Gounaridis, Athènes 1994, p. 208-209.

7. *Peira*, XV, § 8. Cette pratique de fondation d'une église avec le concours de simples villageois est encore attestée à l'époque des Paléologues : en 1278, les habitants du village de Polémitas, dans le Magne, rappellent par un inscription qu'ils ont contribué collectivement à la construction et au décor d'une église dédiée à l'archange Michel. L'un deux a aussi donné une terre à titre de *psychikon* pour la commémoraison de l'empereur [Michel VIII Paléologue] (D. Feissel et A. Philippidis-Braat, Inventaires en vue d'un recueil des inscriptions historiques de Byzance. III. Inscriptions du Péloponnèse, *Travaux et Mémoires* 9, 1985, p. 314-317).

8. A. Laiou, Marriage Prohibitions, Marriage Strategies and the Dowry in the Thirteenth-Century Byzantium, dans Beaucamp-Dagron, *Transmission* (cité n. 1), p. 129-160.

sans descendance[9]. Pour cette raison, les Byzantins consacraient une partie de leurs biens à assurer le salut de leur âme par des fondations pieuses, église ou monastère, selon des modalités qui pouvaient différer[10]. Ils y établissaient, en fonction de leurs moyens, un personnel plus ou moins nombreux chargé de la liturgie[11]. Les plus grandes précautions juridiques étaient prises pour éviter les risques de contestation. Kalè, l'épouse de Symbatios, membre de la famille géorgienne des Pakourianoi qui connut son apogée sous Alexis Comnène, fut son exécutrice testamentaire. Lorsqu'elle-même rédigea ses dernières volontés, elle mentionna les reçus (*apodeixeis*) que les bénéficiaires des legs accordés par Symbatios, y compris le monastère d'Iviron, lui avaient remis pour attester qu'ils avaient bien recueilli, après la mort de son époux, les donations prévues[12].

Cette partie du patrimoine, en dépit des précautions, était souvent la plus menacée, car d'un côté, la famille pouvait chercher à réduire la part donnée à Dieu et, à l'inverse, l'Eglise tentait d'intégrer à ses propres biens les donations ainsi constituées et, éventuellement, de les accroître. La tâche lui était facilitée par la situation démographique de l'époque qui faisait que nombre de familles restaient sans descendance ou sans enfant parvenu à l'âge adulte.

Différents cas de figure se présentaient donc, qui tous pouvaient conduire à des conflits. Des héritiers directs trouvaient trop importante le lot offert à l'Eglise. Les biens donnés à une fondation religieuse étaient susceptibles d'être détournés de leur but premier par des collatéraux ou par les autorités ecclésiastiques, notamment les évêques, qui avaient déjà, selon les canons, un droit de regard spirituel. Tel grand monastère pouvait en absorber un autre, plus modeste ou moins prospère. Les querelles éclataient souvent lorsque des membres de la belle-famille visaient à mettre la main sur des propriétés, notamment lorsqu'aucun héritier direct ne subsistait. L'entrée des femmes au monastère constituait un moment crucial dans la dévolution des patrimoines. Les filles recevaient à ce moment-là leur part d'héritage, si elles n'étaient pas mariées, ou reprenaient leurs biens dotaux dans le cas contraire, sauf si elles étaient convaincues d'adultère, et les fausses accusations se répandaient à dessein pour capter le patrimoine de la fautive. La situation se compliquait si elle laissait des enfants. Les biens donnés par testament étaient parfois réclamés par des sujets extérieurs, l'Etat, mais aussi des voisins, des vendeurs de mauvaise foi, etc. Enfin, lorsque les circonstances s'y prêtaient, invasions ennemies, soubresauts politiques, les usurpations sans titre n'étaient pas rares.

9. Nous ne disposons d'exemples de telles listes de commémoraisons que pour des familles de sang impérial : par exemple, P. GAUTIER, L'obituaire du typikon du Pantocrator, *Revue des études byzantines* (= *REB*) 27, 1969, p. 235-262 ou M. KOUROUPOU et J.-Fr. VANNIER, Commémoraisons des Comnènes dans le *typikon* liturgique du monastère du Christ Philanthrope (*ms. Panaghia Kamariotissa* 29), *REB* 63, 2005, p. 41-69.

10. Sur le rôle du don à Byzance, cf. Ch. GIROS, Le statut de la donation à Byzance : rhétorique et actes de la pratique (xe-xve siècle) dans *Donateurs et donations dans le monde byzantin*, éd. J.-M. SPIESER et E. YOTA, Paris 2012, p. 97-106.

11. G. DAGRON, Hériter de soi-même, dans BEAUCAMP-DAGRON, *Transmission* (cité n. 1), p. 80- 99.

12. *Actes d'Iviron. 2, Du milieu du XIe siècle à 1204*, éd. diplomatique par J. LEFORT, N. OIKONOMIDÈS, D. PAPACHRYSSANTHOU, avec la collab. de V. KRAVARI et H. MÉTRÉVÉLI (Archives de l'Athos 16), Paris 1990, acte no 47 (1098).

Les fondations familiales

Les biens consacrés à Dieu étaient inaliénables, mais les églises et monastères, qui étaient dotés de biens pour l'entretien du clergé ou des moines, pouvaient appartenir à des personnes privées. Cette pratique constituait même une des façons de sauvegarder un patrimoine familial, face aux menaces de confiscation. La fondation était transmise à un héritier, parfois unique. Ce choix n'était pas sans risque, car il fallait maintenir sur la longue durée le contrôle des biens. Plusieurs *typika*, dont le plus éclairant est celui de Michel Attaleiatès, comportaient ainsi des clauses de maintien de l'établissement au sein de la famille fondatrice. Rappelons cependant que la durée de vie des monastères était assez brève à Byzance, sauf en ce qui concernait les fondations impériales ou celles des proches parents des *basileis*. Ce point est étudié par ailleurs. Le monastère fondé par Attaleiatès ne comptait que cinq moines à son origine[13] et il semble avoir perdu son indépendance après la mort du *ktètôr* et de son fils, Théodore[14].

Les fondations familiales sont attestées dès le XIe siècle au sein de l'aristocratie provinciale, mais elles paraissent peu nombreuses comparées à celles instituées à l'époque des Comnènes où elles se multiplient, toutefois, il peut s'agir d'un effet d'optique de nos sources qui sont plus développées pour le XIIe siècle[15]. Les *ktètôres* sont très souvent des hommes d'Eglise, des eunuques ou des personnages sans descendants directs[16], ce qui réduisait les contestations possibles, sinon par des collatéraux ou éventuellement par des ascendants. Même lorsque la fondation était familiale, la crainte de laisser s'introduire un tiers ambitieux était clairement exprimée : « Que celui, empereur, fonctionnaire (*archôn*), simple sujet (*archoménos*), évêque, prêtre, qui entreprendra de faire quoi que ce soit à l'encontre de mes dispositions, ou de transgresser une des prescriptions qu'il m'a plu de prendre, ou de placer la fondation sous un éphore, ou de lui imposer un charisticaire ou un curateur, en dehors de ceux que je vais mentionner, ou une anaphore, ou la nomination d'une quelconque autorité ... soit maudit par Dieu tout-puissant, que son souvenir soit extirpé du milieu des hommes, qu'il soit frappé par le deuil et la douleur, ... »[17]. Attaleiatès résume bien tout ce qui menace potentiellement une fondation : les autorités politiques[18] et religieuses et même le simple particulier[19]. Les donations conditionnelles entraînaient souvent le détournement de biens au profit d'un bénéficiaire qui n'était plus choisi par les héritiers du fondateur et qui avait parfois la tentation de faire passer les biens de l'établissement dans son propre patrimoine. C'était un des reproches adressés au charisticariat. Les exemples ci-dessous prouvent que ces inquiétudes n'étaient pas infondées. Michel Attaleiatès revint sur les malversations possibles en se prémunissant autant que possible contre les parents en ligne collatérale qui intenteraient un procès ou monteraient une machination contre le représentant de la

13. P. Gautier, La diataxis de Michel Attaliate, *REB* 39, 1981, p. 59.

14. *Ibid.*, p. 15.

15. Ainsi, la fondation des Argyroi dans le Charsianon (J.-F. Vannier, *Familles byzantines : les Argyroi (IXe-XIIe siècles)* [Publications de la Sorbonne. Série Byzantina 1), Paris 1975, p. 20 et J. Ferluga, Les débuts d'une famille aristocratique byzantine – les Argyroi, *Зборник Филозофског факултета Универзитета у Београду*, XII-1, 1974, p. 154-157.

16. A titre d'exemple, on peut consulter la liste des fondations au XIe siècle donnée par J. Darrouzès Le mouvement des fondations monastiques au XIe siècle, *Travaux et Mémoires* 6, 1976, p. 159-176.

17. Gautier, *Diataxis* (cité n. 13), p. 33.

18. Toutefois, Attaleiatès fait appel à l'empereur pour chasser quiconque serait intervenu frauduleusement dans les affaires de son monastère (Gautier, *Diataxis* (cité n. 13), p. 80).

19. Pour un commentaire plus complet, cf. Dagron, Hériter de soi-même (cité n. 1), p. 90-91.

ligne directe[20]. Si la ligne directe s'éteint, le monastère et l'hospice deviennent autonomes. L'higoumène sera choisi parmi les moines les plus vertueux et sera béni par l'higoumène de Stoudios, mais ce dernier n'aura aucune autre prérogative sur la fondation[21]. Cette frénésie de précautions vient sans doute de l'instabilité des temps, alors que les confiscations se multiplient au gré des nombreux changements d'empereur, et de la pratique triomphante du charisticariat.

Un des exemples les plus anciens de ces fondations familiales, hors du cercle impérial, est offert par le testament d'Eustathe Boïlas. Cet aristocrate cappadocien, qui avait perdu son fils et son épouse, légua ses biens à ses deux filles. Cependant, comme l'avait déjà noté P. Lemerle, l'héritier véritable de Boïlas était l'église de la Théotokos Salem qu'il avait fondée[22]. Cette église restait la propriété de ses deux filles, mais pour autant qu'elles respectassent les instructions de leur père en matière de commémoraison. Cette clause supposait l'entente des filles et plus largement des couples qu'elles formaient avec leurs époux. Si cette entente venait à être rompue ou si les filles cherchaient à compromettre les commémoraisons, par exemple par l'aliénation des biens servant à entretenir le clergé de l'église, elles seraient aussitôt privées d'un des principaux villages qui leur avait été légué, au profit de l'église. Ce testament montre bien le peu de confiance qu'Eustathe accordait à ses filles et sans doute à ses gendres et quelle était sa vraie obsession, son propre salut, celui de son épouse et de son fils, mort prématurément à l'âge de trois ans. Il n'oublie même pas de laisser quelques *nomismata* pour une église, Saint-Modestos, établie dans sa patrie d'origine, où était commémorée la mémoire de sa propre mère.

Dans les *typika*, la répétition des clauses qui mettent en garde les higoumènes contre les revendications des membres de la famille suggèrent que le cas se produisait fréquemment. Le *typikon* rédigé par Grégoire Pakourianos représente admirablement les oppositions que le fondateur d'un monastère craignait de rencontrer. « Je veux que notre monastère soit à l'abri de tous ceux qui entendraient lui nuire, personnes étrangères ou de notre parenté... » Si un de nos parents est resté hors de l'héritage par oubli ou pour une autre raison et qu'il se démène pour recevoir une part, nous le mettons résolument en garde contre cette mauvaise démarche et nous ordonnons qu'il reçoive de nos épitropes à titre d'héritage seulement douze *folleis*. » La somme donnée marque ici le mépris dans lequel sera tenu le parent saisi « d'une honteuse convoitise ». Pakourianos veille à se différencier des « gens qui instituent des monastères et d'autres établissements pieux et qui les placent après la mort du fondateur sous l'autorité héréditaire de leurs parents ». Pakourianos distinguait donc son type de fondation de celui presque contemporain de Michel Attaleiatès. Le grand domestique voulait éviter de « susciter des inimitiés et des prétextes à recourir aux tribunaux, chacun des exclus se prétendant le maître et le propriétaire des biens du monastère. » La démarche des protestataires était parfois couronnée de succès, car « dans de telles affaires, la sentence des juges donne souvent la préférence aux indignes sur les personnes méritantes et des filous sont préférés aux ayants-droit. » Enfin, Pakourianos prévoyait le cas où le bénéficiaire d'un legs, un parent ou l'un de ses hommes, chercherait à recevoir plus que son dû, il perdrait alors tout le bénéfice de la donation[23].

20. Gautier, *Diataxis* (cité n. 13), p. 80.

21. Gautier, *Diataxis* (cité n. 13), p. 75.

22. P. Lemerle, *Cinq études sur le XIe siècle byzantin* (Le Monde byzantin), Paris 1977, p. 55.

23. P. Gautier, Le *typikon* du sébaste Grégoire Pakourianos, *REB* 42, 1984, p. 89-91. La traduction citée est celle de Paul Gautier.

Un professionnel de la justice ne donnait pas un avis différent. Eustathe Rhômaios avait eu à se prononcer sur un conflit concernant une femme qui désirait entrer au monastère, en accordant différents legs sur sa part d'héritage. Devait-elle prendre ses disposions avant d'entrer au couvent ou après ? Eustathe favorisait la première solution dans ce désaccord qui se présentait souvent, car dans le cas contraire, le juge affirmait que « celle qui n'a pas reçu la dot avant d'embrasser la vie monastique courra sûrement plus tard le risque de passer ses jours dans des embarras, des tumultes, et devant les tribunaux »[24].

Les réserves sur la bonne utilisation du patrimoine familial se manifestaient souvent dès l'origine du projet. Dans la haute aristocratie, les premières réticences apparaissent lorsque l'enfant décide, contre la volonté des parents, d'embrasser la carrière monastique[25]. Michel Maléïnos dut ainsi se cacher de son père pour entrer au monastère, *topos* hagiographique, mais aussi réalité sociale, car ce dernier envisageait pour son fils une brillante carrière, que la position éminente de la famille depuis plusieurs générations semblait pouvoir lui assurer. La perte était donc double, l'espoir d'une augmentation du patrimoine était déçu et la fortune présente se trouvait divisée, la part de Michel risquant d'aller au monastère où il aspirait à entrer ou, plus tard, à l'établissement qu'il serait susceptible de fonder. Malgré tout, la position sociale des Maléïnoi se maintint. Constantin, frère de Michel, conserva, semble-t-il, l'unité de la fortune immobilière de la famille, en rachetant la part de son frère. Il redistribua pour moitié le numéraire ainsi obtenu pour le donner à son père spirituel qui put agrandir son monastère et se montrer généreux envers les pauvres[26]. Des empereurs, qui voyaient disparaître une partie de la fortune foncière des laïcs en faveur des monastères, manifestèrent leur hostilité en décrétant par des novelles qu'il fallait cesser de donner des terres aux monastères[27]. La crainte d'une dilapidation des patrimoines au profit d'actions pieuses est clairement présente. Selon la *Peira*, les donations supérieures à cinq cents pièces d'or, qu'elles fussent destinées à l'Eglise, à un établissement pieux, aux pauvres ou à la ville, devaient faire l'objet d'un document officiel (*hypomnèma*), afin d'être connues de tous et éventuellement soumises à une contestation[28].

Pour qui n'avait pas accès au palais impérial, l'entrée au monastère d'un fils était susceptible de compromettre le niveau de fortune. Le décès du chef de famille entraînait un partage des biens à chaque génération, mais, en principe, les héritiers se rétablissaient en épousant une aristocrate richement dotée et en accomplissant une belle carrière au service de l'empereur, mais l'entrée au monastère interdisait l'une et l'autre des voies de reconstitution d'une fortune[29].

24. *Peira*, XXIV § 5, traduction et commentaire dans A. LAIOU, *Mariage, amour et parenté à Byzance aux XIe-XIIIe siècles* (*TM*, Monogr. 7), Paris 1992, p. 113-115.

25. Ces réticences à l'entrée précoce d'un enfant dans un monastère n'étaient pas l'apanage des hautes classes. Pour tous, l'entrée d'un garçon ôtait l'espérance d'une lignée et, chez les plus pauvres, l'espoir d'avoir un secours dans leur vieillesse. Pour quelques exemples, cf. A.-M. TALBOT, The Byzantine Family and the Monastery, *Dumbarton Oaks Papers* (= *DOP*) 44, 1990, p. 126-127, repris dans EADEM, *Women and Religious Life in Byzantium*, Aldershot 2001, n° XIII.

26. Sur Michel Maléïnos, voir en dernier lieu, A. LAIOU, The General and the Saint: Michael Maleinos and Nikephoros Phokas, *Eupsychia. Mélanges offerts à Hélène Ahrweiler*, Paris 1998, t. 2, p. 399-412.

27. Novelle de Nicéphore Phocas, en 963/964 (N. SVORONOS, *Les novelles des empereurs macédoniens concernant la terre et les stratiotes. Introduction – édition – commentaires*, éd. posthume par P. GOUNARIDIS, Athènes 1994, p. 151-p.161). Manuel Comnène était dans le même état d'esprit lorsqu'il fonda le monastère de Katasképè sur le Bosphore (P. MAGDALINO, *The Empire of Manuel I Komnenos 1143-1180*, Cambridge 1993, p. 298-299).

28. *Peira*, LIII § 1, p. 220.

Le fondateur d'un monastère avait le droit d'abandonner la plus grande part de sa fortune à l'établissement alors qu'il laissait des descendants encore actifs au moment de la mort de leur père. Ainsi, nous avons conservé des éloges funèbres rédigés par Grégoire Antiochos, rhéteur et haut fonctionnaire dans la seconde moitié du XIIe siècle, dédiés à la mémoire de son père. Nous y apprenons que ce personnage, qui avait de hautes relations et avait acquis une fortune notable, décida de restaurer une église donnée par le patriarche, en y consacrant tous ses biens, et d'y adjoindre un monastère où seraient accueillies jusqu'à douze moniales dont dix sachant lire. Il dut cependant faire appel, avec succès, à l'empereur Manuel Comnène pour compléter ses ressources. Grégoire, bien qu'il se présentât en fils affectueux et blessé par la mort de son père bien-aimé, avoua qu'il s'était plaint de la décision de celui-ci. Dans l'un des discours, Grégoire prétendit que c'était par souci pour la santé de son père qui consacrait tout son temps à cette tâche, mais dans un autre il confessait que la construction du monastère obérait le niveau de vie, déjà modeste, de la famille et que les dépenses engagées auraient mieux convenu à de plus riches qu'eux. Cependant, Grégoire respecta toutes les volontés de son père. Il est vrai que le monastère reçut la dépouille paternelle et que le tombeau de Grégoire y était aussi préparé. On peut se demander quelle était la nature de cette fondation familiale. Etait-ce une manière de mettre à l'abri les biens de la famille ? Mais rien ne nous dit que Grégoire tirait un revenu de ce monastère qui semble tout juste doté pour subvenir aux besoins des moniales, puisqu'il fallut construire des logements dont les loyers contribuaient à l'entretien des moniales. Tout au contraire, dans un autre discours, Grégoire affirme que son père n'exigeait aucun service des moniales et que, si l'un de ses descendants essayait de tirer le moindre avantage matériel de ce monastère, il devrait être expulsé[30]. Autre curiosité, ce sont des femmes qui sont chargées de commémorer le père d'Antiochos et son fils, mais il n'est jamais fait allusion ni à l'épouse du fondateur ni à ses autres enfants, peut-être des filles. La mère et les filles devaient-elles finir leurs jours dans le monastère ? L'art oratoire est peu propice à la description des conditions juridiques de la fondation. Nous ignorons, par exemple, si le père de Grégoire utilisa aussi, avec son accord, la dot de son épouse. En tout cas, le testament du père ne fut apparemment pas contesté par ses descendants, et la privation de cet héritage n'a nullement interdit à Grégoire Anchiochos d'accomplir une brillante carrière – il fut juge du Velum, grand drongaire – [31] et donc, bien que nous n'en ayons aucune preuve formelle, de reconstituer un patrimoine.

Grégoire laissait entendre que son père consacrait à sa fondation toute sa fortune, ce qui serait contraire à la législation. Lorsqu'un testament, en effet, ne respectait pas la loi, il perdait toute autorité. Nous avons dans la *Peira* des exemples de l'application de la loi. Contrairement à la *lex Falcidia*, reprise dans les *Basiliques*, qui oblige à laisser une part réservataire aux enfants, mais aussi aux ascendants. Un fils avait légué par testament tout ce qu'il possédait, pour être commémoré, sans doute à des institutions ecclésiastiques qui assumaient traditionnellement ce rôle. Or, à sa

29. J.-Cl. CHEYNET, Aristocratie et héritage (XIe-XIIIe siècle), dans BEAUCAMP-DAGRON, *Transmission*, (cité n. 1), p. 53-80, repris dans IDEM, *The Byzantine Aristocracy and its Military Function* (Variorum Reprints), Aldershot 2006, no IV.

30. GRÉGOIRE ANTIOCHOS, *Éloge du patriarche Basile Kamatèros*, texte, trad., commentaire, suivis d'une analyse des œuvres de Grégoire Antiochos par M. LOUKAKI (Byzantina Sorbonensia 13), Paris 1996 ; l'analyse des discours se trouve aux pages 123-128.

31. Il était drongaire de la Veille en 1196 (*Actes de Lavra*. 1, *Des origines à 1204*, éd. diplomatique par P. LEMERLE, A. GUILLOU, N. SVORONOS, avec la collab. de D. PAPACHRYSSANTHOU (Archives de l'Athos 5), Paris 1970, p. 356.

mort, ses parents étaient encore vivants et le juge Eustathe Rhomaios décida qu'ils devaient recevoir un tiers de la fortune de leur enfant[32]. Cette part était donc perdue par les bénéficiaires des legs. Le même juge cassa d'autres dispositions testamentaires[33]. D'une manière plus générale, le juge affirmait qu'il fallait éviter de confier l'épitropie à un moine, s'il y avait des héritiers mineurs[34].

Nous rencontrons un autre exemple, beaucoup plus tardif, de ces réticences familiales, lorsqu'Irène Choumnaina, entrée au monastère qu'elle avait fondé, décida, sur les conseils de son père spirituel, Théoleptos de Philadelphie, de donner tous ses biens aux pauvres et à la restauration du monastère du Christ-Philanthrope à Constantinople. Son père biologique, Nicéphore Choumnos, *mésazôn* de l'empereur Andronic II Paléologue, qui s'était considérablement enrichi dans cette fonction, protesta devant la dilapidation de cette fortune, vainement, semble-t-il, ce qui prouve que sa fille restait maîtresse de ses biens. La résistance de la parenté à la transmission des biens familiaux à un moine ou une moniale vaut aussi lorsque l'intéressé est entré de longue date au monastère. Les femmes sont peut-être particulièrement visées, en raison de la menace systématique qui pèse sur leurs biens dotaux, y compris lorsqu'elles sont encore dans le siècle.

Contestations d'héritage par les parents

Quels sont les cas de figure où des héritiers pouvaient entrer en conflit avec des institutions religieuses ? Le cas le plus simple est celui où un héritier du défunt conteste la donation ; il apparaît peu dans les documents conservés, car il est difficile d'aller contre des dispositions testamentaires rédigées devant témoin. La question se complique quand la légitimité de la possession du bien donné est attaquée devant les tribunaux. Si le bien, en effet, n'appartient pas vraiment au testateur, il ne peut légitimement le donner. Cette situation se présente lorsque le défunt, sans enfant, offre des biens qui lui venaient de son épouse, elle-même décédée. Ce cas vaut aussi lorsqu'il s'agit de la vente à un monastère d'un bien immobilier dont la possession est remise en cause. Enfin, citons le cas exceptionnel d'un *proasteion* illégalement arraché à Saint-Paul du Latros par Léon Karantènos, dont le nom de famille suggère qu'il appartenait à l'aristocratie. Ce domaine fut restitué au temps d'Isaac II, puis à nouveau saisi par Léon, peut-être à l'occasion du coup d'Etat de 1195, qui vit la chute d'Isaac II. Puis le domaine fut légué par Léon à un autre monastère. L'higoumène de Saint-Paul fit appel au tribunal impérial, qui lui donna raison en janvier 1204[35].

Eustathe Rhômaios eut à trancher une contestation, déjà présentée devant le tribunal patriarcal, qui opposait une héritière à un monastère, celui de Saint-Lazare. Un testateur avait prévu que sa fortune irait à ses enfants, mais, si son fils décédait, sa part, qui se comptait en livres d'or, irait au monastère à titre de *psychikon*. Le père mourut, mais le fils demeura introuvable et le monastère, après un certain délai, rentra en possession de sa part. La sœur conduisit une action en justice pour s'emparer de l'héritage de son frère, que les moines avaient utilisé pour acheter un bien immobilier, jadis propriété du père. Elle fut déboutée et la précipitation des moines

32. *Peira*, XIV, § 10, p. 45.
33. Cf. Howard-Johnston, *supra*, p. 264-267.
34. *Ibid.*, XVI, § 3, p. 55.
35. *Acta et diplomata Graeca medii aevi sacra et profana*, collecta ediderunt F. Miklosich et I. Müller t. IV, Vienne 1871, p. 327-329. Résumé dans R. Janin, *Les Églises et les monastères des grands centres byzantins*, Paris 1975, p. 449.

à s'emparer du *psychikon* dans un délai trop bref, condamnée. Le frère réapparut et recouvra sa part[36]. Cette affaire pourrait concerner une famille d'officiers supérieurs, compte tenu des sommes en jeu et du fait que l'absence du fils pourrait s'expliquer par une captivité chez l'ennemi. Cette mésaventure, qui éliminait temporairement des héritiers potentiels, mais pour de nombreuses années parfois, était assez fréquente et dut provoquer de nombreux conflits. Cet épisode met admirablement en valeur la nécessité de la *prostasia*, même chez les puissants.

Les cas les plus abondants sont présentés dans le recueil de jugements du plus célèbre patriarche de Bulgarie, Dèmètrios Chômatianos, lui-même fin juriste, auquel s'ajoutent quelques actes conservés dans la correspondance du métropolite contemporain de Naupacte, Jean Apokaukos. L'un des intérêts du dossier est de faire apparaître aux procès des personnes de condition modeste aux côtés de l'habituelle élite aristocratique, elle-même moins impressionnante, car elle est constituée de provinciaux de souche et de rescapés de l'effondrement de 1204. Elle était à l'échelle du modeste Etat des maîtres grecs de l'Epire. Cette documentation nous permet d'observer les conflits que ces intérêts contradictoires ont pu générer au sein de la société épirote du début du XIIIe siècle. Les procès les plus nombreux, qui se comptent par dizaines, concernent surtout les différends que suscitent les remariages lorsqu'il y a des enfants des deux lits. Les cas où des biens ecclésiastiques sont en jeu sont plutôt rares. Il semble en effet que ces procès sont le plus souvent intentés par des familles de condition assez modeste, or celles-ci ont peu de biens à distraire, même pour le salut de leur âme. Il n'est pas toujours facile de discerner l'importance économique des enjeux, faute d'éléments sur ce point. Toutefois les ressources de la prosopographie et, plus rarement, la mention de titres ou de fonctions, pallient en partie cette lacune et on remarque alors que les plaideurs les plus actifs appartiennent au milieu de l'aristocratie provinciale.

Le premier exemple est caractéristique[37], car il engage les familles Pakourianos, Kounalès et Skoutariôtès. Grégoire Pakourianos n'était pas un descendant direct de son homonyme, grand domestique de l'empereur Alexis Comnène, mort sans enfants, mais il appartenait sans aucun doute à une lignée collatérale, le prénom Grégoire étant très prisé dans cette famille d'origine géorgienne et arménienne. Le père des deux sœurs dont il est question dans le procès était archonte à Berrhoè de Thessalie[38], mais la ville passa sous la domination des Bulgares au moment de la prise de Constantinople vers 1204 et ne fut pas reconquise par Théodore Ange Doukas avant 1215. C'est à ces événements que le jugement fait allusion.

Les deux autres familles sont aussi établies à Berrhoè. La plaignante, l'une des filles de Grégoire Pakourianos, dont le prénom n'est pas donné, porte le nom de son époux, un certain Skoutariôtès. Or, dans un acte délivré par Chômatianos, lorsque Andronic Skoutariôtès se présente au tribunal, il est qualifié de *mégalodoxotatos archôn* de Berrhoè[39]. La famille est connue essentiellement par les sceaux qui permettent d'attester son importance dès le XIe siècle[40].

36. *Peira*, XXXI, § 5.

37. PRINZING, *Demetrii Chomateni* (cité n. 3), Acte 48, p. 177-180.

38. On aurait pu penser à l'autre Berrhoè, l'actuelle Stara Zagora, plus proche de Philippoupolis où s'était constitué le gros du patrimoine du grand domestique d'Alexis Comnène, mais la ville, prise aussi par les Bulgares, ne fut pas reconquise par les Grecs.

39. PRINZING, *Demetrii Chomateni* (cité n. 3), Acte 25, p. 96

40. Ch. STAVRAKOS, *Die byzantinischen Bleisiegel mit Familiennamen aus der Sammlung des Numismatischen Museums Athen* (Mainzer Veröffentlichungen zur Byzantinistik 4), Wiesbaden 2000, n° 238 ; J.-Cl. CHEYNET, V. BULGURLU, T. GOKYILDIRIM, *Les sceaux byzantins du Musée archéologique d'Istanbul*, Istanbul 2012, n° 5.241.

Elle comprenait des dignitaires, patrice, vestarque, etc. et, à partir du XIIe siècle, des ecclésiastiques[41]. Le défenseur, Nicéphore Kounalès, est issu d'une famille moins illustre. Cependant, Syméon Kounalès négociait en 1210 pour le compte de Michel Ange d'Epire avec les Vénitiens[42]. Peut-être était-il le grand-père de l'enfant Syméon, mort en bas âge, qui est mentionné dans cet acte, et en ce cas, Nicéphore serait son fils. Constantin Kounalès appartenait au groupe d'*apographeis* qui, en 1317, rédigèrent le *praktikon* des biens du monastère d'Iviron. Il a laissé un sceau collectif où il figure, porteur de la dignité modeste de sébaste, avec ses collègues[43]. Une autre branche de la famille était établie en Asie Mineure : Jean fut domestique, puis *taboullarios* et *prôtekdikos* de la métropole de Smyrne sous les Lascarides[44].

Nicéphore Kounalès épousa en secondes noces Hélène, fille légitime du défunt Grégoire Pakourianos, archonte de Berrhoè, avant que la ville ne passe sous l'autorité des Bulgares. Il y eut un contrat par lequel elle reçut les cadeaux prénuptiaux, elle-même apportait une dot, puis son patrimoine s'accrut de maisons et d'une église consacrée à la Vierge Eléousa qui lui étaient parvenus par voie d'héritage. De ce couple naquit un garçon, Syméon. Deux ans après la naissance de Syméon, Hélène mourut. Elle ne fit pas mention de tous les biens reçus du côté de Kounalès, car ils étaient inaccessibles puisque Berrhoé se trouvait sous la domination des Bulgares. Parmi ses biens immobiliers, elle mettait de côté l'église de la Vierge qu'elle divisait en trois parts, une part pour effectuer des donations, une autre pour sa sœur, l'épouse de Skoutariôtès, et une troisième part, destinée aux dépenses assurant sa commémoraison. Le reste de ses biens immobiliers allaient à son fils Syméon. Elle faisait exécuteur testamentaire et tuteur de son fils, son époux Nicéphore Kounalès et une autre personne de qualité.

Peu de temps après, Syméon mourut à son tour et son malheureux père se trouva hériter selon la loi. Un terrible tremblement de terre à Berrhoè abattit l'église de la Vierge. Kounalès, au prix de graves difficultés et d'une dépense en numéraire, rebâtit l'église et y installa un hiéromoine chargé de chanter et accomplir la liturgie, puis il construisit un monastère d'hommes pour la commémoraison de son épouse, de ses parents et de Syméon. Il appliquait ainsi le testament d'Hélène.

La belle-sœur Skoutariotissa contesta ces dispositions et réclama l'héritage de sa sœur. Le tribunal rejeta sa demande. Chômatianos s'appuyait sur la loi, car, selon les *Basiliques*, nous l'avons vu, le père hérite des biens de ses enfants, or Syméon avait lui-même reçu les biens de sa mère. De plus, en 1210, le père s'était parfaitement acquitté des souhaits de sa femme, en reconstruisant l'église de la Vierge. La Skoutariotissa ne pouvait donc plus, ni maintenant ni plus tard, contester l'héritage, car, en tant que tante maternelle du défunt, elle figurait au quatrième rang de succession alors que le père venait en second. Quelle pouvait être la motivation de la Skoutariotissa ? Elle estimait sans doute qu'une fois les biens immobiliers venant de sa famille intégrés au patrimoine de Kounalès, ces derniers seraient définitivement perdus pour les Pakourianoi. Dans cette affaire, Grégoire Pakourianos n'aurait eu, semble-t-il, que deux filles et pas de fils. La dernière fille survivante cherchait à reconstituer le patrimoine familial,

41. K. Zafeiris, The issue of the authorship of the Synopsis Chronike and Theodore Skoutariotes, *REB* 69, 2011 p. 253-263.

42. G. L. F. Tafel – G. M. Thomas, *Urkunden zur älteren Handels- und Staatsgeschichte der Republik Venedig* I, Vienna 1856, p. 120.

43. Stavrakos, *Bleisiegel* (cité n. 40), no 133.

44. Miklosich – Müller IV (cité n. 35), p. 55, 69, 72, 153, 158.

sa sœur n'ayant plus de descendant vivant et leur père étant décédé. Il est probable que si le droit était du côté de Kounalès, le fait que ce dernier ait respecté la volonté d'Hélène, en reconstruisant l'église abattue par le séisme, a aussi joué en sa faveur. Faute de descendance, en effet, cette église et le monastère attenant étaient les seuls moyens d'assurer le salut de l'âme de la défunte.

Un autre cas, plus simple, fut aussi tranché par Chômatianos. Kalos, fils de Tzantzès, contesta le don d'une vigne que son père avait offerte à un monastère, après la mort de son épouse. Cette vigne avait été acquise en commun par ses parents, sans que le nom de la mère fût mentionné dans l'acte. Chômatianos condamna cependant le père, privant ainsi de la vigne le monastère bénéficiaire non nommé. Le métropolite usa de deux arguments. D'une part, un père doit prendre soin de ses enfants sans ressources, ce qui était, semble-t-il, le cas de Kalos et, d'autre part, Kalos était l'héritier légitime de sa mère. Le monastère ne pouvait donc disposer que de la part de vigne appartenant au père[45].

Chômatianos jugea aussi une querelle portant sur un don par testament en faveur d'une église, qui serait transformée si possible en monastère[46]. L'affaire s'étend sur plusieurs générations. Alexis Arrabônitès[47] vint se plaindre du comportement de Michel Salérinos, époux de la grand-mère maternelle de sa propre femme. Irène, morte sans enfant, légua à l'église Saint-Nicolas des terrains, dans l'espoir d'y établir aussi un monastère où elle serait commémorée. Michel Salérinos ne respecta pas les volontés de son épouse, mais acquit pour lui-même lesdits terrains, en ayant de plus obtenu l'approbation du défunt métropolite de Corfou, Basile Pédiatitès. Chômatianos confirma bien que l'action de Salérinos était contraire à la loi. Toutes ces affaires confirment la réticence des parents survivants à transférer des biens familiaux à l'Eglise, à un moment où les noms, qui paraissent dans ces procès, montrent qu'il s'agit sans doute, en bonne part, de réfugiés de Constantinople. Ces conflits étaient évidemment exacerbés lorsque de grands mouvements de réfugiés se produisaient du fait des invasions qui réduisaient les biens disponibles ou invitaient à remplacer ceux qui avaient été perdus. C'est également pour cette raison que les procès aux enjeux assez modestes semblent se multiplier devant le tribunal patriarcal dans la seconde moitié du XIVe siècle.

Non seulement les *psychika* en faveur des établissements religieux étaient contrôlés, mais les monastères aussi étaient parfois l'objet de disputes. Dans la première moitié du XIVe siècle, l'Empire est encore assez prospère et étendu dans sa partie européenne et les sommes engagées peuvent être considérables.

Marie Palaiologina, princesse des Mongols, avait acheté à Ta Panagiou du Phanarion des immeubles, dont une église, pour fonder un monastère. Ces biens étaient considérables puisque Marie avait versé quatre mille hyperpères. Elle éleva le monastère prévu, puis décéda, laissant une fille, Théodora, qu'elle confia à son frère, l'empereur Andronic II, ainsi que son monastère. Andronic donna en mariage Théodora au panhypersébaste Isaac Paléologue Asanès. Après quelques années de vie commune, Théodora mourut sans enfant et son époux se vit confier l'éphorie du couvent, qui fut, semble-t-il, une institution pro-

45. PRINZING, *Demetrii Chomateni* (cité n. 3), acte n° 24, p. 93-96.

46. *Ibidem*, n° 101, p. 330-333.

47. Ce nom de famille ne semble attesté que dans une seule source, qui mentionne un protospathaire et stratège, Jean, qui fit campagne contre un émir arabe sous Romain Lécapène (CONSTANTINE PORPHYROGENITUS, *De administrando imperio*, Greek text ed. by Gy. MORAVCSIK; English transl. by R. J. H. JENKINS (*Corpus Fontium Historiae Byzantinae* 1), Washington DC 1967[2], p. 212.

fitable. Ce dernier fut accusé de piller le monastère, en augmentant à l'excès le nombre de moniales, exigeant deux mille hyperpères en *adelphata*, allant même jusqu'à s'emparer du matériau des bâtiments monastiques pour construire les siens. Ensuite, par un document écrit, il fit transférer le monastère à sa fille, Irène Asanina Philanthôpénè, et des immeubles à son fils, Andronic Asanès. Les moniales devaient prier pour le salut de l'âme du panhypersébaste, décédé entre-temps. Les moniales, lésées, se plaignirent à l'empereur qui renvoya l'affaire devant le tribunal patriarcal. Celui-ci fit examiner le chrysobulle, qu'Irène avait envoyé ; les spécialistes désignés par le patriarche révélèrent qu'il avait été trafiqué. Le couvent retrouva donc sa pleine indépendance, la restitution de ses biens fut ordonnée, mais les prières pour le salut du panhypersébaste furent sauvegardées, le tribunal n'ayant pas voulu un châtiment trop dur[48].

Cette affaire, qui touche de près la famille impériale, met en jeu des intérêts considérables. Elle illustre à quel point la tentation de détourner l'héritage d'une femme sans enfant par son époux, d'autant plus s'il a lui-même a des enfants d'un second lit, était forte et que s'opposer à cette captation d'héritage impliquait des actions en justice d'une très longue durée.

Un second exemple touche également la très haute aristocratie. Le domestique de la table impériale, Phôkas Maroulès[49], avait élevé, près de la porte Saint-Romain, une église dédiée à la Vierge, puis un monastère de femmes consacré au repos de son épouse et de ses filles, selon un témoignage. Jean Synadènos, grand fauconnier, fils de Maroulès, décida de transformer le monastère en y accueillant désormais des hommes. Il prétendit avoir le consentement de sa mère, puis exhiba un testament de son père manifestant son désir d'un tel changement. Le synode acquiesça à cette demande. Le fils mourut et sa mère avoua qu'elle avait été contrainte de donner son accord et le testament de Maroulès fut aussi reconnu comme un faux. De plus, à partir du moment où le monastère avait été consacré et une abbesse intronisée, un changement de destination était contraire aux canons[50]. En 1341, le synode décida donc, après une enquête auprès de témoins, que le monastère fût rendu aux moniales et que la veuve de Maroulès et ses filles jouissent du droit des fondateurs[51].

L'arrière-plan du procès n'est pas explicité, mais l'enjeu semble bien un détournement des biens maternels et de l'héritage des sœurs du grand fauconnier, au profit de ce dernier. Cette affaire illustre aussi l'influence d'un familier de l'empereur qui peut se permettre de tricher sur les documents et faire une pression efficace sur sa propre mère. Il faut attendre sa mort pour qu'une action réparatrice soit engagée.

48. J. DARROUZÈS, *Les Regestes des actes du patriarcat de Constantinople*. 1, *Les Actes des patriarches*, Fasc. V, *Les Regestes de 1310 à 1376*, Paris 1977, n° 2330. *Register des Patriarcats* III, n° 184, p. 62-76 .

49. Le premier Maroulès connu, Olbianos, commandait le *tagma* des Hicanates contre Syméon de Bulgarie (*Ioannis Scylitzae Synopsis historiarum*, rec. I. THURN (*Corpus Fontium Historiae Byzantinae*. Series Berolinensis 5), Berlin – New York 1973, p. 203).

50. Sur la conversion de couvents d'hommes en établissements destinés à des moniales et vice versa, cf. A.-M. TALBOT, Affirmative Action in the 12th c. : An Act of John Apokaukos concerning the Blachernitissa Monastery in Arta, dans *Philellen : in Honor of Robert Browning*, éd. C. CONSTANTINIDES *et alii*, Venise 1996, p. 399-409, repris dans EADEM, *Women and Religious Life in Byzantium*, n° XVI. EADEM, The conversion of Byzantine monasteries from male to female and vice-versa, dans *Polupleuros Nous : Miscellanea für Peter Schreiner zu seinem 60. Geburtstag*, éd. C. SCHOLTZ et G. MAKRIS, Munich 2000, p. 360-364.

51. *Regestes du patriarcat* V, n° 2207, *Register des Patriarcats* II, n° 135.

Les procès ne concernent pas seulement des biens immobiliers, mais aussi d'autres sources de revenus. Un évêque de Kernitsa dans le Péloponnèse et sa sœur, la moniale Euphrosynè, avaient hérité d'une icône de la Vierge Hodèghètria, dont ils devaient se partager par moitié les revenus qu'elle engendrait[52]. L'évêque avait, une première fois, tenté de s'approprier la majorité des revenus et un jugement l'avait débouté. Cependant, le métropolite de Patras s'était emparé de l'icône avant d'être obligé de la rendre. Euphrosynè fit alors construire une église, avec l'appui d'Andronic Paléologue Asanès, gouverneur du Péloponnèse, et elle y plaça l'icône. Mais un nouveau métropolite de Patras s'empara de nouveau de l'icône. Finalement, le synode décida que celle-ci devrait être restituée et que l'évêque et sa sœur se partageraient par moitié les revenus[53].

L'entrée d'une épouse au monastère

Lorsqu'une femme entre dans un monastère, le conflit reste familial, cependant il ne porte pas sur l'héritage, mais le devenir d'une dot. Manuel Exakoustos avait obtenu, lors d'un procès en divorce, de conserver toute la dot de son épouse, qui avait l'intention de se faire nonne. Le tribunal avait considéré que l'épouse, qui était encline à d'autres amours, avait commis une faute grave qui lui faisait ainsi perdre sa dot. Le beau-père, qui était prêtre, s'était emparé des immeubles donnés en complément de la dot pour, prétendait-il, les offrir au monastère où sa fille entrerait. Le tribunal, qui avait apparemment des doutes sur la vocation de la femme, décida que tout devait revenir à Exakoustos. Toutefois, si son ancienne épouse entrait vraiment au couvent, celui-ci devait recevoir cinquante hyperpères à titre de dot de la nouvelle moniale[54]. Le montant en jeu, qui ne représente qu'une partie de la fortune de Exakoustos, montre que nous sommes dans un milieu aisé. Dans ce jugement, le patriarche, conformément au droit, préserve les intérêts du mari, mais aussi ceux du monastère, l'ancien époux se trouvant dans l'obligation de doter l'épouse répudiée d'une donation non négligeable en faveur du couvent.

Détournement par autrui

La menace sur les héritages ne venait pas nécessairement du côté d'autres membres de la famille. Ainsi, un jugement de 1330 rapporte l'affaire suivante : un moine, Théodose, fuyant la région du Scamandre en Bithynie, menacée par les Turcs, avait construit à Héraclée, de l'autre côté de la Propontide, un monastère dédié à la Vierge Krionéritissa. Il y accueillit sa sœur Anastasie, elle aussi moniale, et sa nièce Agathonikè, fille de cette dernière. Sur le point de mourir, Théodose exprima, devant témoins, dont l'évêque de Daneion, son intention de laisser son monastère à ses parentes et de rédiger un testament. Visiblement, il n'en eut pas le temps, car un certain Georges Kounalès s'y opposa, qui fit rédiger par son propre fils un

52. Sur les revenus procurés par les icônes, cf. N. Oikonomides, The Holy Icon as an Asset, *DOP* 45, 1991, p. 35-44.

53. *Regestes du patriarcat* V, n° 2064, *Register des Patriarcats* I, n° 35, p. 274-278.

54. *Regestes du patriarcat* V, n° 2075, *Register des Patriarcats* I, n° 46, p. 316-318.

autre testament en faveur de *l'épi tou kanikleiou* défunt, non nommé, mais dont chacun savait qu'il s'agissait de Nicéphore Choumnos, très puissant personnage, jadis principal ministre (*mésazôn*) d'Andronic II. C'est probablement en raison de la mort de Choumnos, en 1327, que les moniales eurent gain de cause[55] et que, sur le testament présenté par la partie adverse, la signature de l'évêque de Daneion fut déclarée fausse. Ici, droit et politique sont liés dans le dénouement de l'affaire. Traditionnellement, les *épi tou kanikleiou* sont nommés protecteurs de grands monastères. On voit, par l'exemple de Kounalès, que le protecteur potentiel pouvait se muer en prédateur.

Il est possible que ce même monastère ait encore fait l'objet, en 1338, d'un procès. Un monastère de la Vierge est revendiqué par droit d'héritage par le *hiéromnèmon* de l'évêché d'Hexamilion, Manuel Artamas, et un lecteur, Michel Kryonéritès. Le nom du lecteur et le fait que l'évêché d'Hexamilion dépendait d'Héraclée de Thrace où se trouvait le monastère, suggèrent qu'il s'agit bien de la Théotokos Kryonéritissa. L'évêque d'Hexamilion prétend qu'il lui appartient. Il est finalement débouté. Dans l'affaire, on note que les grands-parents des héritiers avaient obtenu un *prostagma* impérial, signe de la crainte que la possession de leurs biens pût être remise en cause[56].

En 1342, Constantin Prasinos, familier de l'empereur, revendiqua par droit d'héritage le monastère Saint-Pantéléèmôn, l'église Saint-Nicolas et quelques *monydria*, biens situés dans l'île de Chios. Le métropolite de l'île fut accusé de percevoir les revenus de ces biens. Il le confessa, mais affirma que c'était pour faire vivre ces établissements. Par injonction patriarcale, le métropolite ne devait plus en toucher les revenus, mais ceux qui héritaient du droit du fondateur ne devaient pas non plus en tirer le moindre profit et il leur fallait donc se contenter des commémoraisons[57].

Querelles sur des biens appartenant à des monastères

Les querelles d'héritages provoquent également l'instabilité du patrimoine des monastères. Les registres du patriarcat constituent à nouveau la source la plus riche concernant ces procès.

Nous disposons cependant de deux lettres, antérieures à 956, de Théodore, métropolite de Nicée, à Théodore, patrice et éparque. Une dispute est évoquée, à propos d'un domaine (*proasteion*) de l'Eglise, mais de façon en partie allusive. Le métropolite protestait pour deux raisons : d'une part le *proasteion* avait été donné en dot à sa fille par un notable, nommé Bardas, d'autre part, l'époux de la fille refusait d'acquitter la part d'impôts qu'il devait, par héritage de son beau-père, donner à l'Eglise, allant jusqu'à s'approprier le *proasteion* comme un bien personnel. Il n'est pas aisé, à partir de ces seules informations, de reconstituer l'affaire. Il semble qu'un bien de la métropole pour lequel le métropolite devait aussi payer l'impôt ait été privatisé. La seconde lettre nous apprend qu'un monastère est aussi l'objet du litige, ce qui conduit à penser qu'il était construit dans le *proasteion*. Bardas en était-il le charisticaire et aura-t-il confondu son patrimoine et celui du monastère, comme beaucoup de charisticaires

55. *Regestes du patriarcat* V, n° 2157, *Register des Patriarcats* I, n° 103, p. 584-588.
56. *Regestes du patriarcat* V, n° 2182, *Register des Patriarcats* II, n° 112, p. 118-122.
57. *Regestes du patriarcat* V, n° 2234. *Register des Patriarcats* II, n° 139, p. 302-306.

qui furent accusés de pareils détournements ? L'Eglise, qui payait une part d'impôt, devait avoir conservé des terrains dans le *proasteion*[58]. La transmission du bien provoqua le conflit.

Une série de décisions du tribunal patriarcal nous fait connaître une intrigue aux aspects rocambolesques, en partie liée, quoiqu'il n'y soit pas fait allusion, aux troubles des guerres civiles, puisque le jugement définitif date de 1360, alors que l'affaire a commencé au moins trente-quatre ans auparavant. Une fois encore, c'est le milieu aristocratique qui est concerné, d'après les noms cités: Magistros, Bryennios, Triphyllios[59]. Toutefois ces personnages n'appartiennent pas à l'entourage impérial.

Magistrina, fille de Kékalesménos, avait une cousine germaine Bryennissa. Elle dut perdre ses parents jeunes. En tout cas, sa cousine reconstitua le patrimoine familial et compléta l'opération en adoptant Magistrina, ce qui laisse entendre qu'elle-même n'avait pas d'enfant. Elle la donna en mariage, en la dotant, en plus du patrimoine personnel de la future épouse de Michel Magistros, d'immeubles, d'ateliers, lui appartenant en bien propre du côté de sa mère. Magistrina devait hériter à sa mort du reste de ses biens, ce qui arriva quelques années plus tard. Cette dernière prétendit qu'une autre cousine, peut-être aussi germaine, Triphyllina, sous le fallacieux prétexte de son décès à l'étranger, s'empara des ateliers qui lui avaient été donnés par Bryennissa. Triphyllina les céda au monastère de Saint-Paul du Latros. Les moines, à leur tour, les revendirent à Synadèna qui les intégra à la dot de sa fille, lorsqu'elle la maria à Perdikarès. Un premier jugement fut rendu, assez promptement, semble-t-il, par le patriarche qui restitua à Magistrina les ateliers perdus. Nous ignorons comment Perdikarès devait être dédommagé, le monastère Saint-Paul n'ayant pas été lésé, dans la mesure où il avait reçu une somme d'argent en échange du terrain. L'absence de Magistrina, prétexte à croire qu'elle était défunte, peut s'expliquer si elle était engagée dans la querelle entre Jean VI et Jean V, le perdant, de quelque côté qu'il fût, devant laisser la place au vainqueur.

Cependant un second procès éveilla les soupçons, lorsque Magistrina essaya de reprendre une boulangerie, en prétendant qu'elle était incluse dans l'héritage de Bryennissa. Des témoins dignes de foi, des moines, attestèrent que Magistrina, accompagnée de son époux, avait signé l'acte de vente de cette boulangerie. Même si celle-ci provenait de la dot de Magistrina, la présence de l'époux au moment de la transaction la rendait valide.

Perdikarès, qui s'estimait lésé, mena une enquête pour rejeter les arguments de Magistrina puis prétendit, après cette recherche, qu'il avait découvert des documents prouvant que les moines étaient effectivement propriétaires du bien et l'avaient donc vendu à bon escient. Cette démarche montre que les archives publiques et privées avaient souffert des troubles civils. Selon Perdikarès, Triphyllina détenait les ateliers du vivant de Bryennissa, car elle en avait hérité. Le père et l'époux de Magistrina tentèrent de faire croire que Triphyllina était une fille bâtarde du frère de Kékalesménos, prétention qui fut rejetée par le tribunal.

Il ressort de cette affaire que Bryennissa, devenue moniale, rédigea un testament par lequel elle légua ses biens au monastère de Kyra Maria, mais aussi des maisons venant de l'héritage de Triphyllina. Cette dernière attaqua alors les moniales de Kyra Maria, et obtint gain de

58. J. Darrouzès, *Épistoliers byzantins du Xe siècle* (Archives de l'Orient chrétien 6), Paris 1960, p. 280 et p. 289-290.

59. Sur les trois noms des protagonistes du conflit, deux évoquent d'illustres et anciennes lignées (Bryennios et Triphyllios) et le troisième, Magistros, une famille bien connue sous les Paléologues, notamment par les écrits de Thomas Magistros.

cause au tribunal. Magistros ne protesta pas, mais il reçut de Triphyllina vingt hyperpères. Il avait signé aussi l'acte de vente des maisons par les moines à Synadèna.

À tous ces arguments, Magistrina présenta un document, dont le tribunal put, en observant le papier, montrer que c'était un faux récent. En résumé, depuis trente-quatre ans, grâce à des témoins, tous moines, Triphyllina prouvait qu'elle disposait des immeubles, sans entraîner de protestations de la part de Bryennissa. Triphyllina était dès lors bien fondée à donner des ateliers, qui lui appartenaient légitimement, à son gendre, Syropoulos, aujourd'hui défunt[60].

Que révèle cette affaire à rebondissements ? La structure familiale est simple. Le grand-père, dont le nom de famille n'est pas donné, disposait de biens importants, qui furent partagés, vers 1326 probablement après sa mort, et transmis à ses enfants, des garçons sans doute au nombre de trois, qui les transmirent à leurs propres descendants : Magistrina, Bryennissa et Triphyllina. Ces trois petites-filles avaient épousé des membres de l'élite constantinopolitaine. Bryennissa, qui n'avait sans doute pas d'enfant, adopta pour cette raison Magistrina, fille d'un de ses oncles. Restait la part de l'autre oncle, dont on peut supposer qu'il était le père de Triphyllina. En déclarant cette filiation illégitime, Magistrina souhaitait priver Triphyllina de sa part d'héritage et la récupérer à titre de plus proche parente, l'idée étant sans doute de reconstituer dans une seule lignée l'ensemble du patrimoine du grand-père, en profitant de la stérilité d'au moins une branche et de l'instabilité des temps.

Pour ce faire, Magistrina a commis en fait plusieurs irrégularités. D'une part, elle a accusé sa cousine Triphyllina d'être une fille bâtarde. Elle a été déboutée. D'autre part, elle a présenté un faux qui lui donnait l'héritage de Bryennissa, alors que cette dernière avait déjà inclus, de façon illégale, des propriétés qui n'étaient pas à elle.

Parfois les usurpations ne tournaient pas toujours au détriment complet du coupable. En 1325, Jean Triakontaphyllos, haut fonctionnaire, rappelle que son défunt père Monomachos, héritier du monastère de la Théotokos Pachniôtissa, situé en province près de la forteresse d'Hexamilion, l'avait laissé en héritage à un proche, peut-être son frère, le moine Barlaam. Barlaam concéda le droit de fondation à Jean Philanthropènos, familier de l'empereur, mais qui était étranger à la famille. En fait, ce geste cachait la vente déguisée du petit monastère contre soixante-douze hyperpères. Philanthropènos avait exploité la terre du monastère et fait d'importantes améliorations. Cette vente, contraire au droit, puisque les biens d'Eglise sont inaliénables, fut annulée. Pour éviter le renouvellement d'une pareille mésaventure, les deux plaignants perdirent tout droit sur le monastère, qui devient autodespote, mais Philanthropènos fut partiellement remboursé de ses dépenses[61].

Les biens d'un monastère pouvaient être captés par un éphore ou ses descendants. Le petit monastère de la Vierge des Varanges fut concédé par le couvent de Plynaria, dont on supposera qu'il en dépendait, à Gèraios Mikroképhalos pour qu'il l'entretienne et l'améliore. À sa mort, la concession passa à une moniale de la famille des Maroulai. Cette dernière avait promis des ateliers qu'elle détenait par ailleurs. Les héritiers de Mikroképhalos, ses petits-fils, réclamèrent le monastère par droit d'héritage du bien dont ils prétendaient que le grand-père avait la pleine propriété. Pour des raisons politiques, Maroulina ne put conserver le monas-

60. *Regestes du patriarcat* V, n°s 2424-2427.

61. *Regestes du patriarcat* V, n° 2126, *Register des Patriarcats* I, n° 93, p. 526-530.

tère, car elle avait soutenu Barlaam, et la concession fut transmise à Alexis Sophianos en 1361. Ce dernier bénéficiera du droit de fondateur, afin d'y être commémoré. À sa mort, le monastère devait revenir à la Grande-Eglise[62].

L'enjeu du conflit est relativement modeste et caractéristique des disputes à propos de revenus médiocres, mais indispensables dans un moment où l'Empire décline profondément, entraînant un amenuisement des ressources. Un bien concédé pendant une longue durée, – ce sont les petits-fils du premier bénéficiaire qui tentent de le conserver – en vient à être considéré comme une propriété familiale. C'est une démarche assez proche de celle des pronoiaires qui tentaient de transmettre leur concession à leurs héritiers. La décision du patriarche illustre aussi le poids de la politique puisque la Maroulina est dépossédée de son bien sans qu'elle ait été accusée de malversations, simplement pour avoir soutenu la partie perdante d'un conflit politico-religieux.

Enfin, dernier cas de figure, des héritages échappaient parfois au bénéficiaire désigné, au profit d'un monastère qui avait pris soin du testateur[63]. Ainsi, avant 1401, Dèmètrios Boullôtès, familier de l'empereur, avait été désigné par une cousine de sa femme, Irène Apokaukissa, comme l'héritier de cette dernière et gérant de tous les biens de son fils absent. Parmi les biens se trouvait une icône de culte de la Panagia Blachernitissa, qui procurait un revenu. Les moniales du couvent Saint-Cyprien recueillent Irène qui est très malade et demande à être admise au monastère après avoir été tonsurée. Auparavant, une des moniales ayant averti Boullôtès de la volonté d'Irène, ce dernier exprime clairement sa décision de ne pas s'occuper d'Irène et indique où se trouve son testament. Une moniale déchire alors le testament et Irène en fait un autre, au profit du couvent Saint-Cyprien, avant d'y être admise. À sa mort, le couvent, qui l'avait accueillie pour ses derniers instants et payé ses funérailles, garda donc ses biens. Boullôtès fut débouté pour deux raisons : premièrement il était pleinement informé du changement de testament et, en second lieu, il avait refusé de prendre soin d'Irène à la fin de sa vie. On supposera que la fortune d'Irène n'était pas très importante et qu'elle avait été largement entamée pendant son court séjour au couvent. Dans une certaine mesure, le tribunal a implicitement considéré que la modeste fortune d'Irène était en quelque sorte un *adelphaton*, destiné à qui prendrait soin d'elle.

Les *adelphata* eux-mêmes pouvaient être contestés. En 1400, la mère de Dèmètrios Kallistos avait vendu un *adelphaton* à un monastère de femmes à Constantinople. Le fils s'opposa à cet acte car, selon lui, l'*adelphaton* venait de son père et il en était donc l'héritier légitime. Les moniales prétendirent que le père s'était associé à la vente et avait ainsi consenti à cet abandon de patrimoine[64].

62. *Regestes du patriarcat* V, n°s 2386 et 2433, *Register der Patriarcats* III, n° 258, p. 514-520.

63. Le cas de Boullôtès est signalé par R. MACRIDÈS, The Transmission of Property in the Patriarcal Register, dans BEAUCAMP-DAGRON, *Transmission* (cité n. 1), p. 182, celui de Kallistos, p. 188.

64. J. DARROUZÈS, *Les Regestes des actes du patriarcat de Constantinople*. 1, *Les Actes des patriarches*, Fasc. VI, *Les Regestes de 1377 à 1410*, Paris 1979, n° 3161, jugement daté de 1400, durant le blocus de Constantinople par les Ottomans.

Conclusion

Les différends où des monastères étaient directement opposés à des laïcs étaient finalement assez peu nombreux ; les querelles entre les monastères athonites fournissent un dossier beaucoup plus fourni. Souvent l'appel aux tribunaux était déclenché par le fait que des héritiers sans enfants donnaient la totalité ou presque de leurs biens et qu'à ce moment les lignées collatérales se manifestaient. Elles étaient, en règle générale, déboutées. Le moment de tension le plus intense, c'est lorsqu'un jeune, homme ou femme, entrait au monastère, en réclamant sa part d'héritage. En conséquence, les monastères se trouvaient engagés dans des conflits de propriété lorsqu'ils avaient hérité de biens que le propriétaire antérieur avait acquis par une transaction douteuse, mais, dans ce cas, le couvent n'était qu'un plaideur comme les autres.

Par ailleurs, s'il est vrai que les grandes fondations impériales constituaient des fondations pieuses produisant des revenus considérables, beaucoup d'établissements plus modestes ne visaient pas à fournir des surplus, mais à accueillir éventuellement le fondateur et ses descendants et surtout à répondre à l'anxiété suprême des Byzantins, l'assurance que des prières pour le salut de leur âme seraient assurées pour l'éternité. Ce vœu rencontre parfois l'opposition des héritiers quand ils s'estiment privés de biens indispensables à leur train de vie ou lorsqu'ils croient déceler une irrégularité dans l'acquisition des biens donnés. Notre documentation ne permet pas de distinguer entre les petits patrimoines sur lesquels tout prélèvement est mal ressenti, notamment s'il y a des héritiers directs, et les très grands, venus de familles très influentes, qui avaient les moyens de les reconstituer par leur proximité avec le pouvoir.

Une double évolution se dessine entre les Xe et XVe siècles. Probablement, jusqu'en 1204 – le XIIe siècle ne nous a pas laissé de documentation exploitable – les enjeux des procès étaient considérables, se comptant en livres, voire en dizaines de livres. Il étaient jugés par les tribunaux laïcs, comme en témoigne la *Peira*. Il ne faut pas en déduire qu'à un niveau social plus modeste aucune contestation ne s'élevait, mais les plaignants n'accédaient pas aux tribunaux impériaux, sauf rares exceptions, dues à de puissants protecteurs. Toutefois, nous n'avons pas conservé de décisions émanant des juges de thème, à l'exception de celles qui furent ensuite contestées en appel, à Constantinople.

Après 1204, le tableau est différent. Les tribunaux sollicités étaient dirigés par des clercs : celui de Chômatianos, archevêque de toute la Bulgarie, celui du patriarcat ensuite, dont les registres sont sauvegardés depuis 1315. Au cours des procédures, on découvre qu'un grand nombre de faux étaient présentés au tribunal : faux chrysobulles, faux testaments. Ces documents ne semblaient pas scandaliser considérablement le tribunal du patriarcat. Fait également remarquable, l'instabilité politique fournissait l'occasion de revenir sur des décisions déjà obtenues.

L'abondance de la documentation n'explique pas entièrement la multiplication des procès aux enjeux modestes, à l'exception de ceux qui étaient engagés par des proches, parents ou familiers, de l'empereur. Les tentatives d'appropriation indue d'un établissement religieux se multiplièrent au XIVe siècle et concernent des biens d'une valeur de plus en plus modeste, reflétant la rareté progressive des biens fonciers. Plus encore que les propriétés, c'étaient les revenus, comme les *adelphata*, qui étaient âprement recherchés. Enfin, le blocus de Constantinople par le sultan Bayezid, entre 1394 et 1402, accentua encore la pénurie et provoqua l'augmentation des conflits autour des dernières ressources disponibles, traduisant l'appauvrissement, de plus en plus marqué, des sujets du *basileus*.

INHERITING POWER

UNEQUAL BROTHERS: AN EXPLORATION OF A SUCCESSION STRATEGY OF AUGUSTUS

Amber Gartrell

The process leading up to the first imperial succession was not smooth, but marred by scandals and deaths. Great care must be taken when exploring the 'succession policy', as the term itself misrepresents its developing nature. The terminology used to refer to different kinds of inheritance is also difficult. I shall therefore refer to those who receive legal and testamentary inheritance, for example property or wealth, which might be passed from the deceased to another person through legal means, as 'heirs'. However concerning the transfer of less tangible legacies such as political alliances, debts or influences, I shall use the term 'successor' to denote the beneficiary of such bequests. For Augustus' own position as *princeps* was in reality an honorific one which had evolved gradually with the accumulation of honours, offices and titles. His potential successors also needed to undergo a similar process to gain both honours and popularity.[1] The imperial succession should not be seen as a fixed policy which was conceived early in Augustus' reign and remained unchanged except for the particular potential successor upon whom it focused. Rather it should be regarded as an evolving process, adapting and changing as the circumstances demanded.[2] This process also falls into two parts. The first concerns what powers, honours and experiences were necessary to establish a successor in this or a similar position.[3] The second aspect, upon which this paper shall focus, concerns how the young men of the imperial family, itself a constantly changing group, might be selected and promoted as successors to the *princeps*.

1. W. Eder, Augustus and the Power of Tradition: The Augustan Principate as Binding Link between Republic and Empire, in *Between Republic and Empire: Interpretations of Augustus and his Principate*, ed. by K. A. Raaflaub and M. Toher, Berkley—London 1993, pp. 120–121, highlights the importance of this accumulation of honours to preserve the illusion of the Republic.
2. On the issues of applying a modern view and term of 'succession' to ancient events see A. G. G. Gibson, 'Introduction', in *The Julio-Claudian Succession: Reality and Perception of the "Augustan model"*, ed. by A. G. G. Gibson, Mnemosyne Supplement 349, Leiden 2012, p. 1; J. Osgood, 'Suetonius and the Succession to Augustus', in *Julio-Claudian Succession*, pp. 19, 31–32.
3. W. Eder, *Augustus* (quoted n. 1), pp. 120–121.

Inheritance, Law and Religions in the Ancient and Mediaeval Worlds, ed. by B. Caseau and S. R. Huebner (Centre de recherche d'Histoire et Civilisation de Byzance, Monographies 45), Paris 2014.

To complicate matters, Augustus had no sons of his own, only a daughter, Julia the Elder from his marriage to Scribonia.[4] His wife Livia had two sons, Tiberius and Drusus the Elder, from her earlier marriage to Nero Drusus. Augustus therefore turned to his closest male relatives to seek a successor, including his grandsons Gaius and Lucius Caesar whom he adopted. In this paper, I shall focus on the strategy which partnered young men of the imperial family of similar ages.[5] This strategy may have developed from Augustus' own relationship with Marcus Agrippa, his long-time friend and second in command.[6] Although this strategy did possess certain benefits, including the attempt to negate the impact of the death of one or both potential successors, it also brought its own possible conflicts: crucially how a pair might struggle between themselves for prominence.[7] I shall argue that a further strategy was developed to lessen at least the appearance of any such conflicts: the comparison of the paired potential successors with two brother gods famed for their fraternal piety; Castor and Pollux, the Dioscuri.

However, before analysing the creation and effectiveness of this strategy, it will be beneficial to briefly explore how inheritance and succession operated in the Roman Republic. Since the expulsion of the kings it had been against the Republican constitution to have hereditary positions of power.[8] The highest ordinary office during the Republic, the consulate, was explicitly non-hereditary. It was an annual office and held by two men simultaneously, who acted as checks and balances upon each other.[9] Restrictions were also placed upon successive consulships.[10] After they had completed their year in office, the magistrates could be prosecuted and thus held accountable for their actions. A son could not, in theory at least, inherit his father's political position. Instead he had to prove his own credentials, progressing through the offices of the *cursus honorum*, holding the junior posts before he might stand for election for the higher magistracies. However we do possess examples of families who held the much coveted consulship generation after generation. The family of the Servilli Caepiones, for example, held the consulship for six successive generations from 253 BC.[11] By the end of the Republic, it could even be said of an offspring of one of these prominent families that

4. Suetonius, *Augustus* 63.1.

5. E. Kornemann, *Doppelprinzipat und Reichsteilung im Imperium Romanum*, Leipzig 1930; G. Rowe, *Princes and Political Cultures: The New Tiberian Senatorial Decrees*, Ann Arbour 2002, pp. 17–18.

6. Cassius Dio 54.31.1; Tacitus, *Annales* 1.3.

7. As we see, for example, in the pairings of Caligula and Tiberius Gemellus (Cassius Dio 59.1.1-3, 59.8.1; Suetonius, *Caligula* 23.3), Nero and Britannicus (Cassius Dio 61.1.1, 61.7.4; Suetonius *Nero* 7.1), and Titus and Domitian (Suetonius, *Domitian* 2.3). C. Bannon, *The Brothers of Romulus*, Princeton 1997, p. 178.

8. Livy 2.1.

9. *Consuls and Res Publica, Holding high office in the Roman Republic*, ed. by H. Beck, Cambridge 2011; S. Marastoni, L'eredità come strumento di legittimazioni di diritti politici. Introduzione al Problema, in *Hereditas, Adoptio e potere politico in Roma Antica*, ed. by S. Marastoni, A. Mastrocinque and B. Poletti, Rome 2011, p. 1.

10. T. J. Cornell, *The Beginnings of Rome: Italy and Rome from the Bronze Age to the Punic Wars (c. 1000-264 BC)*, London 1995, pp. 226–227, 371.

11. M.-H. Prevost, *Les adoptions politiques à Rome sous la Républic et le Principat*, Paris 1949, p. 28; this sequence also included adopted sons. An opposing view is K. Hopkins and G. Burton, 'Political Succession in the Late Republic (246-50 BC)', in *Death and Renewal: Sociological Studies in Roman History vol 2*, ed. by K. Hopkins, Cambridge 1983, pp. 32–33, 42–43, 55–60.

Lucius Domitius was 'consul designate from the cradle'.[12] It is not until the late Republic that regulations governing the successive holding of offices by an individual began to disintegrate, as demonstrated by the seven consulships of Gaius Marius, five of which were held in succession[13] and the four successive consulships of Julius Caesar, who would eventually become dictator for life.[14] The beginning of a trend can therefore be seen in which the restrictions on political offices were beginning to weaken, particularly in the case of prominent individuals.

A son might more easily take his father's vacated place in a religious college however.[15] This is probably owing to the different methods of selection for political and religious offices. Vacancies in priestly colleges were usually filled by co-option, in which the members of the college would nominate someone to fill the newly vacant space.[16] Even the office of *pontifex maximus*, Rome's highest priestly office, might remain in a family: in 141 BC it passed from father to son[17] and in 130 BC between brothers.[18] Although from the third century BC the candidates for *pontifex maximus* did stand for election before an assembly, the nominees were selected by the pontifical college who thus expressed their preferences.[19] This means that the position could not pass directly between relatives with no mediation, but rather that such a transfer had to be approved by both the *pontifices* and the people. It would not be surprising however, if a candidate whose relative, such as brother or father, had held the position of *pontifex maximus*, particularly if he had been admired, might gain an advantage over his competitors. Therefore although not common, it was certainly possible that a priestly office could be held by relatives in succession.[20]

In order to have a chance to bestow his position on another, a man needed someone who could inherit his accumulated property and succeed to his alliances. A son would usually be the first choice, but on occasion this was not possible. If he had no living sons, he might, like Augustus, choose another close male relative, such as a nephew or grandson.[21] If that option was not available, he might choose to adopt an heir from another family. During the Republic, adoptions appear to have possessed three primary functions: first, to provide an heir for the adoptive father's possessions, wealth and clients; second, to bind two families together;

12. Cicero, *Epistulae ad Atticum* 4.8a.2, translation after Shackleton Bailey (1999).

13. Plutarch, *Marius* 45.1; Appian, *Bella Civilia* 1.75.

14. Suetonius, *Divus Iulius* 76.1-2.

15. Servius, *Aeneid* 11.768; Cicero, *Orationes Philippicae* 13.12; Livy 27.6.12; F. PRESCENDI, Children and the Transmission of Religious Knowledge, in *Children, Memory and Family Identity in Roman Culture*, eds. by V. DASEN and T. SPÄTH, Oxford 2010, p. 87, suggests that such successions were atypical.

16. M. BEARD, Priesthood in the Roman Republic, in *Pagan Priests: Religion and Power in the Ancient World*, eds. by M. BEARD and J. NORTH, London 1990, pp. 22–24, after the *Lex Domitia* in 104 BC some colleges began selecting members by public election rather than co-option, however the colleges still compiled a shortlist of candidates who were then voted upon.

17. G. SZEMLER, *The Priests of the Roman Republic: A study of interactions between Priesthoods and magistracies* (Collection Latomus 127), Bruxelles 1972, cat. no. 28.

18. G. SZEMLER, *Priests of the Roman Republic* cat. no. 30 p. 122.

19. L. R. TAYLOR, The Election of the *Pontifex Maximus* in the Late Republic, *Classical Philology* 37.4, 1942, p. 421.

20. G. SZEMLER, *Priests of the Roman Republic* cat. nos. 2, 8, 14, 20, 33, 35, 37. There may of course be more such 'successions' about which we do not know.

21. H. LINDSAY, *Adoption in the Roman World*, Cambridge 2009, p. 355.

and third, to increase the adoptive son's status, perhaps allowing him to pursue a career which his natural parents could not support.[22] Adoption removed the adoptee from his biological family, severing all legal ties between them and recreated those legal relationships within his adoptive family.[23] An adoptive son therefore held the same status and rights within his adoptive family as if he had been born into it.[24]

This was the situation in which Octavian found himself following the assassination of his great-uncle Julius Caesar in 44 BC, having been adopted by Caesar posthumously in his will.[25] Upon his acceptance of Caesar's legacy Octavian gave a speech in the Forum Romanum, in which he extended his hand towards a statue of Julius Caesar and prayed 'that he might be able to obtain to the honours of his father (*parentis honores*)'.[26] As his new father's honours had included, among many others, the consulship and dictatorship, this would be an unusual bequest.[27] Octavian's suggestion that because he was now the adopted son of Caesar he might hope to attain a similar position to his father is extraordinary.[28]

In fact, it was possible for testamentary adoptions to be refused by the heir, as Octavian was advised to do by his mother and stepfather.[29] As demonstrated by Caesar's will, it was sometimes a stipulation of the will that to take up his inheritance, the adopted son also had to take his adoptive father's name.[30] Octavian duly did so, reportedly using Caesar as his name at once to promote himself as he embarked upon a political career.[31] Octavian demanded that his adoption be verified by the *lex curiata*, which usually ratified full adoptions. This ceremony, by sanctioning the adoption, entitled him to the full rights of a biological child of Caesar: his wealth, name, and rich and influential freedmen and possibly clients as well.[32] His eagerness for this decree was surely an attempt to legitimise his position as Caesar's heir and successor, particularly in comparison to Caesarion, the biological son of Caesar and Cleopatra.[33]

22. J. F. GARDNER, *Family and Familia in Roman Law and Life*, Oxford 1998, p. 141; M. CORBIER, Constructing Kinship in Rome: Marriage and Divorce, Filiation and Adoption, in *The Family in Italy from Antiquity to the Present*, eds. by D. KERTZER and R. SALLER, New Haven—London 1991, p. 142; M.-H. PREVOST, *Les Adoptions Politiques* (quoted n. 11), pp. 39–40; K. HOPKINS and G. BURTON, *Political Succession in the Late Republic* pp. 49–50.

23. J. F. GARDNER, *Family and Familia*, pp. 117, 119; M. PEPPARD, *The Son of God in the Roman World: Divinity and Divine Sonship in its Social and Political Context*, New York—Oxford 2011, p. 54.

24. Aulus Gellius, *Noctes Atticae* 5.19; GARDNER, *Family and Familia* (quoted n. 22) pp. 117, 119; PEPPARD, *The Son of God* (quoted n. 23), p. 54.

25. Suetonius, *Divus Iulius* 83.2. J. F. GARDNER, The Dictator, in *A Companion to Julius Caesar*, ed. by M. GRIFFIN, Chichester 2009, pp. 67–68.

26. Cicero, *Epistulae ad Atticum* 16.15.3, translation after Shackleton Bailey (1999).

27. Suetonius, *Divus Iulius* 76.1.

28. On testamentary adoption see LINDSAY, *Adoption* (quoted n. 21), ch. 5.

29. LINDSAY, *Adoption* (cited in n. 21), p. 80; Suetonius, *Divus Augustus* 8.2.

30. Suetonius, *Divus Iulius* 83.2, *Divus Augustus* 7.2; Appian, *Bella Civilia* 3.11; GARDNER, The Dictator (quoted n. 25), pp. 67–69; LINDSAY, *Adoption* (quoted n. 21), pp. 83–84 argues that testamentary adoption involved no more than the obligation to take the testator's name.

31. Appian, *Bella Civilia* 3.11; Cassius Dio 45.3; LINDSAY, *Adoption* (quoted n. 21), p. 183; GARDNER, *The Dictator* (quoted n. 25), pp. 67–68, argues that Caesar did not intend to adopt Octavian, just to pass on his name.

32. Appian, *Bella Civilia* 3.94.

33. Suetonius, *Divus Iulius* 52.1-2.

After Cleopatra and Mark Antony were defeated in 30 BC, Octavian wasted little time in eliminating his rival as the son (and potential successor) of Caesar, according to Plutarch following the advice of the philosopher Areius that 'not a good thing were a Caesar too many'.[34]

It can therefore be seen that from the very beginning of the empire adoption played a pivotal role in the imperial succession. Octavian's adoption by Caesar helped pave his way to becoming *princeps* many years later. It is perhaps not surprising that adoption therefore continued to be used as a tool to manipulate the status of members of Augustus' family, promoting some above the rest. In particular, such promotions often focused upon young men of a similar age, who I shall argue were promoted together and as a potential pair of successors. However the fact that these pairs were promoted together does not mean that they were always promoted equally. Such inequality within the pairing created potential conflicts between both the young men, but also possibly with their supporters.[35] I shall argue that one of the ways in which this potential conflict was alleviated or at least its appearance was minimised, was through the comparison of these mortal pairs with a pair of gods who were renowned for their fraternal piety and harmony.

Castor and Pollux, the Dioscuri, were the sons of Leda, the Queen of Sparta. Their fathers differed, as Leda was impregnated by both the god Zeus (in the form of a swan) and her husband Tyndareus during the same night. Owing to their different fathers Pollux, the son of Zeus, was immortal, while Castor, the son of Tyndareus, was mortal. However, the brothers were so devoted to each other that when Castor was fatally wounded, Pollux begged his father to share his immortality between them, so that he would not have to live without his brother. Zeus, in recognition of his son's fraternal piety, agreed, making both immortal.[36]

Of importance for my argument is that in Rome the brothers were often perceived as being unequal. This inequality is indicated by a complaint uttered by Marcus Bibulus, Julius Caesar's co-consul in 59 BC; that he shared the same fate as Pollux, for 'just as the temple erected in the Forum to the twin brethren, bears only the name of Castor, so the joint liberality of Caesar and myself is credited to Caesar alone'.[37] The brothers are also commonly both depicted as horsemen, Castor's attribute, while Pollux was known for his skill at boxing.[38] This perceived inequality between the brother gods is mirrored in the imperial pairs as well, who were often linked to the Dioscuri in Augustan ideology. The first pair to be compared with Castor and Pollux were Augustus' grandsons from the marriage of his daughter Julia to Marcus Agrippa. Gaius and Lucius were adopted by their grandfather soon after Lucius' birth in 17 BC.[39] They received their most significant titles, although not at the same time, at the same age, when each was fifteen years old, being named *consul designatus* by the Senate

34. Plutarch, *Antony* 81.2, translation after Perrin (1920); Suetonius, *Divus Augustus* 17.5; Cassius Dio 49.41.1-2.

35. Tacitus, *Annales* 2.43 suggests that although the court was divided by their preferences for Germanicus and Drusus, the brothers remained close and loyal to each other.

36. Ovid, *Fasti* 5.693-720; Homerica, *Cypria* 1, 12; Lucian, *Dialogues of the Gods* 26.281-287; Pindar, *Nemean Odes* 10.55-90; Plutarch, *De Fraterno Amore* 12.

37. Suetonius, *Divus Iulius* 10, translation after Rolfe, rev. Hurley (1998).

38. Homer, *Iliad* 3.236-238; Horace, *Satirae* 2.1.26-27; Ovid, *Amores* 3.2.54, *Metamorphoses* 8.301-302; Plutarch, *De Fraterno Amore* 15; Propertius 3.14.17-20.

39. Cassius Dio 54.8.5, 54.18.1; Suetonius, *Divus Augustus* 64.1.

and acclaimed *princeps iuventutis* by the *equites*.[40] The knights also presented the pair with silver shields and spears, representations of traditional cavalry weapons.[41] It was this title in particular which singled out the brothers as being in line for the imperial succession, as a link can be seen between their primarily honorific titles of *principes iuventutis*, with Augustus' own position as *princeps*. Such parallels were seen at the time, as demonstrated by references in contemporary literature, such as Ovid's description of Gaius as '*nunc iuvenum princeps, deinde future senum*'.[42]

As *principes iuventutis* Gaius and Lucius were linked to Castor and Pollux, who were the patrons of the *equites*.[43] The annual parade of the knights, the *transvectio equitum*, which was revived by Augustus, occurred on the 15th July, the date of the Battle of Lake Regillus.[44] Castor and Pollux were said to have appeared at this battle and led the Roman cavalry to victory against the Latins.[45] Gaius and Lucius, as *principes iuventutis*, on at least one occasion may have taken part in the procession of the knights, carrying their silver shields and spears, as they passed through the city, past the temple of Castor and Pollux in the Forum Romanum to the Capitoline Hill.[46] This parallel was perhaps drawn more explicitly outside Rome, for an inscription from Ephesus reveals that the city possessed a cult worshipping Gaius and Lucius alongside the Dioscuri and Alexander the Great.[47]

However Gaius and Lucius were not always promoted equally. Following Gaius' birth annual sacrifices were voted, whereas no such honour is noted at Lucius' birth.[48] As both boys were adopted by Augustus shortly after Lucius was born, our sources often focus upon their adoption rather than Lucius' birth, which may explain the lack of references to any honours for Lucius. In addition Gaius, as the first-born may have received honours in his own right, whereas Lucius, being the younger, may only have been honoured as one of a pair. In some instances the pair also received different positions, for example Gaius was elected among the *pontifices*, whilst Lucius became an augur.[49] Although Gaius and Lucius did receive the majority of their commands, honours and titles either at the same time, or at the same age, they can thus still be seen as being unequally promoted in some aspects of their careers. Their adoption by Augustus and the subsequent honours voted to them, receiving offices

40. Augustus, *Res Gestae Divi Augusti* 14.1-2; KORNEMANN, *Doppelprinzipat* (quoted n. 5), pp. 29–30.

41. Cassius Dio 55.12.1; Augustus, *Res Gestae Divi Augusti* 14.2.

42. Ovid, *Ars Amatoria* 1.194.

43. B. POULSEN, The Dioscuri and Ruler Ideology, *Symbolae Osloenses* 66, 1991, p. 123; B. SEVERY, *Augustus and the Family at the Birth of the Roman Empire*, New York—London 2003, p. 164.

44. Dionysius of Halicarnassus, *Antiquitates Romanae* 6.3.14.

45. Livy 2.19; Dionysius of Halicarnassus, *Antiquitates Romanae* 6.13.1-5; Plutarch, *Aemilius Paullus* 25.1.

46. Dionysius of Halicarnassus, *Antiquitates Romanae* 6.13.4-5.

47. POULSEN, *Dioscuri* (quoted n. 43), p. 125; *SEG* IV.521. Although this cult is only attested in a second century AD inscription, it would probably have been founded when the brothers were alive rather than two centuries after their deaths. Contra: E. CHAMPLIN, Tiberius and the Heavenly Twins, *JRS* 101, 2011, pp. 99–100.

48. Cassius Dio 54.8.5 (Gaius), 54.18.1 (Lucius).

49. *CIL* 11.1420; the difference may be explained by a desire to spread his family's influence widely, but it may be indicative that it was Gaius who joined the *pontifices* while Lucius became an augur, although augury was important in Augustan ideology.

under the minimum required age, were necessary to distinguish the pair as potential heirs. As they were brothers, related to Augustus to the same degree, perhaps the inequality in this pairing derives from the greater age of Gaius. Three years older than Lucius, he possessed the benefit of primogeniture, always having more titles, powers and honours than his younger brother. We are not told by the sources of any great conflict between the brothers and thus the comparison of the potential successors with the Dioscuri served to promote both and to suggest that they too possessed great fraternal harmony.

Following the deaths of Lucius in AD 2 and then Gaius in AD 4, Augustus appears to have developed the programme further, creating two pairs in the adoptions of AD 4. Augustus himself adopted his remaining grandson, Agrippa Postumus, and his stepson Tiberius. In turn, Tiberius adopted Germanicus, Augustus' great-nephew, pairing him with Tiberius' biological son Drusus the Younger.[50] Tiberius and Agrippa do not appear to have been linked as a pair during the three years before Agrippa was exiled owing to his violent temperament.[51] Furthermore, in AD 4 Tiberius would have been forty-five while Agrippa would have been only sixteen, perhaps stretching the idea of a fraternal relationship to the extreme. Tiberius had a brother, Drusus the Elder, who had died in 9 BC whilst on campaign in Germany.[52] The perceived prominence of these brothers may have been affected by their eventual fates: Drusus' early death and Tiberius' accession as emperor. However the evidence of their honours during life suggests that Tiberius was the more prominent in life. Both, similarly to Gaius and Lucius, received equal honours at the same age, for example both were permitted to stand for office five years before the legal age at nineteen years old.[53] However it was Tiberius who was ordered to divorce Vipsania, his beloved wife, and marry the newly widowed daughter of Augustus, Julia.[54]

It is this pairing which is most explicitly linked to the Dioscuri, as Tiberius and Drusus were also famous for their fraternal harmony, for example Ovid writes in the *Fasti* '*hac sunt Ledaeis templa dicata deis: / fratribus illa deis fratres de gente deorum / circa Iuturnae composuere lacus*', explicitly drawing a parallel between the two sets of brothers.[55] However it must be asked when the comparison between the Dioscuri and the Claudian brothers began to be publicised, for while Drusus was alive, Gaius and Lucius were still the most prominent potential heirs for Augustus. It would thus be somewhat strange at this stage for Tiberius and Drusus, who were older and not biologically related to Augustus, to be linked with the Dioscuri rather than Gaius and Lucius. It has been suggested by Champlin that the comparison of Tiberius and his brother to the Dioscuri was only promoted following Tiberius' unexpected rise to prominence follow-

50. Cassius Dio 55.13.1-3; Suetonius, *Tiberius* 15.2.

51. Cassius Dio 55.32.1-2; Suetonius, *Divus Augustus* 65.1.

52. Cassius Dio 55.1.3-2.3; Valerius Maximus 5.5.3.

53. Cassius Dio 53.28.3 (Tiberius), 54.10.4 (Drusus); G. V. Sumner, Germanicus and Drusus Caesar, *Latomus* 26, 1967, pp. 424–425.

54. Cassius Dio 54.6.5, 54.31.2; Suetonius, *Tiberius* 7.2; Severy, *Augustus and the Family* (quoted n. 43), p. 67, argues that this marriage was more concerned with Julia's status and Augustus' marriage legislation than the succession. I would agree with this, as Gaius and Lucius were still alive, but nonetheless, I believe that the choice of Tiberius remains significant.

55. Ovid, *Fasti* 1.705-708.

ing the deaths of Gaius and Lucius.[56] This would perhaps explain why the most explicit links between Castor and Pollux and the sons of Livia tend to be later than the deaths of Gaius and Lucius. In some ways therefore, this comparison may have primarily been a retrospective one and thus not have been promoted when both members of the pair were alive.

In fact it was perhaps Drusus' death which cemented their connection with Castor and Pollux. For, as Drusus was dying in Germany, shooting stars and two young men were seen riding on horseback through the camp.[57] Two of the key attributes of Castor and Pollux were stars and horses, thus these riders were perhaps identified as the Dioscuri escorting one of their mortal counterparts from life. Upon hearing of his brother's illness, Tiberius travelled to the camp, arriving just before Drusus died. Tiberius then escorted his body to Rome, walking before it the entire way.[58] Valerius Maximus concludes his account with the statement that 'no example of kindred affection can be suitably added save Castor and Pollux'.[59] Furthermore in AD 6 Tiberius rededicated the Temple of Castor and Pollux in the Forum Romanum.[60] This dedication was performed in his and Drusus' name at the same time as his rededication of the Temple of Concordia Augusta.[61] These two temples thus alluded to their fraternal harmony and piety even fifteen years after Drusus' death and should perhaps be seen as the context for the publication of their parallel to Castor and Pollux.[62] The anonymous author of the *Consolatio ad Liviam* highlights the parallel between the mortal and divine brothers, emphasising the pathos of Tiberius' dedication of a temple to the immortal brother gods after the death of his own brother.[63]

We are told that it was a condition of Tiberius' adoption in AD 4 that he adopted Germanicus, Augustus' great-nephew.[64] Tiberius however had a son of his own, Drusus, who was younger than Germanicus and thus supplanted in the line of succession.[65] A potential conflict was therefore created- what did it mean for the succession policy when Tiberius had two sons, one adoptive and one biological? Legally, as I have earlier stated, there was no difference between Germanicus and Drusus, any testamentary inheritance would usually be shared between siblings, either biological or adoptive.[66] However the role of the *princeps* as

56. Champlin, *Tiberius and the Heavenly Twins* (quoted n. 47), p. 92, argues that there is no evidence for a parallel being drawn between the Dioscuri and Gaius and Lucius. Although I acknowledge that there are no explicit references in Rome, references can be found in the provinces, although these are not unproblematic. The less explicit nature of this relationship is perhaps due to the succession policy still developing at this early stage.

57. Valerius Maximus 5.5.3; Cassius Dio 55.1.3-2.3; K. Scott, Drusus, nicknamed 'Castor', *CPh*, 25.2, 1930, pp. 158–159.

58. Cassius Dio 55.1.3-2.3; Suetonius, *Tiberius* 7.3; Valerius Maximus 5.5.3.

59. Valerius Maximus 5.5.3, translation after Shackleton Bailey (2000).

60. Cassius Dio 55.27.4; Suetonius, *Tiberius* 20.1; G. S. Sumi, Monuments and Memory: The *Aedes Castoris* in the formation of Augustan Ideology, *CQ* 59.1, 2009, p. 186.

61. Suetonius, *Tiberius* 20.1; Cassius Dio 55.8.1-2, 55.27.3-4; *Consolatio ad Liviam* 283-290.

62. Ovid, *Fasti* 1.705-708.

63. *Consolatio ad Liviam* 283-290.

64. Suetonius, *Tiberius* 15.2.

65. On Germanicus and Drusus' ages B. Levick, Drusus Caesar and the Adoptions of AD 4, *Latomus* 25, 1966, pp. 236–237; on adoption when the adopter already had a son, M. Corbier, Divorce and Adoption as Roman familial strategies, in *Marriage, Divorce, and Children in Ancient Rome*, ed. by B. Rawson, Oxford 1996, p. 66.

primus inter pares could not be shared and thus the very nature of the imperial family perhaps increased the potential for conflict between imperial brothers.[67]

Germanicus was the elder of the two and also was related by blood to Augustus, being his grand-nephew, while Drusus (prior to Tiberius' adoption) was Augustus' grandson only by marriage. It is therefore perhaps unsurprising that Germanicus should be promoted faster than Drusus, as in the case of both earlier examined pairings, primogeniture seems to have been an advantage. The relative importance of this pair of adoptive brothers is demonstrated by their wives: Germanicus married Agrippina the Elder, Augustus' granddaughter,[68] while Drusus, although he married at a younger age, was given Claudia Livilla, Germanicus' sister and Augustus' great-niece.[69] Tacitus, describing the situation in Tiberius' reign, states that it was Germanicus' grander genealogy and closer relationship to Augustus, as well as those of his wife, which led to his greater popularity.[70] Germanicus continued to receive further promotions, becoming consul and being commended to the Senate by Augustus in AD 12.[71] He was two years younger than Drusus was when he received the same honour. It therefore appears that Germanicus received greater emphasis, receiving honours first and at a younger age than his adoptive brother.

After the death of Augustus and the accession of Tiberius, the first successful imperial succession, the succession policy perhaps began to develop a clearer and more cohesive programme, learning from the earlier attempts of Augustus. For example, when Tiberius became emperor, Drusus, the biological son of the new Emperor, began to rise faster in prominence.[72] That this was a concern of Tiberius' is suggested by an incident when Germanicus was on campaign in Germany and requested another year to conclude the campaign, Tiberius summoned him to return to Rome, adding that 'if the war must be continued, he might leave his brother, Drusus, the material for a reputation'.[73] However, in addition to a second consulship, which he shared with Tiberius, Germanicus received *imperium maius* over the eastern provinces, a significant advancement.[74] These relative positions suggest that Tiberius was continuing to follow Augustus' succession policy; distinguishing Germanicus as the more prominent heir, but also increasing Drusus' prestige, lessening the distance in prominence between the two.[75]

66. Lindsay, *Adoption* (quoted n. 21), pp. 65, 112–113.

67. S. Dixon, *The Roman Family*, Baltimore—London 1992, p. 142; J. Bellemore, The Identity of Drusus: The Making of a *Princeps*, in *The Julio-Claudian Succession* (quoted n. 2), p. 79; C. Bannon, *Romulus* (quoted n. 7), pp. 176 n. 3, 179–180, notes that this rivalry was extended even beyond brothers, drawing distant relatives of Augustus into the conflict.

68. Suetonius, *Divus Augustus* 64.1, *Caligula* 7.1.

69. Sumner, Germanicus and Drusus Caesar (quoted n. 53), pp. 431–432; Levick, Drusus Caesar (quoted n. 65), pp. 233–234.

70. Tacitus *Annales* 2.43.

71. Cassius Dio 56.26.1-2; Levick, Drusus Caesar (quoted n. 65), pp. 240–241, suggests that Germanicus had a talent for warfare, which Drusus might have lacked, thus explaining his relative lack of military honours. She does however note that Drusus did still take on military responsibilities; Bellemore, *Identity of Drusus* (quoted n. 67), p. 81.

72. Tacitus, *Annales* 3.56; Bannon, *Brothers of Romulus* (quoted n. 7), p. 180.

73. Tacitus, *Annales* 2.26, translation after Jackson (1937).

74. Tacitus, *Annales* 2.43.

75. R. Seager, *Tiberius*, London 1972, pp. 110–111.

I have thus far argued that not only were the potential successors linked to the Dioscuri, but that both pairs, mortal and immortal, were perceived as being unequal in status. Should we then expect to see parallels being drawn not only between the two pairs, but also between individual heirs and gods? In Rome it appears that Castor was perceived as being the more prominent divine brother.[76] If such specific parallels were drawn, we should therefore expect to see Castor being connected to Gaius, Tiberius and Germanicus, whilst Pollux is linked to Lucius, Drusus the Elder and Drusus the Younger.

No such specific connection is evident in the first pairing of imperial princes, that of Gaius and Lucius. Instead, they are linked as a pair with both of the Dioscuri. Stronger specific parallels can however be seen in the second and third pairings. I have highlighted how Drusus' tragic death and Tiberius' devotion might have influenced the depiction of the brothers. However, if we were to follow the myth closely, Castor was the mortal twin and thus, logically, should perhaps be linked to Drusus, the deceased brother. This would then cast Tiberius in the role of Pollux, the devoted surviving brother. This does not appear to correlate with the more prominent role of Tiberius. However it should be noted that we do not possess a great deal of contemporary evidence for the comparative status of the brothers whilst both were alive. Tiberius, as the elder brother, and the one who would later become emperor, naturally has a greater role in our sources. It would not be unexpected for him to be later cast in the role of the more prominent member of the pairing, simply on account of his survival and later accession. It was perhaps Drusus' death which cast him in the role of the originally mortal Castor, rather than his prominence. I would therefore suggest that any such direct identification of a god with a specific member of an imperial pair was fluid, adapting to changing circumstances as required.

The pairing of Germanicus and Drusus the Younger is certainly linked to the Dioscuri as a pair, for example the adoptive brothers were described by Ovid as '*sidus iuvenale*'[77] echoing descriptions of the Dioscuri, as well as 'like unto the brethren dwelling in the neighbouring temple [of Castor and Pollux]'.[78] However, this pairing is the only instance in which a member of an imperial pairing is explicitly linked to one of the Dioscuri alone. Cassius Dio records an event in which Drusus fought a well known equestrian and was afterwards given the nickname 'Castor'.[79] If we take into account the role of the Dioscuri as patrons of the equestrian order, and Drusus' animosity to this particular member, it is likely that this name was bestowed sarcastically.[80] As seen in the case of Tiberius and Drusus, this parallel does not equate with the relative prominences of the adoptive brothers, as explored above. There is also another discrepancy here, although one of the Dioscuri was famed as a boxer, it was Pollux, not Castor who instead was known as a horseman.[81] This could however indicate the primacy of Castor over Pollux in the Roman consciousness: although Pollux might

76. Suetonius, *Divus Iulius* 10.

77. Ovid, *Tristia* 2.167-168; the Dioscuri are described as '*sidera*' by Statius, *Silvae* 3.2.9 and '*lucida sidera*' by Horace, *Carmina* 1.3.2; K. Scott, The Dioscuri and the Imperial Cult, *Classical Philology* 25.4, 1930, p. 379.

78. Ovid, *Epistulae ex Ponto* 2.2.81-84, translation after Wheeler (1924).

79. Cassius Dio 57.14.9; A. Stein, Drusus Castor, *Hermes* 53.2, 1918, p. 217.

80. Scott, Drusus, nicknamed 'Castor' (quoted 57) p. 161; Stein, Drusus Castor (quoted 79), p. 219.

81. Homer, *Iliad* 3.236-238; Horace, *Satirae* 2.1.26-27; Ovid, *Amores* 3.2.54, *Metamorphoses* 8.301-302; Plutarch, *De Fraterno Amore* 15; Propertius 3.14.17-20.

have been a better comparison for Drusus' actions, Castor was the twin whom the Romans thought of first. At the very least, this tale certainly suggests that there was a familiarity with the concept of comparing individual gods with specific mortals.

The pairing of Germanicus and Drusus straddled the reigns of Augustus and Tiberius, thus their relative statuses are somewhat difficult to discover, as their treatment differed under each emperor. Perhaps significantly, there is no evidence which links Germanicus to Castor exclusively. Rather all references during Germanicus' life link both princes with both gods.[82] However, following Germanicus' death, which would, as in the case of his father Drusus the Elder, perhaps link him even more strongly with the mortal Dioscurus, it was in fact Drusus, the surviving heir, who received the nickname Castor. Once again then, this succession policy in which an imperial prince and a Dioscurus might be specifically linked appears to remain fluid and adapting to the changing circumstances.

In conclusion, I have attempted to demonstrate ways in which the imperial succession policy drew upon or adapted a Republican succession strategy. Adoption had long been a method by which a man might restructure his family and dictate who would inherit his status, wealth and property. Augustus adapted this method to both consolidate his own position and those of his family members, by focusing more on internal adoptions and alliances. His adoption of Gaius and Lucius in 17 BC, followed by that of Tiberius and Agrippa Postumus, and Germanicus by Tiberius in AD 4, served to create a succession pattern of pairs, through which he intended his position and power to pass to those he selected.

It was the nature of this policy of unequal promotions and the singular nature of the position to which they aspired which might have caused conflict between the members of these pairings.[83] The comparison between the unequal mortal pairs and the Dioscuri perhaps should be read as an attempt to justify the inequality between the potential successors. For if the Dioscuri, although unequal, were still devoted to each other, why should the same not be true of the imperial heirs? Inequality between Castor and Pollux did not create conflict between them, thus such comparisons could be seen as an attempt to reassure many different facets of Roman society that the same was true of these imperial pairs. That this was an on-going concern requiring reassurance is suggested by complaints of the citizens in Tiberius' reign that they were 'to be slaves… to two half grown boys Germanicus and Drusus. First they will be a burden to the state and then they will tear it in two'.[84]

Augustus' succession policy therefore can be seen as both creating the potential for conflict between the unequal imperial pairs and attempting to diminish at least the appearance of this conflict through the comparisons drawn between the potential successors and the Dioscuri, famed for their fraternal piety. However what long term roles Augustus intended for these pairs after his death remain unknown. For, on account of the early deaths of the majority of the members of these pairs, it was Tiberius alone, without a partner in power, who eventually succeeded Augustus to become Emperor.

82. Ovid, *Epistulae ex Ponto* 2.2.81-84.

83. Bannon, *Brothers of Romulus* (quoted n. 7), p. 178.

84. Tacitus, *Annales* 1.4, translation after Jackson (1937). Tacitus' perception of the imperial succession and depiction of common attitudes towards Germanicus and Drusus is probably coloured by his contemporary experience of the succession, in which Domitian is suggested to have plotted against his brother Titus (Cassius Dio 66.26.2-4; Suetonius, *Domitian* 2.3).

POUVOIR, RELIGION ET CONFLITS FAMILIAUX À BYZANCE AUTOUR DU IXe SIÈCLE[1]

Christian SETTIPANI

Les Byzantins ont toujours eu l'obsession de la mort et ont donc pris un soin très particulier à préparer leur succession. La transmission des biens, mais également de la renommée d'une famille faisait l'objet d'une préparation spécifique aux différents stages de la vie. Le mariage[2], la conception et l'éducation des enfants puis la dévolution de l'héritage sont des étapes rigoureusement planifiées, au moins dans les hautes classes de la société, les seules dont il sera question ici[3].

Il ne nous est malheureusement parvenu que très peu de testaments byzantins se rapportant à l'aristocratie et la plupart sont d'époque relativement tardive et ne sont pas pertinents pour la période qui fera l'objet de cette étude, le IXe siècle, siècle charnière qui voit se succéder notamment trois dynasties importantes et s'imposer définitivement le culte des images. À défaut, j'ai donc choisi d'examiner les conflits familiaux liés à l'héritage au travers d'un prisme très particulier, mais qui a l'avantage d'être suffisamment documenté, celui de la transmission du pouvoir impérial.

1. Je remercie ici chaleureusement Béatrice Caseau d'avoir bien voulu accueillir cette contribution dans son volume. Dans la suite de l'article, j'utiliserai les abréviations suivantes : *Prosopographie der mittelbyzantinisches Zeit* (= *PmBZ*) : 7 vol. Berlin 1998-2002 ; *Prosopographie der mittelbyzantinisches Zeit. Zweite Abteilung (867-1025)* (= *PmBZ*²) : 8 vol. Berlin 2013 ; *Prosopography of the Byzantine Empire, CD-Rom* (= *PBE*) : Londres 2001.

2. La transmission des biens à sa descendance passe en premier lieu par le choix du conjoint, préliminaire à la conservation ou l'extension du patrimoine. L'organisation de l'union entre Théophane et son épouse Mégalo est exemplaire. Méthode raconte que la mère de Théophane négocie le mariage de son fils, âgé de dix ans avec une jeune fille de huit ans issue d'une famille très riche avec laquelle elle établit des contrats garantissant la propriété de la fortune du futur couple. L'intérêt ultime déclaré, aussi bien pour la mère de Théophane que pour le père de la fiancée, étant à terme d'avoir une descendance. Voir P. YANNOPOULOS, *Théophane de Sigriani le Confesseur (759-818). Un héros orthodoxe du second iconoclasme*, Bruxelles 2013, p. 87-88. Il arrive cependant que les deux familles ayant ainsi contracté alliance rentrent ensuite en conflit, en raison d'intérêts politiques ou financiers divergents. Dans ces conditions, l'aristocratie apprendra à utiliser à son avantage les règles progressivement plus contraignantes des canons ecclésiastiques en se rappelant opportunément des liens de parenté prohibés pour défaire une union devenue indésirable. Voir par exemple A. SCHMINCK, Vier eherechtliche Entscheidung aus dem 11. Jahrhundert, *Fontes Minores* III, 1979, p. 221-279.

3. J. BEAUCAMP et G. DAGRON, *La transmission du patrimoine. Byzance et l'aire méditerranéenne*, Paris 1998.

Inheritance, Law and Religions in the Ancient and Mediaeval Worlds, ed. by B. CASEAU and S. R. HUEBNER (Centre de recherche d'Histoire et Civilisation de Byzance, Monographies 45), Paris 2014.

Même si l'on a pu écrire que le système dynastique ne s'est jamais réellement imposé à Byzance, il est clair pourtant que le premier héritier légal du souverain en titre était également considéré comme l'héritier présomptif du trône. Cela a bien été souligné par Peter Schreiner qui pense pourtant encore que l'idée de dynastie n'apparaît réellement qu'avec les Macédoniens[4], ce qui certainement faux : les empereurs ont toujours eu la volonté de transmettre leur dignité à leurs descendants directs et n'ont pas hésité à le faire savoir[5]. Les raisons de famille se mêlent ici aux raisons d'Etat pour un enjeu qui concerne tant l'un que l'autre. Bien entendu, les risques étant démultipliés, on ne saurait affirmer qu'il n'y a pas un phénomène de résonnance qui provoque une surreprésentation des dissensions par rapport à un cadre aristocratique « simple »[6]. Pour autant, l'étude reste pertinente dans la mesure où, du point de vue de l'héritier potentiel, il s'agissait de toute façon de récupérer un héritage auquel il pensait avoir légitimement droit. Qu'il s'agisse d'un trône plutôt que d'un domaine aristocratique ne changeait pas fondamentalement ce principe essentiel. J'en trouve une confirmation dans une historiette figurant dans un contexte qui, à défaut d'être réellement byzantin n'en est pas moins rapporté par un auteur byzantin. Il s'agit de Procope qui raconte comment le roi d'Arménie Arsace, ayant par testament laissé son héritage à ses deux fils, mécontenta grandement le plus jeune parce qu'il laissait une part quatre fois plus importante à l'aîné[7]. Le cadet, se sentant lésé par ce partage trop inégal en appela à l'empereur pour faire valoir ses droits. Aussitôt l'aîné se tourna, lui, vers les Perses pour chercher leur protection, de sorte qu'à l'arrivée les Perses récupérèrent la part de l'aîné et les Byzantins celle du cadet. L'histoire n'est probablement qu'une invention destinée à expliquer, ou justifier, la situation politique particulière de l'Arménie à l'époque de Procope, déchirée entre les Perses, pour l'essentiel, et les Byzantins. Mais ce caractère imaginaire rend l'histoire d'autant plus intéressante pour notre propos, puisqu'on peut admettre sans hésiter qu'elle a été fabriquée dans un cadre byzantin. Or, ce qui ressort de cette anecdote c'est la traduction en termes d'héritage « normal » des biens d'un aristocrate, fut-il roi, et l'analyse des conséquences néfastes que le déséquilibre dans la dévolution des biens est susceptible d'apporter chez les héritiers inégalement pourvus. On voit donc que dès le VIe siècle, le trône est considéré dans l'imaginaire byzantin comme un élément du patrimoine paternel qui doit revenir naturellement à ses héritiers légitimes.

4. P. SCHREINER, Réflexions sur la famille impériale à Byzance (VIIIe-Xe siècle), *Byzantion* 61, 1991, p. 181-193, p. 184-185.

5. Il suffirait de rappeler que Maurice donne le nom de Théodose à son fils aîné pour souligner sa naissance porphyrogénète et son rang dans la succession, ou encore les manœuvres qui entourent la succession d'Héraclius et après lui le soin avec lequel ses descendants associeront leurs frères sur leurs monnaies pour bien marquer le caractère dynastique de leur pouvoir, ce qu'on retrouve encore jusque chez les empereurs Amoriens. Basile, parvenu sur le trône en 867 associe peu après (869) son fils aîné Constantin et l'année suivante son deuxième fils, Léon.

6. Ainsi, on soulignera les mises en garde de SCHREINER, Réflexions (cité n. 4), p. 182, qui rappelle que l'on doit considérer la famille impériale de façon différente.

7. PROC., *BP*, II, 3, 35 : « Arsakès, roi des Arméniens eut deux fils nommés Tigranès et Arsakès ... il fit un testament par lequel il fit de ses deux fils les successeurs du royaume ... laissant une portion quatre fois plus grande à Tigranès ... mais son fils Arsakès, mécontent et blessé ... présenta l'affaire à l'empereur des Romains ... Théodose, le fils d'Arcadius ... encore tout jeune garçon ... Alors Tigranès ... se rendit aux Perses et leur abandonna son royaume ... et Arsakès ... rendit son propre royaume à l'empereur Théodose ... Pendant un certain temps, les Romains et les Perses se disputèrent le territoire des Arméniens ; puis, enfin, ils arrivèrent à un accord selon lequel les Perses auraient la part de Tigranès, et les Romains, celle d'Arsakès » (éd. et trad. angl. H. Br. DEWING, *Procopius, History of the Wars*, Londres 1914, II, p. 278-280).

Dans les faits, la question de l'héritage impérial s'est évidemment posée aussitôt qu'un empereur a occupé le trône suffisamment longtemps pour avoir pérennisé son pouvoir et envisagé de le transmettre. Dans ce cas, l'absence totale d'héritier ou au contraire la multiplicité de ceux-ci sont l'objet de stratégies, et dans certains cas de disputes exacerbées.

Dans le cadre de la fourchette chronologique considérée, je ne m'intéresserai pas ici aux simples complots[8] quand bien même ils impliqueraient des membres de la famille impériale, mais plutôt aux conflits nés d'une conception familiale de l'Empire. Lorsque la famille devient un instrument dont le détenteur du trône ou ses opposants usent au mieux de leurs intérêts respectifs. L'empereur peut décider dans un but de propagande de mettre en avant sa proche parenté, ou dans un but politique, d'occulter celle-ci[9]. Mais en retour, la famille intervient dans des moments essentiels comme le mariage de l'empereur, le sort des différents enfants et gère, le cas échéant, la régence et donc l'Empire. L'importance des relations familiales dans l'entourage du trône est bien connue à partir du XIIe siècle dans la mesure où les sources nous livrent alors le nom de famille de la plupart des aristocrates, ce qui permet d'étudier en détail les relations de parenté à un moment où les Comnènes en font un véritable instrument du pouvoir. Mais avant le XIe siècle, la plupart des Byzantins ne sont connus que par leur seul prénom, ce qui rendait pratiquement impossible jusqu'à une époque récente toute tentative d'interprétation familiale des conflits politiques[10]. La publication d'ouvrages prosopographiques étendus et de monographies familiales permet aujourd'hui une première approche[11] et démontre que la famille jouait un rôle bien plus important que le silence des sources ne le laisse supposer de prime abord[12].

Si l'héritage du trône est vraisemblablement la première cause de conflit au sein d'une dynastie impériale ou des familles qui lui sont proches, ce n'est pas la seule. La question des images, comme autrefois la conversion à la chrétienté, a nécessairement été à l'origine de bien des querelles entre les membres d'une même famille aristocratique, les uns adoptant le point de vue officiel, les autres s'accrochant absolument au culte des images. Le positionnement religieux a poussé bien des familles à se déchirer entre partisans et opposants des images.

La dynastie impériale n'est pas épargnée. Irène, la jeune aristocrate athénienne que Constantin choisit pour épouser son jeune fils Léon le Khazare, était très certainement iconoclaste en apparence puisque destinée à régner sur un Empire iconoclaste. Mais aussitôt son époux disparu, Irène s'empresse de restaurer le culte des images. Le calcul politique qui consiste à s'appuyer sur d'autres élites que celles en place pour assoir un pouvoir chancelant reste possible, mais l'impératrice semble avoir été réellement une adepte des images.

8. Pour ceux-là on se référera évidemment au travail fondamental de J.-Cl. CHEYNET, *Pouvoir et contestation à Byzance (963-1210)*, Paris 1990, mais qui couvre une époque postérieure à celle envisagée ici.

9. Ainsi, les souverains de la dynastie héraclide mettent systématiquement en exergue leurs fils ou leurs frères sur leurs monnaies pour souligner la dimension familiale, donc dynastique, de leur pouvoir, quitte à les effacer ensuite en cas de conflit ou d'intérêts divergents.

10. Voir les réflexions de Cl. LUDWIG, Social Mobility in Byzantium? Families Ties in the Middle Byzantine Period, dans *Approaches to the Byzantine Family*, éd. L. BRUBACKER et Sh. TOUGHER, Birmingham, 2013, p. 234-245, p. 234-235.

11. En dehors de la *PBE* et de la *PmbZ* on doit au moins citer M. HERLONG, *Kinship and Social Mobility in Byzantium, 717-959*, diss. Catholic Univ. of America 1986.

12. LUDWIG, Social Mobility (cité n. 10), p. 240-242.

On peut soit croire qu'elle était fille d'un dignitaire impérial et d'une aristocrate iconophile, ou, plutôt, que son père appartenait à une vieille lignée aristocratique et iconophile que l'empereur a cherché à s'attacher[13]. Quoi qu'il en soit, il est certain que cette divergence, puisqu'elle était secrète, était susceptible d'être le nid probable de disputes dont on ignore la forme qu'elles prirent. Ainsi, Irène avait pour beau-frère (plutôt que pour frère) le patrice Constantin Sérantapèchos, lequel était le petit-fils probable de Béser Sérantapèchos, patrice et stratège de Léon III en 717, et surtout l'un des principaux artisans de l'instauration de l'iconoclasme à Byzance. Tout comme son proche parent David, comte de l'Opsikion en 766, fils ou petit-fils de Béser, Constantin Sérantapèchos, était nécessairement iconoclaste au début de sa carrière. On ignore si les Sérantapéchoi ont accompagné ou subi la réforme imposée par Irène. Mais la question religieuse est peut-être intervenue dans le choix de Léon Sérantapèchos, questeur en 802[14], de rallier les conspirateurs qui ont détrôné sa tante Irène.

La famille de Théodore le Studite offre un meilleur exemple encore de la dissension entre membres d'une même famille causée par les convictions religieuses. Pour autant qu'on puisse en juger, la famille s'est scindée en deux branches distinctes à partir des trois enfants du couple Sergios et Euphémia. Tandis que Platon et les enfants de sa sœur Théoctistè, Théodore, Joseph, Euthyme et une fille anonyme, s'engagent dans une carrière ecclésiastique, une partie au moins des descendants de la seconde sœur, Anna, Sergios et ses deux fils, occupent des positions importantes dans le siècle et donc professent, peut-on admettre, des positions iconoclastes jusqu'au règne de Léon IV[15]. Mais, c'est la question du second mariage de l'empereur Constantin VI qui va entraîner un conflit très violent entre les deux rameaux. En effet, après s'être séparé, au mépris des lois de l'Eglise, de son épouse Maria d'Amnia, Constantin VI cherche à épouser une dame de la suite de l'impératrice déchue, une certaine Théodotè. Celle-ci est la sœur de deux patrices de la cour, mais surtout, elle est la petite-fille d'Anna, sœur de Platon et de Théoctistè. Pourtant Platon et ses neveux vont se dresser de toutes leurs forces contre la conclusion de cette union qu'ils jugent absolument illégitime[16]. Les lois ecclésiastiques passent alors avant la solidarité du lignage, puisque la nouvelle fiancée n'est autre que leur petite-nièce (pour Platon) ou la fille de leur cousin germain (pour Théodore et ses frères).

En dépit de l'opposition irréductible de Théodore et des autres moines, Constantin n'en parviendra pas moins à ses fins et relègue Maria dans un monastère avant d'épouser Théodotè. Avec Maria s'éclipse l'ensemble de sa parentèle dont la *Vie de Philarète* nous offre un tableau d'une rare précision[17]. Pour autant, cette éclipse ne sera pas définitive. De son éphé-

13. D. Barbe, *Irène de Byzance. La femme empereur 752-803*, Paris 1990, p. 66-67.

14. *PmbZ* III, 2000, 4406, p. 37. Pour les Sérantapéchoi : Fr. Winkelmann, *Quellenstudien zur herrschenden Klasse von Byzanz im 8. und 9. Jahrhundert*, Berlin 1987, p. 193.

15. Pour la famille de Théodore Studite, voir Th. Pratsch, *Theodoros Studites (759-826). Zwischen Dogma und Pragma*, Francfort 1998, p. 17-62 ; R. Cholij, *Theodore the Stoudite. The Ordering of Holiness*, Oxford 2002, p. 15-19.

16. Sur le second mariage de Constantin VI et l'opposition de Théodore, voir notamment J. A. Fuentes Alonso, *El divorcio de Constantino VI y la doctrina matrimonial de San Teodoro Estudita*, Pamplona 1984.

17. *Vie du noble Philarètos le miséricordieux*, éd. et trad. franç. : M.-H. Fourmy et M. Leroy, *Byzantion* 9, 1934, p. 85-170 ; L. Rydén, *The Life of St Philaretos the Merciful, written by his grandson Niketas*, Uppsala 2002. Voir Winkelmann, *Quellenstudien* (cité n. 14), p. 192-193.

mère union avec Constantin VI, Maria avait eu deux filles, elles aussi envoyées au couvent, probablement lors de la chute d'Irène en 802. Mais nous retrouverons l'une d'elle comme impératrice quelques décennies plus tard. Nous y reviendrons.

Après la chute d'Irène, l'Empire traverse une période trouble qui voit naître plusieurs tentatives d'usurpation. Au début de l'année 803, le stratège des Anatoliques Bardanios, membre d'une ancienne lignée sénatoriale ralliée à Irène, a pour principaux lieutenants Thomas le Slave, Léon l'Arménien et Michel d'Amorium. Selon un récit qui pourrait remonter au contemporain Théognostos de Sicile[18], les quatre hommes auraient rendu visite à un moine respecté avant d'entreprendre une rébellion. Le moine prédit alors l'échec de la tentative mais affirme quand même que le second se rebellera à son tour puis que les deux derniers régneraient malgré tout comme empereurs[19]. Cette prophétie, rapportée par un contemporain, proche du trône, occulte pourtant un aspect important. Un peu avant sa tentative d'usurpation, Bardanios avait marié deux de ses subordonnés à ses filles. Par ailleurs, les deux versions, écrites par des contemporains, de la *Vie de Iohannikios* nous informent que le troisième subordonné, Léon l'Arménien, était le cousin germain du fils de Bardanios, donc le neveu de ce dernier[20]. Enfin, Génésios affirme que Léon l'Arménien était le parrain du fils de Michel d'Amorion[21]. Cet éclairage nouveau permet de voir la rébellion de 803 comme une entreprise familiale avec à sa tête un groupe d'hommes étroitement apparentés. Mais une cohésion familiale n'est pas synonyme de cohésion politique. Lorsqu'il devient clair que la fortune des armes ne favorisait pas Bardanios, ses complices et proches parents l'abandonnèrent en échange de leur amnistie. La solidarité du groupe ne résiste pas aux contraintes militaires. Pour autant, les trois officiers de Bardanios restent dans un premier temps soudés et lorsque l'un d'entre eux, Léon l'Arménien, obtient finalement la pourpre en 813, une de ses premières mesures est de promouvoir ses anciens compagnons d'armes : Michel devient patrice et chef des excubites et Thomas est nommé tourmarque des Fédérés[22]. D'autres parents de Léon bénéficient également de ses faveurs puisque deux cousins et le mari d'une cousine obtiennent des commandements importants sous son règne[23].

18. W. Treadgold, *The Middle Byzantine Historians*, Basingstoke 2013, p. 79-90.

19. A. Kaldellis, *Genesios. On the reigns of the Emperors* (= Gén.) I, 6, Canberra 1998, p. 8-10. Sur cette prophétie, voir en dernier lieu A. Timotin, *Visions, prophéties et pouvoir à Byzance. Etude sur l'hagiographie méso-byzantine (ixe-xie siècles)*, Paris 2010, p. 129-131.

20. Pierre, *Vita Iohannikios I*, 16 (trad. angl. : *Byzantine Defenders of Images. Eight Saints' Lives in English Translation*, éd. A.-M. Talbot, Washington 1998, p. 270). Bryenès, fils de Tourkos est présenté comme l'ἐξαδελφος de Léon V. Dans la seconde *Vie*, elle aussi contemporaine, rédigée par Sabas, la parenté est traduite par le mot ἀδελφιδος, ce qui signifie donc cousin germain et certainement pas beau-frère comme l'a cru W. Treadgold, *The Byzantine Revival 780-842*, Stanford 1988, p. 414-5, n. 263 : voir le commentaire détaillé chez Chr. Settipani, *Continuité des élites à Byzance durant les siècles obscurs*, Paris 2006, p. 234, n. 4.

21. Gén. I (cité n. 19), 11, p. 13. Cette précision ne prouve nullement, quoi qu'on en ait dit, que le fils de Michel avait été baptisé précisément en 813.

22. Gén. I (cité n. 19), 8 & I, 11, p. 11, 13 ; Theoph. cont., p. 24 Bonn.

23. Grégorios (*PmbZ* II, 2000, 2477, p. 86-87) et Bardas (*PmbZ* I, 1999, 789, p. 260-261), cousins germains de Léon du côté paternel et Léon Sklèros (*PmbZ* III, 2000, 4409, p. 38-39), époux d'Irène, cousine germaine de Léon du côté maternel (*PmbZ* III, 2000, 1443, p. 460-461 = ? 1446, p. 462-463). Un autre Bardas, σύγγαμβρος de Léon V, stratège des Thracésiens, auquel Théodore le Stoudite prédit la mort prochaine en 819 selon la *Vita Theodori*, est certainement distinct de Bardas, ἀνεψιός de Léon V, auquel le patriarche Nicéphore prédit la

On observe ainsi que bien avant l'époque des Comnènes, les empereurs byzantins favorisent leurs proches parents et leur octroient des positions avantageuses. Mais la popularité de Léon s'étiole rapidement et provoque la constitution d'une conspiration à laquelle se rallie son cousin par alliance Michel d'Amorium. Arrêté, il est condamné à mort par Léon V, et sur le point d'être exécuté lorsque l'impératrice supplie son époux de surseoir à la mise à mort en raison des fêtes de Noël. On ignore les raisons qui ont poussé l'impératrice à intervenir avec autant de véhémence, mais sa proche parenté avec Michel, parrain d'un de ses fils, pourrait bien avoir joué un rôle essentiel. Comme la suite le montre, il s'agissait non seulement de surseoir à l'exécution, mais probablement aussi de la commuer. Léon souscrit de mauvaise grâce aux injonctions de son épouse. Michel en profite alors pour faire intervenir des complices qui surprennent Léon dans la chapelle où il communiait pour Noël et l'égorgent au pied de l'autel[24]. Aussitôt Michel couronné, son beau-frère Thomas le Slave entreprend, pour venger la mort de Léon, une révolte qui durera trois ans et affaiblira considérablement l'Empire[25].

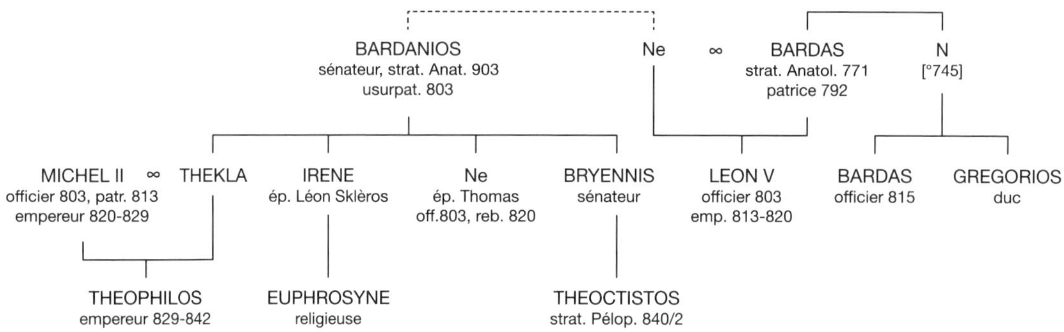

Il est probable que les liens de parenté ont joué un rôle non négligeable dans ces événements. Les chroniqueurs précisent que Léon avait refusé de tenir compte de présages montrant que Michel lui succéderait et que, loin de l'écarter, il l'avait alors promu et titré patrice. Quant à la révolte de Thomas, elle prend tout son sens si l'empereur défunt était uni à lui par des liens étroits de parenté. C'est ce lien qui fournissait à Thomas sa légitimité et le confortait dans son rôle de vengeur de l'empereur assassiné. Pour autant, aucune des sources qui rapportent ces faits ne mentionne de tels liens. La raison tient essentiellement à l'origine com-

mutilation en 815, ce qui arriva quatre ans plus tard selon la *Vita Nicephori*. La coïncidence de nom et de date est frappante, mais selon la *Vita Nicephori*, le second Bardas est toujours vivant au moment de la rédaction de l'ouvrage, en 828 dans sa première version. Voir la discussion chez Timotin, *Visions* (cité n. 19), p. 150-158, qui pense plutôt que l'auteur de la *Vita Theodori* a repris et déformé l'histoire du premier Bardas pour faire une allusion à la fin du plus fameux des Bardas, le césar oncle de Michel III, hypothèse possible mais peut-être inutilement complexe.

24. D. E. Afinogenov, The Conspiracy of Michael Traulos and the Assassination of Leo V: History and Fiction, *Dumbarton Oaks Papers* (= *DOP*) 55, 2001, p. 329-338.

25. Pour la révolte de Thomas, l'analyse moderne la plus pertinente reste celle de P. Lemerle, Thomas le Slave, *Travaux et memoires* I, 1965, p. 255-297. Voir aussi Treadgold, *The Byzantine Revival* (cité n. 20), p. 225-244; *PmbZ* V, 2001, 8459, p. 33-38.

mune de ces sources, sans doute la chronique de Théognostos, précepteur du fils de Léon V selon toute apparence, et qui écrivait au début du règne de Théophile[26]. Grâce à une lettre fort précieuse envoyée par Michel à l'empereur Louis le Pieux en 824, nous savons que la version officielle à Byzance était que Thomas, homme sorti du rang, adultère et ensuite apostat, s'était révolté avant la mort de Léon et que celui-ci avait été assassiné en raison de son incapacité à circonscrire la rébellion, Michel étant alors appelé sur le trône pour vaincre l'usurpateur[27]. Cette trame est reprise pour l'essentiel par Théognostos, fidèle partisan de Michel, pour lequel faire état de ces parentés aurait rendu encore plus abominable le crime de son suzerain. La dimension familiale de l'entreprise a donc été volontairement gommée de façon à effacer toute légitimité à la tentative de Thomas et tout opprobre sur les actions de Michel.

Aussitôt parvenu au pouvoir, Michel II se met en quête d'assurer à la fois la légitimité et la continuité de sa dynastie. Pour ce faire, il fera sortir du couvent Euphrosyne, l'aînée des filles de Maria, afin d'en faire son épouse[28]. Par ailleurs, il a aussi cherché à marier très vite son fils Théophile afin d'assurer le futur. Les chroniqueurs byzantins affirment que ce fut à travers un concours de beauté, ce que plusieurs historiens modernes contestent[29]. Mais quoi qu'il en soit, le choix s'est porté sur une certaine Théodora, jeune fille issue d'une famille aristocratique de Paphlagonie, et d'origine arménienne par son père. Loin d'être innocent ou fondé sur les seules qualités morales ou physiques de la jeune fiancée, Syméon logothète affirme que ce choix est celui de l'impératrice Euphrosyne, mère de Théophile[30]. Ce témoignage reste vraisemblable, même s'il n'est pas exempt de confusions : Euphrosyne n'était pas la mère de Théophile et il n'est pas certain qu'elle était déjà devenue impératrice au moment du mariage de Théodora[31].

26. TREADGOLD, *Middle Byzantine Historians* (cité n. 18), p. 84.

27. *MGH*, p. 476-478. Voir LEMERLE, Thomas (cité n. 25), p. 256-259.

28. *PmbZ* I, 1999, 1705, p. 540-541.

29. Voir la bibliographie sur la question dans les articles de L. RYDÉN, The Bride-shows at the Byzantine Court – History or Fiction?, *Eranos* 83, 1985, p. 175-191, partisan d'une invention, et de W. TREADGOLD, The historicity of imperial Bride-Shows, *Jahrbuch der Österreichischen* (= *JÖB*) 54, 2004, p. 39-52, favorable à l'authenticité des concours.

30. SYM. MAG., 129 (éd. St. Wahlgren, *Symeonis magistri et logothetae Chronicon*, Berlin 2006, p. 214).

31. La date du mariage de Théophile et de Théodora a été longuement débattue. Selon la chronique de Syméon et ses avatars, la veuve de Michel, Euphrosyne, organise un concours de beauté et Théophile choisit Théodora, de préférence à Kassia. Nous sommes donc en 830. Mais le texte original de la chronique (voir l'édition de WAHLGREN, p. 216-217) précisait que le mariage de Théophile a eu lieu le même jour que son couronnement, à la pentecôte 821 donc. En conséquence, E. W. BROOK, The marriage of the Emperor Theophilos, *Byzantinische Zeitschrift* 10, 1901, p. 540-545, a établi que la version de Syméon résulte d'une confusion entre le couronnement de Théophile (821) et son accession comme seul empereur (829). Pourtant W. TREADGOLD, The problem of the marriage of the Emperor Theophilus, *Greek, Roman, and Byzantine Studies* 16, 1975, p. 325-341, et ID., The chronological accuracy of the chronicle of Syméon the Logothète for the Years 813-845, *DOP* 33, 1979, p. 157-197, p. 171-174, souvent suivi, maintient fortement qu'il faut préférer la date de 829. Toutefois, cette chronologie soulève de trop nombreuses difficultés pour qu'on puisse la retenir, en dépit du maintien indéfectible de TREADGOLD, The historicity (cité n. 29), p. 42-45. Voir C. MANGO, On Re-reading the Life of St. Gregory the Decapolite, *Buzantina* 13, 1985, p. 633-646, p. 639-64; *PmbZ* IV, 2000, 7286, p. 344-350; SETTIPANI, *Continuité* (cité n. 20), p. 159-166. Le seul problème avec la date de 821, c'est qu'à ce moment l'instigatrice du mariage ne pourrait être Euphrosyne qui n'épouserait Michel II qu'en 824 admet-on et vivait auparavant recluse dans un couvent loin du palais. Cette difficulté n'est pas forcément dirimante. En effet, la date de 824 pour le mariage de Michel II et d'Euphrosyne est tout sauf assurée : même si elle est généralement acceptée

Elle n'en était pas moins à ce moment princesse impériale et a bien pu avoir une influence considérable à la cour même avant d'épouser Michel II[32]. On a pu s'étonner de l'absence de tout soutien familial autour d'Euphrosyne que ce soit durant ses années en tant que religieuse ou comme impératrice[33]. En fait, il est probable que ses nombreux parents qui avaient accompagné à Constantinople sa mère Maria lors de son mariage avec Constantin VI étaient retournés dans leur province d'origine au moment de la répudiation de celle-ci. C'est donc en Paphlagonie qu'il faut espérer retrouver la trace d'une éventuelle parentèle d'Euphrosyne. Or, c'est bien de Paphlagonie que vient la jeune Théodora, d'une famille alliée aux Arméniens, tout comme celle d'Euphrosyne[34]. En choisissant comme épouse pour l'héritier du trône une jeune femme issue du même milieu qu'elle, et peut-être même sa parente[35], Euphrosyne exerçait aussi une revanche sur le destin qui avait privé sa famille du trône après la destitution de son aïeule Irène en 802. Si elle-même est à nouveau écartée du pouvoir en 830, Théodora en revanche, donnera naissance à l'héritier de Théophile. Lorsque celui-ci succède à son père, son premier geste, largement commenté, sera de faire exécuter une partie des anciens complices de son père au prétexte qu'en tuant Léon V, ils avaient attenté à la majesté impériale. Les historiens qui ont cherché les vraies raisons de cette purge n'ont pas mis en avant parmi les motifs possibles le fait que la mère de Théophile était la cousine germaine de Léon V. Loin de renier son propre lignage au profit d'une dynastie précédente, Théophile pouvait mettre en avant pour se débarrasser de dignitaires devenus gênants la solidarité envers le meurtre d'un proche parent.

(*e. g.* par J. Signes Codoñer, *El periodo del segundo iconoclasmo en Theophanes continuatus. Analisis y comentario de los tres primeros libros de la Cronica*, Amsterdam 1995, p. 320), elle n'est donnée que par Michel le Syrien (III, 72) qui affirme qu'il eut lieu la quatrième année du règne de Michel, donc en 824/5. Certes, Michel le Syrien dépend ici de la chronique syriaque perdue du contemporain Dionysios de Tell Mahré, mais son récit est trop émaillé d'erreurs et d'anachronismes pour être retenu tel quel (je souligne en italiques les erreurs): Michel *Juif d'Amorium*, tue Léon V le *vendredi saint*; sa femme Thécla meurt après quatre ans et il épouse alors la *petite-fille* de Constantin VI, religieuse ; *il abdique alors en faveur de son fils* et vit encore quatre ans ; *sa nouvelle épouse assassine alors leur fils, Juif par son père*, et retourne au couvent. On n'insistera donc pas sur la méfiance qui doit entourer une précision connue par ce seul texte. Plusieurs historiens estiment en conséquence qu'il faut plutôt avancer le mariage d'Euphrosyne à 823 ou 822 : voir Rydén, *The Life of St Philaretos* (cité n. 17), p. 46-47, n. 103, au moment où Michel, en lutte contre Thomas, avait un impérieux besoin de légitimité. Mais ne serait-il absolument impossible alors d'aller jusqu'à 821 ?

32. Pour Euphrosyne et sa famille, voir notamment M.-Fr. Auzépy, De Philarète, de sa famille et de certains monastères de Constantinople, dans *Les saints et leurs sanctuaires à Byzance*, éd. C. Jolivet-Lévy, M. Kaplan et J.-P. Sodini, Paris 1993, p. 117-135 (= Ead., *L'histoire des iconoclastes*, Paris 2007, p. 179-198) ; J. Herrin, *Women in Purple*, Londres 2001, p. 130-184 ; Chr. Angelidi, Family Ties, Bonds of Kinship (9th-11th Centuries), dans *Authority in Byzantium*, éd. P. Armstrong, Londres 2013, p. 155-165, p. 155-159.

33. Herrin, *Women* (cité n. 32), p. 140 ; Angelidi, Family Ties (cité n. 32), p. 157.

34. Ce dont témoigne le nom de Bardas, porté par le cousin germain de la mère d'Euphrosyne.

35. Récemment, Ludwig, Social Mobility (cité n. 10), p. 241, souligne l'origine géographique commune de Maria d'Amnia et de Théodora aussi bien que la similitude de leur arrivée sur le trône. On peut sans doute aller plus loin. Même si aucune source ne permet de l'affirmer, il n'est pas exclu que Théodora soit alliée à Euphrosyne. La mère de Théodora, la noble paphlagonienne Théoctistè, devient religieuse et sera enterrée dans le couvent fondé et dirigé par Euphrosyne, dont elle était donc une proche. Les deux familles partagent plusieurs noms communs. Enfin, le patrice Nicétas Monomaque est donné par une des versions de sa vie comme le parent de Théodora, et par l'autre comme le parent d'Irène et il peut donc bien avoir été apparenté à l'une *et* à l'autre. Voir Settipani, *Continuité* (cité n. 20), p. 213-216.

À la mort de Théophile le 20 janvier 842, son unique fils Michel est encore mineur[36] et un conseil de régence est donc constitué pour gérer les affaires de l'Empire[37]. La constitution de ce conseil n'est toutefois pas donnée de façon complète par une source unique. Bien au contraire, certaines de nos sources principales n'y font simplement aucune référence.

Génésios[38] :

Les rênes ancestrales du pouvoir furent ainsi laissées sous la direction de Michel et de sa pieuse mère Théodora, l'année 6350, la cinquième indiction. La régence était confiée au patrice Théoctistos et au protomagistre Manuel.

Théophane Continué[39] :

À la mort de Théophile, son fils Michel, son successeur recueille l'Empire, alors âgé de trois ans, sous la direction de sa mère Théodora. La direction des affaires est donnée à un conseil de régence, désigné par son père Théophile : l'eunuque Théoctistos, à ce moment *kanikléios* et logothète du drome, le patrice Bardas, frère de l'impératrice, ainsi que le magistre Manuel, originaire d'Arménie et oncle paternel de l'impératrice.

Acta Davidis[40] :

Lorsque le rétablissement du culte des images est discuté, le conseil d'État réuni pour l'occasion autour de l'impératrice Théodora et de Méthode est composé de « Serge le Nicétiate, Théoctistos, Bardas et Pétronas, hommes très orthodoxes et membres du sénat, les premiers du conseil ».

Henri Grégoire a su rendre vie à la figure obscure (pour nous) du dénommé Sergios le Nicétiate qui ouvre la liste des membres du conseil impérial selon les *Acta Davidis*, avant même le tout puissant Théoctistos et les deux frères de l'impératrice. Grâce à une notice du synaxaire de Constantinople, il établit que Sergios était le parent par le sang de l'impératrice Théodora et de son fils Michel[41].

36. Michel était né le 19 janvier 840 : *PmbZ* III, 2000, 4991, p. 259.

37. La réalité de ce conseil de régence est discutée dans la mesure où il n'est pas mentionné par tous les chroniqueurs et où la liste de ses membres n'est jamais donnée de façon exhaustive : voir par exemple A. Vasiliev, *Byzance et les Arabes. I La dynastie amorienne*, édition française par M. Canard et H. Grégoire, Bruxelles 1935, p. 191-192, n. 2, et plus récemment P. Varona Codeso, *Miguel III (842-867) : Construcción histórica y literaria de un reinado*, Madrid 2009, p. 59-63. Mais à tout prendre, je crois plus probable d'en accepter l'existence que de la rejeter.

38. Gén IV, 55 (p. 71 Kaldellis). Son récit est repris par Skylitzès, 81 : « Après que Théophile eut quitté cette vie, son fils Michel, avec sa mère Théodora, hérite des sceptres impériaux. Il avait comme tuteurs, pour le diriger, ceux-là même que son père avait institués pour lui dans son testament : le magistre Manuel, qui était domestique des scholes, et le patrice Théoctistos, logothète du drome » (trad. franç. B. Flusin et J.-Cl. Cheynet, *Jean Skylitzès. Empereurs de Constantinople*, Paris 2003, p. 73).

39. Theoph. Cont., p. 148 Bonn.

40. *Acta graeca SS. Davidis, Symeonis et Georgii, Mitylenae in insula Lesbo*, éd. J. Van den Gheyn, *AB* 18, 1899, p. 211-259, p. 245-246 (trad. angl. : Treadgold, *Byzantine Defenders* (cité n. 20), p. 216-217).

41. Synax. Cple, 28 juin (*AASS, Nov.*, p. 777) : « Sergios le *magistros* ..., fondateur du ... monastère du Nicétiate ... originaire du pays des Paphlagoniens, d'un village appelé Nicétia, tout près d'Amastris ... fils de parents excellents ... parent (« σύγγενες ») de l'impératrice Théodora ... et de l'empereur Michel son fils, lutta vaillamment pour faire proclamer l'orthodoxie des saintes et vénérées icônes » (éd. et trad. franç. : Henri Grégoire, Études sur le neuvième siècle. Un grand homme inconnu : le magistre et logothète Serge le Nicétiate, *Byzantion* 8, 1933, p. 515-550, p. 519).

Quand bien même il s'agit de l'Empire, on voit que l'héritage de Théophile est confié en raison du très jeune âge de son seul fils à un conseil composé exclusivement, ou presque, de membres proches de la famille :

- Théodora, épouse de Théophile et mère de Michel III[42] ;
- Sergios le Nicétiate, parent de Théodora et de Michel, probablement l'un des oncles maternels de Théodora[43] ;
- Théoctistos, eunuque, logothète du drome, peut-être proche parent de Théodora[44] ;
- Bardas, patrice, frère de Théodora[45] ;
- Pétronas, frère de Théodora[46] ;
- Manuel, magistre, oncle paternel de Théodora[47]
- Thécla, fille aînée de Théodora[48] ;

42. *PmbZ* IV, 2001, 6286, p. 344-350.

43. *PmbZ* IV, 2001, 6664, p. 124-125. La nature de la parenté entre Sergios et Théodora n'est pas précisée par le Synaxaire. H. Grégoire avait cru qu'il pouvait s'agir du frère homonyme de Photios, effectivement apparenté à l'impératrice, opinion encore rappelée avec faveur par Varona, Miguel III (cité n. 37), p. 60 (entérinée dans l'index, s. v.). Mais elle a ensuite convenu qu'il s'agissait d'une erreur (P. Varona Codeso et Ó. Prieto Domínguez, Deconstructing Photios : Family relationship and political kinship in Middle Byzantium, *Revue des études byzantines* 71, 2013, p. 105-148, p. 135-137) comme je l'avais signalé précédemment : Settipani, *Continuité* (cité n. 20), p. 174. Selon Skylitzès, Théodora a restauré les images « parce qu'elle y était incitée constamment par sa mère et par ses oncles maternels, les patrices » (p. 74 Flusin-Cheynet). Theoctistè, mère de Théodora, était en effet une iconodule convaincue. Mais on ne lui connaît pas de frères, aussi J.-Cl. Cheynet, *ad. loc.*, se demande s'il ne s'agit pas plutôt des oncles maternels de Michel III, Bardas et Pétronas. Mais qu'on ne connaisse pas d'oncles maternels à Théodora n'empêche pas qu'elle ait pu en avoir (d'ailleurs J.-Cl. Cheynet admet que Sergios devait en effet en être un). La mention de la mère de Théodora est cohérente et confirme l'action d'oncles maternels. Or, pour autant que l'on sache les deux principaux artisans de la restauration des icones dans l'entourage de Théodora sont le logothète Théoctistos et Sergios le Nicétiate. Sergios est d'abord attesté comme « patrice, protospathaire impérial et logothète du drome » puis comme « magistre, patrice, protospathaire impérial et logothète du drome ». On ignore à quel moment est intervenue la promotion à la dignité de magistre, mais on voit qu'elle est postérieure à la nomination comme logothète du drome, donc à la mort de Théoctistos en 855. À la mort de Théophile, Sergios n'était donc encore que patrice. Par ailleurs Sergios venait de Paphlagonie, tout comme la mère de Théodora. Lui de Nicètia près d'Amastris, elle d'Ebissa, dont on ignore la localisation, mais qui pourrait s'identifier à Abysiano où eut en 863 lieu une grande bataille entre Byzantins et Bulgares et qui se situait à l'ouest de l'Halys, à 500 milles d'Amisos, donc peut-être pas si loin d'Amastris (voir Grégoire, Études sur le neuvième siècle (cité n. 41), p. 535-536). Enfin, on comprend mieux la confusion commise par les chroniqueurs entre lui et Manuel, oncle paternel de Théodora s'il était, lui, son oncle maternel. Voir Settipani, *Continuité* (cité n. 20), p. 171-172, dont les vues sont entérinées par Varona Codeso et Prieto Domínguez, *op. cit.*, p. 135. Reste à identifier l'autre patrice, oncle maternel de Théodora. On l'a vu, à part Sergios, le principal instrument de la restauration des images a été Théoctistos. Mais celui-ci ne peut intervenir ici. D'une part, contrairement à Sergios, il apparaît dans le récit des chroniqueurs, et ne peut donc prendre la place d'un personnage non nommé, et surtout, en tant qu'eunuque, il ne pouvait évidemment pas être patrice.

44. *PmbZ* IV, 2001, 8050, p. 578-581.

45. *PmbZ* I, 1999, 791, p. 261-267.

46. *PmbZ* III, 2000, 5929, p. 565-567.

47. *PmbZ* III, 2000, 4707, p. 136-141. Grégoire, Études sur le neuvième siècle (cité n. 41) et Id., Manuel et Théophobe ou la concurrence de deux monastères, *Byzantion* 9, 1934, p. 183-204, a tenté de prouver que Manuel était mort avant la fin du règne de Théophile, et que les sources qui le font survivre à ses blessures et devenir l'un des tuteurs de Michel III ont simplement ressuscité le défunt pour lui donner une carrière iconophile et lui ont

À l'exception de Théoctistos, pour lequel il ne s'agit que d'une conjecture[49], tous les membres de ce conseil sont des proches parents de l'héritier. Mais on soulignera qu'il ne s'agit que de parents du côté maternel du jeune empereur. Aucun proche de Théophile n'y figure[50]. Il subsistait encore pourtant des alliés de la dynastie amorienne, mais aucun ne joue de rôle important à la mort de Théophile[51]. On peut évidemment en conclure que le « clan » arménien de Théodora avait réussi une sorte de coup d'État au détriment du reste de la parentèle impériale. Et c'est probablement exact en partie. Mais la réalité est probablement plus complexe. Tout d'abord on ne peut opposer simplement les « Arméniens » de la famille de Théodora aux « Amoriens » de la famille de Théophile. En effet la mère de Théophile était une Arménienne elle aussi, fille de Bardanios, belle-sœur de l'Arménien Léon Sklèros et cousine germaine de Léon V l'Arménien. Il n'est pas davantage évident qu'on puisse opposer deux « clans » arméniens, celui de Théodora et celui issu de Bardanios et de Léon V. Une des sœurs de Théodora avait épousé Arsaber, neveu de Théodosia, femme de Léon V[52]. Ce clan arménien qui entoure Théodora n'est pas nécessairement homogène non plus. L'époux d'une des sœurs de Théodora, le Perse Théophobe[53] est exécuté par Théophile peu avant son propre décès pour prévenir tout remous dans la succession. Il est transparent que sa chute et son exécution sont le fait des manœuvres de la famille de Théodora puisque Théophobe a été en

---

attribué à cet effet les actions d'un autre oncle de l'impératrice, Sergios le Nicétiate. Mais la découverte d'un sceau au nom de « Manuel, patrice, protospathaire impérial, magistre et bagylos de l'empereur » est venue prouver définitivement la présence de Manuel comme tuteur « bagylos » de Michel III : voir SETTIPANI, *Continuité* (cité n. 20), p. 148, n. 8, qui répond aux objections de TREADGOLD, The historicity (cité n. 29), p. 44, n. 22 (que l'auteur a répétées sans changement : W. TREADGOLD, The lost Secret History of Nicetas the Paphlagonian, dans *The Steppe Lands and the World beyond Them. Studies in honor of Victor Spinei on his 70th birthday*, éd. Fl. CURTA, B.-P. MALEON, Iaşi 2013, p. 662, n. 51). Depuis, J. SIGNES CODOÑER, Dead or Alive ? Manuel the Armenian's (after)life after 838, dans *Pour l'Amour de Byzance. Hommage à Paolo Odorico*, éd. Chr. GASTGEBER et *alii*, Francfort, 2010, p. 231-242, s'élevant contre (d'après lui) la totale unanimité des historiens modernes, a montré qu'on pouvait reconstituer le contenu de deux *Vitae* de Manuel, l'une étant en fait un éloge écrit de son vivant et la seconde une œuvre hagiographique rédigée après sa mort. Il explique ainsi les incohérences de nos sources sans recourir aux explications extrêmes de H. Grégoire et nier l'existence de Manuel après 838.

48. VASILIEV, *Byzance et les Arabes* (cité n. 37), p. 191.

49. On a vu que Théoctistos n'est probablement pas un oncle de Théodora, mais en revanche, il pourrait s'agir de son cousin germain du côté maternel. La précision nous échappera toujours.

50. Il est possible que Manuel ait été l'époux d'une sœur de Théophile, mais c'est sa qualité d'oncle de Théodora qui prime ici. Dans les récits confus concernant Théophobe et qui, en partie, mélangent ses actions et celles de Manuel, on trouve que Théophobe avait épousé Hélène, sœur de Théophile. Ce qui est faux puisque Théophobe avait épousé en réalité une sœur de l'impératrice Théodora. Cette Hélène, sœur de Théophile, est peut-être identique à Hélène épouse de Manuel connue par la *Vie de Nicolas le Studite* : SETTIPANI, *Continuité* (cité n. 20), p. 172, n. 1 ; VARONA CODESO et PRIETO DOMÍNGUEZ, Deconstructing Photios (cité n. 43), p. 134.

51. Théodosios Baboutzikos (*PmbZ* IV, 2001, 7874), ambassadeur chez les Francs en 839 et à Venise en 840, proche parent de Théophile selon GEN., III, 18, n'entre pas en compte parce qu'il est en réalité le probable beau-frère de Théodora, dont une sœur était mariée à un Constantin Baboutzikos. D'ailleurs Génésios utilise le mot ἀγχιστέα qui traduit le plus souvent une parenté par alliance.

52. On pourrait certes ajouter que Théodora appartenait par son père à la grande famille arménienne des Mamikonians, et que tel devait être le cas aussi de Bardanios. Mais cette communauté d'origine n'a probablement pas joué un grand rôle en la circonstance dans la mesure où il s'agit de deux branches fort éloignées de la famille Mamikonian (voir la généalogie chez SETTIPANI, *Continuité* (cité n. 20), p. 309-310).

53. *PmbZ* IV, 2001, 8237, p. 656-659.

compétition permanente avec Manuel, oncle de l'impératrice, qui le jalousait férocement[54]. Dans au moins une des versions de la mort de Théophobe, c'est le frère de l'impératrice, Pétronas, et un logothète non cité mais certainement identique à Théoctistos, qui sont désignés comme les exécuteurs envoyés par Théophile[55].

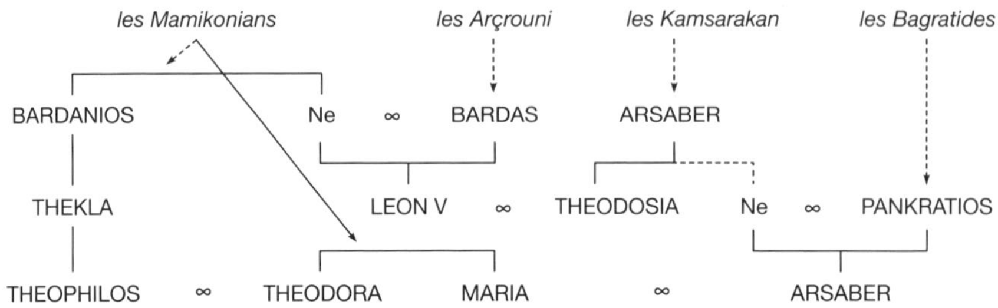

Par ailleurs, il semble que c'est Théophile lui-même qui a écarté une partie de ses parents. On a vu qu'il a fait exécuter un des beaux-frères de l'impératrice. La famille arménienne des Mousélé, dont un membre, Alexis, avait épousé une fille de Théophile, et avait même reçu le titre de césar et été envisagé un temps comme successeur potentiel, était encore représentée. Mais Alexis avait été relégué dans un monastère en 839 en dépit de sa proximité de sang avec les ancêtres de Théodora. Pareillement, les Martinakioi, qui devaient donner deux impératrices à la dynastie des Macédoniens, eux aussi étroitement apparentés à Théophile[56], mais suspects, avaient été éloignés par Théophile. Enfin, on ignore si le patrice Katakylas, comte de l'Opsikion en 822[57], neveu (ou cousin ?) de Michel II[58], était encore en vie en 842, mais il avait de toute façon des descendants qu'on retrouve par la suite occupant de hautes fonctions[59].

54. Cf. Théoph. cont., III, 22, 31-32.

55. Léon gram., p. 228 ; Georg. Mon., p. 810.

56. Un Martinakios, cousin germain ou beau-frère de Théophile, est exilé par celui-ci sous le soupçon de conspiration : Settipani, *Continuité* (cité n. 20), p. 268, n. 3.

57. *PmbZ* II, 2000, 3639, p. 464 ; M. Nichanian, *Aristocratie et pouvoir impérial à Byzance VIIe-IXe siècle*, thèse doct. Paris IV 2004, p. 267-268.

58. Gén. II (cité n. 19), 3 : Κατακύλας αὐτοῦ Μιχαὴλ Βασιλέως ἐξαδέλφος καὶ πατρίκιος. Le mot signifie le plus souvent neveu (compris ainsi dans *PmbZ* 3639), mais quelquefois cousin (compris ainsi dans *PBE*, s. v. Katakylas 1).

59. Léon Katakylas, ou Katakalos ou Katakalon, *gambros* ou *syngénès* de Photios, est drongaire de la Veille en 886, puis domestique des scholes, magistros et exarque contre les Bulgares en 896 (*PmbZ*² III, 2013, 24329, p. 51 ; Timotin, *Visions* (cité n. 19), p. 200-202). Il est probablement identique (ou étroitement apparenté) au patrice Léon Katakalitès attesté en 913 (*PmbZ*² IV, 2013, 24404, p. 100) et évidemment identique à Katakylas, beau-père [et non père] de Gabalas dont la fille Anna épouse en 934 Stéphanos Lécapène, fils de l'empereur Romain Ier (*PmbZ*² III, 2013, 23690, p. 464). Voir aussi les individus nommés Katakalon : *PmbZ*² III, 2013, 23684-23689. Pour la famille Katakalon aux XIe/XIIe s., voir A. Avramea – D. Feissel, Inventaires en vue d'un recueil des inscriptions historiques de Byzance, *Travaux et Mémoires* 10, 1987, p. 357-398, p. 370-372 ; J.-Cl. Cheynet – D. Theodoridis, *Sceaux byzantins de la collection D. Theodoridis. Les sceaux patronymiques*, Paris 2010, p. 112-113. Elle s'alliera ensuite avec les Euphorbénoi, les Comnènes, les Bryennioi et les Paléologues : K. Varzos, Η Γενεαλογια των Κομνηνων, Thessalonique 1980-1984, I, K33, p. 198-203, K69-K73, p. 331-339, II, K120-122b, p. 108-117 ; J.-Cl. Cheynet et J.-F. Vannier, *Etudes prosopographiques*, Paris 1986, p. 160-161 ; M. Kouroupou et J.-Fr. Vannier, Commémoration des Comnènes dans le Typikon liturgique du monastère du Christ Philanthrope, *Revue des études byzantines* 63, 2005, p. 41-69, p. 53, n° 12.

Aucun toutefois qui intervienne au moment de la mort de Théophile. Il est donc clair que le clan de Théodora avait réussi, du vivant même de l'empereur, à monopoliser la première place autour du trône et à se débarrasser un à un de tous les parents propres des Amoriens.

La solidarité du groupe ne résistera finalement pas à son accession au pouvoir[60]. On ne sait pour quelle raison Bardas sera d'abord exilé. Puis Théoctistos écartera le vieux Manuel qui passera alors l'essentiel de son temps dans sa maison transformée en monastère[61]. Bardas, revenu à la cour grâce au concours d'amis bien placés, réussi à convaincre son neveu de se débarrasser de Théoctistos. Le 20 novembre 855, Bardas avec la complicité de sa sœur Kalé Maria et l'aval du jeune Michel III, fait arrêter puis assassiner peu après le ministre, ce qui provoquera une rupture définitive entre eux et Théodora. Celle-ci sera donc déposée le 15 mars 856 avant d'être reléguée dans un couvent en 858 avec ses filles[62]. Même Manuel, semble avoir rompu avec Bardas à la suite du meurtre de Théoctistos[63].

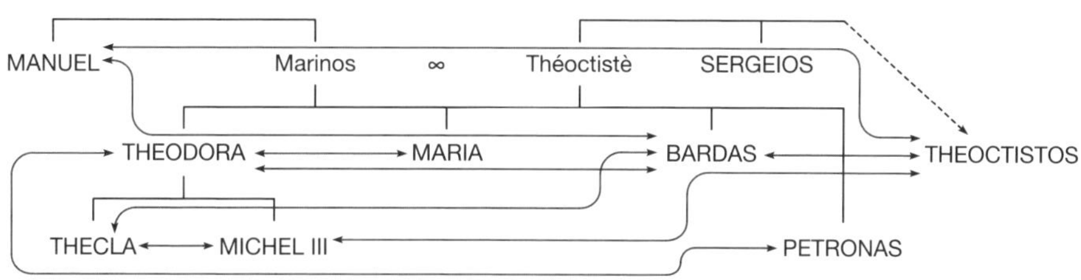

Les antagonismes au sein du conseil de régence (en majuscules) de 843 (←→ indique un conflit).

On assiste ici à la désagrégation d'un groupe familial sous la pression des ambitions politiques et de la soif du pouvoir. Les questions religieuses ont certes pu jouer un rôle, mais cela n'apparaît pas de façon probante. Ainsi, si Théophobe est réputé avoir été orthodoxe, donc iconophile et Manuel un iconoclaste, il faut relativiser en tenant compte des opportunismes et des contraintes politiques. L'un des deux assassins de Théophobe est le logothète Théoctistos, lui aussi iconophile. Les sources subsistantes, iconophiles pour la plupart[64], nous expliquent bien volontiers que leur champion professait secrètement la vraie foi sous un em-

60. Les événements concernant la dislocation du groupe ont été analysés de façon détaillée par P. Karlin Hayter, Etude sur les deux histoires du règne de Michel III, *Byzantion* 41, 1971, p. 452-496 (= Ead., *Studies in Byzantine Political History*, Londres 1981, n° IV) étude extrêmement pertinente pour l'essentiel mais viciée par l'acceptation de la thèse de Henri Grégoire concernant la mort de Manuel en 838.

61. Théoph. cont., IV, 18 (p. 168 Bonn).

62. Pour la chronologie de l'effacement du pouvoir de Théodora, voir P. Varona Codeso, Contribución al problema de la cronología y las fuentes de la *Vita Basilii*, *Byzantinische Zeitschrift* 102, 2009, p. 739-775, p. 745, n. 34.

63. Manuel, venu au palais juste après la mort de Théoctistos, prédit à Bardas, que puisqu'il avait tué le ministre, lui-même devrait désormais vivre dans la crainte d'être assassiné à son tour : Théoph. cont., IV, 19 (p. 170-171 Bonn) ; Skyl., V, 9 (p. 84-85 Flusin-Cheynet).

64. Pour l'hagiographie iconoclaste, voir M.-F. Auzépy, L'analyse littéraire et l'historien : l'exemple des vies de saints iconoclastes, *Byzantinoslavica* 53, 1992, p. 57-67 (= Ead., *L'histoire des iconoclastes*, Paris 2007, 329-340).

pereur impie avant de la faire éclater au grand jour sous un règne plus favorable[65]. Ce qui est une autre façon de dire que bien des aristocrates proches du trône étaient iconoclastes sous un prince iconoclaste et iconophiles sous un prince iconophile.

D'autres, peut-on le supposer, avaient une conviction plus profonde, ou un sens plus aigu de l'opportunisme politique. L'un des principaux acteurs de la restauration des icones semble avoir été le patrice, puis magistre, Sergios le Nicétiate, probablement oncle de l'impératrice Théodora. Sa biographie est quelque peu obscure dans la mesure où les chroniqueurs l'ont écarté de l'histoire officielle, pour des motifs qui restent ignorés mais qui seraient liés selon Henri Grégoire à une confusion entre ses actions et celles d'un autre magistre, lui aussi oncle de l'impératrice, Manuel. En conséquence, les historiens ont quelque peu hésité pour parvenir à reconstituer une biographie raisonnable de Sergios. Parmi les difficultés qu'il a fallu lever se trouve la confusion qu'on a pu introduire à certains moments avec un autre Sergios, également iconophile et également apparenté à Théodora. Mais une analyse plus serrée des textes et l'apport de la sigillographie permettent désormais de bien distinguer les deux homonymes. Le second Sergios, surnommé le Confesseur, est l'auteur d'une histoire inachevée qui couvrait la période de 769 à 735 environ, date de sa propre mort. Cette chronique a disparu et n'est plus connue à présent que par deux fragments assez étendus et des emprunts par d'autres auteurs[66]. Il nous reste également une notice de Photios qui nous permet d'avoir une idée de son style et de son contenu[67] :

« J'ai lu un ouvrage de Sergios le Confesseur. Il commence aux faits et gestes de Michel, puis revient aux crimes horribles du Copronyme et repart de là pour une revue continue des événements jusqu'à la huitième année du règne du même Michel ... Dans son style, il a, plus que tout autre, les ornements de la clarté et de la simplicité tant dans les mots, dont le sens est net, que dans la construction et les autres détails de l'ordonnance du discours, si bien qu'il semble avoir écrit dans une sorte d'improvisation. En effet, son langage est fleuri d'une grâce naturelle et ne porte l'empreinte d'aucune recherche exagérée. C'est pourquoi son style convient surtout à l'histoire ecclésiastique ; c'était d'ailleurs ce qu'il cherchait ».

Ces restes suffisent à montrer que Sergios était un iconophile convaincu qui dénonce avec force la politique iconoclaste des empereurs de Constantin V à Michel II[68]. Il n'épargne

65. C'est, par exemple, le cas de Théodora elle-même : Ps.-Symeon, p. 629-630 ; Théoph. cont., III, 6. Aussi bien Manuel que Théophobe ont fondé des monastères qui se sont chargés de faire leur propagande posthume.

66. Pour l'œuvre de Sergios, voir notamment Treadgold, *Middle Byzantine Historians* (cité n. 18), p. 90-100, qui propose de reconnaître des fragments de son *Histoire* notamment dans le *Scripor Incertus* et dans la *Chronique de 811*.

67. Photios, *Bibl.*, cod. 67 (éd. R. Henry, *Photius. Bibliothèque*, Paris 1959, I, p. 99).

68. Il descendait pourtant de certains de ces empereurs. Un passage du pseudo-Syméon donne l'information suivante : « Ce Photios était le fils du *spatharios* Sergios, fils de Zacharias ... qui eut pour fils Léon l'emp(ereur) ... Sergios, d'origine étrangère [ou païenne] ... lequel enleva par la violence une femme d'un monastère de religieuses et en fit son épouse » (Ps.-Syméon, p. 668). Cet extrait, dont la lecture a depuis été confirmée à partir de l'unique manuscrit de la chronique pose problème. Il s'agit évidemment pour le pseudo-Syméon, anti-Photien convaincu, de rattacher le père de celui-ci à un abominable empereur iconoclaste. Mais dans la mesure où l'une de ses sources est la chronique perdue de Sergios le Confesseur (Treadgold, *Middle Byzantine Historians* (cité n. 18), p. 218-219), fils de Zacharias et père de Photios, il y a certainement trouvé des renseignements de première main sur leur famille. Comment Zacharias peut-il alors passer pour le père de Léon V dont on sait bien qu'il était fils d'un Bardas ? Varona Codeso et Prieto Domínguez, Deconstructing Photios (cité n. 43), p. 117-119, qui ont vérifié le manuscrit, suggèrent que le Ps. Syméon a peut-être confondu Léon V avec Léon III, dont le père se serait appelé Zacharias.

pas davantage, et même charge particulièrement, le patriarche Jean VII le Grammairien. Or, il est pratiquement assuré que Sergios le Confesseur n'est autre que le père homonyme du patriarche Photios. Dans ces conditions, le patriarche Jean le Grammairien est son beau-frère, le frère de son épouse, Irène[69]. Au moment du mariage de Sergios et de la sœur de Jean, vers 815 probablement, Jean devait être encore iconophile et donc sa sœur appartenir à une famille tout à fait recommandable pour un neveu du patriarche Tarasios. Mais l'évolution de la position de Léon V qui s'est progressivement tourné vers l'iconoclasme, entraînant évidemment dans son sillage une partie de la cour, a modifié les convictions de Jean et provoqué une rupture profonde entre Sergios et Jean.

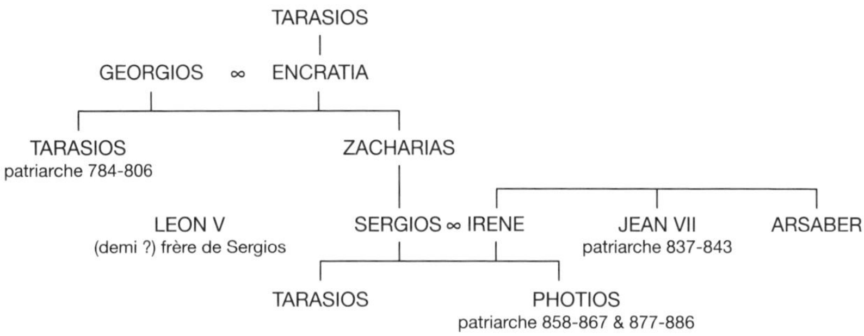

Hypothèse à mon sens désespérée dans la mesure où on ignore le patronyme de Léon III (notons quand même qu'une source arabe invérifiable le dit fils d'un Constantin : St. Gero, *Byzantine Iconoclasm during the Reign of Leo III, with particular Attention to the Oriental Sources*, Louvain 1973, p. 11, n. 43) et où Syméon tient ses renseignements du propre fils de Zacharias. J. Signes Codoñer – F. J. Andrés Santos, *La introducción al derecho (eisagoge) del patriarca Focio*, Madrid, 2007, p. 4, n. 7, pensent pour sa part qu'un échelon intermédiaire manque peut-être dans le texte qui nous est parvenu, ou encore qu'il faut peut-être écarter Sergios et Zacharias si on veut absolument conserver Léon V comme oncle paternel de Photios. Mais, comme ils le reconnaissent, Zacharias paraît bien intégré à la généalogie. Treadgold, *Middle Byzantine Historians* (cité n. 18), p. 91, n. 45, préfère quant à lui corriger le mot υἱὸν en θεῖον, ce qui ferait de Zacharias le neveu (fils d'une sœur) d'un empereur Léon qui serait cette fois Léon IV le Khazar. Cette solution aurait l'avantage d'expliquer l'allusion à l'ascendance khazare de Photios. Mais elle n'est guère probable dans la mesure où l'on sait que Zacharias était le frère du patriarche Tarasios, fils de Georgios et d'Enkratia, fille d'un précédent Tarasios, dont le nom s'est transmis dans la famille de Photios, montrant que Zacharias était bien né d'Enkratia. Si Zacharias est bien lié à Léon IV, ce ne peut être que par son épouse, qui serait une fille ou nièce de l'empereur. Sauf que la correction qu'il faudrait apporter au texte du pseudo-Syméon devient cette fois drastique. Par ailleurs, si Léon IV a bien eu une sœur, celle-ci est connue, il s'agit d'Anthousa, qui est demeurée vierge (Herlong, *Kinship and Social Mobility* (cité n. 11), p. 37). Et Léon IV lui-même n'a évidemment pas pu avoir de fille inconnue avec l'impératrice Irène. Enfin, j'avais proposé moi-même que Léon V aurait pu être en réalité le frère utérin de Sergios (Settipani, *Continuité* (cité n. 20), p. 180-181). J'admets que cela n'est pas exactement ce qu'écrit Syméon, mais il a pu facilement commettre cette confusion si sa source parlait simplement de Sergios frère de Léon.

69. Pour tout ce qui touche à la famille de Photios, voir désormais l'article très fouillé de Varona Codeso et Prieto Domínguez (cité n. 43), p. 105-148, avec l'arbre généalogique p. 142-143. Toutefois, la totalité des conclusions généalogiques et ajustements chronologiques de ce travail se trouvent déjà dans Settipani, *Continuité* (cité n. 20), p. 167-184 et 206. D'un autre côté, on doit signaler que Signes Codoñer, *La introducción al derecho*, cité *supra* n. 68, p. 7, n. 16, a suggéré que Photios n'était peut-être pas fils de Sergios. Tout récemment, lors d'une communication à Paris, il va même plus loin et propose de corriger la lecture « Sergios », qui serait fautive, et de donner au père de Photios un nom différent. En attendant la publication de son travail, je me borne à en mentionner l'existence.

La dynastie amorienne s'achève avec le meurtre sordide de Michel III dans la nuit du 23 septembre 867 par son co-empereur Basile. A priori, rien qui touche à la parenté donc. Mais un examen plus approfondi va nous permettre d'y déceler des influences familiales. Sa légende présente Basile comme un pauvre paysan venu chercher fortune à Byzance pour sortir du dénuement le plus complet dans lequel croupissait sa famille. Remarqué par sa force et sa beauté, il grimpe rapidement les échelons et de proche en proche devient familier de l'empereur Michel III, qui en fera son coempereur et l'unira à sa maîtresse, Eudocie. À la fin, la méfiance s'installant, comme il se doit, entre les deux compères, Basile est le plus rapide et assassine son maître, ce qui lui permet d'accéder au trône.

Si la famille semble absente de ce récit, il faut faire intervenir en réalité les relations intimes qui unissent Michel III, sa maîtresse en titre Eudocie et celui qui deviendra l'époux de celle-ci, Basile. Et alors, une trame familiale se laisse entrevoir sous le tissu légendaire. Tous les textes, même ceux qui lui sont favorables, et dont certains sont contemporains de Basile[70], s'accordent à voir en Basile un aventurier d'origine arménienne venu d'Andrinople chercher fortune à la capitale[71]. Mais en même temps, et de façon qui peut nous paraître contradictoire mais ne pose apparemment pas de problème aux contemporains, certains de ces textes mentionnent l'ascendance royale arménienne de Basile[72]. D'autres en revanche sont bien plus critiques. Notamment Nicétas David, dans sa *Vie d'Ignace*, qui tient à préciser, à l'inverse des courtisans, que cette filiation est totalement fictive. Selon lui, ce serait le patriarche Photios, soucieux de revenir en grâce après sa déposition en 867, qui aurait fabriqué cette généalogie fabuleuse faisant de Basile un rejeton direct des rois d'Arménie auquel la couronne impériale aurait été promise[73].

70. En particulier un poème anonyme rédigé entre 867 et 872, du vivant même de l'empereur et au début de son règne, compare Basile « à David, qui lui aussi parvint de la position de berger à celle de roi » (A. Markopoulos, An anonymous laudatory poem in honour of Basil I, *DOP* 46, 1992, p. 225-232 (= Id., *History and Literature of Byzantium in the 9th – 10th Centuries*, Aldershot 2004, ch. XIV). Pareillement, cette humble origine est transcrite en filigrane dans la *Vita Ignatii*, écrite sous le règne de Basile et dans son oraison funèbre publiée deux ans après sa mort.

71. L'origine arménienne de Basile me semble être absolument hors de doute et est admise sans hésitation par la quasi-totalité des historiens modernes depuis longtemps. À une époque récente, seul A. Schminck, « The beginnings and origins of the 'Macedonian' dynasty », *Byzantine Macedonia*, 2000, p. 61-68, a cru devoir la contester, mais avec des arguments totalement insuffisants : voir Settipani, , *Continuité* (cité n. 20), p. 254, n. 5.

72. Cette ascendance royale est mentionnée dans l'oraison funèbre de Basile par son fils Léon VI, ainsi que dans la chronique de Génésios et la *Vita Basilii*, rédigés sous la houlette de Constantin Porphyrogénète, petit-fils de Basile. La *Chronique* de Syméon et ses dérivés, hostiles aux Macédoniens, n'en parlent pas, tandis que Nicétas David (*Vie d'Ignace* 89, cité note suivante) et, plus tard, Zonaras (XVI, 6), ne la mentionne que pour la rejeter fermement.

73. Nicétas David, *Vie d'Ignace* 89 : « Photios ... exilé au monastère de Sképé ... ayant observé les noms de l'empereur Basile, de son épouse l'*Augusta* Eudocie et de leurs fils Constantin, Léon, Alexandre et Stéphane, il eut l'idée, avec la première lettre de chaque nom, d'une fraude ingénieuse. Il fabriqua une histoire ou plutôt une généalogie, qui n'existait pas et n'avait jamais existé, partant du fameux Tiridatès, le grand roi d'Arménie contemporain du martyr Grégorios [l'Illuminateur]. Ce récit fabuleux donnait une suite descendante arbitraire de différentes personnes et différents ancêtres ; arrivé au père de Basile, il écrivit que celui-ci devrait engendrer un homme tel que Basile lui-même, et son nom serait Béklas et prédisant qu'il deviendrait le plus glorieux des empereurs de tous les temps » (éd. et trad. angl. A. Smithies et J. M. Duffy, Washington 2013, p. 118-121). Voir aussi le récit parallèle du pseudo-Syméon, p. 689.

À sa suite, les historiens modernes adoptent de façon assez unanime la position suivante : Basile est un paysan de la naissance la plus obscure qui soit et ce n'est que tardivement que Photios lui forge une ascendance royale fantaisiste. Mais dans le même temps, ils admettent que la Vie de Basile n'est qu'un tissu de légendes assemblées de façon plus ou moins habile[74]. Cela n'est pas nécessairement cohérent puisque si la *Vita Basilii* est fantaisiste, cela vaut pour ses origines humbles. La publication des recueils prosopographiques a montré désormais que la société byzantine était, comme la société médiévale occidentale, très fermée et que la mobilité sociale y était très faible. Bien des familles ont été classées trop vite comme « nouvelles » par les historiens modernes en raison de sources insuffisantes ou biaisées[75], alors que des recherches plus approfondies, fondées sur une étude plus critique et sur l'apport des sceaux et des sources étrangères notamment, prouvent leur appartenance à l'aristocratie provinciale ou même de la capitale[76]. Le cas de Basile serait une anomalie curieuse. Très tôt, Basile a cherché à s'identifier à un nouveau David. Il a donc probablement exagéré l'obscurité de ses débuts pour rendre la ressemblance plus parfaite et encore plus éclatante la protection divine dont il a profité tout au long de sa vie[77]. Quant à sa généalogie et à la façon dont elle a été fabriquée par Photios, il convient de regarder de plus près la valeur de la *Vita Ignatii* source éminemment polémique[78] : l'histoire du livre ancien inventé afin de regagner la grâce de l'empereur est déjà rapportée à propos de Méthode[79] et n'est donc ni originale ni, probablement, crédible[80]. Par ailleurs, il semble bien que la filiation légendaire de Basile est déjà admise au

74. Le travail de référence reste celui de G. Moravcsik, Sagen und Legenden über Kaiser Basileios I, *DOP* 15, 1961, p. 61-126 (= Id., *Studia Byzantina*, Amsterdam 1967, p. 147-220). Voir aussi N. Tobias, *Basil I, Founder of the Macedonian Dynasty. À Study of the Political and Military History of the Byzantine Empire in the Ninth Century*, New York 2007, p. 25-62. On trouvera une très bonne analyse de la *Vita Basilii* chez Sp. Vryonis Jr., The Vita Basilii of Constantine Porphyrogenitus and the absorption of Armenians in Byzantine Society, dans *Euphrosynon : Aphieroma ston Manole Chatzidake*, Athènes 1991, I, p. 677-691, et une étude récente de ses sources chez Varona Codeso, Contribución (cité n. 62) et Treadgold, *Middle Byzantine Historians* (cité n. 18), p. 165-180 (qui ignore malheureusement le premier travail).

75. Le dénigrement des origines d'un adversaire, politique ou religieux, était une pratique courante chez les historiens byzantins et s'avère bien souvent purement fantaisiste. Voir quelques exemples chez Settipani, *Continuité* (cité n. 20), p. 88-89.

76. Voir la synthèse éclairante de Ludwig, Social Mobility (cité n. 10), p. 240.

77. Basile n'est pas le premier empereur dont les origines auront été abaissées par les auteurs postérieurs. Ainsi, Maurice, Léon III ou Thomas le Slave ont été décrits comme issus de rien alors que ce n'était pas le cas. Ce qui est nouveau ici, c'est que ces origines obscures sont assumées par la dynastie elle-même.

78. On sait que l'auteur de la *Vita Ignatii*, Nicétas David de Paphlagonie était un anti-photien convaincu, probablement auteur d'une *Histoire secrète* source des passages anti-photiens de la *Chronique* de Syméon Magister : S. A. Paschalidès, From Hagiography to Historiography : the Case of the *Vita Ignatii* (*BHG* 817) by Nicetas David the Paphlagonian, dans *Les* Vies des Saints *à Byzance. Genre littéraire ou biographies historique*, éd. P. Odorico et P. Agapitos, Paris 2004, p. 161-173 ; Treadgold, *Middle Byzantine Historians* (cité n. 18), p. 134-151.

79. Ps. Sym., p. 643 Bonn.

80. Voir N. Adontz, L'âge et l'origine de Basile I (deuxième partie), *Byzantion* 9, 1934, p. 223-260, p. 234-235 (= Id., *Notes arméno-byzantines*, Lisbonne 1965, p. 82-83). Curieusement, la plupart des auteurs modernes se réfèrent à N. Adontz pour justifier que la généalogie de Basile n'est qu'une grossière invention, alors que N. Adontz, s'il récuse la filiation arsacide directe de Basile, admet malgré tout qu'il descendait des Mamikonian, et donc en effet du roi Tiridate par les femmes (Id., *ibid.*, p. 243 : « le père de Basile avait encore quelques raisons de faire remonter son origine à Tiridate »).

palais lorsque l'empereur nomme son quatrième fils Alexandre, en référence à Alexandre le Grand selon toute probabilité[81]. Or, Alexandre est né en novembre 870[82], avant que Photios, exilé à la fin 867, ne revienne en grâce, autour de 872[83]. Enfin, l'existence d'une version concurrente de l'astuce employée par Photios pour revenir à la cour qui ne fait plus du tout intervenir la généalogie impériale rend suspecte l'invention de celle-ci telle qu'elle est rapportée par Nicétas David[84]. Quelle que soit la nature de l'ouvrage rédigé à propos de la généalogie de Basile, et son auteur, Photios ou un autre, nous ne connaîtrons jamais son contenu ni son propos exact[85].

Quelques traces de la situation réelle de Basile survivent parfois au détour d'une phrase. À défaut de donner son patronyme[86], la biographie de Basile livre le nom de son aïeul et celui de son bisaïeul : son grand-père, Maiktès, apparemment encore natif d'Arménie, ayant épousé la fille d'un certain arménien nommé Léon, natif d'Andrinople, alors qu'il était venu faire des affaires à Byzance[87]. On n'est pas dans un milieu paysan exclusivement provincial.

81. *Cf.* Gén. III (cité n. 19), 85-89 : « Basile lui-même appartenait à la race de l'ancien Arsace le Parthe qui conquit l'empire d'Assyrie ... et à celle de Tiridate, roi descendant du précédent, ainsi qu'à celle des très nobles princes Philippe et Alexandre. Il naquit en Macédoine de parents obscurs mais non pas indignes ».

82. Voir N. Adontz, La portée historique de l'oraison funèbre de Basile par son fils Léon VI le Sage, *Byzantion* 8, 1933, p. 501-513, p. 504, 508 ; *PmbZ*[2] I, 2013, 20228, p. 138-139.

83. Pour la date, voir par exemple Treadgold, *Middle Byzantine Historians* (cité n. 18), p. 116, n. 125.

84. Ps. Sym., p. 689 : Photios aurait soudoyé un des chambellans de l'empereur pour qu'il asperge son lit d'une eau miraculeuse préparée par Théodore Santabarènos ce qui aurait fait changer instantanément les sentiments de Basile à son égard. Très certainement les contemporains ont laissé errer leur imagination quant aux raisons du retour de Photios.

85. Photios, dont la mère appartenait à l'une des plus grandes familles princières d'Arménie, ne devait pas être en peine de connaître la filiation des grandes familles de cette nation. Par ailleurs, on peut croire, à partir des données de l'*Oraison funèbre de Basile* rédigée par Léon VI et celles fournies par Génèsios, que l'ouvrage généalogique en question ne s'arrêtait pas à Tiridate mais poussait au-delà, même de façon allusive ou rapide, et embrassait la généalogie des Arsacides arméniens jusqu'aux Arsacides parthes, et à partir de ceux-ci jusqu'aux Achéménides et à Artaxerxès II d'une part, aux Séleucides et à Alexandre le Grand d'autre part.

86. Treadgold, *Middle Byzantine Historians* (cité n. 18), p. 169, par exemple pense que l'omission du nom du père de Basile est liée à la généalogie fabriquée par Photios selon laquelle son père se serait appelé Béclas, ce que j'avais proposé également (Settipani, *Continuité* (cité n. 20), p. 252). W. Treadgold suggère alors (*op. cit.*, p. 169, n. 55) que le père de Basile devait s'appelait Constantin, puisque c'est le nom donné par Basile à son fils aîné. En réalité, cette hypothèse avait déjà été formulée par C. Toumanoff, *Manuel de généalogie et de chronologie pour l'histoire de la Caucasie chrétienne*, Rome 1976, p. 344. Mais surtout, il a manqué ma propre observation qui souligne que le véritable premier né de Basile était en fait Bardas, et que c'est donc ce nom que l'on doit supposer avoir été celui du père de Basile. Certes, Basile a un frère nommé Bardas et l'on ne donne pas à Byzance à un enfant le nom d'un de ses parents. Mais cette règle ne s'applique pas en cas de naissance posthume et Basile lui-même étant tout jeune à la mort de son père, son plus jeune frère a bien pu être posthume. L'hypothèse a en outre l'avantage que le nom Bardas est plus proche de celui de Béclas (ΒΕΚΛΑΣ/ΒΑΡΔΑΣ), ce qui justifierait l'invention. Pour l'intérêt de la précision concernant l'écriture alexandrine, voir G. Cavallo, Γράμματα Ἀλεξανδρῖνα, *JÖB* 24, 1975, p. 23–54, p. 23-27.

87. *Vita Basilii*, 3 : « Plusieurs années plus tard, alors que Constantin régnait avec sa mère Irène, Maiktès de bonne réputation, vint dans notre admirable ville de Constantinople en raison d'une ambassade ou d'une quelconque autre affaire ; lui aussi était du sang arsacide. Par chance, il rencontra un compatriote nommé Léon, et constata par son apparence soignée et son équipage distingué qu'il ne s'agissait pas d'une personne de rien, mais plutôt d'un noble et d'un homme d'importance. Maiktès passa quelque temps avec Léon et le trouva avenant. Lorsqu'il apprit qu'elles étaient les origines de Léon et entendu parler de la communauté arsacide qui vivait à

Quel que soit le statut exact de cet Arménien nommé Léon, il semble disposer d'une certaine aisance[88]. Il en va de même de Basile : selon la *Vita Basilii*, Basile, seul soutient de famille après la mort de son père, quitte la ferme familiale qui n'arrive plus à les nourrir et arrive à Byzance comme un pauvre hère. Il rencontre bientôt Théophilos, dit le « petit Théophilos » ou Théophilitzès, parent de l'impératrice et de Bardas, qui en fait aussitôt son *stratôr*. Peu après, à l'occasion d'un voyage d'Etat à Patras, Basile, séparé de Théophilos par une maladie, rencontre une riche veuve, Danèlis, qui y reconnaît grâce à une prédiction le futur empereur, et lui cède une part de sa fortune. De sorte que, lorsque Basile revient à Byzance, une fois guéri, il est riche et propriétaire de nombreux domaines dans sa province d'origine. Mais à part cela, sa situation reste la même « il demeura auprès de son maître et continua à le servir »[89]. Il y a une incohérence certaine dans cette présentation[90]. Et il y a mieux, ou pire. Dans sa version de l'histoire de Basile, Génèsios laisse échapper, par fierté familiale sans doute, un renseignement omis par les autres sources : alors qu'il était encore au service de Théophilos, Basile se fait remarquer au cour d'un dîner organisé par Antigonos, fils du césar Bardas, lors d'un combat de lutteurs, au cours duquel il reçoit l'aide de Constantin Maniakès, *qui était son parent* (et accessoirement, le grand-père de Génèsios)[91]. Ainsi, un an à peine après son arrivée à la capitale, le jeune parvenu y apparaît comme relativement fortuné et on apprend en outre qu'il est apparenté à l'un des plus grands personnages de l'État : voilà qui contredit

---

Andrinople, il choisit une contrée étrangère plutôt que sa patrie à cause des vertus de cet homme ; et il devint le gendre de Léon en épousant une de ses filles. Le fruit de ce mariage est le père de l'homme qui est le sujet de récit » (éd. I. Ševčenko, *Chronographiae quae Theophanis continuati nomine fertur. Liber quo Vita Basilii imperatoris amplectitur*, Berlin 2011, p. 17). Si l'on se fie à ce récit, Maiktès, lui aussi arsacide, donc comme ceux d'Andrinople dont il est question juste avant, vient en terre byzantine où il rencontre Léon, membre de la communauté arsacide d'Andrinople. Et après avoir épousé une fille de Léon, Maiktès/Hmayeak, change de patrie et s'installe à Andrinople. C'est donc Léon qui descend de la lignée arsacide détaillée auparavant, et Maiktès, même s'il a aussi du sang arsacide, vient d'un autre endroit. Evidemment d'Arménie. Selon Açołik de Taron, II, 5, la famille de Basile était originaire de la province du Taron, du village de T'il. C'est-à-dire au cœur des possessions de la famille des Mamikonian, dont les chefs avaient fui à Byzance après la défaite de Bagrévand en 775, notamment leur chef Artavazd, fils d'un Hmayeak.

88. Le simple fait qu'il mène des affaires dans la capitale le suggère. On ne saurait aller au-delà et j'ai imprudemment suivi ADONTZ, L'âge et l'origine (cité n. 80), p. 243, en accordant trop de faveur à l'hypothèse de cet historien qui propose d'identifier l'Arménien Léon, beau-père d'Hmayeak, à Léon l'Arménien, futur empereur. Cette suggestion, fondée sur de multiples rapprochements onomastiques entre les deux familles, entraîne malgré tout de nombreuses complications chronologiques (l'Arménien Léon, père d'une fille nubile sous le règne de Constantin VI, semble antérieur d'une génération à Léon l'Arménien) ou historiques (proche parenté qui en résulterait entre Basile et ses prédécesseurs, invraisemblance d'une fille de Léon V mère d'un simple paysan, invraisemblance de petits-enfants de Léon V laissés en captivité durant tout son règne, etc).

89. *Vita Basilii*, 9-11 (p. 35-47 ŠEVČENKO).

90. Même si A. VOGT, *Basile Ier empereur de Byzance (867-886) et la civilisation Byzantine à la fin du IXe siècle*, Paris 1908, p. 28, pense que Basile fut en cela particulièrement habile et ne se laissa pas griser par sa nouvelle fortune, on reconnaîtra que, soit les présents de Danèlis ont été en réalité fort modestes, soit la décision de Basile de ne rien changer à sa situation subalterne est incompréhensible.

91. GÉN. IV (cité n. 19), 26 : « les lutteurs de l'empereur et du césar furent victorieux, Basile ne participant pas aux joutes. Mais alors, il participa au combat et fut mis en face du vainqueur de l'équipe opposé. Constantin était favorablement disposé envers lui en raison de leur parenté », p. 97. Sur cette mention, voir notamment A. KALDELLIS, *ad. loc.*, p. XIX-XX ; TREADGOLD, *Middle Byzantine Historians* (cité n. 18), p. 187. Dans la *Vita Basilii*, la parenté entre Basile et Constantin est supprimée.

singulièrement sa soi-disant condition si modeste. Ce n'est d'ailleurs pas la seule défaillance d'une biographie qui accumule les silences[92], les anachronismes[93], les contradictions[94] ou les ajouts merveilleux empruntés au folklore ou à la Bible[95].

Parent pauvre d'un aristocrate arménien, la progression de Basile vers le sommet s'apparente davantage à l'ascension d'un cadet ruiné qu'à celle d'un homme du peuple. Et cette ascension qui doit certainement beaucoup à ses prouesses physiques, ne repose pas que sur elles. Elle n'est pas non plus si rapide : il se passe plusieurs années entre son départ de la ferme et son arrivée à Byzance, puis au moins dix ans entre cette arrivée et son élévation spectaculaire, peut-être due à ses charmes[96] mais favorisée par des liens familiaux avec des aristocrates proches du trône. Son ascension est l'occasion d'un nouvel affrontement entre groupes familiaux apparentés. La première étape de cette conquête du pouvoir a été l'assassinat du césar Bardas. Les principaux complices de Basile sont en effet : Pierre le Bulgare, Jean Chaldos, Jacobitzès, Marianos, Symbatios, Asyléon, Bardas, Constantin Toxaras, Marianos, fils de Pétronas[97]. Si Marianos, Symbatios, Bardas et Asyléon sont des proches de Basile (ses frères et un cousin germain)[98], le deuxième Marianos en revanche n'est autre que le cousin germain de Michel III, fils de son oncle maternel Pétronas. Parmi les généraux fidèles, du moins au départ, à Basile, figurait aussi Symbatios, qui avait épousé une fille du césar Bardas, oncle de Michel III. L'officier qui leur donne les clés du palais de Marina, l'hétairiarque Artabasdos est un Arménien homonyme du grand-père de l'impératrice Théodora, et peut-être alors un cousin de celle-ci[99]. Sans oublier bien sûr la propre épouse de Basile, Eudocie, qui non contente d'être alors la maîtresse de Michel III avait

92. Ainsi, la *Vita Basilii* omet de raconter qu'en quittant sa famille, Basile entre d'abord au service de Zantzès, chef des Macédoniens d'Andrinople, épisode qui n'est rapporté que dans la *Chronique* du Logothète et qui doit durer un certain temps puisque Basile quitte sa famille à peine sorti de l'adolescence mais ne parvient à Byzance qu'à 25 ans environ.

93. La question de la date de naissance de Basile, de l'exil de ses parents et de leur retour est définitivement embrouillée : voir, par exemple TOBIAS, *Basil I* (cité n. 74), p. 26-36.

94. La *Vita Basilii* peine à expliquer que Basile descendait d'un sang royal arsacide resté pur à travers les siècles, tout en concédant que des mariages avaient eu lieu avec les peuples voisins, et qu'ainsi né d'un rameau royal il n'en est pas moins l'artisan de sa noblesse ; que Basile était né de parents d'une ascendance illustre et non sans illustration ou fortune, mais que lui-même est parti de moins que rien ; que rendu immensément riche par Danèlis peu après son arrivée à Byzance, il reste malgré tout au service d'un courtisan, etc.

95. Basile ne peut pas faire un pas sans que sa mère (à différentes reprises), des moines (à l'église Saint-Diomède, à Patras) ou de grands personnages (Constantin Maniakès, l'impératrice Théodora, puis Bardas) lui prédisent sa prochaine accession au trône. Les emprunts à la légende orientale du berger devenu conquérant (cf. Sargon, Cyrus) voire à Romulus sont évidents et plus encore à l'histoire biblique du roi David auquel Basile veut très tôt être comparé.

96. Pour la nature de la relation entre Michel et Basile, amants pour R. J. H. Jenkins, simples confidents pour P. Karlin Hayter, voir en dernier lieu S. TOUGHER, Michael III and Basil the Macedonian : just good friends ?, dans *Desire and denial in Byzantium : papers from the 31st Spring Symposium of Byzantine Studies, éd. L.* JAMES, Aldershot 1999, p. 149-158, qui conclut ... qu'on ne peut conclure.

97. Cette liste a été abondamment commentée par ADONTZ, L'âge et l'origine (cité n. 80), p. 229-232, mais avec des conclusions fantaisistes quant à l'origine des conspirateurs dont il affirme qu'ils étaient tous des Arméniens, au mépris du témoignage clair de leurs patronymes.

98. Pour la parenté de ces personnages avec Basile, voir en dernier lieu SETTIPANI, *Continuité* (cité n. 20), p. 259-264.

99. *PmbZ*[2] I, 2013, 20627, p. 361-362. Pour annoncer à Artabasdos la mort de Michel III, Basile lui envoie le Perse Eulogios qui lui parle dans sa propre langue, évidemment l'Arménien (plutôt que le Perse comme le suggère la *PmbZ* : *cf. PBE* I, s. v. Artabasdos 1 ; WINKELMANN, *Quellenstudien* (cité n. 14), p. 198).

été auparavant celle de Bardas et l'épouse du fils de celui-ci, Antigonos. En outre, en tant que membre de la famille Martinakios, Eudocie était également une proche parente par le sang de l'empereur Théophile, père de Michel III.

La révolution de 867 n'est pas la seule victoire d'un intriguant venu de rien, c'est l'arrivée au premier plan d'un groupe de parents de l'ancienne dynastie aux détriments d'un autre. Constantin Maniakès, Théophylitzès et Artabasdos sans doute, Marianos, fils de Pétronas, Symbatios et Eudocie, déçus de leur position précédente, parient sur un candidat dont ils espèrent davantage. Et Basile lui-même n'est pas isolé : ses frères et son cousin occupent tous de hautes positions à la cour. Surtout, marié à Eudocie, il est de cette façon au moins apparenté à Michel III. En tant qu'associé au trône il est en outre l'héritier légitime de Michel, au moins tant que celui-ci n'est pas pourvu d'un fils reconnu.

C'est d'ailleurs en réalité tout l'enjeu de cette histoire d'association sur le trône : trouver un héritier à l'Empire qui soit un rejeton de la dynastie amorienne. Car la victoire finale de Basile ne doit pas faire oublier pour autant les préparatifs de Michel III. Celui-ci, depuis longtemps amant d'Eudocie Ingerina, mais empêché de l'épouser en raison de l'irréductible hostilité de sa mère Théodora, avait été contraint de se marier avec Eudocie Décapolitissa qu'il détestait. Pour poursuivre ses relations avec Eudocie Ingerina, il imagine de la marier vers 865 avec son favori Basile[100], étant entendu que Basile n'aurait pas de commerce avec son épouse officielle, qui continuerait à fréquenter son impérial amant, et qu'en contrepartie, Basile bénéficierait des faveurs de Thécla, sœur de Michel[101]. Le 26 mai 866, lorsque Michel fait de Basile son associé sur le trône, la femme de ce dernier, Eudocie, était notoirement enceinte puisqu'elle accoucha de Léon le 19 septembre 866[102]. C. Mango a donc suggéré avec

100. La date du mariage n'est pas certaine et les considérations récentes de N. Tobias à ce propos sont tout à fait négligeables. La date de 865 n'est donnée que par le pseudo-Syméon (voir note suivante). Mais les ajouts de date chez cet auteur sont souvent fantaisistes (voir en dernier lieu TREADGOLD, *Middle Byzantine Historians* (cité n. 18), p. 220). Toutefois, dans ce cas précis, il ne doit pas être loin de la vérité puisque ce mariage a lieu après la nomination de Basile comme parakoimomène qui succédait, après un délai de vacance, à Damianos tombé en disgrâce après la nomination de Bardas comme césar le 12 avril 864. Voir la discussion de S. TOUGHER, *The Reign of Leo VI (886-912). Politics and People*, Leiden 1997, p. 44, n. 9.

101. SYM. MAG., 131, 32 : « La onzième année de son règne, Michel ordonna à Basile de répudier son épouse Maria, et de prendre Eudocie Ingerina comme épouse et lui prescrivit de la tenir pour sa souveraine. Elle était, en effet, la concubine de l'empereur et il l'aimait beaucoup car elle était belle. Auparavant, il renvoya son ancienne épouse Maria chez elle en avec une grosse somme d'argent. Il offrit également à Basile sa sœur Thécla, pour qu'il en fasse sa maîtresse » (p. 248 WAHLGREN). P. KARLIN HAYTER, L'enjeu d'une rumeur. Opinion et imaginaire à Byzance au IXe s., *Byzantion* 41, 1991, p. 85-111,p. 89, croit qu'on peut comprendre « lui prescrivit de la prendre comme épouse légitime », mais c'est contraire au contexte et aussi, quoi qu'elle en dise, à la version parallèle d'EUTYCHIUS D'ALEX., *Le cordon de pierres précieuses*, II, 67 : « Michel avait un général nommé Basile à qui il avait donné le premier rang ... Basile n'était pas de la famille royale, il était d'origine slave. On lui dit 'Pourquoi as-tu trouvé licite de tuer le roi ?' – 'Michel, répondit-il, aimait une femme qu'il m'a ordonné d'épouser, mais sans l'approcher, de façon qu'elle ne fut ma femme que de nom et que lui cohabitât avec elle. C'est parce qu'il craignait que sa femme légitime ne vint à apprendre cela et qu'il ne lui était pas permis d'épouser une autre femme que son épouse. J'ai accepté, puis j'ai regretté et j'ai craint Dieu. Alors, j'ai considéré qu'il m'était permis de tuer le roi' » (édit. et trad . franç. A. VASILIEV, *Byzance et les Arabes. II La dynastie macédonienne*, édition française M. CANARD, Bruxelles 1950, II, p. 25).

102. V. GRUMEL, Notes de chronologie byzantine : la date de naissance de Léon VI le Sage, *Echos d'Orient* 35, 1935, p. 331-335, p. 331-333, suivi par TOUGHER, *The Reign of Leo VI* (cité n. 100), p. 42, n. 3. La notice de la *PmbZ*² IV, 2013, 24311, p. 26, 35, est plus hésitante (fin septembre/début octobre).

vraisemblance que l'intronisation de Basile faisait partie d'un plan de Michel qui avait pour but de faire du futur fils d'Eudocie un héritier légitime du trône[103]. Basile étant alors voué à disparaître à terme, ce qui faillit en effet arriver. Même si cette interprétation n'est pas certaine[104], elle reste à ce jour la meilleure explication des événements et des comportements des principaux protagonistes. La dévolution du pouvoir apparaît encore une fois au cœur des stratégies et des manipulations familiales.

La combinaison de Michel quant à son héritage trouvera un lointain écho deux décennies plus tard au moment de l'héritage de Basile. De ses deux mariages, Basile a eu neuf enfants : deux fils et une fille de sa première épouse, Maria (Bardas, Constantin et Anastasia)[105] et trois fils et trois filles d'Eudocia Ingerina (Léon VI, Etienne, Alexandre, Anne, Hélène et Maria)[106]. Imitant la politique de son prédécesseur, il a confiné ses filles au couvent de sainte Euphémia où elles furent ensuite enterrées[107]. Mais l'aînée n'en avait pas moins été mariée précédemment à un certain Christophe, qui avait succédé avant 872 comme domestique des scholes à

103. C. MANGO, Eudocia Ingerina, the Normans and the Macedonian Dynasty, *ZRVI* 14/5, 1973, p. 17-27 [= ID., *Byzantium and its Image. History and Culture of the Byzantine Empire and its Heritage*, Aldershot 1984, n° XV] ; C. I. TOUL, Περὶ τῆς νοθογενείας τοῦ Λέοντος τοῦ Σοφοῦ, *Parnassos* 21, 1979, p. 15-35 ; E. KISLINGER, Eudokia Ingerina, Basileios I. und Michel III, *JÖB* 33, 1983, p. 119-136.

104. TOUGHER, *The Reign of Leo VI* (cité n. 100), p. 45, est sceptique parce que, d'une part, Constantin aussi était le fils de Michel d'après la chronique de Syméon, et d'autre part, parce que la disgrâce de Basile aurait dû intervenir dans la logique de C. Mango peu après la naissance de Léon, alors qu'elle n'a lieu que beaucoup plus tard. En réalité, ce dernier point n'est pas dirimant. Les jeux organisés par Michel à l'issue desquels la disgrâce de Basile est consommée, ont forcément lieu juste avant le meurtre de Michel le 23 septembre. Or, Léon était né le 19 septembre. De toute évidence, Michel a donc logiquement attendu que Léon ait un an avant d'agir. Quant à la filiation de Constantin, il est clair qu'il s'agit à coup sûr d'un simple lapsus, son nom ayant malencontreusement été mis à la place de celui de Léon. En effet, voilà ce qu'écrit SYM. MAG., 132, 18 : « naissance de Constantin, fils de l'empereur Michel et d'Eudocia, mais qu'on disait fils de Basile » (p. 266 WAHLGREN). Toutefois, on trouve chez PS. SYM., c. 46 : « Au mois de septembre, indiction XV, naît Constantin, fils de l'empereur Michel et d'Eudocie Ingerina, alors que Michel était encore vivant » (p. 686D Bonn). Ces précisions suffisent à prouver, comme on l'a vu depuis longtemps, qu'il est ici question de Léon : GRUMEL, La date de naissance (cité n. 102), p. 331 ; *PmbZ*² IV, 2013, p. 35, n. 2. Pour Constantin, fils de Basile, voir *PmbZ*² III, 2013, 23742, p. 541-543.

105. Pour Constantin comme fils de Maria, voir la démonstration de ADONTZ, La portée historique (cité n. 82), p. 508-509. Constantin apparaît comme apte à diriger des armées dès 878 et son père veut le marier vers 870. Certes, TOUGHER, *The Reign of Leo VI* (cité n. 100), p. 45, argue qu'on connaît des cas d'enfants dirigeant nominativement des armées et aussi des mariages dynastiques d'enfants. Mais pourquoi accumuler les anomalies ? Le plus naturel reste de faire naître Constantin bien avant 864/5 (ainsi, *PmbZ*² III, 2013, 23742, p. 542). Pour Anastasia et Bardas, voir SETTIPANI, *Continuité* (cité n. 20), p. 279-280. TOUGHER, *op. cit.*, p. 26, 45, croit que Maria, qui n'est pas mentionnée par la *Vita Basilii* ou l'*Oraison funèbre de Basile* a été inventée par les chroniqueurs de la famille de Syméon. Mais quoi de plus normal que l'omission de Maria dans la vision idéalisée de la vie familiale de Basile que cherchent à véhiculer son fils et son petit-fils ? Voir ce qu'écrivait déjà VOGT, *Basile Ier* (cité n. 90), p. 57, n. 3 : « La *Vita Basilii* ignore, naturellement, toute cette histoire. Elle ne connaît qu'Eudocie Ingerina, femme très belle, très noble, très vertueuse, modèle de toutes les impératrices, épouse légitime et unique de Basile, mère de Constantin et de Léon ... de même Génésios ».

106. Pour la généalogie de la dynastie macédonienne, voir SETTIPANI, *Continuité* (cité n. 20), p. 246-309. Voir aussi la synthèse récente de Sh. TOUGHER, Imperial families : The case of the Macedonians, dans L. BRUBACKER et Sh. TOUGHER, *Approaches* (cité n. 10), p. 303-326, mais qui ne fait que survoler les problèmes généalogiques.

107. *Vita Basilii*, p. 249 ; Anastasia est enterrée en face de ses sœurs : CONST. PORPH., *De Cer.*, II, 42 (éd. & trad. angl. A. MOFFAT et M. TALL, *Constantine Porphyrogennetos, The Book of Ceremonies*, Canberra 2012, II, p. 648).

Marianos, frère de Basile[108]. Si on ignore somme toute les relations que Basile a pu avoir avec ses filles[109], on connaît en revanche ce qu'il en est de ses liens avec ses fils. Bardas étant rapidement disparu, il a reporté, semble-t-il, toute son affection sur son fils aîné, Constantin, et a voué au suivant, Léon, une inimitié féroce. Quelles que soient les raisons de cette inimitié, d'ailleurs réciproque, sur lesquelles les historiens ont beaucoup épilogué, il reste qu'en raison du décès prématuré de Constantin, elle sera la cause d'une situation très particulière : la dévolution du trône à un héritier qui n'est pas celui qu'aurait choisi son père. Et c'est le moins qu'on puisse dire puisqu'il paraît que dans un accès de colère Basile aurait même failli tuer Léon. Pour autant, alors même qu'il avait deux autres fils, dont l'un, Alexandre, n'était ni ecclésiastique ni encore un enfant, à aucun moment semble-t-il Basile n'a songé a écarter Léon du trône. Il l'avait associé dès le 6 janvier 870 et ne semble pas être revenu sur cette décision, même lorsque Léon sera emprisonné (ou en résidence surveillée) de 883 à 886. Le trône lui revenait légitimement par ordre de primogéniture après la mort de Bardas et de Constantin. En contrepartie de cette haine affichée, Léon aura comme premier geste après la disparition de Basile d'honorer la dépouille de Michel III, et ses rapports avec ses frères, notamment Alexandre qu'il tentera même d'assassiner[110], seront toujours conflictuels[111].

108. Sur la nature de la parenté entre Basile et son *gambros* Christophe (*PmbZ*² I, 2013, 21258, p. 757-759), voir la discussion chez Settipani, *Continuité* (cité n. 20), p. 278. De l'union d'Anastasia avec Christophe ont pu naître deux filles, l'aînée dénommée Maria comme son aïeule, serait la première épouse de Romain Lécapène, mère de son fils aîné Christophe (ainsi : O. Kresten et A. E. Müller, *Samtherrschaft, Legitimationsprinzip und kaiserlicher Urkundentitel in Byzanz in der ersten Hälfte des 10. Jarhunderts*, Vienne 1995, p. 49, n. 149, dont je retiens le tableau mais pas la correction textuelle), et la seconde, qui reste anonyme, pourrait être la mère de Panthérios Sklèros, devenu domestique des scholes en 944 grâce à sa parenté avec Romain Lécapène (*PmbZ*² V, 2013, 26243, p. 274) : Settipani, *Continuité* (cité n. 20), p. 237-238. La famille de ce Christophe reste inconnue mais elle devait être particulièrement illustre si Romain Lécapène a choisi de donner ce nom à son fils aîné plutôt que celui de son propre père, Théophylacte. Peut-être doit-on faire alors le rapprochement avec Christophe, patrice et comte de l'Opsikion, devenu magistre, l'une des plus hautes dignités auliques, fidèle de l'empereur Michel II (*PmbZ* I, 1999, 1126 & 1138, 1139, p. 368 & 371) et qui était probablement d'origine arménienne ou arabe si l'on en croit le nom de ses fils, les patrices Barsacios [Varšak] (*PmbZ* I, 1999, 816, 814 ?, 815 ?, p. 272-273) et Basileios (= Nasar) (*PmbZ* III, 2000, 5227, p. 335-336. Il faut certainement distinguer cependant les fils de Christophe, ayant déjà le rang élevé de patrices en 822, des homonymes stratèges cités de 863 à 894 : *PmbZ* I, 1999, 814 ?, 815 ?, p. 272 = *PmbZ*² I, 2013, 20819, p. 518-519 ; *PmbZ*² IV, 2013, 25490, p. 624-626.

109. Rapports qui n'étaient pas forcément mauvais, même s'il les a reléguées au couvent, puisque le jour de la bataille de Téphrikè, il était en leur compagnie (*Vita Basilii*, 43, p. 156 Ševčenko).

110. Voir B. Flusin, Un fragment inédit de la vie d'Euthyme le patriarche ? II Vie d'Euthyme ou vie de Nitétas ?, *Travaux et memoires* 10, 1989, p. 233-260, p. 237.

111. Voir Tougher, *The Reign of Leo VI* (cité n. 100), p. 219-232.

Conclusion

Ce tour d'horizon rapide des aléas de la politique au sommet de l' État byzantin montre, d'une part, que l'exercice du pouvoir et surtout sa transmission sont bien une affaire de famille depuis le début de l'Empire, comme on pouvait s'y attendre. D'autre part, que ces familles étaient loin d'avoir adopté en toutes circonstances des comportements monolithiques. Entre mouvements de masse, ou de classe, et destins individuels, il fallait que l'historien trouve une place pour la dynamique des groupes familiaux à l'œuvre dans l'exercice du pouvoir. Grâce à la progression des études prosopographiques et à la publication de monographies familiales, nous sommes désormais en mesure de distinguer des rapports familiaux peu ou pas du tout explicités par les sources les plus courantes. Les événements qui déchirent la politique impériale aux VIIIe et IXe siècle peuvent également recevoir une lecture en termes de conflits au sein de la parentèle où chacun se positionne en fonction de l'héritage impérial futur. Non en termes de « clans » regroupant plusieurs familles qui s'affrontent entre eux, mais au niveau de la cellule familiale la plus étroite elle-même. Contrairement à une approche simpliste de la prosopographie, qui n'a plus guère court, on observe alors que la cohésion familiale n'intervient somme toute qu'avant la conquête du pouvoir et se dilue assez rapidement ensuite dans les luttes qui entourent le détenteur du trône. Par ailleurs, il est assez difficile de classer une famille comme absolument « iconoclaste » ou « iconodule ». La plupart des grandes familles aristocratiques devaient pouvoir arborer un champion de l'un ou l'autre camp susceptible de lui fournir le certificat d'orthodoxie utile en temps de crise, ou *a posteriori*[112]. Il ne s'agissait pas en effet nécessairement d'un calcul réfléchi et d'une stratégie objective de ne pas mettre tous ses œufs dans le même panier. Les luttes entre proches parents de l'un ou l'autre bord, les exils, privations de biens voire exécutions dont ont eu à souffrir certaines familles témoignent dans bien des cas d'engagements sincères et de convictions défendues en dépit de réels périls. Le paroxysme de ces affrontements se retrouve naturellement dans les moments qui entourent la succession. Alors qu'on pourrait s'attendre à ce que celle-ci soit réglée en premier lieu par des dignitaires choisis pour leur position au sommet de l'État ou de l'Église, on constate qu'en réalité, elle est essentiellement gérée par des membres de la famille, qui manœuvrent de façon collégiale ou en faveur de l'un d'entre eux en particulier. L'Empire apparaît ainsi comme un bien aristocratique qu'il est licite de se transmettre au sein de la parenté proche.

112. C'est ce que montre bien par exemple, la famille de Théodora de Thessalonique (M. Kaplan, La *vie de Théodora de Thessalonique*. Un écrit familial, dans L. Brubacker et Sh. Tougher, *Approaches* (cité n. 106), p. 285-301).

INCESTE, MEURTRE EN FAMILLE ET GUERRES CIVILES. L'HÉRITIER, LA FAMILLE ET LA DYNASTIE MÉROVINGIENS AU DÉBUT DU VIe SIÈCLE

Gerhard LUBICH

Dans les années 1950, l'écrivain autrichien Heimito von Doderer publia son roman «Les Mérovingiens ou la famille totale», satire mordante de la psychanalyse et en même temps le portrait grotesque d'une famille noble au milieu du XXe siècle[1]. Le récit commence avec le moment où le protagoniste irascible, Childéric III, fait face à un problème : son père, veuf depuis longtemps, s'épanouit de façon inattendue dans sa 9ème décennie : il se marie avec une jeune femme. Ce mariage met en danger l'héritage de Childéric, jusque-là seul héritier. Le Mérovingien, lui aussi veuf, trouve un moyen pour résoudre ce problème : après la mort de son père, il épouse la veuve de celui-ci ; cette femme était légalement – (mais) non pas biologiquement – sa mère, sa belle-mère. Par ce mariage Childéric devient, si l'on veut, son propre père et le tuteur de sa femme-mère. Jusque-là, le passage des biens, donc l'héritage, ne pose aucun problème.

Or, l'histoire continue : après la mort de sa femme peu de temps après, Childéric commence à exploiter systématiquement cette politique matrimoniale. Comme il disposait d'une virilité extraordinaire, il épouse et épuise toutes les héritières disponibles les unes après les autres, en succession rapide, au point de se trouver, en fin de compte, à l'intersection de toutes les lignes d'héritage possibles. Ainsi, Childéric devient le centre de la famille entière, centre généalogique aussi bien que politique – il est « la famille totale », dans le sens de « La famille, c'est moi ». Mentionnons que cet état ne dura pas très longtemps – Childéric est destitué et émasculé par ses parents jaloux, qui divisent l'héritage et sont dorénavant forcés de vivre dans les limites étroites de la bourgeoisie[2].

1. La publication la plus récente sur le roman avec les références sur les études actuelles : C. DEUPMANN et K. LUEHRS-KAISER éd., *« Die Wut des Zeitalters ist tief », « Die Merowinger » und die Kunst des Grotesken bei Heimito von Doderer* (Schriften der Heimito von Doderer-Gesellschaft 4), Würzburg 2010.

2. S. NIEBERLE, « Wer sich in Familie begibt, kommt darin um. » Genealogische Verfilzung und narrativer Ovismus bei Heimito von Doderer, dans T. MARTINEC et C. NITSCHKE éd., *Familie und Identität in der deutschen Literatur* (Regensburger Beiträge zur Sprach- und Literaturwissenschaft 95), Frankfurt 2009, p. 17-34.

Inheritance, Law and Religions in the Ancient and Mediaeval Worlds, ed. by B. CASEAU and S. R. HUEBNER (Centre de recherche d'Histoire et Civilisation de Byzance, Monographies 45), Paris 2014.

Cette construction littéraire d'une « famille totale » diffère en même temps de notre conception de la famille moderne et de nos idées reçues sur l'héritage et le mariage aristocratiques, au moins sur deux points : d'abord, cette construction suppose que l'héritage soit transmis par les femmes. De plus, cette construction ne tient pas compte des obstacles du mariage par parenté – dans ce monde fictif, la notion de l'inceste ne semble pas exister. Aurait-on donc à voir ici avec une fiction littéraire sans relation avec l'histoire mérovingienne évoquée dans le titre du livre ? Le comportement de protagoniste correspond au monis aux idées reçues sur les rois germaniques-barbares de l'antiquité tardive. En plus, il faut tenir compte du fait que Heimito von Doderer a rédigé une thèse de doctorat sur un sujet médiéval[3] et il a suivi le cours prestigieux de l'Institut autrichien pour la recherche historique qui portait sur le Haut Moyen Âge[4]. Donc, on soupçonnera au moins l'existence de quelques renvois aux Mérovingiens historiques dans ce récit, que Doderer en tant qu'auteur averti pensait pouvoir transmettre[5]. Mais les perspectives scientifiques sur le monde du bas Moyen Âge ne sont plus les mêmes que ceux du temps de Doderer – voilà le point de départ de cet exposé : dans quelle mesure le regard de l'auteur correspond-il à l'opinion actuelle ? Voit-on toujours les Mérovingiens comme famille extraordinaire, hors des conventions sociales, surtout ce qui concerne le rôle du mariage et de l'héritage dans les conflits familiaux correspond-t-il aux données historiques ?

Un modèle possible pour le personnage littéraire de Childéric III et son comportement est sans doute Clotaire I, archétype et personnification du mode de vie mérovingien[6]. Clotaire dirigea, à la fin de sa vie, un royaume franc unifié, ayant commencé comme un des plusieurs gérants d'un royaume particulier à la suite d'un partage successoral. Il était le survivant d'un nombre considérable de conflits autour de cet héritage, de quelques guerres civiles et d'intrigues nombreuses. Il atteignit l'âge d'environ 60 ans, ce qui constitue à peu près le double de la durée de vie moyenne d'un roi mérovingien[7]. Il eut au moins sept femmes (dont deux sœurs en même temps, la veuve d'un frère, puis une sainte) et au moins neuf enfants. Voilà un Mérovingien à succès, même si cette qualité se traduit par le fait assez banal (au moins à nos yeux) d'avoir survécu. Clotaire était simplement, pour reprendre une expression américaine « the last man standing », devenant ainsi l'ancêtre de tous les Mérovingiens après lui, formant l'image de la dynastie pour la postérité.

3. H. von Doderer, *Zur bürgerlichen Geschichtsschreibung in Wien während des 15. Jahrhunderts*, 3 tomes, Wien 1925.

4. Doderer s'inscrit à l'institut en octobre 1948; W. Fleischer, *Das verleugnete Leben. Die Biographie des Heimito von Doderer*, Wien 1996, p. 373-375, p. 380, p. 386. E. Király, Der Autor als Mediävist: Der Fall Heimito von Doderer: « Swer sînen vriunt behaltet, daz ist lobelîch », dans A. Vizkelety éd., *Festschrift für András Vizkelety zum 70. Geburtstag* (Budapester Beiträge zur Germanistik; Bd. 37), Piliscsaba 2001, p. 455. Doderer finit ses études en mars 1950 par un travail de diplomatique (*Die Abtwahlformel in den Herrscherurkunden bis zum 10. Jahrhundert*, Wien 1950).

5. M. Meyer, Genealogie, Geschichte und Gregor. Zur Funktion von Geschichtlichem in Doderers Merowingern, dans K. Luehrs-Kaiser éd. *„Excentrische Einsätze". Studien und Essays zum Werk Heimito von Doderers*, Berlin 1998, p. 206-224.

6. La seule biographie monographique est par I. Gobry, *Clotaire Ier* (Histoire des rois de France), Paris 2004; M. Hartmann, *Die Merowinger*, München 2012, p. 27-32; E. Ewig, *Die Merowinger und das Frankenreich*, Stuttgart 1993, p. 33-40.

7. E. Ewig, Studien zur merowingischen Dynastie, dans M. Becher, T. Kölzer et U. Nonn éd., *Spätantikes und Fränkisches Gallien. Eugen Ewig: Gesammelte Schriften (1974-2007) Band 3* (Beihefte der Francia 3/3), Ostfildern 2009, p. 213-257, p. 248-250.

D'un regard près, ce n'est qu'avec l'ascension de Clotaire que la violence dans la famille nucléaire des Mérovingiens éclate. Comparés avec cette troisième génération royale des Mérovingiens[8], les mariages et les cas de succession des prédécesseurs, de Childéric I et de Clovis, paraissent peu exemplaires et nullement spectaculaires. Bien sûr, Grégoire de Tours, notre source presque unique, ne s'abstient pas d'esquisser les circonstances avec des anecdotes d'un caractère archaïque ou bien « archaïsant » afin de faire des Mérovingiens des rois païens ce que se, pour lui, se traduisait en « barbares ». Mais même si la légende, selon laquelle Childéric aurait enlevé sa femme à un roi de Thuringe[9], correspond à un évènement historique, ce rapt ne semble pas résulter d'une tradition germanique, ni établit-il une coutume. En ce qui concerne Clovis, il était apparemment fils unique, et ses sœurs ou ses parents plus éloignés[10] n'étaient pas considérés pour l'héritage ; la succession de Childéric par Clovis ne posait donc pas de problème, sans obstacles, sans conflits.

Les choses deviennent plus compliquées et plus intéressantes pour la succession de Clovis, qui avait plusieurs fils. Le plus ainé d'entre eux, Thierry, était issu d'un concubinage[11], si Grégoire de Tours ne nous trompe pas, et ne disparut pas de l'entourage royal alors que Clovis se mariait avec Clotilde, descendante du clan royal burgonde[12]. Ce mariage, une connexion dont on ne peut que vaguement déterminer le caractère politique[13], produisit trois fils,

8. La désignation de Clovis comme *primus rex Francorum* dans un prologue de la loi Salique est repris par Ewig, *Merowinger* (cité n. 6), p. 18 et 30 dans un sens figuré.

9. Grégoire de Tours, X *libri historiarum*, lib. II cap. 12 ; M. Hartmann, Sage, Klischee, Fiktion? Zum Bild der merowingischen Königinnen in den frühmittelalterlichen erzählenden Quellen, dans E. Dewes et S. Duhem éd., *Kulturelles Gedächtnis und interkulturelle Rezeption im europäischen Kontext* (Vice Versa 1), Berlin 2008, p. 23-32, surtout p. 23-24.; S. Joye, Basine, Radegonde et la Thuringie chez Grégoire de Tours, *Francia* 32, 2005, p. 1–18 surtout p. 2-9.

10. Les rois des autres royaumes francs figurent désignés comme *parentes* dans le *Liber Historiæ Francorum*, cap. 9 et comme *propinqui* dans Grégoire de Tours, X *libri historiarum*, lib. II cap. 42 ; sur la terminologie des relations de parenté cf. G. Lubich, *Verwandtsein. Lesarten einer politisch-sozialen Beziehung im Frühmittelalter (6.-11. Jahrhundert)* (Europäische Geschichtsdarstellungen 16), Köln 2008, p. 105-107 et 149-150 ; il est impossible d'établir une généalogie fiable avec les renseignements transmis par les quelques sources dont nous disposons.

11. Grégoire de Tours, X *libri historiarum*, lib. II cap. 28. L'appartenance de cette première femme de Clovis à une famille (royale) de la région du Rhin a été suggérée E. Ewig, Die Namengebung bei den ältesten Frankenkönigen und im merowingischen Königshaus, *Francia* 18/1, 1991, p. 21-69, surtout p. 49 et C. Settipani et P. van Kerrebrouck, *La préhistoire des Capétiens* (= Nouvelle histoire généalogique de l'Auguste Maison de France. t. 1). 1ère partie : Mérovingiens, Carolingiens et Robertiens, Villeneuve-d'Ascq 1993, p. 56 à la base d'indices anthroponymiques.

12. H.-H. Anton, Lemma « Chrodichilde », *Reallexikon der Germanischen Altertumskunde* 4, 1981, p. 604-605; sur la situation (avec la discussion des sources et les dernières hypothèses généalogiques). De la perspective de Clovis M. Becher, *Chlodwig I. Der Aufstieg der Merowinger und das Ende der antiken Welt*, München 2011, p. 167-173 ; plus sommairement M. Hartmann, *Die Königin im frühen Mittelalter*, Stuttgart 2009, p. 10-11 et p. 63.

13. Une certaine réserve à l'encontre du roi burgonde Gondebaud est sensible dans le récit de Grégoire de Tours, X *libri historiarum*, lib. II cap. 28. L'appréciation moderne repose sur I. Wood, Gregory of Tours and Clovis, *Revue belge de philologie et d'histoire* 63/2, 1985. p. 249-272 = http://www.persee.fr, p. 253, qui démontre les « inconsistances » logiques de la construction grégorienne. En ce qui concerne le caractère politique, on fait face au même problème que la datation du baptême de Clovis attribuée à l'influence de Clotilde : Tout dépend de la datation de ce mariage, pour laquelle on n'a pas d'indication incontestable dans les sources. Si on le date vers 493/494, une relation avec le système des alliances initié par Théodoric semble probable ; si on le date vers 496/7 on y peut voir un souhait de distance à l'égard du roi ostrogoth. Sous presse sur le mariage de Clovis : G. Lubich, Schwierige Schwiegersöhne. Entwicklungen, Grenzen und Probleme frühmittelalterlicher „Heiratspolitik" am Beispiel des Frankenreichs, dans H. Mierau éd., *Der Schwiegersohn* (Beihefte zur ZHF) Berlin 2015.

dont le plus jeune fut Clotaire. Pour la répartition de l'héritage de Clovis, la division du royaume franc en 511, tous les fils furent pris en compte ; Thierry, le *filius naturalis* de Clovis ne fut pas désavantagé par rapport à ses frères, les fils de Clotilde[14]. Au contraire : si on compare les dimensions des royaumes qui furent attribués aux héritiers, c'est précisément le « bâtard » Thierry qui obtint le plus grand (ou au moins une part d'héritage qui n'était pas inférieure)[15] ; cette contradiction apparente avec la division dite *aequa lantia* (= à parts égales) annoncée par Grégoire de Tours[16] s'explique peut-être par le fait que le règne sur la plupart des territoires attribués à Clotaire était encore à établir (surtout en Aquitaine)[17]. Les filles ou les parents par alliance ne bénéficièrent d'aucune part et ne jouèrent d'ailleurs aucun rôle[18].

L'explication traditionnelle des modalités de cette division combine deux lignes d'argumentation. Premièrement, la dynastie mérovingienne aurait suivi une règle de succession qui ne discriminait pas entre des fils nés d'un concubinage et ceux issus d'un mariage légitime ; mais la seule preuve d'une telle coutume nous vient encore des *X libri historiarum* de Grégoire de Tours[19]. Deuxièmement, on attribue la division *aequa lantia* (i.e. à parts égales)s aux lois des Francs comme la *Lex salica* ou le plus ancien *Pactus legis salicae*, partant de la supposition que le royaume fut traité comme *allodium* (alleu, c'est-à-dire des terres possédées en pleine propriété)[20]. En 511 on aurait donc agi en faisant un mélange entre des normes

14. Une égalité qualitative en dépit de quelques différences territoriales E. Ewig, Die fränkischen Teilungen und Teilreiche (511-613), dans H. Atsma éd., *Spätantikes und Fränkisches Gallien. Eugen Ewig, Gesammelte Schriften, Band 1* (Beihefte der Francia 3/1), München 1976, p. 114-171, en détail sur ce cas p. 115-123; récapitulé dans Id., *Merowinger* (cité n. 6), p. 31-32. Sur le rôle de Clotilde et le caractère politique de le division I. Wood, Kings, Kingdoms and Consent, dans P. Sawyer et I. Wood éd., Early Medieval Kingship, Leeds 1977, p. 6-99, surtout p. 25-26; plus sommairement B. Kasten, *Königssöhne und Königsherrschaft. Untersuchungen zur Teilhabe am Reich in der Merowinger- und Karolingerzeit* (MGH Schriften 44), Hannover 1997 p. 13-14 et T. Offergeld, *Reges pueri. Das Königtum Minderjähriger im frühen Mittelalter* (MGH Schriften 50), Hannover 2001, p. 186-192. Un point de vue différent est offert par M. Widdowson, Merovingian Partitions. A « Genealogical Charter » ?, *Early Medieval Europe 17*, 2009, p. 1-22. B. Dumézil, *La reine Brunehaut*, Paris 2008, p. 82-83.

15. L'opinion traditionnelle d'y voir une divisio *aequa lantia* Ewig, Teilungen und Teilreiche (cité n. 14), p. 122-123 ; pour une division en faveur de Thierry B. Kasten, *Königssöhne und Königsherrschaft* (cité n. 14, avec la littérature plus ancienne), p. 11-12.

16. Grégoire de Tours, X *libri historiarum*, lib. III cap. 1.

17. Ewig, Teilungen und Teilreiche (cité n. 14), p. 123. Selon Kasten, *Königssöhne und Königsherrschaft* (cité n. 14), p. 50, l'Aquitaine, royaume périphérique à l'époque, était souvent attribué aux « Unterkönige », donc les héritiers prévus agissaient en tant que partenaires juniors.

18. Selon Grégoire de Tours, X *libri historiarum*, lib. III cap. 23 Sigivald et Mundéric réclamaient une partie du royaume de Clovis sans mentionner une raison généalogique. Widdowson, Merovingian Partitions (cité n. 14), p. 3-4, suggère de les regarder comme frères de Thierry. M. Mitterauer, *Traditionen der Namengebung. Namenkunde als interdisziplinäres Forschungsgebiet*, Wien 2011, p. 79 n. 23 se prononce contre une affiliation de Sigivald aux Mérovingiens à cause de son rang (inférieur) comme duc d'Aquitaine : cf. la dernière note. C. Settipani, *Les ancêtres de Charlemagne*, Paris 1989, p. 96 voit en Mundéric un descendant des rois francs de Cologne ; sans faire mention de ce travail, mais avec un résultat similaire H. Grahn-Hoek, *Gundulfus subregulus – eine genealogische Brücke zwischen Merowingern und Karolingern?, Deutsches Archiv für Erforschung des Mittelalters* 59, 2003, p. 1-48, p. 40-45.

19. Grégoire de Tours, X *libri historiarum*, lib. V, cap. 20 ; M. da Silva, *Reges pro publicis utilitatibus, le problème de la légitimité royale sous les Mérovingiens de Clovis à Clotaire II* (*fin* ve*-début* viie *siècle*), Lyon 2002.

20. La notion d'une division des bien propres entre les fils du testateur comme forme typiquement germanique de l'héritage est dérivée de Tacite, *Germania* c. 20 ; G. Köbler, Lemma « Erbrecht », *Reallexikon für Germanische Altertumskunde* 7, 1986, p. 430-433 ; pour les divisions mérovingiennes cf. les positions classiques

familiales et publiques, créant ainsi un précédent pour des divisions ultérieures. Mais les deux éléments de cette explication sont problématiques : Comme on le verra, il existait en fait des princes royaux qui furent exclus de l'héritage ; et en ce qui concerne le partage à parts égales, les mots *aequae lantie* ne se trouvent pas dans les textes des lois proprement dites, mais seulement dans quelques *formulae* (formules), donc dans les collections des actes et des chartes exemplaires, et là-dedans, de préférence, en référence à des transmissions de l'héritage plutôt rares (à une veuve, à une fille en excluant les fils etc.)[21]. Somme toute, au sujet des divisions du royaume, une norme (soit-elle familiale ou emprunte de la société) est difficile à supposer.

Face à toutes ces incertitudes (et à d'autres, encore plus fondamentales, en ce qui concerne la sphère du droit au Haut Moyen Âge[22]), on considéra l'hypothèse, que la division de 511 n'était pas le résultat d'une pratique établie, mais le résultat d'une négociation politique[23]. Surtout si on jette un regard critique sur le témoignage de Grégoire de Tours – une activité très en vogue parmi les historiens depuis deux décennies[24] – on découvre rapidement

citées par KASTEN, *Königssöhne und Königsherrschaft* (cité n. 14), p. 9-10 ; R. LE JAN, *Famille et pouvoir dans le monde franc (VIIe-Xe siècle) : Essai d'anthropologie sociale* (Publications de la Sorbonne), Paris, 1995, p. 239 : « Cependant, les lois germaniques prévoyaient le partage de l'héritage, *aequa lantie*, entre tous les fils et accessoirement les filles », omet que cela n'est pas forcément le cas pour la *Lex salica* en question dans notre contexte.

21. Dans la collection encore importante de K. ZEUMER, *Formulae Merowingici et Karolini aevi, accedunt Ordines iudiciorum Dei* (MGH LL V), Hannover 1886, on trouve la formule dans : *Formulae Andecavenses* n° 37 p. 17 (*equalis lanciae*) ; Marculf. *Formulae* II n° 12 p. 83; n° 14, p. 84 (*equo lante*); dans un mot – *equalentia* – dans les *Cartae Senonicae* n° 29 p. 197 et 198; n° 42, p. 204; n° 45, p. 205; *Formulae Salicae Bignonianae* n° 19, p. 235; quelques fragments encore dans le *Formularium Pithoei*, p. 597.

22. Presque toutes les circonstances autour de la *Lex Salica* sont encore en discussion : Caractère, genèse et évolution (J.-P. POLY, Le premier roi des francs. La loi Salique et le pouvoir royal à la fin de l'empire, dans G. CONSTABLE, et M. ROUCHE éd., Auctoritas. Mélanges offerts au professeur Olivier Guillot, Paris 2006, p. 97-128 ; É. VIENNOT, La France, *Les femmes et le pouvoir, Volume 1, L'invention de la loi Salique (Ve-XVIe siècle)*, Paris 2006 ; E. SEEBOLD, Zur Entstehung der « Lex Salica », *Beiträge zur Geschichte der deutschen Sprache und Literatur* 129, 2007, p. 387-401 ; K. BAYERLE, Einsatzfelder des weltlichen Bannes im Frühmittelalter, dans T. GUTMANNM H.-G. HERMANN et al. éd., *Von den Leges Barbarorum bis zum ius barbarum des Nationalsozialismus: Festschrift für Hermann Nehlsen zum 70. Geburtstag*, Cologne/Weimar/Wien 2008, p. 24-29), l'efficacité (A. RIO, *Legal Practice and the Written World in the Early Middle Ages. Frankish Formulae, c. 500-1000* (Cambridge Studies in Medieval Life and Thought. Fourth Series), Cambridge 2011), la dimension politique (H.-W. GOETZ, Gens-Regnum-Lex: das Beispiel der Franken, dans G. DILCHER, E.-M. DISTLER éd., *Leges – Gentes – Regna. Zur Rolle von germanischen Rechtsgewohnheiten und lateinischer Schrifttradition bei der Ausbildung der frühmittelalterlichen Rechtskultur*. Berlin 2006, p. 537-542) ou l'arrangement linguistique entre le latin des juristes et le vernaculaire (R. SCHMID-WIEGAND, Sprache, Recht, Rechtssprache bei Franken und Alemannen vom 6.–8. Jahrhundert, dans *Ibid.*, p. 141-158, ou ID., Der *sermo rusticus* und die *Lex Salica* dans A. GREULE, E. MEINEKE, C. THIM-MABREY éd., *Entstehung des Deutschen: Festschrift für Heinrich Tiefenbach* (Jenaer germanistische Forschungen / NF 17), Heidelberg 2004, p. 427-432).

23. La discussion sur la base légale M. BECHER, Vater, Sohn und Enkel. Die Bedeutung von Eintritts- und Anwachsungsrecht für die Herrschaftsnachfolge im Frankenreich, dans B. KASTEN éd., *Herrscher- und Fürstentestamente im westeuropäischen Mittelalter* (Norm und Stuktur 29), Cologne/Weimar/Vienne 2008, p. 301-320; avec un examen de chaque division mérovingienne KASTEN, *Königssöhne und Königsherrschaft* (cité n. 14), p. 9-57.

24. D'une recherche sur « Gregor », « Grégoire » et « Tours » dans l'OPAC des Regesta Imperii (opac.regesta-imperii.de) résultent plus de 120 articles et livres pour la décennie passée. La discussion récente sur l'historiographie du Haut Moyen Âge, pour laquelle l'œuvre W. GOFFART, *The Narrators of Barbarian History (A.D. 550–800). Jordanes, Gregory of Tours, Bede, and Paul the Deacon*, Princeton NJ 1988 est crucial, est marquée par plusieurs monographies sur Grégoire, surtout A. H. B. BREUKELAAR, *Historiography and Episcopal Authority in Sixth-Century Gaul. The Histories of Gregory of Tours interpreted in their historical context* (Forschungen zur

quelques indices prouvant que la situation en 511 n'était pas du tout claire. Le prétendu « bâtard » Thierry était vraisemblablement un de deux, sinon le seul des cinq fils de Clovis qui avait atteint la majorité[25]; ses frères étaient en toute probabilité représentés par leur mère Clotilde[26]. Grégoire n'a pas écrit en faveur de Thierry, mais il a une attitude favorable, peut-être trop favorable envers Clotilde : elle était, aux yeux de Grégoire, un facteur décisif pour le baptême de Clovis, la christianisation des Francs et, dans la logique de son œuvre, l'amélioration du monde entier[27]. Mis à part cette estime fondamentale, il faut mentionner la connaissance personnelle qu'avait Grégoire de Clothilde, qui fut l'une des sources de l'évêque sur le passé merovingien[28]. On peut se demander si la dénonciation – justifiée ou pas – de l'origine illégitime de Thierry provenait de la reine elle-même; notons aussi une tradition littéraire qui fait, dans une situation comparable auprès les Wisigoths, du premier mariage de Théodoric un concubinage[29]. Finalement, l'absence quasi-totale de conflits entre les héritiers de Clovis pendant plus qu'une vingtaine d'années démontre la stabilité de la construction de 511, une stabilité qu'on attribuera avec plus de conviction à un compromis politique qu'à un règlement suivant des normes traditionnelles sans considération de la situation des parties intéressées.

Kirchen- und Dogmengeschichte 57) , Göttingen 1994; M. HEINZELMANN, *Gregor von Tours (538-594), Zehn Bücher Geschichte: Historiographie und Geschichtskonzept im 6. Jahrhundert*, Darmstadt 1994; K. MITCHELL, I. WOOD éd., *The World of Gregory of Tours* (Cultures, Beliefs, and Traditions 8), Leiden 2002.

25. Les sources ne disent rien sur ce point, mais beaucoup dépend de la datation du mariage de Clovis avec Clotilde (cf. n. 13) : Si on se prononce pour une date tardive autour de 496, il n'y a qu'un ou deux des quatre fils pour qui la majorité serait possible par voie de calcul, surtout si on estime à 12 ans l'âge de la majorité, comme le fait EWIG, *Merowinger* (cité n. 6), p. 30, qui fait du Clothaire le seul héritier mineur, ce qu'expliquerait sa part moins grande du royaume divisé. Le débat est retracé par R. KAISER, *Das römische Erbe und das Merowingerreich* (Enzyklopädie deutscher Geschichte 26), München 2004, p. 89-90. Le calcul ne diffère pas trop si on fixe l'âge de la majorité à 15 ans et une date de mariage vers 493, comme le font E. EWIG. Studien zur merowingischen Dynastie (cité n. 7), p. 220-222; KASTEN, *Königssöhne und Königsherrschaft* (cité n. 14), p. 10-11; OFFERGELD, *Reges pueri* (cité n. 14), p. 187-188. La minorité de la plupart des fils de Clotilde expliquerait leur passivité : Les sources ne parlent d'eux que vers 522/523, cf. WIDDOWSON, Merovingian partitions (cité n. 14), p. 5.

26. L'idée d'un partage entre deux clans, l'un formé par Clotilde représentante de leurs fils, l'autre par Thierry, a été établi par I. WOOD, Kings, Kingdoms and Consent (cité n. 14), p. 25-26; la discussion est récapitulée par OFFERGELD, *Reges pueri* (cité n. 14), p. 186-192; une perspective plus traditionnelle dans BECHER, *Chlodwig I* (cité n. 12), p. 270-274. Sur le rôle de Clotilde et le problème de la régence (laquelle – ou un statut comparable – elle maintenait au moins pour ses petits-fils orphélins selon Grégoire de Tours, X *libri historiarum*, lib. III cap. 18). C. NOLTE, Die Königinwitwe Chrodichilde. Familie und Politik im frühen 6. Jahrhundert, dans MICHEL PARISSE éd., *Veuves et veuvages dans le haut Moyen-Age : Table ronde organisée à Göttingen par la Mission Historique Française en Allemagne*, Paris 1993, p. 177-185; sommairement HARTMANN, *Königin* (cité n. 12), p. 63-65. DUMÉZIL, *La reine Brunehaut* (cité n. 14), p. 132 : Si un héritier masculin était disponible, la mère « pouvait conserver certaines de ses prérogatives à la cour et même espérer participer à la régence ».

27. Sur ce point HEINZELMANN, *Gregor von Tours* (cité n. 24), p. 141-166.

28. WOOD, Gregory of Tours and Clovis (cité n. 13), p. 253, supporte cette idée de G. TESSIER, *Le Baptême de Clovis*, Paris 1964, p. 74; BECHER, *Chlodwig I* (cité n. 12), p. 177, juge les informations comme provenant « aus zweiter Hand », donc sans transmission directe.

29. Jordanes, *Getica* 296. Le débat sur le personnage de Jordanes et la valeur de son récit n'est pas encore décidé, cf. W. GOFFART, *Barbarian Tides. The Migration Age and the Later Roman Empire*, Philadelphia 2006, p. 56-72, l'opinion duquel est maintenant au moins discutée par W. LIEBESCHÜTZ, Why did Jordanes write the Getica, *Antiquité tardive* 19, 2011, p. 295-302 qui persiste dans l'opinion traditionnelle.

Retenons un premier point : dans la famille mérovingienne, au moment de la première division du royaume franc en 511, l'héritage ne se limitait pas aux descendants d'une seule femme, mais on tenait compte de tous les descendants masculins, sans que le statut de la mère et du type d'union ait joué un rôle perceptible. Même si la manière d'organiser la succession semble suivre l'idéal de l'égalité, un règlement de plein droit n'est pas encore établi ce que rend la division sujette à la négociation ; le compromis politique stabilisait la situation politique et était donc un moyen approprié à éviter les conflits autour de l'héritage.

En ce qui concerne Clotaire, notre Mérovingien historique exemplaire, le compromis de 511 le mettait dans une situation difficile. Selon les sources peu abondantes, son royaume se composait des deux zones périphériques (la Gaule belgique autour et au nord de Soissons ; l'Aquitaine au sud-ouest côtoyant les Pyrénées), juxtaposées et – surtout en Aquitaine – pas encore totalement intégrées dans le royaume franc. Même si la somme des deux territoires faisait de la part de Clotaire la plus grande, les fils autres de Clotilde avaient toujours la possibilité de couper la communication entre les deux parties de son royaume. Si la division était donc plutôt défavorable pour Clotaire, elle le poussa à faire des efforts pour compenser son désavantage structurel. Mais le conflit imminent n'était pas immédiat. Au contraire, pendant une vingtaine d'années, les accords de division établirent un *modus vivendi* assez solide[30]. Durant cette période, les relations entre les frères furent sans conflits, parfois même empreintes de solidarité, en particulier en ce qui concerne les campagnes à l'extérieur[31]. En tant que chefs militaires, les fils de Clovis achevaient l'œuvre d'expansion de leur père en repoussant, dans les années 30 du VIe siècle, les frontières du royaume franc à une distance impressionnante surpassée seulement par les conquêtes de Charlemagne plus que deux siècles plus tard.

Des conflits entre les frères surgirent seulement à la mort de l'un d'entre eux. Apparemment, la question de l'héritage n'était pas tout à fait claire, même si on peut partir du principe de la transmission des biens du défunt à ses fils et de leur division (de préférence *aequa lantia*). En 524, Clodomir, fils de Clotilde et roi du royaume central d'Orléans, mourut pendant une expédition de tous les fils de Clovis, laissant une veuve, Gondioque, et trois fils mineurs. Clotaire prit l'initiative de s'emparer du royaume de Clodomir – par des moyens que l'on va évoquer tout de suite -, mais une solution ne fut trouvée que huit ans plus tard quand ce royaume fut partagé entre les fils de Clovis survivants, ce qui donne encore un exemple d'une division par négociation[32]. En 531, une mauvaise information sur la mort de Thierry en Thuringe avait amené Childebert à envahir son royaume – puis à rediriger son armée contre les Wisigoths, quand il apprit la vérité[33]. En 533, après la mort de Thierry, ses oncles Clotaire

30. EWIG, Teilungen und Teilreiche (cité n. 14), p. 128-130.

31. En ce qui concerne les liens de parenté et leur valeur politique, on notera le comportement de Thierry, qui ne faisait pas partie d'une première campagne contre le royaume des Burgondes étant le beau-fils du roi Sigismond (qu'il ne supportait pas contre ses demi-frères), mais qui était présent pour la deuxième campagne, quand le frère de Sigismond défunt l'avait remplacé ; cf. Grégoire de Tours, X *libri historiarum*, lib. III cap. 6 p. 108; la solidarité entre parents est expliquée par M. HARTMANN, *Aufbruch ins Mittelalter. Die Zeit der Merowinger*, Darmstadt 2003, p. 49 ; des opinions opposées sont citées par R. KAISER, *Die Burgunder*, Stuttgart 2004, p.70-71.

32. EWIG, Teilungen und Teilreiche (cité n. 14), p. 128-129 en corrigeant Grégoire de Tours, X *libri historiarum*, lib. III cap. 18. WIDDOWSON, Merovingian partitions (cité n. 14), ne s'occupe pas de cette division.

33. EWIG, Teilungen und Teilreiche (cité n. 14), p. 129, est sceptique envers ce tableau présenté par Grégoire de Tours, X *libri historiarum*, lib. III cap. 10 et cite (n. 79) des sources complémentaires (surtout wisigothes) qui ne disent rien sur cette motivation prétendue.

et Childebert, se tournèrent contre Theudebert, unique fils de Thierry, apparemment majeur, en essayant de lui interdire de succéder à son père[34].

Le comportement des fils de Clovis démontre qu'un schéma différent pouvait s'appliquer : dans le cas du décès de l'un d'entre eux, les frères survivants réclament au moins une partie sinon l'ensemble de l'héritage du défunt, sans considération d'un accès à l'héritage pour les descendants. L'héritage des biens et des fonctions n'était donc pas l'affaire de la famille du testateur, mais était réclamé par la génération précédente, la dynastie dont le testateur faisait partie. Il est difficile d'affirmer qu'il y avait un fondement légal ou traditionnel pour ce comportement en raison de l'histoire relativement brève des Mérovingiens, mais la tendance de plutôt garder l'héritage dans la génération du testateur que de le passer à la génération des fils est tout à fait comparable à la succession par séniorat si répandue dans l'Europe orientale du Moyen Âge. De quelque manière qu'on juge cette configuration, on prendra soin de n'attribuer trop vite les réactions des frères d'un défunt à un instinct prédateur (comme l'a fait Doderer), si elle résultait de la perception que l'héritage était une affaire de la dynastie, et, ainsi, soumis à une entité plus grande que la famille étroite. Cette explication rend les actions de Clotaire, notre protagoniste exemplaire, peut-être un peu plus compréhensibles. Mais à nos yeux, le récit que Clotaire a tué deux fils de Clodomir, âgés de sept et dix ans, de ses propres mains pour obtenir ses buts[35], reste quand même choquant, étrange et barbare.

Ce verdict résulte, bien sûr, d'une moralité moderne. Mais le comportement de Clotaire transgressait aussi les normes contemporaines, par sa brutalité dan la sphère politique, mais surtout, par son immodération, dans le domaine du mariage. Quand Clotaire épouse Gondioque, la veuve de son frère défunt Clodomir, il se trouve dans une liaison incestueuse. Selon l'idéologie de l'« una caro » du droit canonique, deux époux sont regardés comme « une seule chair » ; le mariage transforme donc le lien social en un lien biologique. La femme de son frère était regardée comme sa sœur, même après la mort de celui-ci – inceste classique, qualifié de crime et de péché à l'époque – une source possible des conflits avec les évêques gaulois[36].

Les raisons, pour lesquelles Clotaire a choisi de courir ce risque, ne sont pas tout à fait claires et sont peut-être multiples. Si Gondioque, comme on l'a suggéré sur la base de considérations onomastiques, était une descendante du clan royal bourguignon, ce lien aurait permis des prétentions sur le royaume des Burgondes[37]. Mais ces prétentions étaient encore à réaliser en 524, la date présumée du mariage, puisque Clodomir, mari défunt de Gondioque fut une victime de la victoire des Burgondes cette année-là[38]. D'un autre coté, surtout pour les alliances matrimoniales de la première moitié du VIe siècle, on n'arrive pas toujours à attri-

34. Ewig, Teilungen und Teilreiche (cité n. 14), p. 130.

35. Grégoire de Tours, X *libri historiarum*, lib. III cap. 18 ; Dumézil, *La reine Brunehaut* (cité n. 14), p. 309, indique la situation exceptionnelle d'une régence conduite par la grand-mère des enfants.

36. Pour les preuves concernant l'interdiction du sororat et du lévirat à l'époque cf. K. Ubl, *Inzestverbot und Gesetzgebung. Die Konstruktion eines Verbrechens (300–1100)* (Millenium-Studien 20), Berlin 2008, p. 50-57 et sur les cas du temps mérovingien et leur jugement selon le droit canon ibid. p. 93-97.

37. Settipani et van Kerrebrouck, *La préhistoire des Capétiens* (cité n. 11), p. 66.

38. Grégoire de Tours, X *libri historiarum*, lib. III cap. 6 ; sur les circonstances et les conséquences Hartmann, *Aufbruch ins Mittelalter* (cité n. 31), p. 50.

buer une raison concrète (politique ou légale) à tous les liens tissés entre les familles royales. Pourquoi Audoin, roi lombard, épouse-t-il la veuve du roi de Thuringe alors que le royaume de celui-ci était déjà conquis par les Francs[39] ? Pourquoi Clotaire épouse-t-il Radégonde, une des petites-filles de celui-ci[40], tout comme Alboin se marie avec Rosamonde, princesse d'un royaume disparu[41] ? Les exemples ne se limitent à ces cas, et outre l'hypothèse d'un gain de légitimité, du prestige ou du « capital social », on ne trouvera pas les réponses dans la logique de l'échange des parents établi par C. Lévi-Strauss et on ne découvrira probablement aucun modèle méditerranéen (« mediterranean pattern »).

Le mariage avec Gondioque servait-il à créer des prétentions sur le royaume de son mari défunt ? Cette hypothèse touche à la question de la minorité des rois et par là à la question de la régence, qui était gérée par la mère, le nouveau *pater familias* ou un parent proche, non par une loi mais de manière coutumière[42]. Toutefois, comme démontre le cas de Clotilde ou les régences de Brunehaut, la régence devait être imposée contre les intérêts des grands dans un processus parfois d'assez longue durée[43]. Pour le cas de Clotaire, une telle intention est à exclure : l'assassinat des fils de Clodomir l'aurait privé des héritiers possibles ou, si le mariage était déjà conclu (la chronologie n'est pas très claire[44]), il aurait tué ses beaux-fils qui – par « una caro » – étaient au sens strict devenu ses propres fils. Si Clotaire visait à devenir – en tant que mari de la veuve – l'héritier du royaume de son frère, il se trompa ; en 532 une nouvelle division eut lieu, qui encore une fois ne donnait pas la préférence à Clotaire[45]. Le parallèle de cette union avec le mariage de Clotaire avec la princesse provençale Vuldetrade, veuve de son petit-neveu Thibaut, est évident. Manque d'enfants, un problème de l'héritage ne se posait pas, et le mariage fut dénoncé comme incestueux et une séparation imposée, sans que Clotaire ait protesté[46].

Somme toute, les motifs pour les mariages de Clotaire et de ses contemporains nous échappent pour la plupart des cas présentés. Même si on est tenté de supposer un souci de la transmission des biens ou des fonctions – fut-ce de manière vague sous forme d'un avantage légitimateur -, l'inefficacité économique de ces unions face à une pratique politique des

39. Le cas devient plus compliqué par une intermédiation byzantine HARTMANN, *Königin* (cité n. 12), p. 41-42.

40. Le mariage est à dater d'après 540 selon EWIG, Studien zur merowingischen Dynastie (cité n. 7), p. 254-255, mais les sources sont assez vagues; sur ce point; cf. G. HUBER-REBENICH, Die thüringische Prinzessin Radegunde in der zeitgenössischen Überlieferung, dans H. CASTRITIUS, D. GEUENICH et M. WERNER éd., *Die Frühzeit der Thüringer. Archäologie, Sprache, Geschichte* (Reallexikon der germanischen Altertumskunde; Ergänzungsbde. 63) Berlin / New York 2009, p. 235-252 ; JOYE, Basine, Radegonde et la Thuringie (cité n. 9), p. 9-18.

41. Pour le contexte, voir S. DICK, *Langobardi per annos decem regem non habentes, sub ducibus fuerunt. Formen und Entwicklung der Herrschaftsorganisation bei den Langobarden. Eine Skizze*, dans W. POHL et P. ERHART éd., Die Langobarden: Herrschaft und Identität (Denkschriften. Akademie der Wissenschaften in Wien, Philosophisch-Historische Klasse 329 = Forschungen zur Geschichte des Mittelalters 9),Wien 2005 p. 335-344, p. 340-341. (avec les sources).

42. OFFERGELD, *Reges pueri* (cité n. 14), p. 36-39.

43. DUMÉZIL, *La reine Brunehaut* (cité n. 14), p. 181-214, parle de « la conquête de la régence».

44. Grégoire de Tours, X *libri historiarum*, lib. III cap. 6 et cap. 18 ne donne pas d'indications et les autres sources de l'époque, extrêmement rares et d'habitude brèves, ne mentionnent pas l'affaire.

45. EWIG, Teilungen und Teilreiche (cité n. 14), p. 130-131.

46. HARTMANN, *Königin* (cité n. 12), p. 68-71 et p. 151 ; UBL, *Inzestverbot* (cité n. 36), p. 93.

divisions est stupéfiante. Si l'on tient compte du fait, qu'aucun lien politique ne fut établi au-delà du royaume franc, on se posera des questions sur l'existence d'une véritable conception politique et économique du mariage princier[47].

Pourquoi donc Clotaire s'est-il marié en fait ? Même la réponse la plus facile à concevoir est fausse dans le cas de Clotaire : aucun de ces mariages ne produisait un enfant, un fils héritier[48]. Tous les héritiers descendaient de la liaison entre Clotaire et les sœurs Ingonde et Aregonde, dont les sources de la période (comme la plupart des historiens modernes) parlent beaucoup plus de l'élément de la polygamie que de celui de l'inceste impliqué[49]. Même si on a du mal à s'imaginer une origine plus compromettante que celle des héritiers issus de cet étrange ménage à trois, c'est le fils d'une autre liaison qui fut exclu de l'héritage ; ce qui aboutit, bien entendu, à des conflits. Ce fils, nommé Chramn (« le corbeau »), n'était pas envoyé en exil. Nous le voyons comme *dux* et confident de son père dans des missions importantes. Mais Chramn – sans qu'on en connaisse la raison – fut exclu ou privé du titre royal que tous ses demi-frères portaient et, par-là, de l'héritage royal. Chramn, on le devine, n'en était pas content et essaya de s'émanciper. À la fin de sa seconde conspiration, Clotaire le fit étrangler et fit brûler son corps avec l'épouse et les enfants de Chramn encore vivants[50].

Dans ce contexte, on remarquera le pouvoir du *pater familias* de traiter ses héritiers potentiels d'une manière inégale, contrairement à l'affirmation de Grégoire de Tours déjà cité[51], outre que la radicalité quasi biblique d'éteindre toute la famille de son fils rebelle et avec elle tous ceux ayant droit à sa succession[52]. Mais ce qui est frappant aussi – dans le cas de Chramn comme dans les autres exemples –, c'est que jamais on n'entend parler des familles des

47. Dans « Schwierige Schwiegersöhne » (cité n. 13) je suggère l'idée d'un développement, partant d'un emploi des mariages pour une politique visant à des buts á courts termes au temps des Mérovingiens, qui est relayé au IX siècle par une politique voyant plus loin, causée par la nécessité d'affronter les nouvelles réalités de la monogamie et d'une noblesse établie.

48. Ce que ne fut pas nécessairement une coïncidence, mais un but recherché selon HARTMANN, *Aufbruch ins Mittelalter* (cité n. 31), p. 53 : « Es mutet nicht wie ein Zufall an, dass gerade Chlothars Ehen mit den «erbeuteten» Königinnen Guntheuca und Waldrada bzw. der Prinzessin Radegunde kinderlos geblieben sind ».

49. Grégoire de Tours, X *libri historiarum*, lib. IV cap. 3 ; UBL, *Inzestverbot* (cité n. 36), p. 93 ; HARTMANN, *Aufbruch ins Mittelalter* (cité n. 31), p. 52-53.

50. KASTEN, *Königssöhne und Königsherrschaft* (cité n. 14), p. 37-43, avec les sources qui diffèrent sur le sexe des enfants laissant l'interprétation ouverte si l'annihilation de la famille visait à éliminer des héritiers possibles ou faisait partie d'une pénalisation radicale.

51. KASTEN, *Königssöhne und Königsherrschaft* (cité n. 14), p. 13 avec une liste des cas probables ; sur « l'affaire Gundovald » exemplaire cf. W. GOFFART, Byzantine Policy in the West under Tiberius II and Maurice: The Pretenders Hermenegild and Gundovald (579–585), *Traditio* 13, 1957, p. 73–118 ; B. S. BACHRACH, *The Anatomy of a Little War. A Diplomatic and Military History of the Gundovald Affair* (*568–586*), Boulder 1994; les faits essentiels récapitulés par HARTMANN, *Aufbruch ins Mittelalter* (cité n. 31), p. 63-65. Parfois les limites à l'usurpation sont assez vagues – les usurpateurs réclamaient toujours l'appartenance à la dynastie, cf. I. WOOD, Usurpers and Merovingian Kingship, dans M. BECHER et J. JARNUT éd., Der Dynastiewechsel von 751. Vorgeschichte, Legitimationsstrategien und Erinnerung, Münster 2004, p. 15-31.

52. La répétition à la carolingienne – donc : moins sanglante et spectaculaire – est le traitement de Tassilon par Charlemagne : la grâce accordée à son neveu condamné à mort menait à l'entrée de la famille entière au monastère, y compris les fils de Tassilon, héritiers possibles ; sur cet aspect, complétant le travail de M. BECHER, *Eid und Herrschaft. Untersuchungen zum Herrscherethos Karls des Grossen* (Vorträge und Forschungen/Konstanzer Arbeitskreis für Mittelalterliche Geschichte. Sonderband 39), Sigmaringen 1993, p. 64-72 voir LUBICH, *Verwandtsein* (cité n. 10, avec les sources principales), p. 175-176.

épouses mérovingiennes : jamais un père d'une mariée ne supporte son beau-fils, jamais une grand-mère maternelle ne prend soin de ses petits-fils, jamais un gendre ne se trouve à côté ou contre un roi mérovingien. La parenté par mariage, semble-t-il, n'était pas forcément une parenté d'alliance, si on comprend le terme « alliance » dans le sens politique de « pacte ». Mais, dans la perspective des Mérovingiens, ce manque de renfort signifia en même temps l'absence d'exigences de la part des parents par alliance. Des filles mérovingiennes, pas une ne semble semble être mariée avec un Franc, ce que complète l'image. Voilà l'explication du phénomène que, dans les sources, on ne trouve pas une seule personne désignée comme « parent » des Mérovingiens[53]. Si on n'était pas le fils reconnu d'un Mérovingien, on n'était pas Mérovingien ; une proximité par la parenté n'existait pas pour les Mérovingiens. Cette stratégie d'isolation, qui accentuait la prééminence agnatique mais niait tout autre lien de parenté, disjoignait les Mérovingiens généalogiquement de la société et s'ajoutait à l'apparence de l'intangibilité propre à cette dynastie[54].

Avant de conclure, encore deux brèves remarques complémentaires :

En ce qui concerne la question d'un développement de cette structure esquissée, il semble que les Mérovingiens ne changèrent pas leur comportement caractéristique du tout au tout. Mais les divisions après la mort de Clotaire, surtout celle de 561, étaient mal négociées ou fondées sur une base légale insuffisante[55], d'où s'ensuivirent des conflits qui dépassèrent vite le contexte local ou régional. De cette situation résultèrent des coalitions fragiles et de courte vie entre les héritiers, puis des conflits aussi intenses que sanglants, qualifiés par Grégoire de Tours de *bella civilia*, ce qui, outre notre concept de « guerres civiles » signifie la débâcle pour la société tout entière par la dissolution de l'ordre primordial de la famille royale[56] ce qui permettait aux grands du royaume d'améliorer leur position. Cette décadence de la famille royale ne doit pas être considérée comme le résultat inévitable d'une pratique malheureuse de la transmission des biens et du pouvoir mais s'explique aussi bien comme la conséquence d'une maladresse politique au moment du mort de Clotaire.

Deuxièmement, le comportement des Mérovingiens semble être effectivement singulier et diffère du reste de la société. L'enquête d'Isabelle Réal sur la famille franque à travers l'hagiographie démontre, que la famille « moyenne » (c'est-à-dire : noble) de l'époque res-

53. LUBICH, *Verwandtsein* (cité n. 10), p. 26-127, pour les termes désignant le fait « d'être parent » comme *consanguineus*, *propinquus* etc.; en outre, il n'existe pas une dénomination concrète indiquant le degré (plus ou moins concret) de parenté comme *nepos*, *avus*, *gener* etc.

54. Sur la sacralité du roi, cf. R. LE JAN, La sacralité de la royauté mérovingienne, *Annales* 58, 2003, p. 1217-1241 ; F.-R. ERKENS, *Herrschersakralität im Mittelalter. Von den Anfängen bis zum Investiturstreit*, Stuttgart 2006, p. 102-109.

55. EWIG, Teilungen und Teilreiche (cité n. 14), p. 135-138. KASTEN, *Königssöhne und Königsherrschaft* (cité n. 14), p. 16, indique le tirage au sort par lequel on aurait distribué les parties du royaume selon Grégoire de Tours, X *libri historiarum*, lib. IV cap. 22. WIDDOWSON, Merovingian Partitions (cité n. 14, aussi sur les conflits après la division), p. 6-15, suggère une sorte de succession individuelle à laquelle aurait aspiré Chilpéric qui n'aurait pas accepté de base légale pour une division. DUMÉZIL, *La reine Brunehaut* (cité n. 14), p. 108-112.

56. Grégoire de Tours, X *libri historiarum*, Préface au livre IV – Les conflits ne commencèrent qu'après la mort de Charibert (567), cf. EWIG, Teilungen und Teilreiche (cité n. 14), p. 138 ; le chapitre IV de DUMÉZIL, *La reine Brunehaut* (cité n. 14), p. 153-180, est intitulé « L'entrée dans la guerre civile (568-575) ». Mon essai portant sur la conception de la « guerre civile » au Haut Moyen Âge est à paraître.

semble plutôt à la famille moderne[57]. Il est ni question de polyginie ni d'inceste ; le modèle familial dominant est plutôt celui de la « famille nucléaire » composée du père, de la mère et des enfants, qui démontrent au moins de l'affection sinon de l'amour ; les conflits autour de l'héritage n'existent guère – un comportement fondamentalement différent de celui des Mérovingiens.

Somme toute, il faut constater que les Mérovingiens du début du VIe siècle étaient un groupe à part, sans relation apparente au reste de la société, avec laquelle aucun lien de parenté ne les liait, et dont les lois, les normes et les règles ne comptaient pas pour eux. On peut bien observer quelques traits caractéristiques : la prépondérance de la lignée agnatique, soit en ce qui concerne la dominance du *pater familias*, soit dans la considération exclusive des fils comme héritiers, par exemple. Mais du côté de la dynastie, la famille n'était pas traitée d'unité indépendante ; dans le cas d'un héritage, les parents proches ne respectaient pas la sphère familiale. Voilà la racine des conflits, qui sont marqués par la confrontation du cercle familial avec celui de la dynastie.

L'« auto-suffisance » et l'auto-referérentialité de la dynastie mérovingienne coupèrent, en fin de compte, tous les liens avec la société. Ainsi les Mérovingiens devinrent une famille à part, une famille « absolue », détachée du reste de la société[58]. Pour en revenir à la « famille totale » construite par Heimito von Doderer, la différence fondamentale entre ses Mérovingiens fictifs et les Mérovingiens historiques consiste dans le fait que les premiers acceptèrent et exploitèrent les lois d'héritage de la société environnante, alors que les Mérovingiens du VIe siècle vivaient plus ou moins selon leurs propres lois et coutumes dans un monde qui nous peut paraître barbare, sombre et sans perspectives. Mais n'oublions cependant pas que la dynastie mérovingienne, en dépit de ces qualifications peu flatteuses, resta au pouvoir près de trois siècles.

57. I. Réal, *Vies de saints, vie de famille. Représentation et système de la parenté dans le Royaume mérovingien (481-751) d'après les sources hagiographiques* (Hagiologica 2), Turnhout 2001.

58. J'ai suggérée cette terminologie dans LUBICH, *Verwandtsein* (cité n. 10), p. 153-155.

TESTAMENTS

THE LATE ROMAN LAW OF INHERITANCE: THE TESTAMENT OF FIVE OR SEVEN WITNESSES*

Carlos SÁNCHEZ-MORENO ELLART

Qui non familiarissimi quemque signandis adhibet, cum extrema conducuntur?
Sym. *Rel.* XLI.4

Where post-classical Roman law and Byzantine law are concerned, talking about inheritance and family conflicts necessarily involves a discussion on the new forms of testament, primarily because during this period the transformation of the traditional form of a will had an impact on the certainty that a will was understood to have or in other words on the perception of its validity. Forms (and consequently formularies) are normally what make people confident that the acts performed according to the proper rituals shall have the expected effect, to ensure the validity of their wishes.[1] This effect is especially important to people not qualified in law. Even within the family, the form of a will and its consequences for certainty and confidence can become crucial matters.

One of the main features of the imperial legislation on testament is indeed its expressed intent to protect the will of the deceased against any fraud.[2] In order to reconstruct the context of this legislation we ought to consider how deep the differences between the traditional forms of testament (particularly the 'testament by bronze and scales' or 'libral testament'[3]) and the new types were. This comparison becomes more fruitful when it comes to evaluating the forms of will that arise from the disintegration of the libral testament. Our paper will be focused precisely

* I am indebted to my friends Prof. Elizabeth Anne Meyer (University of Virginia) and Prof. Gianfranco Purpura (University of Palermo) for their comments on previous versions of this paper and their good advice. I am also grateful to Prof. Renzo Lambertini (University of Modena) for his observations on the *Interpretatio* to the Theodosian Code. Of course all mistakes remain my own.

1. E. CHAMPLIN, *Final Judgments. Duty and Emotion in Roman Wills*, 200 B.C.–A.D. 250, Los Angeles 1991, p. 70.

2. CHAMPLIN, *Final Judgments* (quoted n. 1), pp. 82–101.

3. In this paper, since it is focused on post-classical law, I am going to use interchangeably the terms 'libral testament' '*mancipatio familiae*' and 'mancipatory will,' but as F. TERRANOVA (*Ricerche sul testamento per aes et libram* I, Turin 2012, p. 18, n. 7) has shown there are some historical differences where the introduction of the *heredis institutio* is concerned.

Inheritance, Law and Religions in the Ancient and Mediaeval Worlds, ed. by B. CASEAU and S. R. HUEBNER (Centre de recherche d'Histoire et Civilisation de Byzance, Monographies 45), Paris 2014.

on a problem that has occupied scholars a great deal: the meaning and the scope of the testament with five or seven witnesses, which respectively were understood as civil and praetorian or — in other words — we shall question whether there was any particular reason behind this distinction, typical of the late Roman law of inheritance.[4] I wonder whether behind this distinction there exists a specific reason: whether it arose merely in practice, or whether it had an actual origin in imperial legislation. First, after some brief methodological notes, we are going to tackle the texts where both testaments appear. After this we are going to focus our interest on the different theories aimed at solving that riddle, and then to conclude with our own interpretation. Regarding the methodological remarks, they must tackle, in our opinion, the following topics: 1) The concept of vulgar law, which necessarily affects our research; 2) The new conceptions of the law of succession in the postclassical period; and 3) The disintegration and disappearance of the libral testament and its link to the emergence of wills with five or seven witnesses.

As stated above, one element that has some unavoidable consequences for our research is the notion of 'Roman vulgar law.' This ambiguous and multi-directional designation insinuates the inexpert interpretation of the provincials, who in their turn were influenced by misconceptions arising from their own local legal traditions.[5] Some years ago this vulgarism was allegedly detected in the imperial constitutions dated to the late empire, especially those dated to the reign of Constantine, but the broad approach that led to this conclusion, an approach that embraced both practice and imperial legislation as vulgar law, has been revealed as misleading. In our opinion, the existence of testaments with seven or five witnesses involves a narrow view of the vulgar law — or rather, the question could be answered by appealing to the conflict between practice (deeply influenced by vulgar law concepts) and imperial legislation, trying to channel this practice into clear-cut notions still informed by classical jurisprudence.[6] I understand from the term 'narrow view' of vulgar law that change

4. P. Voci, *Diritto ereditario romano* II, Milan, 1956, p. 76: 'La diferenza diveniva solo numerica' The fusion between both *ius civile* and *ius honorarium* was openly recognized by Justinian himself (I. 2.10.3: *paulatim tam ex usu hominum quam ex constitutionum emendationibus coepit in unam consonantiam ius civile et praetorium iungi*) It is significant that in dealing with the evolution of the testamentary forms Justinian evaluates the importance of both practice and imperial legislation. M. Amelotti, Un ventennio di studi sulle successioni in età tardoantica, *Atti dell'Accademia Romanistica Costantiniana* 17, 2010, pp. 25–42, esp. 31–32 correctly sums up: 'L'antinomia è per vero assurda perchè sarebbero due forme in tutto identiche se non nel numero die testimoni e la forma con numero minore avrebbe massima validità.'

5. The usual explanation of this period is — for good or ill — highly indebted to the theory of the vulgar law coined in the nineteenth century by L. Mitteis, *Reichsrecht und Volksrecht in den östlichen Provinzen des römischen Kaiserreichs*, Leipzig 1891. According to this explanation, the evolution of late Roman law could be analogized to that of classical Latin: the imperial constitutions and the jurists who wrote them played a part comparable to the classical Latin. Practice, on the other hand, developed what could rightly be compared to Vulgar Latin. Indeed people made wills or contracts not always drawn up with the advice of an expert, which implies both free and illegitimate interpretations of the law in force. This comparison could be useful in the same measure as it could be confusing. On these matters, see D. Liebs, Roman Vulgar Law in the Late Antiquity, in A. J. B. Sirks, (ed.) *Aspects of law in Late Antiquity dedicated to A. M. Honoré* Oxford 2008, pp. 35–53; C. Sánchez-Moreno Ellart. Roman Law: Vulgar, in R. S. Bagnall, K. Brodersen, C. B. Champion, A. Erskine, & S. R. Hübner (eds.), *The Encyclopedia of Ancient History*, Oxford 2012, pp. 3975–3978.

6. Concerning the irregular work of the office *a libellis* in this period until the reign of Diocletian, see T. Honoré, *Emperors and Lawyers*, London 1981, p. 104. Honoré's palingenesia of imperial *rescripta* (193-305) belongs to the second edition (Oxford, 1994) but it is now available at [http://www.iuscivile.com].

or pressure merely derives from practice and its misunderstandings, not from actual legal decisions (the broad view of Roman vulgar law). According to my interpretation I think that this distinction — civil and praetorian wills as based on the number of witnesses — was simply borne in mind by the imperial legislation, which had to cope with it.

The late-antique law of inheritance has sometimes been approached through style: the contrast between how classical Roman law and vulgar Roman law were conceived. This starting point is in part correct and in part reductionist. We will try to reduce this strong contrast between classical and vulgar. The usual approach through style identifies some features from late-antique legislation and from late-antique documents as elements of the so-called 'Roman vulgar law'. I insist that this stylistic approach sometimes proves to be insufficient, since it ignores the fact that late imperial legislation developed not only the tendencies incorporated in the late law of succession, but also the tendencies incorporated as early as the beginning of the 1st century AD. At the same time these late imperial constitutions tried to establish some order or in other words to channel chaotic practices into correct directions. I will try to point out the internal logic of this development and to explain in which logical framework some of these legal developments can and should be understood. In this sense I shall try to show how vulgarism could be detected in the praxis but not in the imperial legislation,[7] which tried to cope with a new reality by giving directions in an attempt to re-unify the system.

Tony Honoré has strongly insisted on the role played by the office of *a libellis* in settling the existing tensions between the theory of classical Roman law and the actualities of practice in the courts of the provincial governors. This role could be described in Honoré's words as 'increasingly pedagogical and even ideological'. After the end of the Severan dynasty the evolution of the juristic level of the chancery is not exactly linear: from Pertinax to Probus imperial jurisprudence declined, but the reign of the emperor Carus marked a 'revival in the work of the rescript office which was favoured by Diocletian.'[8] When it comes to analyzing the origin of the postclassical testament we must reckon on both factors, the part played by imperial legislation and the reality of practice. Seeing change as a consequence of a dialectical relationship is an improvement on the previous way of approaching this problem, which seemed to say that only imperial legislation was relevant. Its role, in our opinion, was to cope with the irregularities of practice. Legislation was not, however, able to construct a solution that resembled the classical law for every problem and must have had to ignore some behaviours spawned by practice.

7. The change in imperial legislation from the reign of Diocletian to the reign of Constantine is not as radical as the old literature thought. In fact there is no gap between Constantine and his predecessors but an evolution that followed classical principles. In this sense, see D. SIMON, Marginalien zur Vulgarismusdiskussion, in *Festschrift für Franz Wieacker*, Göttingen 1978, pp. 154–174; S. CORCORAN, *The Empire of the Tetrarchs. Imperial Pronouncements and Government AD 284-324*, Oxford 2000, p. 3.

8. HONORÉ, *Emperors and Lawyers* (quoted n. 6), p. 54. M. AMELOTTI, Reichsrecht, Volksrecht, Provinzialrecht. Vechi problemi e nuovi documenti, *Studia et documenta historiae et iuris* 65, 1995, pp. 210–215, esp. 214: 'L'attenzione cade particolarmente su Diocleziano, che si oppone a molte pratiche provinciali nel quadro del suo tentativo di restaurazione del antico impero romano e pagano, e in nome di una più rigorosa osservanza del diritto ufficiale. Ma i suoi risultati vanno poco oltre un limitato ritorno al latino e un esteriore adeguamento a requisiti formali. Altre volte deve cedere egli stesso'.

The second methodological issue is yet more difficult to summarise. Some new conceptions appearing in the late Roman law of inheritance stressed a contrast with classical principles to such an extent that the later law modified or even altered the classical law's defining elements. Specifically, the law of succession (in a way) lost its autonomous nature for it was placed on the same footing as donations. The Theodosian Code shows the use of this combinational concept, for it included in a confusing way both succession and donation. A will is just a kind of *donatio* as *CTh* 16.2.20 (Valentinian, Valens and Gratian 370 AD) clearly expresses: *ut nec per subiectam personam valeant aliquid vel donatione vel testamento percipere*. In the same constitution we can confirm that the testament was conceived mainly as the will of the testament-maker. That is why in late law it is also called *extremum iudicium*, i.e. 'final judgement': *Quin etiam, si forte post admonitionem legis nostrae aliquid isdem eae feminae vel donatione vel extremo iudicio putaverint relinquendum, id fiscus usurpet*. This is the last stage of an evolution that started some centuries before, not exactly a symptom of vulgarism.[9]

To draw a preliminary conclusion from the two remarks above, the Roman law of succession at the final stage of its evolution loses its conceptual autonomy (in fact, the clear-cut classical notion of succession totally vanishes) and consequently diverse para-testamentary acts (such as *donationes mortis causa*) appear in the place previously monopolized by the Roman classical will.[10] Both *legata* and *fideicommissa* became both mixed in a general category, and codicils, which in classical law had also their conceptual autonomy and which normally included *fideicommissa*, became acts hardly distinguishable from wills.[11] Many of these differences from the classical system of succession started in the classical period, but during those centuries imperial jurisprudence was able to maintain the difference between these categories. For many years thereafter the imperial chancery lacked the effective power to regulate these complicated questions.[12] After the reconstruction of the classical chancery under Diocletian this decline was halted but obviously the classical system had to be legally modified to be adapted to the new realities of practice. The imperial constitutions enacted in this period are good examples of the above-described evolution that encompassed both practice and legislative response.

9. P. Merêa, Sobre o testamento hispánico no século VI, *Anuario de Historia del Derecho Español* 16, 1945, pp. 86–99 = *Estudos de direito visigótico*, Coimbra, 1948, pp. 105–119; F. Samper Polo, La disposición *mortis causa* en el Derecho romano vulgar, *ibid.* 38, 1968, pp. 87–227, esp. 112–123. This scholar rightly points out this development but he understands it as a vulgar element. The problem is perhaps more complicated because it is not exactly stylistic. Imperial legislation just confirms this last stage of a long evolution, which started in the classical law although that later legislation probably still had knowledge of the classical legal concepts.

10. This expression has been rightly used by M. Amelotti, Testamenti e atti paratestamentari nei papiri bizantini, *RIDA* (= *Revue internationale des droits de l'antiquité*) 16, 1969, pp 211–214. Some of these paratestamentary acts were technically poor. R. S. Bagnall, Two Byzantine Legal Papyri, in R. S. Bagnall & W. V. Harris (eds.), *Studies in Roman Law in Memory of A. Arthur Schiller*, Leiden 1986, pp. 1–9, esp. 2, accepts this idea but on the other hand he is reluctant to endorse Amelotti's stylistic approach.

11. Merêa, Sobre o testamento (quoted n. 9), p. 106.

12. M. Amelotti, *Il testamento romano attraverso la prassi documentale*, Florence 1966, pp. 226–237. Legal practice became confused as the wills documented after AD 235 demonstrate: *P.NYU* II 39 is the last example of the use of the *mancipatio* in the Egyptian papyri (AD 335 or 345), but the presence of the mancipatory clause is normally missing starting from AD 235.

The decadence of the so-called classical Roman will (the 'libral testament' or the will by bronze and scales) favours the emergence of a will defined mainly by imperial constitutions and as enacted in the fourth century AD free from its traditional requirements. We cannot treat the contrast between the civil and the praetorian succession in classical law in depth, but are persuaded by Amelotti that in classical law there was no direct contrast between the two kinds of testament. It is widely known that in the classical period, the praetor and imperial pronouncements gave priority to the document over the required formalism of the *ius civile*. The so-called *testamentum praetorium* was actually not a kind of testament in itself but merely an invalid testament according to the *ius civile* that was deemed valid by the praetor when some formalities required by the *ius civile* had not been correctly observed.[13] All that was required by praetorian law was the written document with the seals of seven witnesses. Even this remedy however — the drawing up of a document under some requirements — was by no means free from ritualism. In other words, relaxing the requirements for the old formalism does not necessarily mean the elimination of formalism.[14] Constantine's legislation is a typical example of this paradox,[15] one of the main characteristics of the Roman postclassical law: praxis, unable to work without some formalism handles this formalism erroneously and the consequence of this careless or uninformed praxis was generally treated in imperial legislation by the removal of these formalities. Yet as a result new problems arose, as for instance those posed by the new contrast between the civil and the praetorian will.

The transformation or rather degeneration of the 'will by copper and scales' could explain many of the novelties introduced by imperial legislation of the late empire, and especially could justify the new role played by witnesses. From at least the end of the first century BC and especially at the end of the Principate the *mancipatio* was a historical remnant from earlier times that was being used in an instrumental way for several different purposes — marriage, transfer of ownership, emancipation, will — with little if any thought to its original meaning. In the Principate the *mancipatio* was hardly ever performed and became only a stylistic device, a clause of style in the documents. But this stylistic device proved to be significant since in classical law the libral testament was the theoretical framework handled by the jurists,[16]

13. V. ARANGIO-RUIZ, Intorno alla forma scritta del *testamentum per aes et libram*, *Atti del Congresso internazionale di diritto romano e di storia del diritto Verona 27, 28 e 29 di setiembre 1948* III, Milan 1953, p. 81 = *Scritti di diritto romano*, IV, Naples 1977, p. 184. This distinguished Italian scholar considered testaments as dispositive documents: I romani testavano, insomma, scrivendo; e questa e non altra è la caratteristica del documento dispositivo, p. 188.

14. According to E. A. MEYER, *Legitimacy and Law in the Roman World*, Cambridge 2004, the drawing up of legal documents on wax tablets meant also ritual unitary acts with magical connotations which were in some way preserved until Late Antiquity. Some old *ius civile* institutions such as *mancipatio* or *stipulatio* contained elements that are easily susceptible of being interpreted as supernatural or magical. For example, certain precise words had to be uttered or some ritual acts had to be performed. It should be stressed that these requirements were both a guarantee (public rituals offered publicity and some certainty) and, on the other hand, an obstacle that had to be gotten over by the praetor or the imperial legislation.

15. AMELOTTI, *Il testamento* (quoted n. 12), p. 243: The new legislation enacted by Constantine meant, in Amelotti's words, an acceptance of 'le esigenze della prassi' which entailed the elimination of formalism.

16. The phrase *quando minus scriptus, plus nuncupatus videtur*, present in one constitution of the emperor Diocletian (*CJ* 6.23.7) but with good classical background (*Dig.* 31.67.9 Pap. 19 *quaest.*; *Dig.* 28.5.9.2 Ulp. 5 *ad Sab.*; *Dig.* 28.1.5, Ulp. 1 *ad Sab.*) deals with the problems arising from the difference between what a will-maker

regardless of its actual use in practice. Of course we must simplify, but when the libral testament collapsed its elements stopped working as a coherent system and its main pieces (*mancipatio*, *nuncupatio*, witnesses) started working by themselves in an uncoordinated way.

Formalism in testaments, practically removed by Constantine the Great, included or might have included the *mancipatio*. *CJ* 6.23.15 pr. and *Vita Const.* IV.26 have been the main foundation of such a theory.[17]

> *Imperator Constantinus. Quoniam indignum est ob inanem observationem irritas fieri tabulas et iudicia mortuorum, placuit ademptis his, quorum imaginarius usus est, institutioni heredis verborum non esse necessariam observantiam, utrum imperativis et directis verbis fiat an inflexa.*
>
> (*CJ* 6.23.15)

> Κἄπειτα τῶν τὸν βίον μεταλλαττόντων ὁμοίως παλαιοὶ μὲν νόμοι ἐπ' αὐτῆς ἐσχάτης ἀναπνοῆς ἀκριβολογεῖσθαι ῥημάτων λέξεσι τὰς συνταττομένας διαθήκας τρόπους τε τίνας καὶ ποίας δεῖ φωνὰς ἐπιλέγεσθαι ὥριζον, καὶ πολλὰ ἐκ τούτων ἐκακουργεῖτο ἐπὶ περιγραφῇ τῆς τῶν κατοιχομένων προαιρέσεως. ἃ δὴ συνιδὼν βασιλεὺς καὶ τοῦτον μετεποίει τὸν νόμον, ψιλοῖς ῥηματίοις καὶ ταῖς τυχούσαις φωναῖς τὸν τελευτῶντα δεῖν τὰ κατὰ γνώμην διατάττεσθαι φήσας κἂν τῷ τυχόντι γράμματι τὴν αὐτοῦ δόξαν ἐκτίθεσθαι, κἂν ἀγράφως ἐθέλῃ, μόνον ἐπὶ μαρτύρων τοῦτο πράττειν ἀξιοχρέων, τὴν πίστιν δυνατῶν σὺν ἀληθείᾳ φυλάττειν.
>
> (*Vita Const.* IV.26)

According to the explanation given by Eusebius there was a decision of Constantine about protecting the will of the deceased against any fraudulent attempt, since the old legislation had ordered that the last will ought to be stated in a prearranged set of words or rather 'some ways of expression and precise words' (τρόπους τε τίνας καὶ ποίας...φωνὰς) and that this requirement had allowed fraud. The emperor abrogated this enactment (μετεποιεῖτο τὸν νόμον) and bestowed the freedom to make a will without those formal requirements, as long as the testament was made in the presence of witnesses. Apart from these references to a formal set of words and witnesses there is no clear mention of an abrogation of the *mancipatio* or of the libral testament as such.

---

really intended and what he had actually stated in the written document. It is significant in my opinion that the reference to the *nuncupatio* apparently could have something to do with a mancipatory will, which at this moment had fallen into disuse. In fact both the emperor and the jurists used the framework of the libral testament as a working hypothesis, regardless of whether it was actually in use or not. About this phrase, see, on the different interpretations O. E. Tellegen-Couperus, The Origin of *quando minus scriptum plus nuncupatum videtur* used by Diocletian in *CJ* 6.23.7, *RIDA* 27, 1980, pp. 313–331. G. Dulckeit's approach (Plus nuncupatum, minus scriptum, *Zeitschrift der Savigny-Stiftung für Rechtsgeschichte* 70, 1953, pp. 200–213) is in my opinion too interpolationist. On the other hand many recent studies have insisted on this view, while accepting a classical basis e.g. P. Müller-Eiselt, *Divus Pius contituit: kaiserlicher Erbrecht*, Berlin 1982, pp. 30–32.

17. As B. Albanese, rightly states (L'abolizione postclassica delle forme solemni nei negozi testamentari, *Scritti giuridici* II, Palermo 1991, pp. 1637–1654, esp. 1648) Eusebius makes a paraphrase of the aforementioned constitution.

Traditionally[18] this ambiguous notice, given by Eusebius of Caesarea (*Vita Const.* IV.26) has been interpreted to mean that the *mancipatio* had been expressly abolished by this emperor and this interpretation has been mostly accepted by scholars,[19] but there is likely not enough evidence to be sure. The *Vita Constantini* explains that the emperor abolished formalities in making a will, in effect abolishing the use of some words, on the grounds that they had been used to undermine the actual will of the deceased. Yet no clear mention of the *mancipatio* is made in this citation. The consequence of this elimination of the need for formalities was that witnesses became the only way of guaranteeing the will.[20]

Apart from *CJ* 6.23.15 pr., where *mancipatio* could be understood to be behind the words *imaginarius usus*, some intervention of Constantine might also be presumed on the basis of even more indirect evidence, albeit with an even lesser degree of certainty. For example, some consequences of accepting this traditional thesis, i.e. the abolition of the *mancipatio* by Constantine, seems to match the misunderstanding of identifying a testament of five witnesses with a civil testament, because the elimination of the *libripens* and of the *familiae* emptor in the formularies could have generated confusion: it is under Constantine that imperial legislation first concerned itself with the problem of testaments with seven or five witnesses and through an indirect question, a codicil (*CTh* 4.4.1). The misidentification (i.e., the civil will with a five witness will) is for the first time attested to in a constitution by Constantine and it could be the case that this problem arose directly from the suppression of this ritual, but this is not a decisive argument, for the essential event was the prior dissolution of the libral testament, which produced extreme uncertainty. The libral testament is not clearly attested under Constantine, who could have simply been legislating on this topic in response to controversial cases submitted to him.

In any case the suppression of the *mancipatio* may have been not a radical decision but rather only a pronouncement in which its role was downplayed or reduced to the same footing as that of other formal requirements, more or less as in *CJ* 6.23.15 pr. This kind of regulation, which is not exactly a clear abrogation of the *mancipatio*, would distort the actual meaning of the mancipatory testament, as for instance in *CTh* 8.12.4, in which the same emperor stated that a donation could be valid regardless of whether the *mancipatio* had been executed or not. I insist on the idea that his enactment could have been not exactly a formal abrogation (as the traditional theory affirms) but an act with an equivalent effect, at least where practice and its formularies were concerned: the removal of the need for the *mancipatio* in particular

18. E.g. ALBANESE, L'abolizione postclassica (quoted n. 17), pp. 1636–1650; F. STURM, *Das Absterben der* mancipatio, in S. BUCHHOLZ, P. MIKAT & D. WERKMÜLLER, *Überlieferung, Bewahrung und Gestaltung in der rechtsgeschichtlichen Forschung*, Paderborn 1993, pp. 347–356.

19. My friend Maria Nowack devotes an interesting article to this question, *Mancipatio* and its Life in Late Roman Law, *Journal of juristic papyrology* 41, 2011, pp. 103–122. She rightly states that there is no direct evidence in *Vit. Const.* IV.26, that Constantine had expressly abrogated the *mancipatio* but on the other hand her exegesis of *CJ* 6.23.15 pr. seems dubious to me. *Imaginarius* has perhaps never been used in relation to *mancipatio* in other fragment in the Theodosian Code or in the Justinianic Code but considering the decadence of this ritual this fact could not be entirely significant. It is difficult to discover the function and the meaning of *imaginarius* in the aforesaid constitution if it does not refer to *mancipatio*.

20. AMELOTTI, *Il testamento* (quoted n. 12), p. 247, links the elimination of the *mancipatio* to the 'persistente e autonoma necessità die testimoni' in *CTh* 4.4.1. (see infra). Recently M. NOWAK, The Function of Witnesses in the Wills from Late Antique Egypt, in P. SCHUBERT (ed.), *Actes du 26e Congrès international de papyrologie*, Geneva 2012, pp. 573–580.

cases and in some rescripts could have entailed the elimination of the *libripens* and of the *familiae* emptor in some formularies with consequent confusion.[21]

The *mancipatio*, as it is widely known, required formally seven witnesses or to be more precise, five witnesses in addition to a *familiae emptor* and a *libripens*. This is of course the origin of the contrast between five and seven witnesses, since the so-called civil will became a will of five witnesses while the so-called praetorian will preserved a requirement for seven. It is irrelevant whether the *mancipatio* was actually performed or not or whether it was removed or not by the lost constitution of Constantine known through the *Vita Constantini* IV.26 or by *CJ* 6.23.15 pr., for its role had become merely a part of a theoretical framework, as Kreller recognized in his seminal book: the document in which the libral testament was recorded implied only a presumption of its actual performance.[22] The jurists assumed that the libral testament was the only legitimate testament, apart of course from the military one and in their answers they accepted this theoretical framework, which did not fit with practice. The *nuncupatio*, which had been simply an inherent part of the *mancipatio*, became the name used to designate an autonomous oral testament in post-classical law[23] and the witnesses became the main or even the only element by which a distinction could be drawn between civil and praetorian wills. In our opinion, under the Principate the mention of the *mancipatio* in the documents is a mere presumption and pertains to the conception of the will rather than to its actual performance: as stated before, the conceptual framework in which the jurists worked included *mancipatio* as a formal theoretical requirement because the only acknowledged and regular form of testament was the libral one. No matter if Constantine officially abrogated it or not, this ceremony stopped probably being performed in the 1st century AD but the formularies mentioned it regularly until AD 235 and it occasionally survived even in the formularies after this date.

21. Under the Principate all the testaments preserved are shaped on the pattern of the libral testament, regardless their origin. R. S. O. TOMLIN, A Roman Will from North Wales, *Archaeologia Cambrensis* 150, 2001, pp. 143–156, publishes a will in which the mancipatory clause is lost, but the pattern is the same. We have no direct evidence for formularies of a civil testament with only five witnesses, but the elimination of the *mancipatio* necessarily implied the elimination of the *familiae emptor* and the *libripens*. The evidence is confusing after AD 235. In the Western part of the empire, the *mancipatio* in the documents, such as the sixth-century testaments from Ravenna, seems to be used as a clause of style, exactly as it had been the case in Egypt. In Egypt, however, the formularies of libral testament disappear — as Amelotti points out — after a constitution by Alexander Severus suppressed the mandatory requirement to draw up wills in Latin; thereafter, when people barely familiar with Roman forms were granted Roman citizenship, the old forms of Hellenistic testaments experienced a revival. Sometimes the use of the mancipatory clause shows no knowledge of its actual meaning: in *P.NYU* II 39, the last dated example from Egypt (AD 335), the *emptio nummo uno* was not understood, but this also happened in the 2nd century AD: *BGU* VII 165 (AD 169). Probably after *Nov. Theod.* 16 the contrast between five and seven witnesses survived in the Western part of the empire but our evidence shows the confusion of will-makers as to the meaning of such a formulary.

22. H. KRELLER, *Erbrechtliche Untersuchungen auf Grund der gräko-ägyptischen Papyrusurkunden*, Leipzig 1919 (repr. Aalen 1970), p. 329.

23. This problem has been explored by G. G. ARCHI, Oralità e scrittura nel '*testamentum per aes et libram*,' in *Studi in onore di P. De Francisci* IV, Milan 1956, pp. 285–316 (=*Scritti di diritto romano* II, Milan 1981, pp. 735–770). This Italian scholar (768-770) comments on different sources (*CTh* 4.4.2.1; 4.4.7; *Nov. Theod.* 16.2; *Nov. Val.* 21.1; Int. *CTh* 4.4.7) in order to emphasize the contrast between written testament and *nuncupatio*. MEYER, *Legitimacy and Law* (quoted n. 14), p. 274 points out the 'Within the fifth-century classifications the separation of writing and nuncupation was pronounced, and the writing itself increasingly stressed as authoritative.'

Accepting and developing Amelotti's theory[24] of the libral testament as the only legitimate will in classical law we can then affirm that while the contrast between *hereditas* and *bonorum possessio* is typically classical, the contrast between the civil and praetorian wills is typically postclassical and the main consequence of the disappearance of the libral testament. In general, the philological background of a concept such as vulgar law could help to explain this phenomenon, i.e. the new relevance of the praetorian or civil nature to characterize a will. It is possible to compare the evolution of the will with the evolution of the ten-vowel system in Vulgar Latin. The classical Latin vowel system, which had relied on phonemic vowel length, was modelled into a different one — the Vulgar Latin vowel system in which vowel length distinctions lost phonemic importance, and qualitative distinctions of height (which already existed but did not imply a way of distinguishing one vowel from another) became more prominent, so much so that height came to be the touchstone for distinguishing one vowel from the other. Something similar happened to the role played by witnesses in the testaments: they were essential but in classical law the theoretical framework was still the libral testament, based — dare we say — on an unstable equilibrium among its three main elements: *mancipatio*, *nuncupatio*, and witnesses.[25] This equilibrium was preserved by the skill of the classical jurisprudents but also by a practice based on formularies that contributed to keep the illusion of a libral testament in force.[26] The breakup of the union of those elements led to the appearance of a law of succession constructed on only two different forms of testament that were based in their turn on the number of witnesses:[27] subsequently witnesses became the only way of telling wills apart.

24. Amelotti, *Il testamento* (quoted n. 12), pp. 191–200; ID *Le forme classiche di testamento* II, Turin 1967 5-26. Some scholars who had defended the classical nature of the praetorian will have changed their minds, for example V. Arangio-Ruiz, *Istituzioni di diritto romano*, Naples 1960[11], p. 524: 'Tuttavia questa indulgenza (scil., to accept the sealed tables as testament) non fu considerate dai giureconsulti classici come fonte di un nuovo tipo di testamento (test. *Praetorium* è terminologia postclassica)'. Contra, P. Voci, Testamento pretorio, *Labeo* 13, 1967, pp. 319–340.

25. I should point out that this approach is not necessarily contradictory with that of E. A. Meyer. The same reality could be seen from a theoretical point of view and from the prospective of the performative acts (in Austin's words 'conventional procedure having a certain conventional effect,' see, *Legitimacy and Law* (quoted n. 14), pp. 73–74). The unitary nature of testaments (also outlined by *Nov. Theod.* 16) has something to do with what Meyer calls 'traditional beliefs' (*Legitimacy and Law*, 275). Also in what the dissolution of the mancipatory testament is concerned, this approach proves to be fruitful. Meyer notes that the post-classical jurists of the fourth century AD found themselves 'writing in a context of traditional beliefs about the mancipatory will — beliefs about its unitary structure and the necessity for formal, ceremonial performance — that were assumed also by the body of juristic opinion they inherited, and especially by its definitions and methods of argumentation'. The author also stresses that in the fifth century new 'categories of definition' that were 'logically dependent on the old understandings.' These traditional beliefs are in some way assumed and re-interpreted within the theoretical framework lying beneath the work of jurists, regardless the actual evaluation of these beliefs by them.

26. Champlin, *Final Judgments* (quoted n. 1), pp. 70–71. The role played by those 'humble drawers-up of documents' is more important than scholars had realized. The Digest hardly ever mentions them as *testamentarii* (*Dig.* 28.5.9.3; 28.5.9.6; 29.6.1 pr.; 36.1.3.5; 48.10.15.6; 48.10.22.10) and some inscriptions do not add much information (see e.g. *ILS* 7749; 7763), but their role in preserving and consolidating the formularies employed to draw up a will is in our opinion decisive.

27. This comparison is based on the explanation on the Latin vowel system by V. Väänänen, *Introduction au Latin vulgaire*, Paris[4] 1981, pp. 20–25. On the classical vowel system see Ph. Bandi, *The Foundations of Latin*, Berlin—NewYork 1999, p. 250.

Apart from a reference in one literary source[28] (Isid. Or. 5.24: *Testamentum iuris civilis est quinque testium subscriptione firmatum. Testamentum iuris praetorii est septem testium signis signatus*) the testament of seven or five witnesses appears only a handful of times — not all of them clearly dated but all of them enacted in the late empire: in the Theodosian Code[29] (*CTh* 4.4.1; 4.4.3; 4.4.7.2) and the *Interpretatio* of the Theodosian Code itself, dated much later, near the end of the 5th century or the beginning of the 6th century; in the *Novellae Theodosiani* (*Nov. Theod.* 16) and in the *Novellae Valentiniani* (*Nov. Val.* 21.1) as well. This classification then reappears in some texts excerpted from the barbarian laws, the *Lex Romana Burgundionum* (45.2) and the *Edictum Theodorici* (*Ed. Theod.* 28). These references ought to be interpreted by starting from the contrast between the *testamentum civile* (five witnesses) and the *testamentum praetorium* (seven witnesses) in the post-classical law, in which this distinction apart from its historical background lacked any meaning.[30]

Behind each of these pieces of legislation one personal answer of the emperor to a particular case can be discovered.[31] The evidence is in this sense misleading. On the one hand it is true that the compilers of the Theodosian Code included in it imperial constitutions of general scope.[32] This criterion based on that general scope implies that these constitutions themselves were likely conceived for a particular case, which in its turn encouraged the enactment of a general treatment of the problem or rather the selection of this constitution to be included in the Code because of its general value. We must bear in mind that it is exactly this procedure that makes our evidence confusing: first the labour of excerpting imperial constitutions carried out by the codifiers of the Theodosian Code followed by the excerpting of those constitutions by the compilers of the barbarian laws. For example, it is widely known that book four of the Theodosian Code, whence these fragments come (*CTh* 4.4.1; 4.4.3; 4.4.7.2), has been reconstructed[33] by means of the excerpts included in the *Breviarium Alarici*. That entails of course a focus on the Western part of the empire[34] in which some Roman institutions survived but we lack other data regard-

28. On the ignorance of Saint Isidorus on the actual meaning of many institutions of classical law, see MERÊA, Sobre o testamento (quoted n. 9), p. 107.

29. The website of the Volterra Project: includes Honoré's revision of the first eight books of the Mommsen edition [http://www.ucl.ac.uk]. We quote according to this version.

30. M. KASER, *Das römische Privatrecht* II. *Die nachklassischen Entwicklungen*, Munich² 1975, p. 479

31. C. HUMFRESS, Cracking the Codex. Late Roman Legal Practice in Context, *Bulletin of the Institute of Classical Studies* 47, 2011, pp. 251–264.

32. The meaning of late Roman codification is clearly different from our present concepts, see e.g., W. TURPIN, The Purpose of the Roman Law Codes, *Zeitschrift der Savigny-Stiftung für Rechtsgeschichte* 104, 1987, pp. 620–630; P. JAILLETTE, Le Code Théodosien. De sa promulgation à son entreprise de traduction française, in S. CROGIEZ-PÉTREQUIN et al. (eds.), *Le Code théodosien : diversité des approches et nouvelles perspectives*, Rome 2009, pp. 15–36, esp. 15–26.

33. We cannot offer an extended commentary on these problems (i.e., the lack of an original text, the fact that only a third of its contents has survived and the editorial practices of the compilers). These questions have been recently tackled: J. F. MATTHEWS, *Laying Down the Law: A Study of the Theodosian Code*, New Haven 2000, pp. 85–98; A. J. B. SIRKS, *The Theodosian Code, a Study*, Norderstedt 2007, pp. 61–62.

34. At this historical moment juristic expertise and the supremacy of the courts are phenomena concentrated mainly in the east (vid e.g. J. HARRIES, *Law and Empire in Late Antiquity*, Cambridge, 1999 p. 16) but some particularities of classical Roman law survived in the west regardless of legal competence or an accurate knowledge of the classical legal system.

ing their original context.[35] In other words, we cannot say for sure what the difference between civil and praetorian will meant for the compilers and what its scope in the original Theodosian Code was, which although far from a modern and systematic code was more systematic than its forerunners.[36] The emperor perhaps coped with a misunderstanding of practice and behind this misunderstanding there were more than one theory . Many theories have been proposed but their actual content is difficult to discover by taking resort to *Nov. Theod.* 16, an attempt to re-order the system ex novo. In the following texts we shall try to point this difficulty.

CTh 4.4.1 [= *Brev.* 4.4.1]
Imp. Constantinus A. et Constantius Caes. pf. Urbis In codicillis, quos testamentum non praecedit, sicut in voluntatibus testamenti septem testium vel quinque interventum non deesse oportet: sic enim fiet, ut testantium successiones sine aliqua captione serventur. Si quando igitur testium numerus defecerit, instrumentum codicilli habeatur infirmum. Quod et in ceteris voluntatibus placuit observari. Dat. xi. kal. ian. Constantino a. vii. et Constantio caes. coss.

Interpretatio. *Si quis non fecerit testamentum, sed vice testamenti fecerit codicillum, in quo codicillo legitima heredis institutio teneatur, et hunc ipsum eodem numero testium, hoc est septem aut quinque subscriptionibus faciat confirmari: si minus quam quinque, valere non poterit, sicuti et ceterae voluntates. nam secundum superiorem legem, si condito testamento postea factus fuerit codicillus, et in eo alium, quam in testamento fecerat, heredem voluerit nominare, in eo codicillo heredis institutio non valebit.*

It is significant indeed that the oldest evidence in the Theodosian Code relating to the number of witnesses was enacted by the chancery of Constantine and that it is related to the *codicillum*. *CTh* 4.4.1, dated around AD 326, proves to be coherent with Constantine's other legislation:[37] formalism had been essentially abolished,[38] even the institution of heir (*CJ* 6.23.15), called by Gaius (2.229) *caput et fundamentum testamenti*.[39] In this context the role played by witnesses becomes more and more important as a guarantee of certainty or — in other words — to ensure that the document was a clear reflection of the testator's last will.[40]

35. This fact has been recently stressed as a way of evaluating other problems, such as the original meaning of *fideicommissa* in the Theodosian Code (see J. C. TATE, Codification of Late Roman Inheritance Law: *Fideicommissa* and the Theodosian Code, *Tijdschrift voor rechtsgeschiedenis* 76, 2008, pp. 237–248).

36. T. HONORÉ, *Law in the Crisis of the Empire*, Oxford 1998, p. 12.

37. M. AMELOTTI, Reichsrecht, Volksrecht, Provinzialrecht. Vecchi problemi e nuovi documenti, *Studia et Documenta Historiae et Iuris* 65, p. 214: Constantine's legislation is more pragmatic and more open to provincial views.

38. This question was treated at length by Jacobus GOTHOFREDUS [Jacques Godefroy] *Codex Theodosianus cum perpetuis commentariis*, vol. I, Leipzig 1708, p. 377 The main problem has been however whether the author of that unpreserved constitution had been Constantine himself or his successor, Constantius II. see AMELOTTI, *Il testamento* (quoted n. 12), pp. 249–250.

39. Where the *testamentum porcelli* is concerned, E. CHAMPLIN (The Testament of the Piglet, *Phoenix* 11 1987, pp. 174–183, esp. 178) points out that 'Far more serious than a breach of the law (since it concerns not just people but property) is the fact that after the perfectly normal *Ille testamentum fecit*, the testator begins with the distribution of legacies: that is, the will is immediately invalid in Roman law for omitting the *heredis institutio*, hence it has been dismissed by philologists as an unknown. But the omission of the heir's name is a sign rather of authorial sophistication than of ignorance, as legal historians have realized.'

40. CHAMPLIN, *Final Judgments* (quoted n. 1), p. 64

This constitution deals with *ab intestato* codicils (*quos testamentum non praecedit*) and states that the presence of seven or five witnesses is a requirement founded on the fact that the intervention of these witnesses could protect the last will from any fraud. The legislator extends the scope of this rule, i.e. to actual testaments and codicils, by using a general category called, in a postclassical way, *ceterae voluntates*.[41]

Where *ab intestato* codicils are concerned five or seven witnesses were needed according to the type of testament, civil or praetorian (*In codicillis, quos testamentum non praecedit, sicut in voluntatibus testamenti septem testium vel quinque interventum non deesse oportet*). Amelotti points out this 'equivoco scolastico' of identifying a praetorian will with a seven-witness testament and civil testament with five-witness testament and emphasizes that this postclassical conception implies a common regime for all the testamentary and paratestamentary forms, since by virtue of this constitution, the freedom of form that had been up to this moment typical for a codicil is abolished. A codicil ought to meet the same requirements of a will:[42] this regulation is a total novelty,[43] since codicils had always been distinguished by their freedom from formalism. In so far as the codicil was nearer to being a form of testament[44] (or at least a minor testament) some control was needed. On these grounds imperial legislation decided to reinforce the requirement for witnesses.

The *interpretatio*, dated (as known) later than the Code,[45] does not add much new data to this question. It only generalises the aforesaid rule that an *ab intestato* codicil must be attested by the same number of witnesses as a will. Yet the commentary also tackles a text later edited in *CJ* 6.36.7 and referred to here as *secundum superiorem legem* by virtue of which if a will had been duly executed and thereafter a codicil had been drawn up which appointed another heir, then in this case the institution of the heir made in this codicil would not be valid. This statement implies that the boundaries between codicils and testaments have become more and more blurred.

41. AMELOTTI, *Il testamento* (quoted n. 12), p. 247 and n. 1.

42. AMELOTTI, *Il testamento* (quoted n. 12), p. 248. The author quotes *CJ* 6.36.7, enacted also by Constantine to insist on the idea that codicils were put on the same footing as wills with two particularities: codicils could include neither *heredis institutio* nor *substitutiones*.

43. In Roman classical law an *ab intestato* codicil could not contain provisions related to *ius civile*. The Theodosian Code does not offer any exceptions of this type: it was the liberty of form that became limited.

44. GOTHOFREDUS, *Codex Theodosianus* (quoted n. 38), vol. I, p. 376: 'Quia scilicet huiusquemodi codicilli vicem testamenti obtinent et ad vicem testamentum fiunt'.

45. The date and the utility of the *Interpretatio* as a source has been a problem for scholarship (see on the old theories H. NEHLSEN, Alarichs II. als Gesetzgeber, in G. LANDWEHR (ed.), *Studien zu den germanischen Volksrechten Gedächtnisschrift für Wilhelm Ebel* 1, Frankfurt 1982, pp. 143–202, esp. 144–146). Today (see eg. R. LAMBERTINI, *La codificazione di Alarico II*, Turin 1991, pp. 57–59) it seems clear that the *Interpretatio* must be understood as a commentary in which many contemporary novelties (5th and 6th centuries) were mixed to those included in the Theosodian Code, but in any case its contents could hardly ever offer good information on how those institutions worked in the 4th century AD. That is why the contrast between written and dictated will emphasized by the *Interpretatio* is perhaps not the best way to understand the basis of the contrast between praetorian and civil testament at that moment, but probably only a way of recognizing a new interpretation that arose later.

CTh 4.4.3 [= Brev.4.4.3]

*Impp. Arcadius et Honorius AA. Aeternali proconsuli Asiae. Testamentum non ideo infirmari debebit, quod diversis hoc deficiens nominibus appellavit, cum superflua non noceant. Praetermissa namque necessaria, non abundans cautela vel contractus imminuit vel testatoris officit voluntati.*1*Nec patimur fidem conditi arbitrii ob hoc debere convelli, si aut maiorem in principio signatorum aut minorem aut nullum numerum conditor suae praedixerit voluntati, cum quinque huic non ignari subscripserint testamento, licet non eisdem series fuerit recensita, sed hic, qui extremum disponit arbitrium, obsignandum porrexerit testamentum.*

Interpretatio. *Si moriens, cum scribit aut dictat chartulam testamenti, praetermiserit forsitan vocabulum ponere, aut civilis, id est, quod quinque testium, aut praetorii iuris, quod septem testium erit subscriptione firmandum; aut si maiorem vel minorem testium numerum se testator in principio dixerit evocasse, usque ad quinque subscriptorum numerum, etiamsi non relegant testamentum, valere permissum est, ita ut, sicut minor numerus impedit voluntatem, sic, quicquid superfuerit, non noceat testamento: quia et lex ipsa constituit, quod superflua iuri impedire non debeant. Hoc etiam observandum, ut testator signandum testibus offerat testamentum, nec ideo habeatur infirmum, si alicui de subscriptoribus testator aliquid legati nomine derelinquit.*

Arcadius and Honorius, in a constitution later also integrated in the Codex of Justinian (*CJ* 23.17) and dated around AD 396, decided on the importance to be given to the number of witnesses. The text does not directly tackle the problem of the civil — five — or praetorian — seven — will or rather does not explicitly relate this question to the number of witnesses but the link could be presumed since under the term *diversis* both names (civil and praetorian) are implied.[46] The Interpretation is clear on this matter.

This constitution starts from the abovementioned general concept of testament in which the clear-cut classical notion has totally vanished. In this sense the emperors state that a testament shall not be invalid because of the name (civil or praetorian) used by the will maker and to strengthen this idea points to *Pauli Sent.* 3.4a.10.

Pauli Sent. 3.4a.10

Plures quam septem ad testamentum adhibiti non nocent superflua enim facta prodesse iuri tantum, nocere non possunt.

In my opinion it is significant indeed that the quoted source assesses a testament with more than seven witnesses, a type of will that cannot be not directly related to our problem. This constitution deals with the question of the witnesses by stating that a superfluous number of witnesses does not invalidate the will as long as the (minimum) number of five had been respected. The problem is to determine whether the emperors referred to a praetorian will or to a civil will this possibility of lessening the number of witnesses. The exegesis carried out by Ferrari dalle Spade aims to overcome this problem by concluding that

46. M. David, Über die Form des ordentlichen, schriftlich abgefaßten Privattestaments zur Zeit des Dominats, *Zeitschrift der Savigny-Stiftung für Rechtsgeschichte* 52, 1932, pp. 314–325, esp. 315 and n. 4. Gothofredus, *Codex Theodosianus* (quoted n. 38), vol. I, p. 380 interprets this text as assuming that the testator had drawn up a testament but called it by a name such as codicil.

with this constitution both kinds of testament were regulated, since a praetorian will with five witnesses would be still valid since the other possibility, a civil will with five witnesses is not a lessening.[47] D'Ors points to the *interpretatio*, which actually mentions both civil and praetorian will (*aut civilis, id est, quod quinque testium, aut praetorii iuris, quod septem testium*), which the text of the constitution does not.[48] In his opinion the text of this constitution does not make clear the requirements of the praetorian will but only confirms that the civil testament required five witnesses and that a higher number of witnesses mentioned did not invalidate the act. According to him if this difference was practically removed by this constitution of Arcadius and Honorius, the existence of testaments with seven or five witnesses in subsequent texts would not make sense. D'Ors is right where the importance of this question is concerned, since this problem does not disappear from the legal texts after Arcadius and Honorius,[49] but at the same time the link between this decision and the civil testament proves to be problematic according to the systematic order of the Theodosian Code.[50] The reference in passing to cases in which only three witnesses were needed is today lost but in a way this phenomenon proves that there was a tendency in the imperial legislation to dismiss these kinds of problems as superfluous.[51] Probably the treatment of these cases experienced changed from the reign of Constantine to that of Arcadius and Honorius and it is likely that the practice was not always in harmony with imperial legislation.

CTh 4.4.7.2 [=Brev.4.4.7]

Imp. Theod(osius) A. Asclepiodoto P(raefecto) P(raetori)o

Si quis vero ex parentibus utriusque sexus ac liberis usque ad gradum quartum agnationis vinculis alligatus vel cognationis nexu constrictus ad tertium usque scriptus heres fuerit vel nuncupatus, in eo videlicet testamento, quod testator vicem quoque codicillorum voluit obtinere, licebit ei, si de hereditate ex testamento secundum mortui voluntatem agens fuerit forsitan superatus, vel certe ipse sponte voluerit, ad fideicommissi subsidium convolare. Non enim par eademque ratio videtur amittere debita et lucra non capere. In omni autem genere testamenti, sive in praetorio iure sive civili consistat seu codicilli conscribantur sive non scripta voluntas ultima praetendatur, id volumus observari, ut eodem die, quo coeptum quid eorum fuerit, ad perfectum sui plenitudinem sortiatur, nihilque eius in diem

47. G. Ferrari dalle Spade, *Ricerche sul diritto ereditario in Occidente nell'Alto Medioevo con speciale riguardo all'Italia*, Venezia 1914 (C. Carmelo, *Scritti giuridici, storici e politici*, II, Milan 1953, pp. 1–172, esp. 40–43).

48. A. D'Ors, El *Testamentum Porcelli* y su interés para la historia jurídica, *RIDA* 2, 1955, pp. 219–236, esp. 230–231.

49. D'Ors, El *Testamentum* (quoted n. 48), p. 231: 'Por lo demás, la persistencia con que las constituciones siguen distinguiendo ambos tipos de testamento hace poco verosímil que el número de cinco testigos fuera suficiente en todo caso y que careciera de todo sentido seguir hablando de siete testigos para algunos casos'.

50. Matthews, *Laying Down the Law* (quoted n. 33), p. 117 points out a separated treatment of *ius civile* institutions. Book IV and Book V overlap also where successory institutions are concerned. Book IV follows the order of the Edict while Book V covers institutions that have not been covered by the Praetor's task: 'The first title in full, *De hereditatibus legitimis*, may help to make this clear. It refers to rights of succession determined not by the praetor but by ius civile (...). The distinction is made explicitly in the very first extant text of Book 5, declaring that a petition for '*bonorum possessio*' was not required in the circumstances considered, since the benefit rested on the law and not on praetorian action,' see *CTh* 5.1.1.

51. On the rule, of Christian background 'duorum vel trium testium stet omne verbum,' see Merêa, Sobre o testamento (quoted n. 9), p. 107.

alterum differatur; quod quidem nullam habeat firmitatem, nisi aut septem aut quinque vel rogati aut qui fortuito venerint, possint iure testimonium perhibere, videlicet post hanc sanctionem divinis illis quiescentibus apicibus, qui trium testium numero sunt contenti.

Interpretatio. *Si quis per scripturam condiderit testamentum et postmodum sine scriptura, hoc est per nuncupationem suam iterandam crediderit voluntatem, vel si codicillis, quod est fideicommissum, potestatem heredi suo commiserit, ut, ex qua voluerit, testatoris ordinatione succedat: tunc in primordio adeundae hereditatis suam publicare non desinat voluntatem, utrum ex testamento, an per nuncupationem, an per fideicommissum hereditatem sibi eligat vindicandam. Quod si prima electio eius fuerit superata, ad alteram ei transire non liceat: quia unius petitione concessa, de reliquis se noverit excludendum, quia una petitio alias aperte et evidenter excludit. Extrema pars legis istius ideo non habetur scripta vel exposita, quia novella lege calcatur.*

CTh 4.4.7.2, enacted in AD 424 by Theodosius II, covers both civil and praetorian testaments (*In omni autem genere testamenti, sive in praetorio iure sive civili consistat*) and extends the same common requirements to codicils: a codicil must be completed on the same day as that on which a part of it was begun with no part postponed for the next day and with the required number of witnesses — five or seven. As we shall see this idea will be developed in *Nov. Theod.* 16. Evidently it has classical background.

Significantly both the text of the constitution (*heres fuerit vel nuncupatus*) and the *interpretatio* start from the postclassical concept of oral will as *nuncupatio*, (*scriptus heres fuerit vel nuncupatus*) as Archi rightly pointed out, but neither the constitution nor its interpretation explicitly relates the civil testament to the oral one (*In omni autem genere testamenti, sive in praetorio iure sive civili consistat seu codicilli conscribantur sive non scripta voluntas ultima praetendatur*).[52]

Apart from the aforementioned constitutions included in the Theodosian Code, the postclassical testamentary law and in large part the aforementioned barbarian laws (the *Edictum Theodorici* and the *Lex Romana Burgundionum*) derive from *Nov. Theod.* 16. This enactment, however, does not insist on the difference between seven and five witnesses and even ignores it. The paradox is that this contrast is still present in *Nov. Val.* 21.1.4 (enacted later in AD 446, but in the west) and in *Lex Rom Burg.* 45.2. Do these enactments preserve some elements of the pre-Theodosian testamentary system? For the sake of clarity I shall comment on *Nov. Theod.* 16 along with the barbarian laws, directly derived from it, and compare to *Nov. Val.* 21.1, whose relationship to *Nov. Theod.* 16 is far from clear.

Nov.Theod.16, enacted in AD 439 does not directly mention the contrast between the seven or five witnesses and clearly introduces a new regulation that apparently underestimates the part played by such a question. Although some other aspects of the preceding legislation are traceable in the text of *Nov. Theod.* 16 and in the barbarian laws, they are not the best way to elucidate the legal regime in existence before this constitution. As we shall see, despite this methodological difficulty, interpretations have used this enactment in this way.

As stated above, *Nov. Theod.* 16 brought important novelties in the form of wills or rather it accepted, regulated and unified some practices,[53] especially (*Nov. Theod.* 16.2 and 4)

52. Archi, Oralità e scrittura (quoted n. 23), p. 268.

53. As we have seen, Theodosius II himself established similar principles in *CTh* 4.4.7.2.

the difference between a testament made before witnesses and a testament already made and only signed by them. This is the starting point for a new regulation, mainly conceived for the barbarians who were interested in making wills under the protection of Roman law.[54] As we shall see the testament must be made and attested to and all the witnesses ought to being summoned for the purpose of attesting the will but not necessarily for its drawing up, provided that the procedure of signing and attesting was concluded *uno tempore*. In other words, although one question is not directly related to the other, witnesses do not need to know the content of the will. The only requirement is that the testament must be made *uno tempore*.

These rules — as stated above — by *Nov. Theod.* 16 were codified and made clear rather than actually newly coined. Champlin insists on the idea that in classical law there were no definite rules on the question of the procedure to draw up a will.[55] This assertion is only partially true, since all these matters were treated by classical jurisprudence in its typical casuistic way. For example, that the will was made *uno tempore* is a requirement already outlined by Ulpian, who in his turn refers to the *veteres*.

Dig. 28.120.8 (*Ulp.* 1 *ad Sab.*)
8. *Et veteres putaverunt eos, qui propter sollemnia testamenti adhibentur, durare debere, donec suprema contestatio peragatur.*

9. *Non tamen intellegentiam sermonis exigimus: hoc enim divus Marcus Didio Iuliano in teste, qui Latine non noverat, rescripsit: nam si vel sensu percipiat quis, cui rei adhibitus sit, sufficere.*

On the basis of this rule, that the testament ought to be subscribed *uno tempore*, or, in other words, that the acknowledgment of the seals and the nature of the document (i.e., a testament) ought to be fulfilled by all the witnesses at the same time[56] was conceived *Nov. Theod.* 16. Its text clearly distinguishes the presence of all the witnesses in the procedure of the subscription (*uno tempore*) from the idea — probably a confusion of post-classical times — that they ought to be present during the whole process of making the testament or even that they ought to know its content. Ulpian comments also upon a *rescriptum* of Marcus Aurelius in which someone who did not know Latin could act as a witness, provided he understood by the senses (*nam si vel sensu percipiat quis, cui rei adhibitus sit, sufficere*) the meaning of

54. *Nov. Theod.* 16 pr.: *Ita prodest gentes barbaras nostri numinis imperio mancipari, ita nostrae victoriae videbuntur obedientibus fructuosae, si pacis commoda legum regulis conponantur.* see W. R. Mathisen, *Peregrini, Barbari*, and *Cives Romani*. Concepts of Citizenship and the Legal Identity, *American Historical Review* 111, 2006, pp. 1011–1040, esp. 1033–1034.

55. Champlin, *Final Judgments* (quoted n. 1), pp. 76–81. Champlin seems to assume that the *mancipatio familiae* was actually performed, but from the context it is plain that he means to include also the mere drawing up of a will.

56. Again we can see that the jurist is still assuming the theoretical framework of the libral testament.The term '*suprema contestatio*' is here the word for '*nuncupatio*', bin the sense that 'I *verba* in questione venivano pronunziati a conclusione dell'intero *negotium*' see F. Terranova, Sulla natura testamentaria della cosidetta *mancipatio familiae*, *AUPA* 52, 2007-2008, pp. 229–335, esp. 316, n. 35, relying on B. Albanese, Prospettive negoziali arcaiche, in '*Poteri negotia actiones' nella esperienza romana arcaica, Atti del Convegno di diritto romano, Copanello (12-15 maggio 1982)*, Naples 1984, pp. 109–124, esp. 119 [= *Scritti giuridici*, II, Palermo 1991, pp. 1621–1636, esp. 1631].

that act. In such a case, if he was able to identify a testament he would be entitled to witness it. The question of the being aware of the content is again the question. When we take into account the structure of the so-called 'Doppelurkunde' and the references of some literary sources it is obvious that Theodosius was dealing with a common practice that had been misunderstood: witnesses ought not necessarily to know the provisions of the will.[57] The first paragraph is devoted to this point.

> *Nov. Theod.* 16.1
>
> *Natura talis est hominum, ut quosdam diligant, alios timeant, quibusdam sint officiosae gratiae debitores, alios suspicentur, quorundam fidem intelligant eligendam, aliis nihil credendum existiment nec tamen audeant de singulis quae sentiunt confiteri. Ideo veteres testamenta scripta testibus offerebant oblatarumque eis tabularum perhiberi testimonium postulabant. Sed dum iuris antiqui cautelam paulatim mutat posteritatis inperita praesumptio et testes exigunt omnimodo quae testamento continentur agnoscere, eo res processit, ut, dum sua quisque nonnumquam iudicia publicare formidat, dum testibus testamenti sua non audet secreta committere, ne suis facultatibus inhiantes offendat, intestatus mori quam sua mentis arcana periculose patiatur exprimere.*

Nov. Theod. 16. 1 tackles this question in the sense that classical jurists had previously declared: it makes clear that to witness an act does not necessarily mean to know its specific content. The whole question is developed using a moral approach and especially stressing the part played by trust in the people summoned to witness a testament (*Natura talis est hominum, ut quosdam diligant, alios timeant, quibusdam sint officiosae gratiae debitores, alios suspicentur, quorundam fidem intelligant eligendam, aliis nihil credendum existiment nec tamen audeant de singulis quae sentiunt confiteri.*). Then the emperor contrasts the normal behaviour of the will makers under the classical law with the recent curiosity for knowing the content. This point is developed in the next paragraph.

> *Nov. Theod.* 16.2
>
> *Hac itaque consultissima lege sancimus, licere per scripturam conficientibus testamentum, si nullum scire volunt quae in eo scripta sunt, signatam vel ligatam vel tantum clausam involutamve proferre scripturam vel ipsius testatoris vel cuiuslibet alterius manu conscriptam eamque rogatis testibus septem numero civibus Romanis puberibus omnibus simul offerre signandam et subscribendam, dum tamen testibus praesentibus testator suum esse testamentum dixerit quod offertur eique ipse coram testibus sua manu in reliqua parte testamenti subscripserit: quo facto et testibus uno eodemque die ac tempore subscribentibus et signantibus valere testamentum nec ideo infirmari, quod testes nesciant quae in eo scripta sunt testamento.*

57. Regarding the normal procedure of witnessing a will in the classical period it is significant that Horace (*Sat.* II 5.51-7) in a context in which a testament is offered to the witness to be signed seems to convey that reading or not reading the content was a matter of social etiquette: *Qui testamentum tradet tibi cumque legendum,/ abnuere et tabulas a te removere memento,/ sic tamen, ut limis rapias, quid prima secundo/ cera velit versu; solus multisne coheres,/ veloci percurre oculo. plerumque recoctus* ('if someone hands you his will to read, decline, and remember to push the thing far from you, but snatch a sidelong glance at the second line of page one: run your eye over it quickly to see if you're one of many,' tr. A. S. Kline).

Testators who preferred that no one knew the contents of their will they were allowed to produce a written testament (whether holographic or dictated) already sealed or tied or just closed and folded (*signatam vel ligatam vel tantum clausam involutamve proferre scripturam vel ipsius testatoris vel cuiuslibet alterius manu conscriptam*) — The testament must be offered to seven witnesses in order to be sealed and subscribed by them but with the requirement that the testator stated that the said document was his will and subsequently signed it with his own hand. Both acts (the statement and the subscription) ought to be performed in the presence of the witnesses.[58] Another aspect of witnessing testaments — the requirement *uno eodemque die, nullo actu interveniente*, i.e., on one and the same day and at the same time) is dealt with in the fourth paragraph. The emperor carefully distinguishes the act of witnessing a testament from the acknowledgement of its content, a distinction that had been plain in classical law but that according to the emperor became blurred in the subsequent period.

> *Nov. Theod.* 16.4
>
> *In omnibus autem testamentis, quae vel absentibus vel praesentibus testibus dictantur, superfluum est uno eodemque tempore exigere testatorem et testes adhibere et dictare suum arbitrium et finire testamentum. Sed licet alio tempore dictatum scriptumve proferatur testamentum, sufficiet uno eodemque die nullo actu interveniente testes omnes, videlicet simul nec diversis temporibus, subscribere signareve testamentum.*

The witnesses could of course attend at the moment of the drawing up the will but they could also simply subscribe *uno eodemque die, nullo actu interveniente* the testament elaborated in advance. It is significant, that *Nov. Theod.* 16 does not mention the contrast between five and seven witnesses, perhaps because this constitution was conceived merely for the praetorian will or perhaps because its aim was to eliminate this contrast. Only the *interpretatio* insists on this difference, but it was composed in the west, where this distinction had greater importance. This constitution is at least problematic because the text does not clearly mention the two types and even deals with other problems such as the oral will. We cannot dismiss the idea that the aim of Nov. Theod 16 was to abrogate this contrast between civil and praetorian wills, since the contrast had became confusing and only was based only on historical issues.[59]

58. D'ORS, El *Testamentum* (quoted n. 48), p. 234, insists on the novelty of this requirement, but in practice we know one example of the subscription of the will maker dated before this reign, that of the testament of Saint Gregory of Nazianzus (E. P. J. SPANGENBERG, *Iuris Romani tabulae negotiorum solemnium*, Leipzig 1822, 71=Migna, *Patrologia Graeca* (=*P. G.*) XXXXVIII 389-396), dated to AD 381 That suggests that Theodosius II was again confirming an existing practice.

59. The impact of *Nov. Theod.* 16 could be partly traced in the documentation of Egypt and has been recently studied by L. MIGLIARDI-ZINGALE (Il testamento tardoromano tra oriente e occidente: alcune rifessioni sui documenti della prassi, *Atti dell'Accademia Romanistica Costantiniana* 17, 2010, pp. 43–62). In *FIRA* III 54 (*St. Pal.* I. pp.6–7), l. 31 we can read: κατὰ τὴν θείαν διάταξιν, which obviously refers to this constitution and (l. 4-5). The will was made before by seven witnesses (τὴν διαθήκην τίθημι ἐπ' ὄψεσι τῶν προσκληθέντων [ἑπτὰ] / [νομίμων μαρτύρω]ν) and even the holographic subscription of the testator is preserved (l. 31). Anyway, as MIGLIARDI-ZINGALE (Il testamento, p. 48) has recently shown it is difficult to deduce from the documents whether a clear distinction between a dictated will and a merely subscribed one is made. In *P. Oxy.* XVI 1901 (the 'Will of Flavius Pousi,' 6th century AD) we can read (e.g. l. 77-78: μαρ[τυρῶ τῇδε τῇ διαθήκῃ] / ἀκούσας παρὰ Ποῦσι κούρσο̣ρος τοῦ διαθεμένου ὡς πρόκειται). MIGLIARDI-ZINGALE (p. 49, n. 18) suggests that also

We must again bear in mind that *Nov. Theod.* 16 was enacted in AD 439 as a general pronouncement and *Nov. Val.* 21.1 — enacted later, in 446 and still dealing with such a contrast — was a decision on a particular case, whose relationship to *Nov. Theod.* 16 is far from evident. Significantly *Nov. Theod.* 16 — focused on the difference between a dictated testament subscribed by witnesses and a later testament subscribed by witnesses — is the last enactment on testaments with general scope issued under the late empire and the starting point for a new legal regime which in its turn brought some novelties that, as stated above, probably do not help to interpret the legal regime before AD 439. It is also important that *Nov. Val.* 21 might have ignored the new regulation of *Nov. Theod.* 16 not only because of the peculiarity of the case dealt with in *Nov. Val.* 21 but also — as stated above — because that Theodosian statute became binding in the western empire later than in the eastern part.[60]

Nov. Val. 21.1.4

Idcirco, quia minutiis priscae consuetudinis et obscuritate submota solam defunctorum convenit inspici voluntatem, cui multum roboris erit, si vel septem vel quinque testibus muniatur, et virum spectabilem Leonium praeter fiduciam precum pridem cum uxore communium voluntas quoque alia et subscriptionibus testium munita defendit, apud eundem solida successione Iucundae coniugis suae iugiter permanente, quisquis voluerit delata nobis supplicatione testari, habeat liberam facultatem.

This text of *Nov. Val.* 21.1 (AD 446) does not provide clear information regarding our problem for it merely mentions the contrast between seven and five witnesses.[61] Its content is merely a question put by a married couple, Leonius and Iocunda, first on the *ius liberorum* and second on whether married people can inherit from one another.[62] The requirement of seven or five witnesses is again mentioned in an enactment issued later than *Nov. Theod.* 16 but unfortunately the only conclusion is that this contrast was still current at least in this part of the empire since *Nov. Theod.* 16 was not yet in force there. It is significant that the mention of the contrast between a praetorian will and a civil one appears in a context in which the importance of formal requirements is diminished and only the intention of the deceased is stressed (*quia minutiis priscae consuetudinis et obscuritate submota solam defunctorum convenit inspici voluntatem, cui multum roboris erit, si vel septem vel quinque testibus muniatur*).

in *FIRA* III 54 ἀκούσας must be read instead of αἰτηθείς. The author rightly points out that 'forse ci si potrebbe chiedere se essa (scil.'la formula') voglia indicare sche i testimoni hanno semplicemente ascoltato la dichiarazione con cui il testatore, presentando loro il documento già approntato, ha precisato che quello era appunto il suo testamento, oppure che essi hanno sentito direttamente la volontà testamentarie.' Once more the formularies simplify these legal problems.

60. B. Kübler, s.v. 'Testament (juristisch)', RE VA 1 1934, col. 966-1010, esp. col. 998-999.

61. M. Bianchi Fossati Vanzetti, *Le Novelle di Valentiniano III* I, Padua 1988, p. 37 does not make any comment about this law (4) but emphasizes that there is a personal petition behind *Nov. Val.* 21. On Firminus, who probably was the jurist behind this enactment, see Honoré, *Law in the Crisis* (quoted n. 36) pp. 270–271; D. Liebs, *Hofjuristen der römischen Kaiser bis Justinian*, Munich 2010, pp. 127–129.

62. Humfress, Cracking the Codex (quoted n. 31), p. 253. On the problem of the *ius liberorum* within this context, see e.g. W. Dajczak, Die Aufhebung der Beschrankungen der *capacitas* von Ehegatten in der nachklassischen Periode, *RIDA* 42 (1995) pp. 155–166, esp. 161–164.

The reference to the contrast between seven and five witnesses could be interpreted in the sense that regardless of the number of witnesses (whether five or seven) if the will of the deceased is protected by the subscription of witnesses, it will be valid. Once again the mention of the difference between five or seven witnesses is merely a concession to practice: the imperial chancery must cope with this misunderstanding created by practice, but without stressing its meaning and avoiding developing its original consequences in depth.

The references made by the barbarian laws are at first sight not especially useful in explaining the contents of Nov. Thed. 16 and even less in discovering the regulation binding before the enactment of this constitution, but we must tackle them in order to discuss all the evidence used to explain the contrast between praetorian and civil testament in postclassical law, at least as long as these barbarian laws may perhaps have preserved something of the pre-Theodosian regulation. I am personally sceptical about this possibility, but — as we shall see-some scholars have based their hypotheses on this assumption and that is why some light must be cast on this question.

Ed. Theod. 28

Faciendorum testamentorum omnibus quos testari leges permittunt, damus late licentiam: ita ut septem aut quinque testes ingenui ac puberes in conspectu testatoris, uno tempore, eodem rogante subscribant.

The *Edictum Theodorici* includes two requirements demanded by *CTh* 4.4.7.2, partly included in *Nov. Theod.* 16: first, the presence of witnesses and the signing (*subscribere*) of the will, not necessarily at the moment of the drawing up of the document, but at least *uno tempore*, although this distinction (i.e. presence at the drawing up the will simply in the subscription) is not clearly stated; second, the requirement of the subscription of the will maker (*eodem rogante*).

For its part, the information coming from the *Lex Romana Burgundionum* is as interesting as it is confusing. D'Ors even considered this fragment the solution to the riddle of the number of witnesses, but some other scholars have rightly doubted its value as a source for the Roman postclassical testament.[63]

Lex Rom Burg. 45.2

Si vero testis adhibentur, ante quos testator vel subscribat vel suum testamentum offerat subscribendum, cives Romani testis adhibendi sunt, numero competenti, vel V vel VII, qui ad testamentum iure adhiberi possunt quorumque testimonium recipetur, cum quibus est nobis testamenti factio, secundum legem Theodosii et Valentiniani ad Florentium prafectum preturii datam.

As the text itself declares, it is closely related to *Nov. Theod.* 16 (*secundum legem Theodosii et Valentiniani ad Florentium prafectum preturii datam*),[64] specifically to paragraph 4 but on

63. D'Ors, El *Testamentum* (quoted n. 48), pp. 232–233; David, Über die Form (quoted n. 46), p. 322, n.2. To evaluate the impact of the Roman law on the *Lex Romana Burgundionum* the contribution of K. Fischer Drew is still important, The Barbarian Kings as Lawgivers and Judges, in R. S. Hoyt (ed.) *Life and Thought in the Early Middle Ages*, Minnesota 1967, pp. 7–29.

64. On Favius Florentinus see J. R. Martindale, *The prosopography of the later Roman Empire* II, Cambridge 1980, pp. 428–429. On the ways in which the Theodosian Code and the *Nov. Theod.* 16 are quoted by the Burgundian Law, see M. A. De Dominicis, Su di una redazione Gaiana di *Lex Romana Burgundionum*, Tit. V.

the other hand, as we shall see, some differences are evident: The subscription of the will maker is not required as in *Ed. Theod.* 28 but the difference between a testament dictated in the presence of witnesses or its mere subscription by all of them *uno tempore* is in the Burgundian law clearly made: this nuance, however had been lost in the *Edictum Theodorici*. According to the *Lex Romana Burgundionum*, the witnesses play a role in the presence of the testator, who *vel subscribat vel suum testamentum offerat subscribendum*. As we already know,in this case a distinction is made between witnesses who were present when the will was drawn up and witnesses who only attended at the moment when the will — already prepared-was signed by the testator. In the former, only five witnesses were required; in the latter seven were mandatory.[65]

Bauer-Gerland rightly argues that if this fragment of the *Lex Romana Burgundionum* reflected the legal reality and the state of affairs before Theodosius II, the quotation of the *Novellae Theodosiani* would make no sense.[66] The reference to a subscription of the will maker is missing and probably not because the Burgundian law knew something of the pre-Theodosian testament, but because it did not interpret correctly the text of *Nov. Theod.* 16.4 or simply summarized (or rather simplified) the regulation of this constitution.[67]

Roels for his part thinks that another source in which this question was dealt with has unfortunately been lost.[68] In this case the Burgundian Law would incorporate the difference between seven and five witnesses taken from a source of the pre-Theodosian age. That hypothetical constitution could have been part of the Theodosian Code and then in its turn the basis of *Lex Rom. Burg.* 45.2. If we bear in mind that the laying down of the Theodosian Code was far from systematic and that we are dealing with a text reconstructed according to the constitutions included into the *Breviarium Alarici* his hypothesis seems not totally absurd. In short, the problem in this case is how to relate this solution to *Nov. Theod.* 16.4 and to determine whether the quoted Roman Burgundian Law could provide arguments to explain the role played by those witnesses in the Theodosian Code exactly in the period before the enactment of *Nov. Theod.* 16.

§ 1, (nota minima). *Bullettino dell'Istituto di Diritto Romano 'Vittorio Scialoja.' Terza serie* 72, 1964, pp. 217–219, esp. 218, n. 1.

65. D'Ors, El *Testamentum* (quoted n. 48), p. 232.

66. F. Bauer-Gerland, *Das Erbrecht der Lex Romana Burgundionum*, Berlin 1995, p. 90.

67. This criticism notwithstanding the fragment has value in so far as the scope of the link between this paragraph of the *Lex Romana Burgundionum* (45.2) and the pre-Theodosian law is highly controversial. In fact the only element to such an assumption is that the will maker's subscription is not mentioned in *Nov. Theod.* 16, but it could derive from the purposeof casting this element aside. In Bauer-Gerland this problem is confusingly handled: Bauer-Gerland, *Das Erbrecht* (quoted n. 66), p. 91: D'Ors nimmt an, die RB (scl. *Lex Romana Burgundionum*) behalte die vortheodosianische Rechtslage bei. Warum die RB dann NT 16 zitiert, erklärt D'Ors nicht. D'Ors does not quote *Nov. Theod.* 16 groundlessly In fact D'Ors points out that in his opinion the text of the Burgundian law could have preserved some elements of the pre-Theodosian law, a thesis that is not easily demonstrable, but this is another matter.

68. W. Roels, Praetorisch en civiel testament in twee constituties van 424 en 446, en in de klassieke tijd, *RIDA* 5, 1958, pp. 539–562, esp. 544: 'Waar heeft de Interpretatio de voorstelling gehaald, dat praetorische testamenten zijn met zeven getuigen, civiele testamenten met vijf getuigen? We weten het niet. Uit het hierboven onder nr. 4 opgemerkte (scil. *CTh* 4.4.7.2) volgt, dat het niet waarschijnlijk is dat de voorstelling uit verloren constituties zou genomen zijn.'

The difference between both testaments — i.e. civil and praetorian — is difficult to understand in the context of postclassical law, unless we consider that the contrast *hereditas / bonorum possessio* was still in force in those days, which is difficult to believe.[69] The old terminology indeed was still in use and to be sure *CTh* 4.4.7 pr. does actually refer to *bonorum possessio*. Yet such a reference most likely only indicates the persistence of the conceptual framework of some classical institutions (essentially based on the vanished formulary system) one that does not correspond to actual legal practice but that at the same time gives form to the legal system. As Barry Nicholas summarized, 'the law had taken shape on the mould of the formula.'[70]

We may conclude that a systematic interpretation of the legal evidence — the type of interpretation carried out by Biondi and D'Ors (and albeit only) partially by David — is perhaps not the best way to tackle the problem. We cannot ignore the fact that *Nov. Theod.* 16, as stated above, was a new regulation of the testamentary law and consequently that its provisions cannot legitimately be put forward to reconstruct the testamentary law binding before its enactment. We can confirm that *Nov. Theod.* 16 tried to unify the way of drawing up a testament and from some of its provisions we can more or less figure out some defects of common practice that this statute tried to cope with. It is troublesome, however, to use this statute to reconstruct the legal background of testaments before its enactment. That *Nov. Theod.* 16.6 forbade an oral testament without seven witnesses does not help us to find out whether this kind of testament was possible before.

An approach that incorporates a likely historical development and a systematic interpretation, would be better, especially if such an interpretation bears in mind that with the compilation of the Theodosian Code and its state nowadays, our sources are incomplete. Among the different scholars analyzing the meaning of the testament with seven or five witnesses only David actually takes into account the documentary evidence, although he himself recognizes that it does not decisively clarify the question. Other scholars are only concerned with imperial legislation, which casts light on some aspects of the problem but obscures others. At the same time it could be argued that this approach relies on legal evidence, which in its turn is — a part from incomplete — far from systematic.

As stated above, Martin David tried to give some unity to this confusing panorama by citing both imperial constitutions and documentary evidence. In his opinion the correct reason why

69. P. Jörs—W. Kunkel, *Römisches Privatrecht*, Berlin 1935², p. 320, n. 1: Kunkel, precisely on the grounds of *CTh* 4.4.7, believes that *bonorum possessio* still survived in those days. C. Dupont, Les successions dans les constitutions de Constantin, *Iura* l5, l964, pp. 57–116, rightly states (89) that the distinction between *hereditas* and *bonorum possessio* that survives in Constantine's legislation is 'beaucoup plus formelle que substantielle'. According to her analysis of the sources (89-109) related to both institutions dated on this reign (e.g. *CTh* 2.16.2; 2.19.1) she concludes that « au début du ɪᴠᵉ siècle l'assimilation des successeurs *jure civile* aux successeurs *jure praetorio* se trouvait très avancée ; elle l'était tellement que le législateur oubliait souvent d'ajouter à la mention de *l'heres* celle du *bonorum possessor* ».

70. B. Nicholas, *An Introduction to Roman Law*, Oxford 1962 (repr. 1969), p. 28. In a way this is similar to the use in English law of terminology — and the systematic framework of the forms of action dating from the period before the enacting of the Judicature Acts 1873-75. So the greater part of Justinian's law is intelligible only in terms that had lost their practical importance two hundred and fifty years earlier. This affirmation — the survival of the old conceptual framework in Justinian law — could of course be extrapolated to post-classical law. This persistence would provide a parallel to the use of the conceptual framework of the libral testament in a context in which this ritual was hardly ever — if it at all — performed.

the law continued to distinguish between the praetorian and civil testaments (five and seven witnesses) was that the former was holographic (entirely handwritten, dated and signed by the testator) while the latter had been dictated to a third person and signed by witnesses.[71] At first sight the documentary evidence seems to fit with this conclusion, although its late date cannot offer firm support.[72] The legal evidence is rightly interpreted on the basis of the historical outline of I. 2.10.1, which confirms that the old distinction between *ius civile* and *ius praetorium* was at that moment without legal foundation. The available sources — such as *CTh* 4.4.2.1; 4.4.3.1; 4.4.5 pr. — mention a written testament, in which the *mancipatio* and consequently the

71. David, Über die Form (quoted n. 46), pp. 314–325. This theory is mainly based on the *Interpretatio* to *CTh* 4.4.3.

72. David, Über die Form (quoted n. 46), pp. 318 n. 1; 319 n. 1. The papyrological sources quoted by David are mostly dated to the Byzantine period and consequently do not cast any light on the situation existing in the fourth or the beginnings of the fifth century. The author cited it merely in order to demonstrate that the difference between a dictated testament and a handwritten one was mentioned in the sources. David himself recognises this fact (318-319): 'Sollen wir uns für eine dieser beiden Auslegungen entscheiden (scil., civil or praetorian testament as handwritten or dictated testament), so werden wir kein Gewicht darauf legen können, daß die uns erhaltenen Testamente aus byzantinischer Zeit, sowohl diejenigen aus Ägypten wie diejenigen aus dem West des Reiches, fast durchgängig einen Vermerkt darüber erhalten ob das Testament diktiert oder eigenhändig niedergeschrieben worden ist.' The evidence is, as stated above, misleading as well as scarcely significant, but on the other hand it is obvious that the mention of the fact that a testament (and even documents in which this fact was irrelevant, such as in donations or sales) was handwritten or dictated was present in many examples. As for the eastern sample, David quotes — among others — the already mentioned *FIRA* III 52 (=*SPP* I p 6-7,1) dated at the end of 5th century and the oldest example: dictated and with seven witnesses ἥνπερ ἐν Ἑλληνικο[ῖς]/[ῥήμασι ὑπηγόρευσα]. The also already quoted *P. Oxy.* XVI 1901 (6th century) could be a reason to discard D'Ors' hypothesis, since it is clearly a dictated will but with seven witnesses. Only the late date could play down this objection. The rest of the eastern evidence is clearly dated after *Nov. Theod.* 16, apart from Spangenberg, *Tabulae* (quoted n. 58) 71 (=*P. Gen.* XXXXVIII 389-396), the famous testament of Saint Gregory of Nazianzus (AD 381) again dictated and with seven witnesses, the first example of a will subscribed by the will maker, which demonstrates that this practice was known before *Nov. Theod.* 16. One interesting case is *P. Lond.* I 77 (*Mitt. Chr.* 319, totally complete at the end), dictated but with only five witnesses, which has been explained as a testament *rure conditum* (Kreller, *Erbrechtliche Untersuchungen* (quoted n. 22), p. 336; David, Über die Form (quoted n. 46), p. 319 n. 1). As for the western sample the results are still more disappointing: the oldest examples are not well preserved and the number of witnesses cannot be read (Spangenberg 80, 475 AD); It is the interesting will of Saint Aredius and his mother Pelagia (*Testamentum Aredii Abbatis Attanensis et Pelagiae matris eius*, 571 AD Spangenberg 112-113 = J. M. Pardessus et al., *Diplomata, chartae, epistolae, leges aliaque instrumenta*, Paris 1852, 180 *quem ego ipse Aredius manu propria scripsi*),. It is holographic with five witnesses but, because of its date, the meaning of those five witnesses is not enough significant enough to decide in favour of David's hypothesis (on the economic context of this will, see Ch. Wickham, *Framing the Early Middle Ages 400-800*, Oxford 2006, pp. 153–158). The text says: testamentum hoc manu mea subscripsi. As we can see, the holographic nature is limited to the subscription, but evidently this document is not a good evidence to discover how a will before Nov. Theod 16 was drawn up and to decide if the holographic was the civil one with five witnesses. The testaments included in the Ravenna documents do not offer anything new: some are difficult to read but all are dictated and have more that five witnesses (testamentum NN: Spangenberg 95-98 = *P. Marini* 110-111—testamentum Constantii Spangenberg 100-101 = *P. Marini* 112-113). It is possible on the other hand that a civil testament was understood in some period as a hand-written testament needing only five witnesses but the evidence is meagre and as David himself recognizes this phenomenon is not exclusively present in the testaments, but also in other kind of documents, such as donations. On this question, but without direct reference to this problem see Bagnall, Two Byzantine (quoted n. 10), p. 2–3. The published will by Bagnall in this article is *SB* XVIII 13740, apparently with five witnesses (ll. 21-31 four witnesses plus the person to helping in the writing of the will), and dated to the 6th or even 7th cent.

libripens (the 'holder of the scales') and the *familiae emptor* (the 'property purchaser') were no longer present. The aforementioned *interpretatio* to *CTh* 4.4.3 gives an important clue perhaps also overvalued by David, to affirm that a civil testament was holographic:

> Int. *CTh* 4.4.3
> *Si moriens, cum scribit aut dictat chartulam testamenti, praetermiserit forsitan vocabulum ponere, aut civilis, id est, quod quinque testium, aut praetorii iuris, quod septem testium erit subscriptione firmandum*

It is actually the *Interpretatio*, not the Theodosian Code itself that makes a contrast between the verbs *scribit* and *dictat*, which corresponds to the distinction between a handwritten testament (holographic) and a dictated one, not exactly what *Nov. Theod.* 16 had decreed. The former — holographic — could be understood as a civil testament and the latter as — dictated — a praetorian one. In any event, according to David's critics, the existence of a holographic will in which witnesses were not required (*Nov. Val.* 21.2.1: *si holographa manu testamenta condantur, testes necessarios non putamus*) does not entirely fit with this theory and has been the strongest argument against it.[73] It is also possible that this decision was only conceived as a particular solution for a particular case: Micce wanted to dictate her will, but she did not have witnesses to. So she declared her will to Pelagia, her heir, and entrusted the document to Cesarius her nephew.[74] In my opinion the text of *Nov. Val.* 21.2 pr. clearly conveys the emperor were dealing with an exceptional case.

Biondi for his part defended that the basis of this distinction between civil and praetorian will was that the civil testament was nothing more than an oral testament and conversely that the praetorian, was a written testament.[75] The main obstacle to accepting this interpretation is that there was an oral testament — called a *nuncupatio* — with seven witnesses according to *Nov. Theod.* 16.6 (= *CJ* 6.23.21.4), but the criticism could be the same as in the preceding case: this source is a poor argument to explain the constitutions included in the Theodosian Code that preserve the contrast.[76]

73. D'Ors, El *Testamentum* (quoted n. 48), p. 231. David (Über die Form (quoted n. 46), pp. 324–325) thinks that the holographic will in *Nov. Val.* 21.2 is an exceptional case handled by the imperial chancery (*Nov. Val.* 21.2 pr.)

74. *Nov. Val.* 21.2 pr. *Inlustrem feminam pelagiam cum Micce inlustris femina dictare vellet heredem, sed testium copiam non haberet, per holografam scripturam votum circa praedictam supremae prodidit voluntatis. Nam, quod solum potuit secretius licere morienti, indicem iudicii sui paginam Caesario viro spectabili tribuno et notario fratris sui filio secura commisit, quem natalium decus et propinquitatis religio fidem cogerent servare defunctae.* G. Bassanelli-Sommariva, La legge di Valenctiniano III del 7 novembre 426, *Labeo* 29, 1983, pp. 280–313: this decision must be understood in the framework of a judicial case heard in a *cognitio*. On the difficult problem of the relationship between the particular pronouncement and its normative general value, see M. Bianchini, 'Orientamenti di politica normative nelle duae partes imperii allíndomani della codificazione teodosiana', *Atti dell'Accademia Romanistica Costantiniana* 4, 1981, pp. 283–304, esp. 297–298. Bianchini believes that this particular pronouncement had no general value. Recently, see Humfress, Cracking the Codex (quoted n. 31), pp. 247–248.

75. B. Biondi, *Successione testamentaria-Donazione*, Milan², 1955, p. 53; Amelotti, Testamenti (quoted n. 10), p. 213, n. 7: The oral will does not disappear, even in Byzantine cases such as *P. Oxy.* I 131, dated to the 5th or 6th century, a petition to an unnamed official on the division of an estate. The will had been made by word of mouth.

76. D'Ors, El *Testamentum* (quoted n. 48), p. 231.

Nov. Theod. 16.6 (= *CJ* 6.23.21.4)

Per nuncupationem quoque, hoc est sine scriptura, testamenta non alias valere sancimus, nisi septem testes, ut supra dictum est, simul uno eodemque tempore collecti testatoris voluntatem ut testamentum sine scriptura facientis audierint, non ut suum, ut adsolet fieri, narrantis arbitrium, hoc est ut manifeste testari se sub isdem testibus sine scriptura eo ipso tempore dicat, non futurum suae voluntatis promittat arbitrium.

Again however, D'Ors criticism overlooks the fact that *Nov. Theod.* 16 is a new regulation that could have modified some previous requirements. On the other hand, it is plausible that since the context of *Nov. Theod.* 16 is the praetorian testament, its regulation does not serve to indicate the meaning of the contrast between the civil and praetorian wills, in the sense of what this terminology could have meant before the enactment of this constitution.

Max Kaser suggested an interesting solution that he unfortunately did not develop in full: he thought that the contrast between five and seven witnesses and the equivalent contrast between civil and praetorian was nothing but an expression to complete a legal form ('Formularpraxis').[77] This contrast is compatible with the aforesaid apparent survival of the categories of the vanished classical system, such as the contrast between *hereditas* and *bonorum possessio*. In our opinion the difference — totally empty of actual meaning — could have arisen from the collapse of the libral testament, and specifically from the confusing new forms used to draw up a will. In other words, the problem originally arose from what Kaser called the 'Formularpraxis.'

We have emphasized the irregular presence of the *mancipatio* clause after AD 235 in the Egyptian documentation but also its presence in later dated documents, in which it played a misleading role. This is obviously a symptom of confusion.[78] The *Mancipatio* was a requirement either explicitly abolished or in fact diminished by Constantine I. It is likely that Constantine's decision (whether direct or indirect) simply accepted reality since probably *mancipatio* had simply disappeared through disuse. In this confusion petitioners looked for some certainty. I must insist on that the merely possible abrogation of the *mancipatio* by Constantine (we have briefly dealt with this subject) is only a possibility, according to our obscure sources.[79] On the other hand we must bear in mind that the evidence in Book IV

77. M. Kaser, *Das römische Privatrecht* II (quoted n. 30), p. 479.

78. That is confusion in exactly the same sense as in *P.Cairo Masp.* II 67151 = *FIRA* III 66 (570 AD) where we can read (l.44) the term πολιτικοπραιτωρίαν οὖσαν which alludes to the validity of the will *iure civili et praetorio*, but it is mentioned just in case there is a problem to compensate for whatever differences there may have been between both kinds of will, see Kreller, *Erbrechtliche Untersuchungen* (quoted n. 22), p. 334. In the western empire precisely in *P.Marini* 74 (*P.Ital.* I, 4-5 = *ChLa* XVII, 653) we can read the so called '*clausula codicillaris*' according to the following version *quod si quo casu iure civili aut praetorio hoc testamentum manu valere non potuerit, etiam tamquam ab intestato vice codicillorum mecum in perpetuum valeat*, see J. O. Tjäder, *Die nichtliterarischen lateinischen Papyri Italiens aus der Zeit 445-100* I, Lund 1955, pp. 4–5.

79. We could put forward at the same time a tempting hypothesis that if Constantine had abrogated mancipation this decision would correspond with the first mention of the two different numbers of witnesses by this emperor in *CTh* 4.4.3, which may have something to do with the vanished *mancipatio* and the consequent confusion of the will makers who looked to create some certainty in a context in which the old formalities have practically disappeared and in which only witnesses became relevant to give evidence of the last will of the deceased. At the same time it could also be argued that Constantine simply coped with this difficulty which had been normal since at least the 3rd century AD, mainly as a consequence of the dissolution of the libral testament.

of the Theodosian Code is also subject to limitations, which is why we cannot ascertain the actual scope of the problem of the five or seven witnesses in its original context. As recent scholarship on the Theodosian Code has established,[80] behind the general pronouncement of one imperial constitution there is always with some degree of probability an individual problem, a problem of legal certainty in this case. Only in this context of legal uncertainty was the emperor, and the jurists who worked for him, able to shape a new law of succession and to construct new kinds of testament out of the ruin of the classical libral one.

The resulting theories of the abovementioned scholars were focused on discovering the actual meaning of a civil or praetorian will in the fourth century AD and they laboured to extract a coherent development from the existing legal texts. The problem, however, and I must insist on this idea, is that we are not dealing with a systematic Code, but rather with some fragments from a Code that itself had never been conceived as a systematic body. Our approach tries to take this setting into account and also aims to distinguish among different periods — the turning point being AD 439, the date of the enactment of *Nov. Theod.* 16 — and tries to emphasize that there was no unique answer to the problem of the number of witnesses for every case and for every period. We have pointed out, for example, that the solution given in *Nov. Theod.* 16.6 is not a good reason to discard a theory about the texts included in the Theodosian Code.

1) The distinction of the testaments according to the contrast civil (five witnesses) and praetorian (seven witnesses) corresponds more to practice and its disorientation than to imperial legislation. This differentiation is typical of Roman vulgar law in what we have called 'its narrow sense,' since according to the available sources this confusion arose from practice and was never directly tackled, much less developed by imperial constitutions.

2) In *CTh* 4.4.1 Constantine responds to a case in which the problem of the two kinds of testaments is not his main concern: rather the decision imposes on the codicil the same requirements as for the testament. On the other hand it implies that at least from the point of view of practice there was some difference between both kinds of testaments but probably this difference or contrast was of little significance. The emperor just accepted the framework in which the petition to him has been drawn up and showed little interest in explaining such a distinction.

3) Probably in one constitution — today lost or perhaps *CJ* 6.23.15 pr. itself — Constantine downplayed the importance of the *mancipatio*, but did not necessarily formally abrogate it as a requirement. In this context — or perhaps before Constantine's reign, since *mancipatio* was hardly ever performed — some formularies probably emerged in which the roles of the *libripens* and the *familiae emptor* had disappeared. Such formularies thereby created confusion for the heirs and uncertainty for the will makers, who had two different formularies whose only apparent difference was their historical origin. Likely the initial difference between the praetorian and the civil will was only a consequence of this confusion and had no actual legal basis and, in this period there

80. see e.g. HONORÉ, *Emperors and Lawyers* (quoted n. 6), pp. 104–107; *Law in the Crisis*, 12-33; MATTHEWS, *Laying Down the Law* (quoted n. 33), pp. 85–98; HUMFRESS, Cracking the Codex (quoted n. 31), pp. 251–254.

was in fact no coherent theory about it. The emperor just coped with this problem but did not give a general answer to the question (itself, at least in our sources not directly stated) of the basis of this distinction. Probably the emperor tried to ignore the confusions of the practice, which were difficult to reduce to a unified order. The new reinforcing role played by witnesses made witnesses the criterion of choice by which both kinds of testaments could be distinguished.

4) In my opinion *CTh*.4.4.3, enacted by Arcadius and Honorius in AD 396 or perhaps in 402, could be interpreted as Ferrari dalle Spade did: a superfluous number of witnesses does not invalidate the will as long as the number of five witnesses had been respected. That confirms that the distinction, which could be important in the popular perception of practice, was of little importance to the imperial chancery. In fact *Nov. Val.* 21.1 pr. refers to this pronouncement in a context in which formalism is diminished. Where the order of the Theodosian Code was concerned, Book IV dealt with the praetorian will, which required seven witnesses. From this fact we can deduce that the distinction was considered as a trivial problem in this period. The imperial answer is once more not intended as a theoretical one conceived to explicate the grounds of this distinction or to express the framework in which the legislator was working. And it is plausible that there were different interpretations in practice. *CTh* 4.4.3 only grants the *favor testamenti* in a controversial case by downplaying the importance of such a distinction, while, on the other hand admitting its existence. It is obvious that we are dealing with an alternative interpretation to *CTh* 4.4.1 that tried to ignore the foundation of the discussion. This imperial interpretation reduces the importance of the contrast between seven and five witnesses as long as at least the number of five is preserved.

5) *CTh* 4.4.7.2 is a pronouncement of Theodosius II, enacted in AD 424, on both kinds of testament that does not draw any practical distinction between civil and praetorian wills: both as well as the codicils ought to be completed within the same day. Once again it is plain that the distinction in types of wills has no great consequences in practice but was still in force. In accordance with the reinforced role played by the witnesses in the new forms of testament this requirement must have meant to stress their importance in the making of a will.

6) The Theodosian Novel 16 (partially included in *CJ* 6.23.21), issued in AD 439 is a new regulation of testaments with general scope, although according to the *Interpretatio* it focused on the praetorian one. The contrast between a will with seven or five witnesses is not mentioned and considering the general scope of this new regulation we cannot dismiss the possibility that this difference could be considered as abrogated. Although up to that time the difference between both kinds of testament had probably been only a matter of formularies, the text of *Nov. Theod.* 16 distinguishes between the testament dictated before witnesses (*testibus praesentibus testator suum testamentum dixerit*) and the testament only signed by the testator before them. Such a distinction was significantly drawn by the text of *Interpretatio* to the abovementioned constitutions included in the Theodosian Code. This demonstrates that the authors of the *Interpretatio* took into account this context — that created by *Nov. Theod.* 16 — and not only the context of the Theodosian Code.

7) On the other hand, *Nov. Theod.* 16 established a kind of testament with the presence of seven witnesses and their subscription, including that of the testator (*ipse coram testibus sua manu in reliqua parte subscripserit*), which implies some small change in this matter. *Lex Rom. Burg.* 45.2, which derives from Nov. Theod 16 does not include this new requirement (i.e. the subscription of the will-maker), but it does not necessarily mean that its regulation was based on pre-Theodosian law and not just on a simplification or distorted interpretation of *Nov. Theod.* 16.

8) From the fact that *Lex Rom. Burg.* 45.2 does not include the requirement of the subscription of the testator D'Ors deduced that this law might have preserved some elements of the pre-Theodosian regulation. This theory could offer a basis for the distinction between civil or praetorian will by understanding the former as a dictated testament and the latter as a merely subscribed one. Nevertheless we must affirm that this sound hypothesis has not support in the sources. In other words we cannot be certain whether this solution of the Burgundian law could be dated before Theodosius II or rather if it was merely an interpretation ventured by this statute or indeed simply a reflection of the practice of some parts of the empire. D'Ors deduces that the presence of witnesses could be typical of civil wills while in the case of praetorian wills the witnesses were not present at the moment of actually drawing up the will. The name of 'civil will' would be for the testament drawn up in the presence of witnesses. Of course we cannot rule out the possibility that the distinction was between a testament in which only five witnesses needed to be present and a testament in which seven witnesses only signed and sealed a drawn up text, but the evidence is in the best of cases slight, especially when we admit — as D'Ors did — that *Nov. Theod.* 16 was devoted chiefly to the praetorian will. In this context the alleged contrast between civil testament (testament dictated in the presence of witnesses) and praetorian testament (that subscribed in the presence of witnesses) makes in my opinion no sense at all.

9) Nov. Theod 16 in fact simply says *in omnibus autem testamentis quae vel absentibus vel praesentibus* with no difference drawn on the basis of the number of witnesses or on which kind of role those witnesses played in the testament. As stated above, the actual distinction between a dictated will and a handwritten one is made only by the *interpretatio*, not exactly by the constitutions included in the Theodosian Code. This could make the reading of the laws enacted before *Nov. Theod.* 16 along the lines suggested by this constitution — as reflecting a difference between written and dictated — a little suspect. The treatment of witnesses in the period before AD 439 is a mystery that perhaps did not always find the same solution in practice, since the material we have preserved is limited and the Burgundian law cannot offer a clue to how this distinction was treated in other areas. The ruin of the libral testament and the new formularies probably did not have the same impact on all of the subjects of the empire. Apparently imperial legislation did not attempt a general response to this problem of confusion before AD 439, or if it did, that response is not preserved. The surviving interventions of the emperors before this year respond only to particular cases and do not state the basis of the difference between the types of will, probably because this difference was only a residual formal requirement that had lost its actual meaning.

10) Reading the relevant constitutions of the Theodosian Code in light of *Nov. Theod.* 16 and the meagre documentary evidence — and all according to the later *interpretatio* — is the basis of David's theory and in some ways also of D'Ors. There is not enough of a basis for this hypothesis — that the foundation of the contrast between the civil and praetorian testament corresponded to a contrast between the handwritten testament and the dictated testament — but on the other hand it cannot be totally discarded. It is possible that the civil will had been understood by some practitioners as an holographic will (probably in the east) but the mention of these facts in the documentation is not limited to wills, as David recognizes, and the main proofs to support such a hypothesis (both the documentary evidence and the *interpretatio*) significantly are dated after the redaction of the Theodosian Code. On the other hand, Biondi's hypothesis — that a civil will was interpreted as an oral one — cannot totally be discarded at least according to the evidence. The only basis to reject such a theory is *Nov. Theod.* 16.4 and we have insisted on the limits of this source. We have no foundation, however in its favour.

To conclude, the testament of five or seven witnesses was nothing but the consequence of seeking in practice new forms to give certainty to the procedure of drawing up a will. Its origin is the contrast between *testamentum civile* and *testamentum praetorium*, a contrast that has no actual roots in classical Roman law. This development occurred in a context in which the old differences between civil and praetorian succession had definitively vanished with the result that the difference between the number of witnesses was based only on two different formularies. The imperial chancery probably encountered this problem, a mere consequence of the dissolution of the libral or mancipatory will, but had not developed any established theory about it, probably because practice was not uniform at all. Only under Theodosian II can we find an attempt with some internal coherence to regulate the new forms of testament but the solution that he gave to this problem entailed a new regulation based on the contrast between a dictated testament before witnesses and a will merely subscribed in their presence. This outline has nothing to do with a handwritten or dictated testament as the *Interpretatio* seems misleadingly to convey. The documentary evidence is also misleading, since no clear link between a handwritten testament — conceived as a civil testament — has been be discovered.

A solution that connects the testament dictated before witnesses (*Nov. Theod.* 16.4) to a civil testament could only be hypothesised through the evidence given in the Burgundian law, and only provided that this solution actually came from this period and not from a subsequent interpretation, what is difficult to demonstrate. The main difficulties for such a deduction are that the mention of *Nov. Theod.* 16 in the text of the Burgundian law does not exactly match its content as otherwise known and that there is no actual evidence of surviving of pre-Theodosian law elements in the *lex Romana Burgundionum*. The survival of testaments with five and seven witnesses does not prove by itself that behind them there was a clear concept, which dictated a difference between them.

PARTITIVE INHERITANCE IN PRINCIPLE AND IN PRACTICE IN ELEVENTH-CENTURY BYZANTIUM

James Howard-Johnston

The *Peira*, which is preserved in a compendium of Byzantine legal texts written in the first half of the fifteenth century, runs to 300 pages in the critical edition by C. E. Zachariä von Lingenthal, published in 1856.[1] It has come in for severe criticism, above all from the German legal historian, Dieter Simon. The reputation of the great high court judge, Eustathios Romaios, whose opinions and decisions are collected in the *Peira*, was badly damaged. He was portrayed as a wayward judge who culled whatever he needed to back his own judgement from the transmitted corpus of Roman law, rather than basing it on a full and careful analysis of the law.[2]

The text consists almost entirely of legal material. Virtually nothing has been preserved of the rhetoric customary in the courtroom. The legal material comprises opinions of Eustathius together with arguments for and against, plus 1) excerpts from the authoritative compendium of Byzantine law, the *Basilica* produced in the reigns of Basil I and Leo VI, and 2) — this is what makes the *Peira* a text to be treasured — summaries of cases which came before the high court. Many of the debates, which culminated in decisions in favour of Eustathios' position, took place during court hearings, but others were moots, disputations about imaginary cases and theoretical issues, involving senior members of the judiciary. Between them they establish contemporary Byzantine case law, part practical, part theoretical. The practical component takes up approximately one third of the text. It consists of some 200-300 of the formal legal opinions (*hypomnemata*) on which judgements (*semeiomata* or *semeioseis*) were based.[3]

The editor, who was devoted to Eustathios, seems often to have been in his company. He puts questions which the great judge answers. He carries out research.[4] He gives good summaries of the memoranda expounding Eustathios' legal opinions, whatever the degree

1. C. E. Zachariä von Lingenthal, *Jus Graeco-Romanum*, I *Practica ex actis Eustathii Romani*, Leipzig 1856.
2. D. Simon, *Rechtsfindung am byzantinischen Reichsgericht*, Frankfurt 1973.
3. N. Oikonomides, The 'Peira' of Eustathios Romaios: An Abortive Attempt to Innovate in Byzantine Law, *Fontes Minores* 7, 1986, p. 177, repr. in N. Oikonomides, *Byzantium from the Ninth Century to the Fourth Crusade*, Aldershot 1992, no. XII. The figure given for *hypomnemata* is Ludwig Burgmann's.
4. *Peira*, 6.15-16, 14.20, 17.14 *etc.* (questions), 15.10 (research).

Inheritance, Law and Religions in the Ancient and Mediaeval Worlds, ed. by B. Caseau and S. R. Huebner (Centre de recherche d'Histoire et Civilisation de Byzance, Monographies 45), Paris 2014.

of condensation sought. He conveys the substance of the opinion, while excising extraneous details. To the summaries of *hypomnemata* he normally appends supporting legal material in the form of excerpts from the *Basilica*. This excerpted material, which provides the solid foundations of the judge's arguments, may well have been filed together with the relevant *hypomnemata*. He also takes care to excise many personal names, partly perhaps to avoid embarrassing or antagonising powerful families but usually, it may be conjectured, because the individuals in question were not well known and no purpose would have been served by giving names when a simple 'someone' (*tis*) could be written.

The *Peira* is divided into 75 chapters (*titloi*), each devoted to a specific legal topic. There is no obvious principle guiding the order of chapters, which may therefore reflect in part the order in which the issues came up in cases heard by Eustathios. Family law is treated in seventeen chapters (nos. 1, 12, 14, 16-17, 24-5, 41, 43, 48-9, 54, 62, 65-6, 67, 71).

Eustathius may well have belonged to a family of lawyers. He mentioned, in an aside to his assistant, the anonymous editor, that his great-grandfather had been a judge and had appeared before the imperial court (30.76). He started practising law in the reign of Basil II (an occasion when he appeared before him is recalled [64.1]) and reached the apogee of his career in the reign of Romanos III Argyros (1028-1034), when he rose swiftly to become Chief Justice, Drungar of the Watch. At the same time he was raised in rank, first to Vestes, then, after his appointment as Chief Justice, to Magistros. He probably retired or was retired soon after the death of Romanos in April. The *Peira* was then put together by his admirer, it seems most likely in the later 1030s.[5]

The autocratic power of the *paterfamilias*, most evident in death, in his freedom to leave his estate to whomsoever he chose, was curbed by the Lex Falcidia issued in 40 B.C. This established, for the first time in Roman law, the right of children, male and female, to a share of their father's estate. This reserved portion amounted to one quarter of the estate, to be divided equally between the children. It remained possible for the *paterfamilias* to disinherit a child, but this involved the drawing up of a special deed of *exheredatio*, in which the targeted child was named or otherwise clearly identified.[6] The law of inheritance remained substantially the same through the heyday of the Roman empire and into late antiquity, until Justinian turned his attention to the west and to legal reform, after the failure of his first policy initiative in the east (527-531). Apart from the perennial need to adapt laws to changing circumstances, the reformers' prime concern was to meld law and Christian morality together. This was as evident in the sphere of family law as in any other.[7]

Justinian — or rather his team of legal advisers, if, as I incline to think, Justinian was a relatively ill-educated but charismatic military man — issued five major pieces of new legislation about the legal portion reserved for children, the Falcidium. Novel 1, issued in 535, was concerned with the execution of wills: the heir was responsible for having an

5. Oikonomides, Eustathios Romaios (quoted n. 3), pp. 171–176; R.-J. Lilie, C. Ludwig, T. Pratsch, B. Zielke *et al.*, *Prosopographie der mittelbyzantinischen Zeit, Zweite Abteilung (867-1025)*, vol. 2, Berlin 2013, pp. 294–298 (Eustathios 21870).

6. J. A. Crook, 'The Development of Roman Private Law', in J. A. Crook, A. Lintott & E. Rawson (eds.), *Cambridge Ancient History*, vol. 9, Cambridge 1994, pp. 538–540.

7. H. F. Jolowicz and B. Nicholas, *Historical Introduction to the Study of Roman Law* (3rd ed.), Cambridge 1972, pp. 506–509.

inventory made of the estate, for reserving the Falcidium, for paying off debts owed by the estate and for distributing legacies, within a year of the notification of the will to the court.[8] The main reforming piece of legislation, novel 18, was issued in 536. This raised the reserved portion of an estate from one quarter to one third, if the testator had up to four children, and to a half, if he had more than four. In cases where a man died intestate and without legitimate issue, children by a concubine were entitled to one sixth of the estate — this did not apply if the deceased had been a philanderer, with many such liaisons.[9] Moral concerns were being brought to bear on questions of inheritance, in this last provision. A concern to strengthen the bonds of the nuclear family probably also underlay the significant increase in the size of the reserved portion, which entailed a further restriction on the freedom of the *paterfamilias*. In this the government may have been responding to a general shift in public opinion, or hoping to strengthen its standing in society at large. What is plain, though, is that it was not part of a conscious policy of stabilising the social order, like that being pursued in the 530s by Justinian's Sasanian rival, Khusro I Anushirwan.[10] Justinian explicitly broke with the traditional bias of Roman law in favour of those of higher social status (the *honestiores*), when he annulled a recent law reserving three quarters of estates for children of *curialis* status.[11]

Novel 18 also introduced rules to ensure that children benefitted forthwith from their entitlement to their share of the Falcidium — so there was no question of a widow's continuing to enjoy the usufruct of the reserved portion of an estate. For the avoidance of confusion and potential dissension, it was laid down that the allocation of shares of the estate among the testator's offspring should be recorded in writing in a duly witnessed deed, either drawn up during his lifetime in the presence of all his children (who then signed it) or in his will.[12] Other practical matters were dealt with in the following two novels, nos. 66 of 538 and 92 of 539: the date when the new level of the Falcidium came into force (there had been confusion about this in 536), the continuing validity of wills drawn up before the new date of enforcement, and the closing of a loophole which allowed a father to channel a disproportionately large part of his estate to a favourite child or children through lifetime gifts.[13] Finally, three years later, in 542, at a time when plague was threatening to tear apart the social fabric of the empire, the traditional rules for the formal disinheritance of named children were tightened in novel 115.3, removing from the testator the right to disinherit a child without good reason. Fourteen grounds for disinheritance were itemised, including physical and mental abuse, slander, attempted murder, sex with a step-mother or a father's mistress, failure to come to a parent's help in need and failure to attend Orthodox church services.[14]

8. *Nov.*, 1, in R. Schöll and G. Kroll (eds.), *Corpus Iuris Civilis. Volumen Tertium. Novellae*, Berlin 1954, pp. 1–10.

9. *Nov.*, 18.1 & 5 in Schöll and Kroll, *Corpus Iuris Civilis* (quoted n. 8), pp. 128–129, 130–132.

10. A. Christensen, *L'Iran sous les Sassanides*, Copenhagen 1944, pp. 363–366; Z. Rubin, The Reforms of Khusro Anūshirwān, in A. Cameron (ed.), *The Byzantine and Early Islamic Near East III. States, Resources and Armies*, Princeton 1995, pp. 227–297.

11. *Nov.*, 18.2, in Schöll and Kroll, *Corpus Iuris Civilis* (quoted n. 8), p. 129.

12. *Nov.*, 18.3 & 7, in Schöll and Kroll, *Corpus Iuris Civilis* (quoted n. 8), pp. 129–130, 133–134.

13. *Nov.*, 66 & 92, in Schöll and Kroll, *Corpus Iuris Civilis* (quoted n. 8), pp. 340–343, 457–458.

14. *Nov.*, 115.3, in Schöll and Kroll, *Corpus Iuris Civilis* (quoted n. 8), pp. 536–544.

The Justinianic system of inheritance was picked up in the *Ecloga*, issued by Leo III at the end of his reign in 741.[15] This very basic manual of law, short and intelligible (being written in Greek unlike the great mass of inherited law codified under Justinian), produced for the guidance of provincial courts, took account of changed circumstances. Thus the number of witnesses required for a valid will (in theory seven) was reduced to five or three, if, as might be the case in specific localities, it was hard to find more. As regards the substance of a will, local magistrates (*akroatai*) were given discretion to determine whether the omission of a child from a will was or was not justified, on the basis of evidence about the nature of the offense given by the child.[16] The bonds of the family had probably grown stronger in an age of declining population, increasing empoverishment and unceasing warfare.

A hundred and fifty years later, the bare bones of the Roman law of inheritance were once more fleshed out with the full body of law codified and updated by Justinian, which was transmitted in the form of Greek translations, summaries commentaries by the *antecessores* (law professors of the sixth and early seventh century). This variegated material was collected and re-arranged in sixty thematically distinct books. It was an imperial project, overseen by Leo VI before and after his accession in 886, and the finished work was designated the *Basilica* after Basil I, Leo's father.[17] Leo completed this legal work with his Novels, which tidied up the law, purging it of extraneous, archaic rules. More important was a series of novels issued in the tenth century to counter the emergence of a powerful group of secular postholders and ex-postholders as well as churchmen and abbots who were building up their landholdings at the expense of peasant villagers. This new legislation imposed further restrictions on the freedom of the property-owner to bequeath the unreserved portion of his estate, where it took the form of land or other fixed property. No person of power might inherit from a so-called poor person (*i.e.* someone who was not and had not been a soldier, state official, bishop or abbot) — a particular instance of a general ban on alienation of any sort, by sale or gift, in life or after death, to the 'powerful' by such persons.[18]

This then was the body of law on which the courts were required to base their judgements at the time when Eustathios embarked on his legal career. The nuclear family was plainly the prime unit of society. It was tightly bound together by the Falcidium and the prohibition of disinheritance in normal circumstances, when there was no breakdown of relations within the family. The threat of predatory magnates and other persons of influence, with connections to the local apparatus of government, had probably further strengthened familial ties. The inheritance rights which underpinned them, it should be stressed, were not confined to the male issue of testators. Daughters enjoyed equal rights to the Falcidium, which normally came in the form of their dowry — *i.e.* a donation of property and other assets from father to daughter made in the former's lifetime. This entailed the steady alienation of individual families' property generation after generation and a compensating accumulation over time

15. L. BURGMANN (ed. & trans.), *Ecloga: Das Gesetzbuch Leons III. und Konstantinos' V.*, Frankfurt 1983.

16. *Ecloga* (quoted n. 15) 5.4-5, pp. 190–191.

17. P. E. PIELER, Rechtsliteratur, in H. HUNGER (ed.), *Die hochsprachliche profane Literatur der Byzantiner*, vol. 2, Munich 1978, pp. 343–480.

18. N. SVORONOS, *Les novelles des empereurs macédoniens concernant la terre et les stratiotes*, Athens 1994; E. MCGEER, *The Land Legislation of the Macedonian Emperors*, Toronto 2000.

of pieces of property belonging to other families acquired in the form of dowries. This intermingling of properties is likely to have led to increasing solidarity at the level of village society and, to a lesser extent, at that of provincial notables with access to power.

Eustathios was thoroughly *au fait* with the Roman law of inheritance and rigorous in applying it. In this legal sphere, the criticisms of Simon can be rebutted without hesitation. Eustathios allowed for certain demands on the testator's estate to be met before its valuation for the purpose of calculating the Falcidium. Three types of expenditure were accepted as justified deductions (41.1, 8, 22), as in the Justinianic corpus — debts incurred by the testator in his lifetime, funeral expenses and the cost of the manumission of slaves laid down in his will (again an act of his which took effect posthumously).[19] The Falcidium continued to be extracted at the higher, Justinianic level. The legal portion of an individual child, as a share of the whole estate, was correctly specified for families with one to four or more than four children (41.3, 4, 22). In cases where legacies reduced the residue available for the Falcidium below the legal minimum, the missing sum was to be clawed back from heirs and legatees. How this should be done was shown by an illustrative example: an estate worth twenty pounds is bequeathed to four of the testator's five children (receiving three, four, five and six pounds respectively) and to other legatees (two pounds in total); the omitted child is entitled to two pounds (a fifth of a half of the estate), made up by taking a sixth of the bequests surplus to his/her siblings' legal portions as of the two pounds left to other legatees (41.3).[20]

There was no discrimination against daughters, presumably on the Justinianic ground that God had made women as necessary as men for procreation (*Nov.*, 18.4).[21] The legal minimum for a dowry was set at the Falcidium (41.12). Dowries were recorded and duly witnessed in marriage deeds, which could not be overturned in a will (45.11). As long as they were at or above the Falcidium, they would not be drawn into litigation about a will (nor would they cause the sort of confusion feared by the Justinianic reformers, when they outlawed piecemeal lifetime distribution of legal portions [*Nov.*, 18.7]). It was only in the case of a spendthrift father (probably a real case, given the unrounded figures quoted), who wasted his property after giving a dowry of two pounds, twelve nomismata to a daughter, and left an estate worth twelve nomismata less than his wife's dowry, that the generous provision for the daughter was reduced to make up the missing twelve nomismata from her mother's dowry as well as the *theoretron*, the balance then being subject to the claw-back mechanism to ensure an equitable distribution of a much reduced Falcidium. Only presents from the mother were exempt (24.4).[22]

Eustathios brought a clear, analytic intelligence to bear on inheritance law, and refined it in several respects. With respect to what should be deducted from the estate or added to it before the Falcidium was calculated, he ruled that none of the cost of commemorative rites taking place *after* the testator's funeral, on the third, ninth and fortieth days, should fall on

19. A 5% tax (*vicesima manumissionum*) was payable on the price of each slave freed, a price which varied according to the sex, age and qualifications of the slave — see the tariff at *Peira*, 28.21.

20. Two other complex calculations are made for cases of intestacy without direct issue (48.10 & 11).

21. J.-C. Cheynet, Aristocratie et héritage (xie-xiiie siècle), in J. Beaucamp & G. Dagron (eds.), *La transmission du patrimoine: Byzance et l'aire méditerranéenne*, Paris 1998, pp. 63–67.

22. The *theoretron*, worth one twelfth of the dowry, was presented by the husband to the wife on marriage (*Peira*, 25.18).

the Falcidium (41.10). On the other hand, he ruled that any increase in the value of an estate which occurred between the writing of a will and the testator's death should be included in the estate before the calculation was made. Otherwise new wills would have to be made with every increase or decrease in an individual's wealth (14.4). He was staunch in upholding the Justinianic prohibition on the giving of excessively large presents to favourite children. In the case of a father who might give away half his wealth (amounting to thirty pounds) to two sons in his lifetime, and would leave the other two in his will their shares of the Falcidium (one twelfth each of the remaining thirty pounds, two and a half pounds), he ruled that the thirty pounds previously given away should be included in the calculation of the Falcidium, thereby doubling individual shares of the Falcidium to five pounds (41.24).

Eustathios upheld the status of the Falcidium as a legal requirement, immune to the wishes of testators. It followed that an under-age son was entitled to receive his Falcidium forthwith on his mother's death. If she stipulated in her will that what she bequeathed him should be kept under seal (until he came of age), this could only apply to what was surplus to the Falcidium (41.5). Equally a child who predeceased his parents could not specify in advance the beneficiaries of his future Falcidium, since his entitlement to it lapsed at death and would automatically pass to his children, if he had any by then (41.7). On the other hand, Eustathios did nothing to restrict the freedom of individuals to dispose of the unreserved portions of their estates as they chose, thereby upholding the fundamental property rights of citizens. So he did not require a mother, who gave half her property to one child without encumbrances and the other half to her remaining children with encumbrances, to compensate the latter for the encumbrances, unless she had specified the value of the land and housing which she was giving them (54.8). This concern of his for individual testators' rights as well as the legal requirement to provide for close kin underlies his judgement in the specific cases which came up before him and which are summarised in the *Peira*. He was not immune to the pull of equity, but it was always subject to the law where the law was explicit and precise (51.3).

Let us then take a look at some of the cases which came up before Eustathios. We should remember, though, that it is a far from simple task to discern what was really going on from the often highly condensed summaries given in the *Peira*. For the summaries are skewed towards the key legal point at issue, leaving much to be inferred about the case argued in court, and even more about the social realities and personal interests behind the case. It is therefore all too easy to overlook legal niceties which are not highlighted and to go astray when compelled, by the elliptical character of a summary, to make inferences about a case and the principal considerations in the judge's mind.

1 & 2. Eustathios was strict in enforcing the *Lex Falcidia*, which, in cases where a son died without issue, allocated the reserved third of his estate to his parents in the first instance. In two cases, it was extracted from the estates of sons, who had evidently amassed some capital in the course of their careers. No names are given, nor any indication about the sources of the sons' earnings. We are just told that one of them justified his bequeathing of only small legacies to his parents, on the ground that he had never received anything from them (not a legally acceptable justification for *exheredatio*), and that the other simply divided his estate between charitable donations (for the sake of his soul) and legacies, saying nothing about his parents and leaving them nothing (14.9 & 10).

3. A third case where a testator was forced to yield up the Falcidium concerned a woman, who left most of her estate to her second husband, thereby depriving her grandson by the daughter (deceased) of her first marriage of all but a small inheritance. She had not behaved dishonestly or irresponsibly. Nothing had been concealed in the inventory of the first husband's assets, and she had lived frugally between marriages. So her grandson was entitled to his mother's Falcidium, which she had received as her dowry and which amounted to two pounds. In addition, he was entitled to the minimum legal portion of his father's estate, of which his grandmother had been *curator*. As a result he was awarded a Falcidium which amounted to one third of his grandmother's (whole) estate, after the usual deductions (41.27).[23]

4. A very different case was that of a distinguished foreign Patrician (the name is again withheld), who left the great majority of his estate to his second wife, and only a little to the daughter of his first marriage. Under Roman law, that daughter was as entitled as any son would have been to the legal portion of a third. The Patrician claimed the right to dispose of his assets according to his own ancestral law. The Magistros clearly attached some importance to this argument, but countered it with the observation that the Patrician had risen high in Byzantine service and had been well rewarded. He should therefore observe the Roman law of inheritance (14.16).

5. Different issues were raised by the suit brought by the daughter of the Magistros Gorgoploutos against the executors of her father's will. It was a complicated will. There was a debt (clearly substantial) to be repaid (probably after lengthy negotiations). Apart from the daughter's Falcidium and the debt, the estate was to be given out in legacies, bequests, *fideicommissa* and charitable spending for the benefit of Gorgoploutos' soul. The executors calculated the Falcidium and handed it over to the daughter, before tackling the rest of their business. They had done their best to estimate it correctly. In the event, they miscalculated, according to the daughter, who came to court demanding an additional sum. Presumably they had managed to reduce the creditors' claim on the estate below their initial estimate. The daughter's suit was rejected, the Magistros arguing that the executors had calculated the Falcidium fairly (evidently at an early stage in the year allowed for the execution of will after its notification to a court) and that the sort of exactitude demanded by the plaintiff would have impeded the efficient discharge by the executors of their obligations. The sum involved is likely to have been trivial, leading the Magistros to dismiss the daughter's case as vexatious, especially as she was in effect demanding money which would otherwise contribute to her father's salvation (16.11).

6. The Magistros' judgements clearly took account of the character of plaintiffs. Hence in another case he leaned decisively in the opposite direction, seeking to maximise the legal portion of the only son of a certain Hexamylitas. In his will Hexamylitas bequeathed the required third of his estate to his son and no more, leaving the remaining two thirds for the executors to spend on legacies and other things. The issue which came before the high court concerned the repayment of debts incurred by Hexamylitas, in particular whether the son's third should or should not bear its share of the cost. Many judges, we are told

23. *Cf.* B. Sirks, The Peira: Roman Law in Greek Setting, in *Studi in onore di Remo Martini*, vol. 3, Milan 2009, pp. 588–590.

(probably a large majority), were of the opinion that the law should be applied, hence that the son should receive a third of the estate *after* the repayment of the debt. The Magistros demurred, his sense of fairness perhaps roused by the father's meanness to his son. He came up with a rather sophistic argument, relying on the exact phrasing in the will: Hexamylitas had left his son a third of his estate *in a first clause*, and had then gone on, *in a second clause*, to give instructions to his executors about what to do with the other two thirds; the third should therefore be extracted before they began their work as executors (41.9).[24]

7. A similar concern to maximise the legal entitlement of a child can be seen in the Magistros' judgement in the case of a divorcée who had become a nun and sued the guarantor of her dowry for its return, her husband having fallen into poverty and being unable to do so himself. The Magistros ruled (1) that her young daughter was entitled to her Falcidium, namely eight pounds, fifty-two nomismata, a third of the dowry of twenty-six pounds, twelve nomismata, (2) that the Falcidium should take the form of liquid assets, and (3) that there should be a good rate of return on the capital while the girl was under age, her Falcidium being loaned out at the orphan's (high) rate of interest (41.11).[25]

8. In a case heard when Eustathios was Vestes, he again exercised discretion, *oikonomia*, in his application of the Roman law of inheritance. The Patrician David the Iberian left his estate to his son, with the stipulation that it should revert to his brothers if the son died without issue and intestate, as he did. The stipulation flouted the Lex Falcidia, and, when the case came to court, the Vestes ruled that the boy's mother should receive a third of the estate. Noting that the son was 20 years old when he died, he observed that he was legally competent to make a will about his whole estate (so that the Patrician David's stipulation lapsed and the whole estate should, strictly speaking, go to the boy's nearest ascendant, his mother). Nonetheless he allowed the uncles to keep two thirds of the estate, on the grounds that the young man was *ethnikos*, of foreign extraction (and therefore likely to have agreed with his father's stipulation) (54.6).

9. Eustathios made his mark as upholder of the Lex Falcidia at an early stage in his career, when he was still a plain judge (*dikastes*). An argument was put forward by some unspecified people (other judges? advocates? members of the deceased's family?) that the third (Falcidium) from the estate of a son who died in *patria potestate* should be spent on alms for the benefit of his soul. Eustathios rejected it out of hand, as it was neither sanctioned by law nor by long usage (54.10).

10. The paramount need to conserve the Falcidium was in the forefront of his mind, when he produced a judgement, which went against a literal reading of the will of one David Saronites. He had left his whole estate to his wife, stressing that she should have complete control over it and should be answerable to no-one for its management on behalf of their son, who was to inherit everything after her death. When the will was read out in court, many judges, as well as the Protoasecretis, were of the opinion that the crops and revenue of all the landholdings were at the widow's disposal during her lifetime and that she need give no account of her management of the estate beyond showing that she was conserving its capital

24. *Cf.* SIRKS, The Peira (quoted n. 23), pp. 584–585.
25. *Cf.* SIRKS, The Peira (quoted n. 23), pp. 586–587.

value and was not acting fraudulently. The Magistros disagreed, arguing that she should be accountable for her handling of the revenue as well as the principal (*i.e.* the landholdings) and that she should preserve crops (*i.e.* the income which they generated) for her son. She was not entitled to indulge in wanton extravagance or to profit for herself. It was only against specific errors of management, with respect to planting, ploughing, propagation of vines, tax payment, land purchase or wages, where no fraud was involved, that she was protected (43.8).

11. Finally, there was a case where the testator (not named), a widower with a single daughter, was taken, by the Magistros, to be flouting the tenth-century legislation banning the alienation of fixed property to persons or institutions of power. The testator had appointed the abbot of the Nea Kome monastery executor of his will and had left his daughter's (and deceased wife's) estate to the monastery. The Magistros overruled another leading judge, called Xeros, who had approved the will. He classified the abbot among the powerful (quite rightly), and the testator implicitly among the poor (presumably because he derived all his wealth from his wife and daughter). As such he was prohibited from leaving property of his own to the abbot, let alone that of an orphaned girl. In his judgement, the Magistros made her grandfather and grandmother responsible for its management (14.22).

These eleven cases of litigation over inheritance form a very small proportion of the cases summarised in the *Peira*. They are nonetheless representative in showing how Eustathios' concern for justice shaped all his judgements. He applied the law, taking due account of ever-varying circumstances, and strove to ensure that law and equity coincided or overlapped as much as possible. In normal circumstances, he simply enforced compliance with the Lex Falcidia on wills which flouted it, as in cases 1-4, 9 and 11 enumerated above. In others, if he felt one of the contending parties was the more deserving, he exploited whatever room there was for the exercise of judicial discretion, for *oikonomia*, so as to achieve what he judged to be the fairest outcome — maximising the Falcidium in cases 6, 7 and 10, limiting it when he attached weight to other considerations as in cases 5 (a grasping daughter) and 8 (primacy of paternal kin in Iberian law).

It is noticeable that no case of *exheredatio* features in the *Peira*. It is not as if the issues likely to arise in such case were simple, as if no such cases would be referred to the high court on appeal. There was plenty of room for argument as to whether the behaviour of a son or daughter constituted *acharistia* (ingratitude) of a level and type (falling under one of the fourteen headings listed by Justinian) which would justify disinheritance.[26] There does not seem to have been any significant loosening of the bonds of the family in the nearly three centuries which had passed since the issue of the *Ecloga*. Indeed it looks as if it was taken for granted at all levels of Byzantine society in the early eleventh century that property belonging to parents should be passed on to their children and should be equitably divided between them. There is no hint of primogeniture, taking the form, say, of a double share for the eldest son as in Roman Egypt.[27] The two cases where the Lex Falcidia was completely disregarded (nos. 1 and 2 above) involved sons and their parents rather than *vice versa*, while it was a grandmother's mistake and the pull of non-Roman inheritance law which reduced the Falcidium well below the legal level in cases 3 and 4.

26. *Nov.*, 115.3, in Schöll and Kroll, *Corpus Iuris Civilis* (quoted n. 8), pp. 536–544.
27. Sabine Huebner in this volume.

We may conclude tentatively that it had become customary for the great bulk of an estate to be handed on in equal shares to the children, in the form of dowries for daughters (which might have to be topped up in the will) and bequests for sons, with a relatively small portion left over for legacies outside the family and for alms for the soul of the deceased.[28] There is nothing surprising in this after nearly two and a half centuries of beleaguered existence, from the 630s to the 860s. All strata of society had had to contribute to the guerrilla war of defence. All suffered a significant decline in living standards. Orthodoxy finally secured a dominant position in the lives and imaginative world of Byzantines, adding moral lustre to the nuclear family. The *Peira* is one of several sources which provide evidence, direct and indirect, of a lasting reinforcement of social bonds from the upper echelons of the administration down to the level of the village (the latter recognised by the Crown as the basic unit of the state) and the families which constituted village society.[29]

Not that there was any ossification of the social order in tenth- and eleventh-century Byzantium. It was an era of success abroad, as army and navy projected Byzantine power further afield, into the Middle East and the central Mediterranean, and of increased confidence and growing population at home.[30] The strong links forged during the dark age struggle for survival between those who took the lead in the affairs of state at the centre and in the provinces (designated the 'powerful') and the population at large began to fray. There was more money around, in an age of sustained economic growth. Liquid assets and investments in urban property, commercial and residential, formed an increasingly significant part of the property portfolios of established aristocratic and rising bureaucratic families.[31] Economic growth as well as the new confidence led to more fluidity in the social order. The threat of the 'powerful' to the property of the 'poor', driven by the increasing prevalence of family interest over that of the wider political community, is very evident in the *Peira*. Eustathios was stalwart in upholding the old order, in curbing the expansion of larger landholdings at the expense of peasant villagers, but could not but take account of the changed economic circumstances of an age when wealth could be built up or lost more swiftly than in the past. He was well aware of the different levels of income generated by different sorts of assets (41.19), and ensured, in the case of under-age children, that their Falcidia were invested and generated income at the highest legal rate (that of orphans) until they came of age and could take charge of their affairs (41.11). He also regarded himself as justified in requiring someone with usufruct of an estate, however insistent the testator might on his managerial power free of accountability, to behave responsibly, not merely safeguarding the capital value but ploughing back the revenue. There was probably nothing fanciful about a scenario in which income was frittered away or fixed assets were run down by the individual granted usufruct (43.8).

In terms of horizontal social relations, within kin groups of similar status and with approximately the same amount of property, stability was programmed into the social order

28. Leo VI viewed such even-handed treatment of children as coming naturally to the parents who had borne them — P. Noailles & A. Dain (ed. & trans.), *Les novelles de Léon VI le Sage*, Paris 1944, pp. 72–77 (*Nov.*, 19).

29. M. Whittow, *The Making of Orthodox Byzantium, 600-1025*, London 1996, pp. 82–95, 134–193.

30. J. Howard-Johnston, Byzantium and Its Neighbours, in E. Jeffreys, J. Haldon & R. Cormack (eds.), *Oxford Handbook of Byzantine Studies*, Oxford 2008, pp. 948–954.

31. J.-C. Cheynet, Fortune et puissance de l'aristocratie (x^e^-xiie siècle), in V. Kravari, J. Lefort, C. Morrisson (eds.), *Hommes et richesses dans l'Empire byzantin*, II *VIIIe-XVe siècle*, Paris 1991, pp. 199–205; M. Kaplan, *Les hommes et la terre à Byzance du VIe au XIe siècle*, Paris 1992, pp. 359–573.

by Roman family law. As can be inferred from what is reported in the *Peira*, children inherited most of their parents' assets, which normally were divided equally between them. Lineage, grand or humble, was underpinned by property transfers down the generations from father to son. As important in its social consequences was the parity accorded to daughters. With each marriage, a daughter carried off to another family a share of her parents' assets as her dowry, the proportion of land probably increasing towards the base of the social order. With each passing generation the links between families created by daughters multiplied, and, if memories endured, developed into increasingly ramified networks of connections, themselves underpinned by property.

At the level of the village, with children keen to have shares of each type of fixed asset (garden, meadow, orchard, arable), the properties of individual families were mixed together by the outflow and inflow of dowries. The pattern of landholding in a village was that of a complex, ever-changing mosaic of parcels of land owned by different families, the average size of the parcel increasing or decreasing according to the population trend.[32] A strong sense of communal solidarity was forced willy nilly on the Byzantine village by partitive inheritance. Individual parcels could not be farmed without the co-operation of the owners of adjoining parcels. Far from being imposed from above by a tax system of collective fiscal responsibility, the cohesion of families within the village was probably an important factor in the development of a fiscal system which designated the village as its basic unit. Fiscal downreach to the village and, within the village, to individual families was one of the secrets of Byzantium's survival in its dark age.[33]

Village society was endowed with great natural resilience *vis à vis* the outside world by the solidarity produced by partitive inheritance in normal circumstances, *i.e.* if the population was reasonably stable and the pressure from without was not raised too high. Neither of these conditions obtained in the era of Byzantine revival, stretching from the late ninth to the middle of the eleventh century. The demographic trend was upwards. Economic growth was significant, to judge by the increase in the money supply in the middle of the eleventh century achieved by a deliberate, staged debasement of the gold coinage.[34] Social and moral responsibilities were increasingly disregarded by members and ex-members of the apparatus of government, who developed a voracious appetite for solid, durable assets in the form of land and were ready to use strong-arm tactics to get them.[35] At the same time the defences of village communities were being weakened, not simply because the military skills once widespread when the peasantry was called up to serve in the infantry were being lost in the interior of the empire, but also because villages were growing in size. Individual parcels of land were becoming smaller and less viable. Families, mainly those

32. W. Ashburner, The Farmer's Law, *Journal of Hellenic Studies* 30, 1910, pp. 85–108 and 32, 1912, pp. 68–95; I. P. Medvedev, *Византийский земледельческий закон*, Leningrad 1984.

33. N. Oikonomidès, *Fiscalité et exemption fiscale à Byzance* (*IXe-XIe s.*), Athens 1996, pp. 24–56. *Cf.* A. E. Laiou, The Byzantine Village (5th-14th century), in J. Lefort, C. Morrisson & J.-P. Sodini (eds.), *Les villages dans l'Empire byzantin* (*IVe-XVe siècle*), Paris 2005, pp. 46–47 and 51–52.

34. C. Morrisson, Byzantine Money: Its Production and Circulation, in A. E. Laiou (ed.) *Economic History of Byzantium* (DOS 39), vol. 3, Washington D.C. 2002, pp. 930–932. *Cf.* A. Harvey, *Economic Expansion in the Byzantine Empire 900-1200*, Cambridge 1989, pp. 47–67.

35. N. Svoronos (ed.), *Les novelles des empereurs macédoniens concernant la terre et les stratiotes*, Athens 1994, *Nov.* 2.62-71 & 3.50-69, trans. E. McGeer, *The Land Legislation of the Macedonian Emperors*, Toronto 2000, pp. 46, 48, 54–55.

which were better off, began to move out of the village and establish their own farmsteads in its territory, thus detracting from the sense of the village as a single community marked off from the world outside.[36]

The most effective response to the problems created by demographic growth would have been a shift to a system of primogeniture, most of a family's property being passed on to the oldest son. Landless younger brothers would then have found themselves in the position of younger sons in archaic Greece, with little option but to leave their home community and to seek their fortunes elsewhere. Their unmarried sisters too would have begun to slip away, to earn their living, if only as domestic servants, in towns and cities. It was the sort of process, sustained migration from country to town, from the interior to the coastlands, which might have given an extra boost to Byzantium's economic growth. The law of partitive inheritance, however, ruled this out. Sons and daughters were treated equally, irrespective of gender or age, and village society as a whole was rendered all too vulnerable to external predators.

If we turn our attention to the predators, the 'powerful', we can again see that partitive inheritance, equal division of property among sons together with the generally accepted right of daughters to a share of their parents' assets equal in value to the inheritances of their brothers, contributed significantly to a tightening of links within and between families. The chief influence on the changing social order at this higher level was that of time rather than demographic trend. As generation followed generation, from the first rooting of a nascent aristocracy in the countryside in the middle and late eighth century, estates grew in size but were increasingly broken up as sons, grandsons, great-grandsons ... each inherited their fair share of paternal lands. The intermingling of plots characteristic of the village was replicated on a grander scale at this higher social level. At the same time dowries, the chief form of conveyance of assets from parents to daughters, transferred land from family to family. The transfer was on a lesser scale than that between fathers and sons, because of a concern to keep land within the family (noted at 17.8). But it was seldom possible to constitute a dowry entirely from cash, jewelry and other moveable assets. A combination of fixed property and moveable wealth was viewed as the norm in the *Peira* (*e.g.* 24.5, 25.66), although there were exceptional cases where the intention was to provide cash only (17.8, 65.5) or where the dowry consisted primarily of landed estates (25.60)[37]

Inheritance and intermarriage thus gradually wove together the landholdings of individual aristocratic families and of other up-and-coming families which joined their ranks. By the middle of the tenth century the intermingling of aristocratic estates was such as to turn the Crown's most effective instrument for controlling its overmighty subjects, confiscation of property, into a dangerous weapon. For it was not possible to expropriate the lands of a refractory aristocrat by a clean surgical excision which would not antagonise a large swathe of local society. Individual estates would have be torn out of the landscape, like bodily organs out of the surrounding tissue to which they were linked by all sorts of filaments, nerves and blood vessels. Other members of the immediate family of the targeted individual and more distant relatives, by blood and by marriage, would suffer as his dispersed estates were seized

36. *Fiscal Treatise*, ed. F. DÖLGER, *Beiträge zur Geschichte der byzantinischen Finanzverwaltung besonders des 10. und 11. Jahrhunderts* (Byz. Archiv 9), Leipzig-Berlin 1927, p. 115.21-38.

37. CHEYNET, Aristocratie et heritage (quoted n. 21), pp. 56–61.

and imperial bailiffs made their appearance. So cases of wholesale expropriation were very rare. One features in the *Peira*, the victim being the most senior of three Bourtzai cousins who rebelled against Romanos III Argyros in 1029 (60.1). The most notable case, though, was that of Bardas Phokas, leader of an Anatolian uprising which threatened to dethrone Basil II in 986-9. After his death and the failure of the rebellion, the Phokas family sank into obscurity, almost certainly because Bardas' immediate family and any relatives implicated in the rebellion were stripped of their lands.[38]

Partitive inheritance can thus be seen to have buttressed the power of the aristocracy in the face of an imperial authority which had not relinquished its right to assign titles as well as offices to postholders. The absolute power exercised by emperors, for long only constrained by the moral strictures of faith, by the need to maintain the loyalty of the court and the support of the armed forces, and by the bargaining power of great servants of state, had now come up against an ineradicable countervailing power, that of a country-based aristocracy. In the course of the late tenth and the following eleventh century, something akin to the solidarity of the village in the eighth century was created at a high social level. Increasingly interrelated by marriage, individual families became more conscious of their membership of aristocratic clans, a consciousness which manifested itself in the increasing use of surnames from the late tenth century. Two or three generations on, nexuses of allied families, all landed, some grander and taking a leading role, took shape in the provinces and consolidated their positions by drawing other families into their clientages and extending their affinities. One such nexus provided the base from which a leading figure with charisma, the young Alexios Komnenos, was able to bid for power not just in the localities but at the centre.[39]

The law of inheritance can thus be seen to have played a key part in bringing about the most profound constitutional change in Byzantine history, the shift from a system of government which was ultimately rooted in military power and which strove to keep careers open to talent, irrespective of lineage, to one where lineage and landed power came to the fore in determining who held supreme power and other great offices of state. Of course, there had been imperial dynasties before the rise of the Komnenoi, but dynastic succession, it was agreed, ran against the grain in a state where the person most fitted to rule should be picked out as God's vice-gerent on earth and where the apparatus of government continued to be run by a coalition of men who had made their way up through the ranks in the army, navy and various department of state.[40] But it was with the advent of the Komnenoi that the dynastic element became predominant and the wider affinity of the ruling family seized firm control of the state apparatus. Komnenoi would be followed by Angeloi, Kantakouzenoi and Palaiologoi.

In one respect at least, Byzantium would begin to converge on the model of rule general in the contemporary west. Its careful adherence to Roman law, one of its key inheritances from classical antiquity, had the paradoxical effect of pulling Byzantium away from its Roman past and the Roman model of rule, and transforming it into a typical Christian medieval state.

38. *Cf.* J.-C. Cheynet, *Pouvoir et contestations à Byzance (963-1210)*, Paris 1990, pp. 331–335.
39. Cheynet, *Pouvoir et contestations* (quoted n. 38), pp. 261–301.
40. G. Dagron, *Empereur et prêtre: étude sur le 'césaropapisme' byzantin*, Paris 1996, pp. 33–73.